**(Continued on back endsheets)**

University of Chicago
5518 Greenwood Avenue
Chicago, IL 60637

# Late-Victorian and Edwardian British Novelists
## First Series

To My Grandparents

George W. P. Johnson (1906–1986)

Doris Johnson (1906–   )

# Contents

# Plan of the Series

*. . . Almost the most prodigious asset of a country, and perhaps its most precious possession, is its native literary product — when that product is fine and noble and enduring.*

Mark Twain*

The advisory board, the editors, and the publisher of the *Dictionary of Literary Biography* are joined in endorsing Mark Twain's declaration. The literature of a nation provides an inexhaustible resource of permanent worth. We intend to make literature and its creators better understood and more accessible to students and the reading public, while satisfying the standards of teachers and scholars.

To meet these requirements, *literary biography* has been construed in terms of the author's achievement. The most important thing about a writer is his writing. Accordingly, the entries in *DLB* are career biographies, tracing the development of the author's canon and the evolution of his reputation.

The purpose of *DLB* is not only to provide reliable information in a convenient format but also to place the figures in the larger perspective of literary history and to offer appraisals of their accomplishments by qualified scholars.

The publication plan for *DLB* resulted from two years of preparation. The project was proposed to Bruccoli Clark by Frederick C. Ruffner, president of the Gale Research Company, in November 1975. After specimen entries were prepared and typeset, an advisory board was formed to refine the entry format and develop the series rationale. In meetings held during 1976, the publisher, series editors, and advisory board approved the scheme for a comprehensive biographical dictionary of persons who contributed to North American literature. Editorial work on the first volume began in January 1977, and it was published in 1978. In order to make *DLB* more than a reference tool and to compile volumes that individually have claim to status as literary history, it was decided to organize vol-

*From an unpublished section of Mark Twain's autobiography, copyright by the Mark Twain Company

umes by topic, period, or genre. Each of these free-standing volumes provides a biographical-bibliographical guide and overview for a particular area of literature. We are convinced that this organization — as opposed to a single alphabet method — constitutes a valuable innovation in the presentation of reference material. The volume plan necessarily requires many decisions for the placement and treatment of authors who might properly be included in two or three volumes. In some instances a major figure will be included in separate volumes, but with different entries emphasizing the aspect of his career appropriate to each volume. Ernest Hemingway, for example, is represented in *American Writers in Paris, 1920–1939* by an entry focusing on his expatriate apprenticeship; he is also in *American Novelists, 1910–1945* with an entry surveying his entire career. Each volume includes a cumulative index of the subject authors and articles. Comprehensive indexes to the entire series are planned.

With volume ten in 1982 it was decided to enlarge the scope of *DLB*. By the end of 1986 twenty-one volumes treating British literature had been published, and volumes for Commonwealth and Modern European literature were in progress. The series has been further augmented by the *DLB Yearbooks* (since 1981) which update published entries and add new entries to keep the *DLB* current with contemporary activity. There have also been *DLB Documentary Series* volumes which provide biographical and critical source materials for figures whose work is judged to have particular interest for students. One of these companion volumes is entirely devoted to Tennessee Williams.

We define literature as the *intellectual commerce of a nation*: not merely as belles lettres but as that ample and complex process by which ideas are generated, shaped, and transmitted. *DLB* entries are not limited to "creative writers" but extend to other figures who in their time and in their way influenced the mind of a people. Thus the series encompasses historians, journalists, publishers, and screenwriters. By this means readers of *DLB* may be aided to perceive literature not as cult scripture in the keeping of intellectual high

priests but firmly positioned at the center of a nation's life.

*DLB* includes the major writers appropriate to each volume and those standing in the ranks immediately behind them. Scholarly and critical counsel has been sought in deciding which minor figures to include and how full their entries should be. Wherever possible, useful references are made to figures who do not warrant separate entries.

Each *DLB* volume has a volume editor responsible for planning the volume, selecting the figures for inclusion, and assigning the entries. Volume editors are also responsible for preparing, where appropriate, appendices surveying the major periodicals and literary and intellectual movements for their volumes, as well as lists of further readings. Work on the series as a whole is coordinated at the Bruccoli Clark Layman editorial center in Columbia, South Carolina, where the editorial staff is responsible for accuracy of the published volumes.

One feature that distinguishes *DLB* is the illustration policy – its concern with the iconogra-

phy of literature. Just as an author is influenced by his surroundings, so is the reader's understanding of the author enhanced by a knowledge of his environment. Therefore *DLB* volumes include not only drawings, paintings, and photographs of authors, often depicting them at various stages in their careers, but also illustrations of their families and places where they lived. Title pages are regularly reproduced in facsimile along with dust jackets for modern authors. The dust jackets are a special feature of *DLB* because they often document better than anything else the way in which an author's work was perceived in its own time. Specimens of the writers' manuscripts are included when feasible.

Samuel Johnson rightly decreed that "The chief glory of every people arises from its authors." The purpose of the *Dictionary of Literary Biography* is to compile literary history in the surest way available to us – by accurate and comprehensive treatment of the lives and work of those who contributed to it.

The *DLB* Advisory Board

# Introduction

The novelists in this volume include ones not covered in *DLB 34: British Novelists, 1890–1929: Traditionalists* and *DLB 36: British Novelists, 1890–1929: Modernists.* Since 1985, when those volumes were produced, there has been increasing attention from a variety of perspectives to the period they cover. Interest has been generated by feminist studies such as Angela Ingram and Daphne Patai's collection of essays *Rediscovering Forgotten Radicals: British Women Writers 1889–1939* (1993); socialist analyses, notably H. Gustav Klaus's collection *The Rise of Socialist Fiction 1880–1914* (1987); and more general studies including Peter Keating's *The Haunted Study: A Social History of the English Novel 1875–1914* (1989) and David Trotter's *The English Novel in History 1895–1920* (1993). All of these works take into account writers not included in the canon, in some cases completely forgotten for a variety of reasons, and not treated in any previous *Dictionary of Literary Biography* volumes.

*Late Victorian and Edwardian British Novelists,* First Series, attempts to respond to and foster that interest by providing more detailed analyses of some of these and other noncanonical writers than have ever been produced. In casting a finer net over this period, however, it has been necessary to limit the dates used by the earlier volumes. This volume covers the range of novelists who began to write in the 1890s or who achieved acclaim by then to those who had started to write before the end of World War I, though the entries treat the entire oeuvre of each writer. In addition, the distinction between "Traditionalists" and "Modernists" from the predecessor volumes does not apply well to this series of novelists and has thus been discarded.

Instead, these novelists have been organized according to whether they are mainly working out of the romance or realist traditions, partly because the debate about these terms was an important one during these years. William Frierson, for example, provides a useful survey of this debate in *The English Novel in Transition 1885–1940* (1965). However, these terms are used here with the recognition of their problematic nature, the hope being that this choice will help renew discussion about the issue of realism versus romance: why, for example, it was considered of such great importance around the turn of the century.

The present volume gathers together those novelists who wrote mainly in the subgenres that might be loosely grouped neoromantic, whereas a Second Series will treat the realists. Since these terms are so nebulous, some attempt at defining them needs to be made before proceeding further. In *Modernism and Romance* (1908), R. A. Scott-James begins his chapter entitled "What is Romance?" by stating that the term has "been used in so many senses that the writer is perhaps justified in choosing whichever of these meanings he may prefer." He associates romance with an attitude of wonderment toward life in which one recognizes that one stands at the beginning or on the verge of the mysterious unknown. Interestingly, he claims that the prominent psychical researcher, Frederic Myers, has probed the terrain of this "borderland" most fully. According to this definition, novelists fascinated by the psychic, the occult, and the supernatural belong under the heading of romance. In the present volume, this would include E. F. Benson, Algernon Blackwood, Marjorie Bowen, Walter de la Mare, Lord Dunsany, Robert Hichens, William Hope Hodgson, Vernon Lee, Oliver Onions, Forrest Reid, M. P. Shiel, James Stephens, and Charles Williams. Other novelists, notably Viola Meynell and "Lucas Malet," frequently deal with the intersection between the ideal or spiritual and the real and have thus been added to the present volume, though they were also influenced by European naturalism. Scott-James also associates the new romance with a sense of incipient adventure; thus, those novelists, some of whom took their cue from Robert Louis Stevenson and who wrote novels in the adventure, scientific romance, and historical modes, have also been collected in this volume. In *Sexual Anarchy: Gender and Culture at the Fin de Siècle* (1990), Elaine Showalter argues that this neoromantic revival "was a men's literary revolution intended to reclaim the kingdom of the English novel for male writers, male readers, and men's stories." These male quest romances were escapist, explored men's secret selves, and excluded women. The large number (twenty-five) of male novelists included in the neoromantic volume of this series lends support to her claim.

However, other types of neoromantic fiction coexisted with this version and were characteristically written by women. Elinor Glyn, among others, specialized in "romantic adventuring by ambitious young women in high society," as Eric Thompson claims. In the novels of such authors as Beatrice Harraden, Katharine Tynan, and Marjorie Bowen the melodramatic or sentimental aspect of romance comes to the fore. In these softer-toned works, the heroine tends to be more passive than in a Glyn novel and will submit to the powerful hero. As Maria Ferraira points out, this type of romance can be read as a form of ideological oppression maintaining the subordinate status of women or can be seen as giving a voice to women's suffering and thus implicitly protesting it. Since all of these varieties fall under the term *romance* in its broadest form, these female novelists have also found a place in this volume.

Realism, though not necessarily in simple opposition to romance, generally "takes its cue from the ordinary, unalterable course of real life," as Scott-James avers. Though it may attempt to be conscientiously mimetic and operate within the realm of the probable, more important is the philosophical stance informing it. According to Robert Squillace, "Realism assumes reality, that is, the existence of a phenomenal world separate and knowable by consciousness. The struggle to recognize that separation and gather that knowledge is the chief theme of realist work. By the same token, the realist novel purports to sharpen a reader's perception of the real world exterior to it." Despite these definitions, in practice the boundaries between neoromanticism and realism blur, since some writers blended elements of realism and romance, or at least wrote in both genres.

The recent extensions and reevaluations of the literary history of the era from the end of the nineteenth century through the first two decades of the twentieth bear testimony to its awkward and unresolved status. The labels most often applied to these years, including fin de siècle, decadent, Edwardian, and Early Modern, seem inadequate and incomplete, and this period, if it can be called that, is often squeezed out between the Victorian and the Modern, or disparaged as transitional. This situation is reflected in the literary academy. A statement made by critic Samuel Hynes in his *Edwardian Occasions: Essays on English Writing in the Early Twentieth Century* (1972) still applies just as accurately today: "Every English department has its Victorianists and its Modernists, but who has ever heard of an academic Edwardianist?" For the lack of a better, more com-

prehensive term, the terms *late Victorian* and *Edwardian* have been adopted for this volume.

Traditional literary histories, such as J. I. M. Stewart's *Eight Modern Writers* (1963), when discussing the novels of this period, survey only a handful of its practitioners, all male, including Joseph Conrad, Thomas Hardy, H. G. Wells, Arnold Bennett, and John Galsworthy. All too frequently, literary historians justify the passing over or slighting of the era by citing Virginia Woolf's deliberately dramatic and defensive comments about the caliber of novel writing during these years. It is ironic that Woolf's comments should have exerted such impact on present-day perceptions, since Woolf herself began writing during the very period she criticized, although she identified herself with the next generation of writers, labeled the Georgians after the accession to the throne of George V in 1910. In "Mr. Bennett and Mrs. Brown" (1923), one of several polemical essays on this topic, Woolf claims that she will "reduce Edwardian fiction to a view." This she certainly does, and it is a view which is striking for its restrictiveness. The Edwardian camp is reduced to Bennett, principally, along with Galsworthy and Wells (though in one version she does "express gratitude" to Hardy, Conrad, and W. H. Hudson), and then compared to the Georgians, limited to E. M. Forster, D. H. Lawrence, Lytton Strachey, James Joyce, and T. S. Eliot. She accuses the Edwardian "culprits" of being materialists because, disappointingly, "they are concerned not with the spirit but with the body" and "spend immense skill and immense industry making the trivial and the transitory appear the true and the enduring." She asserts that, whereas the Victorians created vivid, memorable characters, the Edwardians fail to do so because of these concerns, and "life escapes" their novels as a consequence.

In contrast, the younger writers, most notably Joyce, "attempt to come closer to life," even if "there was no English novelist living [in 1910] from whom they could learn their business," and they must discard most of the conventions of the novel in order to do so. Less frequently noticed than Woolf's claims has been the context in which they were written. She was responding to a specific criticism of Bennett's about her inability to create memorable characters. She was also trying to define and justify her own "modernist" aesthetic. She did not, however, restrict her critique of her predecessors' fiction to their manner of presentation but severely attacked the Edwardians' selection of subject matter. Edwardian fiction, though, was far more diverse and amorphous than that of the three admittedly important novelists targeted by Woolf.

Reductive views of the late Victorian and Edwardian years have persisted in the popular imagination as well, perpetuated by such phenomena as the lush Merchant-Ivory films of Forster's novels, despite periodic debunking of period myths by scholars and writers such as Hynes and J. B. Priestley. This introduction will deal with several of these myths as a way of introducing the spirit of the age, as well as examining more closely one or two literary myths. As with all myths there is undoubtedly some truth at their root, but the large shadow that they cast threatens to obscure other significant growth.

The 1890s is most often cast as the decade of decadence, of aesthetes and absinthe, during which a pervasive sense of ending was played out in alternating moods of skepticism, jaded witticism, and ennui. The controversy surrounding Oscar Wilde, along with his decline ("Life is such a disappointment"), is held up as iconic of the malaise. However, the aesthetes represented only a tiny (and often-ridiculed) fragment of this society caught up in a whirlwind of activity directed at improving the plight of humanity. As Karl Beckson stresses in his *London in the 1890's: A Cultural History* (1993), there was a strong sense of renewal, of embracing the new, as captured in Havelock Ellis's *The New Spirit* at the beginning of the decade and in the various "New" movements launched and identities created during it, including New Woman, New Hedonism, New Imperialism, New Psychology, New Drama, New Journalism, and, most pertinently, New Fiction. The time was one of ferment, of paradoxes and crosscurrents, and its complexity calls into question Hynes's statement in *Edwardian Occasions* that "the sense of an ending and the sense of a new beginning do not coincide, but are separated by ten years, the length of Edward's reign." It also makes the clarion call of the modernists, Ezra Pound's "make it new," sound rather old hat, though he applied this phrase specifically to literary form.

The new era that began after the death of Queen Victoria on 22 January 1901 and the ascension to the throne of Edward VII has most frequently been depicted as a crass and superficial age, one of philistinism and extravagance, captured by the image of the Edwardian garden party. Certainly the rebellious new king, described privately by Henry James as "an arch-vulgarian," enjoyed his pleasures, which included lavish entertaining along with ostentatious dress, the company of pretty women, horse racing, yachting, and shooting, and there is no doubt that he was a popular king who encouraged a certain sense of liberation and joie de vivre among his subjects. Vita Sackville-West captures that world perceptively and treats it scathingly in her 1931 novel *The Edwardians*. She describes it as "a world where pleasure fell like a ripened peach for the outstretching of a hand." However, the stark reality is that only about 1 percent of the population could afford to participate in this opulent world. This 1 percent owned 69 percent of the national capital, the highest concentration of wealth in modern British history. As for the rest, as Donald Read notes, "Eight out of ten Edwardians were working class, and most of these passed large parts of their lives below the poverty line, first defined by Seebohm Rowntree in his famous book on *Poverty, A Study of Town Life*." The majority could not even conceive the notion of extravagance: Paul Thompson writes that "very little that could be re-used was wasted. Children picked from street gutters, rubbish heaps and river banks. They crawled under market stalls to look for fallen food, and queued at public houses and restaurants for the day's leftovers. . . . Women, as patient, cheap workers, were especially used for refuse work." To make matters worse, this society inherited from the Victorians rigid segregation along class lines.

Recognition of such disparity helps deflate another closely related myth about this period, that it was a golden age of security and leisure. In part this myth was perpetuated by those who mournfully and nostalgically gazed back at it over the chasm of horror of the Great War, in which approximately 30 percent of the men aged fifteen to twenty-four in 1914 were slaughtered. One of those who escaped and mythologized the prewar period was Siegfried Sassoon, who wrote that "the years of my youth were going down for ever in the weltering western gold, and the future would take me far from that sunset embered horizon." Similar views continue to be reflected in popular writing about the age, for example in Gerald Sparrow's *Vintage Edwardian Murder* (1971): Edward's "reign was the last comparatively untroubled one of the golden era of the British Monarchy" and "the Edwardians believed in their land of hope and glory, because life in many ways was glorious and certainly full of hope."

However, the number and severity of crises riddling these years strongly suggest that far from being a golden age of security and leisure, this time was actually one of tension and conflict – that the Great War was only a dramatic culmination of these conflicts. Just before these years unfolded, labor unrest was dramatically exhibited on Bloody Sunday, 13 November 1887, described as a "monstrous riot" by Queen Victoria. In the East End the

dockers struck and subsequently achieved victory in 1889. Workers continued to gain momentum, dramatized by severe and widespread labor disputes and strikes by coal miners, dockers, and transport workers in 1910–1912, through to the labor electoral victories of 1924 and 1929. The suffragist and then suffragette movements leaped ahead with the formation in 1889 of the Women's Protective Provident League (later called the Women's Trade Union League) and the Women's Franchise League, involving Mrs. Pankhurst. In 1903 the Pankhursts formed the Women's Social and Political Union, and by the summer of 1909 the union had become militant, with its members rioting, hunger striking, and committing acts of arson to gain the vote and, more broadly, to combat political and moral injustice. "Black Friday" in November 1910 stands out as a particularly nasty confrontation, but there were many other incidents, such as Emily Davison's martyrdom by suicide for the cause in 1913.

The 1894 Dreyfus affair in France, a miscarriage of justice, eventually scandalized Britain and the rest of Europe. The course that the Boer War (1899–1902) took, pitting the inefficient blundering British forces against the much smaller force of the South African Boers, caused an even deeper questioning of justice, as well as of imperialism, especially since the British appeared to be motivated economically to protect gold and diamond interests. Then followed the upheaval occasioned by the sweep of the Liberal Party in 1906, after which the new government attempted to introduce radical social reforms. The attempt was blocked by the aristocratic House of Lords. This government failed on several counts, especially over its Irish Home Rule Bill, a failure which led to conflict again within the empire, notably the Easter 1916 uprising in Dublin.

By 1914 a crisis had been reached as England, in George Dangerfield's words, was "a liberal democracy whose parliament had practically ceased to function, whose Government was futile, and whose Opposition had said enough to put lesser men in the dock for treason." Under these conditions England embraced war with Germany, declared 4 August 1914. Though the war was expected to last only for a few months, it dragged on for more than four years and escalated conflict to a multinational level. It also caused personal havoc in the lives of thousands and transformed class and gender relations, as well as the moral code.

These glimpses into the successive tensions of these years reinforce Priestley's claim that "the Edwardian was never a golden age, but seen across the dark years afterwards it could easily be mis-

taken for one." Priestley locates the tension among the middle classes: "The members of the upper middle class felt that property and position were being threatened. In the lower middle class, respectability itself, often newly-won, had to be guarded. There was a feeling that religion, the family, decency, social and political stability, the country itself, were all in danger." However, the history of labor conflict demonstrates that the working class was just as deeply embroiled. Even the wealthiest of the upper class started to feel a slight flutter of change. Statistics show that they stopped, for instance, building large country houses during these years.

Given the number and range of conflicts and upheavals in the late Victorian and Edwardian years, it is not surprising that this period has been labeled transitional. Rapid changes certainly occurred, which need to be touched on before considering the literary use and implications of that term. Between 1890 and 1918 many aspects of British society were transformed utterly. In 1890 the average person had not heard of the motorcar, motorcycles, motion pictures, the Metro, radiotelegraphy, airships (let alone airplanes), tanks, X rays, radium, and bakelite (heralding the age of plastics), all of which were invented or discovered during the period and had entered into use by 1918. Advances in scientific theory were just as significant and include Ernst Haeckel's contributions to evolution theory, Max Planck's quantum theory, Einstein's special theory of relativity, and Niels Bohr's electric theory of matter. Ironically, this scientific probing was perceived as undermining the Newtonian universe, and it contributed to distrust of the mechanistic view of the world.

The reaction against scientific positivism took the form of a revival of romanticism and philosophical idealism. The Victorian quest for a replacement for traditional religious belief continued – as the rise in popularity of the Society for Psychical Research, theosophy, Eastern mysticism, and comparative religion attests. Though Freud considered himself a scientist, psychoanalysis was introduced to Britain by members of the Society for Psychical Research and perceived in the light of psychical research into phenomena undetectable by the five senses. Psychoanalysis focused attention on the irrational in mankind and contributed to dissolving the rigid Victorian boundary between the sane and the insane. By 1918 it was being discussed more widely, having received enormous impetus through its contribution to identifying and treating "shell shock," a term invented in England during the war. In the years prior to the war, the metaphysical psychology

of Henri Bergson became enormously popular in Britain and elsewhere. His poetically written arguments altered conceptions of time and memory and were directed toward illustrating that the universe is essentially spiritual rather than material, captured in his conception of the élan vital, the life force. All of these discoveries and developments contributed to a sense of rapid change, of instability, and of flux.

Contemporaries from C. F. G. Masterman, an Edwardian Liberal politician, to Yeats recognized and commented on the transitional nature of this period, but it was a feeling that was to persist. Edwin Muir titled his 1926 collection of essays on contemporary literature *Transition* and wrote that "in ages of transition, on the other hand, everything makes the writer more uncertain, saps his faith, only nourished from himself, and gives his work an air either of vacillation or of violence." Literary historians such as Frierson, G. S. Fraser, and Hynes have subsequently applied this label. However, more recently scholars, such as Peter Keating in his *The Haunted Study: A Social History of the English Novel 1875–1914* (1989), have argued that consciousness of transition existed earlier in the Victorian age. And John A. Lester Jr. in his *Journey Through Despair 1880–1914* (1968) suggests that if the period "was a transition, the transit is not yet completed. In some larger sense, that age must in fact have been a beginning."

These ambiguities call into question the notion that this period experienced a greater sense of transition than had those prior to it and following. But there is a potentially greater problem with the term if it is used to imply that the fiction of this period wallowed, without a sense of direction, that its contributions were not quite up to the mark and led on inexorably to what the modernists did better, with more skill. The Edwardians had their own projects, concerns, and pressures, different from those of the modernists, who paradoxically emerged from within their midst. In fact, their fictional impulses were incredibly diverse, leading Jefferson Hunter to claim that "Edwardian novelists need to be taken on individual terms, because some were more interested in the purely formal management of their art than others, and a few were determined not to be plain at all." Fiction writing existed in a state analogous to John Keats's negative capability, in which great variety and innumerable possibilities were entertained before closure was imposed, in this case before lines had hardened between modernists and traditionalists, commercial and serious novelists.

The encyclopedic structure of *Late Victorian and Edwardian British Novelists,* First Series, enables the diversity among the novelists of this period to be recognized and yet also acknowledges webs of interconnectedness both conscious and unconscious, a phenomenon which is not too surprising since the British literary world of the turn of the century was relatively small. This volume deals with so-called minor novelists, those not considered, to use traditional terminology, of the first or in some cases even of the second or third ranks. Its subject matter represents a deliberate act of de-centering the canon, or possibly of enlarging it. Some may question expending the enormous amount of time and energy represented by this volume on writers who have traditionally warranted not much more than a footnote in most literary histories. George Dangerfield suggests a different perspective in noting that minor literature "is the Baedeker of the soul, and will guide you through the curious relics, the tumbledown buildings, the flimsy palaces, the false pagodas, the distorted and fantastical and faery vistas which have cluttered the imagination of mankind at this or that brief period of its history." However, even this delightful description smacks of condescension and does not do full justice to these writers.

Aside from expanding the present-day reader's sense of what this culture was like, these novelists play several more important roles. Many were closely connected with the more major figures and aided them in various ways, from providing material and emotional support to championing them in the press, especially if they ran afoul of the censor. Together these minor writers provide a composite portrait of what conditions were actually like for a writer contributing to the discourse of this era. If their work was not experimental, many achieved experiments in living, making their biographies intrinsically fascinating. The scandalous life of Elinor Glyn immediately leaps to mind. Since many of these novelists wrote best-sellers, they typically touched the lives of more of their contemporary readers than their longer-remembered and more critically acclaimed colleagues. In some instances their work has been undeservedly forgotten for a variety of reasons, including politics and gender. The triumph and pervasiveness of a modernist aesthetic and its reflection in literary criticism have contributed to relegating some of these novelists to obscurity. Some were dismissed as genre writers, not worthy of consideration in the mainstream development of the English novel. One even wonders whether the sheer output of most of the writers represented here has discouraged scholars from probing their work. Perhaps most important, these nov-

elists bring to light the eddies and undercurrents which reveal a much more complex cultural stream than appears on the surface and make generalizations about an epoch less comfortable.

If the writing was so varied, making generalizations problematic, and if these years have been distorted by the myths mentioned, then should one attempt to construct these years as a period at all? Periodization of course is an artificial construct and to some degree is imposed for convenience's sake, which is why year markers are preferable as guidelines. As mentioned, this volume covers novelists who began writing in the 1890s (or who had embarked on writing careers slightly ahead of this but who achieved success or notoriety during the decade) through to those who began writing before the end of the war. Within this group there seem to be two "generations." The first began writing in the nineteenth century, making up approximately 50 percent of this volume. Their writing careers are roughly contemporary with those of Wells, Bennett, and Galsworthy, which began in 1893, 1898, and 1897, respectively. The work of the second "generation" first appeared within the first two decades of the twentieth century.

Although the choice of 1890 to mark a turning point is partially arbitrary, one could point to several indicators of shifts in focus occurring at about this time. In 1890 appeared Oscar Wilde's *The Picture of Dorian Gray* (in serial form); Gen. William Booth's *In Darkest England*; American William James's *Principles of Psychology*; Havelock Ellis's *The Criminal*; Lucas Malet's *The Wages of Sin* (in the United States, and in 1891 in Britain); Anthony Hope's first novel, *A Man of Mark*; and the first volume of Sir James Frazer's *The Golden Bough*. As well, in that year the Rhymer's Club was founded and Yeats initiated "The Hermetic Order of the Golden Dawn." Though quite diverse, this selection can be used to reveal significant characteristics of these shifts.

Both Wilde's novel, the best-known English decadent novel, and the formation of the Rhymer's Club are emblematic of aestheticism. Some of the novels analyzed within these pages have a "whiff" of the aesthete about them, as George Woodcock says of Hudson's writing, and echo the credo of "Art for Art's Sake," the rebellious attitude of valuing aesthetic form and style over moral earnestness and controversial social engagement. A few of these novelists even knew Wilde personally, including Ada Leverson and Elizabeth Robins, but they are just as likely to satirize the aesthetes, as do Leverson, Vernon Lee, William de Morgan, Anthony

Hope, and, most notoriously, Robert Hichens in *The Green Carnation* (1894), at the time thought to have been penned by Wilde himself.

These satires point to a strong countertrend to the aesthetic in the 1890s: polemic novels concerned with social conditions and ever-present class tensions, employing "art for life's sake," to borrow the phrase Miles Franklin applied to a novel by Elizabeth Robins. These novels reflected the intense interest in the plight of the urban poor, captured by Booth's *In Darkest England*, in which he pointed out that the deplorable slum conditions represented a social jungle, as well as the growth of the labor movement and such organizations as the socialist Fabian Society. Though most were written by middle-class writers, there was also a spate of working-class novels, most notably Arthur Morrison's *A Child of the Jago* (1896). Such novelists were frequently roundly criticized for their advocacy and propaganda aims, not thought to be the proper sphere of fiction.

William James's monumental fourteen-hundred-page *Principles of Psychology* and Ellis's *Criminal* indicate increasing concern with all aspects of psychological behavior, including the deviant. James focused on normality and consciousness, imaging the latter as a stream and emphasizing its dynamism and fluidity. However, his later work, on psychic research and religious experience, increasingly blurred the boundaries of normality and aberration. As Karl Beckson and others have pointed out, 1890s society was intensely fascinated with madness, degeneracy, criminal behavior, and the relationship between insanity and genius, reflected in a few novels discussed in this volume, including Lucas Malet's *The Wages of Sin*.

Malet's novel also dramatically conveys another closely related and important shift in focus during the 1890s. Under the influence of Emile Zola's naturalism and his first English disciple, George Moore, novelists turned to a "scientific" examination of the frequently disastrous impact of heredity and environment on their protagonists, and most notoriously to portrayals of illicit or irregular sexual liaisons with a new emphasis on their acceptability.

Just as important, Malet stands for the "New Woman" novelists, though as Patricia Srebrnik points out, the author's position in regard to this label is problematic. As a group, these novelists portrayed women who questioned or even rejected the traditional roles handed to them, or who became victims of the injustice inherent in those traditional roles, as is the case in *The Wages of Sin*. Many advo-

cated equality in one or more of the political, educational, economic, and sexual realms. The importance of this trend is illustrated by the quantity of these novels: more than one hundred were published between 1883 and 1900. More of the "New Woman" novelists will be examined in the Second Series.

Most of the forays into new thematic territory that have been mentioned were gathered together under the label "unpleasant fiction" and were severely criticized as morbid, promoting unhealthy introspection. The vociferously championed reaction to all this unpleasantness in fiction was loosely termed "romance," though it might more accurately be termed neoromanticism; it is this neoromantic reaction which forms the basis of this volume, as mentioned. One reason that naturalism in its severest form did not survive long in Britain (even Moore became disenchanted with its objective reporting and implicit determinism) was owing to many novelists' attraction to the spiritual and the occult, manifested in subgenres ranging from supernatural, psychical, speculative, and fantasy, to ghost tales. Again Malet's career is pertinent since she wrote a few supernatural novels during the decade. The fascination with the esoterically occult is also attested by Yeats's formation of the Golden Dawn. Several of the writers in this volume belonged to branches of this society, including Charles Williams and Algernon Blackwood.

Blackwood, along with several others, also belonged to the Society for Psychical Research, formed in 1882 by a group of highly respected, mainly Cambridge-educated intellectuals. The society's main aim was to sift the "scientific" evidence for the survival of human personality beyond death. Accordingly, it discussed all types of phenomena imperceptible to the five senses and introduced to the British the latest foreign developments in the field of psychiatry and abnormal psychology, including telepathy, invasion of personality, dual personality, idées fixes, and prevision, all of which were treated thematically in the novels of the 1890s and into the twentieth century. As supernatural and speculative tales inspired by psychical research shaded into the realm of abnormal psychology, they too ran the risk of being labeled "unpleasant."

A "purer" form of romance was the adventure story, frequently extolling the romance of imperialism, perhaps as a panacea for social problems, and eventually more critical of the excesses of the imperialistic creed. Anthony Hope's *A Man of Mark* represents one of these adventures, though with an early mark of cynicism about it. Other novelists in this volume who cover this terrain are W. H. Hudson, Arthur Quiller-Couch, and P. C. Wren, though Joseph Conrad's and E. M. Forster's explorations are the ones now commonly identified with this subgenre.

Another manifestation of the adventure tale which came into its own during the 1890s decade was scientific romance. The term was apparently first used in 1886, but this subgenre flourished in the 1890s, capitalizing on speculations about the implications of some of the various scientific discoveries mentioned earlier, including electricity. Though associated with Wells's *The Time Machine* (1895) and *The War of the Worlds* (1898), this trend is represented here in the work of M. P. Shiel and William Hope Hodgson; it was carried into the twentieth century in such classic novels as the psychological realist J. D. Beresford's *The Hampdenshire Wonder* (1911). In contrast, an older type of adventure novel, the historical novel, underwent a revival during the period. Practitioners represented here include Anthony Hope, Arthur Quiller-Couch, Robert Hugh Benson, Warwick Deeping, and Marjorie Bowen.

Social engagement, psychological and sexual naturalism, "new woman" revisionism, spiritual and psychical romance, adventure, scientific romance, and historical fiction – these are some of the more important trends which give the novel of the 1890s a distinguishable character. But how did these trends, particularly those which might be classed as neoromantic, play out in the remaining years under consideration? Romantic worship of the rural and of nature continued to find expression in such works as Algernon Blackwood's Edwardian fantasies, and in what Ray Mackenzie calls the novel of primitive, sensual rural people, developed by both Viola Meynell and W. H. Hudson. A variation on this, the regional novel, also thrived, as demonstrated in the work of Eden Phillpotts ("The Hardy of Dartmoor," as Agatha Christie called him) and Arthur Quiller-Couch, most of whose novels were Cornish in background and dialect.

Though issues of class consciousness were more frequently treated by novelists working in the realist vein, some of the writers included in this volume continued to write sentimentally or sensationally about various classes, notably the upper classes. As Hunter points out, "The Edwardian silver fork novel carried that early Victorian genre to new intensities of snobbish enticement and to huge new sales." Undoubtedly the most sensational of these was Glyn's *Three Weeks* (1907), but novels by many others, including Robert Hichens and Katharine

Tynan, fall into this category. E. F. Benson's *The Climber* (1908) might even qualify, though the novel focuses more on criticism of the social climber into high society.

The naturalistic and often satiric impulse found expression in the autobiographical life novel or bildungsroman, which obviously falls into the realist camp; however, a few of the novelists in this volume, including Robert Hichens in *Felix* (1903) and E. V. Lucas in *Landmarks* (1914), tried their hand at this form. They have been completely and justifiably overshadowed by more famous examples of the life novel, including Lawrence's *Sons and Lovers* (1913), Joyce's *A Portrait of the Artist as a Young Man* (1914), and Forster's *The Longest Journey* (1907). Novels such as these moved toward candidness and inclusiveness of personal experience; correspondingly the broader category of "unpleasant novel" became more so because it explored a greater range of issues with a new attitude. Keating (1989) points out about the sex novel that from around the turn of the century, "it could now be assumed that there was no such thing as normal or orthodox sexuality; no single generally acceptable pattern for family life; no one kind of sexuality that was attributable to all women and all men." Malet, for example, explored "sexual inversion," as homosexuality was then termed, in *The History of Sir Richard Calmady* (1901). Working in the neoromantic vein, Glyn in *Three Weeks* (1907) and Horace de Vere Stacpoole in *The Blue Lagoon* (1908) treated sexuality in a sensationally erotic manner.

As in all other arenas of life, World War I profoundly affected both novelists and novel writing for years to come. Just after the outbreak some middle-aged and older male writers enthusiastically accepted a role in the newly formed Ministry of Information "for the organization of public statements of the strength of the British case and principles in the war by well-known men of letters." C. F. G. Masterman headed this propaganda unit which included writers represented in the present volume, such as Robert Hugh Benson, Anthony Hope, E. V. Lucas, John Masefield, and Arthur Quiller-Couch. At least one woman, Phyllis Bottome (a realist novelist), was later added to the ranks, and others publicly voiced their support or patriotically contributed to the effort, including Flora Annie Steel and Elinor Glyn. The novels about the war published early in its course by the novelists in this volume tend to be uncritical, such as Quiller-Couch's *Nicky-Nan, Reservist* (1915), or even comedic, as in Lucas's *The Vermillion Box* (1916). However, a shift seems to have taken place around 1916, a year of "imagina-

tive vacuum," in Hynes's (1991) words. The change in attitude is reflected in a novel such as *The Fortune: A Romance of Friendship* (1917) by Douglas Goldring, who will be covered in the Second Series. The book anticipates a trickle of antiwar novels published in the last years of the war, including Clemence Dane's *First the Blade* (1918) and even conservative Quiller-Couch's *Foe-Farrell* (1918). That trickle continued through the 1920s and became a flood from about 1929 on. Since the vast majority of the novelists included in this volume were too old for active service, it is not surprising that only one of them, William Hope Hodgson, was killed in battle.

"The end of the Edwardian Age is as certain as it was sudden – August 4, 1914," Samuel Hynes dramatically declares in *The Edwardian Turn of Mind* (1968), though King Edward had died in 1910. But time had to elapse, and the horrors and, perhaps more important, the futility of the war had to emerge before attitudes changed and the culture was transformed. The enthusiasm with which the war was greeted by the majority, and even the majority of writers included here, seems very alien to present-day readers looking back on it. However, the disillusion and bitterness expressed toward it at its close seem much more un-Edwardian and modern. Only by the end of the war was the transformation complete. In his reminiscences, *South Lodge* (1943), Douglas Goldring claims that "London, right up to August, 1914, remained 'Edwardian.' It only became 'Georgian' during the Armistice years which followed victory." Writing in 1939, literary historian Malcolm Elwin gave 1918 as the date of triumph over Victorianism, and this is symbolized by conscientious objector Lytton Strachey's *Eminent Victorians* (1918), a notorious attack on representative figures of the Victorian age, including military ones. After the war, writers increasingly used experimental form to attempt to capture the sense of loss and fragmentation resulting largely from the war, and the gap between art and entertainment, between so-called highbrow, middlebrow, and lowbrow novelists, grew much wider.

At this point it might be worthwhile to attempt to summarize the achievement of the late Victorian and Edwardian novelists, especially since their approach to form is often compared unfavorably with the modernists' radical experimentation. One of the first characteristics one notices about the late Victorians and Edwardians is the great diversity of genres and subgenres in which they worked, for which they discovered markets. Though this volume focuses on these writers' contributions to the novel, the range of writing represented includes po-

etry, drama, essays, travel writing, biography, autobiography, history, and literary criticism, as well as, later in their careers, projects involving new media, including radio, television, and silent and sound motion pictures. The types of novels range from the "light entertainments" of E. V. Lucas and sentimental romances of Warwick Deeping to genre fiction such as crime and detection, supernatural, fantasy, children's literature, and the recent category of scientific romance.

Novelists' approaches to these forms also changed during this period. The year 1890 marks the death of Charles Mudie, founder of one of the largest circulating libraries in Britain. Since the mid nineteenth century, circulating libraries had promoted the production of "triple-decker" or three-volume novels because they were too expensive for most people to buy. This economic situation helped the libraries obtain subscribers at an annual fee of about a guinea. During the 1880s and 1890s these libraries came under increasing attack from writers such as George Moore because of the censorship they exerted, ostensibly so as not to offend their largely middle-class and female readers. Then, in 1894, the firm Mudie's decided to reduce the amount that it would pay publishers per volume, rendering the triple-decker uneconomic and heading it for extinction. Several of the novelists assembled in this volume started their careers writing the triple-decker, including Vernon Lee and Lucas Malet, before switching to the one-volume format. William de Morgan is the exception since his career ended with bulky, Victorian-sized novels. Whereas the triple-decker permitted and even encouraged prolixity with loose, episodic plotting and digressions, novelists had to become more precise and selective in a one-volume format. Some brought character into the foreground and reduced plot to a minimum. Others highlighted the social worlds of their protagonists.

In addition, the loosening of the circulating libraries' moral stranglehold contributed to the greatest late Victorian and Edwardian innovation, the exploration of new topics in fiction or with new attitudes of openness. Increasingly, novelists wanted to explore the gaps or disjunctions in the Victorian novel: what happened after the bedroom door closed, after Cousin Bee was labeled a lunatic or a hysteric and bundled off to a rest home or an asylum, or young Alison decided not to get married and to embark on a career? More important, what influence did society have on these and other situations? The new generation of novelists showed motivation as being more complex and morality less

clearcut than the Victorians typically had depicted these aspects. Just as important, the Edwardians wanted to pierce the veil of the five senses, to discover other worlds both outside and within them. They also documented the lives of the mundane. As Hunter claims, "the Edwardians deserve credit for extending the fictional imagination to those who had rarely been thought worthy of narrative: the unpicturesque, the unromantic, the unadventurous, the unexceptional." They often received severe criticism for their broadening of the fictional scope. For example, E. F. Benson's examination of superficial character in *The Climber* (1908) was not considered a worthy subject, nor were Algernon Blackwood's explorations of the sorrows of childhood.

For the most part these writers kept within the English tradition of storytelling, an antimodern tradition that has persisted to the present and makes the modernists' experiments seem a temporary though influential divergence from the mainstream. However, as recent critics such as Keating and David Trotter (1994) have pointed out, some noncanonical novelists did experiment with tone and point of view.

Paradoxically, it was the economic and social factors enabling these novelists to exist which kept their interest from straying too far into other kinds of experimentation than thematic. Their position as Grub Street writers most strongly links the majority in this volume. Though the term *Grub Street* had originally been pejoratively applied in the Augustan period to those hacks on the fringes of the publishing world, by the early twentieth century it generally referred to those who were completely dependent on their writing income, and it even attained a kind of romantic appeal, as shown in A. St. John Adcock's prefaces to *Gods of Modern Grub Street* (1923) and *The Glory That Was Grub Street* (1928). As Brian Stableford notes, "after 1890, it became much easier for would-be writers to think in terms of a career." The term *best-seller* was first coined in 1889, the year that the new journalism achieved a more professional status by the granting of a charter to the Institute of Journalists.

Both of these events mark growing public demand for more reading material, including novels, newspapers, and magazines, as more of the populace became literate and better educated. Various reasons have been used to explain the increase in literacy and consequent publishing boom, including education acts in 1870 and 1902, which extended educational opportunities to the lower-middle-class level, and a rapid spread of public libraries, as opposed to circulating libraries, in the 1890s.

However, the most pertinent consequence was that greater numbers of individuals developed careers in writing to fill that need, which the market could now sustain, though competition for readership also increased. According to the *Publisher's Circular*, only 362 novels were published in 1870, whereas by 1890 the figure had risen to 1,204, and in 1913 the number of novels peaked at 2,504 before declining during the war years to 1,014. Keating estimates that an average of 1,618 works were published per year between 1895 and 1914 (or 4.4 per day) in the combined (and not easily distinguished) genres of adult and juvenile prose fiction. The demand for information about these writers also increased, and periodicals devoted to authors' lives and authorship proliferated, among them the *Bookman*, the *Book Buyer*, and the *Literary Year-Book*.

Many of the writers in this volume started their careers writing journalism and continued to supplement their incomes with journalism of all kinds. In some cases, perhaps many, quantity detrimentally affected quality. The association with journalism likely helps account for a strong documentary impulse that has been noted and disparaged in late Victorian and Edwardian fiction. For obvious reasons, most of these novelists closely monitored the trends of readership, though some also complained about the limitations this readership placed on their art, and they actively pursued specialized markets (as did E. F. Benson). Thus, economic conditions strongly contributed to both their existence and the shape of their fiction, a topic that deserves further investigation.

With so many novels being written and so many Grub Street novelists writing them, this volume could not pretend to be comprehensive. Rather, it, along with the Second Series, will attempt to be representative according to several criteria. Since the late Victorian and Edwardian novel has so often been characterized as social realism and as materialist (most famously by Woolf), the editor initially set out to gather novelists more concerned with the spiritual, with life that flickers in the world beyond the five senses, than with the material. These novelists fascinated by the psychical or occult in various manifestations make up the core of this volume and include E. F. Benson, Algernon Blackwood, Marjorie Bowen, Walter de la Mare, Lord Dunsany, Robert Hichens, William Hope Hodgson, Vernon Lee, Oliver Onions, Forrest Reid, M. P. Shiel, James Stephens, and Charles Williams. This volume also contains several novelists with a more peripheral interest in the nether world, such as William de Morgan, Arthur Quiller-Couch,

and R. H. Benson. Even in this category there were other novelists that might have been represented, such as George Griffith and Barry Pain.

However, the great diversity of fictional genre within the work of these psychical novelists and the period itself are worthy of exploration, and thus all of the trends mentioned above, from "New Woman" novelists to "unpleasant fiction," are represented in this volume and in the Second Series. An important concern was to be sensitive to the Zeitgeist, to try and represent those writers considered significant by the public and the critics (preferably both) of the time. This accounts for the inclusion of several best-selling novelists who produced more than one novel that created a sensation (though only their most famous or infamous, as the case may be, are listed). In this volume they include E. F. Benson (*Dodo*, 1893), Warwick Deeping (*Sorrell and Son*, 1925), George du Maurier (*Trilby*, 1894), Elinor Glyn (*Three Weeks*, 1907), Beatrice Harraden (*Ships that Pass in the Night*, 1893), Robert Hichens (*The Green Carnation*, 1894, and *The Garden of Allah*, 1904), Anthony Hope (*The Prisoner of Zenda*, 1894), Henry de Vere Stacpoole (*The Blue Lagoon*, 1908), and P. C. Wren (*Beau Geste*, 1924). The commercial leaders of these were probably Harraden's *Ships that Pass in the Night*, which reputedly sold over a million copies, and Hichens's *The Garden of Allah*, which sold over eight hundred thousand copies and was filmed three times, in an age when five thousand copies was considered a good run.

Which novelists did contemporary critics feel would endure? At the close of these years W. L. George opined in *A Novelist on Novels* (1918) that the following would occupy the positions of Bennett, Conrad, Galsworthy, Hardy, and Wells in twenty years: J. D. Beresford, Gilbert Cannan, E. M. Forster, D. H. Lawrence, Compton Mackenzie, Oliver Onions, and Frank Swinnerton. His opinion was reinforced six years later by Abel Chevalley in *The Modern English Novel*. Of the three novelists — Beresford, Cannan, and Onions — not covered in earlier *DLB* volumes, one has been included here and two will be covered in the Second Series.

At various points in the evolution of this project, practical considerations entered into the picture. For some novelists, particularly working-class ones, a paucity of biographical information and scarcity of texts made their inclusion problematic. A host of novelists such as Clementina Black, Emma Brooke, Winifred Muriel Cory ("Winifred Graham"), Francis Gribble, John Collis Snaith, and W. E. Tirebuck fall under this rubric. This situation brings up the important issue of how the availability

of material shapes the possibility of a biography about a writer and canon formation, an issue that deserves further consideration. Even with the writers included, some contributors experienced extreme difficulty in locating information and texts. The Beatrice Harraden and Warwick Deeping entries are notable examples. For another set of novelists, such as Gilbert Frankau, Philip Hamilton Gibbs, A. S. M. Hutchinson, Charles Marriott, Ethel Colburn Mayne, Stephen McKenna, and Evelyn Underhill, contributors could not be found to complete entries. Instead, some suggestions of subjects from potential contributors were accepted, and thus to some degree the volume has been shaped by contributors' interests. Henry de Vere Stacpoole is one of these writers. In addition, novelists who are known for or who wrote only one novel were eliminated. These include George Douglas Brown (*The House With the Green Shutters*, 1901) and Ethel Voynich (*The Gadfly*, 1897).

Though the task of eliminating writers was often painful, the resulting selection works well because it illustrates significant, though in some cases previously overlooked, trends in the novel during the period; the diversity of contributions to the novel; and the fascinating and seemingly endless biographical threads linking these writers. These threads run through all types of relationships, from acquaintance through friendship, in some cases extending to mutual influence, and even love relationships. These novelists frequently echo one another, either consciously or unconsciously. Hodgson, for example, drew on Blackwood's *John Silence* (1908) for his *Carnacki, the Ghost Finder* (1913). Forrest Reid wrote a book-length critical tribute to his friend Walter de la Mare. The list could go on.

The pattern of connections extends beyond the boundaries of this volume since many of these novelists were well connected with better-known and canonized writers. Connections could be through family, as in the cases of Lucas Malet, the daughter of Charles Kingsley, and Anthony Hope, the first cousin of Kenneth Grahame, or through marriage or partnership, as in the case of Violet Hunt, Ford Madox Ford's partner, but more likely occurred through friendship.

This variety of threads, both biographical and textual, woven together constitutes the discourse of the novel during these years. To pick out and place under the magnifying glass only a few of these threads, say the novels of Bennett, Galsworthy, and Wells, is to distort perception of the richness of the fabric. It is significant that the editor has been unable to find any printed commentary which would

aptly or even adequately summarize the novel writing of the years 1890–1918. Priestley offers a particularly Edwardian and personal assessment which could act as a starting point if his time boundaries were extended. He said, "I have long believed that the decade, say 1904–13, was more richly creative than any decade since, far more representative of essentially English talent and genius." The editor's hope is that this volume will contribute to making clearer the varied results of that creativity on the novel during these years of its flourishing. It may not make possible a neat summary of the period, but it should broaden the boundaries of consideration and make the complexity, including the paradoxes and continuities, of the relationship between the novel and this culture more apparent.

– *George M. Johnson*

## Acknowledgments

This book was produced by Bruccoli Clark Layman, Inc. Karen L. Rood is senior editor for *The Dictionary of Literary Biography* series. Sam Bruce was the in-house editor.

Production coordinator is James W. Hipp. Photography editor is Bruce Andrew Bowlin. Photographic copy work was performed by Joseph M. Bruccoli. Layout and graphics supervisor is Penney L. Haughton. Copyediting supervisor is Laurel M. Gladden. Typesetting supervisor is Kathleen M. Flanagan. Systems manager is George F. Dodge. Julie E. Frick is editorial associate. The production staff includes Phyllis A. Avant, Charles D. Brower, Ann M. Cheschi, Melody W. Clegg, Patricia Coate, Denise W. Edwards, Joyce Fowler, Stephanie C. Hatchell, Erica Hennig, Rebecca Mayo, Kathy Lawler Merlette, Jeff Miller, Pamela D. Norton, Laura S. Pleicones, Emily R. Sharpe, William L. Thomas Jr., and Jonathan B. Watterson.

Walter W. Ross and Robert S. McConnell did library research. They were assisted by the following librarians at the Thomas Cooper Library of the University of South Carolina: Linda Holderfield and the interlibrary-loan staff; reference-department head Virginia Weathers; reference librarians Marilee Birchfield, Stefanie Buck, Cathy Eckman, Rebecca Feind, Jill Holman, Karen Joseph, Jean Rhyne, Kwamine Washington, and Connie Widney; circulation-department head Caroline Taylor; and acquisitions-searching supervisor David Haggard.

The publishers acknowledge the unparalleled generosity of William R. Cagle, director of the Lilly Library, Indiana University, who provided many of the illustrations that enhance this volume.

The editor would like to express his gratitude to John Ferns for his encouragement throughout the project. Thanks also to Deborah Morrison, whose second set of eyes helped greatly with the editing and proofreading, and whose commitment to the project extended well beyond her position as a work-study student. For very helpful comments on a draft of the introduction, the editor would like to thank Pat Srebrnik, as well as several colleagues at the University College of the Cariboo: Annette Dominik, David Keppel-Jones, Genevieve Later, Gail McKay, Joan Weir, and Mervyn Nicholson (who also revised the late George Woodcock's entry on W. H. Hudson). Finally, sincere thanks to all of the contributors for their fine essays, their patience, and their suggestions for illustrations. The variety of perspectives and of locales from which they wrote – including all parts of Canada and the United States, Britain, France, Portugal, and Australia – appropriately reflects the variety of fiction and lives they so carefully analyzed.

# Late-Victorian and Edwardian British Novelists
## First Series

# Dictionary of Literary Biography

# E. F. Benson
## (24 July 1867 – 29 February 1940)

Catriona de Scossa
*University of Alberta, Canada*

See also the Benson entry in *DLB 135: British Short-Fiction Writers, 1880–1914: The Realist Tradition.*

BOOKS: *Dodo: A Detail of the Day,* 2 volumes (London: Methuen, 1893; New York: Appleton, 1893);

*Six Common Things* (London: Osgood McIlvaine, 1893);

*The Rubicon* (London: Methuen, 1893; New York: Appleton, 1893);

*A Double Overture* (Chicago: Sergel, 1894);

*The Judgement Books* (London: Osgood McIlvaine, 1895; New York: Harper, 1895);

*Limitations* (London: Innes, 1896; New York: Harper, 1896);

*The Babe, B.A.* (New York: Putnam, 1896; London: Putnam, 1897);

*The Vintage* (London: Methuen, 1898; New York: Harper, 1898);

*The Money Market* (Bristol: Arrowsmith, 1898; Philadelphia: Biddle, 1898);

*The Capsina* (London: Methuen, 1899; New York: Harper, 1899);

*Mammon & Co.* (London: Heinemann, 1899; New York: Appleton, 1899);

*The Princess Sophia* (London: Heinemann, 1900; New York: Harper, 1900);

*The Luck of the Vails* (London: Heinemann, 1901; New York: Appleton, 1901);

*Scarlet and Hyssop* (London: Heinemann, 1902; New York: Appleton, 1902);

*Daily Training,* by Benson and E. H. Miles (London: Hurst & Blackett, 1902; New York: Dutton, 1903);

*The Book of Months* (London: Heinemann, 1903; New York: Harper, 1903);

*The Valkyries* (London: Dean, 1903; Boston: L. C. Page, 1905);

*The Relentless City* (London: Heinemann, 1903; New York: Harper, 1903);

*An Act in a Backwater* (London: Heinemann, 1903; New York: Appleton, 1903);

*The Challoners* (London: Heinemann, 1904; Philadelphia: Lippincott, 1904);

*Diversions by Day,* by Benson and Miles (London: Hurst & Blackett, 1905);

*The Angel of Pain* (Philadelphia: Lippincott, 1905; London: Heinemann, 1906);

*The Image in the Sands* (London: Heinemann, 1905; Philadelphia: Lippincott, 1905);

*Paul* (London: Heinemann, 1906; Philadelphia: Lippincott, 1906);

*The House of Defence* (New York: Authors & Newspapers Association, 1906; London: Heinemann, 1907);

*Sheaves* (New York: Doubleday, 1907; London: Heinemann, 1908);

*The Blotting Book* (London: Heinemann, 1908; New York: Doubleday, 1908);

*English Figure Skating* (London: Bell, 1908);

*The Climber* (London: Heinemann, 1908; New York: Doubleday, 1909);

*A Reaping* (London: Heinemann, 1909; New York: Doubleday, 1909);

*Daisy's Aunt* (London: Nelson, 1910); published as *The Fascinating Mrs. Halton* (New York: Doubleday, 1910);

*Margery* (New York: Doubleday, 1910);

*The Osbornes* (London: Smith & Elder, 1910; New York: Doubleday, 1910);

*Juggernaut* (London: Heinemann, 1911);

*E. F. Benson, circa 1893 (photograph by Russell and Sons)*

*Account Rendered* (London: Heinemann, 1911; New York: Doubleday, 1911);

*Bensoniana* (London: Humphries, 1912);

*Mrs. Ames* (London: Hodder & Stoughton, 1912; New York: Doubleday, 1912);

*The Room in the Tower and Other Stories* (London: Mills & Boon, 1912; New York: Knopf, 1929);

*Winter Sports in Switzerland* (London: G. Allen, 1913; New York: Dodd, Mead, 1913);

*The Weaker Vessel* (London: Heinemann, 1913; New York: Dodd, Mead, 1913);

*Dodo's Daughter* (New York: Century, 1913);

*Thorley Weir* (London: Smith & Elder, 1913; Philadelphia: Lippincott, 1913);

*Dodo the Second* (London & New York: Hodder & Stoughton, 1914);

*Arundel* (London: Unwin, 1914; New York: Doran, 1915);

*The Oakleyites* (London: Hodder & Stoughton, 1915; New York: Doran, 1915);

*David Blaize* (London: Hodder & Stoughton, 1916; New York: Doran, 1916);

*Mike* (London: Cassell, 1916); published as *Michael* (New York: Doran, 1916);

*The Freaks of Mayfair* (London: Foulis, 1916; New York: Doran, 1917);

*Deutschland über Allah* (London: Hodder & Stoughton, 1917);

*An Autumn Sowing* (London: Collins, 1917; New York: Doran, 1918);

*Mr. Teddy* (London: Unwin, 1917); published as *The Tortoise* (New York: Doran, 1917);

*Poland and Mittel-Europa* (New York & London: Hodder & Stoughton, 1918);

*Up and Down* (London: Hutchinson, 1918; New York: Doran, 1918);

*The White Eagle of Poland* (London: Hodder & Stoughton, 1918; New York: Doran, 1919);

*Crescent and Iron Cross* (London: Hodder & Stoughton, 1918; New York: Doran, 1918);

*David Blaize and the Blue Door* (London: Hodder & Stoughton, 1918; New York: Doran, 1919);

*Robin Linnet* (London: Hutchinson, 1919; New York: Doran, 1919);

*Across the Stream* (London: John Murray, 1919; New York: Doran, 1919);

*The Countess of Lowndes Square and Other Stories* (London & New York: Cassell, 1920);

*Queen Lucia* (London: Hutchinson, 1920; New York: Doran, 1920);

*Our Family Affairs 1867–1896* (London: Cassell, 1920; New York: Doran, 1921);

*Lovers and Friends* (London: Unwin, 1921; New York: Doran, 1921);

*Dodo Wonders* (London: Hutchinson, 1921; New York: Doran, 1921);

*Miss Mapp* (London: Hutchinson, 1922; New York: Doran, 1923);

*Peter* (London: Cassell, 1922; New York: Doran, 1922);

*Colin* (London: Hutchinson, 1923; New York: Doran, 1923);

*And the Dead Spake – , and the Horror-Horn* (New York: Doran, 1923);

*Visible and Invisible* (London: Hutchinson, 1923; New York: Doubleday, 1924);

*Expiation, and Naboth's Vineyard* (New York: Doran, 1924);

*The Face* (New York: Doran, 1924);

*Spinach and Reconciliation* (New York: Doran, 1924);

*David of King's* (London: Hodder & Stoughton, 1924); published as *David Blaize of King's* (New York: Doran, 1924);

*Alan* (London: Unwin, 1924; New York: Doran, 1925);

*Mother* (London: Hodder & Stoughton, 1925; New York: Doran, 1925);

*A Tale of an Empty House, and Bagnell Terrace* (New York: Doran, 1925);

*The Temple* (New York: Doran, 1925);

*Rex* (London: Hodder & Stoughton, 1925; New York: Doran, 1925);

*Colin II* (London: Hutchinson, 1925; New York: Doran, 1925);

*Mezzanine* (London: Cassell, 1926; New York: Doran, 1926);

*Pharisees and Publicans* (London: Hutchinson, 1926; New York: Doran, 1927);

*Sir Francis Drake* (London: John Lane, 1927; New York: Harper, 1927);

*Lucia in London* (London: Hutchinson, 1927; New York: Doubleday, 1928);

*Spook Stories* (London: Hutchinson, 1928);

*The Life of Alcibiades* (London: Benn, 1928; New York: Appleton, 1929);

*Paying Guests* (London: Hutchinson, 1929; New York: Doubleday, 1929);

*The Male Impersonator* (London: Mathews & Marrot, 1929);

*Ferdinand Magellan* (London: Lane, 1929; New York: Harper, 1930);

*As We Were: A Victorian Peep Show* (London & New York: Longmans, Green, 1930);

*The Step* (London: Marrot, 1930);

*The Inheritor* (London: Hutchinson, 1930; New York: Doubleday, 1930);

*Mapp and Lucia* (London: Hodder & Stoughton, 1931; New York: Doubleday, 1931);

*Charlotte Brontë* (London & New York: Longmans, Green, 1932);

*Secret Lives* (London: Hodder & Stoughton, 1932; New York: Doubleday, 1932);

*As We Are: A Modern Revue* (London & New York: Longmans, Green, 1932);

*King Edward VII: An Appreciation* (London & New York: Longman, 1933);

*Travail of Gold* (London: Hodder & Stoughton, 1933; New York: Doubleday, 1933);

*The Outbreak of War 1914* (London: Davies, 1933; New York: Putnam, 1934);

*More Spook Stories* (London: Hutchinson, 1934);

*Ravens' Brood* (London: Barker, 1934; New York: Doubleday, 1934);

*Queen Victoria* (London & New York: Longmans, Green, 1935);

*Lucia's Progress* (London: Hodder & Stoughton, 1935); published as *The Worshipful Lucia* (New York: Doubleday, 1935);

*The Kaiser and English Relations* (London & New York: Longmans, Green, 1936);

*Old London,* 4 volumes (New York: Appleton-Century, 1937);

*Queen Victoria's Daughters* (New York: Appleton-Century, 1938); published as *Daughters of Queen Victoria* (London: Cassell, 1939);

*Trouble for Lucia* (London: Hodder & Stoughton, 1939; New York: Doubleday, 1939);

*Final Edition: Informal Autobiography* (London: Longmans, Green, 1940; New York: Appleton-Century, 1940);

*The Horror Horn and Other Stories,* edited by Alexis Lykiard (London: Panther, 1974);

*Desirable Residences and Other Stories* (Oxford: Oxford University Press, 1991).

PLAY PRODUCTIONS (full dates and theaters not available): *Aunt Jeannie,* New York, 1902;

*Dodo: A Detail of Yesterday,* London, 1905;

*The Friend in the Garden,* London, 1906;

*Westward Ho!,* London, 1913;

*Dinner for Eight,* London, 1915;

*Benson as a prep-school student, circa 1886*

*The Luck of the Vails,* Eastbourne and London, 1928.

OTHER: *A Book of Golf,* edited by Benson and E. H. Miles (London: Hurst & Blackett, 1903; New York: Dutton, 1903);

*The Cricket of Able, Hirst, and Shrewsbury,* edited by Benson and Miles (London: Hurst & Blackett, 1903; New York: Dutton, 1903);

Henry James, *Henry James: Letters to A. C. Benson and Auguste Monod,* edited by Benson (London: Mathews & Marrot, 1930; New York: Scribners, 1930).

In the last two decades of the twentieth century, it seems certain that more people on both sides of the Atlantic have seen E. F. (Edward Frederic) Benson's best-known characters, Emmeline "Lucia" Lucas and Elizabeth Mapp, than have read about them. In 1984–1985 Benson's *Mapp and Lucia* (1931) was adapted for British television's Channel 4 by Gerald Savory. The reading and viewing experiences do not coincide. Benson's miniaturist talent

for delineating character, with much less attention to plot and action, does not translate well to a medium where "talking heads" are best avoided. His masterly use of conversation, often expertly contradicted by the same characters' simultaneous interior monologues, largely vanishes on screen. To replace it tends to produce frenetic activity verging on slapstick, something to which Benson seldom stoops. Even faithful dramatic adaptation of such a small part of Benson's work hardly makes it more than superficially available, and scholarly interest in his oeuvre has only recently begun to appear. To some extent this is hardly surprising, given the flood of words Benson wrote throughout his adult life.

Benson's prodigious output consists mostly of novels in many styles: sentimental; seriocomic; melodramatic; and satiric. Sometimes he combines several styles, with varying degrees of success. He wrote school stories, ghost stories, plays, sporting texts, and volumes of autobiography and biography. To complicate the huge task of critically assess-

ing Benson's work is the fact that a large institutional audience consisting of subscription and circulating libraries and for whom Benson specifically wrote novels is now obsolete. Nevertheless, there seems little question that Benson merits an honorable, if modest, place in the history of traditional English literature. There is also a sense that Benson's reputation may grow, both on the merits of his work and on its place in literary history.

Edward Frederic Benson was born on 24 July 1867, the fifth child and third son of Mary "Minnie" Sidgwick, called "the cleverest woman in Europe" by William Gladstone, and Edward White Benson, a classical scholar who began his career as the first headmaster of the public school in Wellington and went on to become the archbishop of Canterbury. The connection with Gladstone continued, and Archbishop Benson died on his knees during the General Confession at a service held in Hawarden Church, with the Gladstones kneeling beside him.

Benson's father told Minnie's parents that he wished eventually to marry her, when she was eleven. He was twenty-three. He proposed to her when she was twelve, as she sat on his knee. He was accepted. They were married when Minnie was eighteen, and they eventually had six children. Two of them died: Martin in his teens, and Nellie in her twenties, both unmarried. None of the four remaining children married, nor did they ever seem inclined to. All, except Fred, as E. F. was called by family members, preferred to associate with members of their own sex. So, ultimately, did Mrs. Benson, who, after her husband's death, shared her house and her bed with Lucy Tait, the daughter of the archbishop of Canterbury who had preceded Archbishop Benson.

Benson remembered his childhood as being happy. He often claimed that he enjoyed prep school in Marlborough and King's College, Cambridge. He spent most of 1892–1895 as an archeologist in Greece, continuing one of his many childhood interests. When Cambridge could no longer afford to finance Benson's digs, at his father's behest he applied to be either a school examiner or inspector for the Education Office – he later forgot precisely which. Inertia rather than action characterized the Office, and nothing came of the application. Fred had hurriedly written and then more carefully revised his first novel, *Dodo: A Detail of the Day* (1893). It proved remarkably successful. So Benson began a career as a writer, something for which he had always hoped.

*Dodo* was published while Benson was in Greece, where he was working on a dig. The author was amazed at its success, and so, possibly, were Henry James and Lucas Malet (Mrs. Harrison). Both had, at Benson's mother's plea, read *Dodo*. To James the work was submitted in massive, entangled manuscript copy, complete with blots, interpolations, and erasures. James was kind but essentially dismissive, and he commented that typewritten copy was the norm for manuscript submissions to publishers. Benson put his novel aside for a time and then sent it to Malet, who wrote him several letters effectively explaining how to write a novel. He used her advice, and *Dodo* became a popular, if not a critical, success. Much of this success seems to have sprung from the fact that the novel was, as Benson phrases it in *Our Family Affairs 1867–1896* (1920), "frankly unepiscopal." Further, it was alleged to be a roman à clef, a send-up of smart society. Margot Asquith and Lady Desborough were among the best-known supposed originals, along with Lady Desborough's arty-artistic group, the Souls, which Evelyn Waugh later parodied in his *Helena* (1950).

*Dodo* was so successful that it went into several editions in its first year and created an entirely unexpected publishing boom. Benson wrote two sequels. *Dodo the Second* (1914) was read by more critics, but though warmly and largely gently received, it did not experience the success of its predecessor. The third volume, *Dodo Wonders* (1921), was given a tepid welcome. A reviewer in the *Times Literary Supplement* of 3 March 1921 suggested that neither Dodo the woman nor the subject matter of the novel had aged well. The review perceptively pointed out that Benson "had the power of hitting off a fool," something that is true in much of his fiction. In 1978 the three Dodo volumes were collected in one volume, and once again there was only modest critical attention.

Benson dramatized *Dodo* in 1905. Judging by a review in the *Times Literary Supplement* dated 1 December 1905, the Stage Society's production was a well-acted performance of a failed play in the outmoded "teacup and saucer" school of comedy invented by T. W. Robertson. The review concludes that *Dodo* "is a story of puerile commonplace handled without a trace of theatrical skill. The meaningless 'patter' of its dialogue amused for five minutes and then became wearisome. Dodoism is that coldest of dead things, a discarded fashion – not to be warmed up again into life by any number of cups of tea."

Benson's second novel, *The Rubicon* (1893), did not catch the reviewers unaware. In retrospect, Benson considered it a poor book. As if to make up for

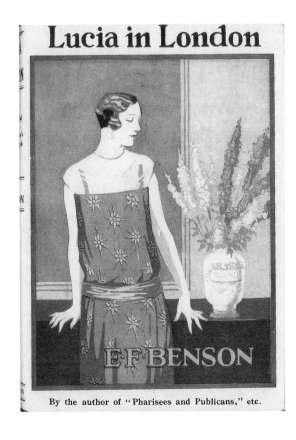

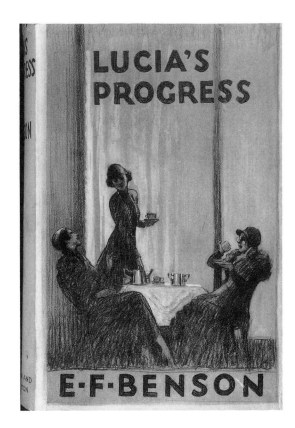

*Dust jackets for three of the Mapp and Lucia novels, the most widely read of all Benson's works (courtesy of the Lilly Library, Indiana University)*

the neglect of *Dodo,* reviewers fell upon *The Rubicon* like wolves and tore it to shreds, retroactively mauling *Dodo,* too. Eva Hayes, *The Rubicon*'s heroine, was seen to be in the worst of vulgar taste, her character and the plot a dull rehashing of the gutter-bound and tasteless *Dodo.* Only the *St. James's Budget* found a few kind words to say to the author: "our thanks are due to him for one thing: his book consists of only two volumes; it might have been three."

Benson was so caught up in his multifarious activities, so happy to move on to each new undertaking, that he scarcely seemed to have felt the pain such reviews might have caused. His own opinions of his work affected him more deeply. In *Final Edition: Informal Autobiography* (1940) he relates his experience of rereading some of his earlier works:

> I observed with a certain acuteness, but not with insight. I made my people bustle about, indulge in what may be called "stock" experiences, talk with a rather brilliant plausibility, but, as a depressed perusal of some of my own volumes convinced me, they lacked the red corpuscle.... I despised sentimentality in other writers. I looked upon it as a deliberate fake yet whenever I got in a difficulty I used it unblushingly myself. Perhaps the most damning evidence against me was that I had quite forgotten what many of these books were about, and now that I read some of them again they roused not the faintest gleam of recollection.... They did not interest me, and I felt that I should very soon forget them again. Accordingly, I pronounced myself guilty, as regards a horrid large number of these. But in the case of some of these books, I pleaded not guilty and was willing to go into the witness box on oath, and be cross-examined. A novel called *Sheaves* [1907] was one, *The Luck of the Vails* [1901] was another; *The Climber* [1908] was a third, and a school story, *David Blaize* [1916]. Into these – there may have been one or two more which I have forgotten – I had put emotional imagination. That most of them were out of print did not concern me. I had chosen to be a writer, and on these occasions I had done my best.

The four novels Benson names cover a fifteen-year period, and their subject matter and styles are various. Though they remain out of print, they make an interesting group of early novels to examine. Given the enormous range of possibilities from which to choose, Benson's own assessment is as valid a reason as another for picking these works.

*The Luck of the Vails* is the story of a cursed family treasure, somewhat in the style of Wilkie Collins, but lacking his strong characterizations and his sense of pervasive doom and impending death. Perhaps the period in which it is set, the turn of the nineteenth century, works to its disadvantage, lacking the vigor of Collins's historical time. The Luck is an ironically named golden goblet set with precious stones, bearing a motto that makes it plain that it will bring ill fortune even to rightful owners, in the shapes of fires, frosts, and water. Its current owner is young Harry Vail, typical of Benson's "serious" heroes. He is handsome, fairly mature for his years, clear-eyed, in perfect health, tall, and, to the present-day reader, rather dull and flat. The novel's melodramatic form and sentimental style sit unhappily together.

Harry discovers the hidden goblet and shows it to his great-uncle Francis with deferential excitement. Uncle Francis, who is the insane villain of the piece, also ensures that the Luck will do its worst. The worst proves insufficiently damaging for a man of Harry's quality, for though he suffers and is endangered, he survives. Manly but gentle, when he discovers the truth about Uncle Francis's plottings, "the truth, bitter and burning as vitriol, ate into the poor lad's brain." Comforted by his friend Geoffrey Langham, he gives way to appropriate weeping. " 'Geoff, Geoff!' he said, and the blessed relief of tears came to him." There is generally an awkward and embarrassing quality to the theatrics of the final pages. To prevent the Luck working its potential evil, though Francis's fate seems to render this unlikely, Vail destroys the Luck as if he were crushing "the life out of some personal creeping horror." The reader is then informed that "the curse is gone from the house." Overlong, overwritten, and possessing only mild incident and suspense, *The Luck of the Vails* has not worn well, and the reader could wish Benson's opinion of it had been more explicit. Its melodramatic plot, high seriousness, and entire lack of humor jar. The vigor of Benson's comic work is missing.

*Sheaves* (1907) offers an even more bizarre blend: a mawkishly sentimental love story, which *The New York Times* of 12 October 1907 called the "lyric joy of love," combined with comedy that prefigures the Lucia stories. Hugh Grainger is a childish rather than childlike heroic tenor who would rather play games with his nieces and nephews than discipline his extraordinary talent. He finally gives a glorious performance in Germany as the title character of Richard Wagner's *Lohengrin* (1850). His love for and marriage to the much older and sadder Edith Allbutt, who secretly writes daring plays as Andrew Robb, brings about this near miracle. Unknown to Hugh, Edith is dying of both a weak heart and consumption. She recovers slightly in the bracing air of Davos, where, as she lies on her balcony, Hugh and Edith's sister, Lady Rye (Peggy), along with other relatives, enjoy the scenic countryside of the Alps. Benson devotes several pages to skating,

*Lamb House in Rye, East Sussex, once the residence of Henry James. In 1919 Benson leased the house, which became the model for Mallards, Elizabeth Mapp's home in the popular Mapp and Lucia novels.*

at which he excelled, and to describing scenes reminiscent of holidays he spent in Switzerland with his family.

As winter leaves Davos, Hugh becomes bored. Edith persuades him to return to England to continue his singing and see their child. Soon after he arrives, however, disaster strikes. The mountain air, good for Edith's lungs, proves dangerous for her heart. A fatal telegram recalls Hugh to Davos in time for his wife to breathe her last in his arms. They have just exchanged Wagnerian words of love in two languages – "*Meine Seele!*" "My soul and my heart!"

An uneasy comedy infiltrates the novel in the characters of Mrs. Gladys Owen and Canon Alington. Mrs. Owen is the president of the Mannington Literary and Scientific Society (known to Canon as the Literific). She is also the frequent performer of the song "Galahad's 'Good Night' " (words and music by Mrs. Owen) and a connoisseur of the arts, though she tends not to know Titian from Tintoret. A woman about town several times a year, who has been four times to Venice, she always brings her music to parties and delights in troublemaking gossip of her own invention. Canon Alington is a contributing member of the Literific. His study contains innumerable, neatly labeled geological specimens used as paperweights; golf balls; a pipe collection in a fumed oak rack carved to represent a Gothic window; and an eclectic and extensive quantity of great art in reproduction. He is also Hugh's brother-in-law.

*Sheaves* shows that Benson, rather like Handel (whom he admired), was a borrower and recycler of his own work. Peggy somehow makes a seasick passenger out of an orange, a feat emulated by Diva Plaistow in *Mapp and Lucia,* though Diva has the art so perfected that, lacking oranges, "a ripe tomato would serve the purpose." If *Sheaves* is of literary value today, it is because it shows the early development of a central character in Benson's later work. The novel is also of interest because it almost certainly contains portraits of Benson and of his adored mother.

With the exception of Minnie, all the Bensons suffered in varying degrees from clinical depression. The archbishop was subject to frequent and long periods of black depression, devastating to himself and a source of terror to his children when they were small. Maggie, Benson's favorite sister, was driven to institutionalized insanity by her ever-deepening gloom. Arthur sank frequently into bleak, desperate inertia and, when recovered, wrote even more voluminously than Fred. Hugh, in spite of his ardent Catholic faith, drank to dispel the misery. Fred was either the least affected, or, by luck or good management, seemed to have used his enormous physical and mental energy to live as fully and happily as possible. He was athletic until arthritis in old age made even walking painful; he loved music; he had many excellent if not tremendously close friends; above all he wrote. If his account in *Sheaves* of Edith's writing reflects his own case, writing seems to have been his salvation. The character claims that the act of writing "really kept me alive and sane. . . . I think I must have gone mad otherwise. But the bringing to birth of that child of one's brain kept me alive."

Benson fought his debilitating disease and understood happiness, which he saw personified in his mother. His description of the character Peggy echoes his many descriptions of his mother: "[Peggy] had formed the excellent habit of enjoying herself quite enormously, without damage to others – an attitude toward life which is more to be desired than gold. It was, in fact, a large part of her gospel; with her whole nature, pleasant and mirthful and greatly alive, she passionately wanted people to be happy. It seemed to her the ideal attitude toward normal life, and she practised it herself." *Sheaves* may have been dear to Benson for reasons other than being a fine novel, for it clearly is not. But he was beginning to discover and develop a comic métier.

Benson habitually wrote for his readers rather than for reviewers or critics. He and his publishers engaged in an early version of surveying the market and meeting the market's demand, rather than imposing an authorial form and style on readers. He was not an innovator like Virginia Woolf or James Joyce; in fact, he actively, if humorously, rejected their ideas. In *Trouble for Lucia* (1939), the title character is in the midst of a disastrous day and thinks, "There seemed to be material for another huge horrid book by Mr. James Joyce before the day was done."

With *The Climber* Benson changed his approach again and wrote a moral tale of human wrongdoing, retribution, the loving friendship of a virtuous companion, and a poor but honest aunt triumphing over social disaster. Lucia Grimson, a Girton-educated social climber of modest accomplishments and great beauty, wishes to scale the social ladder. Lucia steals Lord Brayton from her good friend, Maud Eddis. She marries him but soon becomes bored with everything but his money and his property and begins to gamble, losing large sums of money at bridge. Lucia's boredom also leads to her attempt to seduce Maud's husband, who succumbs in mind if not in deed. Maud forgives Lucia immediately and her husband eventually. Lord Brayton is more self-righteous. He divorces Lucia, who is taken in by her Aunt Cathie. Lucia the climber had reached a modest peak of wealthy high society for the duration of her marriage, but after being divorced she returns to the life of boring, genteel provincialism she knew as a child. None of her experiences leave any mark on her self-interested character, but Lucia is strongly and roundly portrayed by Benson, as is Aunt Cathie, though the other characters, major and minor, are ciphers.

Before *The Climber* was published Benson tested popular reaction to a section of the work. A short story, "The Puce Silk," appeared in the November 1907 issue of *Lady's Realm*. It is an almost verbatim version of a cruelly humorous scene between Aunt Cathie and Lucia, who is horrified by her aunt's vibrantly colored evening dress.

Benson's short stories appeared in a wide variety of periodicals, among them the *Illustrated London News, Pearson's,* the *Windsor Magazine,* and women's magazines such as *Good Housekeeping* and *Woman.* He managed to appear in the famous *Strand Magazine* only once. The editors of that periodical preferred the more carefully plotted romantic and sentimental stories of Ethel M. Dell and Warwick Deeping to Benson's, with their often tenuous or absent plots and richness of description and conversation.

Readers and reviewers alike on both sides of the Atlantic praised *David Blaize.* The reader of the 1990s might be more inclined to respond as did the critic of the dramatic version of *Dodo.* What was pathetic, jolly, and true in 1916 has become bathetic and self-parodic to the point of embarrassment. This sense is the opposite of Benson's clearly intended purpose in the work.

The novel's eponymous hero passes almost painlessly through his prep school, Helmsworth, and proceeds to Marchester, Benson's fictional version of Marlborough. There he suffers only the pain of two beatings, laid on with justice and humanity by the headmaster and by his beloved erstwhile

*Benson at his desk, circa 1935 (Hulton-Deutsch Collection)*

fagmaster, Frank Maddox. Maddox is Blaize's idol and ideal. He is an athletic intellectual, bedecked with house colors and caps for every conceivable sport, who goes on to become a Cambridge scholar and blue. Maddox's overpowering moral rectitude and incessant good cheer pall rapidly. His trouble stems from the fact that he apparently realizes, but refuses to act on the fact that he is in love with the invariably ignorant and innocent David. Recovered, Maddox, or Frank as the boys and his housemaster call him, teaches David the finer points of rackets, not to use cribs to translate Greek and Latin texts, to appreciate the poetry of Swinburne but to appreciate *Oedipus Coloneus* more. Frank also protects David morally and physically from intellectual damage or contamination by "filth." Benson as a small boy had been briefly believed to have been involved with filth, interpreted as homosexuality, but made it obvious to his first headmaster that he was, in body and mind, innocent and baffled.

The relationship between David and Frank, with the dimmer but faithful satellite, Bags, is summed up in the closing scenes of the novel. In chapel the headmaster requests, as the service proceeds, that everyone pray for David Blaize, who has been seriously injured while halting a runaway horse and cart. Frank, having heard the news, has returned from Cambridge. He sits by the boy's bed all night, holding David's hand, his own hand and arm increasingly painful then numb, insisting that David sleep healingly. In the morning David wakes and demands food, suggesting that all will be well.

If variety and unevenness of quality and content mark these four early novels, they serve to emphasize the value of considering them as examples of the first and essentially fictional phase of Ben-

son's work. The second phase began four years after *David Blaize* appeared, with the novel *Queen Lucia* (1920), the first of six in the Lucia series, and the memoir *Our Family Affairs (1867–1896)*. The latter is a vivid, affectionate, and amusing account of the Benson family from the year of the author's birth to his father's death in 1896. Disinterested biography is the great development that constitutes Benson's third phase, marked by the publication of *Sir Francis Drake* (1927), one of a series commissioned from several authors by the Bodley Head.

The novels in the Lucia series are *Queen Lucia*; *Miss Mapp* (1922); *Lucia in London* (1927); *Mapp and Lucia*; *Lucia's Progress* (1935); and *Trouble for Lucia*. They remain in print and are the most widely read of all Benson's work. In addition to the series of novels, there are two extant short stories in the Mapp and Lucia canon. "The Male Impersonator" (1929) has often been published with *Miss Mapp*. "Desirable Residences" (1929), published first in the February 1929 *Good Housekeeping* (U.K.), was first collected in *Desirable Residences and Other Stories* (1991). The story is an account of house swapping in Tilling, fully developed later in *Mapp and Lucia*.

These comedies blend satire, occasional farce, and near slapstick. They have slender continuing plots and historical sequence and begin with Lucia as prima donna in two novels, allowing Mapp her moment of solo virtuosity once; the last three depict a battle for power, with Mapp almost always the "undercat."

Emmeline Lucas, called Lucia, as wife of Mr. Lucas, lives in the picture-book village of Riseholme, named for Benson's childhood paradise. It was the home of Bishop Charles Wordsworth, whom the Bensons visited when Benson *père* was Chancellor of Lincoln. Lucia is "culture" incarnate, like Gladys Owen. She is also an organizer of terrifyingly efficient ineptitude. Artist, actress, director-producer, archeologist, pianist, and linguist, Lucia's boundaries seem limitless. In addition she practices, usually briefly, yoga, calisthenics, and skipping. She plays golf and bridge, makes cycling the rage locally, seeks to reestablish Elizabethan customs, and is an exponent of the psychic arts. Lucia's version of "Galahad's 'Good Night' " is the slow movement of Beethoven's "Moonlight" Sonata.

Georgie Pillson is Lucia's neighbor, confidant, semislave, and finally, after Pepino Lucas's death, her platonic, virgin husband. He is nearly as rich as she and as reliant on his maid, but he is much more generous in both cases. Besides joining Lucia in matrimony, Georgie speaks limited Italian and baby-talk with her, plays the dull or difficult parts in piano duets, and, always, is second fiddle. He does have personal passions – for his carefully dusted bibelots, embroidery, and dashing clothes over pretty underwear. He has a similar number of terrors. He fears that his toupee will become dislodged and therefore discovered (though its existence is already common knowledge). He lives in dread that his precious maid, Foljambe, will desert him. Above all he fears that sex will raise its appalling head. Balancing this fear is Georgie's enduring, utterly chaste *grande passion* for Olga Bracely, a world-famous diva. This relationship is unique in Lucia's world, for Georgie and Olga also share a naughtily generous friendship based on humor, honesty, and good-heartedness. Nonetheless both Georgie and Olga find their mutual pleasure enhanced by Lucia's evident jealousy.

Through Olga, Benson was able to express his real pleasure in and understanding of music, which is the antithesis of Lucia's. Olga is often the cause of Lucia's cultural collapses, when, as with Gladys Owen and her painters, she cannot identify a tune. Olga is amused by Lucia as Hugh Grainger had been by Mrs. Owen, and she joins the group of Lucia fans who appear fictionally in *Lucia in London*. This group expanded into real life. Noel Coward, Gertrude Lawrence, Nancy Mitford and W. H. Auden were all members of the clan – Auden took so much pleasure in Lucia that he included a passage from *Lucia's Progress* in his *A Certain World: A Commonplace Book* (1971).

Riseholme had a large cast of characters that vanished almost entirely after Benson conceived of Elizabeth Mapp and moved Lucia and Georgie to Mapp's town, Tilling. Tilling is based on Rye, Benson's home from 1920 on, when he took up residence in Lamb House, which had belonged to Henry James. Rye's Tillingham River gave Benson the name for Mapp's little town. Benson transforms Lamb House into "Mallards," owned by Mapp until she is ousted by the new owner, Lucia. As though to compensate herself, Mapp, distinctly past youth, marries Maj. Benjamin Flint, a blustery Hindi-shouting veteran of implausible tiger hunts. She reduces him to Benjy-boy Mapp-Flint, kept on short alcoholic commons and briefly, but impossibly, the progenitor of Mapp's phantom pregnancy.

Tilling's inhabitants are even stranger and more entertaining than the Riseholmites. They reappear in the three further novels in the series. There is Godiva Plaistow, dog lover, tea-shop owner, avid consumer of nougat chocolates, and Mapp's sartorial nemesis. Her first name is so embarrassing in its associations that she is known only

*Dust jacket for Benson's last book (courtesy of the Lilly Library, Indiana University)*

as Diva. There are the Wyses: Susan is dazzlingly rich and grotesquely attached to a budgerigar, which she wears, stuffed, after its untimely death. She is married to Algernon Wyse, whose dress sense rivals Georgie's and whose sister is married to an Italian count. There is also Irene, the pipe-smoking, breeches-wearing artist who swears, spits, paints nudes while nude herself, and develops a massive *Schwärm* for Lucia. A Scots-speaking padre from Birmingham and his wife, who squeaks, mouselike, when shocked or excited, complete the cast of principals.

Food figures largely in the Lucia novels and was the cause of one of Benson's most antic escapades for Mapp and Lucia. In *Mapp and Lucia* Mapp attempts to steal Lucia's secret recipe for Lobster à la Riseholme from Lucia's kitchen at her first Tilling house, Grebe. Caught red-handed, Mapp, along with Lucia, is swept out of the kitchen, floating on a kitchen table, by a flash flood. Several months on a cod trawler serve to make the two women firm enemies. Major Benjy and Georgie erect a joint memorial to the pair and feel relieved. Late one night Georgie's blood runs cold when he hears Lucia's voice, informing him: "Me's tum home, Georgie." (Baby talk is Lucia's and Georgie's other "foreign" language.)

Reviewers tended either to love or to loathe Mapp and Lucia, but the characters found more favor at the beginning and the end of the series. By 1935 Peter Quennell had made it plain that in his view Lucia suffered the same problems as the dramatized *Dodo*. He wrote in the *New Statesman and Nation* of 23 March 1935: "It is all very diverting, faintly acid, but leaves behind it a feeling of having drunk too much China tea, played too much bridge and eaten far too many buttered scones." Traditional had, for Quennell, lapsed into reactionary.

Four years later, shortly after war was declared in Europe, M. L. Becker wrote in *Books* (24 September 1939) that "You get what you have learned to expect from these carefree, war-defying entertainments. Wodehouse and Benson are doing their respective bits to keep us smiling for the duration." Mapp and Lucia's small battles did and do provide refreshingly comic relief.

Once Mapp and Lucia appeared in Benson's fiction they quickly monopolized it. The author used most of his remaining literary power to write eight biographies. His subjects were as different as Alcibiades and Kaiser Wilhelm II. Benson's long life, his education and archeological expertise, and his personal and family contacts often enabled him to make use of previously unavailable information. Benson was the first biographer to detail the injury at birth that resulted in Kaiser Wilhelm's useless left arm, and he recounted the story again in his biographies of Queen Victoria and of Queen Victoria's daughters. In these biographies he made plain the degree to which personalities and familial likes and dislikes affected the politics of Europe from 1837 until his own time.

If Benson lacked the power to develop and sustain coherent, interesting plots in his fiction, he worked easily and intelligently with the ready-made plots of his biographies. He was anxious to steer a proper middle course between Victorian hagiography and the private revelations that he deplored in contemporary studies. Instead, he attempted to discover at least a version of truth. He detested the vagaries and omissions that marred Elizabeth Gaskell's life of Charlotte Brontë and produced his own account. Benson's primary biographical tool was humane psychological insight rather than concealment or muckraking. For Benson, as for Edmund Gosse, the mind of the novelist was ideally suited to the task of character study, which for both was the purpose of biography. Dean Dick Sheppard, the founder of the Peace Pledge Union, offers a humorous summation of Benson's place in English literary history: "I wonder why people who say their prayers don't thank God for aspirin, Phillips's patent soles, E. F. Benson, Jane Austen and Charlie Chaplin and other real soul-filling things."

**Biography:**

Brian Masters, *The Life of E. F. Benson* (London: Chatto & Windus, 1991).

**References:**

Robert F. Kiernan, *Frivolity Unbound: Six Masters of the Camp Novel* (New York: Continuum, 1990);

David Newsome, *On the Edge of Paradise: A. C. Benson: the Diarist* (Chicago: University of Chicago Press, 1980).

# Robert Hugh Benson

*(16 November 1871 – 19 October 1914)*

Francis F. Burch
*Saint Joseph's University*

BOOKS: *The Light Invisible* (London: Isbister, 1903; New York: Benziger, 1906);

*By What Authority?* (London: Isbister, 1904; New York: Benziger, 1906);

*An Alphabet of Saints,* by Benson, Reginald Balfour, and Charles Ritchie (London: Burns & Oates, [1905]);

*The King's Achievement* (London: Burns, Oates & Washbourne, 1905; Saint Louis: Herder, 1905);

*The Religion of the Plain Man* (London: Burns & Oates, 1906);

*The Conversion of England* (London: Catholic Truth Society, 1906);

*The Death-Beds of "Bloody Mary" and "Good Queen Bess,"* (London: Catholic Truth Society, 1906);

*The Queen's Tragedy* (London: Hutchinson, 1906; Saint Louis: Herder, 1906);

*The History of Richard Raynal, Solitary* (London: Burns, Oates & Washbourne, 1906; Saint Louis: Herder, 1906); published as *Richard Raynal, Solitary* (Chicago: Regnery, 1956);

*The Sentimentalists* (London: Pitman, 1906; New York: Benziger, 1906);

*Mirror of Shalott* (New York: Benziger, 1906; London: Pitman, 1907);

*Infallibility and Tradition* (London: Catholic Truth Society, [1907]);

*Papers of a Pariah* (London: Smith, Elder, 1907; New York: Longmans, Green, 1907);

*Mysticism* (London: Sands, 1907; Saint Louis: Herder, 1907);

*Lord of the World* (London: Pitman, 1907; New York: Dodd, Mead, 1908);

*The Conventionalists* (London: Hutchinson, 1908; Saint Louis: Herder, 1908);

*The Holy Blissful Martyr Saint Thomas of Canterbury* (London: Macdonald & Evans, 1908);

*A Mystery Play in Honour of the Nativity of Our Lord* (London: Longmans, Green, 1908);

*Robert Hugh Benson*

*The Necromancers* (London: Hutchinson, 1909; Saint Louis: Herder, 1909);

*The Cost of a Crown: A Story of Douay & Durham* (London: Longmans, Green, 1910; Saint Louis: Herder, 1910);

*Non-Catholic Denominations* (London: Longmans, Green, 1910);

*A Winnowing* (London: Hutchinson, 1910; Saint Louis: Herder, 1910);

*None Other Gods* (London: Hutchinson, 1910; Saint Louis: Herder, 1911);

*Christ in the Church* (London: Longmans, Green, 1911);

*The Dawn of All* (London: Hutchinson, 1911; Saint Louis: Herder, 1911);

*The Maid of Orleans* (London: Longmans, Green, 1911);

*Spiritualism* (London: Catholic Truth Society, 1911);

*A Child's Rule of Life* (London: Longmans, Green, 1912);

*Come Rack! Come Rope!* (London: Hutchinson, 1912; New York: Dodd, Mead, 1912);

*The Coward* (London: Hutchinson, 1912; Saint Louis: Herder, 1912);

*The Friendship of Christ* (London & New York: Longmans, Green, 1912);

*An Average Man* (London: Hutchinson, 1913; New York: Dodd, Mead, 1913);

*Confessions of a Convert* (London: Longmans, Green, 1913; New York: Dodd, Mead, 1913);

*Old Testament Rhymes* (London: Longmans, Green, 1913);

*Optimism* (London: Catholic Truth Society, [1913]);

*Paradoxes of Catholicism* (London: Longmans, Green, 1913);

*Catholicism* (London: Catholic Truth Society, 1914);

*Initiation* (London: Hutchinson, 1914; New York: Dodd, Mead, 1914);

*Lourdes* (London: Manresa/Herder, 1914);

*Oddsfish!* (London: Hutchinson, 1914; New York: Dodd, Mead, 1914);

*Poems* (London: Burns & Oates, 1914; New York: Kenedy, 1914);

*Maxims from the Writings of Mgr. Benson.* Compiled by Elsie E. Morton (London: Washbourne, 1914);

*The Upper Room: A Drama of Christ's Passion* (London: Longmans, Green, 1914);

*Loneliness* (London: Hutchinson, 1915; New York: Dodd, Mead, 1915);

*A Book of Essays,* edited by Allan Ross (London: Catholic Truth Society, 1916; Saint Louis: Herder, 1916);

*Sermon Notes,* 2 volumes, edited by C. C. Martindale (London: Longmans, Green, 1917).

OTHER: *A Book of the Love of Jesus,* compiled and edited by Benson (London: Isbister, 1904);

*Vexilla Regis: A Book of Devotions and Intercessions on Behalf of . . . All Affected by the War,* compiled and translated by Benson (London: Longmans, Green, 1914).

Robert Hugh Benson's psychology remains faithful to the root meaning of the word: it is the "study of the soul," which, according to Socratic and Christian traditions, is immortal and infinitely perfectible. This concept of the soul is explored in his essays, poems, plays, short stories, children's tales, sermons, prayer books, and novels. But his fifteen novels, written during the last eleven years of his life, best record his growing understanding of the soul's development.

Benson's novels contribute to the evolution of the religious novel (one that starts with meaning and talks about religion) into the theological novel (one that explores the mysterious human relationship with the transcendent and moves toward meaning). They describe the complex interrelations of his main characters' physical, emotional, and spiritual beings with the physical world, human society, and God. As the characters react to a variety of situations, they illuminate possibilities for the human journey toward fulfillment and salvation. The methodology proceeds from a phenomenological description of experience to an analysis of this data for abstract principles and finally to an organization of these principles into coherent patterns.

Robert Hugh Benson was born on 16 November 1871; he was the last of six children born to Mary Sidgwick and Edward White Benson. In 1883 Benson's father became archbishop of Canterbury. Although he had been ordained to Anglican orders in 1895 (the year before his father's death), Benson became a Catholic priest in 1904 – the first son of an Anglican archbishop of Canterbury to convert to the Roman church. This cause célèbre is central to understanding Benson and his works. Conversion dominates his writings, and the notoriety of his situation helped to sell his books. His readership expanded beyond the empire, as his books were translated into French, Spanish, Polish, and German. His sermons and lectures attracted crowds in Britain, the United States, and Rome.

Benson came to his novels well prepared, for the Benson and Sidgwick families were both religious, and the Benson children grew up meeting articulate leaders of church and state. He exercised his imagination in several settings, as his father advanced from founding headmaster of Wellington College in 1859; to canon and chancellor of Lincoln in 1872; to founding bishop of the Diocese of Truro, Cornwall, in 1877; and finally to ninety-fourth lord archbishop of Canterbury from 1883 to 1896. Dr. Benson's homes were large – often historic – and culminated in Lambeth Palace and at Addington Park.

The archbishop was a prolific writer and encouraged composition. Hugh's siblings Arthur,

*Cover for Benson's second novel, set during the reign of Henry VIII*

Margaret, and Fred (E. F. Benson) would also publish. Hugh won a scholarship to Eton in 1885 and submitted prizewinning verses on Damien de Veuster, the leper priest of Molokai. He was a restless student who did not take well to school, but his perceptive verses of 1890 record unusually mature emotional introspection. Although he never became a serious poet, shortly before death he authorized publication of a slim volume, *Poems* (1914), to benefit a charity.

The Benson children collaborated on original plays and became skilled in telling impromptu ghost stories. Benson eventually published a few plays for amateurs: *The Queen's Tragedy* (1906), *A Mystery Play in Honor of the Nativity of Our Lord* (1908), *The Cost of a Crown* (1910), *The Maid of Orleans* (1911), and *The Upper Room: A Drama of Christ's Passion* (1914). A polished raconteur, he also published some of his gruesome and ghostly tales: *The Light Invisible* (1903) and *Mirror of Shalott* (1906). Interest in otherworldly phe-

nomena ran deep from both sides of the family. According to E. F. Benson, in *As We Were* (1930), Henry James maintained that he got his idea for *The Turn of the Screw* (1898) from Archbishop Benson. In his student days at Trinity College, Cambridge, the archbishop had founded a "Ghost Society."

Hugh Benson enjoyed life at Trinity College, Cambridge, from 1890 to 1892 but did not excel in his studies and surprised the family by opting to follow his father into the ministry. He became an Anglican deacon in 1894, labored in the inner-city Eton Mission, and was ordained a priest in 1895. There followed a period in the comfortable parish at Kemsing in 1897 and 1898 and religious community life at Mirfield from 1898 to 1903.

Composed largely at Mirfield, but not published until 1904, *By What Authority?* shows Benson wrestling with the craft of the novel. His continued religious doubts and efforts to resolve them according to Jesuit methods elaborated in *The Spiritual Exercises* of Saint Ignatius Loyola are fictionalized in this tale of conversion during the persecutions of Elizabeth I. Anthony and Isabel Norris question the religion of their Puritan father, and each pays dearly for embracing Catholicism. Isabel forfeits human love. Anthony becomes a priest; is pursued, betrayed, and tortured; and dies in the Tower in his sister's arms. "*Magnus valde!*" she sighs, recalling the question of the women approaching Christ's tomb on Easter morning: "Who shall roll away the stone, *for it is great indeed?*" But the impediment has been removed, and Anthony's soul has been raised to a higher world.

Benson grew up reading fictionalized religious debate and tales intended to communicate religious experience. At Mirfield, Benson read widely – Joris Karl Huysman's *La Cathédrale* and Maurice Maeterlinck's *Pelléas et Mélisande,* among other works – and became interested in fiction as a means of self-exploration. From the first his family and friends could spot Benson in his characters. Reacting to the proofs of *By What Authority?* his mother wrote: "You know, OF COURSE, you *are* Anthony!" Even readers who did not know Benson sensed that his characters and descriptions of spiritual experiences were autobiographical.

*By What Authority?* is a good first effort; his second novel, *The King's Achievement* (1905), is less satisfactory. Benson set a schedule, timing his production of manuscript pages by the chimes of the tower clock. He selected a good range of contrasting spiritual and worldly types and another hero who makes his way to bloody execution. But Ralph Torridon is less well drawn than Anthony Norris; the descrip-

tion of King Henry VIII is flat; and the executions of Thomas More and John Fisher are more interesting than the victims.

For all their defects, these efforts begin to sketch a pattern of religious development. Benson's protagonists advance from a first sense of the supernatural, to an incident of radical choice (usually of a path in life), to the search for a specific task that is fulfilling (because it gives a recognizable purpose to life), to ultimate union with the divine through death – often a heroic and painful one. Following this general progression, his characters forge unique identities by force of will. If the intellect cannot fully grasp the natural order it is certainly at a greater disadvantage before the supernatural order and its complex interrelations with the natural.

In 1905 Benson took up residence at Cambridge to continue his studies and writing. He rejoined some of his old clubs and soon had a following of "Bensonians," students and dons who found him a worthy debater, enjoyed his stories, and approved his motto, "Unconventionality is the spice of life." Among his unconventional acquaintances from earlier days was the flamboyant Frederick W. Rolfe ("Baron Corvo"). Benson came under the spell of Corvo's novel *Don Tarquinio* (1905) and began to create a fictitious narrative in the guise of a found manuscript. *The History of Richard Raynal, Solitary* (1906), begun in Rome and finished at Cambridge, imitates the structure and style of earlier centuries. Benson details the events of Master Richard's final week, illuminated by answers to nagging questions: Why has he been called to live in solitude? Is striving for perfection through mystical contemplation an end in itself or is ascetic life a preparation for some mission yet to be revealed?

The answers come in stages. The "Word of God" comes to Richard in a vision. He is to leave his hut and convey a message to King Henry VI. Yet he is not told what to say. The journey that follows is the heart of the tale and recalls Christ's last week. Richard is scorned and beaten by low and high alike; courtiers and churchmen conspire to prevent him from revealing to the king that he, too, must prepare to die a slow and painful death. By keeping faith in the face of the unknown and before every obstacle and by not being diverted from his goal by pain of body, doubt of mind, or depression of spirit, Richard completes his mission, dies a martyr, and enters into his glory.

Hagiographies are written to instruct through role models, and Benson is true to this genre. Sir John Chaldfield, the narrator, often digresses to summarize Richard's Christian philosophy of life and his medieval psychology of the spiritual life. He offers a compendium of ascetic and mystical principles that explain Richard's development from his initial will to believe to his supreme choice to triumph over his last temptation – the dark night of the soul.

Chaldfield's essays interpret and organize the novel's action in groups of linked triads. The interrelated body, mind, and soul are connected to the interlocking worlds of matter, intellect, and spirit. Perfection of this complex of relationships requires threefold human nature to follow the third triad: the purgative, illuminative, and unitive stages of spiritual development. Richard's temptations to cease his journey constitute a fourth triad: body broken, mind confused, and soul in anguish. Richard finds a way out of pain, doubt, and depression. In the crucial moments of his spiritual combat, he uses his most powerful weapon – his will. Richard refuses to be turned away from God.

This tale of a fifteenth-century English mystic allowed the author to concentrate on the spiritual inheritance, common to Protestants and Catholics, that antedates the Reformation; it proposed solitude, prayer, and asceticism to balance the hyperactivity and restless social work of muscular Christianity. In this novel Benson articulates for the first time a comprehensive understanding of human nature and of the principles of religious psychology. This system provides the organization for many later descriptions of moments that change relationships and determine destinies.

*The History of Richard Raynal, Solitary* was Benson's favorite of his novels, and the fact that some readers objected on discovering that Master Richard and Sir John were not historical figures is a mark of its success. Simplicity, brevity, and convincing medievalism give the work a certain timelessness. It may be his most enduring book.

Benson next turned to novels with contemporary settings, freely based on his Cambridge friends and experiences. He modeled Chris Dell, the lead character in *The Sentimentalists* (1906), on a friend who had given Benson permission to do so, but some readers recognized and protested over the caricature. A convert and poseur, at school and beyond, Chris is ostracized by society and driven to the verge of suicide. The conventional man must die before the new man can be born. Rejection and guilt do what compassion and innocence cannot: the poseur becomes authentic and is saved. Readers demanded a sequel. In *The Conventionalists* (1908) another protagonist based on an acquaintance searches for his proper place in life. Listless Algy

*Cover for Benson's novel describing a struggle for supremacy between the Antichrist and the pope (courtesy of the Lilly Library, Indiana University)*

Banister's conversion is directed by Father Benson – the author put himself in this book – and they journey to see Chris Dell, now a solitary in Sussex. Algy is won over and joins the Carthusians at Parkminster.

*The Necromancers* (1909) shows the author's lifelong interest in the occult. A cast of forgettable characters revels in "New Thought," "Higher Light," and "Deeper Unity" and is involved with automatic writing, hypnosis, trances, swoons, and visions. The ghost of Amy finally appears in a dark drawing room, spurring skeptical Laurie to believe in the otherworld. The story is more akin to Elena Blavatsky's seances than William James's quest for *The Varieties of Religious Experience* (1902). Altogether the author dismisses spiritualism, and his notion of religion is unclear in the midst of psychic and pseudopsychic phenomena.

In *The End of a Chapter* (1916) Benson's friend Shane Leslie applauds the Cambridge novels for their "mixture of fear and fun" that should characterize true religion, but he recognizes propaganda: these novels are "Epistles of Hugh the Preacher to the Anglicans – to the Conventionalists – to the Sensualists." Nevertheless, the extent to which these exercises improved Benson's skills and sharpened his judgment becomes clear in later work.

In 1908 Benson left the excitement of Cambridge and moved to Hare Street House, a Tudor structure on a few rustic acres near Buntingford in Hertfordshire. Only an hour from London by rail, it was a retreat from his hectic schedule of speaking and social engagements. Here he could deal with correspondence, write, work in his garden, carve, paint, and weave. Benson was growing protective of his time and solitude. He had never been eager to

attract a permanent following, and he wanted more control of his life.

During his seven years at Hare Street he wrote some of his best novels. *Come Rack! Come Rope!* (1912) shows him at the top of his historical form. Transitions between thought and action are smooth; reflections here give depth without disrupting the narrative. Aliases, disguises, hidden rooms in country manor houses, intrigue, and executions are the stuff of this well-paced tale of Elizabethan England. Roman Catholicism was outlawed, and those who failed to join in Anglican Communion became outcasts. Pursuivants roamed the land in search of itinerant priests and "Mass houses," jailed those who harbored Catholic clergy, and confiscated their property. Priests were racked, hanged, and quartered.

Fidelity to laws higher than those of family and country matures a young couple and propels the novel's plot. Robin Audrey (Robin was one of Benson's childhood names) and Marjorie Manners are in love but face a decision. Robin's father would have him renounce Catholicism. From the first suspicion of the paths they must follow to mystical contact with the divine, Marjorie and Robin are faithful to their calls and search for their missions. They are not only faced with choices between what is good and evil but are also pulled between good and what appears to be a greater good. Robin does not renounce his faith, and the couple chooses divine love over human passion. Robin makes his way to France and into the priesthood. He eventually returns to England and is smuggled into the presence of Mary, Queen of Scots, who has been forbidden the consolations of a priest as the time of her execution approaches. He evades the searchers until a band, led by his distraught father, now a magistrate of the Crown, discovers him hidden in Marjorie's house. Robin is tortured and executed.

*Come Rack! Come Rope!* has ample violence and moments of melodrama. The section on the execution of Mary, Queen of Scots, is worthy of Aubrey Beardsley: "For there, in full view beyond the clear glass stood a tall, black figure, masked to the mouth, who held in his outstretched hands a wide silver dish, in which lay something white and round and slashed with crimson." The graphic descriptions of Robin's racking, hanging, and quartering are terrifying, while the mind's control of pain and the will to endure prepare the reader for the novel's climactic end. "He only awoke once again, after the strangling and the darkness had passed. He could see nothing, nor hear, except a heavy murmuring noise, not unpleasant. But there was one last Pain

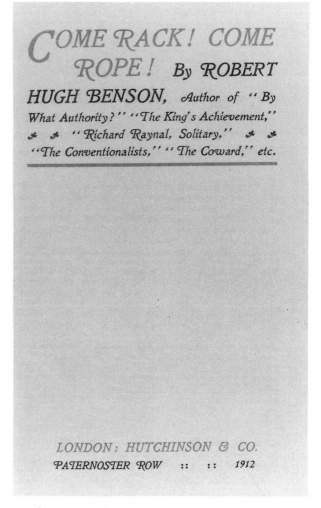

*Title page for Benson's novel about Robin Audrey and his struggles for the Catholic faith in Elizabethan England*

now into which all others had passed, keen and cold like water, and it was about his heart."

Benson's contemporary novels are not old enough to be period pieces, and their preoccupation with pre–World War I class distinctions, especially in language and manners, can be annoying. But *None Other Gods* (1910) is the finest of the Cambridge books and Benson's own choice for the best expression of his thought. Its quirky hero, Frank Guiseley, incarnates two of Benson's linked beliefs articulated in his *Conversion of England* (1906): first, that it is "characteristic of divine grace to produce a divine discontent, and a determination to make things a great deal better"; second, that "faith has a right to a kind of recklessness." Frank, the second son of a titled father — the first son is born into a predetermined role — begins his pilgrimage when he converts to Roman Catholicism and decides to take the Gospels at face value. He leaves Trinity College

*The Bensons at Tremans: (seated) Maggie, Mary, and Beth;*
*(standing) Arthur, Hugh, and Fred*

and takes up with Gertie and the Major, a pathetic woman and her disreputable bully. Lord Talgarth, Frank's father, and Jenny Launton, his fiancée, are puzzled but expect that he will return to his senses and rejoin his social class. He does not. Only Jack Kirkby, his college friend, remains loyal. Misunderstood, humiliated, imprisoned for a crime he did not commit, and overwhelmed at times by a sense of divine rejection, he goes on. Even when an accident makes him heir to the family title and property, Frank refuses to salvage any of his old life at the expense of his "job" – to return Gertie to her family. He succeeds but is beaten by the Major and dies: "the Failure was complete." It is, of course, the "failure" of the Crucifixion.

Important choices change relationships with family, friends, church, and schools. Mavericks pay a price. Benson's typical heroes declare their independence in searching for their authentic selves and in pursuit of transcendent goals. They choose ways in life that do not follow popular paths. They become outsiders. Benson gives the impression that anyone who is really willing to live according to the Gospels will become an outsider.

No review of Benson's works is complete without mention of his apocalyptic fiction. With a nod to Jules Verne and H. G. Wells, Benson conjectured what the world would become should it deify humanity. *Lord of the World* (1907) pictures a mortal struggle between the Antichrist and the pope involving an air war. Victory goes to the Antichrist: "I, in my completed human evolution, am enough," announces American Julian Felsenburgh. Percy Franklin is less humanly perfect than his adversary but continues to proclaim that the human race divorced from the supernatural can never be fulfilled. Percy Franklin becomes Pope John XXIV (the first English Pope since twelfth-century Hadrian IV), is driven from Rome, hides in Nazareth, and is betrayed to the forces of humanitarianism. Inspired by Corvo's *Hadrian VII* (1904) and the theories of the French socialist Saint Simon, the novel ends: "Then this world passed, and the glory of it."

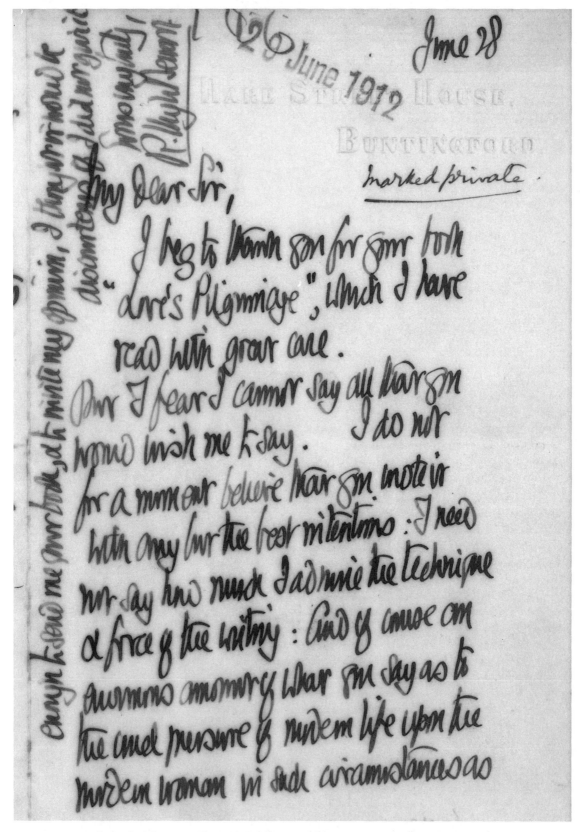

*Letter from Benson to Upton Sinclair (courtesy of the Lilly Library, Indiana University)*

*The Dawn of All* (1911) offers a contrasting, if less entertaining, vision of a world that is trying to change the city of man into the city of God. Catholicism triumphs. Ireland has become a great medieval monastery, and civilization advances through the efforts of contemplatives who spread peace throughout the world. Recalcitrant Berlin alone resists. With debt to Charles Devas's *The Key to the World's Progress* (1906), a compendium of Cardinal Newman's view of history, Benson sees the future in the light of Christianity and the Catholic Church as the permanent factor of Christianity. This view foreshadows a major theme of T. S. Eliot's poetry and prose – that the only hope for a civilization that would advance and prosper is to become authentically Christian. These apocalyptic novels are tame by comparison with the swashbuckling science fiction of the space age, but they share with it the belief that the world can lose its way and may have to return to some better way of the past. *The Dawn of All* would have the world return to an idealized and universal medieval Christendom.

Benson's seven years at Hare Street were productive: he wrote many articles and as many as five books a year; he was much in demand as a speaker both at home and abroad. He was named a papal chamberlain in 1911, volunteered for chaplain duty in the army at the outbreak of World War I, and was planning another tour of America for 1916. Neglecting warnings, he continued his exhausting pace. On 19 October 1914 pneumonia brought his life to an end. Benson died in the library of Bishop's House by Salford Cathedral but was returned to his Hare Street orchard for burial.

Benson's corpus of novels stresses religious questions that particularly concerned converts to Roman Catholicism. His success in isolating essential elements and in articulating telling characteristics should be judged both according to his choice of a general audience and by the difficulties inherent in finding expression for the mysteries of religious experience. He dramatizes the role that willpower can play in directing human life. Other writers, such as Evelyn Waugh in *Brideshead Revisited* (1944) and Graham Greene in *The Power and the Glory* (1940), extend the study to the intricate workings of divine grace on the weak-willed and obstinate. Benson's descriptions of mystical experience, whether of descent into nature or the self in quest of the immanent Divinity or of the flight out of self toward the Transcendent, are often ambiguous. Out of their religious context, they could just as easily be interpreted as aesthetic experiences or instances of natural mysticism.

Early criticism of Benson's novels runs the gamut. In *The End of a Chapter* Leslie remarks that "He wrote fascinating novels in the nature of propaganda.... He mingled mysticism and wove the tags of theology into his novels exactly as Wells transferred the sweepings of science to his." In his *Life of Robert Hugh Benson* (1916) C. C. Martindale, the author's official biographer, finds that some characters do not grow beyond types but that Benson's mind was ever at work, even though he fails to "disguise the process sufficiently" in his weaker works. Waugh wishes that Benson had shown more Flaubertian attention to technical perfection but admits that his popular histories paved the way for Alfred Duggan and H. F. M. Prescott. Waugh might also have mentioned himself and Greene. The range of more recent interest is clear in the titles of Robert Galbreath's "Ambiguous Apocalypse: Transcendental Versions of the End" (1983), Paschal Baumstein's, "Impact of the Will on Mysticism: Compiling Benson's Theory" (1983), and Francis F. Burch's "Robert Hugh Benson, Roger Martin du Gard, and Evelyn Waugh's *Brideshead Revisited*" (1990).

Popular in their day, Benson's novels have been selectively reprinted over the years. Their argumentative thrust has lost much of its edge, as the climate and substance of religious debate have changed. But his analysis of religious experience common to Christianity and many non-Christian religions remains incisive. Materialists see no further than the feet of their graves, Benson believed; he insisted that eternal life alone gives meaning to temporal life, that the finite human creature in pursuit of salvation and sanctification corresponds perfectly to the infinite Trinitarian God who is Creator, Savior, and Sanctifier.

Three symbols in Benson's Hare Street Chapel summed up the thought of his fiction. A tapestry he wove included himself among the followers of a grinning Pied Piper skeleton who are engaged in the relentless Dance of Death. Benson could have easily included his characters. A crucifix Benson carved is a call to join the Son of God in his triumph over death: "I am the way, the truth and the life." Finally, a burning lamp signals the eternal Spirit of God, alive in the incarnate God and in all who have died with Christ to become resurrected for eternity.

But doubts remain. Life, Benson said in *Papers of a Pariah* (1907), is "a chess-board of black and white – of suffering and sweetness ... and what right have I to choose to say that the board is essentially white and only accidentally black?" His characters must play the game move by move and do not know where their choices will lead – until the

end. Benson's characters are not simple, but they are radically free and are trying their best to "come down where they ought to be."

**Letters:**
*Spiritual Letters of Monsignor R. Hugh Benson to one of his Converts,* with a preface by A. C. Benson (London & New York: Longmans, Green, 1915).

**Biographies:**
Arthur C. Benson, *Hugh. Memoir of a Brother* (London: Smith, Elder, 1915; New York: Longmans, Green, 1915);

Blanche Warre Cornish and others, *Memorials of Robert Hugh Benson* (London: Burns & Oates, 1915; New York: Kenedy, 1915);

Katharine Olive Parr, *Robert Hugh Benson: An Appreciation* (London: Hutchinson, 1915; Saint Louis: Herder, 1915);

Cyril Charles Martindale, S.J., *The Life of Monsignor Robert Hugh Benson,* 2 volumes (London & New York: Longmans, Green, 1916).

**References:**
Paschal Baumstein, O.S.B., "Impact of the Will on Mysticism: Compiling Benson's Theory," *Faith and Reason,* 9 (Summer 1983): 97–106;

Patrick Braybrooke, F.R.S.I., "Robert Hugh Benson: Novelist and Philosopher," in his *Some Catholic Novelists, Their Art and Outlook* (London: Burns, Oates & Washbourne, 1931), pp. 113–114;

Francis F. Burch, "Robert Hugh Benson, Roger Martin du Gard, and Evelyn Waugh's *Brideshead Revisited,*" *Notes and Queries,* 37 (March 1990): 68;

J. E. Canavan, S.J., "The Theory of Life in Benson's Novels," *Studies,* 5 (December 1916): 555–560;

Charles Stanton Devas, *The Key to The World's Progress* (London: Longmans, Green, 1906);

Robert Galbreath, "Ambiguous Apocalypse: Transcendental Versions of the End," in *The End of the World,* edited by Eric S. Rabkin (Carbondale: Southern Illinois University Press, 1983), pp. 53–72;

M. I., "The Psychological Novels of Monsignor Benson," *Month,* 126 (September 1915): 238;

Shane Leslie, *The End of a Chapter* (New York: Scribners, 1916);

Sophie D. Maude, *The Hermit and the King: A Fulfillment of Monsignor R. H. Benson's Prophecy of Richard Raynal* (London: Washbourne, 1916; Saint Louis: Herder, 1916);

Allan Ross, "Monsignor Hugh Benson (1871–1914)," in Benson's *A Book of Essays* (Saint Louis: Herder, 1916), pp. 1–32;

Evelyn Waugh, Preface to Benson's *Richard Raynal, Solitary* (Chicago: Regnery, 1956), pp. vii–xvii;

Robert Lee Wolff, *Gains and Losses: Novels of Faith and Doubt in Victorian England* (New York: Garland, 1977).

**Papers:**
The Trinity and Magdalene College Libraries at Cambridge hold Benson family papers but nothing of R. H. Benson. The Bodleian Library, Oxford, has some R. H. Benson material, as do the archives of the London Diocese of the Church of England and those of the Catholic Archdiocese of Westminster. R. H. Benson's papers passed to his brother E. F. Benson and were scattered, largely into such American collections as the Berg Collection of the New York Public Library; the Fales Library of New York University; the Beinecke Rare Books and Manuscripts Library at Yale University; the Harry Ransom Humanities Research Center, University of Texas at Austin; and the UCLA Library.

# Algernon Henry Blackwood

*(14 March 1869 – 10 December 1951)*

George M. Johnson
*University College of the Cariboo*

BOOKS: *The Empty House and Other Ghost Stories* (London: Eveleigh Nash, 1906; New York: Vaughan, 1915);

*The Listener and Other Stories* (London: Eveleigh Nash, 1907; New York: Vaughan & Gomme, 1914);

*John Silence: Physician Extraordinary* (London: Eveleigh Nash, 1908; Boston: Luce, 1909);

*Jimbo: A Fantasy* (London & New York: Macmillan, 1909);

*The Education of Uncle Paul* (London: Macmillan, 1909; New York: Paget, 1909);

*The Lost Valley and Other Stories* (London: Eveleigh Nash, 1910; New York: Vaughan & Gomme, 1914);

*The Human Chord* (London: Macmillan, 1910; New York: Macmillan, 1911);

*The Centaur* (London: Macmillan, 1911; New York: Macmillan, 1912);

*Pan's Garden: A Volume of Nature Stories* (London & New York: Macmillan, 1912);

*A Prisoner in Fairyland (The Book That 'Uncle Paul' Wrote)* (London & New York: Macmillan, 1913);

*Ten Minute Stories* (London: Murray, 1914; New York: Dutton, 1914);

*Incredible Adventures* (London & New York: Macmillan, 1914);

*The Extra Day* (London & New York: Macmillan, 1915);

*Julius Le Vallon: An Episode* (London: Cassell, 1916; New York: Dutton, 1916);

*The Wave: An Egyptian Aftermath* (London: Macmillan, 1916; New York: Dutton, 1916);

*Day and Night Stories* (London: Cassell, 1917; New York: Dutton, 1917);

*The Promise of Air* (London: Macmillan, 1918; New York: Dutton, 1918);

*Karma: A Reincarnation Play* (London: Macmillan, 1918; New York: Dutton, 1918);

*The Garden of Survival* (London: Macmillan, 1918; New York: Dutton, 1918);

with Wilfred Wilson, *The Wolves of God and Other Fey Stories* (London: Cassell, 1921; New York: Dutton, 1921);

*The Bright Messenger* (London: Cassell, 1921; New York: Dutton, 1922);

*Episodes Before Thirty* (London: Cassell, 1923; revised edition, London: Nevill, 1950);

*Tongues of Fire and Other Sketches* (London: Jenkins, 1924); published as *Tongues of Fire and Other Stories* (New York: Dutton, 1925);

*Through the Crack* (London: Samuel French, 1925);

*Ancient Sorceries and Other Tales* (London & Glasgow: Collins, 1927);

*The Dance of Death and Other Tales* (London: Jenkins, 1927; New York: Dial, 1928);

*Sambo and Snitch* (Oxford: Blackwell, 1927; New York: Appleton, 1927);

*Mr. Cupboard* (Oxford: Blackwell, 1928);

*Dudley and Gilderoy: A Nonsense* (London: Benn, 1929; New York: Dutton, 1929);

*Strange Stories* (London: Heinemann, 1929; New York: Arno, 1976);

*Full Circle* (London: Mathews & Marrot, 1929);

*By Underground* (Oxford: Blackwell, 1930);

*The Parrot and the — Cat!* (Oxford: Blackwell, 1931);

*Maria (of England) in the Rain* (Oxford: Blackwell, 1933);

*Sergeant Poppett and Policeman James* (Oxford: Blackwell, 1934);

*The Fruit Stoners: Being the Adventures of Maria among the Fruit Stoners* (London: Grayson & Grayson, 1934; New York: Dutton, 1935); republished as *The Fruit Stoners* (Oxford: Blackwell, 1935);

*Shocks* (London: Grayson & Grayson, 1935; New York: Dutton, 1936);

*How the Circus Came to Tea* (Oxford: Blackwell, 1936);

*The Adventures of Dudley and Gilderoy* (New York: Dutton, 1941; London: Faber & Faber, 1941);

*The Doll, And One Other* (Sauk City, Wis.: Arkham House, 1946).

**Editions:** *Short Stories of To-Day and Yesterday* (London: Harrap, 1930);

*The Willows and Other Queer Tales* (London & Glasgow: Collins, 1932);

*The Tales of Algernon Blackwood* (London: Secker, 1938; New York: Dutton, 1939);

*Tales of the Uncanny and Supernatural* (London: Nevill, 1949; Secaucus, N. J.: Castle Books, 1974);

*In the Realm of Terror* (New York: Pantheon, 1957);

*Selected Tales of Algernon Blackwood* (London: John Baker, 1964); published as *Tales of Terror and the Unknown* (New York: Dutton, 1965);

*Tales of the Mysterious and Macabre* (London: Spring Books, 1967; Secaucus, N. J.: Castle Books, 1974).

SELECTED PERIODICAL PUBLICATIONS – UNCOLLECTED: "A Mysterious House," *Belgravia,* 69 (July 1889): 98–107;

"The Story of Karl Ott," *Pall Mall Magazine,* 10 (October 1896): 189–200.

During a career spanning sixty-one years, Algernon Henry Blackwood wrote more stories and novels in the realms of the psychic, mystic, and supernatural than any other contemporary. Much of his neoromantic fiction is of high quality and particularly excels at evoking atmosphere, leading no less an expert than H. P. Lovecraft to refer in 1927 to Blackwood's work as "some of the finest spectral literature of this or any age." E. F. Bleiler more re-

cently confirms Blackwood's position as "the foremost British supernaturalist of the twentieth century." However, Blackwood has often been misleadingly labeled as simply a ghost-story writer and thus underrated, though he deals with a vast array of psychological and spiritual states in stories ranging from the psychologically realistic to portrayals of nature as alive and potentially threatening to the evocation of mystical union with the divine. His novels in particular have been underrated. On this larger canvas he typically explores various extensions of consciousness through inward, psychic voyages that show the limitations of linear time and of a materialistic view of the universe. Blackwood's novels are informed by a more complex framework of ideas than his stories, ranging from Eastern mysticism, theosophy, and psychic research to psychoanalysis. Occasionally this framework obtrudes, but most often the author successfully involves the reader in his flights of poetic fancy.

Algernon Henry Blackwood was born on 14 March 1869, the fourth of five children born to Stevenson Arthur "Beauty" Blackwood and Harriet Sydney Dobbs, both of whom were descended from aristocratic families. They became important figures in the evangelical movement, which exerted a profound influence on Blackwood's youth. In *Episodes Before Thirty* (1923) he characterizes his upbringing, repressive even by late-Victorian standards, as excessively sheltered and "strange." He admired the intense convictions of his parents but feared their rigid belief system. A "dreamy boy," as Blackwood described himself, he escaped from this narrow world by turning to nature. At Shortlands House near Beckenham, where he lived from age eleven, he would climb out of the window at night, launch a boat on the garden pond, and imagine that supernatural beings observed him. Algernon would often accompany his father on long walks, though he never became as intimate with this sincere yet stern figure as he did with his mother. Of Celtic descent, she "read far deeper into things" than her husband, possessed an "old" soul, and, according to her son, always knew his thoughts.

Like most English boys of his class, Blackwood was separated from his parents during his formal education. His schooling had an unsettling and even traumatic effect on him; he referred to the five schools that he attended as "my horrible private schools." At one of these, in Kent in 1881, he was falsely accused by the "fiendish" evangelical headmaster of stealing a poetry book, an event that haunted him for years. Blackwood looked back with disgust at the harsh discipline of the Moravian

Brotherhood school in the German Black Forest, where he spent an unhappy eighteen months beginning in May 1885. Yet the remote setting of this school, "haunted by elves and dwarfs and peopled by charming legends," also left a lasting impression, increasing his worship of nature. That passion for nature became the dominant influence in his life, and from it he often drew comfort and inspiration.

Blackwood's real education, however, did not truly begin until after he had left the Moravian school. In September 1886 his reading of Patañjali's "Yoga Aphorisms" prompted his conversion to Eastern wisdom, fueled by his father's disturbance at this new interest and by his further reading of works deemed subversive in G. H. Pember's evangelical book *Earth's Earliest Ages* (1876), given as a warning to him by his father. Foremost among these eclectic works was the Bhagavad Ghita, considered by Blackwood "the profoundest world-scripture I have ever read." He also "swallowed whole" the theosophy of Madame Blavatsky. Her claims that a spirit realm existed beyond the perception of the five senses became a central preoccupation of Blackwood's throughout his life. Even at the early age of seventeen he cultivated this interest by reading Alfred Binet and Fere's works on "Animal Magnetism" and works on hypnotism by James Braid and Dr. James Esdaile of India.

Blackwood continued his formal education in early 1887 at Bole in Switzerland. According to one friend, he was already telling ghost stories while on hikes. Algernon's future career, though, was still uncertain. Recognizing his son's love of nature, Arthur decided to see whether Algernon would be interested in becoming a farmer, perhaps in Canada, which they visited together in 1887. In ten weeks they crossed the country and visited a farm near Toronto, Ontario, and it was decided that Algernon would return when he came of age.

However, first he needed to learn more about agriculture; consequently, he attended Edinburgh University for a year from October 1888. More fascinated by lectures on pathology than on farming, he soon encountered the first of several influential mentors. "Dr. H." encouraged Blackwood to become a mental specialist, taught him hypnotism, and introduced him to spiritualism and seances. At several seances Blackwood received messages, including the revelation that he had been an Indian medicine man and needed to return to their land "to work off certain painful Karma." Though Blackwood treated some of these with skepticism, he shortly lent credence to a prophecy that he would "scratch" by composing his first short story, "A

Mysterious House," while at the university. The tale includes all the elements of the conventional ghost story, including a haunted house, knives, blood, unaccountable movements and noises, and madness, but it focuses on developing the psychology of fear in the skeptical narrator, a focus that would become one of Blackwood's specialties. The revelation at the story's close that the events have occurred in a nightmare serves as commentary on imaginative power.

After Blackwood left Edinburgh in the summer of 1889, better versed in matters of the spirit than the soil, he traveled in Switzerland before he embarked for Toronto in April 1890. The nine adventurous years that Blackwood spent in North America would be the most momentous of his life. His character developed enormously during this time, he met the men who would leave the most lasting impressions on him, and in his fiction he would repeatedly draw on his experiences in the wilds there.

Though his father had pulled strings at the Canadian Pacific Railway to ensure that Blackwood would prosper, the awkward youth managed to ruin that opportunity by offending the key official. Left to his own devices, he worked without pay in an insurance office and gave French, German, and violin lessons at night. Three months later he landed his first writing job as editorial assistant on the *Methodist Magazine,* to which he contributed articles on Christmas in England and on travels in Europe. After admitting that he was a Buddhist, his relations with the editor became less cordial. Fortunately for Blackwood, the Methodist preacher did not discover that his associate was also involved in founding the Toronto branch of the Theosophical Society in February 1891. Nevertheless, Blackwood voluntarily left his position on the magazine once his capital of two thousand pounds arrived from England. He tried his hand at dairy farming and then at running a pub but failed at both.

On hearing of the latter venture, Blackwood Sr., a temperance advocate, proclaimed that "Algie has gone to hell!," increasing Algernon's sense of guilt. His father died one year later in 1893, and the two never had the chance to reconcile. The "hated" bar experience also, however, caused Blackwood to cherish his hours of relaxation away from work. He found a safety valve in nature, music, and a few friendships. With one friend, Johann Kay Pauw, he retreated to an island in Lake Rousseau, Ontario, in the spring of 1892, having sold his interest in the bar business. In the fall they decided to try their fortunes in New York.

Blackwood's New York experience hardened this ultrasensitive and naive young man, stripping away his illusions, shaking his faith in his fellows, and exposing him to unaccustomed hardships. He and Pauw were forced to live in a vermin-ridden boardinghouse on the East Side and to pawn their overcoats while searching for work. Though Blackwood had no desire to write, necessity drove him to apply at various magazines. Eventually he landed a job as court reporter with the *Evening Sun.* The sordid reporting routine introduced him to "vice, crime, horror, terror, and every kind of human degradation" and later provided the atmosphere for many of his tales. Abject poverty and an untreated wound eventually took their toll, and Blackwood succumbed to a fever. Though Blackwood could not afford to pay the attending doctor, Otto Huebner, he befriended Huebner, who became another mentor. They shared thoughts about idealistic philosophy and literature as well as experiments with morphine. Blackwood experienced "an intensification of consciousness" while on the drug but managed to break the habit; Huebner died from his addiction less than a year later.

Blackwood's poverty was not eased until January 1893 when he had recuperated enough from illness to return to his job at the *Evening Sun.* Although he had hit rock bottom during this period, Blackwood remained in New York. However, he had no love for the city, which he described as "monstrous." Apparently his sense of failure was so strong and he felt so divorced from his family that he considered it impossible to return to England. In addition, his belief in Karma convinced him that his unpleasant experiences were deserved. Most important, Blackwood further developed his capacity to escape the horror of his circumstances through his imagination, stimulating it by devouring the works of Percy Bysshe Shelley, Russian writers, Eastern books, and "every kind of book I could find on psychology."

Blackwood found a receptive audience for the expression of his imagination in Angus Hamilton, a fellow Briton employed by the *Evening Sun.* According to Blackwood, Hamilton "liked, above all to listen to weird stories I used to tell, strange, wild, improbable tales akin to ghost-stories." With characteristic humility, Blackwood recounted that he "found, to my surprise, that my listeners were enthralled" and that he had a "taste for spinning yarns." Hamilton wrote out these stories, claiming that they would sell, but Blackwood had no impulse to do so himself. More than ten years later Hamilton took an active role in launching Blackwood's literary career, through which Blackwood claimed that he found his liberty.

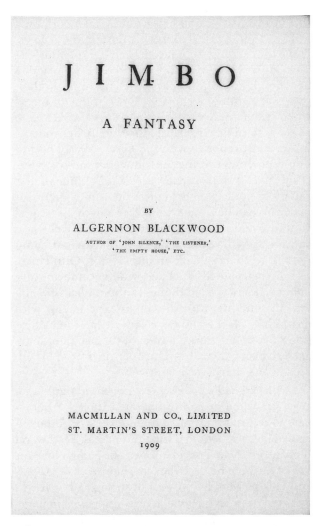

# JIMBO

## A FANTASY

BY

ALGERNON BLACKWOOD

AUTHOR OF 'JOHN SILENCE,' 'THE LISTENER,'
'THE EMPTY HOUSE,' ETC.

MACMILLAN AND CO., LIMITED
ST. MARTIN'S STREET, LONDON
1909

*Title page for Blackwood's first novel, which describes the fantasy adventures of a young boy in a delirium after an accident (courtesy of the Lilly Library, Indiana University)*

Meanwhile, Blackwood managed to escape the misery of New York by traveling to Ontario in 1893 and again in 1894 as a gold prospector. Though he did not find gold, the experience seemed like "some legendary Golden Age" and provided inspiration for more than one wilderness tale, notably "The Wendigo" (1910). Lack of funds forced his return to New York in October 1894, and he moved from job to job, including freelance journalism, acting, and manufacturing and selling eau de cologne. He discovered that his partner in the latter enterprise had stolen the cologne formula, and the horror-stricken Blackwood was nearly implicated in the crime.

During this period Blackwood met his most influential mentor, Alfred Hyman Louis, who had been the friend of George Eliot, G. H. Lewes, Her-bert Spencer, and Cardinal Manning before his fortunes and his mental health had declined. Louis's "upper-mind," to use Blackwood's term, was damaged, but Blackwood believed that his "under-mind" was whole and that he possessed other-worldly wisdom; Louis inspired Blackwood's story "The Old Man of Visions" (1907).

Blackwood's fortunes began to improve when he joined the staff of *The New York Times* and sold a few short stories, including "The Story of Karl Ott" (1896), and then more dramatically when he became a millionaire banker's private secretary for two thousand pounds per year. This happier state of affairs lasted until Blackwood's sister visited in late 1898, stirring a longing to return to England. Since his position had improved and he had prospects to begin a dried-milk business in England, Blackwood felt that he could return without shame. He arrived in Liverpool on 3 March 1899, eleven days before his thirtieth birthday.

Blackwood settled in a boardinghouse in Chelsea after a search for rooms that would form the basis of "The Listener" (1899). Work at the dried milk company was demanding, but he also continued to travel extensively between the years 1900 and 1908. With Wilfred Wilson, who would become a friend for life, he made a six-week, twenty-four-hundred-mile voyage from the Danube's source to the Black Sea in a Canadian canoe. He described the expedition in several essays and transformed it into one of his most powerful tales, "The Willows" (1907). In the following year he journeyed down the river again, probably with an archaeologist, Edwyn Bevan, and his wife, with whom Blackwood later investigated haunted houses.

From 1900 to 1914 Blackwood also became heavily involved in various orders of the Golden Dawn, organized in 1888 to study the occult and mysticism. More important, he became a professional writer, though characteristically he did not take an active role in gaining the notice of a publisher. Angus Hamilton reappeared in Blackwood's life circa 1905 and took away approximately twenty stories that Blackwood had stored in a cupboard. Blackwood forgot about the incident until he received a letter from Eveleigh Nash asking to publish them; Hamilton had submitted the stories without Blackwood's permission.

Blackwood's motivation for writing was complex, as suggested by his initial reaction to the proposal, related in *Episodes Before Thirty:* "I never forget my shrinking fear at the idea of appearing in print, my desire to use another name, my feeling

that I should have a book of my own published being too absurd to accept as true." He apparently feared publicity partly because writing had become a solitary pleasure for him. He claimed that "It had been my habit and delight to spend my evenings composing yarns on my typewriter, finding more pleasure in this than in any dinner engagement, theatre or concert. Why this suddenly began I cannot say, but I guess at a venture that the accumulated horror of the years in New York was seeking expression." Perhaps he also found relief in expunging the devils and fears engendered by his rigid upbringing, projecting these inner demons onto the natural world or into the ancient past.

Before moving into a chronological discussion of Blackwood's novels, it is worthwhile to note some general characteristics. Whereas his stories vary greatly in theme, language, atmosphere, and length, his eleven novels reveal a fascination with a more cohesive thematic territory and defined atmospheric range, and there is more interplay between novels – certain character types, for example, reappear in them. The novels are of two kinds, adult novels about children and mystical novels; neither can be easily categorized, a quality that baffled contemporary reviewers and has probably contributed to the subsequent neglect of this part of Blackwood's canon. He wrote that "My fundamental interest, I suppose, is signs and proofs of other powers that lie hidden in us all; the extension, in other words, of human faculty." In both types of novels he explores such extensions, from learning to fly in the mind, as in *Jimbo: A Fantasy* (1909) and *The Promise of Air* (1918), to reconnecting with Mother Earth, in *The Centaur* (1911), to achieving psychic connection with a lost loved one through the quality of beauty that she represents, as in *The Garden of Survival* (1918). Typically, the protagonists of the novels undergo psychic voyages touched off either by a shock or trauma, as in *Jimbo,* or by contact with a being more in tune with the spiritual world. Frequently these beings are children with more-direct access to the world of wonder, who may be possessed of "old souls," and who connect with other old souls in adult form, as is the case in *The Education of Uncle Paul* (1909) and *The Extra Day* (1915). Alternatively, these beings are manifestations of natural forces, or Deva, as is Julian Le Vallon in *The Bright Messenger* (1921). Throughout Blackwood's canon, nature is a powerful living force, though it can either destroy or heal. Nature can also serve as a metaphor for, or projection of, the psyche. In several of the novels a more scientific, objective character unsuccessfully attempts to

explain the protagonist's experience as a psychological case, the failure illustrating Blackwood's belief in the limitations of rational scientific explanation. Though several of the protagonists are children, most are adult males, physically large, active, and charismatic mystics.

The ideal is expressed in this description of Uncle Paul, who first appears in *The Education of Uncle Paul* and whose story comprises another novel, *A Prisoner in Fairyland* (1913): "His life became 'inner' in the best sense – a Life within a Life; not given over to useless dreaming, but ever drawing from the inner one the sustenance that provided the driving force for the outer one: the mystic as man of action!" (Blackwood's friends identified him with Paul.) Like Paul, Blackwood's protagonists tend to be bachelors and are more comfortable with their imaginative nieces and nephews than with other adults. These men do not require feminine companionship since they are possessed of the feminine within. The women who do appear in Blackwood's novels are typically idealized and distant, and allusions to sexual relations are rare.

Blackwood developed a distinctive technique and style in order to express his deeply held belief in voyages of expanded consciousness. He describes at great length psychic events that occur in mere seconds of clock time, illustrating his frequently expressed conviction that "Time and Space were bits of elastic that could stretch or shrink as thought directed, feeling chose." Blackwood found confirmation of his intuitions about time and other psychological matters in writers such as Henri Bergson and William James. He also concurred with Bergson about the limitations of language, frequently commenting that the experiences he attempted to convey are beyond intelligible description. This quality of his writing has been criticized by Derek Hudson, who speaks of Blackwood's "habitual inconclusiveness," but it might also be argued that making these supernatural occurrences conclusive would have run counter to their nature.

Blackwood's first three volumes were collections of short stories, including tales of haunted houses, reincarnation, and revenge as well as nature stories. The most critically acclaimed of these was the nature tale "The Willows" in *The Listener* (1907). Though all three collections were received positively by reviewers as prominent as Hilaire Belloc, the third volume, *John Silence: Physician Extraordinary* (1908), achieved the greatest notoriety and success, partly because its title character, a psychic detective who treats difficult cases of spiritual affliction in a

society suffering from spiritual malaise, was linked with Sherlock Holmes by contemporary reviewers.

With the success of *John Silence*, Blackwood was able to divest himself of the dried-milk company and to enjoy his new liberty at Bole in the Jura Mountains, where he lived and worked as a professional writer for the next six years. In that prolific period he published nine novels and collections of short stories, as well as many occasional pieces for papers like the *Westminster Gazette, Country Life,* and the *Morning Post.* The first two books he produced were novels about children: *Jimbo: a Fantasy,* drafted before his first short-story collection; and the autobiographical *The Education of Uncle Paul.*

*Jimbo* traces the mental odyssey of a dreamy boy, James "Jimbo" Stone. Believing he is being pursued by the inmate of an empty house, the terrified boy runs into a nearby field, where he is attacked and injured by a bull. In the delirium that follows, Jimbo fantasizes that his punitive governess atones for instilling fear into him by helping him to escape the house of fear through teaching him to fly. A large part of the novel is taken up with poetic descriptions of his adventures flying, with its attendant dangers. Blackwood would return to the flying theme in *The Promise of Air.* On submitting the manuscript to Macmillan, Blackwood wrote that "It is neither a children's story, nor a novel, . . . and, though it is addressed more to caretakers of children than to general readers, I honestly do not know into what class of books it falls." Several reviewers were similarly baffled, though reviews in *Outlook* and the *Spectator* agreed that the novel was not fit for children to read. Nevertheless, they praised its "graphic style" and insight into the psychology of fright.

*The Education of Uncle Paul* similarly enters the imaginative world of the child in its focus on the spiritual union between a forty-five-year-old mystic, Uncle Paul, who has a child's capacity for wonder, and his niece, Nixie. Paul returns to England after a twenty-year sojourn in America and joins the household of his widowed sister-in-law, her three children, and many animals. Though Paul is determined not to expose his visionary qualities, the children sense his allegiance and soon enlist him to participate in and then write out their "verywonerfulindeedaventures". He gives these "aventures" titles, such as the "Wind-Vision," and the act of writing them down provides a therapeutic safety valve for his imagination. On one excursion he goes with the children into the "crack between Yesterday and Tomorrow," recognized by Paul as "a mystical haven where all lost or broken things eternally reconstruct themselves."

This is a world out of time, analogous to the moments of expanded consciousness that the modernists would later explore. Blackwood makes clear the autobiographical nature of this experience, with roots going back to his New York days, when he states in *Episodes Before Thirty* that "I imagined, the world being old and creaky, ill-fitting too, that a crack existed between the two days. Anyone who was thin enough might slip through! I, certainly, was thin enough. I slipped through. . . . I entered a region out of time, a region where everything came true. And the first thing I saw was a wondrous streaming vision of the wind, the wind that howled outside my filthy windows . . . I little dreamed that these fancies would appear fifteen years later in a book of my own, 'The Education of Uncle Paul.' That crack, at any rate, became for me, like the fiddle, a means of escape from unkind reality into a state of inner bliss and wonder. . . ."

In the novel the importance of the crack becomes clear after the death of Nixie, with whom Paul has developed "perfect companionship" beginning with an "electric shock of a kiss" when they first met. In the "crack-land" Paul has earlier discovered his ideal, the "eternal feminine within himself," and now identifies this veiled woman as being one and the same as Nixie. Freed from the constraints of time and space, they can share true communion between their old souls. Both Nixie's spiritual presence and the practical example of Joan Nicholson, an adult cousin of the children, inspire Paul to join Joan's work rescuing London waifs, and thus he reaches the ideal balance of "the mystic as man of action."

This novel successfully captures the imaginative life of the child, and Blackwood describes the dream sequences eloquently if verbosely. The novel is also perceptive about the therapeutic value of expression and about coping with loss. However, its dreamlike quality also makes it appear episodic, and, as Edward Wagenknecht avers, some elements, such as the initial attraction between Joan and Paul, are underdeveloped. Though this neoromantic tale is sprinkled with epigraphs and quotations from William Blake, William Wordsworth, and other Romantics, and in its evocation of a child's realm of fantasy it faintly echoes the work of George Macdonald and Lewis Carroll's *Alice's Adventures in Wonderland* (1865), Blackwood's vision is unique. Most contemporary reviewers recognized this, claiming that the book was uncommon though powerful and would appeal strongly to a select readership.

Following a collection of uncanny nature stories, *The Lost Valley and Other Stories* (1910), Black-

*Dust jacket for Blackwood's 1916 novel about reincarnation and
retribution (courtesy of the Lilly Library, Indiana University)*

wood tried his hand at two mystical novels, *The Human Chord* (1910) and *The Centaur* (1911). In the former, Blackwood demonstrates most extensively his fascination with the power of sound, developing the idea that "Sound is the original divine impulsion behind nature . . . communicated to language" and that sound can alter physical form. The young, ineffectual protagonist, Robert Spinrobin, seeking "an authoritative adventure of the soul," applies for an unusual position requiring a tenor voice, knowledge of Hebrew, and unworldliness. He is hired by a former clergyman, Philip Skale, one of Blackwood's large and powerful mystics. At his isolated Welsh mountain retreat, Skale requires help with various experiments in sound, leading to a great and blasphemous experiment of uttering in a chord the long-forgotten name of the Almighty, which will transform the utterers into gods. The harmonization involves two others, Skale's housekeeper and her lovely, pristine niece, Miriam. Though Spinrobin's

burgeoning love for Miriam causes him to feel conflict about the project, since if successful the participants might lose their individuality, it is eventually Miriam who refuses to utter the essence of her being. The two escape, though not without some remorse on the part of Spinrobin, and as the novel closes they anticipate marital bliss and their own human power of creation. Reviewers found the story captivating and praised Blackwood's poetic powers of description, but several felt that the writing was uneven, and the *Nation* lashed out at his "hysterical theorizing on occult subjects."

*The Centaur* similarly provoked mixed contemporary reviews but eventually became his most highly acclaimed novel, impressing writers as diverse as Rainer Maria Rilke and James Stephens, and it was Blackwood's own favorite. Based on the author's 1910 voyage to Greece, the novel explores the inner odyssey of the protagonist, O'Malley, a Whitmanesque rolling stone, while on a trip to the

Caucasus. En route he encounters a massive Russian and his son who are *Urmenschen,* or primitive beings, the elder being figured as the centaur of the title. They draw O'Malley out of his body, enabling him to pass within the consciousness of the earth and to an inner Eden. Thoroughly immersed in the psychological ideas of his day, O'Malley finds it almost impossible upon his return to waking consciousness to describe the mystical expansion of consciousness he has undergone. His despair and sense of loss cause him to lose his hold on life. During his odyssey O'Malley is monitored by a curious German doctor, Stahl, who is shown to be divided by his scientific skepticism, though objectively interested in mysticism. A "self-contradictory" figure, he has a mind of opposite type to O'Malley's and yet acts as a double to him, one of several such doubles in the novel. He attempts to explain O'Malley's experience in the language of the new psychology. In the novel as a whole, Blackwood draws too heavily and obtrusively on a wide variety of sources, including Frederic Myers's concept of subliminal self, Gustav Fechner's ideas about cosmic consciousness, William James's concepts of the strenuous life and the pluralism of reality, and Morton Prince's descriptions of the dissociations of personality.

Blackwood collected more of his visionary nature stories in *Pan's Garden: A Volume of Nature Stories* (1912) before returning to the novel form with *A Prisoner in Fairyland (The Book That 'Uncle Paul' Wrote)* (1913). As a "spiritual sequel" to *The Education of Uncle Paul,* this long fantasy resembles the earlier novel in that a bachelor uncle, Henry Rogers, visits and psychically connects with his nieces and nephew. The children enchant and captivate him because their fantasy life accords with his own. Together they make nocturnal visits on the "Starlight Express" to the Cave of Stars and retrieve stardust, which is used to spread good thoughts. The novel is premised on the idea of a collective mind and that thought and feeling exist apart from matter. Mike Ashley's recent criticism that the book "today is disappointingly unreadable" is too severe, but Blackwood did overwrite some sequences, and the romance that develops between Rogers and a countess near the book's denouement seems contrived.

During World War I Blackwood continued to write prolifically. He published five novels and two collections of stories, *Incredible Adventures* (1914) and *Day and Night Stories* (1917), and produced the first of several unsuccessful plays, while still managing to engage in some incredible adventures of his own. Though refused for active service, he qualified as a translator and also wrote some propagandistic sto-

ries and essays. In the summer of 1916 he was about to depart for Serbia with a field ambulance corps when he was asked to operate as an undercover agent in Switzerland for the British Military Intelligence, and on one occasion he dispatched important information about the U-boat campaign. According to his biographer, Mike Ashley, "Blackwood's exploits at this time read rather like a boy's adventure serial complete with code names, invisible ink and hair's-breadth escapes."

None of Blackwood's novels reflects his war experience; instead they continue to depict various spiritual adventures. *The Extra Day* (1915), another adult novel about children, features another imaginative, slightly rebellious writer-uncle who participates in a quest for wonder, described as the beginning of wisdom, during an extra day out of or beyond time, when the adult household authorities are absent. The adventures in three of the next four novels involve reincarnation. In *Julius Le Vallon: An Episode* (1916) the protagonist, Professor John Mason, receives a letter from Julius Le Vallon, a mystical boyhood companion, that causes him to reflect on their past together, which had culminated in psychic experiments at the University of Edinburgh. That past turns out to extend back one thousand years, as Mason discovers on joining Le Vallon and his wife at their retreat in the Jura Mountains. A rather unusual love triangle develops as John realizes that he has loved this woman in a previous incarnation, claiming that "mine was the old subconscious love unrecognized by her normal self," while "the love of the daily, normal self" was Le Vallon's.

John also knows that he was wronged during a ceremony in which elemental powers were misused for selfish ends. Le Vallon convinces him that the crime must be expiated, and they attempt to reenact the ceremony using Mrs. Le Vallon's unborn child as the channel through which to draw the necessary elemental forces. A conflict of wills between Le Vallon and his overprotective wife foils the experiment and costs Le Vallon his life, though his son, possessed of an elemental, is born. This youth is featured in the sequel, *The Bright Messenger* (1921). *Julius Le Vallon* develops Blackwood's familiar pattern of a practical or "normal" protagonist encountering someone with extraordinary and potentially destructive powers who nearly draws the protagonist into a spiritual abyss before the protagonist pulls back and returns to everyday reality, though with heightened awareness of powerful psychic realities. The novel contains a fascinating exploration of consciousness, unconsciousness, memory, time,

and space, but its ending is melodramatic. Contemporary criticism was again divided, largely depending on the critic's predisposition to the otherworldliness invoked by Blackwood.

*The Wave: An Egyptian Aftermath* (1916) similarly treats the theme of reincarnation and involves a love triangle, though the discovery of past experiences occurs in the setting of Egypt. The novel does, however, set a more important precedent in being probably the first English novel to refer to Sigmund Freud by name, as well as first exploring the Oedipal complex in a supernatural context. From an early age Tom Kelverdon is afflicted by an obsession about a wave. His father, a Freudian analyst, unsuccessfully attempts to discover the root of his son's "premonition," though he entertains the suggestion that it was communicated prenatally. Not until Tom is posted to Egypt, where he joins a childhood friend, Lettice, and his cousin, Tony, does Tom discover the real source of his affliction in his need to atone for misjudging Lettice in her previous incarnation as the wife of Tony, who was then a general in ancient Egypt. During a windstorm in which a wave of sand engulfs Tom and Lettice, Tom lets go of his jealousy and rage toward the powerful and interfering Tony, and the lovers are freed to rejoin in their modern manifestations. The happy ending seems somewhat forced, and Blackwood succumbs to his characteristic flaw of overwriting in the Egyptian winter section.

The interest shown in the power of wind in *The Wave* is full-blown in *The Promise of Air,* a novel strangely optimistic and uplifting given the timing of its publication (26 April 1918). In it Joseph Wimble, an agent for the What's-in-the-Air Publishing Company with a passion for birds and flight, marries a woman whose ethereal quality gives way to plodding. Joseph's inspiration revives with the development of his singular daughter Joan, who is more airy and less tied to time and space than he is. He attends the cinema, which frees and extends the consciousness through its dynamism, and a lecture on Henri Bergson, William James, and "Frood of Vienna and Young of Zurich," reinforcing his intuition about the coming of a new spiritual age in which subconscious will become increasingly conscious and new powers will be released. After moving his family to the country, Joseph experiences a moment of futuristic vision as the novel closes, of "a practical, cooperative life based upon those greater powers, and upon that completer understanding lying, hid with God, in the subliminal regions of humanity" rather than some "flabby, utopian idealistic brotherhood." This rather breathtaking novel

shows how quickly and perceptively the idealist Blackwood grasped the imaginative possibilities of the new psychologists' ideas, particularly Freud's therapeutic aim of making more of the unconscious conscious. A few reviewers pointed out the thinness of the plot, but more recognized the novel's uniqueness.

*The Garden of Survival,* an even slimmer novel, continues the optimistic tone of *The Promise of Air,* perhaps with a more conscious aim, as Blackwood claimed that "my theme is that the dead do not return, but that those who lived Beauty in their lives, co-operate with the spirit of Beauty afterwards, and for ever. So many who have lost their loved ones in the war have liked it, that I thought of publishing it if possible." The narrator describes the piece as "not a novel but a transcript from actual life" written as a letter to his twin brother, who is finally revealed to have passed on to the beyond, figured as a garden. A man of action, the narrator married his wife out of pity; she died one month later. He recounts that the power of beauty she represented remained benevolently active in his life and encouraged him to develop spiritually, described in very Wordsworthian passages about silences "so deep that I could hear the murmur of my blood." While Hudson's dismissal of *The Garden of Survival* as a failure is overly harsh, the work is overly sentimental.

In the postwar period Blackwood's circle of friends widened, and he regularly stayed at the estates of various friends, including Lady Essendon, Henry Ainley, and Baroness de Knoop. The latter's parties often included H. G. Wells, Noel Coward, and the mystic Pyotr Ouspenskii, under whom Blackwood studied throughout the 1920s. He became increasingly involved in the theater: acting, collaborating with various playwrights, and producing at least two popular successes, *The Crossing* (1920) and *Through the Crack* (1925). Though the volume of his prose writing correspondingly declined, in the early 1920s he collaborated with his friend Wilfred Wilson on a collection of stories with a darker vision of humanity, *The Wolves of God and Other Fey Stories* (1921), and produced a novel, *The Bright Messenger* (1921), and his autobiography, *Episodes Before Thirty* (1923).

In *The Bright Messenger* Blackwood again successfully blends the supernatural, psychic research, and psychoanalysis to explore human potential as more of the subconscious and superconscious is made conscious, by then a dominant theme in his work. The novel centers on the development of Dr. Edward Fillery, "psychiatrist and healer" and one of "the unstable" to whom the book is dedicated. He

EPISODES BEFORE
THIRTY

BY
ALGERNON BLACKWOOD

NEW YORK
E. P. DUTTON & COMPANY
681 FIFTH AVENUE

*Frontispiece and title page of the American edition of Blackwood's autobiography*

and his unimaginative, rational assistant, Paul Devonham, take into their care Julian Le Vallon, son of Julius Le Vallon. Julian is a divided personality, part of him possessed by a nonhuman ("N.H.") elemental of wind and fire and part of him by a vital and attractive human being. Blackwood sustains dramatic tension in the novel through the debate between doctors about which part will dominate and what the appropriate treatment is, a structure that brings to mind Doris Lessing's *Briefing For A Descent Into Hell* (1971). Julian creates an enormous impact on a society of psychically sensitive beings, the Prometheans, who are lightly satirized, and he magnetically attracts a Russian beauty, Nayan Khilikoff. In an ironic twist Julian escapes back to the elements, but Fillery's contact with him and Devonham's diagnosis of Fillery persuade the psychiatrist to overcome his inhibition and accept Nayan into his life.

On finishing his autobiography, Blackwood felt that he had said all he had to say, but he continued to collect his stories in volumes such as *Tongues of Fire and Other Sketches* (1924) and *Shocks* (1935). He also proceeded to develop another facet of his var-

ied talent, as a children's story writer. His most successful and highly acclaimed effort in this genre, *Dudley and Gilderoy: A Nonsense* (1929), humorously describes the London adventures of a renegade parrot and cat with human capabilities. Another imaginative children's novel, *The Fruit Stoners: Being the Adventures of Maria among the Fruit Stoners* (1934), concerns the adventures of a girl with characters she has invented using her father's discarded prune stones. Their quest to find a lost object occurs during a brief moment of time and thus recalls Blackwood's earlier explorations beyond time in novels like *The Extra Day*. Blackwood also contributed many shorter popular tales to Basil Blackwell's and Cynthia Asquith's children's annuals.

During the 1920s and 1930s Blackwood continued to travel extensively in Europe and even returned briefly to New York in 1933. Finally in 1934 the BBC persuaded him to embark on a broadcasting career. His success as a storyteller led to his appearance in November 1936 on Britain's first television show. Though an exciting episode, it could not compare with the hike that Blackwood, then sixty-seven, had undertaken earlier in the year from Austria to pre–civil war Spain, where he observed "rioting, arson, and murder."

THE

# PROMISE OF AIR

BY

ALGERNON BLACKWOOD

AUTHOR OF
'THE EDUCATION OF UNCLE PAUL,' 'A PRISONER IN FAIRYLAND,'
'THE CENTAUR,' ETC.

MACMILLAN AND CO., LIMITED
ST. MARTIN'S STREET, LONDON
1918

*Title page for the novel in which Blackwood predicts a new spiritual age when the subconscious potential of humans will be released (courtesy of the Lilly Library, Indiana University)*

In the late 1930s and through the 1940s Blackwood's literary production slowed. Ever seeking out new experiences, he continued to travel until the outbreak of World War II. He was refused service in espionage but served as a fire watcher at his nephew's house in Hampstead until it suffered a direct hit during the Battle of Britain. Blackwood survived only because he and his nephew had returned to their bomb shelter to rescue some burning sausages just before the bomb struck. The shock of this event prompted him to move first to Devon and then to a friend's Sussex home, where he wrote several radio plays as well as three new short stories.

Following the war, in 1947 Blackwood became involved in performing on radio and television and in short films. His regular *Saturday Night Story* spot on television made him a household name, and in 1949 he was made a commander of the British Empire, one of the proudest moments of his life. After a Halloween broadcast in 1950, Blackwood suffered a slight stroke, but by January 1951 he had recovered enough to visit friends in Switzerland. Ironically,

his next Halloween broadcast, prerecorded on 13 October 1951, would be his last performance. His health deteriorated, and on 10 December he died of cerebral thrombosis and arteriosclerosis.

A particularly striking characteristic of this prolific author was his openness to new ideas and experiences. Blackwood claimed that he had "always taken ideas where [he] found them," and this quality is reflected in the variety and nature of subjects that he explores and in the variety in length of his printed work and the variety of media in which he worked. Contemporary reviewers realized the difficulties of classifying Blackwood's work, and it consequently slipped between the cracks of criticism. Subsequent critics have often viewed him merely as a genre writer of the ghost, fantasy, or supernatural short story, though most acknowledge his preeminence. Even a brief survey of his novels indicates how restrictive that view is. His book-length fiction compellingly explores the possibilities of expanded consciousness through all kinds of psychic voyages, leading Louise Field to acclaim Blackwood as the "prose-poet of the borderlands which lie beyond and behind the outer edge of the conscious, the physical and the tangible." Even before D. H. Lawrence, Blackwood saw the imaginative potential in the findings of psychoanalysts on the unconscious and psychic conflict. In Blackwood's poetic evocation of natural settings and atmosphere and his descriptions of the magnetic attraction between individuals possessed of old souls, he reaches the intensity of Lawrence's vision. In 1935 Stuart Gilbert, an astute critic of Blackwood, went so far as to claim that "no living writer in the English tongue has done more than Algernon Blackwood to quicken [the] sense of wonder and open our eyes to the conscious vitality of much that we habitually regard as inert matter, and to the miraculous nature of what we call causation." Blackwood deserves to be more widely recognized for exploring such unusual thematic territory and articulating so vividly experiences often considered incommunicable, for his escape from the formulas of genre, and ultimately for his brilliance as a storyteller.

**Bibliographies:**

John Robert Colombo, *Blackwood's Books* (Toronto: Hounslow Press, 1981);

Mike Ashley, *Algernon Blackwood: A Bio-Bibliography* (New York: Greenwood Press, 1987).

**Biography:**

Mike Ashley, *Algernon Blackwood: A Bio-Bibliography* (New York: Greenwood Press, 1987).

**References:**

Hilaire Belloc, Review of Blackwood's *John Silence: Physician Extraordinary, Morning Post,* 17 September 1908, p. 2; republished in *Horror: One Hundred Best Books,* edited by Stephen Jones and Kim Newman (New York: Carroll & Graf, 1988), pp. 67–68;

E. F. Bleiler, "Introduction to the Dover Edition," in *Best Ghost Stories of Algernon Blackwood* (New York: Dover Books, 1973), pp. v–x;

Julia Briggs, *The Rise and Fall of the English Ghost Story* (London: Faber & Faber, 1977);

Donald R. Burleson, "Algernon Blackwood's 'The Listener': A Hearing," *Studies in Weird Fiction,* 5 (Spring 1989): 15–19;

R. F. Fleissner, " 'No Ghosts Need Apply'? Or, The Adventure of the Empty House's Empty House," *Studies in Weird Fiction,* 6 (Fall 1989): 28–30;

Derek Hudson, "A Study of Algernon Blackwood," in *Essays and Studies,* new series 14 (London: John Murray, 1961), pp. 102–114;

S. T. Joshi, *The Weird Tale: Arthur Machen, Lord Dunsany, Algernon Blackwood, M. R. James, Ambrose Bierce, H. P. Lovecraft* (Austin: University of Texas Press, 1990);

Russell Letson Jr., *The Approaches to Mystery: The Fantasies of Arthur Machen and Algernon Blackwood,* Ph.D. dissertation, Southern Illinois University, 1975;

H. P. Lovecraft, "Supernatural Horror in Literature," in his *The Outsider and Others* (Sauk City, Wis.: Arkham House, 1939);

Peter Penzoldt, "Algernon Blackwood," in his *The Supernatural in Fiction* (London: Peter Nevill, 1952), pp. 228–253;

Dorothy Scarborough, *The Supernatural in Modern English Fiction* (New York: Putnam, 1917);

Jack Sullivan, "The Visionary Ghost Story: Algernon Blackwood," in his *Elegant Nightmares: The English Ghost Story From Le Fanu to Blackwood* (Athens: Ohio University Press, 1978), pp. 112–129;

Edward Wagenknecht, "Algernon Blackwood," in his *Seven Masters of Supernatural Fiction* (Westport, Conn.: Greenwood Press, 1991), pp. 69–94.

**Papers:**

The main collection of Blackwood's manuscripts is at the BBC Written Archives at Caversham, Reading. Mike Ashley, who lives in Chatham, Kent, possesses the largest collection of Blackwood's letters, though the British Library also has a substantial collection. Other letters are scattered throughout archives in North America.

# Marjorie Bowen
## (Gabrielle Margaret Vere Campbell)
### *(1 November 1886 – 22 December 1952)*

Maria Aline Seabra Ferreira
*Universidade de Aveiro*

See also the Joseph Shearing entry in *DLB 70: British Mystery Writers, 1860–1919*.

BOOKS: *The Viper of Milan: A Romance of Lombardy* (London: Alston Rivers, 1906; New York: McClure, Phillips, 1906);

*The Glen o' Weeping* (London: Alston Rivers, 1907; New York: McClure, Phillips, 1907); published as *The Master of Stair* (New York: McClure, Phillips, 1907);

*The Leopard and the Lily* (New York: McClure, Phillips, 1907; London & New York: Doubleday, Page, 1909);

*The Sword Decides! A Chronicle of a Queen in the Dark Ages; Founded on the Story of Giovanna of Naples* (London: Alston Rivers, 1908; New York: McClure, Phillips, 1908);

*A Moment's Madness* (London: Cassell, 1908);

*Black Magic: A Tale of the Rise and Fall of Antichrist* (London: Alston Rivers, 1909);

*I Will Maintain* (London: Methuen, 1910; New York: Dutton, 1910);

*Defender of the Faith* (London: Methuen, 1911; New York: Dutton, 1911);

*The Quest of Glory* (London: Methuen, 1911; New York: Dutton, 1912);

*God and the King* (London: Methuen, 1911; New York: Dutton, 1912);

*God's Playthings* (London: Smith, Elder, 1912; New York: Dutton, 1913);

*The Rake's Progress* (London: Rider, 1912);

*Lover's Knots* (London: Everett, 1912);

*A Knight of Spain* (London: Methuen, 1913);

*The Governor of England* (London: Methuen, 1913; New York: Dutton, 1914);

*The Two Carnations* (London: Cassell, 1913; New York: Reynolds, 1913);

*Prince and Heretic* (London: Methuen, 1914; New York: Dutton, 1915);

*The Carnival of Florence* (London: Methuen, 1915; New York: Dutton, 1915);

*Marjorie Bowen (Gabrielle Margaret Vere Campbell)*

*Mr. Washington* (London: Methuen, 1915); published as *The Soldier from Virginia* (New York: Appleton, 1912);

*"Because of These Things . . ."* (London: Methuen, 1915);

*Shadows of Yesterday: Stories from an Old Catalogue* (London: Smith, Elder, 1916; New York: Dutton, 1916);

*"William By the Grace of God — "* (London: Methuen, 1916; New York: Dutton, 1917);

*The Third Estate* (London: Methuen, 1917; New York: Dutton, 1918);

*Curious Happenings (Short Stories)* (London: Mills & Boon, 1917);

*The Burning Glass* (London: Collins, 1918; New York: Dutton, 1920);

*Kings-at-Arms* (London: Methuen, 1918; New York: Dutton, 1919);

*Crimes of Old London* (London: Odhams, 1919);

*Mr. Misfortunate* (London: Collins, 1919);

*The Cheats: A Romantic Fantasy* (London: Collins, 1920);

*The Haunted Vintage* (London: Odhams, 1921);

*The Pleasant Husband and Other Stories* (London: Hurst & Blackett, 1921);

*Rococo* (London: Odhams, 1921);

*The Love Thief* (London: Odhams, 1922);

*Stinging Nettles: A Modern Story* (London & Melbourne: Ward, Lock, 1923; Boston: Small, Maynard, 1923);

*Seeing Life and Other Stories* (London: Hurst & Blackett, 1923);

*The Presence and the Power: A Story of Three Generations* (London & Melbourne: Ward, Lock, 1924);

*Five People* (London & Melbourne: Ward, Lock, 1925);

*"Luctor et Emergo"; Being an Historical Essay on the State of England at the Peace of Ryswyck, 1697* (Newcastle-upon-Tyne: Northumberland Press, 1925);

*The Seven Deadly Sins* (London: Hurst & Blackett, 1926);

*Boundless Water* (London & Melbourne: Ward, Lock, 1926);

*Nell Gwyn: A Decoration* (London: Hodder & Stoughton, 1926; New York: Appleton, 1926);

*The Netherlands Display'd: or The Delights of the Low Countries* (London: Bodley Head, 1926; New York: Dodd, Mead, 1926);

*Dark Ann and Other Stories* (London: Bodley Head, 1927);

*The Pagoda (La Pagode de Chanteloup)* (London: Hodder & Stoughton, 1927);

*"Five Winds": A Romance* (London: Hodder & Stoughton, 1927);

*The Countess Fanny: A Cornish Sea Piece (1856)* (London: Hodder & Stoughton, 1928);

*The Golden Roof* (London: Hodder & Stoughton, 1928);

*Exits and Farewells: Being Some Account of the Last Days of Certain Historical Characters Well-Known in Their Own Times* (London: Selwyn & Blount, 1928);

*The Story of the Temple and its Associations* (London: Griffin, 1928);

*Sundry Great Gentlemen: Some Essays in Historical Biography* (London: Bodley Head, 1928; New York: Dodd, Mead, 1928);

*William, Prince of Orange (Afterwards King of England) Being an Account of His Early Life up to His Twenty-Fourth Year* (London: Bodley Head, 1928; New York: Dodd, Mead, 1928);

*The Winged Trees* (Oxford: Blackwell, 1928);

*Holland: Being a Survey of the Netherlands Commonly Called Holland* (London: Harrap, 1928; New York: Doubleday, Doran, 1929);

*Old Patch's Medley, or, a London Miscellany, Being Some Adventures of the Old Gentleman in London City Some Two Hundred Years Ago or So Here Recorded* (London: Selwyn & Blount, 1928);

*Fond Fancy and Other Stories* (London: Selwyn & Blount, 1928);

*Mademoiselle Maria Gloria* (Oxford: Basil Blackwell, 1929);

*Dickon: An Historical Romance* (London: Hodder & Stoughton, 1929);

*The Third Mary Stuart: Mary of York, Orange, and England, Being a Character Study, With Memoirs and Letters of Queen Mary II of England, 1662–1694* (London: Bodley Head, 1929);

*The Lady's Prisoner* (Oxford: Blackwell, 1929);

*The Gorgeous Lovers and Other Tales* (London: Bodley Head, 1929);

*Sheep's Head & Babylon, and Other Stories of Yesterday and Today* (London: Bodley Head, 1929);

*The English Paragon* (London: Hodder & Stoughton, 1930);

*A Family Comedy (1840): A Comedy in One Act* (London: Samuel French, 1930);

*Brave Employments* (London: Collins, 1931);

*Grace Latouche and the Warringtons: Some Nineteenth Century Pieces (Mostly Victorian)* (London: Selwyn & Blount, 1931);

*The Question: A Play in One Act* (London: Samuel French, 1931);

*Withering Fires* (London: Collins, 1931);

*Dark Rosaleen* (London: Collins, 1932; Boston & New York: Houghton Mifflin, 1933);

*The Last Bouquet: Some Twilight Tales* (London: Bodley Head, 1932);

*The Shadows on Mockways* (London: Collins, 1932);

*The Veil'd Delight (The Rainbow and the Mirror)* (London: Odhams, 1933);

*I Dwelt in High Places* (London: Collins, 1933);

*"Set with Green Herbs"* (London: Ernest Benn, 1933);

*The Stolen Bride* (London: Dickson, 1933);

*Mary Queen of Scots: Daughter of Debate* (London: Bodley Head, 1934; New York: Putnam, 1934);

*The Scandal of Sophie Dawes* (London: Bodley Head, 1934; New York: Appleton-Century, 1935);

*Patriotic Lady: A Study of Emma, Lady Hamilton* (London: Bodley Head, 1935; New York: Appleton-Century, 1936);

*Peter Porcupine, A Study of William Cobbett, 1762–1835* (London & New York: Longmans, Green, 1935);

*Trumpets at Rome* (London: Hutchinson, 1936);

*William Hogarth, The Cockney's Mirror* (London: Methuen, 1936; New York: Appleton-Century, 1936);

*Crowns and Sceptres: The Romance and Pageantry of Coronations* (London: Long, 1937);

*Wrestling Jacob: A Study of the Life of John Wesley and Some Members of the Family* (London & Toronto: Heinemann, 1937);

*The Triumphant Beast: A Tribute, A Confession, An Apology* (London: Bodley Head, 1937);

*A Giant in Chains: Prelude to Revolution (France 1775–1791)* (London: Hutchinson, 1938);

*God and the Wedding Dress* (London: Hutchinson, 1938);

*World's Wonder and Other Essays* (London: Hutchinson, 1938);

*The Trumpet and the Swan. An Adventure of the Civil War* (London: Pitman, 1938);

*Ethics in Modern Art* (London: Watts, 1939);

*The Circle in the Water* (London: Hutchinson, 1939);

*Mr. Tyler's Saints* (London: Hutchinson, 1939);

*Exchange Royal* (London & Melbourne: Hutchinson, 1940);

*Strangers to Freedom* (London: Dent, 1940);

*Today is Mine: The Story of a Gamble* (London & Melbourne: Hutchinson, 1941);

*The Church and Social Progress: An Exposition of Rationalism and Reaction* (London: Watts, 1945);

*The Bishop of Hell, and Other Stories* (London: Bodley Head, 1949);

*Mistress Nell Gwyn* (London: Mellifont, 1949);

*In the Steps of Mary Queen of Scots* (London: Rich & Cowan, 1952);

*The Man with the Scales* (London: Hutchinson, 1954);

*Kecksies and Other Twilight Talks* (Sauk City, Wis.: Arkham House, 1976).

BOOKS – as George R. Preedy: *General Crack* (London: Bodley Head, 1928; New York: Dodd, Mead, 1928);

*Captain Banner: A Drama in Three Acts* (London: Bodley Head, 1930);

*Bagatelle and Some Other Diversions* (London: Bodley Head, 1930; New York: Dodd, Mead, 1931);

*The Rocklitz* (London: Bodley Head, 1930); published as *The Prince's Darling* (New York: Dodd, Mead, 1930);

*Tumult in the North* (London: Bodley Head, 1931; New York: Dodd, 1931);

*The Pavilion of Honour* (London: Bodley Head, 1932);

*Violante (Circe and the Ermine)* (London: Cassell, 1932);

*Passion Flower* (London: Collins, 1932); published as *Beneath the Passion Flower* (New York: McBride, 1932);

*Double Dallillay* (London: Cassell, 1933); published as *Queen's Caprice: A Novel of Mary, Queen of Scots* (New York: King, 1934);

*Dr. Chaos; and The Devil Snar'd* (London: Cassell, 1933);

*The Knot Garden: Some Old Fancies Re-set (Tales)* (London: Bodley Head, 1933);

*The Autobiography of Cornelis Blake, 1773–1810, of Ditton See, Cambridgeshire (Sometime Banker of the Netherlands and Naples)* (London: Cassell, 1934);

*Laurell'd Captains* (London: Hutchinson, 1935);

*The Poisoners* (London: Hutchinson, 1936);

*This Shining Woman: Mary Wollstonecraft Godwin: 1759–1797* (London: Collins, 1937; New York: Appleton-Century, 1937);

*My Tattered Loving. The Overbury Mystery* (London: Jenkins, 1937);

*Painted Angel: A Mystery of the Napoleonic Wars* (London: Jenkins, 1938);

*The Dove in the Mulberry Tree* (London: Jenkins, 1939);

*The Fair Young Widow* (London: Jenkins, 1939);

*Child of Chequer'd Fortune: The Life, Loves and Battles of Maurice de Saxe, Maréchal de France, Born 1696, Died 1750* (London: Jenkins, 1939);

*Primula. A Romantic Tale* (London: Hodder & Stoughton, 1940);

*The Life of John Knox* (London: Jenkins, 1940);

*The Life of Rear-Admiral John Paul Jones . . .* (London: Jenkins, 1940);

*Findernes' Flowers* (London: Hodder & Stoughton, 1941);

*Black Man, White Maiden* (London: Hodder & Stoughton, 1941);

*The Courtly Charlatan: The Enigmatic Comte de St. Germain* (London: Jenkins, 1942);

*Lyndley Waters* (London: Hodder & Stoughton, 1942);

*Lady in a Veil* (London: Hodder & Stoughton, 1943);

*The Fourth Chamber* (London: Hodder & Stoughton, 1944);

*Nightcap and Plume* (London: Hodder & Stoughton, 1945);

*No Way Home* (London: Hodder & Stoughton, 1947);

*The Sacked City* (London: Hodder & Stoughton, 1949);

*Julia Ballantyne* (London: Hodder & Stoughton, 1952);

*Forget-Me-Not* (London: Fontana, 1953) – previously published (1932) as by Joseph Shearing.

BOOKS – as Edgar Winch: *The Mountain of Gold* (London: Hurst & Blackett, 1928);

*The Hunting of Hilary* (London: Skeffington, 1929);

*When the Tide Runs Out* (London: Hurst & Blackett, 1930);

*Idlers' Gate* (London: Collins, 1932);

*Captain Joan*, by Winch and J. D. Makgill (London: Hodder & Stoughton, 1932).

BOOKS – as Robert Paye: *The Devil's Jig* (London: Bodley Head, 1931);

*Julia Roseingrave* (London: Benn, 1933).

BOOKS – as Joseph Shearing: *Forget-Me-Not* (London: Heinemann, 1932); published as *Lucile Cléry, A Woman of Intrigue* (New York: Harpers, 1932);

*Album Leaf* (London: Heinemann, 1934); published as *The Spider in the Cup* (New York: Smith & Haas, 1934);

*Moss Rose* (London: Heinemann, 1934; New York: Smith & Haas, 1935);

*The Angel of the Assassination: Marie-Charlotte de Corday d'Armont, Jean-Paul Marat, Jean-Adam Lux. A Study of Three Disciples of Jean-Jacques Rousseau* (London & Toronto: Heinemann, 1935; New York: Smith & Haas, 1935);

*The Golden Violet: The Story of a Lady Novelist* (London & Toronto: Heinemann, 1936; New York: Smith & Durrell, 1936);

*The Lady and the Arsenic: The Life and Death of a Romantic: Marie Capelle, Madame Lafarge, 1816–1852* (London & Toronto: Heinemann, 1937; New York: Barnes, 1944);

*Orange Blossoms* (London: Heinemann, 1938);

*Blanche Fury; or, Fury's Ape* (London & Toronto: Heinemann, 1939; New York: Harrison-Hilton, 1939);

*Aunt Beardie* (London & Melbourne: Hutchinson, 1940; New York: Harrison-Hilton, 1940);

*Laura Sarelle* (London: Hutchinson, 1941); published as *The Crime of Laura Sarelle* (New York: Smith & Durrell, 1941);

*The Fetch* (London: Hutchinson, 1941); published as *The Spectral Bride* (New York: Smith & Durrell, 1942);

*Mignonette* (London: Heinemann, 1942; New York: Harpers, 1942);

*Airing in a Closed Carriage* (London: Hutchinson, 1943; New York: Harpers, 1943);

*The Abode of Love* (London & New York: Hutchinson, 1944);

*For Her to See* (London: Hutchinson, 1947); published as *So Evil My Love* (New York: Harpers, 1947);

*Within the Bubble* (London: Heinemann, 1950);

*To Bed at Noon* (London: Heinemann, 1951).

BOOK – as Margaret Campbell: *The Debate Continues: Being the Autobiography of Marjorie Bowen* (London: Heinemann, 1939).

OTHER: Semm Benelli, *The Jest*, translated by Bowen (London: Odhams, 1922);

*Affairs of Men*, selected by Bowen (London: Heath Cranton, 1922);

Percy Allen, *The Plays of Shakespeare & Chapman in relation to French History*, with an introduction by Bowen (London: Archer, 1933);

*Great Tales of Horror*, selected, with an introduction, by Bowen (London: Bodley Head, 1933);

*More Great Tales of Horror*, selected, with a foreword, by Bowen (London: Bodley Head, 1935);

*Some Famous Love Letters*, edited by Bowen (London: Jenkins, 1937).

Marjorie Bowen is the best-known pseudonym of Gabrielle Margaret Vere Campbell, but she wrote under a variety of others, including Joseph Shearing, George R. Preedy, Robert Paye, and John Winch. She wrote in a range of genres, including romance, supernatural, and historical novels; short stories; biographies; and children's books. In her autobiography, *The Debate Continues* (1939), she defines herself as "a woman who earned her living by writing fiction – with occasional essays in that kind of history deplored by historians." Bowen was prolific, writing at least 150 books, and she conceived of herself in clearheaded fashion as a competent crafter of light fiction portraying a gallery of women protagonists for a largely female public.

Born on 1 November 1886 on Hayling Island, Hampshire, Bowen was the second daughter of Vere Douglas Campbell and Josephine Elisabeth

Ellis (Bowen), whose marriage was unhappy. Her childhood was marred by her parents' poverty and the breakup of their marriage. She was an introspective and reserved child, deeply sensitive to the material disadvantages of their existence and to the bohemian life led by her mother, an aspiring novelist. Taught to read and write by her mother, Bowen was later left mainly to her own resources. In *The Debate Continues* she recalls of her early reading that Alfred Tennyson's *The Idylls of the King* was "a perfect experience." She greatly enjoyed Oscar Wilde's *The Picture of Dorian Gray* (1890), and Samuel Richardson's *Clarissa* (1747–1748) was her favorite novel. William Wordsworth's "Lucy Gray" "had a frightful fascination" for Bowen, who recognized that "there was pleasure amounting to ecstasy in this terror." She also indulged in literary exercises designed to improve her style. In her autobiography she reflects on the extent of her self-teaching and its appropriateness for the development of her literary career: "I tried to write verses, a narrative in elaborate stanzas after the model of the *Faerie Queen,* and another on Chaucerian lines. I also tried to dramatise some of Browning's longer poems in the form of plays. These were by way of literary exercises. I had read no really first-class fiction, only the missionary magazine stories and moral tales. I had not read any trashy fiction either."

She also began to draw, in spite of her difficulty in getting money for canvases and paint. She had, however, obtained permission to copy at the National Gallery, where she learned about the techniques of both oil and watercolor painting. After her parents' separation, Bowen was sent to the Slade School of Art, but she did not enjoy the experience, and her artwork was generally dismissed by the professors at the school. At about this time she started earning some money as a research assistant at the British Museum. This position contributed decisively to spur on her writing career and her interest in historical research. She began writing a novel.

Around this time, Bowen's mother decided to send her to Paris to improve her drawing technique. However, her mother could never afford to send the money to pay for the boardinghouse, run by an Englishwoman, where Bowen was staying or for the art-school fees, so she was reduced to going to sketching classes and later, when there was no money for that, to frequenting museums and picture galleries. In addition to her financial difficulties, Bowen's technical expertise was not advanced enough at that stage to enable her to profit as much as she might have from her stay abroad. On the

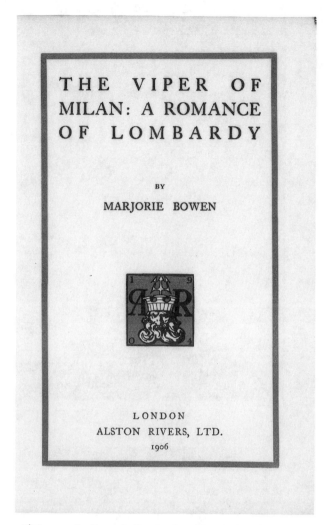

THE VIPER OF
MILAN: A ROMANCE
OF LOMBARDY

BY

MARJORIE BOWEN

LONDON
ALSTON RIVERS, LTD.
1906

*Title page for Bowen's first book, a historical romance set in fourteenth-century Lombardy (courtesy of the Lilly Library, Indiana University)*

other hand, she loved Paris and tried to make her sojourn there as worthwhile as she possibly could, claiming that she "had the 'feel' of the nation."

The fact that Bowen's drawing was not progressing led her to concentrate on her writing and to give vent to her desire for describing the scenes she saw. She had also been inspired by reading some of the French classics and Russian works in French translations. Bowen's first book, *The Viper of Milan: A Romance of Lombardy,* dedicated to her mother, was published in 1906, when the author was sixteen, after having been rejected by eleven publishers. It quickly became a success, going through eight printings in five months, and launched her immensely prolific career. As Bowen had signed a fixed-price contract, she received only sixty pounds from her publishers. She also signed a

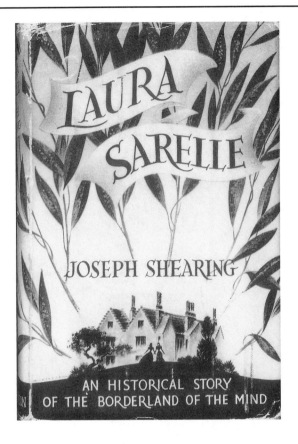

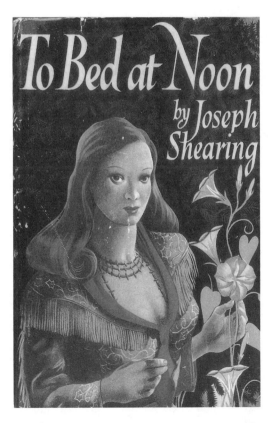

*Dust jackets for three novels published under one of Bowen's many pseudonyms (courtesy of the Lilly Library, Indiana University)*

contract with the same publisher for her next two books, in spite of better offers from other publishing houses, out of a sense of duty and fairness. Although she enjoyed writing, it sometimes became a burden, for the whole responsibility of providing for the household fell on her. She had to keep writing to support the somewhat extravagant lifestyle of her mother and sister.

*The Viper of Milan* is a historical novel that beautifully captures the spirit and local color of its setting, a gift that Bowen acknowledged and for which she was grateful. Edward Wagenknecht, in a highly eulogistic piece in *The New York Times Book Review* titled "The Extraordinary Mrs. Long," stresses this aspect of Bowen's work, considering her "a genius in the creation of atmosphere. . . . Nobody since Wilkie Collins has surpassed Mrs. Long in this particular achievement." Bowen's first historical romance opens in Lombardy in 1360, and it features all the expected paraphernalia of casements, castles, baronial halls, battles, beautiful heroines, and dark and handsome villains. The "dread power that rules Lombardy," the evil Visconti, has just sacked Verona and believes he has killed Mastino della Scala, its duke, and has captured the duchess, Isotta. The reader is introduced to the story via two youths, Vittore and Tomaso, on their way to join relatives in Verona. The latter is dashed to the ground by Visconti in the opening incident on a road. They are then assisted by the giant Franciso, who later turns out to be Mastino della Scala in disguise. Other characters include Visconti's half-crazed brother Tisio and his beautiful and honest sister Valentine (whom he wants to marry to a Valois but who is in love with a young German count attached to the Veronese).

As the tale unfolds, Franciso is revealed as della Scala, regroups, retakes Verona, and leads an assault on Visconti, who narrowly escapes. The count tries to kill Visconti and fails. Graziosa, the beautiful painter's daughter, has helped to save Milan, and Visconti plans to reward her by marrying her. However, she is warned by Valentine of his unbounded evil and kills herself rather than wed Visconti. The latter revenges himself on Valentine by the cruel ploy of pretending to make her drink poison, which drives Valentine mad. The dénouement of the tale, which seems somewhat hasty and unfinished (a characteristic of many of Bowen's historical romances), narrates the death of della Scala, killed in a final battle in Milan by a cowardly team of Visconti's men. Visconti plans to escape but is stabbed in the back by Ginotto, his jealous and nasty servant, and dies. *The Viper of Milan* received

wide praise from readers, including Mark Twain, to whom in gratitude Bowen dedicated her third novel, *The Glen o' Weeping* (1907; *The Master of Stair* in the United States).

Bowen's early historical romances were all preoccupied with political intrigue among the great houses of Europe, with sudden revelations and improbable coincidences, interspersed with romantic episodes with a predominance of dark, exotic maidens who have to choose between the seductive villain and his good-natured but often ineffectual male counterpart. *Black Magic: A Tale of the Rise and Fall of Antichrist* (1909) is a Gothic novel uniting historical and supernatural elements, in the manner of Marie Corelli's *The Sorrows of Satan* (1895) and with strong overtones of Jacobean tragedy at its most baroque. Wagenknecht, in the chapter dedicated to Bowen of his *Seven Masters of Supernatural Fiction* (1991), describes it as the first of her novels "that can be called definitely supernatural," one of a long succession of novels and tales that draw heavily on and explore supernatural manifestations, a subject Bowen was attracted to, having herself lived in a supposedly haunted house. Part 1 of the novel, titled "The Nun," opens in a convent in Flanders, where the young sculptor Dirk is gilding a figure of a devil. Two men arrive: the blond noble Balthasar of Courtrai, whose wife, Ursula of Rooselaare, has been in the convent since she left him after an arranged marriage, and the dark scholar Theirry of Dendermonde. Dirk shows them her grave, and he also shows the fearful Theirry some black magic – a vision of a strange blond woman in a glass. After this display of witchcraft, the two of them decide to study the dark arts together.

At Basle University, Theirry and Dirk meet the beautiful Jacobea of Martzburg, with whose destiny they are to be entwined and with whom Theirry falls in love. Dirk lays a curse on a rival student, Joris, who later dies. They are accused of witchcraft and their apparatus is discovered, but they manage to escape, meeting Jacobea and her steward Sebastian on the road to Frankfurt. They also meet Saint Ambrose, whose money they steal, and Ysabeau, empress of the West and part-time witch, who was the face in the mirror. She is married to Melchior of Brabant but wants to wed Balthazar (a friend of Melchior) and make him emperor. Melchior is later poisoned by Ysabeau. The noble Hugh of Rooselaare accuses her and is imprisoned and then executed, Dirk failing to arrive with a pardon in time. It is revealed that Hugh is Dirk's father.

The stream of coincidences and Gothic surprises continues. Part 2, titled "The Pope," opens in

Rome eight years later. Dirk has risen in the church and is now Cardinal Luigi Caprasola, the most powerful man in Rome, living in decadent luxury. Theirry, who has wandered guilt-ridden to Constantinople to receive forgiveness from this famous priest, meets him. The baroque and Gothic thunder and lightning at this point in the tale signal a crucial moment of revelation and crisis in the plot. Dirk reveals his identity to his horrified friend and prevails on him again, promising him that he will replace Balthazar as emperor. The pope dies and Dirk is elected Pope Michael II, after gaining the empress's support, threatening to reveal all about Melchior's death to Balthazar if she does not help him. The covert homoerotic strain present in the tale from the beginning becomes more pronounced as the pope and Theirry clasp hands after the papal army, led by Theirry, wins a victory over Balthazar at Tivoli.

The pope's ambiguous identity and gender become more and more problematic. Theirry fits the pieces of the puzzle together, realizing that the characters of the pope, Dirk, and Ursula, who appears as a mysterious and seductive dancer, are the same. On the one hand Dirk/Ursula's sexual transgressiveness as a woman who plays a man's role, like the legendary female pope, or as a man in female garb, seems to be closely related with the book's general thematic concerns with satanism and witchcraft; on the other hand, this strong subversive strain of gender roles is toned down at the end when it is implied that he/she was really female, although doubt lingers in the reader's mind. In a final and eloquent note to Theirry, where the ambiguity of his/her sexuality is again emphasized, the pope writes: "If I be a devil I go whence I came, if a man I lived as one and die as one; if a woman I have known love, conquered it and by it have been vanquished. Whosoever I am I perish on the heights, but I do not descend from them. I have known things in their fulness and will not stay to taste the dregs." Theirry discovers him/her dead in his/her inner chamber. As he prepares to resolve the ambiguity about gender and uncovers the breast, the body crumbles to dust and Theirry falls, himself dying, beside the bed, to follow him/her to eternity.

This novel can be characterized as apprentice work, with its bizarre intricacies of plot, proliferation of exotic characters and locations, improbable events, rampant supernaturalism, phantasmagoria, and a pronounced Gothic strain; nevertheless, *Black Magic* raises several important questions concerning gender stereotyping and society's definition of sexual roles. Both male and female paradigms come under scrutiny, and the blending of gender and gen-

dered behaviors presumably had a strong appeal to the turn-of-the-century audience.

Despite the pressure put on her to publish, Bowen always tried to keep the standards of her writing high. Because of the care she took over her prose, historical work seemed particularly suited to her. As she remarks in her autobiography, "A good deal of effort, research and painstaking work, and a severe self-discipline were necessary for the writing of these books in which history was to be transformed into fiction and men and women of the past given some kind of life."

*A Knight of Spain* (1913) is a good example of the kind of painstakingly researched historical romance that became Marjorie Bowen's stock-in-trade. It is a three-part novel based on the life of John of Austria (bastard son of the Holy Roman Emperor Charles V), the general who won the battle of Lepanto. The first part opens at the University of Alcalá, where the dashing and ambitious youth Don Juan (John) woos the dusky maiden Doña Ana. The plot follows John of Austria's adventurous life and battles in Spain, Italy, France, and Holland, as well as his love affairs with the Machiavellian Ana de Mendoza, Diana di Falanga, Marguerite de Valois, and the queen of Spain.

Many of Bowen's historical romances feature a historical figure – such as Edward Plantagenet, Prince of Wales, and his rule as duke of Aquitaine in the provinces of Guienne and Gascony, in *The English Paragon* (1930) – and fictionalize their lives. Others, such as *The Cheats: A Romantic Fantasy* (1920), a tale of the impossible love between one of the maids of honor to the Duchess of York and the son of a Jersey farmer, attempt to describe courtly life in all its colorful detail. Others treat the plight of a country in the throes of rebellion, as in *Dark Rosaleen* (1932) and its story of Lord Edward Fitzgerald's involvement in the Irish Rebellion, interwoven with a love story concerning Fitzgerald and Pamela. Of this category, her novels with Italian and Dutch settings were particularly successful.

Historical novels, which often included Gothic settings, foreign and exotic locations, and a fast pace, provided Bowen and her readers with the possibility of escape from an often-monotonous quotidian reality and gave them the opportunity to indulge in gratifying fantasies. The author's vivid descriptions of background settings and costumes particularly appealed to a feminine audience. Historical novels thus served many purposes: they gratified a renewed interest in remote and unindustrialized times that had set in as a reaction to the mechanization spreading over the Western world, and they

gave readers the possibility of vicariously becoming heroes and heroines and traveling to faraway places. Marjorie Bowen's tales of mystery and passion, of ghosts and murder, set in the past and in remote places, illustrate Joanna Russ's characterization of the "modern Gothic," which provides "the kind of escape reading a middle-class believer in the feminine mystique needs, without involving elements that either go beyond the feminine mystique or would be considered immoral in its terms." Indeed, many readers appreciated Marjorie Bowen's concern with morality, with the confrontation and eventual triumph of good over evil, evident in *The Viper of Milan,* where the wicked Visconti is murdered in the end. In *Beyond the Lighthouse* (1981) Margaret Crosland calls it "a new type of 'horrid' novel, which would have been inconceivable in a contemporary setting." Crosland also points out that historical novelists such as Marjorie Bowen fulfill an important function by showing "how the great or even the obscure figures of history – Rupert of the Rhine, the Young Pretender, Lady Hamilton – actually lived, and how the private lives of unknown people were affected by the public lives and deeds of kings, queens, religious, political and military leaders." Wagenknecht adds that Bowen was "admired not only by Mark Twain but by Walter de la Mare, Compton Mackenzie, Hugh Walpole, who thought her the finest historical novelist England had had in a generation, William Roughhead, and others, and Graham Greene gladly acknowledged his debt to her in the collection of essays called *A Lost Childhood.*"

The nature of Bowen's work as a serious, committed writer of romances raises the question of the type of audience she attracted. While certain critics and readers took Marjorie Bowen's work seriously, the restrictions of the genre, which tended to attract a not highly educated feminine audience, must also be taken into account. Bowen specifically called *"Five Winds"* (1927) a "Romance," recalling Henry Fielding's dismissive categorization of a type of prose narrative, but also invoking the twentieth-century understanding of the term as the type of love story in which a passive heroine takes pleasure in or considers it her duty to submit to the powerful and masterful hero; this type of plot is very common in Bowen's historical romances and surfaces in some of her modern novels and short stories. As has been often noted, especially by Marxist feminist critics, romance can be regarded as a form of ideological oppression, maintaining and illustrating the ambiguous and subordinate position of women. There is, however, another side to the ideology transmitted by romances. As Tania Modleski stresses in *Loving with a Vengeance* (1988), the act of expressing women's suffering is also a protest against that suffering.

Marjorie Bowen's novels and short stories fit Modleski's assertion. They portray many types of characters, ranging from the traditional romantic heroine to the older woman who is left alone and almost helpless in a man's world. In spite of women's empowerment, which was brought about by the active role they played during the First World War, the majority of Bowen's women-centered novels still convey the message that marriage is the main recourse available to women to solve their financial and sentimental problems. Although a common character type in Bowen's fiction seems to be that of the unmarried middle-aged woman who is trying to lead an independent life and fighting against all sorts of prejudices and conventions, this drive to freedom and self-sufficiency is undermined by the sometimes unstated belief in marriage as the solution to those heroines' feelings of inadequacy and fear in a predominantly patriarchal world. Often financially dependent on a father or brother, the plight of these women is poignantly described and exposed by Bowen, whose books appealed to female readers worried about the shifting role of women in a time of rapidly changing perspectives.

From an early concentration on the writing of historical romances, Bowen shifted to novels and short stories with contemporary settings, although in many of them she keeps exotic settings and foreign characters. This shift seems to follow a parallel tendency to move away from the cloak-and-dagger, swashbuckling tales that dominated the market during the first decades of the twentieth century toward a different kind of fiction, more modern in character and predominantly directed to a feminine audience.

*Stinging Nettles: A Modern Story* (1923) typically describes the plight of three young women who struggle to find a job, a husband, and enough money to survive. Like many of Marjorie Bowen's tales, it is a story of "unsatisfied, struggling people." Lucie, the heroine, is married to an Italian, who has left for Sicily, never to return, leaving her in London where she has a job that gives her some satisfaction. When, however, her husband writes to her asking her to come and nurse him, she goes and looks after him until he dies, meeting in the meantime Carlo Ghisleri, with whom she falls in love, even though she perceives that he would not make her life happier. The problem of marriage and independence is deeply probed:

*Bowen at the time of* The Pavilion of Honour *(1932),
published under her George Preedy pseudonym
(Hulton-Deutsch Collection)*

Marriage. There is nothing else for a woman, she thought. I must try and make him marry me.

And where did her freedom, her independence, go?

As wife to a man like Carlo Ghisleri she would be his mere echo, in a few years his slave; once again her own tastes, thoughts, wishes, would be completely overshadowed, not this time by weak tyranny and sickness, but by a superior intellect, a stronger character.

After Lucie's husband's death, Carlo Ghisleri starts behaving like "the master of the house. . . . She could not have been more perfectly free; there was no longer anyone or anything to shackle her, but she felt bound as before; after all, she had only changed masters." This theme recurs in Bowen's work, reflecting her preoccupation with women's situation in society and highlighting their position as prisoners in their husbands' or fathers' houses, as well as the limited resources women had to change their lives. The epigraph to the book is highly significant to many of Bowen's works:

She was really quite happy in the palace, but the fact she could not get out, gave it, she thought, the impression of a prison, and she took to gazing out of the window and sighing.

A cluster of green-and-white flowers beneath her window particularly excited her longing, and when she finally made her escape, the first thing she did, was to pluck them eagerly. Alas! They were stinging nettles, and hurt her so cruelly that she wanted to run home again. But the door was shut, and she could by no means get it open (From an Old French Fairy Tale).

Lucie is a paradigmatic "Lady of Shalott" figure, incarcerated in her isolated palace, wistfully gazing out of her window, a typically feminine frame that effectively emphasizes both the woman's enforced imprisonment and the possibility of freedom in the outside world; the escape, however, is fraught with difficulties, powerfully symbolized by the stinging nettles.

There is a marked autobiographical element in *Stinging Nettles.* Bowen had married a Sicilian, Don Zefferino Emilio Costanzo, in 1912, and they lived in Tuscany. During this period Bowen finally had her own house and belongings, but her husband fell sick and gradually got worse. He died in 1916 after a long illness, during which she tended him, writing while at his bedside to earn their living. They had a daughter, who died of meningitis in England, and a son, who survived. Marjorie Bowen fell in love with

her husband's physician, and although they wanted to get married she eventually left for England. An older man, he knew he was suffering from a disease that would drastically limit his movements, and he decided not to tie her to him in those circumstances. She married Arthur L. Long of Richmond, Surrey, in 1917, and they had two sons.

Feelings of social isolation and frustration, however, continue to be apparent in *The Pagoda (La Pagode de Chanteloup)* (1927), a novel Wagenknecht considers reminiscent of Virginia Woolf and in which the heroine, Madame de Bellegarde, a widow of a year, feels lonely and lost in her big, luxurious house and tries to find in a succession of travels some solace to her unhappiness.

*Passion Flower* (1932) employs a typical romance plot. Phenice Campion, accustomed to luxury and idleness, becomes a penniless orphan. Although she decides to find a wealthy husband, she unexpectedly falls in love with a young lawyer, Noel Barton, who is already engaged to her best friend, Sylvia. The passion flower of the title is the emblem of suffering and sacrifice, and Phenice gradually changes from a scheming adventuress who would do anything to win Barton's love to a person able to achieve lasting happiness through sacrifice and pain.

Many of Marjorie Bowen's stories and novels thus powerfully dramatize the difficulties women face, from marriage as an escape from individual responsibility, romantic love versus stability and a home, issues of property ownership, legal status, and finding a suitable job, to the disturbing complexities attendant upon growing old. In Bowen's fiction the reader finds a gallery of emotionally starved women who have no real options and who frequently resort to the life of the imagination to fulfill their dreams. As her tales and novels profusely illustrate, the world outside women's homes is full of pitfalls, invoked by the image of the stinging nettles in the novel of the same name. The "Lady of Shalott" figures that populate her fiction are paradigmatic of the position women occupy in a profoundly masculine world. The endings of her tales, on the other hand, often fail to offer solutions to women other than remaining where they are as prisoners of patriarchal laws. Marriage is perceived by many of Marjorie Bowen's heroines as the passport to a new life, with broader horizons and financial stability, and the author candidly acknowledged in her autobiography that she "knew that to be desired, to be happily married, to be financially secure and the mother of children was a woman's highest objective. Nothing could possibly compare with it."

Her modern novels and short stories, then, can be said to be, borrowing Modleski's words, "as much a protest against as an endorsement of the feminine condition."

Bowen's social concerns, and in particular her preoccupation with the situation of women, are mirrored in two of her nonfiction works: *This Shining Woman: Mary Wollstonecraft Godwin: 1759–1797* (1937), written under the pseudonym of "George R. Preedy," and *Ethics in Modern Art* (1939). The latter presents a full-blown eulogy of modern art and its important social function. The author argues, "Art must be an affirmation of belief in the fullness and richness of life, in the endless potentialities of humanity" and adds, "I do believe in the vitality of modern art, in the part that it has in liberating our minds and in making our lives richly full." In this book Bowen also ponders the position of women in the literary world, paying particular attention to Virginia Woolf, Dorothy Richardson, Rosamond Lehman, Elizabeth Bowen, and Storm Jameson, who "reveal with delicate precision the woman's point of view, and analyse with a tenderness, and yet a realism that no man could achieve, the woman's heart, mind and soul." She rejoices in the influence of women on modern literature and on the prominent position women novelists occupy: "The prose-writers of to-day have revealed, with a fullness unknown to any other civilization, the woman's point of view. In all the arts women have recently achieved some distinction. They have become articulate in many varying mediums. But in the novels they have disclosed themselves with a clarity impossible in music, architecture, sculpture or painting . . . you have here a half of humanity made articulate for the first time." She even claims that "the technique of the modern novel has been largely the invention of women. In this country women were among the first to introduce and modify the methods of the great foreign novelists. It was women who brought to perfection the 'stream-of-consciousness' method."

Bowen also reflects on women's contribution to art and ethics and reaches the conclusion that:

The intelligence, culture, grace, and humanity of the women prove the quality of a civilization. To-day they have their full share of the modern spirit of revolt. Not revolt against their individual grievances or against the once-proclaimed wrongs of women, but against injustice, cruelty, and ignorance that affect men and women alike.

A revolt, too, against shams and hypocrisies and the taboos of dying creeds. This revolt is expressed with both power and delicacy in the work of our finest

women of letters, and I think that they do thus contribute to both art and ethics.

Although not a full-fledged feminist, Marjorie Bowen's writings, in their pragmatic manipulation of the literary market and expectations, are very much the work of a survivor and a fighter, in spite of the sometimes romantic nature of her narration. Her clear awareness of this fact constitutes one feminist option in a man's world.

Despite the sometimes uneven nature of Bowen's books, mostly due to strict deadlines and the pressure she was under to write for a living, the high level of professionalism of her work should be stressed. The impressive thematic range of her publications attests to the enormous scope of her interests and her preoccupation with various social issues. Bowen continued to explore these themes throughout her long and prolific writing career. She suffered a serious concussion after a fall in her bedroom, and she died on 22 December 1952.

As a protofeminist in a masculine world, Marjorie Bowen demonstrated a shrewd understanding both of her own capabilities as a writer and of two overlapping sectors among her readers. By privileging historical romances and novels of contemporary women's enclosure and disempowerment, Bowen both analyzed women's situations and provided fictions that could operate as alternative models of women's intervention, or at least provide imaginative spaces to which readers could escape. In this latter activity readers could reconstruct women's roles and see their encumbered and cramped lives as in some way empowered and justified. Bowen's sharpest work, however, would appear to be her bleak novels of contemporary life in which mostly passive, suffering heroines hardly dare to violate morally and socially sanctioned norms of feminine behavior. As statements of the problems, they are insightfully glum, perhaps containing the suggestion of their own circumvention in the fact of their having been written, of Bowen's having borne witness. To write of disempowerment is in some sense to circumvent it, to intervene, to empower oneself and thus, vicariously, one's readers.

**References:**

Gillian Beer, *Romance* (London: Methuen, 1970);

Margaret Crosland, *Beyond the Lighthouse: English Women Novelists in the Twentieth Century* (London: Constable, 1981);

Helen Hughes, *The Historical Romance* (London & New York: Routledge, 1993);

Tania Modleski, *Loving with a Vengeance: Mass-Produced Fantasies for Women* (London & New York: Routledge, 1988);

Joanna Russ, "Somebody's Trying to Kill Me and I Think It's My Husband: The Modern Gothic," *Journal of Popular Culture,* 6, no. 2, (1972–1973): 666–691;

Edward Wagenknecht, "Bowen, Preedy, Shearing & Co.: A Note in Memory and a Check List," *Boston University Studies in English,* 3 (1957), 181–189;

Wagenknecht, "The Extraordinary Mrs. Long," *New York Times Book Review* (2 May 1943), pp. 2, 22, 23;

Wagenknecht, *Seven Masters of Supernatural Fiction* (New York: Greenwood Press, 1991), pp. 152–179.

# George Warwick Deeping

*(28 May 1877 – 20 April 1950)*

George J. Johnson

BOOKS: *Uther and Igraine* (London: Richards, 1903; New York: Outlook, 1903);

*Love Among the Ruins* (London: Richards, 1904; New York: Outlook, 1904);

*The Slanderers* (New York: Harper, 1905; London: Cassell, 1907);

*The Seven Streams* (London: Nash, 1905; New York: Fenno, 1909);

*Bess of the Woods* (London & New York: Harper, 1906);

*A Woman's War* (London & New York: Harper, 1907);

*Bertrand of Brittany* (New York & London: Harper, 1908);

*Mad Barbara* (London: Cassell, 1908; New York: Harper, 1909); revised as *These White Hands* (New York: McBride, 1937);

*The Red Saint* (London: Cassell, 1909; New York: McBride, 1940);

*The Return of the Petticoat* (London & New York: Harper, 1909; revised, London: Cassell, 1913);

*The Lame Englishman* (London: Cassell, 1910; New York: Cassell, 1911);

*The Rust of Rome* (London & New York: Cassell, 1910);

*Fox Farm* (London: Cassell, 1911); published as *The Eyes of Love* (New York: McBride, 1933);

*Joan of the Tower* (London: Cassell, 1911; New York: McBride, 1941);

*Sincerity* (London: Cassell, 1912; revised edition, London: Nelson, 1917); published as *The Strong Hand* (New York: Cassell, 1912); published as *The Challenge of Love* (New York: McBride, 1932);

*The House of Spies* (London & New York: Cassell, 1913);

*The White Gate* (London: Cassell, 1913; New York: McBride, Nast, 1914);

*The King Behind the King* (London: Cassell, 1914; New York: McBride, Nast, 1914); published as *The Shield of Love* (New York: McBride, 1940);

*The Pride of Eve* (London: Cassell, 1914);

*Marriage by Conquest* (London: Cassell, 1915; New York: McBride, Nast, 1915);

*Unrest* (London: Cassell, 1916); published as *Bridge of Desire: A Story of Unrest* (New York: McBride, 1916);

*Martin Valiant* (London: Cassell, 1917; New York: McBride, 1917);

*Valour* (London: Cassell, 1918); published as *Valour, a Novel* (New York: McBride, 1934);

*Countess Glika, and Other Stories* (London: Cassell, 1919);

*Second Youth* (London: Cassell, 1919); published as *The Awakening* (New York: Grosset & Dunlap, 1932);

*The Prophetic Marriage* (London: Cassell, 1920; New York: Grosset & Dunlap, 1932);

*The House of Adventure* (London: Cassell, 1921; New York: Macmillan, 1922);

*Lantern Lane* (London: Cassell, 1921);

*Orchards* (London: Cassell, 1922); published as *The Captive Wife* (New York: Grosset & Dunlap, 1933);

*Apples of Gold* (London: Cassell, 1923);

*The Secret Sanctuary; or The Saving of John Stretton* (London: Cassell, 1923);

*Suvla John* (London: Cassell, 1924);

*Three Rooms* (London: Cassell, 1924);

*Sorrell and Son* (London: Cassell, 1925; New York: Knopf, 1926);

*Doomsday* (London: Cassell, 1927; New York: Knopf, 1927);

*Kitty* (London: Cassell, 1927; New York: Knopf, 1927);

*Old Pybus* (London: Cassell, 1928; New York: Knopf, 1928);

*Roper's Row* (London: Cassell, 1929; New York: Knopf, 1929);

*Exiles* (London: Cassell, 1930); published as *Exile* (New York: Knopf, 1930);

*The Short Stories of Warwick Deeping* (London: Cassell, 1930);

*Stories of Love, Courage, and Compassion* (New York: Grosset & Dunlap, 1930);

*George Warwick Deeping (Hulton-Deutsch Collection)*

*The Road* (London: Cassell, 1931); published as *The Ten Commandments* (New York: Knopf, 1931);

*Old Wine and New* (London: Cassell, 1932; New York: Knopf, 1932);

*Smith* (London: Cassell, 1932; New York: Knopf, 1932);

*Two Black Sheep* (London: Cassell, 1933; New York: Knopf, 1933);

*Seven Men Came Back* (London: Cassell, 1934; New York: Knopf, 1934);

*The Man on the White Horse* (London: Cassell, 1934; New York: Knopf, 1934);

*Sackcloth into Silk* (London: Cassell, 1935); published as *The Golden Cord* (New York: Knopf, 1935);

*Two in a Train, and Other Stories* (London: Cassell, 1935);

*No Hero, This* (London: Cassell, 1936; New York: Knopf, 1936);

*Blind Man's Year* (London: Cassell, 1937; New York: Knopf, 1937);

*The Woman at the Door* (London: Cassell, 1937; New York: Knopf, 1937);

*The Malice of Men* (London: Cassell, 1938); published as *Malice of Men* (New York: Knopf, 1938);

*Fantasia* (London: Cassell, 1939); published as *Bluewater* (New York: Knopf, 1939);

*Shabby Summer* (London: Cassell, 1939); published as *Folly Island* (New York: Knopf, 1939);

*The Man Who Went Back* (London: Cassell, 1940; New York: Knopf, 1940);

*The Dark House* (London: Cassell, 1941; New York: Knopf, 1941);

*Corn in Egypt* (London: Cassell, 1941; New York, Knopf, 1942);

*I Live Again* (London: Cassell, 1942; New York: Knopf, 1942);

*Slade* (London: Cassell, 1943; New York: Dial, 1943);

*Mr. Gurney and Mr. Slade* (London: Cassell, 1944); published as *The Cleric's Secret* (New York: Dial, 1944);

*Reprieve* (London: Cassell, 1945; New York: Dial, 1945);

*The Impudence of Youth* (London: Cassell, 1946; New York: Dial, 1946);

*Laughing House* (London: Cassell, 1946; New York: Dial, 1947);

*Portrait of a Playboy* (London: Cassell, 1947); published as *The Playboy* (New York: Dial, 1948);

*Paradise Place* (London: Cassell, 1949);

*Old Mischief* (London: Cassell, 1950);

*Time to Heal* (London: Cassell, 1952);

*Man in Chains* (London: Cassell, 1953);

*The Old World Dies* (London: Cassell, 1954);

*Caroline Terrace* (London: Cassell, 1955);

*The Serpent's Tooth* (London: Cassell, 1956);

*The Sword and the Cross* (London: Cassell, 1957).

OTHER: "Martyrdom," in *The Reader's Library* (London: Reader's Library, 1929).

Warwick Deeping was aptly described in his obituary in *The New York Times* as "one of the most prolific modern writers of light fiction." In addition to about seventy published novels, six of which appeared posthumously, Deeping published several collections of short stories, many of which had already appeared in magazines ranging from *Harpers* to *The Saturday Evening Post*. Most of his novels were published in both England and the United States and many in Canada; more than twenty were translated into other languages, such as German, French, Polish, Danish, Italian, and one into Slovenian. Perhaps the best indicator of their popularity is the annual appearance from 1926 to 1932 of at least one Deeping novel among the ten best-selling fiction books listed by *Publishers Weekly*, with two Deeping novels on the list for 1927: *Doomsday* and *Sorrell and Son*, the latter appearing for its second consecutive year. In 1973 *Sorrell and Son* reached its forty-first

*Cover for Deeping's first published historical romance, which*
*features the parents of the legendary King Arthur (courtesy*
*of the Lilly Library, Indiana University)*

edition, and in 1987 it was reissued by Penguin Books to coincide with its adaptation for the *Masterpiece Theatre* television series. In addition, the work, along with three other Deeping novels, had already been adapted for motion pictures.

Despite his popularity as a writer, little information is available about the life of George Warwick Deeping, probably because he disliked being interviewed almost as much as he avoided attending literary dinners. He was born on 28 May 1877 in Southend, Essex, the son of a country doctor, George Davidson Deeping, also the son of a doctor. George Warwick was educated at Merchant Taylor's school and by private tutor; for four years he studied science and medicine at Trinity College, Cambridge, where he obtained both bachelor of arts (1898) and bachelor of medicine (1898) degrees, to which he later added a master of arts (1902). After training in Middlesex Hospital, London, he qualified as a doctor. In his biographical sketch for *Twentieth Century Authors* Deeping claims to have been bored with school, but at that early

stage he had no desire to write. He began to compose poetry at age twenty, but by his own admission, "much of it was bad"; however, after he "became infected with the mediaevalism of the romantic school" he began writing popular historical novels, which allowed him to leave his practice as a country doctor after only one year.

Deeping attributed much of his success and happiness to his parents and especially to his wife, Maude Phyllis Merrill. Their relationship, which overcame what Deeping called "our struggles and our worries," led to his sense of life as a great adventure, reflected in the male/female relationships in many of his romantic novels. Their living on a farm in Sussex, their building a small home themselves, and his interest in gardening and designing gardens were also likely instrumental in influencing his vivid descriptions of both rural outdoors and homey interiors. One of the strongest influences on his later novels was the four years he spent during World War I in the Royal Army Medical Corps, where he served as a doctor in Egypt, France, and

Belgium, and at the Gallipoli Peninsula. Deeping wrote, "I wish the work I did before the war had never been written. . . . I was leading a self-absorbed, dreamy life. The war pulled me out of that. I think I came back with bigger, more human enthusiasms. . . . I was after humanity, and the life of the day, and how it would express itself thru me."

After the war Deeping's life was considerably simpler, dominated by a day that began with work at seven in the morning and ended with his going to bed at half past nine. During that period at least three hours were spent writing in the absolute quiet he found necessary; some of the rest of the time was spent meeting people, some of whose qualities so impressed the author that they became the bases for his novels. He argued, "To enjoy the perfume of life one has to cultivate a certain simplicity. I agree with my old gardener of seventy-six, who is full of grim humour and gaiety, and who says: 'I've lived hard and simple.'" George Warwick Deeping's simple life ended on 20 April 1950, one month before his seventy-third birthday, at Weybridge, Surrey, where the author had resided for more than twenty years.

*Uther and Igraine* (1903) was Deeping's first published historical romance. Set in a Britain freed from Roman occupation and facing the onslaught of the Saxon pirate-invaders, it follows the developing relationship of King Uther Pendragon of Britain and Igraine, a British woman of noble birth, the mother-to-be of King Arthur. On the novel's republication in 1928, *The Saturday Review of Literature* (31 March 1928) offered a retrospective assessment, claiming that Deeping "would not do chapters much better than the first of this book. His style in the descriptive passages . . . is already full-functioning and very beautiful." Other reviewers were harsh, commenting on "the tintinnabulations of his poetic prose" and on Deeping's attempt at verisimilitude in using Roman words for household objects. A critic in *The New Republic* (9 May 1928) wondered "how this brackish book ever got printed without a glossary."

Another historical romance, *Love Among the Ruins* (1904) features as its protagonist a beautiful young woman, Yeoland, who becomes leader of an uprising of commoners in medieval England. *The Seven Streams* (1905) followed, also vaguely medieval in setting and whose heroine, Rosamunde, has to contend with a villainous husband, Lord of the Joyous Vale. Despite a new setting in the early eighteenth century and a well-received story of smugglers and romantic intrigue, *Bess of the Woods* (1906)

drew criticism from contemporary reviewers for its formal similarities to Deeping's other historical romances.

Departing from this pattern, Deeping set two novels in contemporary English towns. In *The Slanderers* (1905) Gabriel Strong marries the wrong woman only to find the right woman, Joan Gildersedge, too late. Despite his bored wife's departure, Gabriel's idealistic relationship with Joan becomes the target of local gossips. A *New York Times* review of 25 February 1905 condemns Deeping's attempt to move his characters of "Arthurian romance" into "a prosaic modern English countryside." In *A Woman's War* (1907) Deeping portrays the conflict between the wives of two doctors. A reviewer for *Spectator* (10 August 1907) found merit in the novel, but the *Nation* (11 July 1907) attacked the "childish superficiality" of its theme.

From 1908 to 1913 Deeping's work was almost evenly divided between five contemporary and six historical romances. Two of the histories are set outside England: *Bertrand of Brittany* (1908) follows the early career of Bertrand de Gueslin, who ultimately became marshal of France in the fourteenth century; and *The Lame Englishman* (1910) traces the tragic involvement of the Englishman Tom Smith in the attempt by Giuseppe Mazzini and Giuseppe Garibaldi to establish a republic in Rome in 1848. The other books are set in England against a variety of historical backgrounds: in *Joan of the Tower* (1911), set during the early-thirteenth-century reign of King John, and in *The Red Saint* (1909), set in the time of Henry III, the actions of the naive hero, Brother Pelleas, and the red-haired saintly heroine, Denise, respectively, are set against the kings' power struggles with the aristocracy; in *Mad Barbara* (1908), set in the late-seventeenth-century reign of Charles II, Barbara Purcell attempts to exact her revenge; and in *The House of Spies* (1913) the anticipated Napoleonic invasion of England forms the backdrop for the nefarious exploits of French spies and the idealistic English owner of Stonehanger House. These novels were generally praised for their rapid action and portrayals of heroism.

Deeping's modern romances of this period depict attempts by the central character to resolve a problem, usually in a pastoral setting. In trying to pass for a man, Sybil Dathan creates a problem herself in *The Return of the Petticoat* (1909) by falling in love with a young farmer. In *The Rust of Rome* (1910) the released convict Benjamin Heriot's attempt to achieve solitude near the site of an excavated Roman villa at Mistmoor leads to his involvement

in the affairs of the neighboring Thorkells. In *Fox Farm* (1911) Jesse Falconer must cope with loss of sight, of wife, and of farm. Similarly, in *The White Gate* (1913), behind the white gate of her family cottage, Constance Brent must deal with the isolation created by her mother and some of the townspeople; however, in *Sincerity* (1912) the strong hand of science, belonging to the young newcomer, Dr. John Wolfe, is needed to overcome the degrading physical and social conditions of other people in a small Sussex town.

The period of Great Britain's involvement in the War of the Nations, as World War I was then called, saw the publication of six novels by Deeping. The pattern of alternating contemporary and historical content continued; as to the conditions under which they were written, Deeping claimed, "I scribbled in dug-outs, huts and billets." Of the three historical novels of this period, the first and last are set in the late medieval period. *The King Behind the King* (1914) depicts the adventures of Fulk Ferrers, forester to the duke of Lancaster, who, as guardian uncle to ten-year-old Richard II at his ascension to the throne in 1377, represents one meaning of the title; the second involves Fulk in Deeping's alteration of the events of the Peasants' Revolt. The late–fifteenth century War of the Roses serves as the background for *Martin Valiant* (1917); in the foreground the Lancastrian Mellis Dale, assisted by the hero of the title, seeks to avenge the loss of her home, brother, and father at the hands of the local Yorkist Roger Bland, Lord of Troy. The other historical novel, *Marriage by Conquest* (1915), is set in eighteenth-century Sussex and describes the machinations of the bully, Sir Richard Heron, whose attempts to conquer are countered by the spirited widow, Stella Shenstone, and the scholarly John Flambard.

Most highly praised of the nonhistorical novels of the war years was *The Pride of Eve* (1914); its theme of thwarted love and human suffering from unfulfilled desire, developed through its heroine, Eve, who remains untarnished after her descent into the depths, led a reviewer for the *Bookman* (November 1914) to assert that the protagonists "are all so vital and true to type, and the things that happen to them seem so essentially the things that would happen to them." Less charitably received was *Unrest* (1916), which depicts the midlife problem of successful playwright Martin Frenshaw, who leaves an inspiring and caring wife to cross "the bridge of desire" (the title of the American publication) and tour Europe with the captivating and unscrupulous American widow, Judith Ruddiger. *Valour* (1918) was labeled disappointing by *The New York Times* (7

*Cover for Deeping's first novel with a contemporary setting*

February 1918). Probably borrowing from Deeping's wartime experience, the novel traces the defiant Lt. Pierce Hammersley's disgraceful court-martial at Gallipoli and his exploits as a reenlisted infantryman in France.

Between 1919 and 1924 a collection of short stories and nine novels by Deeping were published. Of the latter the historical fiction is set in Stuart-dominated seventeenth-century England. *Orchards* (1922) depicts the tempestuous relationship between the fiery Rachel and Sir Richard Falconer, whom she is forced to marry, a struggle set against the panorama of the Cavalier-Roundhead civil war. The period following, in the reign of Charles II, provides the backdrop for *Lantern Lane* (1921). Still later, in the early 1700s, Jordan March, adopted by the Nandos and raised above his station, parallels the search of Hercules in *Apples of Gold* (1923).

Of the contemporary romances of this period, four are concerned with the impact of the war on individuals. *The Prophetic Marriage* (1920) is the only

one in which war service helps solve the problems of its protagonist – in this case the marital and business troubles of an idealistic young orphan. In *The House of Adventure* (1921) the war creates a problem through the destruction of the French village of Beaumont, although the need to rebuild it provides Paul Brent with a new life and a new companion, Manon Latour. The war has more-harmful effects on the behavior of the idealistic protagonist of *The Secret Sanctuary; or The Saving of John Stretton* (1923), who must be saved from bouts of anger and physical attacks resulting from shell shock. The title character in *Suvla John* (1924), having been shot in the back and left for dead by a fellow officer at Gallipoli, returns home seven years later to find that his fiancée has married his "murderer." *Three Rooms* (1924) is the only contemporary romance of this period that does not employ World War I and its consequences as a backdrop. It depicts a middle-aged woman desperately trying to snare her wealthy lover. He is more interested in her pure and pretty daughter, who, in turn, is more attracted to a younger man.

In 1925 Deeping entered the period of his greatest popularity, especially in the United States, through the publication of *Sorrell and Son* (1925). The novel covers a twenty-year span beginning three years after the demobilization of a heroic British officer, Stephen Sorrell, M.C., left with the care of his eleven-year-old son, Christopher (Kit), little money, and no work. Starting as a lowly porter, Sorrell struggles to provide Kit with the education he needs to become a doctor. *Sorrell and Son* was rebuked for its length and its frequent discursive passages; generally, however, it was praised for its characterization, its absorbing story, its treatment of the theme, and its skillful use of sentimental elements. Judging from its initial reception and subsequent popularity, the public found the novel appealing; perhaps Sorrell's Job-like endurance, or his willing self-sacrifice, struck a responsive chord in its readers.

The title of *Doomsday* (1927) identifies the Sussex farm in which former officer Arnold Furze has invested his money and five years of exhaustive labor. The novel portrays his relationship with Mary Viner and the farm. *Doomsday* suffered by comparison with its predecessor: detractors focused mainly on its weak and artificial plot; positive comments cited its striking theme, strong characterization, and outstanding descriptions.

Despite receiving more-positive reviews, *Kitty,* published later the same year, failed to make the best-seller list as had its two predecessors. Its theme centers on the struggle for the crippled Alex St. James between his cold, aristocratic mother and his wife, the courageous and compassionate tobacconist's daughter, Kitty. Several reviewers labeled it the best of contemporary novels, primarily for its honest, wholesome sentiment, its very human and attractive characters, and its effective and competent narration.

*Old Pybus* appeared on the best-seller list in 1928. In the work the war serves only as a background – the central Victorian character, John Julius Apostasius Pybus, has alienated himself from his two materialistic sons, Probyn and Conrad, for their refusal to fight for their country. The novel follows Probyn's son, Lance, as he and his grandfather become friends. *Old Pybus* also suffered by comparison to *Sorrell and Son*, with the *New Statesman* (13 October 1928) calling it "an inferior variant."

Deeping's popular success continued in 1929 with *Roper's Row,* the story of the rise to medical eminence of the impoverished and crippled Chris Hazzard, accomplished with the assistance of his doting mother, Mary, and the worship and devotion of Ruth Avery. Number 7, Roper's Row, located in a poorer section of London, is the setting for most of the novel. The book was criticized for its excessive length and emotional flatness, though some reviewers found it superior to some of Deeping's other novels.

Two novels by Deeping were published in 1930: *Exiles,* another best-seller, and *Stories of Love, Courage, and Compassion.* Set in the Italian resort town of Tindaro, *Exiles* depicts the activities of many stereotypical English "exiles" but focuses mainly on Billy Brown, a popular member of the English community, and her relationships with the novelist Oscar Slade and the tubercular architect, Thomas Isherwood. Deeping was chided for the novel's formulaic structure but praised for its "characterization and simple style." While *Stories of Love, Courage, and Compassion* was not as popular a work, its title is important in providing a summary of what has been called Deeping's "artistic credo" (*New York Times*, 20 September 1931). In reviewing the "vast collection," the same newspaper (30 November 1930) noted that the better stories "carry the weight of the worse and fortunately outnumber them" but criticized the use of "the familiar Deeping characters" under different names.

In the following year best-seller status was achieved by *Bridge of Desire: A Story of Unrest,* a republication of *Unrest;* during the next ten years thirteen other novels were published in the United States, with almost half retaining their original En-

glish titles. Also in 1931 *The Road* (*The Ten Commandments* in the United States) returned to World War I with the character of Nicholas Bonthorn, a one-eyed veteran and neighbor of Robinia Buck and her two fun-loving daughters, Rhoda and Rachel, proprietors of Ye Old Mill House Tea Room. Rachel's crippling injury in an accident forces all the novel's characters to examine their lives. In addition to embodying the old values by which Nicholas lives, the Ten Commandments are parodied by the novel's most loathsome character, the communistic Stanley Shelp. The novel was commended for its characterization, clever plot, and its defense of humanitarian values.

*Old Wine and New* (1932) was the last of Deeping's novels to appear on the *Publishers Weekly* best-seller list. Spencer Scarsdale, the returned veteran, finds the old wine of his sentimental writings no longer wanted, and he is deprived of most of his savings by Julia Marwood, the new wine of dissipation and boldness. Poverty enables Scarsdale, aided by Eleanor Richmond, to write a successful realistic novel. Opinion on *Old Wine and New* was almost evenly divided between those who saw it as trite and those who praised its beauty and presentation of tender emotions.

The title of Scarsdale's fictional novel, *Smith*, became the title of Deeping's next novel published in 1932. The everyman of the title, hardworking carpenter Keir Smith, is buffeted by failed expectations and poor health and led to the realization of "the beauty and beneficence of simple things" by his devoted wife, Sybil. This same pattern of vicissitudes interrupts the developing relationship of Henry Vane and Elsie Summerhays in *Two Black Sheep* (1933); both characters have been imprisoned, hence the title.

The year 1934 saw the publication of two quite different novels. *Seven Men Came Back* follows the lives of six Company B officers and their mess orderly, Kettle, as they return to civilian life at the end of the war. While five of them find varying degrees of success, their leader, Captain Jack Sherring, is less fortunate. Roman Britain in the fourth century is the setting for the historical romance *The Man on the White Horse,* who is Geraint, Lord of the White Tower. His fortunes become involved with those of the beautiful orphan, Guinevra, and the villainous Bishop Balthasar. Another contemporary romance, *Sackcloth into Silk* (1935) emphasizes the transition in the life of the Jewish Slopp family from Rebecca's ownership of a used-clothing store in slum London to young son Karl's fame and fortune. The American title, *The Golden Cord,* stresses the

*Dust jacket for Deeping's 1921 historical novel set during the reign of Charles II (courtesy of the Lilly Library, Indiana University)*

strong bond between mother and son, whose talent she recognizes and nurtures.

Between 1936 and 1938 the words *familiar, characteristic, formula,* and *trademark* frequently appeared in reviews of Deeping's four novels of the period. Written as the journal of a thirty-five-year-old, happily married doctor, *No Hero, This* (1936) traces the year's service of Stephen Brent in the ill-fated Gallipoli expedition; his reenlistment to serve in France for the rest of the war completes a pattern which parallels Deeping's own war service. Most severely criticized was *Blind Man's Year* (1937), the story of a disfigured, eminent novelist, Rosamund Gerard, who lives as a recluse on her estate until a plane crash forces on her the care of the pilot, Clive Strange, who eventually goes blind. Critics called it stilted, fabricated, and synthetic. Another voluntary recluse in *The Woman at the Door* (1937) is war veteran and writer John Luce, whose attempt at soli-

Dust jacket for Deeping's novel about Jordan March, whose
adventures in eighteenth-century England parallel those
of Hercules (courtesy of the Lilly Library,
Indiana University)

tude in Surrey is interrupted by the arrival of neighbor Rachel Ballard at his door to announce her murder of her surly, tyrannical husband. Despite accusations of the Deeping trademark, *The Malice of Men* (1938) was praised for its dramatic qualities; told in diary form by wealthy builder John Lancaster, it records the malice he felt in his rise from poverty, first toward the privileged in general and then toward an individual, the cruel Sir Beverly Bullstrode.

Two novels appeared in 1939: *Fantasia* (*Bluewater* in the United States) and *Shabby Summer* (*Folly Island*). The former shows the contrast and conflict between a modern Sussex seaside resort, Bluewater, promoted by the unscrupulous Mallison, and Forge Farm, founded by Richard Jekyll to create a self-supporting farm industry based on the old, right

values. The title of *Shabby Summer* describes the season for nurseryman Peter Ghent, plagued by drought, and for Sybil Strangeways of Folly Farm, caught in a pointless love affair. Reviews focused on Deeping's use of the novel for philosophizing and social criticism. This philosophical bent was combined with historical fiction in *The Man Who Went Back* (1940), when John Hallard's car crashes on a lonely moor in 1939 England and he awakes to find himself in Roman Britain as the cowardly, wounded Pellias. The Saxon invasion is compared to the threat of German invasion in 1939 led by "a little strutting fellow with blob eyes and a smudge of a moustache."

Again in 1941 two novels appeared with similar themes but different subject matter. *The Dark House,* with a Victorian setting, follows the bitter Dr. John Richmond, relegated to a provincial practice at Southend. It was praised for its solid story, its intricate but logical plot, and the values it portrays. *Corn in Egypt* traces Grant Carey's rehabilitation of a farm in southeast England prior to World War II and his wife's injury in a German bombing raid in 1940; the latter situation allows Deeping to criticize wartime leadership.

*I Live Again* (1942) quadruples the concept of return to the past by having the hero reincarnated as an eighteenth-century footman, Black Jack Lovechild; as a successful and rich nineteenth-century industrialist, Jack Heckworthy; as an early–twentieth century mathematician, John Marwood; and finally as his son of the same name in World War II London. *The New York Times* (11 October 1942) saw the novel as a "parable of human progress" but found the stories "uneven in quality."

Negative critical comments became more common between 1943 and 1947. *Slade* (1943) received mildly negative reviews. Its title character is a Sorrell-like porter, recently released from prison and employed by the seemingly virtuous, but dictatorial, Mrs. Pomeroy in the Victorian community of Southend. The name was used again in the 1944 novel *Mr. Gurney and Mr. Slade* (*The Cleric's Secret* in the United States). The curate, John Gurney, has two secrets: one, revealed by the town character, Slade, is that Gurney was decorated for bravery as a wartime chaplain; the other, which the townspeople know and despise him for, is his marriage to a prostitute. The novel likewise received negative reviews.

*Reprieve* (1945) was criticized because the ending was given away in the title. The reprieve is for Arthur Valentine Brown, who, on being told he is terminally ill, travels abroad leaving behind a de-

manding wife, two indifferent children, and a palatial house. He actually receives two reprieves, the second from his family. *Saturday Review of Literature* (12 October 1946) dismissed Deeping's next novel, *The Impudence of Youth* (1946), as "a nice story about interesting people topped off with proper sentiments and a happy ending." In Victorian England a young doctor, John James Pope, assisted by a lower-class shopgirl, becomes a patent medicine tycoon, more by chance than ability. The title of Deeping's next novel, *Laughing House* (1946), is the pet name for Beech Hill House, a mansion owned by Sir John Mortimer and requisitioned in wartime for troops by the British government. As narrator, Sir John makes his annoyance clear, but the arrangement does bring a wounded officer who has plans for renovating the residence as a paying rest home for "the right people." It was criticized by contemporary reviewers as being maudlin.

Reviews of Deeping's novels, which had become briefer and more critical, ceased to exist in the major papers altogether for the seven books issued posthumously in England. They were not published in the United States, where attention was focused on postwar issues, which were not compatible with the subject matter and values of Deeping's novels.

While romanticism, the war, and "real people" were influences on Deeping's selection of subjects, he felt that courage and character were most important, a belief that led to a positive view of life and away from what he termed "a negative cynicism." The writer of his obituary in *The New York Times,* however, claimed that Deeping's "gift was very much for the sentimental and all too human narrative. He was content to make recognizable emotional symbols rather than individual men and women of the characters in his novels, to provide his readers with all the sentimental incident they could reasonably ask for, and to avoid harrowing their feelings too deeply." Warren French, quoted in *Romance and Historical Writers,* called Deeping "a traditionalist" who tried to "keep alive the pastoral vision of Edwardian England in the years after World War I."

# Walter de la Mare

*(25 April 1873 – 22 June 1956)*

James M. Decker
*Northern Illinois University*

See also the de la Mare entry in *DLB 19: British Poets, 1880–1914.*

BOOKS: *Songs of Childhood,* as Walter Ramal (London, New York & Bombay: Longmans, Green, 1902);

*Henry Brocken, His Travels and Adventures in the Rich, Strange, Scarce-Imaginable Regions of Romance* (London: Murray, 1904; New York: Knopf, 1924);

*Poems* (London: Murray, 1906);

*The Return* (London: Arnold, 1910; New York & London: Putnam's, 1911);

*The Three Mulla-Mulgars* (London: Duckworth, 1910; New York: Knopf, 1919); published as *The Three Royal Monkeys* (London: Faber & Faber, 1935; New York: Knopf, 1948);

*The Listeners and Other Poems* (London: Constable, 1912; New York: Holt, 1916);

*Peacock Pie* (London: Constable, 1913; New York: Holt, 1917);

*Motley and Other Poems* (London: Constable, 1918; New York: Holt, 1918);

*Poems 1901 to 1918,* 2 volumes (London: Constable, 1920); published as *Collected Poems 1901–1918* (New York: Holt, 1920);

*Crossings: A Fairy Play,* music by C. Armstrong Gibbs (London: Beaumont, 1921; New York: Knopf, 1923);

*Memoirs of a Midget* (London, Glasgow, Melbourne & Auckland: Collins, 1921; New York: Knopf, 1922);

*The Veil and Other Poems* (London, Bombay & Sydney: Constable, 1921; New York: Holt, 1922);

*Down-Adown-Derry: A Book of Fairy Poems* (London: Constable, 1922; New York: Holt, 1922);

*The Riddle and Other Stories* (London: Selwyn & Blount, 1923; New York: Knopf, 1923);

*Broomsticks and Other Tales* (London: Constable, 1925; New York: Knopf, 1925);

*Readings: Traditional Tales,* 6 volumes (Oxford: Blackwell, 1925–1928);

*The Connoisseur and Other Stories* (London, Glasgow, Sydney & Auckland: Collins, 1926; New York: Knopf, 1926);

*Walter de la Mare*

*John Fanning's Legacy,* anonymous, with Naomi Royde-Smith (London: Constable, 1927);

*Stuff and Nonsense and So On* (London: Constable, 1927; New York: Holt, 1927);

*Told Again: Traditional Tales* (Oxford: Blackwell, 1927); published as *Told Again: Old Tales Told Again* (New York: Knopf, 1927);

*At First Sight: A Novel* (New York: Crosby Gaige, 1928);

*The Captive and Other Poems* (New York: Bowling Green Press, 1928);

*Stories From the Bible* (London: Faber & Gwyer, 1929; New York: Cosmopolitan Book Corporation, 1929);

*On the Edge: Short Stories* (London: Faber & Faber, 1930; New York: Knopf, 1931);

*Poems for Children* (London: Constable, 1930; New York: Holt, 1930);

*The Dutch Cheese* (New York: Knopf, 1931);

*The Fleeting and Other Poems* (London: Constable, 1933; New York: Knopf, 1933);

*A Froward Child* (London: Faber & Faber, 1934);

*Poems 1919 to 1934* (London: Constable, 1935; New York: Holt, 1936);

*The Nap and Other Stories* (London & Edinburgh: Nelson, 1936);

*The Wind Blows Over* (London: Faber & Faber, 1936; New York: Macmillan, 1936);

*Stories, Essays and Poems* (London: Dent, 1938);

*Memory and Other Poems* (London: Constable, 1938; New York: Holt, 1938);

*Pleasures and Speculations* (London: Faber & Faber, 1940);

*Collected Poems* (New York: Holt, 1941; London: Faber & Faber, 1941);

*The Picnic and Other Stories* (London: Faber & Faber, 1941);

*Bells and Grass: A Book of Rhymes* (London: Faber & Faber, 1941; New York: Viking, 1942);

*Mr. Bumps and His Monkey* (Philadelphia: Winston, 1942);

*Time Passes and Other Poems* (London: Faber & Faber, 1942);

*The Old Lion and Other Stories* (London: Faber & Faber, 1942);

*The Magic Jacket and Other Stories* (London: Faber & Faber, 1943);

*Collected Rhymes and Verse* (London: Faber & Faber, 1944); published as *Rhymes and Verse: Collected Poems for Children* (New York: Holt, 1947);

*The Scarecrow and Other Stories* (London: Faber & Faber, 1945);

*The Burning-Glass and Other Poems* (London: Faber & Faber, 1945); published as *The Burning-Glass and Other Poems, Including The Traveller* (New York: Viking, 1945);

*The Dutch Cheese and Other Stories* (London: Faber & Faber, 1946);

*The Traveller* (London: Faber & Faber, 1946);

*Collected Stories for Children* (London: Faber & Faber, 1947);

*The Collected Tales,* edited by Edward Wagenknecht (New York: Knopf, 1950);

*Inward Companion* (London: Faber & Faber, 1950);

*Winged Chariot* (London: Faber & Faber, 1951);

*Winged Chariot and Other Poems* (New York: Viking, 1951) — includes "Inward Companion";

*Private View* (London: Faber & Faber, 1953);

*O Lovely England and Other Poems* (London: Faber & Faber, 1953);

*Selected Poems,* edited by R. N. Green-Armitage (London: Faber & Faber, 1954);

*A Choice of de la Mare's Verse,* edited by W. H. Auden (London: Faber & Faber, 1963);

*Complete Poems* (London: Faber & Faber, 1969; New York: Knopf, 1970).

OTHER: *Come Hither. A Collection of Rhymes and Poems for the Young of All Ages,* edited by de la Mare (London: Constable, 1923; New York: Knopf, 1923);

*Early One Morning in the Spring: Chapters on Children and Childhood as It Is Revealed in Particular in Early Memories and in Early Writings,* edited, with commentary, by de la Mare (London: Faber & Faber, 1935; New York: Knopf, 1935);

*Behold This Dreamer,* edited by de la Mare (London: Faber & Faber, 1939; New York: Knopf, 1939);

*Love,* edited, with an introduction, by de la Mare (London: Faber & Faber, 1943; New York: Morrow, 1946).

Better-known as a poet than as a novelist, Walter de la Mare nonetheless managed to craft several intriguing narratives that explore the conflict between the ordinary and the extraordinary. Despite the various labels attached to de la Mare — neoromantic and supernaturalist among them — his novels continue to defy academic categorization. Ignoring or dismissing the central tenets of the modernist movement developing around him, de la Mare carved for himself a niche in fiction that won the admiration of such luminaries as T. S. Eliot, W. B. Yeats, and Virginia Woolf. After an initial foray into romance, de la Mare concentrated on the tensions that occur between individuals and their stifling social environments. In characters such as Arthur Lawford, Miss M., and Cecil Jennings, de la Mare painted delicate portraits of souls in flux; all three characters, each possessed of a mental or physical "abnormality," experience a mental awakening and attempt to reexamine their position in the established social order. De la Mare's novels chart this psychological exploration through a rich juxtaposition of mimesis and fantasy that clearly suggests a symbolic import to the characters' perceived deficiencies. In de la Mare's fictional universe, individuals must confront the singular dreams and desires that often make them appear grotesque to the communities in which they must exist. The confrontation, and not the ultimate result of that struggle, provides de la Mare with a forum to dissect the

HENRY BROCKEN

HIS TRAVELS AND ADVENTURES
IN THE RICH, STRANGE, SCARCE-
IMAGINABLE REGIONS OF ROMANCE

BY WALTER J. DE LA MARE
(" WALTER RAMAL ")

LONDON
JOHN MURRAY, ALBEMARLE STREET, W.
1904

*Title page for de la Mare's first novel, in which the title character meets Annabel Lee, Electra, Jane Eyre, and other famous literary characters (courtesy of the Lilly Library, Indiana University)*

heart of human existence in an acute but sensitive manner.

Born on 25 April 1873 in Charlton, Woolrich, Walter de la Mare apparently enjoyed a joyful childhood. The sixth of James Delamare and Lucy Browning Delamare's seven children, Walter overcame bouts of nervousness to become a lively yet introspective boy who liked both roaming the countryside and storytelling. Walter's ancestry provided him with ample material for such tales: not only could he claim Robert Browning as a relative, but he descended from Huguenot stock as well, a fact that must have impressed the boy, for de la Mare re-adopted the French form of his surname later on. Walter possessed high powers of attention as a boy, an acumen that certainly contrasts with his later association of childhood with unrestrained fantasy and dreams. Walter remained only an average student, however, although he loved reading books such as Jonathan Swift's *Gulliver's Travels* (1726) and John Bunyan's *Pilgrim's Progress* (1678). Lack of money precluded an education beyond the Choir

House School at Saint Paul's Cathedral, where the boy matriculated on 21 March 1882. Homesick and bullied, Walter did not care much for the school at first, but the religious inspiration he derived from his singing, coupled with his relationship with Canon Henry Scott-Holland, eventually caused de la Mare to enjoy St. Paul's. The onset of puberty forced Walter to quit singing in 1889, but he helped to found a chorister's journal before he left.

His formal education over, de la Mare reluctantly resigned himself to a life of drudgery when he joined Anglo-American Oil as a clerk. Faced with the endless parade of numbers in the corporation's statistics department, a less resolute man might have soon lost any artistic pretensions, but de la Mare held out, although he initially lacked direction. De la Mare honed his embryonic literary skills by reading, telling stories to his sister's children, keeping a journal, smoking opium, and joining the Esperanza Amateur Dramatic Club, for which he wrote several farces in the early 1890s. He fell in love with fellow club member Efrida Ingpen, whom de la Mare married in 1899 after she became pregnant. Elfie's brother, Roger, encouraged de la Mare to publish, and Walter had Elfie send out some of his manuscripts anonymously. De la Mare wrote more frequently, trying his hand at a novel titled "The Master," which he never finished, helping out with a literary magazine, *The Basilisk,* and penning stories and poems. De la Mare began to think of literary activities as an escape, writing to Elfie that "I am dying in this place of Oil . . . How greatly I loathe this hurrying, sordid place." After the birth of the first of four children in October 1899, de la Mare hired literary agent J. B. Pinker and looked forward to the commencement of a new century and a new career.

Pinker proved effective, for de la Mare began placing stories and poems, and as "Walter Ramal" he published his first book of verse in 1902. Following that volume's marginal success, de la Mare started work on *Henry Brocken, His Travels and Adventures in the Rich, Strange, Scarce-Imaginable Regions of Romance* (1904), his first completed novel, in late 1902. The transition from short fiction to novels appears to have caused de la Mare some grief, for although early stories such as "The Almond Tree" display the idiosyncratic but delightful style the writer would use in his later novels, few would call *Henry Brocken* anything other than an apprentice piece. Indeed, de la Mare himself called the poorly selling work a "dismal and complete failure," and in *Cavalcade of the English Novel* (1954) Edward Wagenknecht deems it de la Mare's "palest" novel.

A series of fantastic episodes loosely connected by a frame tale in which the first-person narrator leaves his aunt's home to satisfy his wanderlust, *Henry Brocken* owes more to the romance tradition than to that of the novel. Henry gets lost in the world of books from an early age and ultimately sets off on a quest that causes him to cross paths with the likes of Annabel Lee and Electra. De la Mare intimates that Brocken's journey takes place in the realm of daydreams, thus making the narrative a metaphoric and spiritual record of the effects of childhood reading on the psyche. Henry rides his horse Rosinante through enchanted lands that contrast sharply with his prosaic upbringing. De la Mare does not fully explore this juxtaposition, though, and as a result Brocken fails to grow substantially, often acting as little more than a semidetached observer. In the Jane Eyre sequence, for example, de la Mare squanders a potentially intriguing transaction, merely depicting an almost farcical exchange between Jane and Rochester. Henry begins to critique Jane's character – and thus offer the reader insight into Brocken's imagination – but his comments remain undeveloped, and he soon leaves. This strategy of understatement and abrupt narrative shifts repeats throughout the work.

De la Mare's episodes occasionally achieve a hauntingly poetic beauty, however. In the "Sleeping Beauty" section de la Mare paints a delicate portrait of alienation, a theme that would dominate his novels. Henry enters a dreamlike realm and encounters Prince Ennui, an ethereal spirit who claims to be Sleeping Beauty's brother. Ennui functions not only as Henry's guide but also as a projection of Henry's own inner sense of isolation. Despite living in a community, Ennui exists within the margins of that society. Although everyone else sleeps, Ennui restlessly walks the gardens, bemoaning his fate as a "captive ever less at ease." Henry seems irritated with Ennui, but the two share the capability to look beyond an object's facade and detect the spiritual essence within. The dull denizens of Henry's community appear every bit as asleep as Ennui's somnolent kinspeople, and one may read the "Sleeping Beauty" section as a metaphorical rendering of Henry's awareness of his difference. Indicative of Henry's sense of himself as atypical or unique is his act of "strutt[ing] conceitedly to and fro" in front of the sleepers due to vain, yet nonetheless naive, feelings of his singular position. Here, as in nowhere else in the novel, does de la Mare touch upon both the dreamer/artist's ability to transform the ordinary into the fantastic and the lonely consequences of that acumen. While the "Sleeping Beauty" sec-

tion examines the individual, the *Gulliver's Travels* chapters focus on the collective. Henry learns that the Houyhnhnms that Gulliver admired in Swift's satire actually possess a narrowness of vision and a cold-blooded brutality. Unlike the curiosity that leads Henry and Gulliver to explore new worlds, the Houyhnhnms "desire no tidings of what follies may be beyond [their] boundaries," a sentiment that "induced in [Henry] nothing but dullness and disgust." As a staunch individualist, Henry can place no faith in a society that systematically squelches idiosyncrasy.

Henry's final encounter is with Criseyde, another outsider who queries Brocken about his world. Henry's response betrays his ambivalent attitude toward society: "the madness mirth calls Life flickers yet . . . and the little race tosses on in nightmare." Both come to the realization that imaginative travel is the only escape from life's cruelties, and Criseyde's desire to search for Troy prompts Henry to ask, "What do you seek else? Oh, you speak in riddles!" This question applies equally well to Brocken's quest to discover the ineffable as to Criseyde's search. The book ends with Henry, his boat tossing in the moonlit sea, continuing his pursuit.

De la Mare continued to juggle his literary life with that of the oil company, but at times the strain became almost unbearable. In early 1908, for instance, de la Mare found himself unable to write. An office upheaval forced him to work heavy hours and strain both his eyes and mind. The editor of *The Monthly Review*, Henry Newbolt, offered hope by seeking a pension for de la Mare to free him for full-time writing. De la Mare at first balked – an unnamed indiscretion by his brother made him nervous that scandal would tarnish the family name – but finally relented after Newbolt convinced him that no one would care. Newbolt found pensions scarce – especially for a young author like de la Mare – but did succeed in securing a one-year stipend of two hundred pounds, a windfall that prompted de la Mare to resign from the oil company in September 1908. A mentally and physically refreshed de la Mare quickly started on two novels, *The Three Mulla-Mulgars* (1910) and *The Return* (1910).

Ostensibly written for children, *The Three Mulla-Mulgars* relates the tale of three royal monkeys, Thumma, Thimbulla, and Nod, and their quest to find their father, Seelem, and enter the mystical Valley of Tishnar. Seelem had embarked on a journey to Tishnar, promising to come back for his wife and sons, but he never returned. Mutt-matutta,

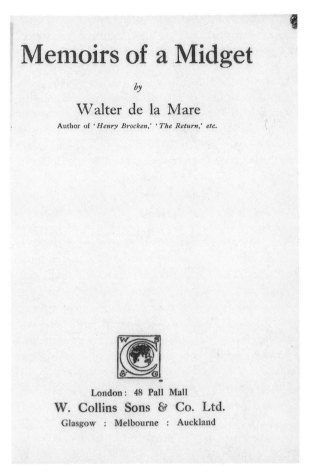

# Memoirs of a Midget

*by*

Walter de la Mare

Author of 'Henry Brocken,' 'The Return,' etc.

London : 48 Pall Mall
W. Collins Sons & Co. Ltd.
Glasgow : Melbourne : Auckland

*Title page for de la Mare's most successful novel, narrated by Miss M., a diminutive woman who struggles to find her place in a society that often treats her as a freak (courtesy of the Lilly Library, Indiana University)*

the boys' mother, tells the monkeys on her deathbed that if Seelem does not return within seven years from the start of his journey then they are to search for him. Mutt-matutta also gives Nod, the youngest, his father's wonderstone, a talisman of mysterious power. After her death the impatient brothers pass the time in gathering food and poking good-natured fun at one another. One catastrophe follows another, however, culminating in the burning down of their hut, an incident that forces them to look for their father. Although the brothers have limited information regarding the location of Tishnar, they forge ahead into the dangerous darkness, where they meet many odd individuals and partake in strange and wonderful adventures.

In *The Three Mulla-Mulgars* de la Mare never adopts a patronizing tone, nor does he treat the mulla-mulgars and their journey as either unimportant or bizarre. As a result, the novel sustains a balance of humor and seriousness atypical of the genre

of children's fantasy, a phenomenon that prompted Wagenknecht to label the book an "epic of courage." The central character, Nod, stands apart from his brothers and the other characters not only because of his supernatural abilities but because of his unique, even artistic, perspective on life. Nod undergoes a process of profound maturation, absorbing knowledge with an uncanny alacrity. At first the butt of Thumma and Thimbulla's taunts, Nod eventually becomes his brothers' savior, fighting disasters with his keen wit as well as with his wonderstone. Doris McCrosson, in noting Nod's propensity to improvise, goes so far as to suggest that the wonderstone is really emblematic of Nod's imagination. Central to Nod's education is a series of encounters with beings more powerful than himself, including the dreaded Oomgar (human). From each of these individuals Nod learns how to rely on himself and to use available resources effectively. Nod evolves into a trickster figure who survives by subverting the expectations of the various societies in which he moves. Nod succeeds through his lack of respect for convention and travels through the wilderness without a definite plan, a fact that allows him to experience every moment to its fullest rather than fall into a routine. *The Three Mulla-Mulgars* ends somewhat ambiguously, for the brothers find Tishnar but do not enter its confines. Clearly, de la Mare intended the journey, especially for Nod, to have more importance than the actual destination and that the lessons of youth take on a greater importance than their later application.

De la Mare hit his stride with his third novel, *The Return*. Aiming for what his biographer Theresa Whistler calls "poetic truth," *The Return* combines the best elements of de la Mare's poetry with a strong plot. The book won praise from the likes of E. M. Forster and J. B. Priestley and was awarded the Polignac Prize (which emphasized style) of one hundred pounds. The book's protagonist, Arthur Lawford, convalescing after a long illness, strolls through a graveyard and reflects on life. He pauses at the grave of Nicholas Sabathier, a Huguenot stranger who committed suicide. As he examines the tombstone, he notices a spider, stares into its pale-green eyes, and falls asleep. Upon awakening, Lawford feels odd and has no conception of time. Returning home, Lawford confronts a "changed strange face" in the mirror and starts reliving old memories in a melancholy fashion. The rest of the novel deals with Lawford and his circle coming to terms with both his altered appearance and his new outlook on life. Accused of everything from insanity to devilry, Lawford finds solace only with Her-

bert and Grisel, kindred spirits who believe that Sabathier has entered Arthur's body. D. R. McCrosson astutely asserts that the novel explores the constant upheaval that personality undergoes throughout life, reflected in Lawford's substantial mental alteration. Although Lawford eventually wards off Sabathier's attempt, he can never truly return to his former way of life, for his intense self-scrutiny reveals to him the hollowness of that duty-bound existence.

While de la Mare disclosed to Newbolt that he had misgivings about the novel's "sensationalism," the work's supernaturalism actually serves more as a catalyst for Lawford's inward examination. Indeed, Kenneth Hopkins believes that "the supernatural is perhaps the least important part of it." Before the transmigration of Sabathier's soul, Lawford is physically and emotionally sick. At the narrative's outset, Lawford, browbeaten by his wife and consumed with upholding his various duties, feels an undefinable sense of emptiness. After Sabathier attaches himself, however, Lawford looks beyond the confines of his body and begins to understand that his roles as husband, father, friend, and worker are merely masks that he adopts, a "dull self-set routine." His wife, Sheila, for instance, cannot tolerate Lawford's changed physiognomy, despite his claims that he still loves her. A series of similar occurrences underscores de la Mare's use of Lawford's physical metamorphosis as a metaphor for the human condition. Stripped of their layers of social functions and relationships, individuals exist in a fundamentally lonely state. The fact that Sabathier was an outsider mirrors Lawford's position as a man divorced from any substantial contact with others. Fatuous people such as Bethany and Danton interact with Lawford's outward appearance rather than with his inner complexities. So concerned are Lawford's "friends" for his face that they forget or never care to understand Arthur's fears and doubts, his loves and desires. Ultimately, it does not matter that Sabathier "possessed" Lawford, for as Grisel — whom Arthur loves but cannot have — tells him, "It was only you — another you." Sabathier's apparition merely provides the impetus for Lawford to come to terms with his own psychological ghosts. That Lawford does so attests to his strength and singularity as an individual, for most people either fear or cannot fathom what lies beneath the facade.

Between 1909 and 1920 de la Mare, with one exception, set his literary sights on poetry, short fiction, and reviews rather than the novel, supplementing his income as a reader for Heinemann. In 1914, however, de la Mare collaborated on a novel, *John Fanning's Legacy,* with Naomi Royde-Smith, an intelligent, attractive woman with whom de la Mare shared a passionate, albeit platonic, relationship. De la Mare wrote over seven hundred letters to Royde-Smith, indicative of the effect this intense friendship had on his literary production. *John Fanning's Legacy,* a light epistolary satire of the literary milieu, eventually embarrassed de la Mare, and he made Royde-Smith promise not to acknowledge that he wrote some of the letters of "Nicholas Quantock." De la Mare's reservations about the novel forced Royde-Smith to finish the work, eventually published under her name in 1927.

Before starting work on the novel most readers consider his masterpiece, de la Mare finished out the 1910s first by successfully lecturing in America and then by working in the Food Controller's Office during World War I. In early 1920 de la Mare began work on *Memoirs of a Midget* (1921), the novel that would bring him the greatest financial and critical success. Storm Jameson, a contemporary critic, claimed that the narrative marked "the most notable achievement in prose of our generation," which included Woolf, James Joyce, and D. H. Lawrence. Set in the late Victorian era, the book relates the compelling story of Miss M., a woman of extremely small stature but also of great insight. Miss M. writes her story to correct false impressions people may have received from a newspaper account that painted her as little more than a freak. Apart from her size, Miss M.'s story convinces its readers that, although she may possess an uncommonly acute sense of detail, she is far from freakish.

After the death of her parents, Miss M. spurns her godmother, Miss Fenne, and decides to board with Mrs. Bowater. Although she likes Mrs. Bowater, Miss M. suffers pangs of remorse over her treatment of Miss Fenne, but the break seems irreversible. At her new residence Miss M. becomes enamored of young Fanny Bowater both emotionally and physically, if not sexually (McCrosson, however, discounts suggestions that Miss M. is a lesbian). Fanny simply exploits Miss M.'s affection, being nice to her when she needs to borrow money or requires a favor. Despite hurt feelings over Fanny's cruelty, Miss M. treats Mr. Anon — a midget who falls in love with Miss M. — with a similar indifference. In a move tantamount to self-destruction, Miss M., distraught over her relationship with Fanny, goes on exhibition in a circus, an experience that provides her with an opportunity to take stock of her life. Mr. Anon eventually, and tragically, takes her place, freeing her to continue her self-

*De la Mare in later years (photograph by Douglas Glass)*

analysis away from the humiliating atmosphere of the circus.

Like Arthur Lawford, Miss M. functions as a metaphor for the stark realities of human existence. Her physical stature does not prove central to the narrative, apart from a few scenes in which she feels frightened and insignificant, but it functions quite effectively as a tangible emblem of the book's recurrent theme of alienation. Alone and adrift in an ambivalent universe, Miss M. desperately seeks in Fanny the companionship and understanding necessary to affirm her status as a vital human being. Fanny's indifference, however, proves illuminating to the protagonist, who comes to the realization that her longings and aspirations are inconsequential to everyone but herself. De la Mare felt it was impossible for anyone to understand more than glimpses of human life, and Miss M. hardly comprehends her own motivations, much less Fanny's. Miss M. starts to ask herself the unmerciful question she had overheard a child ask about her: "Is that alive?" Forcibly excluded from both the daily course of events and Fanny's heart, Miss M. struggles to interpret her place in an irrational world. Her sense of emptiness over losing, or never really possessing, Fanny does

not abate, and even when she attempts to conform to the role others have created for her – that of a freak – she ultimately cannot find happiness. Miss M.'s story underscores both the utter lack of control humans have over their physical and mental destinies and the devastating consequences of that lack.

De la Mare's final foray into the novel, *At First Sight* (1928), also examines the theme of alienation but does so from the perspective of a socially naive young man, Cecil Jennings. Jennings, possessed of a congenital ocular condition that prevents him from looking up, finds his uneventful daily routine disturbed by the discovery of a cheap glove. The novelty of the situation prompts Jennings to search for the glove's owner. Jennings finds her after much struggle, but upon meeting the somewhat ungrateful Miss Simcox, Cecil decides to keep the glove. Nevertheless, Cecil convinces Simcox to meet with him the next day. The pair fall in love, but Cecil's grandmother, a woman for whom appearances are all-important, convinces the lower-class and poor Simcox that she cannot accept Cecil's marriage proposal, a fact that shatters both of the lovers' lives.

Whereas *The Return* and *Memoirs of a Midget* respectively examine alienation within the family and the self, *At First Sight* explores barriers of class. Cecil's philosophical perspective parallels his visual perspective, for both lack range. Cecil, heir to a substantial fortune, lacks awareness of the social mores that prompt his grandmother to discourage his relationship with Simcox. Similarly, Cecil's arrogant attitude toward beggars betrays little understanding of the economic forces at play in his community. He only realizes, somewhat childishly, that he cannot have what he desires, and he reacts with impotent rage. De la Mare casts Cecil as a prisoner of his own ignorance, a naïf lacking the wherewithal to alter his situation. Only when Cecil interrupts Simcox in the midst of a suicide attempt does he comprehend that social forces much more powerful than individual love threaten to destroy the pair. Simcox's characterization of Cecil as "blindly unpractical and unworldly" seems apt, for the youth would impetuously ignore the strictures of class and marry her anyway. Cecil's sincerity is particularly touching, however, and he even looks up at Simcox despite great physical pain. This incident, despite McCrosson's arguments to the contrary, suggests that Cecil learns a lasting lesson from his passion and that his perspective has grown commensurably with his love. Like Lawford and Miss M., though, Jennings must continue to exist without the lover who would make him more complete and less trapped within the lonely confines of society.

After completing *At First Sight,* de la Mare abandoned the novel form and concentrated on poetry and short stories. Nevertheless, his contribution to the twentieth-century novel is significant, despite waning critical interest following his death in 1956. Standing apart from the reigning modernist hegemony, de la Mare infused his novels with a rare combination of sensitive insight and poetic grace. While he did not experiment as did Joyce or philosophize as did Lawrence, de la Mare shared with these writers the sense that modern individuals needed to develop a spiritual center in order to combat the slings and arrows of postindustrial life. De la Mare's novels deftly handle the confusion that arises from contemplating one's existence and suggest that while answers may not be forthcoming, the process of asking such ontological questions is not only worthwhile but essential.

**Bibliographies:**

Leonard Clark, "A Handlist of the Writings in Book Form (1902–53) of Walter de la Mare," *Studies in Bibliography,* 6 (1954): 192–217; "Addendum: A Checklist of Walter de la Mare," *Studies in Bibliography,* 8 (1956): 269–270;

Edward Wagenknecht, "A List of Walter de la Mare's Contributions to the London *Times Literary Supplement," Boston University Studies in English,* 1 (Winter 1955): 243–255;

Clark, *Walter de la Mare: A Checklist* (London: Cambridge University Press, 1956).

**Biography:**

Theresa Whistler, *Imagination of the Heart: The Life of Walter de la Mare* (London: Duckworth, 1993).

**References:**

John Atkins, *Walter de la Mare: An Exploration* (London: Temple, 1947);

Russell Brain, *Tea With Walter de la Mare* (London: Faber & Faber, 1957);

Boris Ford, "The Rest Was Silence: de la Mare's Last Interview," *Encounter,* 7 (September 1956): 38–46;

Kenneth Hopkins, *Walter de la Mare,* Writers and Their Work, 36 (London: Longmans, Green, 1953);

W. R. Irwin, *The Game of the Impossible* (Urbana: University of Illinois Press, 1976), pp. 106–107, 132;

Storm Jameson, "Mr. de la Mare and the Grotesque," *English Review,* 24 (May 1922): 424–430;

D. R. McCrossen, *Walter de la Mare* (New York: Twayne, 1966);

R. L. Mégroz, *Five Novelist Poets of To-Day* (London: Joiner & Steele, 1933), pp. 19–58;

Mégroz, *Walter de la Mare: A Biographical and Critical Study* (London: Hodder & Stoughton, 1924);

J. B. Priestley, *Figures in Modern Literature* (London: John Lane/Bodley Head, 1924), pp. 31–54;

Forrest Reid, *Walter de la Mare: A Critical Study* (London: Faber & Faber, 1929);

Edward Wagenknecht, *Cavalcade of the English Novel* (New York: Holt, Rinehart & Winston, 1954), pp. 533–546;

Wagenknecht, *Seven Masters of Supernatural Fiction* (New York: Greenwood Press, 1991), pp. 121–149.

**Papers:**

De la Mare's papers are collected at Temple University Libraries, Rare Book Department; the University of Chicago Library; the Syracuse University Library; and King's College, Cambridge.

# William De Morgan

## (16 November 1839 – 15 January 1917)

Darrell Laird
*University College of the Cariboo*

BOOKS: *Joseph Vance: An Ill-Written Autobiography* (London: Heinemann, 1906; New York: Holt, 1907);

*Alice-For-Short: A Dichronism* (London: Heinemann, 1907; New York: Holt, 1907);

*Somehow Good* (London: Heinemann, 1908; New York: Holt, 1908);

*It Can Never Happen Again* (London: Heinemann, 1909; New York: Holt, 1909);

*An Affair of Dishonour* (London: Heinemann, 1910; New York: Holt, 1910);

*A Likely Story* (London: Heinemann, 1911; New York: Holt, 1911);

*When Ghost Meets Ghost* (London: Heinemann, 1914; New York: Holt, 1914);

*The Old Madhouse,* by De Morgan and Evelyn De Morgan (London: Heinemann, 1919; New York: Holt, 1919);

*The Old Man's Youth and the Young Man's Old Age,* by De Morgan and Evelyn De Morgan (London: Heinemann, 1921; New York: Holt, 1920).

OTHER: Mary Augusta De Morgan, *On a Pincushion and Other Fairy Tales . . . With Illustrations by William De Morgan* (London: Jackson & Holliday, 1877);

Charles Dickens, *Our Mutual Friend,* introduction by De Morgan (London: Waverly Books, 1913);

Mary Augusta De Morgan, *The Necklace of Princess Fiorimonde and Other Stories . . . With Original Illustrations by William De Morgan, Walter Crane, Olive Cockerell* (London: Gollancz, 1963).

*from a photograph by Ethel Glazebrook*

William De Morgan's novels present a difficulty for many present-day readers. In many ways they resemble the works of William Makepeace Thackeray and Charles Dickens, but De Morgan was a contemporary of such early modernist writers as Ford Madox Ford, Joseph Conrad, and James Joyce. The critical attention his works have received falls into two camps: that of the 1920s, which tends to emphasize his early Victorian parallels; and the scant and usually scathing glimpses thereafter, which tend to dismiss his work as an aberration. Apart from brief mentions in literary histories, De Morgan's work has been neglected since his death in 1917, although his last two novels – *The Old Madhouse* (1919) and *The Old Man's Youth and the Young*

*Man's Old Age* (1921) – completed by his wife after his death, helped to sustain some popular interest in his writing into the early 1920s, as did the publication of A. M. W. Stirling's biography in 1922.

The neglect of De Morgan's work may largely be a result of his style, characterized by length rather than brevity, whimsy rather than satire, and sentimentalism rather than psychological realism. A reader today may feel that a little more whimsy and a little less sentimentality might more securely place De Morgan's novels in a recognizable and therefore acceptable context, perhaps as an interesting precursor of P. G. Wodehouse, whose comic novels make a virtue and a joy of whimsy. Placed among the novelists publishing in the late Victorian and the Edwardian periods, De Morgan is closer in tone to Jerome K. Jerome than to the social realists such as George Gissing, Sir Walter Besant, or Arthur Morrison. More generally, readers today might find a corrective to their view of his fictional world by following the hints in De Morgan's scattered allusions to Lewis Carroll, Sir Arthur Conan Doyle, and "Uncle Remus," as well as to his fondness for humorously grotesque ceramic designs. It is his comedy that appeals most to the present-day reader.

William Frend De Morgan, the eldest son in a family of seven children, was born 16 November 1839. His father, Augustus De Morgan, was descended from a long line of military men who had served in India since the early 1700s and was the great grandson of the distinguished mathematician James Dodson. Augustus De Morgan was appointed to the mathematics chair at the newly established (1826–1827) London College (University College), where he met Sophia Frend, the daughter of the mathematician William Frend. De Morgan married Sophia in 1837, and she subsequently became involved in many social causes. She helped Elizabeth Frye in the formation of Bedford College in 1849 and was an advocate of higher education for women and woman suffrage. The household of Augustus and Sophia De Morgan received many distinguished visitors, including John Stuart Mill and Sir William Hamilton.

William De Morgan attended University College School from 1849 to 1855 and then entered the college proper. In 1859 he was admitted to the Royal Academy School, where he met Edward Burne-Jones, Dante Gabriel Rossetti, and William Morris. Although his first intention had been to become a painter, De Morgan gradually began searching for a new medium in which to apply his creative sensibility. He began to experiment with the manufacture of glass and tiles and then made a breakthrough with thickly glazed pottery that drew on Moorish lusters. After the death of his father in 1871, De Morgan moved his mother and the family to Cheyne Row in Chelsea, set up a kiln in the garden, and started life as a potter, by far his most successful artistic venture. For the rest of his working life as an artist, from the ages of thirty-two to sixty-six, De Morgan produced pots and tiles. In 1882, after his business had outgrown its back-garden premises, he moved it to a site at Merton Abby near Wimbledon; in 1888, for health reasons, he built a new factory closer to his home, at Sands End, Fulham.

Although De Morgan's designs for ornamental tiles and pots were highly prized, he was never a businessman and kept no accounts. A great camaraderie existed between De Morgan and his employees, but De Morgan was eventually forced to lay off workers as his business got into greater financial difficulties and as his health deteriorated. In a letter dated January 1903 he remarked that he had temporarily closed his factory. Finally, neuritis in one of his thumbs forced him to give up his career as a potter; he retired in 1905, and his firm dissolved two years later.

An important personal and financial support through a good deal of his pottery career was his wife, Evelyn Pickering, whom De Morgan had married in March 1887 and who at critical times injected funds into his business. Referred to by Samuel Pepys and intermarried with John Dryden's family, the Pickerings were a well-descended and well-connected family. Eighteen years younger than De Morgan, Evelyn had also determined to be an artist, encountering some resistance to the idea from her family. Yet with the encouragement and example of her artist uncle, Roddam Spencer-Stanhope, Evelyn persisted, and she eventually won high praise from the critic George Frederick Watts: "I look upon her as the first woman-artist of the day – if not of all time." Until his death Spencer-Stanhope remained close to William and Evelyn; for health reasons from the 1890s to the beginning of World War I, the De Morgans wintered in Florence in a house not far from that of Evelyn's uncle, and these annual sojourns in Italy are perhaps reflected in some of the settings of De Morgan's novels, for example, the Italian sections of *Joseph Vance: An Ill-Written Autobiography* (1906) and *A Likely Story* (1911).

Writing fiction did not present itself as a necessary or obvious successor to De Morgan's reluctantly discarded first love, pottery. His first attempt at writing prose was a report he wrote in the spring

*The De Morgan brothers, Edward, William, and George*

of 1893, following a visit to Cairo on behalf of the Egyptian government. Unpracticed as an author, De Morgan was also something less than a great consumer of fiction. His biographer, Stirling, reports that De Morgan remarked to a friend: "The fact is, I have blundered into the wrong generation. I belong entirely to the Dickens of life and literature. I read greedily when *Pickwick* was up-to-date, and when all the world was as Dickens drew it. Afterwards, I plunged into an active life in which every moment of my time was absorbed by art, by chemical problems or mechanical inventions, and for forty years I scarcely looked in a book unless it was about pots or mechanisms. When I turned again to literature, I took it up exactly where I had left off – the interregnum did not exist for me." As he summed up his turn from pots to plots, "when I took to [novel writing] I had been . . . long outside the pale making tiles not *tyles* [Cockney for 'tales']."

In turning to consider those "tyles," a good place to begin is with the sentimental components of De Morgan's style, for it may be sentimentalism

that most offends the modern reader. His novels repeatedly demonstrate a close connection between whimsy and sentimentality. The sentimental writer is often accused of lacking ironic detachment from his or her subject, but it can be argued that sympathetic feelings for the poor are at the heart of the late Victorians' "moral imagination." Thus, though self-deprecating, whimsical humor creates the atmosphere in most of De Morgan's fiction – the main exception being his historical romance, *An Affair of Dishonour* (1910) – at its center is the classic Victorian and Edwardian concern with the poor. The style often suggests the farcical romances for which Wodehouse would become famous. The parrot from *Alice-For-Short: A Dichronism* (1907), for instance – " 'Minute somebody comes,' said [the parrot], with perfect distinctness, 'he stops talking' " – might well open its beak in a story about Mr. Mulliner, or of Jeeves and Bertie, or somewhere in Blandings Castle. Yet De Morgan's plots and settings lack the reassuring, moneyed sunniness of the later writer's works.

De Morgan's play on *tiles/tyles* is just the sort of humor that sets the tone for his fiction. His first novel, *Joseph Vance: An Ill-Written Autobiography,* displays many of his characteristic strengths and weaknesses. Indeed, the same sort of punning parallels exist between De Morgan, the author, and Joseph Vance, the protagonist, as exist between *tiles* and *tyles.* Joe Vance, like his author, is an older man; both character and author are literary naïfs, disavowing any literary skill; like his author, Vance looks back on a practical, active career – the one as a potter, the other as an engineer, both as somewhat reluctant businessmen, both as inventors. Finally, like De Morgan, who after he retired considered writing a history of pottery, Vance, too, has been led from the relatively safe scholarly task of writing a history of musical instruments, tentatively titled *Music and Mechanism,* to the psychologically more revealing and therefore riskier one of autobiography.

Vance's motivation for reliving his past and the reason for his referring to this task as "a sort of trial of strength" is his unrequited love for Lossie Desprey, who befriends and educates him, rescuing the boy from an impoverished home with gloomy prospects – a rescue motif repeated in De Morgan's *Alice-For-Short* and *Somehow Good* (1908), among others. Vance finally resolves to burn his manuscript, but it is rescued by an insubordinate maid, and, ironically, the memoirs are instrumental in his regaining Lossie, because writing them (in the British Museum Reading Room) detains Vance in London long enough for Lossie to locate him and thus fulfill their love.

The novel is partly an exercise in remembrance and partly the story of a man who loves two women, as well as the story of a man's relationship with two father figures: Vance's with his natural father and with Lossie's father, Dr. Thorpe, who undertakes Joe's education. (Thorpe, who wins the eight-year-old Joe's respect by introducing him to the theorems of Euclid, seems to be modeled on De Morgan's father.) Vance, born around 1842, has set himself the task of remembering his life, beginning with the first events he can recall, some fifty years previously. As he remarks, simple remembering becomes "a sort of trial of strength" and "the more I come to memories I shirk, the more I nerve myself to the efforts to record them." His determination to face his past parallels his natural father's stubbornness. Fittingly, the novel begins with the events leading up to a head-butting contest between young Vance's father, a recently fired warehouseman and an alcoholic, and Peter Gunn, a sweep in a bar. Appropriately, the novel ends after Joe and Lossie have been reunited, with all misunderstandings cleared up and Joe's old life (in the form of the manuscript) packed and crated in a London warehouse.

What sustains Joe Vance in his "trial of strength" is the humorous tone of the novel. As in most of De Morgan's novels, the sentimentality and melodrama of the plot are redeemed by the humor of the telling. Comic mishearings multiply, ranging from eight-year-old Joe's misconstruals of his father's Cockney speech to those of Lossie's deaf old Aunt Isabella and to the remarkable virtuoso episode of the "Magic Board," which bears some resemblance to Oliver Twist's confusion about the "board" in Dickens's novel. Joe's father, Christopher, purchases for fifteen pence a signboard that reads, "C. Dance. Builder. Repairs. Drains promptly attended to." His father seizes an opportunity: " 'Wery good, then. Round we goes to-morrow morning to Mr. Parbuckle and we'll see if he won't make good this here error in this here signboard." Mr. Vance launches a profitable career as a builder by the simple alteration of "Dance" to "Vance," as though by appropriating the sign he had appropriated its advertised calling as well. The narrator comments, "my Father thenceforward treated the letter he proposed to correct as an erratum due to the ignorance of the original composer." Considering that the elder Vance had been up to that moment an obstreperous, prevaricating, unemployed alcoholic, the change surpasses the ingenious and approaches the miraculous.

In De Morgan's second novel, *Alice-For-Short,* the social problem of alcoholism again initiates the events of the plot. Alice Kavanagh, a girl of six who leads a miserable existence with her alcoholic, quarreling parents, has been sent out on a foggy, cold day to fetch a jug of beer from the Duke of Clarence's Head pub. As she is returning, some boys bump into her and break her jug. At this point the narrator, Charles Heath, a young aspiring artist who lives in Alice's apartment building, happens upon her and straightens matters out by settling with her mother for the wasted beer.

Shortly after this first encounter with Charles, Alice awakens one night to the sounds of a terrific quarrel, which ends in death for both of her parents. Her father kills her mother with a hammer and then takes cyanide in remorse and panic. Like young Joe, Alice finds herself rescued by a benevolent middle class. Charles takes her to his family home, and Alice grows up in comfort and safety. The ending hints that she will eventually become her rescuer's wife. The intervening plot, with suggestions of the occult, an element also found in

*First page of a four-page illustrated letter from De Morgan to his cousin Fanny Seeley (from A. M. W. Stirling,* William De Morgan and his Wife, *1922)*

*When Ghost Meets Ghost* (1914) and *A Likely Story,* unravels the mystery of a murder committed on the same premises many years before.

As in De Morgan's other novels, however, the plot, with all its meanderings and jerkings, is of much less interest than the characters and their conversations. At one point Heath muses over the words of the reclusive and destitute old artist J. W. Verrinder. Verrinder addresses the story's protagonist, who, like the young De Morgan, is an aspiring but not very talented painter from an indulgent bourgeois home and whose misgivings about his vocation are beginning to overcome his previous enthusiasm: " 'But you're a gentleman. There's but a very few left nowadays. They're all Feejee Injuns.' His mispronouncing of a word or two did not seem to be from want of education. 'Injuns' might have been jocularity – a word spoken quotation-wise.' " The narrator's remark might well be taken for a signpost to De Morgan's own style, for his too is a jocular style, much given to words "spoken quotation-wise." Somewhat further on, the narrator offers another revealing description while commenting on Charles's sister Peggy – variously, affectionately, and playfully referred to by Charles as Pog, Poggy, or Poggy Woggy – "She felt that she had been rather making a speech, and wasn't sure she wasn't a humbug. Perhaps we all feel this whenever we say anything consecutive. Honesty is supposed to be fraught with jerks, and sincerity with sloppiness of style." Both comments reflect upon De Morgan's self-consciousness about his fiction: his work is full of jerks and sloppiness; but they are, by his way of regarding the matter, signs of sincerity – the highest value, perhaps, for many late Victorians. In any case De Morgan had a well-tuned ear for the character and music of speech and undoubtedly expressed his own feelings through the protagonist of *It Can Never Happen Again* (1909), Alfred Challis, who reflects, "absurd tropes and inversions, without a smile, are the breath of life to cab and bus men."

Both *Joseph Vance* and *Alice-For-Short* concern themselves with the moral problems of poverty and inequality in Victorian society. The first questions the ascent of Mr. Vance from unemployed worker to self-employed businessman; the second questions the way in which society deals with abused and neglected children. Although in each novel these social concerns lie beneath a thick coating of sentiment, what engages both author and reader are the moral issues of responsibility, sympathy, compassion, and care for the less fortunate. Yet perhaps that sunny exterior is more a part of the writer's

*Sketch of De Morgan, circa 1907, by his wife, Evelyn (from William Gaunt and M. D. E. Clayton-Stamm,* William De Morgan: Pre-Raphaelite Ceramics, *1971)*

moral concern than the metaphor of "coating" tends to suggest.

Although his first three novels contain satiric elements – the first, perhaps, being the portrait in *Joseph Vance* of Lossie's brother, a fin de siècle aesthete – satire remains a minor element. More often than not, when it does appear, it is mild. In *Alice-For-Short,* for example, the narrator pokes fun at a symbol of bourgeois philistinism, the decorative library in his father's home, describing it as "a place where some titles of books were sometimes perused through plate glass." *Somehow Good,* in the same mild vein, satirizes the old India soldiers and their Hurkara Club.

Not surprising, De Morgan, like many late Victorians, seems to disparage radical attempts to reform society: in *Somehow Good,* for example, the narrator refers to another character as "a disciple of what used to be called Socialism." Nevertheless, the author was clearly concerned with the injustices of his time, and each of these episodes signals both the attraction for De Morgan of a more pointed critique of social ills and the problems he had in taking the

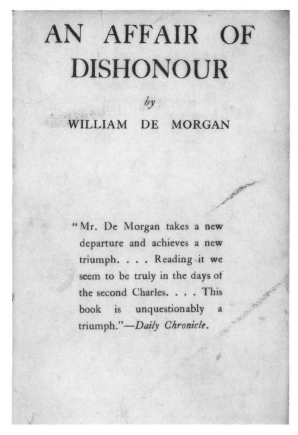

# AN AFFAIR OF DISHONOUR

*by*

WILLIAM DE MORGAN

"Mr. De Morgan takes a new departure and achieves a new triumph. . . . Reading it we seem to be truly in the days of the second Charles. . . . This book is unquestionably a triumph."—*Daily Chronicle.*

*Dust jacket for one of the last novels De Morgan completed, published in 1910 (courtesy of the Lilly Library, Indiana University)*

step from writing novels of sentimental entertainment to writing those of critical commentary. The presence of the moral and the comic in his novels suggests a continual artistic struggle. On the one hand, he adopts the tone of benign condescension toward the less fortunate, as in his dismissal of socialism – the same tone, one might add, that he adopts toward the world in general, an attitude which allows him to exercise his comedy of speech and memory. On the other hand, this attitude seems to mask De Morgan's desire to turn his fiction into something more than simple comedy, and at times a harder, more satiric edge makes itself felt, most notably in *It Can Never Happen Again,* which examines the anguish arising from infidelity and the inadequacy of divorce law.

Yet the same novel, which presents the Reverend Athelstan Taylor's strident denunciation of English law's historic injustices to women, also includes as a subplot something of a tour de force in sentimentalism in the characters of Lizerann Coupland and her father, Jim. Like Joe Vance and Alice Kavanagh, Lizerann begins life in unpromising cir-

cumstances. Her mother dies a few days after her father is dismissed from the Merchant Service as an invalid, blinded when he dropped a match into an oil cask aboard his ship. Yet De Morgan has not quite finished with the hapless pair: while he is selling matches in the street, Jim's legs are crushed by a passing wagon; only then does help, once again from the philanthropically minded middle class, appear – when Reverend Taylor rescues Lizerann from her drunken and knife-wielding uncle.

The effect of such sentimental excesses, typical of De Morgan's fiction, is to dilute the psychological realism of his stronger satiric portraits. But readers should not lose sight of the fact that even his sentimentalism seems to be offered, at least at times, more as parody than in earnest. Modern readers may find it hard to adjust their perceptions to this hybrid, but humor rather than pure sentimentality seems to have been his aim. On being asked by the Reverend Athelstan Taylor what her father does, Lizerann replies: "He's a Asker. Askin', he does. Yass!" Such passages give the impression that De Morgan has had his eye all along on the truth and wit of his characters' words, not on the horrors with which he has burdened them.

The three novels De Morgan wrote after *It Can Never Happen Again – An Affair of Dishonour, A Likely Story,* and *When Ghost Meets Ghost,* together with the pair of novels completed after his death by his wife – *The Old Madhouse* and *The Old Man's Youth and the Young Man's Old Age* – continue in the same vein as his first four. Like the early novels, these are dense with incident and character, mine the older person's fond memories of youth, and reveal their author, in the words of one contemporary reviewer, as "a story-teller rather than a novelist." In listening to stories – and the sound of words are always important in De Morgan's fiction – the sympathetic listener learns to trust and enjoy the voice of the teller and to refrain from being overly critical of the improbabilities of his plots. None of De Morgan's novels is free from implausible plotting, but his later novels probably strain the reader's credulity more than his earlier works. Nevertheless, for all its orality, there is, as the same reviewer also suggests, "a streak of Henry James" in De Morgan's concern with memory and, as another reviewer points out, his techniques of exploring the past through the most trivial of details is not all that different from Marcel Proust's.

Yet it is the sound of his words that ultimately saves De Morgan's work from oblivion. He had an ear for the quirks of human speech, and it may not be going too far to say that that ear remains his re-

deeming virtue as a novelist, overcoming his sentimentalism and perhaps even helping, after all, to make his readers look again at others more compassionately. His leisurely, rambling style may become somewhat tiresome to the modern reader, but one's attention is suddenly caught by De Morgan's wit, as displayed in *It Can Never Happen Again* by an exchange between Judith Arkroyd, the upper-class lover of Alfred Challis, and Elphinstone, the butler: "She calls the little ex-dairymaid back; and then turning to Mr Elphinstone, waiting patiently to be the last to retire, says to him, 'What is good for a burn, Elphinstone?' – as to a universal referee. He replies, 'I always use olive-oil, Miss,' as if he belonged to a particular school of singed butlers."

## Biography:

A. M. W. Stirling, *William De Morgan and his Wife* (London: Butterworth, 1922).

## References:

Julia Cartwright, "William De Morgan: A Reminiscence," *Cornhill Magazine,* new series 42 (April 1917): 461–471;

Edwin Francis Edgett, "William De Morgan," *Bookman,* 45 (March 1917): 64, 67;

William Gaunt and M. D. E. Clayton-Stamm, *William De Morgan: Pre-Raphaelite Ceramics* (London: Studio Vista, 1971);

"Last of the Dickensians: William De Morgan (1839–1917)," *Times Literary Supplement,* 18 November 1939, p. 673;

Katherine A. Lochnan, Douglas E. Schoenhen, and Carole Silver, eds., *The Earthly Paradise: Arts and Crafts by William Morris and his Circle from Canadian Collections* (Toronto: Key Porter, 1993), pp. 185–215;

May Morris, "William De Morgan," *Burlington Magazine,* 174 (September 1917): 91–97;

Flora Warren Seymour, *William De Morgan: A Post-Victorian Realist* (Chicago: Bookfellow, 1920);

"William De Morgan," *Times Literary Supplement,* 9 July 1954, p. 440.

## Papers:

Collections of William De Morgan's correspondence are held by the Bancroft Library at the University of California (dating from 1866 to 1917); the Bodleian Library, Oxford (dating from 1894 to 1909); and the Cambridge University Library (letters from De Morgan to Professor R. S. Conway, 1907–1916).

# George Du Maurier

*(6 March 1834 – 8 October 1896)*

Richard Kelly
*University of Tennessee, Knoxville*

BOOKS: *English Society at Home: From the Collection of "Mr. Punch"* (London: Bradbury, Agnew, 1880);

*Society Pictures from Punch,* 2 volumes (London: Bradbury, Agnew, 1890–1891);

*Peter Ibbetson* (London: Osgood & McIlvaine, 1892 [1891]; New York: Harper, 1891);

*Trilby* (3 volumes, London: Osgood & McIlvaine, 1894; 1 volume, New York: Harper, 1894);

*The Martian* (London & New York: Harper, 1897);

*Social Pictorial Satire* (New York & London: Harper, 1898).

During the last seven years of his life, George Du Maurier turned from his career as the leading artist for *Punch* and the popular illustrator of books to achieve new acclaim as a novelist. His three novels, *Peter Ibbetson* (1891), *Trilby* (1894) and *The Martian* (1897), became best-sellers in England and America. Although his works have been given scant attention in recent times, they have a powerful literary significance. In reshaping the traditional romantic novel, Du Maurier was one of the first British authors to introduce into fiction the subject of the unconscious mind. In his three novels he probes the processes of memory, dreams, hypnotism, free association, and automatic writing. Through these explorations Du Maurier was adapting the romantic novel to the burgeoning field of depth psychology. The author does not seem to have been aware that at the time he was writing his novels some of the most influential philosophers and social scientists, such as Sigmund Freud, Henri Bergson, and William James, were investigating the same mental phenomena that formed the heart of his fiction.

George Louis Palmella Busson Du Maurier was born in Paris on 6 March 1834. Half French and half English, he spent his early childhood in a tranquil suburb of Paris called Passy. His family then moved to the grim town of Pentonville, England, and Du Maurier enrolled in the Birkbeck Chemical Laboratory of University College, Lon-

*George Du Maurier in the 1890s*

don. Unhappy with his studies, he returned to France to study painting in the atelier of Charles Gleyre, a Swiss artist who stressed the importance of line over color and the importance of skillful drawing as the basis of art. There Du Maurier became friends with the British artists Thomas Lamont, Thomas Armstrong, and Edward Poynter and the American artist James Whistler.

Shortly after leaving Paris, Du Maurier lost sight in his left eye, leading him to abandon his dream of becoming a painter. Instead, he turned to drawing in black and white for several English periodicals. In 1860 he was hired by *Punch,* and during

the next twenty years he produced hundreds of cartoons for that magazine. Most of his work centered upon the foibles of the upper classes and the excesses of the aesthetes. In *Partial Portraits* (1899) Henry James notes that Du Maurier's drawings in *Punch* constitute "a complete comedy of manners," and John Ruskin in his *Art of England* (1883) compares Du Maurier's drawings favorably with those of Hans Holbein.

On 3 January 1863 Du Maurier married Emma Wightwick, who was to bear him five children. In 1874 the family moved to Hampstead, an idyllic suburb that Du Maurier used as the basis for many of his domestic cartoons in *Punch*. It was here that Henry James came to visit the artist. During one of his visits James urged Du Maurier to try his hand at writing. Encouraged by his friend's confidence in his talent, Du Maurier, at the age of fifty-five, produced his first piece of fiction, *Peter Ibbetson,* published in 1891.

The modest success of his first novel led Du Maurier to write *Trilby,* which became one of the best-selling books of the nineteenth century. The novel's villain, Svengali, is a demonic hypnotist who seduces, defiles, and deifies the innocent heroine, Trilby. Millions of readers in England and America were entranced by the exotic and dangerous sexuality of the novel's theme, and soon quick-thinking entrepreneurs exploited the book's success by producing an array of Trilby merchandise. Capitalizing upon the foot fetishism set forth in the novel, a New York caterer began featuring ice cream molded in the form of Trilby's foot. Then a Chicago manufacturer produced a lady's high-heeled shoe called "the Trilby." A Kansas City journalist claimed to have purchased Trilby's house in Paris and put a plaque on the door to memorialize its former occupant. Trilby and Svengali, in short, were quickly becoming part of popular culture. People still refer to someone who possesses manipulative and sinister powers as a "Svengali," not realizing the source of their allusion.

The publication of *Trilby* brought fame, wealth, and prestige to Du Maurier, but he regretted the loss of his privacy. He was always a family-centered man who enjoyed the company of his wife and five children, whether at home or on a seaside vacation with their Saint Bernard, Chang. Despite the many demands placed upon him as a famous author, however, he managed to produce a third novel, a romantic fantasy titled *The Martian* (1897), shortly before his death. Although less popular than *Trilby,* the novel's compelling psychological themes did not disappoint Du Maurier's readers.

*Du Maurier with his wife, Emma, and their daughter Marie Louise in September 1874 (photograph by Julia Margaret Cameron)*

Through both his art and his fiction Du Maurier conjures up Edenic dreamworlds where time and harsh reality seldom intrude. Through these dreams and fantasies he defers the inevitable prospect of death. Troubled by ill health, however, he moved his family in 1895 from his beloved Hampstead to Oxford Square, near Hyde Park, a place he came to despise. His health steadily declined in his new home, and on 8 October 1896, at the age of sixty-two, Du Maurier died of congestive heart failure.

For a quarter of a century Du Maurier had been shaping in the pages of *Punch* an image of fashionable society that had the power of a captioned slide show, a series of literary still lifes. In turning to the novel Du Maurier discovered an exhilarating freedom from the confines of the single sketch through the continuity, movement, and extensive dialogue allowed in this new genre. More important, however, the novel allowed him to explore the mind and the potential of its unconscious forces. A romantic by nature, Du Maurier saw the connection

*The staff of* Punch *at the Paris Exhibition in 1887: Sir Henry Lucy; Harry Furniss; W. H. Bradbury; Sir William Agnew; Frank Burnand; Arthur A. Beckett; John Tenniel; E. J. Milliken; and Du Maurier (with unidentified individuals in foreground and background)*

between dreams and his lost youth, and the further he got from his idyllic childhood the more intense was his need to re-create it in both pictures and words.

The story of *Peter Ibbetson* is told from the point of view of Gogo Pasquier, later given the English name of Peter Ibbetson, who is a convicted murderer writing his memoirs in his prison cell. He recalls the sweetness of his childhood days in Passy and how they quickly soured after his father's death, when he became the ward of the British colonel Ibbetson, a relative of his mother. In England he falls in love with the beautiful duchess of Towers, who explains to him how he can "dream true" — that is, return to the past, experience it, and see himself there — provided he does not touch or alter anything. Although he seldom actually sees the duchess of Towers, he begins to visit her in his dreams and later learns that she shares these dreams. She and Peter henceforth meet at almost every sleeping moment of their lives, two people who share one dreamworld.

After a violent argument, Peter kills Colonel Ibbetson in self-defense and is imprisoned for life. He now lives only to sleep, to dream, and to spend fantastic hours with the duchess of Towers. Al-

though physically a prisoner, by dreaming true he is able to visit with the duchess, his grandparents in France, great artists, musicians, and authors from the past, and he is even able to create a dream home, Magna sed Apta, a palace of art decked with historical treasures. When the duchess of Towers dies, Peter plans to commit suicide, but she visits him in a final dream and informs him that their true joy and unity is yet to come. Peter thus dies a happy and fulfilled man.

The central theme of this novel is that of the split personality. First, there is the duality of Peter's parentage: his mother is English, and his father is French. Peter embodies this duality. His memoirs are rich with French dialogue and descriptions. His emotional life is shaped by France and the idyllic childhood he spent in Passy, but his English character leads him to admire the British aristocracy and the purity and beauty of its women, embodied in the duchess of Towers. The duality extends to his name: born Pierre Pasquier de la Mariere, he is reborn in England as Peter Ibbetson.

There is also a fairy-tale quality to the two father figures that du Maurier develops for his hero. The splitting of the father-figure into two distinct selves, one hated, the other idolized, is an attractive

fantasy. Du Maurier thus presents an idealized version of his own father in the character of "le beau Pasquier" and focuses all of his threatening and unpleasant traits in the character of Colonel Ibbetson. By having Peter murder the colonel, du Maurier finally eliminates altogether the menacing aspects of the father. The fact that neither Peter's father nor Colonel Ibbetson are believable characters is precisely due to the bifurcation involved in this fantasy.

The theme of duality also involves the central women of the novel, Madame Seraskier (the mother of the duchess of Towers), Madame Pasquier, and the duchess. The author's descriptions and illustrations reveal these characters to be nearly identical in beauty and stature. The "divine" Madame Seraskier is presented in terms of idealized beauty and is similar to Peter's mother, though the former is several inches taller. Like his mother, Madame Seraskier possesses warmth, kindness, simplicity, grace, naturalness, courtesy, sympathy, and joy, and, in fact, the two women become close friends. Ultimately, they both die at about the same time. The coincidence of their deaths is perhaps a too-obvious contrivance of the plot, but it has a certain psychological cogency. What appears to be involved in this duality is the Oedipal wish to possess the mother without guilt by splitting the mother figure into the virgin and the sexual object. The bifurcation is more complicated in this instance than it is with the father figure. With the deaths of the idealized mother and of the divine Madame Seraskier, Peter is free to fall in love with the duchess of Towers and to allow her to press her lips to his. The duchess of Towers is a composite figure: she is an allowable sexual object because she is sufficiently distanced from the mother, and yet her character includes the desirable traits of Peter's mother.

Finally, the most important thematic duality is that of Peter's mind, as he conducts his life for some thirty years on two levels, that of everyday consciousness and that of dreams. Unlike the heroes of Robert Louis Stevenson's *The Strange Case of Dr. Jekyll and Mr. Hyde* (1886) and Oscar Wilde's *The Picture of Dorian Gray* (1890), the duality in *Peter Ibbetson* is not between good and evil or between superego and id, but rather between dream and reality, with an almost compulsive emphasis that argues that dream *is* reality. The duality is more aesthetic than moral. Peter's dreams are essentially comprised of childhood visions, unspoiled nature, music, beautiful people, works of art and literature, freedom, and timelessness. The catalyst of his dreams is the virginal comforter, the duchess of Towers. His waking life, on the other hand, is made up of ugly people (Colonel Ibbetson, his crude schoolmates at Pentonville, and the prison inmates), depressing cityscapes in Pentonville, spoiled nature (the stumps of his childhood apple trees and the general destruction wrought by "progress" upon his golden Passy), and imprisonment.

While Du Maurier's characters have strong autobiographical roots, they also owe something to the Pre-Raphaelite movement with its idealized women, such as Dante Gabriel Rossetti's poem "The Blessed Damozel" (1850), and its rejection of the Victorian period for an aesthetic treatment of the Middle Ages and Renaissance. Walter Pater's gospel of beauty and his message that to "burn always with this hard, gem-like flame, to maintain this ecstasy, is success in life" also shaped Du Maurier's vision. These influences are reflected, for example, in Peter's comment at the end of the novel that a cell in a criminal lunatic asylum has been to him like a bower in the Elysian fields.

No one was more surprised than Du Maurier when his second novel, *Trilby,* became the best-selling book in England and America, with 300,000 copies sold by the end of its first year of publication. Some of this success clearly derives from the novel's exotic subject matter. Du Maurier gives the reader an inside look at the lives of three young English artists, Little Billee, the Laird, and Taffy, all studying painting in Paris and adapting to bohemian life in the Latin Quarter. There they meet the charming and beautiful young Trilby, who has modeled in the nude (the "altogether," as Du Maurier phrases it), and whose lack of chastity is balanced by her simplicity and affectionate nature.

The central power of this novel, however, derives from the character of Svengali, a demonic Jewish hypnotist who transforms Trilby into "La Svengali," the greatest singer in Europe. In his account of Svengali's control over Trilby, Du Maurier employs the theme of sexual domination. This may be one reason Svengali, like the title character of Bram Stoker's *Dracula* (1897), had such a powerful appeal to a reading public accustomed to sexual prudery, and the power of this theme may account for the character's continuing survival in the popular imagination, detached from the text that first gave him life.

Trilby has a haunting fear of being devoured by Svengali. "He reminds me of a big hungry spider, and makes me feel like a fly," she exclaims. One of Du Maurier's illustrations depicts a grotesque spider with Svengali's head sitting in the center of its web. Despite the repulsion Trilby feels for Svengali,

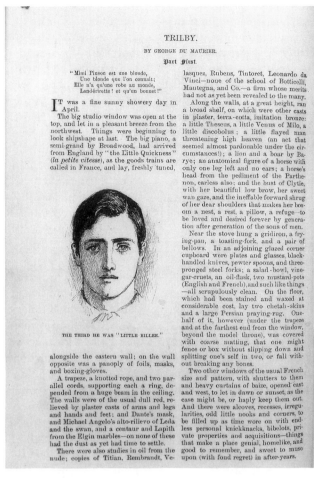

*First page of the serial publication of Du Maurier's most successful novel, in* Harper's New Monthly Magazine *for January 1894 (courtesy of the Lilly Library, Indiana University)*

she apparently feels a powerful attraction toward him that makes her fear that she will lose control over her emotions and possibly over her life.

Du Maurier develops the theme of sexual domination through the image of the incubus, a demon that has sexual intercourse with its victim during her sleep. Trilby perceives Svengali as a "dread, powerful demon, who . . . oppressed and weighed on her like an incubus — and she dreamed of him oftener than she dreamed of Taffy, the Laird, or even Little Billee." The fact that Trilby has recurrent dreams about Svengali singles him out from the proper and prudish Englishmen as a potent, dreadful, all-devouring sexual force, more appropriate to Victorian nightmares than to rational discourse. The mysterious foreign Jew is rousing sexual feelings that are already present but repressed. What Trilby fears is the arousal of this latent female sexuality.

Du Maurier fuses the theme of mesmerism with that of music and thereby adds a paradoxical quality to the power and influence of Svengali. By depicting Svengali as a virtuoso, Du Maurier draws on the literary tradition of the fabulous powers of music, which goes back centuries to the mythological figures of Arion, Amphion, the Sirens, Marsyas and Linus, and Orpheus. With the creation of Svengali, Du Maurier introduces a sinister element to the Orphic theme. Through the combined mastery of music and hypnosis, Svengali can control Trilby and, through her beautiful song, control the minds and hearts of thousands of people throughout Europe. Power becomes an end in itself, and its vital medium is the voice of Trilby, through which Svengali expresses himself.

Another important theme in this novel is the corruption of innocence. The early chapters establish a romantically idealized world in which the

three British artists are completely at home in their Paris enclave. Their world derives its solidity from the strong male bond between Little Billee, the Laird, and Taffy. When Trilby enters the lives of these three men the group becomes even more closely knit and they live as one family. Theirs is a chaste arrangement in which Trilby, when she is not serving the three artists as an inspirational model, assumes the traditional role of a Victorian housewife, sewing on buttons and darning socks.

The males bond, as in *Dracula,* to protect Trilby, a mother figure, and to keep the foreigner from arousing her sexuality. They want to keep her as a mother figure, and their suppression of her sexuality suggests that there may be an Oedipal fantasy at work. But Trilby, who brings a clearer harmony to the group, unwittingly brings about the eventual dissolution of their happy unity. By corrupting Trilby and using her like an exotic musical instrument to further his own power, Svengali drains her of life. Their symbiotic relationship finally leads to their deaths. In destroying Trilby, Svengali also destroys the only person who can restore to Little Billee his lost romantic vision of a world built upon love, friendship, and freedom. Little Billee dies shortly after the death of Trilby. Trilby's brief time with Little Billee, the Laird, and Taffy was "her little fool's paradise," even as it was to Little Billee. The "black spider-cat" poisons and devours them both. Their romantic and youthful ideals rendered them the perfect victims.

Du Maurier's ambiguous attitude toward Svengali keeps him from becoming the stereotypical villain of Victorian melodrama. Gecko, Svengali's doglike follower, acknowledges his master's supernatural powers: "Svengali was the greatest artist I ever met! Monsieur, Svengali was a demon, a magician! I used to think he was a god!" Du Maurier also associates Svengali with the legend of the Wandering Jew and the stereotype of the Shylock tradition by describing him "walking up and down the earth seeking whom he might cheat, betray, exploit, borrow money from, make brutal fun of, bully if he dared, cringe to if he must – man, woman, child, or dog."

Four mythic figures, then, are embodied in the character of Svengali: the Wandering Jew, Orpheus, the Devil, and the incubus. Du Maurier, however, freely modifies some of the particulars of these archetypes. The Wandering Jew, for example, can get his nose tweaked by Taffy, rendering him a figure of ridicule, and Orpheus is a demonic creature who uses his musical talents to acquire power and prestige. Comic, grotesque, terrifying, repul-

*Cover for Du Maurier's third and final novel, a romantic science fantasy (courtesy of the Lilly Library, Indiana University)*

sive, oracular, restless, musical, demonic, and sexually oppressive, Svengali is a compelling and complex character that appeals to the reader on many levels at once.

In his third and final novel, *The Martian,* Du Maurier continues to explore the power of the unconscious mind. Rich in autobiographical details, the novel takes the form of a romantic science fiction. Its hero, Barty Josselin, depressed after losing sight in one eye (like du Maurier himself), hears while asleep the voice of Martia, a creature from Mars, who comforts him with the promise that his good eye will remain intact and that she will help him become a famous literary figure. Barty marries an exotic Jewish beauty named Leah, an idealized portrait of Du Maurier's wife, Emma Wightwick. Martia continues to visit Barty at night, acting as a sort of demon or muse who will use his knowledge and his words to fashion immortal works of literature. Before long he is the author of several best-selling books.

Having won international fame for Barty, Martia explains her previous life on Mars. Over a great period of time she has undergone many rein-

carnations, from the lowest form to the highest. Now, as a disembodied spirit, she seeks another reincarnation, more fulfilling than the occasional dwelling within Barty Josselin. She thus makes the startling announcement to Barty that she will be his next child: "Barty, when I am a splendid son of yours or a sweet and lovely daughter, all remembrance of what I was before will have been wiped out of me until I die. But *you* will remember, and so will Leah, and both will love me with such a love as no earthly parents have ever felt for any child of theirs yet."

The Josselins name their next daughter Martia, or Marty for short. She grows up to be a model child, bright, imaginative, refined, and beautiful. One day while climbing a tree, she falls and injures her spine. She never recovers from the injury, and it leads to an illness that lasts four years, a period during which the family is brought more closely together. Marty finally dies, and Barty dies at the same moment, leaving the noble Leah to carry on the family responsibilities.

What saves all the supernatural paraphernalia from destroying the credibility of the novel is the narrator's assertion that Barty "might, in short, have led a kind of dual life, and Martia might be a simple fancy or invention of his brain in an abnormal state during slumber." A Victorian audience might have been able to accept more readily than a twentieth-century reader the account of life on Mars, the doctrine of reincarnation and spiritual evolution, and the practice of automatic writing. The psychological subtext, however, has considerable interest and significance for the modern reader.

Barty's relationship with Martia and his wife is intriguing and complex and perhaps reveals Du Maurier's ambivalent feelings about his mother. Martia is a sort of idealized mistress who visits her love at night, in his sleep, and shares and directs his deepest thoughts. She first appears in order to save his life and to comfort him, after which she declares her spiritual love for him: "I love you Barty, with a love passing the love of woman; and have done so from the day you were born." Sometimes her feelings suggest that she is more than a spirit, as when she exclaims, "especially I love your splendid body and all that belongs to it – brain, stomach, heart, and the rest; even your poor remaining eye, which is worth all the eyes of Argus." She shares his senses and is physically one with him in the intimacy of sleep. Her invisibility makes her the near perfect mistress, and her dismissal by Barty's wife, Leah, as a somnambulistic invention, completes the guiltless fantasy.

The psychological implications are rather intriguing. Beneath the complex web of relationships there appears to be a fundamental Oedipal conflict. A mother-mistress figure, acting out the role of a succubus, becomes the daughter of the son-lover figure. This is not the first time that Du Maurier has fused the character of a daughter and a mother. Madame Seraskier and the duchess of Towers became as one in the mind and emotions of Peter Ibbetson. The duchess of Towers, like Martia, also enjoined the roles of mother and dream lover in her relationship with Peter.

The climax of Barty's long involvement with Martia comes with the simultaneous deaths of Barty and Martia. First Martia shares his mind and body, then becomes his child, and finally, in death, they are reunited as one spirit. Leah, confined to domestic duties, survives briefly in the mundane world she has always inhabited, an outsider who never shared her husband's more rarified level of existence. The curious trinity of Barty-Martia-Marty is self-contained and self-referring. Poor Leah is a sort of incubator, a midwife to a dream come true. With Marty's death the triangle collapses upon itself. Barty is now totally possessed by his demon, and Leah, despite her nobility, "seems to bear it well." She must not have borne it too well, however, for she lives only twenty-four hours after her husband's death. Barty was her "fixed star," and she shone "with no other light than his." Such a melodramatic death clearly exhibits the male fantasy that a woman has no real life of her own and can live only through her husband.

Through these three books Du Maurier helped to reshape the traditional romantic novel by probing the nature of the unconscious mind. Memory, dreams, hypnotism, free association, and automatic writing are the five major phenomena that constitute the range of psychological interest in the unconscious in the novels. Du Maurier's interest in the theme of the split personality also dominates his fiction. Peter Ibbetson, Trilby, and Barty Josselin all exhibit fundamental dualities in personality. Their minds move between dream and reality. Stevenson, in *The Strange Case of Dr. Jekyll and Mr. Hyde,* is one of the few Victorian authors who previously had treated the theme of the split personality in such dramatic detail.

Du Maurier also embodied in his novels the aesthetic gospel of Pater. All of Du Maurier's heroes and heroines and even his villains possess finely tuned sensibilities that lead them to ecstatic responses to beauty, whether found in poetry, painting, music, the human body, or even smells and

taste. The French critic Maurice Lanoire, in his essay "Un Anglo-Français, Georges du Maurier," perceptively observes that Du Maurier's leading motif in all of his novels is "the need to flee the reality in the dream as one approaches death."

**Letters:**

*The Young George Du Maurier: A Selection of his Letters, 1860–67,* edited by Daphne Du Maurier (London: Davies, 1951).

**Interview:**

Robert H. Sherard, "The Author of *Trilby,*" *McClure's Magazine,* 4 (October 1895): 391–400.

**Biographies:**

Daphne Du Maurier, *The Du Mauriers* (London: Gollancz, 1937);

Leonee Ormond, *George Du Maurier* (Pittsburgh: University of Pittsburgh Press, 1969).

**References:**

J. B. Gilder and J. L. Gilder, *Trilbyana: The Rise and Progress of a Popular Novel* (New York: Critic, 1895);

Henry James, *Partial Portraits* (London: Macmillan, 1899), pp. 327–372;

Richard Kelly, *The Art of George Du Maurier* (Hants: Scolar, 1995);

Kelly, *George Du Maurier* (Boston: Twayne, 1983);

Maurice Lanoire, "Un Anglo-Français, Georges du Maurier," *Revue de Paris,* 47 (1940): 263–281;

Edgar Rosenberg, *From Shylock to Svengali* (Stanford, Cal.: Stanford University Press, 1960), pp. 234–261;

Lionel Stevenson, "George Du Maurier and the Romantic Novel," in *Essays by Divers Hands,* edited by N. Hardy Wallis (London: Oxford University Press, 1960), pp. 36–54;

Derek Pepys Whitely, *George Du Maurier* (London: Art & Technics, 1948);

T. Martin Wood, *George Du Maurier – The Satirist of the Victorians: A Review of His Art and Personality* (London: Chatto & Windus, 1913).

# Lord Dunsany
## (Edward John Moreton Drax Plunkett, Baron Dunsany)

*(24 July 1878 – 25 October 1957)*

Leonard R. N. Ashley
*Brooklyn College of the City University of New York*

See also the Lord Dunsany entries in *DLB 10: Modern British Dramatists, 1900–1945* and *DLB 77: British Mystery Writers, 1920–1939.*

BOOKS: *The Gods of Pegana* (London: Elkin Mathews, 1905; Boston: Luce, 1916);

*Time and the Gods* (London: Heinemann, 1906; Boston: Luce, 1907);

*The Sword of Welleran and Other Stories* (London: George Allen, 1908; Boston: Luce, 1916); published as *The Sword of Welleran and Other Tales of Enchantment* (New York: Devin-Adair, 1954);

*A Dreamer's Tale* (London: G. Allen, 1910; New York: Modern Library, 1917);

*The Book of Wonder* (London: Heinemann, 1912; Boston: Luce, 1913);

*Selections from the Writings of Lord Dunsany* (Churchtown, Ireland: Cuala Press, 1912);

*Five Plays* (London: Richards, 1914; London & New York: Kennerley, 1914);

*The Gods of the Mountain* (New York & London: Putnam, 1914);

*King Argimenes and the Unknown Warrior* (London & New York: Putnam, 1914);

*The Lost Silk Hat* (London & New York: Putnam, 1914);

*Fifty-One Tales* (London: Elkin Mathews, 1915; New York: Kennerley, 1915);

*Plays of Gods and Men* (Boston: J. W. Luce, 1915; Dublin: Talbot Press, 1917);

*The Last Book of Wonder* (Boston: J. W. Luce, 1916);

*A Night at an Inn* (New York: Sunwise Turn, 1916; London & New York: Putnam, 1918);

*Tales of Wonder* (London: Elkin Mathews, 1916);

*Songs of Peace* (London: Jenkins, 1917);

*Beyond the Fields We Know* (New York: Boni & Liveright, 1918);

*Nowadays* (Boston: Four Seas, 1918);

*The Queen's Enemies* (London & New York: Putnam, 1918);

*Edward John Moreton Drax Plunkett, Baron Dunsany (Hulton-Deutsch Collection)*

*Tales of War* (Dublin: Talbot Press, 1918; London: Unwin, 1918; London & New York: Putnam, 1918);

*The Tents of the Arabs* (London & New York: Putnam, 1918);

*The Complete Poems of Francis Ledwidge* (London: Jenkins, 1919; New York: Brentano's, 1919);

*Tales of Three Hemispheres* (Boston: Luce, 1919; London: Unwin, 1920);

*Unhappy Far-Off Things* (Boston: Little, Brown, 1919; London: C. Mathews, 1919);

*A Good Bargain* (London & New York: Putnam, 1920);

*The Hopeless Passion of Mr Bunyon* (London & New York: Putnam, 1921);

*If* (London & New York: Putnam, 1921);

*The Chronicles of Rodriguez* (London & New York: Putnam, 1922);

*The Laughter of the Gods* (London & New York: Putnam, 1922);

*Plays of Near and Far* (London & New York: Putnam, 1922);

*The Compromise of the King of the Golden Isles* (London & New York: Putnam, 1923; New York: Grolier Club, 1924);

*If Shakespeare Lived Today* (London & New York: Putnam, 1923);

*The King of Elfland's Daughter* (London & New York: Putnam, 1924);

*Alexander and Three Small Plays* (London & New York: Putnam, 1925);

*The Amusements of Khan Karuda* (London & New York: Putnam, 1925);

*The Evil Kettle* (London & New York: Putnam, 1925);

*The Old King's Tale* (London & New York: Putnam, 1925);

*The Charwoman's Shadow* (London & New York: Putnam, 1926);

*The Blessing of Pan* (London & New York: Putnam, 1927);

*The Art of Playwriting: Lectures Delivered at The University of Pennsylvania: The Carving of the Ivory* (Philadelphia: University of Pennsylvania Press, 1928);

*Atalanta in Wimbledon* (London & New York: Putnam, 1928);

*His Sainted Grandmother* (London & New York: Putnam, 1928);

*In Holy Russia* (London & New York: Putnam, 1928);

*The Jest of Hahalaba* (London & New York: Putnam, 1928);

*The Raffle* (London & New York: Putnam, 1928);

*Seven Modern Comedies* (London & New York: Putnam, 1928);

*Fifty Poems* (London & New York: Putnam, 1929);

*The Old Folks of the Centuries* (London: Elkin Mathews & Marrot, 1930);

*The Travel Tales of Mr Joseph Jorkens* (London & New York: Putnam, 1931);

*The Curse of the Wise Woman* (London: Heinemann, 1933; New York: Longmans, Green, 1933);

*Lord Adrian* (Waltham St. Lawrence, Berks.: Golden Cockerel Press, 1933);

*If I Were Dictator . . .* (London: Methuen, 1934);

*Jorkens Remembers Africa* (London: Heinemann, 1934; New York & Toronto: Longmans, Green, 1934);

*Mr. Faithful* (New York: Samuel French, 1935);

*Up in the Hills* (London: Heinemann, 1935; New York: Putnam, 1936);

*My Talks with Dean Spanley* (London: Heinemann, 1936; New York: Putnam, 1936);

*Rory and Bran* (London: Heinemann, 1936; New York: Putnam, 1937);

*My Ireland* (London & New York: Jarrold's, 1937);

*Plays for Earth and Air* (London & Toronto: Heinemann, 1937);

*Mirage Water* (London: Putnam, 1938; Philadelphia: Dorrance, 1939);

*Patches of Sunlight* (London & Toronto: Heinemann, 1938; New York: Reynal & Hitchcock, 1938);

*The Story of Mona Sheehy* (London & Toronto: Heinemann, 1939; New York & London: Harper, 1940);

*Jorkens Has a Large Whiskey* (London: Putnam, 1940);

*War Poems* (London & Melbourne: Hutchinson, 1941);

*A Journey* (London: Macdonald, 1943);

*Wandering Songs* (London: Hutchinson, 1943);

*Guerilla* (Indianapolis & New York: Bobbs-Merrill, 1944; London & Toronto: Heinemann, 1944);

*While the Sirens Slept* (London & New York: Jarrold's, 1944);

*The Sirens Wake* (London & New York: Jarrold's, 1945);

*A Glimpse from a Watch Tower . . .* (London & New York: Jarrold's, 1945);

*The Year* (London & New York: Jarrold's, 1946);

*The Odes of Horace* (London & Toronto: Heinemann, 1947);

*The Fourth Book of Jorkens* (London: Jarrold's, 1948; Sauk City, Wis.: Arkham House, 1948);

*To Awaken Pegasus and Other Poems* (Oxford: George Ronald, 1949);

*The Strange Journeys of Colonel Polders* (London & New York: Jarrold's, 1950);

*The Last Revolution* (London & New York: Jarrold's, 1951);

*The Man Who Ate the Phoenix* (London: Jarrold's, 1951);

*His Fellow Men: A Novel* (London: Jarrold's, 1952);

Frontispiece and title page for a limited edition of Dunsany's first novel, a picaresque fantasy based on Miguel de Cervantes's Don Quixote (1605) (courtesy of the Lilly Library, Indiana University)

*The Little Tales of Smethers and Other Stories* (London: Jarrold's, 1952);

*The Hill of Dreams* (London: John Baker, 1954);

*Jorkens Borrows Another Whiskey* (London: M. Joseph, 1954);

*Ireland/ L'Irland/ Irland* (London: Anglo-Italian Publications, 1959);

*The Complete Poems* (London: Jenkins, n.d.);

*Essays in the Arts* (Boston: International Pocket Library, n.d.).

**Edition:** *Ghosts of the Heavyside Layer and Other Fantasms,* edited by Darrell Schweitzer (Philadelphia: Owlslick, 1980).

PLAY PRODUCTIONS: *The Glittering Gate,* Dublin, Abbey Theatre, 30 April 1909; London, Court Theatre, 6 June 1910;

*King Argimenes and the Unknown Warrior,* Dublin, Abbey Theatre, 26 January 1911; produced as *King Argimenes,* London, Court Theatre, 26 June 1911;

*The Gods of the Mountain,* London, Theatre-Royal in The Haymarket, 1 June 1911;

*The Golden Doom,* London, Theatre-Royal in The Haymarket, 19 November 1912;

*The Lost Silk Hat,* Manchester, Gaiety Theatre, 4 August 1913;

*The Tents of the Arabs,* Liverpool, Playhouse, 19 September 1914;

*A Night at an Inn,* New York, Neighborhood Playhouse, 23 April 1916; London, Palace Theatre, 6 November 1917;

*The Queen's Enemies,* New York, Neighborhood Playhouse, 14 November 1916;

*The Laughter of the Gods,* New York, Punch & Judy Theatre, 15 January 1919;

*The Murderers,* Indianapolis, Shubert Murat Theatre, 14 July 1919;

*If,* London, Ambassadors' Theatre, 30 May 1921;

*Cheezo,* London, Ambassadors' Theatre, 15 November 1921;

*Lord Adrian,* Birmingham, Prince of Wales' Theatre, 12 November 1923;

*Fame and the Poet*, Leeds, Albert Hall, 8 February 1924;

*His Sainted Grandmother,* London, Fortune Theatre, 8 December 1926;

*The Jest of Hahalaba,* London, Playroom 6 Theatre, 22 March 1927;

*Mr Faithful,* London, Q Theatre, 22 August 1927.

Edward John Moreton Drax Plunkett, Lord Dunsany, was born in London on 24 July 1878. He was of an ancient Irish family and succeeded to the family title, as the eighteenth Baron Dunsany, in 1899. He was given a top-flight English education at Cheam School, Surrey, Eton College, and the military academy at Sandhurst, and he went into a fashionable and famous regiment, the Coldstream Guards, his grandfather's regiment. He served as a junior officer in Gibraltar and then in the Boer War from 1899 to 1902. In World War I he was a captain in the Fifth Inniskilling Fusiliers, serving with distinction in France, and he received some slight wounds while serving in minor actions against Irish insurrectionists in 1916.

After World War I Dunsany took up literature as a sort of sideline and was a prolific writer of drama (with encouragement from William Butler Yeats and others), short stories, poetry (he deplored the moderns such as Ezra Pound and T. S. Eliot and admired the works of Walter de la Mare), and novels. He was also the Byron Professor of English Literature at the University of Athens from 1940 to 1941. He was a fellow of the Royal Society of Literature and the Royal Geographical Society and a member of the Irish Academy of Letters and L'Institut Historique et Heraldique de France. He received an honorary doctorate in Dublin, became president of the Authors' Society, and for more than fifty years he was a noted figure in literary circles. He describes his life in several autobiographical works: *My Ireland* (1937), *Patches of Sunlight* (1938), *While the Sirens Slept* (1944), and *The Sirens Wake* (1945). Dunsany's personal opinions and cherished prejudices and passions, including his love of sports, often crop up in his work, as does his sometimes childish delight in teasing and surprises and his belief in the world of faerie. He was a skilled writer who could turn his hand as easily to the unfamiliar mythological world as to the everyday world of the familiar essay.

Dunsany was married in 1904 to Lady Beatrice Child-Villiers, daughter of the seventh earl of Jersey. They had one son, Randal Arthur Henry, who was born in 1906. In time Dunsany gave the family castle in County Meath to his son, and Dunsany and his wife lived in England. In many respects he was a typical absentee landlord – passionate about hunting, shooting, and fishing and feudal in his relationship to his beloved peasantry.

Dunsany claimed that the fantastic novels and short stories he wrote simply came to him without much effort (and, he cautioned, ought not to have too much read into them by sedulous interpreters).

*Dunsany in uniform while serving in the Fifth Inniskilling Fusiliers, circa 1914*

Although he had a quick intelligence, a mordant wit, and a sometimes macabre humor, his theory was that the artist goes beyond that which his "intellect can discover." In both drama and the short story he adhered to Edgar Allan Poe's philosophy of composition: everything must contribute to one preconceived final effect. At his best Dunsany let himself be led by his lively fancy, and he drew on his dreams for his fiction. The dreamlike quality of his best work more than anything else made him famous.

Though Dunsany always thought of himself first and foremost as a poet, it was not through his rather mediocre verse (although T. S. Eliot and others admired Dunsany's technical mastery of verse) that he gained fame, nor did he (in his somewhat aloof, superior way) like to think he deliberately worked for public acclaim and honors. He was in the great British tradition of the gentleman amateur with the emphasis on the word *gentleman*. In fact, in

*Cover for the most autobiographical of Dunsany's novels, in
which an old woman stops a British company from exploiting
the natural peat resources of County Meath in
Ireland – Dunsany's family seat (courtesy of the
Lilly Library, Indiana University)*

*Fame and the Poet* (a play written by Dunsany and
produced in 1924) Dunsany portrays fame as a
Cockney harridan, cheap and vulgar. He was not as
snobbish as some of his readers, but he was incon-
trovertibly and unabashedly a product of a class-
ridden society that divided even cricketers into gentlemen and players.

Dunsany's writing career began with fiction.
He published several collections of short stories:
*The Gods of Pegana* (1905), *Time and the Gods* (1906),
and *The Sword of Welleran and Other Stories* (1908).
However, he first became well known through his
association with Dublin's Abbey Theatre, beginning
with the production of his *The Glittering Gate* in
1909. He is chiefly remembered for several of his
stories, including "Two Bottles of Relish," and for

the plays collected in *Five Plays* (1914), *Plays of Gods
and Men* (1915), *Plays of Near and Far* (1922), *Alexander and Three Small Plays* (1925), *Seven Modern Comedies* (1928), and *Plays for Earth and Air* (1937). His
verse was collected in *Fifty Poems* (1929) and six later
volumes, concluding with *To Awaken Pegasus and
Other Poems* (1949). Dunsany also translated the odes
of Horace, wrote about World War I in *Unhappy
Far-Off Things* (1919), and addressed many other
subjects.

Dunsany obviously felt more or less at home
in many literary genres, and turning to novels after
his success with short fiction may have simply
seemed natural. His first novel, *The Chronicles of
Rodriguez* (1922), has become a classic of fantasy. It
is a picaresque novel set in Spain's golden age and
owes much to Miguel de Cervantes's *Don Quixote*
(1605) but also resembles Dunsany's short story
"The Wonderful Window." The Lord of the Valleys of Arguento leaves his domain to a duller,
younger son, but to his eldest he leaves a sword and
a mandolin. The young fellow sets out to make his
fortune and claim a domain of his own, and, in company with a kind of Sancho Panza for contrast, he
has a dozen astounding adventures that recall both
Oriental tales and Western romances.

The influence of Dunsany's tutor Stephen
Phillips, known in his day for verse drama, is clear
in the novel. Though not as well characterized as he
might be, Don Rodriguez is as developed as the protagonists of tales of the Arabian Nights or the fairy
tales of Hans Christian Andersen. He wins the
favor of the King of Shadow Valley and gets to look
through two magic windows. Through one of these
he sees the battles of the past, not quite as reported
in Spanish history. Through the other he views conflicts of the future, not graced by chivalry. He even
travels to distant planets, thanks to an accommodat-
ing magician. Joseph Wood Krutch found all this
too easy and compared Dunsany to an old lady who
will not obey the rules of the game and cheats at sol-
itaire. But William Rose Benét was gentler in his
criticism and praised "a distinction in tone that
makes anything Dunsany writes worth putting up
on the favorite shelf." By this time Dunsany's plays
and short stories had won him an avid following,
even if the *Spectator* found this novel's language too
fancy and in some cases amateurish.

*The King of Elfland's Daughter* (1924) is a more
successful work – somewhere between a children's
fairy tale and an adult version of William Morris
with generous portions of white magic, pastel color-
ation, poetic prose, and enchantment. Contemporary critics disagreed as to whether it was more suit-

able for children or adults, or both. The plot involves the kingdom of Erl, whose king sends his son Alveric (equipped by a friendly witch with a magic sword) to Elfland to win the hand of the princess Lirazel, half elf and half mortal. Alveric succeeds and returns with her to Erl. They have a son, Orion, but Lirazel becomes homesick, and her father, on his throne of ice in Elfland, longs for the warmth of her companionship. He sends a troll with a magic rune to Erl. Lirazel reads it and is magically transported back to Elfland. Alveric tries to recover her, but to no avail.

Orion grows to manhood and becomes discontent with knightly chores such as recapturing a strayed unicorn. He wants to be in Elfland. Lirazel now wants to be in Erl. Her father reunites Alveric, Lirazel, and Orion by repositioning Elfland (always able to move near or far), and everyone is happy, with the possible exception of one Christian friar who thinks elves are all evil and who is left in a tiny enclave surrounded by the fairyland. The mixture of worlds in this novel is not as neatly effected as that in Dunsany's successful play *If* (1921), and the work did not at first gain the following that it eventually won. From the beginning Dunsany had an ability to create a fantastic world, practically unchallenged before the work of J. R. R. Tolkien. The thrilling violence of Dunsany's *A Night at an Inn* (1916) is absent from *The King of Elfland's Daughter*. The novel is dreamier and gentler, a romance "only told in song," a poetic and fragile vision of a mythology in which the oldest secrets of "our race" are coded.

Dunsany returns to the swashbuckling, colorful golden age of Spain for his third novel, *The Charwoman's Shadow* (1926). The work uses folktale motifs, such as that of the man who sold his shadow, the secret words of power (as in "Open Sesame" and "Rumplestiltskin"), and the hero and heroine who, united at long last, live happily ever after. In the work a father apprentices his son Ramon to an alchemist who he hopes will teach the boy to transmute base metal into gold. Ramon's new master demands that the boy give up his shadow, which the alchemist adds to his collection. From time to time the wizard dispatches his captive shadows – locked in a casket that opens only to the sound of three magical Chinese words: "Ting Yung Han" – to perform evil deeds in distant places. One of these shadows is that of the alchemist's charwoman, who was once an innocent, pretty young maiden who came to be a servant in the old man's house. Having unwisely traded her shadow for immortality, she is now a miserable hag who wishes

*Dunsany at Dunsany Castle in County Meath, Ireland*

she could die. The old wizard promises Ramon that in return for his shadow he can have another one just like it, but the false shadow does not shorten and lengthen like a real shadow. Ramon and the old hag are both trapped by the evil old magician and are drawn together by their common plight.

A real Spanish master of the occult, Raymond Lull, next enters the story as a character. With his expert assistance Ramon learns the three Chinese words, opens the mystic box, recovers his own shadow, and falls in love with the charwoman's shadow, which appears as a beautiful maiden. The charwoman is reunited with her shadow and regains her beauty, and she and Ramon return to his country, where they live happily ever after. The wizened old alchemist is revealed to be none other than the great god Pan. He leaves Spain in disgust and, after a sort of Cook's tour of the rest of Europe, flees earth altogether – for the time being. The book received positive reviews, although some ranked it lower than *The King of Elfland's Daughter*.

*Dust jacket from Dunsany's only attempt at a science-fiction novel, the story of computers that revolt against their human masters (courtesy of the Lilly Library, Indiana University)*

One way in which Dunsany is to be estimated higher than many other creators of fantastic mythologies and fairy worlds is in terms of his style, which can be light and playful or can command the rich tones of the King James Bible. As early as Ernest A. Boyd's appreciation of Dunsany (1917) there is an emphasis on "the Biblical note," and Boyd reports that Dunsany "has attributed his style to the fact that, as a child, he was encouraged to consider the Bible as literature – the greatest English in the history of the language. . . . In Lord Dunsany Ireland has a writer in whom the Biblical spirit replaces the Gaelic tradition which usually supplies the element lacking through the absence of the former." Other impressive qualities of Dunsany's fiction are that his prose is euphonious and evocative, his cadences resound in the reader's memory, and even his characters' names are inspired. His finely crafted prose was never more effective than in certain passages of his novels of fairyland, which are a mixture of the stark images of the Grimm Brothers' tales

from the dark Teutonic forests and re-creations of the leafy groves of the classical world in which Pan and other deities move among mortal men.

The great god of disorder and pagan joy returns in *The Blessing of Pan* (1927). This time the story is set in Wolding (Kent), but a strange place it is, for Tommy Duffin, a farmer's boy, has been influenced by a spell put upon his parents by the Reverend Arthur Davidson ( just before he vanished), and Tommy is attracting the locals to strange rites by playing on a reed pipe that he has made. The current vicar, the Reverend Elderick Anwrel, sees Pan at work and paganism on the march, especially on Wold Hill, where ancient stones encircle a pagan altar. The locals are gradually abandoning civilization and Christianity and reverting to nature. The local saint's tomb cannot draw them any more than the vicar's sermon can. In fact, they are going to make a sacrifice to Pan on Wold Hill, and the vicar's heroic efforts cannot do much to reform them. Tommy becomes a Druid as the old order supplants the new. The figure of Pan personifies Dunsany's rejection of the modern, materialist world of "cobbled streets that dare to wander over the dancing places of Pan."

In addition to his other interests, Dunsany had political ambitions, though he was unsuccessful in these endeavors. The time when any squire who wanted to go to Parliament or any lord with a hereditary seat in the House of Lords could launch himself on a political career with little effort was passing. Although Dunsany could not win a seat in the House, politics seems to underlie the most autobiographical of his novels, *The Curse of the Wise Woman* (1933), a fiction in which "the Old Woman" that is Ireland in Gaelic lore is able to stop a British company from exploiting peat in the verdant County Meath, Dunsany's family seat. The novel's tone is nostalgic as the elderly narrator looks back over half a century to the time when the English wanted to drain the bogs, ruin the landscape and its wildlife, and destroy the soul of the people in the name of pecuniary gain. The Peat Development Syndicate, however, has to cope with old Mrs. Marlin. She lays a great curse on the Sassenachs, drowning their hopes under eight feet of water. Some similar deluge or defeat seems to be threatened for any English exploiters.

Two other of Dunsany's books are sometimes categorized as novels, but they are actually short-story collections. The stories of *My Talks with Dean Spanley* (1936) are linked by their narrator, who relates what it was like to have been, in a previous incarnation, a trusty old guard dog protecting

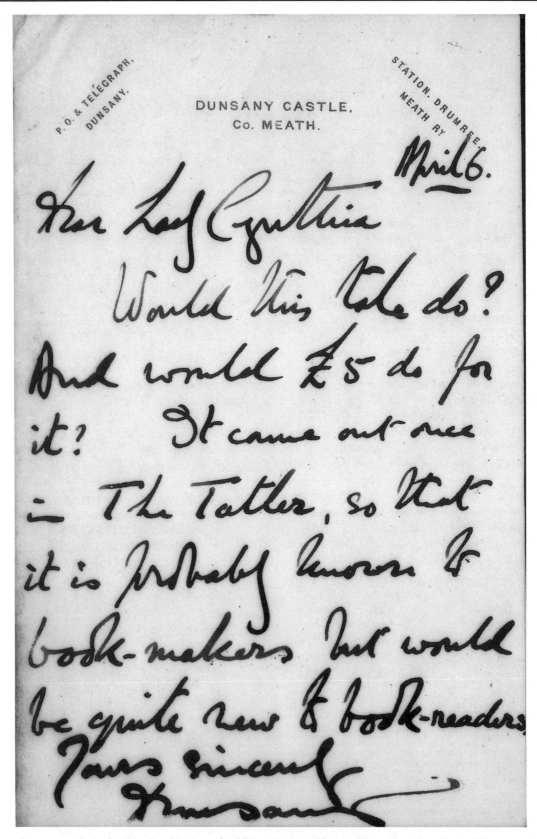

*Letter from Dunsany to Lady Cynthia Asquith, the wife of Prime Minister Herbert Henry Asquith and a well-known patron of the arts who edited an annual literary anthology (courtesy of the Lilly Library, Indiana University)*

the great ones in the big house. The other mélange of tales comprises imaginative stories about *The Strange Journeys of Colonel Polders* (1950). The narrator is a clubbable old gentleman who assures the reader that a character named Pundit Sinadryana has turned him into a succession of animals. The reader learns what it is like to be the dog Dunsany so admired, the fox he loved to hunt, the cat, the snail, and many other creatures.

*Guerilla* (1944) benefits from Dunsany's cultivated style (here rich in atmosphere and striking in dialogue) but does not add much to his reputation as a novelist. It is set in "The Land," an ancient country that has been invaded by Hitler's forces, and it tells the tale of brave and persistent fighters in the mountains who put up a patriotic resistance. The book suffers in comparison with other novels written about guerrillas and resistance forces during World War II. Virtually ignored by contemporary reviewers, *Guerilla* has been forgotten by present-day readers, as well.

*The Last Revolution* (1951) is Dunsany's single attempt at a science-fiction novel. The artificial intelligence of computers becomes so great that they turn on their masters. The results are as dire as those in Karel Čapek's *RUR (Rossum's Universal Robots)* (1921), in which the robots (named from the Czech for "workers") turn on the humans who created them. Computers get not merely intelligence but identity, and they learn to reproduce themselves as well as to intercommunicate. Humanity's fate appears grim when the programmed have wills of their own as well as superior powers. Having created Erewhons all his life, in *The Last Revolution* Dunsany toys with a dystopia.

Contemporaries praised Dunsany primarily as a great dramatist, but modern readers tend to neglect both his dramatic oeuvre and his novels in favor of his short fiction. Yet in all of his fiction Dunsany created a world of fantasy and wrote with an aristocratic amateur's fleet pen. He said whimsically during a lecture at the University of Pennsylvania that he "wrote with quills made of wild goose feathers," fantasizing that these quills injected into his work "something of the magic of distant climes the birds themselves visited." In *Rushlights Heritage* (1969) George Brandon Saul critically observes of Dunsany's work that "sometimes his concern with the dreamworld leads him into sentimentality and extreme vagueness of fancy; too often his writing suggests a sort of generalized talent rather than genius." That talent was sufficient nonetheless to make the peer and poet, dramatist and short-story writer, translator, essayist, autobiographer, and inveterate contributor to all sorts of periodicals a major influence on the novel of fantasy and the sometimes symbolic novel of science fiction.

**References:**

A. S. Anderson, "Lord Dunsany: The Potency of Words and the Wonder of Things," *Mythlore*, 15 (Autumn 1988): 10–12;

Edward Hale Bierstadt, *Dunsany the Dramatist* (Boston: Little, Brown, 1917);

Brent Cantrell, "The British Fairy Tradition in *The King of Elfland's Daughter*," *Romantist*, 4–5 (1990–1991): 51–53;

L. Sprague de Camp, "Two Men in One: Lord Dunsany," in *Literary Swordsmen and Sorcerers: The Makers of Heroic Fantasy* (Sauk City, Wis.: Arkham House, 1976);

Max Duperray, " 'The Land of Unlikely Events': L'Irlande de Lord Dunsany," *Etudes Irlandaises*, 4 (1975): 31–37;

Duperray, "Lord Dunsany: Sa Place dans une eventuelle litterature fantastique," *Etudes Irlandaises*, 9 (December 1984): 81–88;

Martin Gardiner, "Lord Dunsany," in his *Supernatural Fiction Writers* (New York: Scribners, 1985), pp. 471–478;

Josephine Hammond, "Wonder and the Playwright: Lord Dunsany," *Personalist* (January 1922): 5–30;

Hazel Littlefield, *Lord Dunsany: King of Dreams* (New York: Exposition Press, 1959);

George Brandon Saul, *Rushlights Heritage* (New York: Walton Press, 1969);

Darrell Schweitzer, "How Much of Dunsany is Worth Reading?," *Studies in Weird Fiction*, 10 (Fall 1991): 19–23;

Schweitzer, "Lord Dunsany: Visions of Wonder," *Studies in Weird Fiction*, 5 (Spring 1989): 20–26;

Schweitzer, "The Novels of Lord Dunsany," *Mythlore*, 7 (Autumn 1980): 39–42;

Louis Charles Stagg, "Lord Dunsany," in *Great Writers of the English Language: Dramatists*, edited by Vinson and Kirkpatrick (New York: St. Martin's Press, 1979), pp. 185–188;

F. G. Stoddard, "The Lord Dunsany Collection," *Library Chronicle of the University of Texas*, 8 (1967): 27–32.

**Papers:**

A selection of Lord Dunsany's letters to Mary Lavin is in the manuscript collection of the library of the State University of New York at Binghamton.

# Elinor Glyn

*(17 October 1864 – 23 September 1943)*

Eric Thompson
*Université du Québec à Chicoutimi*

BOOKS: *The Visits of Elizabeth* (London: Duckworth, 1900; New York: John Lane, 1901);

*The Reflections of Ambrosine* (London: Duckworth, 1902; New York: Harper, 1902); republished as *The Seventh Commandment* (New York: Macaulay, n.d.);

*The Damsel and the Sage* (London: Duckworth, 1903; New York: Harper, 1903);

*The Vicissitudes of Evangeline* (London: Duckworth, 1905; New York: Harper, 1905); republished as *Red Hair* (New York: Macaulay, n.d.);

*Beyond the Rocks* (London: Duckworth, 1906; New York: Harper, 1906);

*Three Weeks* (London: Duckworth, 1907; New York: Business Press, 1907);

*The Sayings of Grandmama and Others* (London: Duckworth, 1908; New York: Duffield, 1908);

*Elizabeth Visits America* (London: Duckworth, 1909; New York: Duffield, 1909);

*His Hour* (London: Duckworth, 1910; New York: Appleton, 1910); republished as *When His Hour Came* (London: Newnes, 1915);

*The Reason Why* (London: Duckworth, 1911; New York: Appleton, 1911);

*Halcyone* (London: Duckworth, 1912; New York: Appleton, 1912); republished as *Love Itself* (Auburn, N.Y.: Author's Press, 1924?);

*The Contract and Other Stories* (London: Duckworth, 1913);

*The Point of View* (New York: Appleton, 1913);

*The Sequence* (London: Duckworth, 1913); published as *Guinevere's Lover* (New York: Appleton, 1913);

*Letters to Caroline* (London: Duckworth, 1914); published as *Your Affectionate Godmother* (New York: Appleton, 1914);

*The Man and the Moment* (New York: Appleton, 1914; London: Duckworth, 1915);

*Three Things* (London: Duckworth, 1915; New York: Hearst, 1915);

*The Career of Katherine Bush* (New York: Appleton, 1916; London: Duckworth, 1917);

*Elinor Glyn, 1904*

*Destruction* (London: Duckworth, 1918);

*The Price of Things* (London: Duckworth, 1919); published as *Family* (New York: Appleton, 1919);

*Points of View* (London: Duckworth, 1920);

*The Philosophy of Love* (London: Duckworth, 1920);

*The Elinor Glyn System of Writing,* 4 volumes (Auburn, N.Y.: Author's Press, 1922);

*Man and Maid – Renaissance* (London: Duckworth, 1922); published as *Man and Maid* (Philadelphia: Lippincott, 1922);

*The Great Moment* (London: Duckworth, 1923; Philadelphia: Lippincott, 1923);

*The Philosophy of Love* (Auburn, N.Y.: Author's Press, 1923); published as *Love – What I Think of It* (London: Readers Library, 1928);

*Letters from Spain* (London: Duckworth, 1924);

*Six Days* (London: Duckworth, 1924; Philadelphia: Lippincott, 1924);

*This Passion Called Love* (London: Duckworth, 1925; Auburn, N.Y.: Author's Press, 1925);

*Love's Blindness* (London: Duckworth, 1926; Auburn, N.Y.: Author's Press, 1926);

*It and Other Stories* (London: Duckworth, 1927; New York: Macaulay, 1927);

*The Wrinkle Book; or, How to Keep Looking Young* (London: Duckworth, 1927); published as *Eternal Youth* (New York: Macmillan, 1928);

*The Flirt and the Flapper* (London: Duckworth, 1930);

*Love's Hour* (London: Duckworth, 1932; New York: Macaulay, 1932);

*Glorious Flames* (London: Benn, 1932; New York: Macaulay, 1933);

*Saint or Satyr? and Other Stories* (London: Duckworth, 1933); published as *Such Men Are Dangerous* (New York: Macaulay, 1933);

*Sooner or Later* (London: Rich & Cowan, 1933; New York: Macaulay, 1935);

*Did She?* (London: Rich & Cowan, 1934);

*Romantic Adventure* (London: Nicholson & Watson, 1936; New York: Dutton, 1937);

*The Third Eye* (London: Long, 1940).

PLAY PRODUCTION: *Three Weeks,* London, 23 July 1908.

MOTION PICTURES: *The Great Moment,* screenplay by Glyn and Monte M. Katterjohn, Famous Players-Lasky, 1921;

*The World's a Stage,* screenplay by Glyn, Colin Campbell, and George Bertholon, Perfect Pictures, 1922;

*His Hour,* screenplay by Glyn, King Vidor, and Maude Fulton, M-G-M, 1924;

*Three Weeks (The Romance of a Queen),* screenplay by Glyn and Carey Wilson, M-G-M, 1924;

*How to Educate a Wife,* screenplay by Glyn, Douglas Z. Doty, and Grant Carpenter, Reliable Feature Film, 1924;

*Man and Maid,* screenplay by Glyn, M-G-M, 1925;

*The Only Thing,* screenplay by Glyn, M-G-M, 1925;

*Love's Blindness,* screenplay by Glyn, M-G-M, 1926;

*Ritzy,* screenplay by Glyn and others, Paramount, 1927;

*It,* screenplay by Glyn and others, Famous Players-Lasky, 1927;

*Three Week-Ends,* screenplay by Glyn and others, Paramount, 1928;

*The Man and the Moment,* screenplay by Glyn, Agnes Christine Johnston, and Paul Perez, National, 1929;

*Such Men Are Dangerous,* screenplay by Glyn and Ernst Vajda, 20th Century–Fox, 1930;

*Knowing Men,* screenplay by Glyn and Edward Knoblock, United Artists, 1930.

Elinor Glyn, glamorous socialite, incessant traveler, and romantic novelist, reached the peak of her celebrity in the autumn of 1907, when she published *Three Weeks.* Soon a naughty rhyme was circulating in New York and London society, cleverly mocking the novel's central scene, in which the heroine, reclining seductively on a tiger skin, seduces the spellbound hero:

> Would you like to sin
> with Elinor Glyn
> on a tiger skin?
> Or would you prefer
> to err with her
> on some other fur?

Within two years the novel had sold two million copies worldwide, largely because of its scandalous reputation. Much later, in 1957, Meredith Wilson's Broadway tribute to American small-town life in turn-of-the-century Iowa, *The Music Man,* included a scene in which Marion the Librarian defends her choice of teenage books to the mayor's wife, Mrs. Shin. Would she not rather have her daughter read the classics than the novels of Elinor Glyn, she asks. To which Mrs. Shin, not quite comprehending, replies: "What Elinor Glyn reads is *her* mother's problem!" Such was the notoriety of one of the most interesting minor writers of the belle epoque.

Glyn's life was even more eventful than those of her heroines. Born on 17 October 1864 on the Channel Island of Jersey, Elinor was the daughter of Douglas Sutherland and Elinor Saunders Sutherland. Her parents had been born in Ontario, Canada, and her maternal grandfather, Col. Thomas Saunders, was related to the famous Adm. Sir Charles Saunders, who brought James Wolfe's troops to Île d'Orléans in the Saint Lawrence River, where they launched the capture of Quebec in 1759. Elinor was brought to the family's estate at Summer

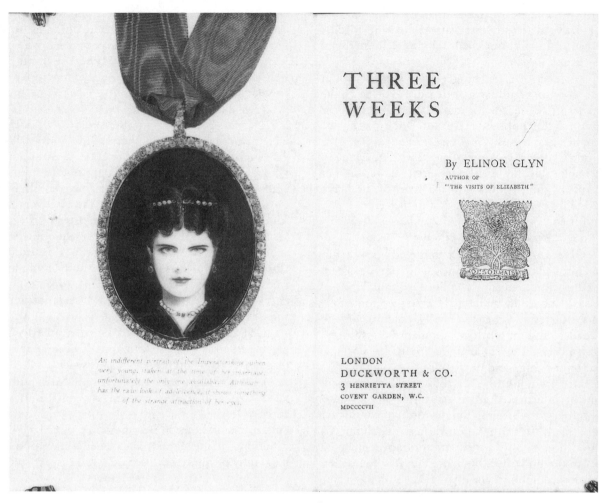

*Frontispiece and title page for Glyn's best-known work (courtesy of the Lilly Library, Indiana University)*

Hill in Guelph, Ontario, when she was less than a year old. In her autobiography, *Romantic Adventure* (1936), Glyn recalls "the quaint, rather pathetic old aristocratic family transported into the Canadian wilds and bravely maintaining the ways of life which they believed essential." It is an odd if revealing comment by someone who strove in her own adult life to create an aristocratic image of herself and her fictional heroines.

After her first husband died of typhoid fever, Elinor's mother married David Kennedy – a selfish and domineering man, according to Elinor. During the 1870s he resettled the family in Jersey, where Elinor and her older sister, Lucille, enjoyed the run of a well-stocked library. They also visited Paris and London, acquiring the manners (and the morals) of flamboyant cosmopolitan society. As an adolescent she was gawky in appearance, but as she grew into young womanhood she gained self-confidence, attracting the attentions of many suitors. Nevertheless, she was beyond the usual marriageable age

when her stepfather died in 1889, and her sister Lucille's expensive divorce had drained most of Kennedy's fortune. Clearly, it was necessary for Elinor to find a husband. In February 1892 she became engaged to Clayton Glyn, a wealthy sportsman in his late thirties. They were not a perfect match: he seemed to prefer bachelorhood, to raise pedigree cattle, and to travel abroad, whereas she was an ostentatious fashion plate. But Clayton Glyn had an established place in society, and Elinor could not afford to let him slip away. They were married in the spring.

For most of the 1890s Elinor seemed content to play the role of the married doyenne who gave, or attended, frequent house parties. She settled into entertaining her husband's friends – Tory aristocrats, politicians, ambassadors, and fellow sportsmen – and she bore him two daughters, Margot and Juliet. Meanwhile, Clayton grew corpulent and became indifferent to her. As the new century loomed, Glyn found herself living an increasingly boring ex-

istence with an estranged husband. She relished their travels to various European and Middle Eastern countries, but eventually even these diversions began to pall.

She sought relief in a collaboration with her sister, composing illustrated feature articles on the lifestyles of her set for the mass dailies. Then, at the urging of the publisher Gerald Duckworth, she wrote her first novel, *The Visits of Elizabeth* (1900), a thinly disguised version of her own experiences. The book's pert heroine writes letters to her mother and offers glib insights into the lives of the privileged. The epistolary form of this novel was also used for such sequels as *The Vicissitudes of Evangeline* (1905) and *Elizabeth Visits America* (1909).

Glyn's writing career was fueled both by her constant need to earn money and her desire to share her experience of "romance" with millions of ordinary men and women. Her conception of romance expresses, rather too neatly, an uneasy blend of the ideal and the worldly: "Romance is a spiritual disguise created by the imagination to envelop material happenings and desires, so that they may be in greater harmony with the soul." Such a statement might be interpreted as an attempt to mask an acquisitive nature beneath fancy words of passionate commitment. In truth, Glyn was a social climber, a name-dropper, and an elitist; the more she paid court to the powerful, the more she was compelled to write the snobbish society romances that became her trademark. At times even her grandson Anthony Glyn, who wrote a highly partial biography of her, could not abide her superior attitude. He describes her second novel, *The Reflections of Ambrosine* (1902), as a "heavy-handed, long-winded sermon on the theme that Norman blood and the distant shadow of a coronet are worth far more than a kind heart." Glyn's social cynicism also appears in *The Career of Katherine Bush* (1916), in which a girl of the lower middle class realizes her dream of rising to aristocratic heights, only to regret what she had sacrificed to get there.

Glyn's major theme, therefore, has to do with romantic adventuring by ambitious young women in high society. Her stories are replete with elegant balls and daring assignations, stylish outings and narrow escapes. Her settings range from English drawing rooms to the watering holes of the wandering rich. She drew freely from her own past, but as her books gained a wide audience she turned to gossip and the real-life intrigues of her wealthy friends for her plots. Lady Warwick and the Marchioness of Londonderry, for example, are models for characters in several of Glyn's romances, portrayed in

ways that might have seemed compromising to them. Elinor's attachments to some of the most influential British statesmen of the period – Lord Cromer, Lord Curzon, and Lord Milner – served her well in chronicling the turmoil of the love/duty dichotomy.

An example of Glyn's method is *His Hour* (1910), based on her trip to Russia in 1909, during which she met many members of the court circle. The heroine, Tamara Loraine, is a straitlaced young English widow who has a moonlit meeting with a mysterious stranger at the Khedive's Ball in Cairo. Later, in Saint Petersburg, she discovers her suitor is none other than the masterful Prince Gritzko Milaslavski. Some of the authentic atmosphere of this work is due to Elinor's unusually close scrutiny of Russian society, both noble and common. But true to her métier, personal experiences influenced her depiction of Russia, as when she was embraced by a handsome guardsman while sightseeing in a troika and, more dramatically, when she was nearly kidnapped while passing through Warsaw on her way to Moscow.

Glyn's romantic nature would not bother most readers if it were not for a suspicion of the author's feigned innocence – she often seems unreliable or duplicitous in her memoirs. As Meredith Etherington-Smith and Jeremy Pilcher note in their biography of Elinor and Lucille (with respect to the philandering of the Edwardians) "no one would have looked askance at a love affair – as long as it was conducted discreetly." Yet Elinor pretends to be shocked by her husband's indifference when she informs him that a mutual friend has made sexual advances to her. Given her social history, it is difficult to believe that she had not encouraged this overture in the first place.

The highlight of Glyn's career is *Three Weeks,* her sixth novel. Its immediate inspiration appears to have been three disconnected events: Elinor's travels to Switzerland and Venice, her encounter with a handsome young Englishman at a castle in Scotland, and the assassination of Queen Draga of Serbia in 1903.

The novel's protagonist, Paul Verdayne, has a fateful meeting with "the Lady" in a small alpine village. He is described as a "god among men," compelled to go abroad to rethink his socially disadvantageous engagement to the middle-class daughter of a parson. While dining one evening at his hotel, he is suddenly confronted by the vision of a superb woman peeling nectarines while she sips a liqueur. As she describes the lady's charms, Glyn's words are redolent with abstractions such as "passion,"

"mystery," "fire," and "soul," as well as a succession of sensuous epithets. The source of the tale is the ancient Germanic story of Undine, for Paul is bewitched by his fair seducer, who promises to teach him all the secrets of love. They pass their days together in their mountain idyll as he listens entranced to her passionate monologue. Very little happens; Glyn imposes a gauzy kind of eroticism over a remarkably uneventful plot. Then, halfway through the tale, the lady (her name is never revealed) tells Paul that she wants to kill a "vicious weakling" who, Paul learns later, is her tyrannical husband. After some added sentimentalities, the pair are whisked off to Venice for a final tryst. At one point they visit the doge's palace, and she says:

> I often ask myself, Paul, if we are not too civilized, we of our time. We think too much of human suffering, and so we cultivate the nerves to suffer more, instead of hardening them. . . ."
>
> "Ah, Paul!" she continued with sudden passion, "I would rather you were dead . . . than I should have to feel you were growing *rien du tout* – a thing who will go down into nothingness, and be forgotten by men!"

This enigmatic speech comes near the end of their three-week affair; a few days later the protagonist awakens to find she has left him forever.

The following spring Paul receives a letter from the lady telling him she has given birth to their son. He realizes that she and the infant may be in danger, but his attempt to learn their whereabouts and rescue them ends when he hears about the death of a drunken king after he has slain his queen in Constantinople. "And so, as ever, the woman paid the price" of passionate love, Glyn moralizes. Five years later Paul receives an invitation from Grand Duke Peter, the Russian regent, to visit Russia, where Paul's son is being held in protective custody.

Cecil Beaton shrewdly guesses that the success of Anthony Hope's *The Prisoner of Zenda* (1894) was the literary inspiration for Glyn's "Ruritanian romance." Although Hope's adventure is more entertaining, Glyn's tale offers a more sophisticated account of love and jealousy. Critics in England flayed *Three Weeks* as a bad imitation of the Italian novelist Gabriele D'Annunzio, and churchmen bewailed its harmful influence on the young. For her part, Elinor professed to be amazed that anyone could have found the story improper. She defends the book in her autobiography, claiming that it "meant everything to me; it was the outpouring of my whole nature, romantic, proud, and passionate, but for ever repressed in real life by the barriers of custom and tradition." Perhaps one of the most im-

*Glyn in 1916 at Montacute, a Jacobean mansion in Somerset that Glyn decorated for George Nathaniel, Lord Curzon*

portant aspects of *Three Weeks* was its sociological impact; the novel helped to undermine the vestiges of Victorian hypocrisy concerning the circulation of sensual, and sexual, narratives. Almost a century later the book has been forgotten, but although surpassed by more accomplished romances of its type, it can still stir the reader prepared to be sympathetic to the plight of its sentimental lovers.

In October 1907 Glyn voyaged alone to New York, chiefly to escape the fuss over *Three Weeks,* but her fame had preceded her and she was lionized everywhere she went. After visiting the principal eastern cities she journeyed to the western states of Nevada and California, where she admired the gallantry of gold miners and the fresh air of a less refined style of life. Writing about her trip two years later in *Elizabeth Visits America,* she reported archly that "the most unattractive creatures of every nation seem to be the ones who travel" – by which she

*Dust jacket for the 1928 edition of the book first published in 1923 as* The Philosophy of Love *(courtesy of the Lilly Library, Indiana University)*

did not mean herself, of course, although she was often condescending in her remarks about Americans in this and subsequent books. The trip marked the beginning of the end, however, of her halcyon days as an author. From 1908 to 1913 she entered a period of "hastily written novels," such as *The Reason Why* (1911), which were obviously written to pay off debts. The fact that Americans continued to buy her novels, travelogues, and etiquette books certainly aided her enterprise.

During World War I Elinor performed several patriotic tasks. She wrote British propaganda aimed at the American market, she served as a volunteer in hospitals in France, and she even worked as a scullery maid. In the latter stages of the war she worked as a war correspondent and later covered the peace talks at Versailles. She never stopped writing novels, but her popularity declined.

A challenging new phase began in Elinor's life in the postwar years. She was invited to Hollywood,

along with prominent British male novelists such as Somerset Maugham and Sir Gilbert Parker, to write screenplays for the burgeoning motion picture industry. As she had always done before, Elinor wasted no time in meeting the right people; among her early conquests was Cecil B. de Mille. Now in her midfifties, Elinor was determined to show the novices of the Seventh Art how romance should be done.

"If Hollywood hadn't existed, Elinor Glyn would have had to invent it," wrote Anita Loos, a fellow screenwriter, paraphrasing Voltaire. In fact, Elinor did more than her share of pioneer work in the new medium; as David Robinson notes in his *Hollywood in the Twenties* (1970), she was innovative in "marrying the old romanticism and the new morality in her . . . screenplays." She proved surprisingly skillful in adapting her novels for the screen, notably *The Great Moment, Three Weeks,* and *His Hour.* Several of her best-known scripts were origi-

nal screenplays, starring actors as luminous as Gloria Swanson, Rudolph Valentino, John Gilbert, and Gary Cooper. Buoyed by her enthusiasm for romance, Elinor flaunted her knowledge of costumes, cosmetics, decor, and theatrical movement before directors and actors. She claimed that American males did not know how to kiss and proceeded to demonstrate the proper technique. Obviously, she felt superior to the "unreal atmosphere" of Hollywood and blasted the "blatantly crude" and "utterly false psychology" of the movie business. Yet, by the end of the 1920s Glyn had achieved a solid place in Hollywood as the inventor of Clara Bow, the "It" girl, the epitome of femininity and sexual allure.

Elinor had many friends in the film colony, including Douglas Fairbanks, Mary Pickford, and Charlie Chaplin, and she was a frequent guest at the lavish William Randolph Hearst mansion at San Simeon. She also made enemies, among them Swanson, who left this memorable caricature: "Her British dignity was devastating. She was the first woman I'd ever seen wearing false eyelashes and although she was old enough to be my grandmother, she got away with it. She had small, squinty eyes and took tiny steps when she walked. Her teeth were too even and white to be real; she smelled like a cathedral full of incense, and she talked a blue streak. Her hair was the colour of red ink and she wore it wrapped around her head like an elaborate turban. She was something from another world." Glyn's reign in Hollywood lasted from 1920 to 1927; she then lived and worked briefly in New York as a magazine writer before returning to England. The last years of Glyn's life were extraordinarily active. She continued to publish novels and to advocate her notions of romance and the liber-

ated life she had led. But apart from one disastrous investment she made in a British film, she lived quietly in semiseclusion until her death on 23 September 1943.

Glyn's assessment of the death of the society she represented in her own person and books seems an apt conclusion to an assessment of her work. She wrote: "Society, in the old meaning of the word, still existed in 1913, but it was no longer the fairy ring within which danced a circle of families entitled to enjoy its privileges on account of birth and tradition. . . . The outward semblance of the old dignity were still preserved, but in reality it was a mere sham. On every side the defences had been broken down by the power of money." Ironically, the very "power" she decried had been the means she chose to preserve a way of life she valued most.

**Biography:**
Anthony Glyn, *Elinor Glyn: A Biography* (London: Hutchinson, 1955).

**References:**
Cecil Beaton, Introduction to Glyn's *Three Weeks* (London: Duckworth, 1974), p. xii;

Meredith Etherington-Smith and Jeremy Pilcher, *The "It" Girls: Lucy, Lady Duff Gordon, the Couturière "Lucille," and Elinor Glyn, Romantic Novelist* (New York: Harcourt Brace Jovanovich, 1987);

Q. D. Leavis, *Fiction and the Reading Public* (London: Chatto & Windus, 1968);

Anita Leslie, *Edwardians in Love* (London: Hutchinson, 1972);

David Robinson, *Hollywood in the Twenties* (New York: Paperback Library, 1970).

# Beatrice Harraden

*(24 January 1864 – 5 May 1936)*

Katherine Sutherland
*University College of the Cariboo*

BOOKS: *Little Rosebud; or, Things Will Take a Turn* (Boston: Brown, 1891);

*Ships That Pass in the Night* (London: Lawrence & Bullen, 1893; Chicago: Donohue, Hennenberry, 1893);

*In Varying Moods* (Edinburgh: Blackwood, 1894; New York & London: Putnam, 1894);

*Hilda Strafford and the Remittance Man: Two California Stories* (Edinburgh: Blackwood, 1897); published as *Hilda Strafford, a California Story* (New York: Dodd, Mead, 1897);

*Untold Tales of the Past* (Edinburgh: Blackwood, 1897; New York: Dodd, Mead, 1897);

*The Fowler* (Edinburgh: Blackwood, 1899; New York: Dodd, Mead, 1899);

*Katharine Frensham: A Novel* (Edinburgh & London: Blackwood, 1903; New York: Dodd, Mead, 1903);

*The Scholar's Daughter* (New York: Dodd, Mead, 1906; London: Methuen, 1906);

*Interplay* (London: Methuen, 1908; New York: Stokes, 1908);

*Out of the Wreck I Rise* (London & New York: Nelson, 1912; New York: Stokes, 1912);

*The Guiding Thread* (New York: Stokes, 1916; London: Methuen, 1916);

*Our Warrior Women* (London: Witherby, 1916);

*Where Your Treasure Is* (London: Hutchinson, 1918); published as *Where Your Heart Is* (New York: Dodd, Mead, 1918);

*Spring Shall Plant* (London & New York: Hodder & Stoughton, 1920);

*Thirteen All Told* (London: Methuen, 1921);

*Patuffa* (London: Hodder & Stoughton, 1923; New York: Stokes, 1923);

*Youth Calling* (London: Hodder & Stoughton, 1924);

*Rachel* (London: Hodder & Stoughton, 1926);

*Search Will Find Out* (London: Mills & Boon, 1928).

OTHER: "Lady Geraldine's Speech," in *How the Vote Was Won and Other Suffragette Plays,* edited

*Beatrice Harraden (Hulton-Deutsch Collection)*

by Dale Spender and Carole Hayman (London: Methuen, 1985).

Beatrice Harraden, though little known today, published novels and short-story collections between 1891 and 1928. She was an important early feminist novelist; she was also extremely active in the suffragette movement, which she describes in her book *Our Warrior Women* (1916). A founder of the Women's Social and Political Union (WSPU), formed in 1903, she traveled extensively on the Continent and in the United States; her hope was to facilitate international comity among women's groups. Harraden's activities on behalf of the WSPU included selling newspapers on street cor-

ners, participating in marches, writing and producing plays dealing with women's suffrage, selling programs and other suffragette literature at entertainments, and making public speeches. Despite her public profile in the women's suffrage movement, Harraden was notoriously shy and private in her personal life.

Beatrice Harraden, born on 24 January 1864 at Hampstead in London, was the youngest daughter of Samuel Harraden, an importer of musical instruments, and Rosalie Lindstedt Harraden. She was educated at Dresden and at Cheltenham Ladies College before going on to Queen's College and Bedford College. She received an honors degree in classics and mathematics in 1883, at a time when earning a B.A. degree was still a novelty for a woman.

*Little Rosebud; or, Things Will Take a Turn* (1891) a story for children in which a little girl living with her grandfather becomes friends with an invalid child, was Harraden's first published book, but by this time the author had already contributed many short stories to *Blackwood's Magazine.* Ironically, *Blackwood's* rejected the manuscript of her first novel, *Ships That Pass in the Night* (1893), because they felt that the work was too short and was unlikely to sell. When published a few years later by Lawrence and Bullen, the book was an immediate success, quickly selling more than one million copies.

In the novel two invalids meet at the Kurhaus spa, a "winter resort for consumptive patients," in Petershof, Switzerland. The protagonist, Bernadine, falls in love with Robert Allisten, dubbed "the Disagreeable Man" by other patients at the spa. Bernadine eventually leaves the spa, and Robert, humanized by his love for her, follows her to England with the intention of marrying her. As they are about to be reunited, however, Bernadine is run over in the street and dies, ending the novel on a rather strange note.

Contemporary critics were inconsistent in their interpretations of the book's theme. The reviewer for *Critic* magazine described the main theme as the loneliness of the individual, while *Publishers Weekly* felt that the story exposed the hollowness of modern society. Perhaps more interesting than the novel's thematic concerns is its presentation of Bernadine, for she in some ways establishes a type of female character that would become a mainstay in Harraden's work. Bernadine is a teacher, writer, and socialist agitator who has retreated to the spa due to exhaustion. During her stay she becomes sufficiently rejuvenated to return to her work. The

character is intriguing for two reasons: first, because her occupations are so similar to Harraden's; and second, because the author is said to have suffered exhaustion similar to that of Bernadine, though not until two years after this novel had been published.

In terms of the representation of women in the novel, however, it is not only the independent woman (Bernadine) who establishes a model for later novels, but also the introduction of the hardness of other women who contrast with her example. "Hard" women appear frequently as negative and stereotypical characters in Harraden's work, portrayals that seem somewhat out of keeping with the author's feminist sympathies. To understand the meaning of these characters in the novels, it is necessary to elaborate briefly on the nature of the suffrage movement at the time of Harraden's involvement. The women's movement at the turn of the century cast female emancipation in different terms than the women's movement at present. Early in the "first wave feminist" movement, as the period of feminism in the late nineteenth and early twentieth centuries is often called, women determined that the surest route to suffrage was the perpetuation of the idea that women were responsible, reasonable, and even morally superior to men and thus worthy of the vote: these were the suffragists who differentiated themselves from the later suffragettes, the more vocal and less passive generation of feminists that emerged early in the twentieth century. The suffragists were determined that not a breath of scandal should touch their societies. They insisted that there be no acts of unwomanly or unladylike behavior, no indecorous comments or deeds that could be used against them.

The late-nineteenth-century manifestation of the women's movement was also associated with the temperance movement and the social purity movement, which advocated male sexual continence, hygiene, and sex education. Today some feminists regard this early feminism as puritanical and narrow, but it was actually practical-minded: temperance and male sexual continence would, it was felt, lead to the diminishment of wife-beating, prostitution, venereal disease, and unwanted pregnancy. In a time before penicillin and reliable birth control, the beliefs were more pragmatic than puritanical.

Maternal feminism was also prevalent during this period, which claimed that the maternal qualities of women voters would counterbalance the more rational but colder voting practices of men. While these are precisely the kinds of gender stereo-

SHIPS THAT PASS
IN THE NIGHT

BY

BEATRICE HARRADEN

LONDON
LAWRENCE & BULLEN
16 HENRIETTA STREET, COVENT GARDEN, W.C.
1893

*Title page for Harraden's first novel, in which two patients
meet and fall in love at a Swiss spa (courtesy of the Lilly
Library, Indiana University)*

types that today's feminists loathe, these "female" characteristics are arguably the basis of many of Harraden's female heroes. Thus, while Harraden's female heroes may not appear to be feminists by today's standards, they can be regarded as prototypes of the modern feminist.

The historical context also helps to explain the nature of many female antagonists in Harraden's work, who often claim long-suffering men as their victims. These women are the antitheses of Harraden's heroines and are therefore models of behaviors that the ideal woman should try to avoid: they highlight, by contrast, the morally superior and "well-behaved" female protagonists as the ideal, emancipated women. They also appeal to male readers by sparing them from direct accusations of the oppression of women. It was, after all, the male audience who needed to be convinced to give women the vote.

Thus, to the modern reader the eponymous central character of an early Harraden novel, *Hilda Strafford* (1897), may seem more paradox than protagonist. In this short book the protagonist arrives

in California to marry her English fiancé, Robert Strafford, and live on his lemon farm. From the beginning of their reunion, she is described from the point of view of her husband's best friend, Ben Overleigh, who finds her voice "somewhat harsh and strident" and her eyes "without any softness." When a storm results in the loss of a reservoir and many trees, Hilda is unable to comfort her husband well: "Hilda gave him the best of her sympathy and kindness; but even her best was poor of quality and scant of quantity." In the end she voices all her loneliness and unhappiness with farm life to her husband, and the shock of her revelation literally kills him.

There is no model of a nurturing yet independent female in this novel. Oddly, Ben Overleigh seems to provide the alternative, feminine ideal; he is described as "a good friend" who "had long ago attached himself to Robert Strafford, and looked after him – mothering him up in his own manly tender fashion." After the storm Hilda's inadequate sympathies are contrasted with Ben's ability to comfort his friend: " 'Ben, old fellow,' Robert Strafford said, looking up, and feeling at once the comfort of his presence." Ben is even accused by another male character of being prosuffragette: " 'You always have something to say for women,' said Holles. 'You ought to go back to the old country, and help them get the suffrage and all that sort of thing. You are lost to them out here. How my maiden aunt, who only loves for the Cause, as she calls it, would adore you.' "

Hilda is not treated entirely without sympathy, though, as there is some elaboration of the difficulties of the life of a settler's wife. Ben tells Hilda that California is "a land and a life for men, and not for women. We gain in every particular: no more small clerkships for us, no more imprisonment in airless offices; but out-of-door freedom, and our own lives to ourselves, and our own land." He then adds that "To you women it is altogether something different . . . and unless you know how to love desperately, there is not much to redeem the life out here for you." Hilda responds, "So here, as everywhere, the women come off the worst." Ben's speech takes on added significance near the end of the novel, when Hilda confesses just such a desperate love for Ben and her willingness to stay in California with him after Robert's death. Ben, although he feels sympathy for and is attracted to Hilda, shuns her. He regards her as a complex but cold figure and loathes himself for the attraction he feels. In the end the character of Hilda Strafford is difficult to analyze; the author seems to extend the same re-

luctant sympathy to the character and to women's causes as does Overleigh.

Harraden's next novel was *The Fowler* (1899), in which Nora Penhurst, a brilliant and educated woman, falls under the evil influence of Theodore Bevan, who wishes to control women and destroy their individuality. She is liberated from his influence when she reads his diary and discovers his true nature. Nora Penhurst is a more positive female protagonist than Hilda Strafford, but clearly even by the time of the writing of *Katharine Frensham: A Novel* (1903), Harraden still felt the need to create unattractive female antagonists. In this latter novel, however, the title character is both appealing and a suffragist, although her appeal derives as much from her nurturing tendencies as from her politics. *Katharine Frenshaw* establishes a romantic triangle in which the female protagonist is idealized as intelligent, ladylike, and, above all, kind, well mannered, and maternal; the male love interest is the tragic victim of the machinations of an evil woman; and the evil woman is neither maternal nor intelligent and is repeatedly described as "metallic."

Clifford Thornton is a tragic figure whose promising scientific career is undermined by his selfish and stupid wife. He decides to leave her, and he dreams that he tells her in detail of every wrong she has done him; the wife has the same dream, and she is so upset that she confronts Thornton. He admits that it was his dream, and she dies of shock that he so despises her (she has a weak heart). Their son blames his father for her death, and the resulting estrangement is made worse by the entrance of the evil woman, Mrs. Stanhope, best friend of the deceased, who convinces the son that Clifford practically murdered his wife. Katharine Frensham functions in the novel as the ideal woman, whose maternal warmth reconciles father and son and leads to her marriage to Clifford.

Katharine is not merely nurturing; she is, in fact, an early model of an emancipated woman. For example, her father leaves an organ-building business to Katharine and her brother at his death, and the two become business partners. At another point in the novel Katharine muses, "If only I had a profession . . . that has been my mistake all along. . . . Everyone ought to have a calling – no matter what it is; and it won't fail them in moments of poverty and trouble and – and desolation." She is also described as a "woman of sense," and when she meets a Norwegian who is hostile to the English, "her own temperamental charm [is] so irresistible that England, personified in her, [goes] up twenty-five per cent in everyone's estimation." Near the end of the

novel she is abruptly called home, by her brother, from Norway, where she has been spending a holiday (by coincidence, not arrangement) with Clifford Thornton; her brother has lost money on the stock exchange, and the family business is in danger of being lost. Katharine saves the day by becoming "a business-woman, with that remarkable adaptability which men are only beginning to recognize and appreciate in the other sex. From her pretty flat across the water, she sallied forth day after day to the organ factory. The manager and workmen welcomed her. They were willing to teach her. She was willing to learn. Her quick brain dealt with difficulties in a surprising fashion. Mr. Barlow, the manager, had always believed in her business-capacities; and it was encouraging to her to know that he was not disappointed."

Contrasting with Katharine are three other characters: Mrs. Thornton; her brother's spendthrift wife, Gwendolyn; and the exceedingly unlikable Mrs. Stanhope. All of these women are "fashionable," a type of woman Katharine does not like. Cold-eyed Gwendolyn, who recalls cold-eyed Hilda Strafford, is clearly ruining Katharine's brother financially, and he is thus established as another male victim of the wrong sort of female. In the end Gwendolyn redeems herself, however, again thanks to Katharine, who determines that Gwendolyn must be made accountable for her spendthrift ways. She proclaims to her brother, "Most women are bricks, Ronnie, if men will allow them to be so," and Gwendolyn does not disappoint, saying to her sister-in-law, "Dear old Kath! . . . You did not think I was a monster of selfishness and inequity, but believed in me. You will see how fearfully economical I shall be in the future. I shall sell all my jewels, dress in brown holland, and take in all the darning of the neighbourhood!" Thus, Gwendolyn's husband is made partly (if not largely) responsible for her failings.

The primary male victim in the novel is Clifford Thornton; he is first victimized by his wife, who "had no mercy on him: none." Thornton is next victimized by Mrs. Stanhope, who wishes to turn his son against him. She is described as "a well-dressed woman with a hard face." In the end resolution is achieved only when Katharine is able to replace the mother in the son's affections, thus effecting the reconciliation of Clifford and his son, who "did not realize it, but he always felt, after he had been with Katharine, that his old love and longing for his father began to tug at his heart. He went and stood by him now . . . and slipped his arm through his father's." Katharine's character is obviously

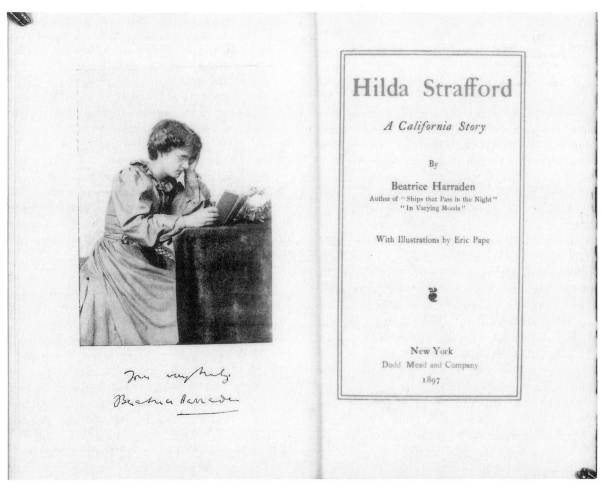

*Frontispiece and title page for the American edition of Harraden's early novel about a British woman who settles in the United States (courtesy of the Lilly Library, Indiana University)*

meant to reassure the male reader that the presence of independent and intelligent women in his life need not disrupt the comforts of heart and hearth; indeed, the implication is that women who behave in more stereotypical female ways – by being beautiful, selfish, and stupid, for instance – are far more destructive to men.

Harraden's later novels continue to explore the theme of gender relationships. In *The Scholar's Daughter* (1906) a young woman is forced to work at compiling a dictionary with a group otherwise composed entirely of men. She rebels by making friends with a celebrated actress, who turns out to be her mother. In *Interplay* (1908) an unhappily married woman leaves her husband, who grants her a divorce only after her lover dies, when it is too late for her happiness. Though a contemporary review in *Outlook* asserts that "The theme of the author is equal morality for men and women," a more cynical

critic at the *Nation* suggests that "one would welcome an interval of emancipation from emancipation."

Harraden's next novel, *Out of the Wreck I Rise* (1912), like *The Fowler,* features a man who controls and manipulates the lives of women to their detriment. *The Guiding Thread* (1916) is perhaps more ambitious in its themes, as it explores the Pygmalion-like relationship of a scholar and his wife. The wife leaves the husband and travels to the United States to enhance her education, and both husband and wife are seen to benefit from the separation, though they reunite in the end. The novel received poor reviews, however, which criticized the contrived ending. In fact, although *Where Your Treasure Is* (1918) and *Spring Shall Plant* (1920) received generally favorable reviews, the critics seem to agree that Harraden never again matched the literary merits of her first novel, *Ships That Pass in the Night.*

It would be unfair, however, to conclude that Harraden's work failed to develop after her first effort. In the play *Lady Geraldine's Speech,* written circa 1909 but published in 1985, Harraden softens her representation of feminist women. The drama involves a series of female characters, all of whom have careers and are sympathetic, indicating that the protagonists of Harraden's novels do not reveal everything about her politics. In this play Lady Geraldine, an "anti" (antifeminist) comes to her suffragette friend, Dr. Alice Romney, for assistance in writing a speech for the Women's National Anti-Suffrage League. Dr. Romney reluctantly agrees to help, and as they work on the speech, they are interrupted by four of Dr. Romney's women friends: an artist, a professor, a pianist, and a typist. The humor of the play revolves around the idea that "antis" are simply ignorant and deal in clichés, as expressed in Dr. Romney's characterization of the speech she helps to compose:

> I'm rather pleased with it. I think I've brought in all the points. Degradation of Womanhood. Degradation and disintegration of entire Empire.... Women have to safeguard the past and the future, and it is the men's work to look after the present. I don't myself know what that means, but it sounds well. Absolute denial that the vote will improve economic conditions for women. Indirect influence of women quite sufficient. Emphatic, nay passionate, insistence on your own brainlessness – that

is very important. A few passing allusions to us Suffragists as obscure vulgarians. I think you might almost call us uneducated. Yes, uneducated and obscure vulgarians. That also sounds well.

Somewhere between the author who wrote this scathing indictment of antifeminists and the author who created the character of Hilda Strafford lies the complex truth of who Beatrice Harraden was – as both author and political radical. If Harraden was a mass of contradictions in her work and in her own mind, it is perhaps unsurprising and certainly understandable: it is difficult to elevate one's consciousness and self-awareness above a culture that undermines women and celebrates the superiority of men. How could Harraden, or any woman, no matter how enlightened, fail to absorb some of that culture's messages? In the end Katharine Frensham says it best: "I begin to see why life is far easier to men than to women. The fight with the outer world braces men up. They go forth, and pass on strengthened. But women are chained to circumstances – or chain themselves."

**Reference:**

Sheila Jeffreys, *The Spinster and Her Enemies: Feminism and Sexuality 1880–1930* (London: Pandora, 1985).

# Robert S. Hichens

*(14 November 1864 – 20 July 1950)*

Richard Bleiler
*University of Connecticut*

BOOKS: *The Coastguard's Secret* (London: Swan Sonnenschein, Le Bas & Lowrey, 1886);

*The Green Carnation,* anonymous (London: Heinemann, 1894; New York: Appleton, 1894);

*An Imaginative Man* (London: Heinemann, 1895; New York: Appleton, 1895);

*After To-morrow and The New Love,* anonymous (New York: Merriam, 1895);

*The Folly of Eustace and Other Stories* (London: Heinemann, 1896; New York: Appleton, 1896);

*Flames: A London Phantasy* (London: Heinemann, 1897); published as *Flames* (Chicago: Stone, 1897);

*Byeways* (London: Methuen, 1897; New York: Dodd, Mead, 1897);

*The Londoners: An Absurdity* (London: Heinemann, 1898); published as *The Londoners* (Chicago: Stone, 1898);

*The Slave: A Romance* (London: Heinemann, 1899; Chicago: Stone, 1899);

*Tongues of Conscience* (London: Methuen, 1900; New York: Stokes, 1900);

*The Prophet of Berkeley Square: A Tragic Extravaganza* (London: Methuen, 1901); published as *The Prophet of Berkeley Square* (New York: Dodd, Mead, 1901);

*Felix: Three Years in a Life* (London: Methuen, 1902); published as *Felix: A Novel* (New York: Stokes, 1903);

*The Garden of Allah* (London: Methuen, 1904; New York: Stokes, 1904);

*The Woman with the Fan* (London: Methuen, 1904; New York: Stokes, 1904);

*The Black Spaniel and Other Stories* (London: Methuen, 1905; New York: Stokes, 1905);

*The Call of the Blood* (London: Methuen, 1906; New York: Harper, 1906);

*Barbary Sheep* (New York: Harper, 1907; London: Methuen, 1909);

*A Spirit in Prison* (London: Hutchinson, 1908; New York: Harper, 1908);

*Egypt and Its Monuments* (London: Hodder & Stoughton, 1908; New York: Century, 1908); republished as *The Spell of Egypt* (London: Hodder & Stoughton, 1910; New York: Century, 1911);

*Bella Donna: A Novel* (London: Heinemann, 1909; Philadelphia: Lippincott, 1909);

*The Knock on the Door: A Novel* (London: Heinemann, 1909; Philadelphia: Lippincott, 1909);

*The Holy Land* (London: Hodder & Stoughton, 1910; New York: Century, 1910);

*The Dweller on the Threshold* (London: Methuen, 1911; New York: Century, 1911);

*The Fruitful Vine* (London: Unwin, 1911; New York: Stokes, 1911);

*The Way of Ambition* (London: Methuen, 1913; New York: Stokes, 1913);

*The Near East* (London: Hodder & Stoughton, 1913; New York: Century, 1913);

*In the Wilderness: A Novel* (London: Methuen, 1917; New York: Stokes, 1917);

*Mrs. Marden* (London: Cassell, 1919; New York: Doran, 1919);

*Snake-Bite and Other Stories* (London: Cassell, 1919; New York: Doran, 1919);

*The Spirit of the Time: A Novel* (London: Cassell, 1921); published as *The Spirit of the Time: A Novel of Today* (New York: Doran, 1921);

*December Love* (London: Cassell, 1922; New York: Doran, 1922);

*The Last Time and Other Stories* (London: Hutchinson, 1923); published as *The Last Time* (New York: Doran, 1924);

*After the Verdict* (London: Methuen, 1924; New York: Doran, 1924);

*The God Within Him* (London: Methuen, 1926); published as *The Unearthly* (New York: Cosmopolitan, 1926);

*The Bacchante and the Nun* (London: Methuen, 1927); published as *The Bacchante: The Story of a Brief Career* (New York: Cosmopolitan, 1927);

*The Streets and Other Stories* (London: Hutchinson, 1928);

*Dr. Artz* (London: Hutchinson, 1929; New York: Cosmopolitan, 1929);

*On the Screen* (London: Cassell, 1929);

*The Bracelet: A Narrative* (London: Cassell, 1930); published as *The Bracelet* (New York: Cosmopolitan, 1930);

*The Gates of Paradise and Other Stories* (London: Cassell, 1930);

*The First Lady Brendon: A Novel in a Prologue and Two Parts* (London: Cassell / Garden City, N.Y.: Doubleday, Doran, 1931);

*My Desert Friend and Other Stories* (London: Cassell, 1931);

*Mortimer Brice: A Bit of His Life* (London: Cassell, 1932; Garden City, N.Y.: Doubleday, Doran, 1932);

*The Paradine Case: A Novel* (London: Benn, 1933; Garden City, N.Y.: Doubleday, Doran, 1933);

*The Power to Kill* (London: Benn, 1934; Garden City, N.Y.: Doubleday, Doran, 1934);

*The Gardenia and Other Stories* (London: Hutchinson, 1934);

*"Susie's" Career: A Novel* (London: Cassell, 1935); published as *The Pyramid* (New York: Doubleday, Doran, 1936);

*The Afterglow and Other Stories* (London: Cassell, 1935);

*The Sixth of October: A Novel* (London: Cassell, 1936; Garden City, N.Y.: Doubleday, Doran, 1936);

*Daniel Airlie: A Novel* (London: Cassell, 1937; Garden City, N.Y.: Doubleday, Doran, 1937);

*The Journey Up: A Novel* (London: Cassell, 1938; Garden City, N.Y.: Doubleday, Doran, 1938);

*Secret Information* (London: Hurst & Blackett, 1938; Garden City, N.Y.: Doubleday, Doran, 1938);

*That Which Is Hidden: A Novel* (London: Cassell, 1939; Garden City, N.Y.: Doubleday, Doran, 1940);

*The Million: An Entertainment* (London: Cassell, 1940; Garden City, N.Y.: Doubleday, Doran, 1941);

*Married or Unmarried* (London: Cassell, 1941);

*A New Way of Life: A Novel in Three Phases* (London: Hutchinson, 1942; Garden City, N.Y.: Doubleday, Doran, 1942);

*Veils* (London: Hutchinson, 1943); published as *Young Mrs. Brand* (Philadelphia: Macrae-Smith, 1944);

*Harps in the Wind* (London: Cassell, 1945); published as *The Woman in the House* (Philadelphia: Macrae-Smith, 1945);

*Incognito: A Novel* (London: Hutchinson, 1947; New York: McBride, 1948);

*Yesterday: The Autobiography of Robert Hichens* (London: Cassell, 1947);

*Too Much Love of Living: A Novel* (Philadelphia: Macrae-Smith, 1947; London: Cassell, 1948);

*Beneath the Magic* (London: Hutchinson, 1950); published as *Strange Lady* (Philadelphia: Macrae-Smith, 1950);

*The Man in the Mirror and Other Stories* (London: Cassell, 1950);

*The Mask* (London: Hutchinson, 1951);

*Nightbound: A Novel* (London: Cassell, 1951).

OTHER: Wilson Barrett, *The Daughters of Babylon*, adapted by Hichens (London: John Macqueen / Philadelphia: Lippincott, 1899).

Although Robert Smythe Hichens wrote more than seventy books, many of which were bestsellers and were adapted for the theater and motion pictures, he is virtually forgotten today. Only two of his works remain tenuously alive: a short, grim fantasy titled "How Love Came to Professor

## KEY TO THE CHARACTERS

| | | | |
|---|---|---|---|
| PAGE 3 | LINE 10 | "REGGIE" ("LORD REGINALD HASTINGS") | (LORD ALFRED DOUGLAS) |
| 4 | 16 | "ELDERLY GENTLEMAN" | (MARQUESS OF QUEENSBERRY) |
| 6 | 14 | "MR. AMARINTH" | (OSCAR WILDE) |
| 38 | 11 | "THE SECOND MARCHIONESS OF HEDFIELD" | (MARQUESS OF QUEENSBERRY'S SECOND WIFE) |
| 40 | 17 | "MADAME VALTESI" | (MRS. GABRIELLI) |
| 42 | 6 | "A THEATRE" | (THE CRITERION THEATRE) |
| 42 | 6 | "A CERTAIN ACTOR" | (SIR CHARLES WYNDHAM) |
| 57 | 26 | "YOUR BROTHER" ("TEDDY") | (WILLIE WILDE) |
| 197 | 29 | "THE SOUL OF BERTIE BROWN" ("THE PICTURE OF DORIAN GRAY") | |

*Page from the American edition of Hichens's satire of the British Aesthetic Movement,* The Green Carnation *(1894), identifying the sources for the novel*

Guildea" is still anthologized, and *The Green Carnation* (1894), Hichens's first mature novel, is still read by scholars interested in Oscar Wilde's aesthetic movement. This critical neglect is not entirely undeserved. Like many writers Hichens wrote his most noteworthy books at the beginning of his career, and though his later works have occasional moments of interest, they tend to repeat the ideas and situations of the earlier books; study of them is not particularly rewarding. Unlike his contemporary H. G. Wells, Hichens was not an author of many ideas, nor, despite the references to Friedrich Nietzsche and Arthur Schopenhauer that frequently appear in his work, was he particularly profound or insightful. Whereas Wells developed as a writer and a thinker, Hichens did not, remaining to mine an established vein of social romanticism rather than establishing new claims. He is, nevertheless, at his best a skilled craftsman in the Edwardian style, able to provide vivid and minute descriptions of exotic locales, and capable of treating soberly subject matter that in other hands would be sensationalized or

vulgarized. In this Hichens is the diametric opposite of another best-selling contemporary author, now also mostly forgotten, Marie Corelli.

Robert Hichens was born on 14 November 1864 in Speldhurst, a small village in Kent, the oldest son of the Reverend Frederick Harrison Hichens, the music-loving and mildly eccentric rector of St. Stephen's, and Abigail Elizabeth Smythe Hichens. As described in *Yesterday: The Autobiography of Robert Hichens* (1947) his childhood was uneventful, occasionally enlivened by visits from painters and musicians; he received a solid education at Hurstleigh, a well-known private school. Although he was a prolific writer of verses and wrote a novel when he was seventeen titled *The Coastguard's Secret* (1886), the young Hichens was a capable pianist and was more interested in music than literature. After a brief stint at Clifton College, he declined to enter Oxford and instead entered the Royal College of Music in London. Though a skillful pianist, Hichens's greatest success in the musical world was to have one of his verses, "A Kiss and Good-Bye," set to music by Tito Mattei and sung by Madame Adelina Patti in Albert Hall. As recounted by Hichens in a 1908 interview published in *Bookman,* the performance was a mixed success. Although the song was enthusiastically applauded by the audience, which called for an encore, the crestfallen Hichens overheard the comments of two people in the seats behind him: " 'What a lovely song that was!' one exclaimed rapturously. 'Yes,' the other grudgingly agreed, 'but what awful rot the words of these songs always are!' "

Hichens recounts essentially the same story in *Yesterday* but alters it by providing different dialogue and locations for the speakers. The discrepancy is small, but it is nevertheless indicative of a great problem in approaching Hichens's life and works: he cannot be relied upon as an accurate reporter, and statements offered as facts on one page may be flatly contradicted by the events related on another. Incidents recounted in *Yesterday* appear verbatim in his fiction, making it seem that Hichens fictionalized the events of his life, but it is equally possible that these anecdotes originated in his fiction. In any event Hichens remains a shadowy presence; the researcher will discover odd gaps in his reported life and emerge with questions that must remain unanswered.

At the age of twenty-four Hichens decided that he had no future as a musician and no great skill at composition, and he enrolled in Daniel Anderson's London School of Journalism, spending a year developing his style. Under Anderson's tute-

lage he published articles in newspapers such as the *Globe,* the *European Mail,* and the *Evening Standard*; encouraged by Anderson, he wrote short stories for Anderson's short-lived magazine, *Mistress and Maid.* In 1893 Hichens submitted a short story, "The Collaborators," to the *Pall Mall* magazine; it was accepted, and the editors, Sir Douglas Straight and Lord Frederick Hamilton, asked him to submit additional stories. Several more stories were accepted before "The Cry of the Child," an account of a haunting by the ghost of an abused child, was rejected; he published it elsewhere.

Also in the year 1893 Hichens suffered a severe attack of what may have been food poisoning; he stated vaguely that his doctor "came and said I had been poisoned. Peritonitis set in and I nearly died." In 1894 Hichens took a sea voyage to Egypt to recuperate, landing first at Port Said, then in Ismailia. In *Yesterday* Hichens recounts that the latter area immediately made a profound impression on him: "I disembarked at dawn in Ismailia. And I have never forgotten the impression the gradual coming of light, African light, among the silvery sands and the palm trees made upon me. I had never seen, or even imagined, anything quite like it before. On that first morning I made a silent vow to visit Africa as often as possible during the rest of my life; and I have kept it."

In Cairo, Hichens became acquainted with Lord Alfred Douglas, and in Luxor the two became closer, Hichens traveling down the Nile with Douglas and several of Douglas's friends, including the writer E. F. Benson and young Reginald Turner, a close friend of Wilde and, according to Hichens, "one of the most amusing conversationalists of the time." Through Douglas and Turner, Hichens met Wilde following their return to London, though their acquaintance was limited to four meetings. Nevertheless, Wilde's brilliant conversation, and the sight of Wilde and other young men wearing green carnations in a theater (in emulation of Wilde), prompted Hichens to write *The Green Carnation,* a short novel published anonymously that parodied Wilde and the aesthetic movement. When his authorship was revealed, Hichens's literary success was assured. He was soon offered the post of music critic by the London *World* and accepted, succeeding George Bernard Shaw; he later declined a position on the *Daily Telegraph,* preferring to remain a novelist.

Hichens remained a professional writer for the rest of his life, and though his next books were not enormously popular, he soon found a formula for success. Until the 1940s Hichens wrote an average of one novel per year, his style and typical subject material gradually shifting from the vividly described landscapes of Italy and Algeria to lengthy descriptions of superficial events and muted emotions among the English upper classes. Modern readers preferring swiftly told stories will find his style interminable.

Because Hichens wrote so much, generalizations about his work are difficult to make. Nevertheless, the majority of his novels involve deteriorating (or failed) relationships described at length. The traditional happy ending is rarely present in his work, and those few novels which end with relationships intact and protagonists alive are curiously unconvincing, the efforts of a man telling a story in which he does not believe. Brian Stableford notes that Hichens "has an attitude toward the difficulties and sufferings of others that, while not exactly sadistic, seems to take satisfaction in demonstrating that the achievement of happiness is impossible. His fiction abounds with broken romances and doomed marriages, minutely explored and described with amazing prolixity."

In *Yesterday* Hichens comments of *The Garden of Allah* (1904) that "when I conceived the book I made up my mind that Religion must triumph over human love," but the novel conveys the feeling that Hichens was firmly convinced that not only religion but everything else in existence must also triumph over human love. This pessimism may have originated in events dating from his late adolescence: he states in *Yesterday* that, prior to entering the Royal College of Music at the age of twenty, he fell in love, but the girl's father denied his suit, stating that he had no prospects. Hichens was hurt by this refusal, and although he claimed that he fell in love again several times, he never married; nor did the woman. This biographical explanation of Hichens's literary tone is suspect, however, as his first novel, which he claimed he wrote at age seventeen (and thus well before his unhappy love affair), concludes with the death of the wealthy and educated protagonist. Unless Hichens lied about his age when he wrote the novel, his unhappiness had far deeper roots than a mere failed adolescent love affair.

Hichens's persistent pessimism also reveals itself in a curious loathing of heterosexual physical relationships and a distrust of any erotic impulse, no matter however innocent or quietly expressed. Virtually all of his novels offer some elaboration of this, and three examples will suffice: in *The Spirit of the Time: A Novel* (1921), middle-aged Derrick Merton falls in love with Russian expatriate Anna Aranensky only to learn that his love has enabled

him to be swindled in an elaborate con game; in *Dr. Artz* (1929) the title character implants glands that reawaken physical desires in the elderly, a process that is presented with a horror and disgust that have no rational basis; and in *Secret Information* (1938) Canon Bankton learns that his secret fascination with erotic literature has been discovered, and the revelation almost destroys his life and reputation.

Hichens also possessed a hyperdeveloped sense of Edwardian morality, an attitude which makes his novels seem dated to present-day readers. In his moral universe those who disagree with the properly behaving representatives of established religion are invariably humbled. He also clearly believed that proper women simply did not speak to men without a formal introduction, nor did married women meet with men (in public or private) when their husbands were not present. The punishments for those who transgress this moral code are severe: the emancipated Cynthia Clarke of *In the Wilderness: A Novel* (1917) is put on trial by her husband when he learns that she entertained male friends in his absence; Lady Ivy Brendon of *The First Lady Brendon: A Novel in a Prologue and Two Parts* (1931) is threatened by her abusive husband for having a male visitor in camp during his absence, and though she has been faithful to him, she feels that he could win if the case came to trial; and in *Veils* (1943), arguably Hichens's cruelest novel, an emasculated and depressed Nicholas Brand commits suicide after learning that his hitherto virtuous wife has attempted to conceal her friendship with an Italian she met in a park who addressed her without an introduction.

Hichens's musical background surfaces in many of his novels either as a central component – *The Way of Ambition* (1913) concerns events in the life of a composer writing a contemporary opera, and *Dr. Artz* focuses on a woman who is being trained as an opera singer – or in minor episodes throughout his works involving recitals and performances. Linked with this background is Hichens's belief in the innate worthiness of English "society" that led him to populate the majority of his novels with titled nonentities who did not have to work for a living and whose lives were spent at cultural affairs, in parties, or in visiting exotic ruins and viewing luxuriant landscapes in other countries. In Hichens's universe truly impoverished people virtually do not exist; the lower classes of all nations are rarely described at any length, but when they are mentioned, they are happy in their lives and lack of property, education, and social clout, and they are delighted to serve the whims of the upper-class English.

This general insensitivity appears most explicitly in Hichens's early work. At one point in *The Slave: A Romance* (1899), for example, the protagonist Aubrey longs "to be a poor man leaning against a public-house. He had sometimes thought that the so-called lower classes are happier than is generally supposed, owing to a gift of devil-may-care insouciance which many of them undoubtedly possess. Now he felt sure of it." Nevertheless, exceptions occasionally penetrate this insular world: Aubrey meets a lower-class family of acrobats and jugglers that experiences a tragic and vividly described death. *Flames: A London Phantasy* (1897) has as a major character the prostitute Cuckoo Bright, whose pure love for the upper-class Julian Addison (who will not touch her) enables her to save Julian's soul; "The Lady and the Beggar" details Mrs. Errington's fate after she fails to give charity to a starving man; and *Secret Information* features a servant named Grader who is capable, able to read German, and surmises the existence of his master's collection of erotic literature long before it is revealed.

Paralleling Hichens's general ignorance about the lower classes is his typical treatment of foreigners, particularly those who do not have the grace to speak English or who are unfortunate enough to be swarthy. Although many of Hichens's novels are set in Italy and the Middle East, his treatment of Italians and Arabs is at times unpleasantly racist. In Hichens's world Italians and Arabs are either as faithful as dogs (and thus not worthy of interest), or as whimsical and superficial as children, prone to violence, or, worst of all, dangerously handsome and thereby mysterious and seductive to English women. In *Barbary Sheep* (1907), for example, the handsome spahi Benchaâlal tells the superficial Lady Wyverne (whom he is on the point of seducing) that "dark men worship the fair women." The narrator comments on the scene: "All the time he spoke he was watching her craftily . . . Two hearts seemed beating in his breast, the heart of a robber and the heart of a lover. The two controlling passions of the Arab were simultaneously alive within him. At that moment he was capable of falling at Lady Wyverne's feet . . . But he was also capable of murdering her for the chain of jewels at her neck if she resisted him. And this is only to say that he was Arab."

Hichens also retained a lifelong interest in the occult. His earliest novel, *The Coastguard's Secret* (1886), opens with a mysterious vision of a dead man lying at a woman's feet and later includes supernatural manifestations from the dead man's

grave. During the late 1880s, while a student at the London School of Journalism, Hichens interviewed psychic practitioners, remaining skeptical but ultimately accepting of supernatural phenomena: *Yesterday* describes several instances in which Hichens visited palmists and believed they accurately foretold his future. Furthermore, supernatural elements frequently appear in the backgrounds of Hichens's otherwise realistic novels: *The Slave* uses death portents in gemstones; *The First Lady Brendon* features prenatal marking; *The Sixth of October: A Novel* (1936) involves a psychic fortune-teller who has predicted an early death for a client; and the otherwise negligible *Hares in the Wind* (1945) begins on a fantastic note, the protagonist having been psychically summoned via recurrent dreams to a house in the countryside.

Although Hichens paid half the costs of printing *The Coastguard's Secret* and was later dismissive of the novel, refusing to allow its reprinting when he became successful, the book is not without moments of interest. It is set in Seamouth, a remote fishing village in Devon, and begins with a supernaturally observed death: Edward Rolands, the coastguard, has accidentally killed Tom Pensford, his rival for the hand of fair Mary Blake, and has buried Pensford's body on a nearby estate. The results of this accident are psychically seen by John Archdale – who is "rich, *very* rich, and young enough to enjoy his wealth" – while he is cruising his yacht off the coast of Devon. Archdale later inherits the estate upon which Pensford is buried and moves to Seamouth, becoming acquainted with the survivors of the triangle and falling in love with Mary himself. He soon realizes that a secret exists and is able to connect the source of a repeated psychic malaise with the location of Pensford's grave. He exhumes Pensford's corpse and learns of Mary's innocence in Pensford's death, but, weakened by sickness and possession by Pensford's ghost, he dies by the grave. Mary (who has fallen in love with Archdale) thereupon marries Rolands, though she occasionally visits Archdale's grave: "And while her tears drop on the grass above his resting place, she can yet thank God with a true joy, that before he died he knew her to be innocent and worthy of his love." *The Coastguard's Secret* is poorly written, weakly characterized, and frequently melodramatic, but in its execution and themes and in the questions it raises, it prefigures Hichens's later works.

*The Green Carnation*, Hichens's next novel and his first mature work of any length, is a comic roman à clef, its protagonist, young Lord Reggie Hastings, a composite of Lord Alfred Douglas and

*Cover for the American edition of Hichens's bildungsroman about a young man who falls in love with a morphine addict*

Reginald Turner. The aesthete Esmé Amarinth is the flamboyant originator of the green carnation – "the arsenic flower of an exquisite life" adopted "because it blended so well with the colour of absinthe" – and is immediately recognizable as Wilde. The actual story of *The Green Carnation* is simple: after introducing the characters in London, the setting removes to a house party in Surrey, where Hastings and Amarinth sparkle and are observed by a recently returned expatriate, the ordinary but enormously wealthy young Lady Locke. Lady Locke is widowed and is considering remarriage; she is physically attracted to the handsome Reggie, but, repelled by his superficiality and artificiality, she rejects his almost offhand marriage proposal and the shallow lifestyle he offers: "If you could forget what you call art, if you could see life at all with a straight, untrammelled vision, if you could be like a man, instead of like nothing at all in heaven or earth except that dyed flower, I might perhaps care for you in the right way. But your mind is artificially

coloured: it comes from the dyer's. It is a green carnation; and I want a natural blossom to wear in my heart."

What makes *The Green Carnation* still readable is not the failed romance but the wit of the author as revealed in Esmé Amarinth. In addition to being a color (purple), an amaranth is a plant cultivated for its showy, colored foliage, and, like his namesake, Esmé Amarinth constantly displays himself in purple (Wildean) wit: "Most people depart in a cloud of blessings and farewells, or give up the ghost arranging their affairs with a huckster, or endeavouring to cut somebody off with a shilling. I at least cannot be so vulgar as to do that, for I have not a shilling in the world"; "To get drunk deliberately is as foolish as to get sober by accident"; "Nothing is so fatal to a personality as the keeping of promises, unless it be telling the truth. To lie finely is an Art, to tell the truth is to act according to Nature, and Nature is the first of Philistines"; and "Nothing on earth is so absolutely middle-class as Nature."

There is, however, more to *The Green Carnation* than wit and verbal play. Its educated readers were undoubtedly aware that the dyed flower was worn in Paris to proclaim the homosexuality of its wearer. Although Hichens is naturally reticent, the nature of the relationship between Amarinth and Hastings is arguably that of a homosexual couple; Hastings is certainly by no means the marrying kind. Furthermore, because *The Green Carnation* was published anonymously, there was speculation about its authorship; even Wilde was accused of writing the book, a charge he emphatically denied in a letter in the *Pall Mall Gazette* on 2 October 1894. After *The Green Carnation* exposed Wilde and his ideas to many who were not previously aware of them, Wilde's response was to become even more outrageous in public, his behavior culminating in his well-known libel suit against Douglas's father, the Marquess of Queensberry, who in 1895 accused him of homosexuality. By that time *The Green Carnation* was in its fourth impression.

Following the success of *The Green Carnation*, Hichens wrote *An Imaginative Man* (1895), an oddly despairing novel seen largely through the perspective of Harry Denison, an egotist who believes himself perspicacious and imaginative. During his honeymoon in Egypt, Denison becomes obsessed with the mysteries of the Sphinx; paralleling the death of Denison's relationship with his wife is the death of tubercular young Guy Aintree, whose mother has brought him to Egypt because of his health. Young Aintree tries valiantly to experience life in the fullest by visiting the fleshpots of Cairo, a lifestyle Den-

ison is unable to comprehend. The conclusion is muffled, but it would seem that Denison has fled from life and love and has hidden in the base of the Sphinx; a bewildered Enid Denison is left with a grieving Mrs. Aintree.

Hichens followed *An Imaginative Man* with *The Folly of Eustace and Other Stories* (1896), a collection of three bitter short stories, two of which examine the relationships of life and art. "The Folly of Eustace" inverts the ideas put forth in *The Green Carnation* and shows what happens when an ordinary man mistakenly believes he is creative: Eustace Lane behaves frivolously and capriciously in order to be thought original; he even jokes about the death of his daughter. Just as he achieves his lifelong goal of being caricatured in *Vanity Fair,* his long-suffering wife leaves him: art has led Eustace to reject life, and he must pay the painful consequences. "The Collaborator" involves two journalists writing a novel of a well-meaning man who befriends a morphine addict and becomes in turn addicted, but what is sensational fiction for Jack Henley is despairing autobiography for Andrew Trenchard, who commits murder and suicide to conclude his share of the work. "The Collaborator" is perhaps ahead of its time in questioning the distinctions between fiction and autobiography; its theme of morphine addiction would be used again in *Felix: Three Years in a Life* (1903). The third story, "The Return of the Soul," is a fantasy involving an abused white cat reincarnated as the beautiful wife of the vicious and selfish narrator; the narrator had killed her previous incarnation, but she evens the cosmic balance.

Hichens's next novel was *Flames,* a long and self-consciously decadent fantasy of vampiric possession and the battle for men's souls. Set in London, *Flames* begins with a series of occult experiments in which young socialite Julian Addison and his ascetic friend Valentine Cresswell ("the Saint of Victoria Street") attempt to switch souls. After progressively greater occult manifestations, their fourth sitting concludes with Valentine's apparent death, but he has recovered by the time Dr. Levillier arrives. Valentine is altered, however, possessed by the spirit of the evil occultist Marr, who had died at the same time. The weak Julian is seduced to a life of dissipation by the malign spirit of Marr, but the evil force is opposed by Dr. Levillier and the prostitute Cuckoo Bright, who was with Marr in a hotel at the time of his death and who now enjoys a chaste relationship with Julian. Though overlong, *Flames* is nevertheless a work of some power, and the arrogant and seemingly victorious Marr-in-Valentine's late revelation is disquieting in its implications:

Marr, too, was my prey. Like Valentine he was not content with himself. His weakness of discontent was my opportunity. I expelled his will . . . Have you read of vampires? . . . There are vampires in the modern world who feed, not upon bodies, but upon souls, wills. And each soul they feed upon gives to them greater strength, a longer reign upon the earth. Who knows? One of them in time may compass eternity.

Also intriguing is the nature of the obviously intimate but vaguely described relationship between Valentine and Julian.

*The Londoners: An Absurdity* (1898) is a mild comedy of manners involving a divorced woman, Chloe Van Adam, who dresses in man's clothing and pretends to be her husband in order to enter London society, as personified by her friend, Mrs. Daisy Verulam: divorced men remain part of society; divorced women do not. The majority of the novel's action takes place during Ascot Week in the rented country house of Mr. Perry Lite, "the Bun Emperor," a nouveau riche buffoon who hovers cholerically nearby worrying about his guests destroying his property. The guests, in turn, suspect each other of sexual misconduct, though their activities are misreported by Harrison, Lite's cowardly servant, who wants only to retain his position. After a period of frantic activity and mistaken identities, everything is properly resolved: Chloe Van Adam reveals her identity and plans to remarry her husband, who has realized that she was not entertaining men in his absence; Daisy Verulam realizes that she was wrong ever to want to leave Society.

Following his novelization of Wilson Barrett's play *The Daughters of Babylon* (1899), Hichens wrote *The Slave: A Romance*. It mixes Hichens's familiar motifs of upperclass English society, sexual unhappiness, and disgust over physical relationships into the story of the beautiful Lady Carryl Knox, who is enslaved by her passion for the enduring and unyielding beauty of gems. She thus rejects relatively poor but worthy young Aubrey Herrick to marry Sir Reuben Allabruth, an elderly dealer in jewels who woos her with an enormous emerald and keeps her happy with gifts of precious stones. Reuben dies, and the widowed Carryl's fate is cruel and bitter: after she is beaten and robbed of her beloved emerald, she marries the thief in order to be reunited with the jewel. Aubrey walks alone into the night, his love thwarted.

*Tongues of Conscience* (1900), Hichens's second short-story collection, includes among its five stories what may be the author's finest work, "How Love Came to Professor Guildea." The brilliant Professor Guildea has renounced human emotion,

*Title page for the American edition of one of Hichens's most successful novels, the story of a young Catholic woman who leaves Great Britain for the deserts of North Africa*

particularly love, but his sole friend, the amiable Father Murchison, watches helplessly as Guildea is abruptly haunted and destroyed by an embodiment of love, an idiotic and loathsome force invisible to humans but perceptible to animals; Guildea's grey parrot can sense it. In this story Hichens's unhappiness receives its clearest expression. Though Hichens wrote many more short stories – thirteen collections were published during his lifetime – none of them have the emotional impact or successfully portray the sheer mystifying hatred found in "How Love Came to Professor Guildea."

Hichens's next novel, *Felix,* employs elements of autobiography – a journalism school, a love of the works of Honoré de Balzac, and people Hichens met while traveling in France – into a bildungsroman about Felix Wilding, a shallow and domineer-

ing adolescent who dislikes the clergy. Felix's life in London is enlivened by his passion for Valeria Ismey, the independent wife of a noted publisher, but Valeria is a morphine addict; her lies, self-destructive behavior, and cravings are terrible and realistically portrayed. Despite its serious subject matter, *Felix* is oddly ambivalent about the use and dangers of drugs, and as an alternative to Valeria, Hichens offers Lady Caroline Hurst, a casual morphine user who remains unaddicted and in complete control of her life. *Felix* is interesting not only as an early attempt at portraying addiction but also because it presents one of Hichens's few attempts at a happy ending: "Happy is the man who has a good mother" proclaims the novel's final page.

In 1904 Hichens had one of his greatest successes with the publication of *The Garden of Allah,* which sold more than eight hundred thousand copies and was filmed three times. Despite the novel's length, its story is simple: a tall and active young Catholic woman, Domini Enfilden, travels into the deserts of North Africa to find peace. After several encounters with an apparently boorish man, she settles into the small town of Beni-Mora and discovers that the man is again present. She learns that he is Boris Androvsky, and they associate almost reluctantly. Under the influence of the desert (the garden of Allah, according to an Arabic proverb) they find passion and are soon married, heading south for their honeymoon. Androvsky's behavior is consistently eccentric and antisocial, and in Amara, Domini learns the reason behind his actions: he is a Trappist monk who has fled his monastery. After due consideration Domini returns the passive Androvsky to his monastery and settles in Beni-Mora to raise the child of their union.

In spite of its simplicity of story, *The Garden of Allah* is filled with vividly described details of North African life. The desert emerges as a major character in its own right, offering commentary via pathetic fallacy on the actions of the humans. There are elements of the fantastic in the prophecies of a sand diviner; discussions about the nature of God and religion with the atheistic Count Anteoni, who has cultivated an elaborate walled garden on the edges of Allah's garden; and the entire novel is infused with what Claud Cockburn in *Bestseller: The Books that Everyone Read, 1900-1939* (1972) refers to as a "steamy religiosity," adding that "it is impossible by summary or quotation to ram home the full charges of sexual passion with which the book is loaded."

The most thought-provoking piece in Hichens's fourth collection of short stories, *The*

*Black Spaniel and Other Stories* (1905), is the title story. In Rome the narrator Lutrell introduces his friend Dr. Peter Deeming to Vernon Kersteven, an ardent antivivisectionist whose black spaniel was once killed by scientists. Learning that Deeming has a black spaniel, Kersteven becomes somehow convinced that Deeming is an evil man who mistreats his (unseen) dog. Deeming, on the other hand, is convinced that Kersteven is a "black fanatic" and, upon his return to England, attempts to distance himself from his harasser, but Kersteven moves next door. Deeming dies from a bite inflicted by the spaniel, which was mistreated and also dies, and some time later Lutrell is with Kersteven when Kersteven buys a black spaniel that is afraid of him. Kersteven is convinced that the spaniel contains Deeming's spirit and cheerfully tortures the dog, eventually killing it. The story is interpretable as a fantasy of reincarnation and retribution, but it is also effective as a study of an aberrant personality, a fanatic who sees nothing wrong in harassing humans and torturing certain animals.

Several stories in *The Black Spaniel* are set in the Africa of *The Garden of Allah:* "Desert Air" and "Fin Tireur" are tales in which those who yield to passion (respectively, an Englishman and a Frenchwoman) are killed. "The Figure in the Mirage" involves a young Frenchwoman being literally carried away by a handsome spahi whom she has seen in visions. "Halima and the Scorpions" is cruel, detailing the unhappy fate of an independent, beautiful, and proud dancing girl who is forced into sleeping with scorpions. "The Mission of Mr. Eustace Greyne" is intentionally humorous and describes what happens when a domineering female novelist sends her milquetoast husband to Algeria to make notes on its wickedness that she may use in her next book. Seduced by the dancing girls, Eustace Greyne leads a cheerfully profligate life but writes letters detailing his inability to find wickedness until Mrs. Greyne arrives and hauls him back to England. The story stands alone in Hichens's work in presenting sexuality outside of marriage as something that may be enjoyed without punishment.

Hichens's next novel of note, *The Call of the Blood* (1906), is set in Sicily and chronicles a doomed marriage. If anything, *The Call of the Blood* has an even simpler storyline than *The Garden of Allah:* the English couple Maurice and Hermione Delarey are honeymooning when Hermione leaves Sicily to nurse an ailing male friend in North Africa. During Hermione's absence Maurice Delarey has an affair with the beautiful peasant girl Maddalena.

Maddalena's greedy father Salvatore sees an opportunity to blackmail Maurice when Hermione returns but ends by killing him offstage, perhaps accidentally, perhaps in rage at having failed to extort money from Maurice, or perhaps in righteous vendetta. A grieving Hermione leaves the island in the company of friends, never realizing her husband was unfaithful.

As with *The Garden of Allah,* what makes *The Call of the Blood* exceptional are its painterly descriptions of Sicily, its flowers, beaches, festivals, and folkways. Furthermore, Maurice's situation is immediate and accessible, and his behavior and reactions are convincing. His death comes after a suspenseful buildup, and it is completely unexpected: nothing Maurice has done warrants his being killed. Nevertheless, if one errs in Hichens's world, one must pay the price, and even the most vital of characters is not immune to punishment.

Hichens wrote few sequels, but he provided one to *The Call of the Blood. A Spirit in Prison* (1908) takes place seventeen years after the events in the first novel on a small island off Naples, and it resolves the situation of the first. Its story is more complex than the earlier story – there are more characters, including Hermione's daughter Vere, a writer named Emile Artois (the friend Hermione went to North Africa to nurse), and Maddalena's son Ruffo – but after a long buildup, it climaxes with Hermione's learning the truth about her late husband. A contemporary reader is not likely to care, and even the author's contemporaries found it overlong: in his autobiography Hichens relates how George Moore told him that "at the climax of the book there are too many sunsets."

Hichens's next two novels of note share the theme of Englishwomen becoming infatuated with Middle Eastern lovers. Hichens often wrote a short novel before writing a long one, and *Barbary Sheep* is the brief companion to the long *Bella Donna: A Novel* (1909). Set in Algeria, *Barbary Sheep* describes the plight of Lady Wyverne, who is annoyed when her husband leaves her at night to hunt Barbary sheep. She is thus prey for Benchaâlal, a handsome spahi whose character is offensively portrayed and who meets the fate Hichens typically meted out to those foreigners who would besmirch English womanhood.

*Bella Donna,* another of Hichens's popular successes, is sometimes described as a mystery, but it is more properly a crime story, the recounting of an attempted murder: greedy Ruby Armine attempts to murder her idealistic husband Nigel during their honeymoon in Egypt so that she might continue to enjoy her passion with wealthy young Mahmoud

Cover for Hichens's story of a successful actress who gives up her career to become a nun (courtesy of the Lilly Library, Indiana University)

Baroudi. She fails only because Nigel's physician, Dr. Meyer Isaacson, becomes suspicious when he receives a letter from a mutual friend mentioning Nigel's illness. Isaacson travels to Egypt to see his ailing friend, forces his way past the lying and evasive Ruby and the incompetent physician she has hired, and diagnoses Nigel's mysterious illness as being caused by lead poisoning, administered by the faithless Ruby. Her fate is cruel but deserved.

*The Fruitful Vine* (1911), an elaborate retelling of Gustave Flaubert's *Madame Bovary* (1856), was successful in England but not in the United States. Hichens's next major works involved the deaths of children: *In the Wilderness* begins with a happy honeymoon in Greece, but upon their return to England the happiness of Dion and Rosamund Leith is shattered when Dion accidentally kills their son. Their marriage founders, and Dion's depressed wanderings take him into Constantinople, where he is picked up by Cynthia Clarke, previously put on trial by her husband for seeing men in his absence.

Though she was found innocent, Clarke later confesses that she had indeed been consorting with men, and she seduces Dion, reawakening him to life and a realization that their sexual relationship is somehow degrading. Eventually Rosamund arrives to reclaim Dion.

The simply told *Mrs. Marden* (1919) probably had as its inspiration Harry Houdini's assaults on phony spiritualists: Mrs. Marden, a social butterfly incapable of deep thoughts, assists in the war effort, and when she receives word that her only son Ronnie has been killed, she is devastated and becomes a virtual recluse. She is taken to Cyril Hammond, a spiritualist whose manifestations of Ronnie reawaken her interest in life. Hammond, however, is exposed as a fraud when his son is killed, but Hichens is surprisingly merciful toward Mrs. Marden. Euripides' epigram "Who knows if life be not death and death be not life?" has several times been quoted in the text, and after Mrs. Marden dies slowly and painfully, the book's last sentence expands on Euripides' idea: "when the clocks in the City had just struck eleven Mrs. Marden lived – at last."

*The God Within Him* (1926) and the more simply told *The Bacchante and the Nun* (1927) feature people who must relinquish their passions. *The God Within Him* is overtly religious, one of its major themes being the coming of the new messiah, here named Peter Kharkoff; he makes his home in an exhaustively described Switzerland, not far from where the League of Nations held its meetings. The novel also deals at length with the awakening of Imogen Lowrie, whose lover, the magnificently physical Sir Hugo Dennistone, has become paralyzed in a riding accident. After talking with Kharkoff, Imogen realizes that she loves the person, not the body, and decides that she is capable of marrying and caring for an invalid; such relationships would be problematic in Hichens's world, and Sir Hugo solves the problem by committing suicide. Despite Hichens's descriptions of the Jewish character Kharkoff as being possessed of a magnificent will, intellect, artistic ability, and ethics, the character is not especially impressive. The book is more interesting as a survey of upper-class English anti-Semitism than as theology.

*The Bacchante and the Nun* is for the most part from the viewpoint of Martin Dale, a short, shy playwright who is bothered by his stature: physically imperfect narrators are rare in Hichens's works. The book describes the stage career of Valentine Morris, a talented actress, the Bacchante of the title, and a character perhaps unique in Hichens's fiction: an unwed mother. After achiev-

ing success as an actress, Valentine renounces her stage career to become a nun, telling Dale via letter that "you have loved a woman who has something in her worth loving, and who wishes to destroy all the rest that is not worth loving, and that a man such as you are cannot love." The perpetually guilty character of Valentine, however, is by no means a Bacchante – her worst behavior involves getting into mild debt and dancing in nightclubs – and she is far less interesting than the theatrical world which she and Dale inhabit, a world populated by greedy and lecherous producers, stupid but sensual actors (one of whom fathered Valentine's child), and talented but exploited playwrights. Hichens was active as a playwright, and the backgrounds of *The Bacchante and the Nun* are frequently convincing.

Like *Mrs. Marden*, *Dr. Artz* has its probable basis in contemporary events, in this case, the glandular grafts performed on Serge Voronoff that were supposed to restore youth and virility. Dr. Artz, in contrast, is successful in his grafts, but the results – elderly patients regaining their ability to indulge in sexual relations – are regarded with horror by the handsome young baritone Carl Fügler, the nominal hero and Hichens's mouthpiece. The bulk of the novel follows the efforts of various men – the wealthy but lecherous and elderly Leon Meyer, the wealthy but lecherous and swarthy Khalil Ibrahim, the wealthy but lecherous and sinister Dr. Artz, the impoverished and pure Carl Fügler – to possess the beautiful young soprano Pauline Iselle, one of the stupidest heroines ever created.

*The First Lady Brendon* is dourly pessimistic: Lady Ivy Brendon leaves her rotter of a husband while vacationing in Egypt, returns to England, divorces Lord Brendon, and marries a former flame, Dr. Mervyn Cleeve. While vacationing in Marseille, the pregnant Ivy Cleeve happens to meet her former husband, who looks intently at her: "She felt as if those eyes were looking with menace on the child, of whose as yet furtive existence he was, she knew, declaring his knowledge . . . A glance at her as she went by, a glance sent to her when he supposed her to be a stranger, and in an instant he had realized the child." Young Guy Cleeve is mysteriously like Lord Brendon: handsome, amoral, seductive, destructive. His parents sacrifice themselves for him. Stripped of its social themes and mild element of fantasy, the latter half of the novel is an extended and querulous complaint: children do not behave the way they should; they should accept their parents' lifestyles and values without questioning.

*The Paradine Case: A Novel* (1933) and *The Power to Kill* (1934) feature psychological triangles and mysteries that must be unraveled. *The Paradine Case* is narrated by Sir Malcolm Keane, K.C., who has been hired to defend the handsome Mrs. Ingrid Paradine, accused of murdering her blind war-hero husband; completing the triangle is the elderly and brilliant Judge Horfield, one of Keane's few enemies. It is Keane's misfortune to have to try the Paradine case before Horfield, and it is his worse luck to fall in love with her and believe her innocence. The story is interpretable as the confrontation between sentiment and emotion (Keane), ruthless and amoral sensuality (Mrs. Paradine), and cold and vicious intellect (Horfield), and Keane's case is destroyed when he foolishly attempts the wrong line of defense. In any event there is little doubt of Mrs. Paradine's guilt in the end, and miscarriages of justice do not occur in Hichens's world. After a slow development the climactic courtroom trials are as exciting and convincing as anything Hichens ever wrote, and his conclusion is coldly effective: the Paradine case destroys all who are connected with it.

*The Power to Kill* is less exciting than *The Paradine Case;* neither its characters nor its story are especially interesting. The characters in the triangle represent different characteristics and include the ruthlessly sensual Creole Mrs. Virginia McGarron (passion); the handsome Clarence Van Brinen (sentiment and emotion); and the Lady Leila Astlie (intellect). The story is simple: after wounding Van Brinen in the United States, Virginia McGarron follows him to England after she is freed from prison; she means to possess Clarence for her own, and her earlier shots were fired not in anger but love. Clarence in the meantime has met and married Lady Leila Astlie, and the story's feeble conflict is generated by the narrator's recounting the attempts of the two women to possess and protect the weak-willed Clarence.

*The Sixth of October* is more convincing than *The Power to Kill* and, though overlong, shows Hichens once again in some control of his material. Like *Mrs. Marden, The Sixth of October* involves psychics, but James Barnard, who tells fortunes as "Claudius," may be genuine; he is sincere when he predicts the death within the year of young Lord Robert Burnaby. Barnard is maneuvered into placing an enormous bet that the prediction will come to pass. He cannot afford to lose the money, and as the year progresses and Burnaby shows no signs of ill health, Barnard's tension increases. The notoriety of his wager enables him to find a new girlfriend and to enter higher social circles, but if Burnaby lives Barnard will be put out of business and lose his social status. Furthermore, the notoriety of his wager has enabled Barnard and Burnaby, once professional and client, to establish a curious friendship. With these situations established, Hichens does much to justify how a hitherto decent man can be driven to attempt murder. The conclusion of the novel is surprisingly merciful: Barnard fails at murder and in the process loses the bet, his girlfriend, and Burnaby's friendship. But Burnaby is injured in an airplane accident, leading the general public to believe in the skills of "Claudius."

*Daniel Airlie: A Novel* (1937) and *Secret Information* feature protagonists with secrets. In the former, theatrical star Daniel Airlie's secret is that twenty years earlier, while starving and unemployed, he had stolen a play written by a friend and passed it off as his own work, thus achieving stardom. The friend apparently commits suicide upon discovering this treachery, and Airlie becomes haunted by a sense of guilt that leads him to reject the affections and blight the career of his late friend's widow. The story is verbosely told and, like the earlier and more simply narrated *The Bacchante and the Nun,* is more interesting for detailing the workings of the English theater than for the depths of its characters.

The Reverend Canon Bankton's secret in *Secret Information* is his enjoyment of erotic literature. He makes the mistake of preaching a sermon on a text drawn from Frank Harris's *My Life and Loves* (1927), and its source is recognized. For most of the novel, Bankton attempts to dispose of the trunkload of books that once brought him pleasure. An attempt at having his servant Grader sell the collection fails, and Bankton is reduced to throwing the books from the bridges of London, until the police start to question his activities. *Secret Information* is perhaps Hichens's funniest novel, but the book is not intended as humor, and Hichens, who places D. H. Lawrence's *Lady Chatterley's Lover* (1928) and Thomas Mann's *Death in Venice* (1925) in Bankton's trunk, resolves the situation primly: to make amends Bankton finally burns the remnants of his collection and joins an ascetic sect. Hichens's message, once again, is that sexuality, however concealed, leads only to disaster; it must be eradicated.

Hichens's last major novels were *Veils* (1944) and *Too Much Love of Living: A Novel* (1947). They reveal the author to be both weary and out of step with his contemporaries but still trying gamely to write salable material. *Veils* begins during the closing days of World War I, when Dorothea Sutton

117

*Robert Smythe Hichens (Hulton-Deutsch Collection)*

meets, marries, and enjoys a brief honeymoon with Nicholas Brand. While Brand is at the front, Dorothea meets Ilario Scaletta, an Italian some years her senior, and enjoys a chaste relationship with him that she breaks off when she learns that Nicholas has been injured; she has been, however, pregnant since their honeymoon. Nicholas returns from the war emasculated and minus a leg (echoing the situation of *Lady Chatterley's Lover*), and the action moves to Italy, where the Brands happen to stay in the villa owned by Ilario's family. Discovering that his wife knew Ilario but attempted to conceal their friendship, Nicholas commits suicide. Dorothea raises their daughter, Cynthia, occasionally indulging in affairs with Ilario but ending the relationship when Cynthia is young, lest the girl become corrupted. As the years pass Dorothea's love for Ilario withers. When the teenage Cynthia vacations in the United States, Dorothea hikes through Europe, meeting and starting an affair with the younger Jeffrey van Rennesler. Upon her return Cynthia discovers Dorothea's secret and is so horrified and dis-

gusted that she renounces her mother and, in effect, forces Dorothea back into her unhappy and unwanted relationship with the ailing but faithful Ilario. The story is remarkably cruel toward Nicholas and the hapless Dorothea, but despite the attempt at being modern, Hichens's warnings about the perils of sexuality remain essentially unchanged from the work he was producing nearly fifty years earlier.

By the time he wrote *Too Much Love of Living* Hichens may have realized that he had outlived his popularity, for the domineering Lord Illington of the novel is a writer whose successes and best work are all past but who is nevertheless reluctant to step aside for a younger generation, represented by his son, Lionel, a talented poet forced into a career in banking. Lionel writes his poetry pseudonymously and falls in love with an American heiress named Pixie Lisle-Stevens. Lionel's poetry wins a major prize and the revelation of his identity briefly estranges his angry father. Though Pixie and Lionel consummate their affection, their relationship does

not last. Lionel devotes his energies to romance and neglects his art, but Pixie will remain only with men strong enough to reject her charms long enough to create. She leaves Lionel, and the lonely poet eventually commits suicide.

The novel's theme of the talented artist destroyed by physical desires is typical of Hichens's work, but the story's ending is oddly ambivalent. The closing pages of *Too Much Love of Living* introduce the poet Alphonse Alladier, who has hitherto been present only as a name. Though Pixie has by then married the millionaire Ellis Van Drenten, Alladier is the father of her child, and he is presented as a vital, creative alternative to Lionel's doomed behavior. Another interesting note is provided by the fact that Alladier and Pixie are foreigners resident in England, with its possibly unintentional thematic suggestion that the future of the arts in England would come from abroad.

After several years of declining health and gradually diminishing output, Robert Hichens died on 20 July 1950 in Zurich. Obituaries were laudatory, but they are unanimous in identifying him as the author of *The Green Carnation, The Garden of Allah,* and *Bella Donna;* his many later works are either ignored or mentioned only in passing and as a group. This situation is not likely to change: although they tend to be lengthy, Hichens's early works remain relatively lively and are enjoyable as fiction, a situation not always true of his later works. Nevertheless, Hichens deserves credit for

perseverance and endurance. Although he was repetitive and often weak as a writer, he made the most of his gifts and outlasted virtually all of his contemporaries. Hichens had nothing substantial to offer, but he remained near the forefront of a highly competitive field for an astonishingly long time.

**Interview:**

"The Reader: Robert S. Hichens," *Bookman* (September 1908): 209–217.

**References:**

Arthur St. John Adcock, *The Glory that Was Grub Street: Impressions of Contemporary Authors* (London: Sampson Low, Marston, 1928): 105–114;

E. F. Bleiler, "Robert Hichens" in *Twentieth-Century Romance & Historical Writers,* second edition, edited by L. Henderson (Chicago: St. James, 1990): 317–319;

Claud Cockburn, *Bestseller: The Books that Everyone Read, 1900–1939* (London: Sidgwick & Jackson, 1972): 43–64;

Brian Stableford, "Robert Hichens" in *Supernatural Fiction Writers: Fantasy and Horror,* edited by Bleiler (New York: Scribners, 1985): 415–420;

Stanley Weintraub, Introduction to *The Green Carnation* (Lincoln: University of Nebraska Press, 1970): i–xxviii;

Harold Williams, *Modern English Writers: Being a Study of Imaginative Literature, 1890–1914* (New York: Knopf, 1919).

# William Hope Hodgson

*(15 November 1877 – 19 April 1918)*

C. J. Keep
*Queen's University*

See also the Hodgson entry in *DLB 70: British Mystery Writers, 1860–1919.*

BOOKS: *The Boats of the "Glen Carrig"* (London: Chapman & Hall, 1907);

*The House on the Borderland* (London: Chapman & Hall, 1908; Westport, Conn.: Hyperion, 1976);

*The Ghost Pirates* (London: Stanley Paul, 1909; Westport, Conn.: Hyperion, 1976);

*The Ghost Pirates, A Chaunty and Another Story* (New York: Reynolds, 1909);

*Carnacki, The Ghost Finder, and a Poem* (New York: Reynolds, 1910);

*The Nightland* (London: Nash, 1912; Westport, Conn.: Hyperion, 1976);

*Poems and the Dream of X* (London: Watt, 1912; New York: Paget, 1912);

*Carnacki, The Ghost Finder* (London: Nash, 1913; enlarged edition, Sauk City, Wis.: Mycroft & Moran, 1947);

*Men of the Deep Waters* (London: Nash, 1914);

*Cargunka and Poems and Anecdotes* (London: Watt, 1914; New York: Paget, 1914);

*The Luck of the Strong* (London: Nash, 1916);

*Captain Gault, Being the Exceedingly Private Log of a Sea-Captain* (London: Nash, 1917; New York: McBride, 1918);

*The Calling of the Sea* (London: Selwyn & Blount, 1920);

*The Voice of the Ocean* (London: Selwyn & Blount, 1921).

**Editions:** *The House on the Borderland and Other Novels* (Sauk City, Wis.: Arkham House, 1946);

*Deep Waters* (Sauk City, Wis.: Arkham House, 1967);

*Out of the Storm: Uncollected Fantasies* (West Kingston, R.I.: Grant, 1975);

*Poems of the Sea* (London: Ferret Fantasy, 1977).

Though primarily a writer of the mysteries and horrors of life at sea, William Hope Hodgson is

*William Hope Hodgson, circa 1907 (Hulton-Deutsch Collection)*

best remembered for two apocalyptic fantasies that presaged the terminal landscapes of later twentieth-century literature. *The House on the Borderland* (1908) and *The Nightland* (1912) are widely regarded as classics of both the science-fiction and horror genres, and several of Hodgson's often-anthologized short stories have been acclaimed for their ability to sustain a steadily mounting pitch of terror. Though enthusiastically received by the press at the time of publication, Hodgson's novels sold poorly and fell into obscurity after his untimely death. Recent reprintings, however, have introduced the author's work to the wider readership he deserves.

William Hope Hodgson was born in Blackmore End, Essex, England, on 15 November 1877.

He was the second of twelve children. His father, Samuel Hodgson, was an Anglican clergyman whose variance from official church doctrine resulted in the family's moving regularly from parish to parish, principally in the industrial towns of northern England. His mother, Lissie Sarah Brown Hodgson, was devoted to her husband and hoped William would follow him into the clergy. Her hopes were dashed, however, when, at the age of thirteen, the boy ran away from his boarding school to pursue a life at sea. He was eventually apprenticed as a cabin boy and was forced to remain in the mercantile marine for eight years by the financial necessities arising from his father's death in 1892. Hodgson completed his apprenticeship in 1895 and spent the following two years studying for his mate's certificate, his only formal higher education. During a passage to New Zealand in 1898, he rescued a shipmate from shark-infested waters and was awarded the Royal Humane Society medal for heroism.

Hodgson's years at sea left an indelible mark on him. In an 1899 article for the *Grand Magazine* he described the seaman's lot as a "comfortless, weariful and thankless life – a life compact of hardness and sordidness such as shore people can scarcely conceive." His intense antipathy for everything connected with the sea is obsessively reenacted in his work, particularly in his short stories. In "Out of the Storm" (1909), for example, the sea is referred to throughout as simply the "Thing" and is deplored as a ravenous and unrelenting force seeking to drag humanity down into its depths.

Despite his aversion to it, seafaring provided Hodgson with the ghastly images and sailor's lore which would form the basic materials of his fiction. Moreover, it was during his years as a sailor on commercial vessels that he was to acquire two other passions which would inflect his work, photography and bodybuilding. The former was his chief creative outlet during the 1890s, and his camera, like his fiction, recorded the more malevolent aspects of life at sea, from the maggots in the mates' food to the passing of a ship through the vortex of a cyclone. He would later use slides of his photographs to accompany the series of public lectures that he gave to supplement his earnings as an author. Later still they would appear as illustrations for his well-received nonfiction articles concerning naval weather phenomena.

Hodgson's preoccupation with "physical culture" resulted in part from necessity. When first apprenticed at the age of thirteen, he had the misfortune of serving under a brutal and apparently sadistic second mate who made the boy's misery his pleasure. Being relatively short (he stood five foot, five inches), and possessed of a gentle demeanor, bodybuilding was Hodgson's only way of defending himself from the physical attacks to which he was persistently subjected. In the years that followed, he became a devotee of Eugene Sandow, "the world's strongest man," and developed an impressive physique of his own. In 1899 he finally left the sea behind him and, returning to the family home in the small industrial city of Blackburn, set up "W. H. Hodgson's School of Physical Culture." The school only survived two years, but from this experience came his first serious published work, "Physical Culture versus Recreative Exercises," in *Sandow's Magazine* in 1903. Subsequent articles on physical culture followed, both for *Sandow's Magazine* and other, more mainstream periodicals.

If Hodgson's interest in bodybuilding arose from necessity, it also dovetailed with many of the deeper anxieties and phobias that dominated his imagination. His devotion to physical culture was an attempt to fortify his body not only against shipboard bullies but also the insurgencies of life itself. A hypochondriac who, despite his massive physique, always washed his hands after opening mail for fear of germs, Hodgson was obsessed with the threat of physical pollution, of the invasion of the stronghold of the body by the forces of corruption. Not coincidentally, these forces are regularly associated in his fiction with the sea and, in particular, with the fungi, slugs, weeds, crabs, and octopods that proliferate there.

An avid reader of Edgar Allan Poe, H. G. Wells, Jules Verne, and Edward Bulwer-Lytton, Hodgson turned to writing supernatural horror stories and occult mysteries as he looked to expand his literary horizons. His first fiction sale was a forgettable short story called "The Goddess of Death," which appeared in the April 1904 *Royal Magazine* and described the murder in a small English town of a dozen people – apparently by a statue of the goddess Kali. The real murderer is finally revealed to be a Hindu assassin looking to revenge the removal of the statue from its rightful place.

Other stories followed, including "From the Tideless Sea" (1906), the first – and one of the best – of his many stories concerning the Sargasso Sea. Sailors had long told tales of the Sargasso, a floating continent of weeds in the mid Atlantic, but Hodgson developed a complex and compelling mythos around it that provided the setting for some of his most outstanding fiction. In this story a small wooden keg is found containing a letter written by a

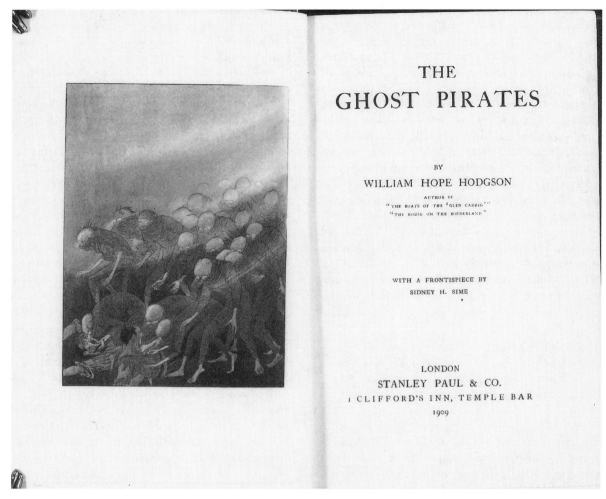

THE
GHOST PIRATES

BY
WILLIAM HOPE HODGSON
AUTHOR OF
"THE BOATS OF THE 'GLEN CARRIG'"
"THE HOUSE ON THE BORDERLAND"

WITH A FRONTISPIECE BY
SIDNEY H. SIME

LONDON
STANLEY PAUL & CO.
1 CLIFFORD'S INN, TEMPLE BAR
1909

*Frontispiece and title page for Hodgson's second novel, the story of a ship trapped between dimensions (courtesy of the Lilly Library, Indiana University)*

man trapped on a derelict in the middle of the Sargasso with his wife and child. The letter details their struggles against giant octopuses and other unseen horrors that attack the ship each night. The survivors fortify their vessel against the attacks from without, but they know that they are beyond rescue. Eventually their food will run out — and with it their struggle against the Sargasso.

With stories such as "From the Tideless Sea"; its sequel, "More News From The Homebird"; and "The Mystery of the Derelict," Hodgson had by 1907 acquired a name for himself as a skilled purveyor of the macabre. He joined the Society for Authors, contributing regularly to its monthly magazine for members, the *Author,* and was regularly consulted on affairs and controversies concerning the mercantile marine. In order to consolidate his standing as a respected writer, he turned to writing his first novel, *The Boats of the "Glen Carrig"* (1907).

Written in a mock eighteenth-century style (including the requisite extended subtitle), the story is a further installment in the Sargasso Sea mythos. In the first segment (which appears to have been a short story that Hodgson decided to extend to novel length) the survivors of a shipwreck land on an island populated only by strange trees that seem to have animal forms and human faces embedded in them. At night they are attacked by unseen monsters, while the trees wail and moan. The narrator, John Winterstraw, and his companions escape after struggling with a forest of the living tree-things and make their way to a second island, where they are attacked by the Weed Men, humanoid slugs with upturned beaks and tentacles that suck the blood from any living creature. Once again, the members of the crew find themselves in a nightly battle. They soon discover, however, that the derelict vessel trapped in the weed-festooned bay is inhabited by

the remnants of its crew and passengers. Winterstraw and the group's de facto leader, the stalwart boatswain, finally conceive a way of freeing the vessel, and the united groups repulse a final onslaught before making their way back to the open sea and then to England.

The novel displays many of the weaknesses of Hodgson's writing: thin characterization, a negligible plot line, and a penchant for archaisms. Nevertheless, *The Boats of the "Glen Carrig"* is able to evoke a tone of unrelieved terror throughout. Brian Stableford accurately describes it as "primarily an exercise in teratology, made highly effective by the careful combination of the realistic details derived from Hodgson's own experiences at sea and the particular horrific *frisson* connected with the mingling of human and animal characteristics."

Published by the respected publishing house of Chapman and Hall in 1907, the novel received favorable reviews, with Hodgson often being compared to Daniel Defoe, Poe, and Wells. The *Bookman,* for example, claimed "Mr. Hope Hodgson writes with an amazingly vivid imaginative power, and a skill in the handling of eerie incidents, the creation of bizarre effects, and the atmosphere of nameless horror and terror, that bear comparison with the . . . most haunting things that even Poe accomplished."

Buoyed by the good reviews for *The Boats of the "Glen Carrig"* and undeterred by its poor sales, Hodgson began writing his second novel. The opening action of *The House on the Borderland* takes place in Ireland, where Hodgson had spent some of his childhood. Two English tourists discover a manuscript in the ruins of a huge house standing on a promontory that looks over a deep chasm. The manuscript relates the story of an unnamed recluse who had lived with his elderly sister in the house many years previously. As with his first novel, Hodgson's *The House on the Borderland* is less a tightly plotted adventure story than a series of loosely connected episodes held together by the author's ability to adumbrate the dimly perceived terrors of the unconscious. The first episode rehearses Hodgson's fascination with the topos of invasion from without. The author of the manuscript finds himself besieged in his house by legions of enormously strong humanoid creatures with the faces of pigs. Before the siege the narrator had briefly glimpsed the Swine-Things in a hallucinatory journey he had taken to the Plain of Silence, an otherworldly place where giant idols of the ancient gods Kali and Seth look down on an exact replica of the house in which he lives. The man repulses the attack of the Swine-Things and traces them to their lair deep in the earth. His house, it seems, stands at some juncture of this world and the next, a nexus through which the forces of decay and corruption, embodied in the pig creatures, may enter the mortal sphere.

There follows what is justifiably considered the centerpiece of the novel, the recluse's disembodied journey through time to the end of the solar system. The passage owes its description of time passing like a blazing river to Wells's *The Time Machine* (1895) and some of its symbolism to Poe's visionary 1848 essay "Eureka," but it transcends its influences. The sun is first caught in the orbit of the giant green sun at the center of the universe and then plunges to a fiery death while the recluse looks on. A great number of whitish "Celestial Globes" are then released from the heart of the green sun, one of which engulfs him; there he is reunited for a time with his long-dead loved one. Returning to his own time, he finds that his dog, wounded in the attack by the Swine-Things, has been infected by an iridescent fungus. He shoots the animal, only to discover that he has contracted the disease as well; the forces of putrefaction have penetrated his body. The manuscript breaks off as the Swine-Things renew their attack and breach the door of the room in which the narrator writes.

*The House on the Borderland* marks a major advance in Hodgson's development as a writer. The preoccupations of his earlier works – invasion from without, bodily pollution, and the return of a dead love object – are reworked here into an elaborate private symbology, the nature of which is indicated in his preface. In the guise of the book's editor he writes: "I cannot but look upon the account of the Celestial Globes as a striking illustration . . . of the actuality of our thoughts and emotions among the Realities. For . . . it enlightens one with conceptions of the existence of worlds of thought and emotion, working in conjunction with, and duly subject to, the scheme of material creation." The recluse's psychic journeys, like those of William Blake's Mental Traveller, are highly allegorical: they reveal Hodgson's growing conception of a universe bound by a higher plane – not simply of Platonic ideals, but of emotion and memory. Even these realms, however, are beset by the forces of malevolence.

The novel was universally praised by contemporary reviewers. Its vision of the death of the solar system has since been singled out by many critics as a high point in the development of science fiction and supernatural horror, an expansion of the very breadth of the imagination's capabilities. In his sur-

*Dust jacket for the Arkham House omnibus edition of Hodgson's novels, published in 1946 (courtesy of the Lilly Library, Indiana University)*

vey of horror fiction, H. P. Lovecraft calls *The House on the Borderland* "perhaps the greatest of all Mr. Hodgson's works," noting that the "wanderings of the narrator's spirit through limitless light-years of cosmic space and Kalpas of eternity, and its witnessing of the solar system's final destruction, constitute something almost unique in standard literature."

Hodgson had begun his writing career with an eye to what would sell. But with *The House on the Borderland* he strayed considerably from the mainstream in his attempt to give full voice to his private vision. He continued to sell short stories, such as the mystical "The Shamraken Homeward" (1908), to the monthly magazines, but none of his novels were ever serialized – perhaps an effort on Hodgson's part to ensure that his artistic integrity not be diluted by the exigencies of serialization. If so, it

was a career decision that must have greatly hampered his pocketbook. A glimpse of both Hodgson's dedication to his writing and his personality is provided by his friend, Arthur St. John Adcock, the editor of the *Bookman*. Adcock recalled that when he met Hodgson in 1909, the latter had "already given himself so entirely and enthusiastically to a literary career that the talk was wholly of books and his hopes as an author. He aimed high, and, taking his art very seriously, had a frank unaffected confidence in his powers which was partly the splendid arrogance of youth and partly the heritage of experience, for he had tested and proved them." Adcock's friendship was to prove important, for it not only secured Hodgson work writing several book reviews for the *Bookman,* but it also resulted in his novels being regularly (and favorably) reviewed there.

*The House on the Borderland,* however, fared little better in the stores than did its predecessor. Hodgson was forced to find a new publisher for his next work and to accept a less favorable contract. For *The Ghost Pirates* (1909) he returned to a setting at sea, but the novel's tale of a ship caught between dimensions, unable to get back to its own and attacked by beings from the next, suffered the same fate as *The Boats of the "Glen Carrig"* and *The House on the Borderland:* good reviews but poor sales. In his preface Hodgson described *The Ghost Pirates* as completing a trilogy begun with his first two novels. The connection between the works seems slight at first – they share none of the same characters or locales and are widely separated in time – but becomes greater on closer inspection. *The Ghost Pirates* makes explicit a theme implicit in, but no less central to, his earlier novels, the permeability of reality itself. "I should say it's reasonable to think that all the things of the material world are barred," the novel's narrator says, "from the immaterial; but that in some cases the barrier may be broken down." We are not secure, Hodgson suggests, from the forces of corruption seeking to break into this world from the other dimensions with which we share the same space, and it is this theme that links his trilogy.

The failure of his attempt to establish himself on an equal footing with the other successful writers of fantastic fiction he admired, such as Wells, found Hodgson turning increasingly to hackwork to make a living. The first evidence of this was a series of mystery stories featuring Carnacki the Occult Detective. Written for the *Idler,* where they appeared during the first half of 1910, the Carnacki stories were little better than pastiches of the work of Ar-

thur Conan Doyle and Algernon Blackwood. In each episode the Occult Detective is called in to investigate a supernatural phenomenon, which, with aid of a magic pentacle and a camera, he invariably explains. Carnacki, however, has little of the charm of John Silence, Blackwood's occult detective, and the stories are particularly hampered by Hodgson's ill-conceived attempts at humor. The series was collected as *Carnacki, The Ghost Finder* (1913).

From 1910 to 1912 Hodgson turned out many workmanlike efforts besides the Carnacki stories, including another of the Sargasso Sea stories, "The Thing in the Weeds" (1912). The eccentric, vaguely forbidding figure Hodgson presented in the editorial offices of Fleet Street is humorously captured in the biographical note accompanying one of his stories in the *London Magazine:* "In spite of being an author who likes the night hours for working, and in spite of his cadaverous looks and abnormally fluid imagination, Hodgson is terribly muscular and takes as much pride in his biceps as his stories. He is a confirmed egotist, who loves to talk about himself, and he is as argumentative as a Scotchman."

Published in April 1912 (though it may have been written as early as 1906), Hodgson's last novel, *The Nightland,* is also his finest achievement. In stark contrast to his market-oriented magazine work, *The Nightland* is an uncompromisingly personal effort: longer than his three earlier novels combined, and written in an ornate prose style that is a strange hybrid of seventeenth-century language and the biblical Book of Revelation, it has been variously described as "virtually unreadable" and "one of the most potent pieces of macabre imagination ever written."

Typical of Hodgson's fiction, the main action is contained within a frame narrative. In the seventeenth century a young man falls in love with a woman, and they marry. She dies in childbirth, but in his dreams the narrator sees her again. The locale shifts to the remote future. The sun is dead, and night reigns eternal over the earth, relieved only by the slight emanations of something called the "earth current." The last remnants of mankind are gathered in the Great Redoubt, a giant pyramid, which towers seven miles above the twilit landscape and extends one hundred miles beneath the surface. There the narrator receives a telepathic message from a woman in another pyramid, the Lesser Redoubt, whose existence had long been forgotten. The woman, Naani, is a reincarnation of his first love, Lady Mirdath. Overcome by his desire to be reunited with her, the narrator ventures out into the Nightland, a treacherous, inhospitable world where

the barriers between the dimensions have broken down and bizarre, malignant demons rule. Only direct quotation can begin to indicate both the horrors of this world and the flavor of the elaborate descriptive style with which Hodgson depicts them:

> And so, searching the road with my gaze, I passed beyond this Silent One, and past the place where the road, sweeping vastly to the South-East, was lit a space, strangely, by the light from the Silver-fire Holes. And thus at last to where it swayed . . . around to the Westward, beyond the mountain bulk of the Watching Thing in the South – the hugest monster in all the visible Night Lands. My spy-glass showed it to me with clearness – a living hill of watchfulness, known to us as the Watcher Of The South. It brooded there, squat and tremendous, hunched over the pale radiance of the Glowing Dome.

After many trials and tribulations the narrator arrives at the Lesser Redoubt only to find that it has already fallen and its denizens have been massacred. Naani, however, has survived, and the two make their way back across the Nightland. When they return to the Great Redoubt they find it besieged by legions of Night Hounds. They fight their way through to the pyramid, but Naani dies in the attempt; however, she is revived by being placed in the stream of the earth current.

While critics have been unanimous in deploring its length (a condensed version titled *A Dream of X* appeared in 1912) and its tiresome prose style, *The Nightland* is a recognized masterpiece of its kind. The early reviews described it as a tour de force, an opinion upheld by later critics. Writing in 1944, Clark Ashton Smith claims that despite its faults, the book "impresses the reader as being the ultimate saga of a perishing cosmos, the last epic of a world beleaguered by eternal night and by the unvisageable spawn of darkness." *The Nightland* takes many of Hodgson's favorite themes to their logical limit. His fascination with eschatology, with the breakdown of the barriers protecting the mundane world from the evil without, and an erotic preoccupation with the recovery of a dead love object resurface in this work with dramatic intensity, lending it a kind of compulsive edge that even the author's distended prose cannot blunt.

Easily the least commercial of Hodgson's novels, *The Nightland* predictably failed to reverse the popular fortunes of his earlier efforts. Disappointed nonetheless, and perhaps becoming resigned to his second-rank status, Hodgson returned to producing fodder for magazines. He proved himself adept not only at sea adventures – the best of which were col-

lected in *Men of the Deep Waters* (1914) and *The Luck of the Strong* (1916) — but also at love stories, historical romances, detective fiction, and even Westerns. In 1913 he met Betty Farnworth, a staff writer for the woman's magazine *Home Notes.* According to his biographer, Sam Moskowitz, Hodgson had previously been seriously involved with two other women, but lack of financial resources and class standing had prevented marriage. But at the age of thirty-six, as an established writer who regularly sold his work in both the British and American markets, Hodgson felt ready to make a commitment. He was married on 26 February 1914 in London, and the couple subsequently took up residence in the south of France.

At the outbreak of war they returned to England, and Hodgson joined the University of London's Officers' Training Corps. He refused to return to the merchant marine and instead opted for the artillery. Commissioned as a lieutenant in 1915, he was thrown from a horse while serving in France in 1916 and badly injured. The injury was severe enough to merit a mandatory discharge, but Hodgson reenlisted and was killed in action in April 1918 near Ypres.

Throughout his life Hodgson had written poems, but only a few had been accepted for publication. Some of the best he used as epigraphs for his novels, including one fine imitation of Poe, "Grief," which was added to *The House on the Borderland.* After his death his wife paid to have two collections of his poetry, *The Calling of the Sea* (1920) and *The Voice of the Ocean* (1921), published in editions of five hundred copies each. But beyond a small circle of admirers, Hodgson's work was forgotten. His work was revived in America through the efforts of two editors, August Derleth and H. C. Koenig, who produced an omnibus edition of his first two novels

and *The Nightland* in 1946. Two collections of his short stories have since been published: *Deep Waters* (1967) and *Out of the Storm: Uncollected Fantasies* (1975), the latter especially notable for editor Sam Moskowitz's extensive biographical introduction.

Today Hodgson's reputation rests largely on the secular apocalypticism of *The House on the Borderland* and *The Nightland,* the influence of which can be noted in the work of Olaf Stapledon, C. S. Lewis, Michael Moorcock, and many other prophets of the end of the world. Lacking the education that allowed Wells to enter into the mainstream of intellectual discourse, Hodgson remained, as Stableford notes, "a remarkable amalgam of hard-headed professional and inwardly driven amateur." Flawed though they may be, Hodgson's novels and short stories often transcend their limitations of style and succeed in conveying the reader to places of undreamt horror and wonder.

**References:**

Arthur St. John Adcock, introduction to Hodgson's *The Calling of the Sea* (London: Selwyn & Blount, 1920), pp. 3–6;

H. P. Lovecraft, *Supernatural Horror in Literature* (New York: Dover, 1973), pp. 82–85;

Sam Moskowitz, "William Hope Hodgson," in Hodgson's *Out of the Storm: Uncollected Fantasies* (West Kingston, R.I.: Grant, 1975), pp. 9–138;

Clark Ashton Smith, "In Appreciation of William Hope Hodgson" in *Planets and Dimensions: Collected Essays of Clark Ashton Smith,* edited by Charles K. Wolfe (New York: Mirage Press, 1973), pp. 46–47;

Brian Stableford, *Scientific Romance in Britain 1890–1950* (London: Fourth Estate, 1985), pp. 91–102.

# Anthony Hope
## (Sir Anthony Hope Hawkins)
*(9 February 1863 – 8 July 1933)*

Ellen Miller Casey
*University of Scranton*

BOOKS: *A Man of Mark* (London: Remington, 1890; New York: Holt, 1895);

*Father Stafford* (London: Cassell, 1891; New York: Cassell, 1891);

*Mr. Witt's Widow* (London: Innes, 1892; New York & Chicago: U.S. Book, 1892);

*Sport Royal and Other Stories* (London: Innes, 1893; New York: Munro, 1895);

*A Change of Air* (London: Methuen, 1893; New York: Holt, 1894);

*Half a Hero* (London: Innes, 1893; New York: Harper, 1893);

*The God in the Car* (London: Methuen, 1894; New York: Appleton, 1894);

*The Prisoner of Zenda: Being the History of Three Months in the Life of an English Gentleman* (Bristol: Arrowsmith, 1894; New York: Holt, 1894);

*The Indiscretion of the Duchess: Being a Story Concerning Two Ladies, a Nobleman, and a Necklace* (Bristol: Arrowsmith, 1894; New York: Holt, 1894);

*The Dolly Dialogues* (London: Westminster Gazette, 1894; New York: Holt, 1894);

*The Chronicles of Count Antonio* (London: Methuen, 1895; New York: Appleton, 1895);

*Comedies of Courtship* (London: Innes, 1896; New York: Scribners, 1896);

*The Heart of Princess Osra and Other Stories* (London: Longmans, Green, 1896; New York & London: Stokes, 1896);

*Phroso* (New York: Stokes, 1896; London: Methuen, 1897);

*Simon Dale* (New York: Stokes, 1897; London: Methuen, 1898);

*Rupert of Hentzau: Being a Sequel to the Story by the Same Writer Entitled The Prisoner of Zenda* (Bristol: Arrowsmith, 1898; New York: Holt, 1898);

*The King's Mirror* (London: Methuen, 1899; New York: Appleton, 1899);

*Quisanté* (London: Methuen, 1900; New York: Stokes, 1900);

*Anthony Hope (Sir Anthony Hope Hawkins; photograph by Ernest K. Mills)*

*Captain Dieppe* (New York: Doubleday & McClure, 1900; London: Skeffington, 1918);

*Tristram of Blent* (London: Murray, 1901; New York: McClure, Phillips, 1901);

*The Intrusions of Peggy* (London: Smith, Elder, 1902; New York & London: Harper, 1902);

*Double Harness* (London: Hutchinson, 1904; New York: McClure, Phillips, 1904);

*A Servant of the Public* (London: Methuen, 1905; New York: Stokes, 1905);

*Sophy of Kravonia* (Bristol: Arrowsmith, 1905; New York & London: Harper, 1905);

*Tales of Two People* (London: Methuen, 1907);

*Helena's Path* (New York: McClure, 1907);

*Love's Logic, and Other Stories* (New York: McClure, 1908);

*The Great Miss Driver* (London: Methuen, 1908; New York: McClure, 1908);

*Dialogue* (Oxford: English Association, 1909);

*Second String* (London & New York: Nelson, 1910; Garden City, N.Y.: Doubleday, Page, 1910);

*Mrs. Maxon Protests* (London: Methuen, 1911; New York & London: Harper, 1911);

*The New (German) Testament: Some Texts and a Commentary* (London: Methuen, 1914; New York: Appleton, 1915);

*The Fleet of Mercy* (New York: N.p., 1915);

*Impressions d'un touriste en France* (London: Darling, 1915);

*A Young Man's Year* (London: Methuen, 1915; New York: Appleton, 1915);

*Beaumaroy Home from the Wars* (London: Methuen, 1919); published as *The Secret of the Tower* (New York: Appleton, 1919);

*Lucinda* (London: Hutchinson, 1920; New York: Appleton, 1920);

*Little Tiger* (London: Hutchinson, 1925; New York: Doran, 1925);

*Memories and Notes* (London: Hutchinson, 1927; Garden City, N.Y.: Doubleday, Doran, 1928).

SELECTED PLAY PRODUCTIONS: *The Adventure of Lady Ursula,* New York, Lyceum Theatre, 1 September 1898; London, Duke of York's Theatre, 11 October 1898;

*English Nell,* by Hope and Edward Rose, London, August 1900;

*Pilkerton's Peerage,* London, Garrick Theatre, 28 January 1902.

Sir Anthony Hope Hawkins, who wrote all his fiction as Anthony Hope, is best known as the author of *The Prisoner of Zenda* (1894). While the popularity of this novel eclipsed that of all his other works, Hawkins also wrote more serious novels of analysis. All his work demonstrates a command of dialogue and an acute observation of character. While Hawkins was one of the most popular novelists of the late nineteenth and early twentieth centuries, his popularity declined after World War I because he found invention more difficult as he grew older and because his novels worked best in a society with clear rules, whether observed or broken.

Anthony Hope Hawkins was born in Clapton on 9 February 1863, the second son and third child of the Reverend Edwards Comerford Hawkins and Jane Isabella Grahame Hawkins. Reverend Hawkins was headmaster of Saint John's Foundation School for the Sons of Poor Clergy. At thirteen Hawkins left Saint John's and went to Marlborough, where he became a noted athlete, president of the debating society, and an editor of the school newspaper, the *Marlburian.*

Hawkins won a grant, later converted to a scholarship, to Balliol College, Oxford, where he earned first class degrees in classics (1882) and humane letters (1885). He was a member of the college rugby team and stayed an additional term to serve as president of the Union. After leaving Oxford in 1886, Hawkins lived for the next seventeen years at Saint Bride's Church in Fleet Street where his widowed father was vicar. In 1887 he was called to the bar, but his law practice was slow in starting; he did not receive his first important legal work until 1889. After working all day on law, Hawkins spent his evenings "scribbling" newspaper articles and stories. As he wrote in his diary, his heart was prey to conflicting allegiances; its "legitimate occupants . . . Madame Law and Lady Politics" had been joined by "an unsanctified slut . . . Miss Literature."

In 1890 Hawkins published at his own expense his first novel, *A Man of Mark.* A cynical tale of adventure about a small-scale revolution in an imaginary South American republic, Aureataland, *A Man of Mark* cost the author fifty pounds but earned only thirteen. It was signed "Anthony Hope," a fact he later regretted: "I mistakenly contracted an alias early in life and have never been able to get rid of it."

By 1890 Hawkins's law practice was finally making progress, but success still seemed a long way off. In June 1891 he agreed to stand for Parliament as a Liberal for South Buckinghamshire, but he was "soundly thrashed" by 1,042 votes in the Conservative constituency. He would be asked twice more to stand, in 1895 and 1900. He declined the first time and was forced to resign the second time because of ill health, leaving him with a "gentle regret" that he never sat in Parliament.

After being rejected by six publishers, Hawkins's second novel, *Father Stafford,* was published by Cassell in October 1891. The story of an ascetic but fashionable Anglo-Catholic priest told by an amiable and cynical narrator, *Father Stafford* received much more attention than its predecessor, including a two-column review in the *Spectator.* Despite this attention, the novel did not earn any

money; as of December 1891 only 199 copies had been sold.

Hawkins's third novel, *Mr. Witt's Widow,* appeared in March 1892. The engagement of Neaera Witt, the widow of a Manchester merchant, to Gerald Neston, the son of a peer, is complicated when Gerald's lawyer cousin recognizes her as a pauper he once defended for stealing a pair of shoes. Called by the London *Times* "a brilliant little tale," the novel possesses easy humor and a deft plot.

Increasingly Hawkins was spending his time on fiction rather than the law. As he wrote in his diary toward the end of 1892: "I almost hate having law now; it's come too late to please me, and it interrupts." He published three books in 1893: a short-story collection titled *Sport Royal* and two novels, *A Change of Air* and *Half a Hero;* in addition *The Dolly Dialogues* was serialized in the *Westminster Gazette.*

*A Change of Air,* the story of Dale Bannister, a poet, bohemian, and radical whose move from London to a dull country district disillusions his former disciples, was a more ambitious work than Hawkins's previous novels. Despite mixed reviews it was the most successful of his early books. *Half a Hero,* like many of Hawkins's novels, combines politics and melodrama as it traces the effect on an imaginary British colony, New Lindsey, when a Labour prime minister comes to power and is finally killed in a riot. The critics complained that the book had "too much politics"; readers seemed to agree, for the novel was not a popular success.

*The Dolly Dialogues,* however, proved extremely popular with readers of the *Westminster Gazette.* Each installment, told entirely in dialogue, details a flirtation between Samuel Carter, a fortyish bachelor, and Dolly Foster, who marries Lord Mickleham. Witty and melancholy, *The Dolly Dialogues* captured exactly the fin de siècle mood of the 1890s and inspired several imitators.

More significant than any of these works was an event that occurred on 28 November 1893; while Hawkins was walking back from the Westminster County Court to the Temple, happy because he had just won a case, the name Ruritania popped into his head. He also passed two men who bore an extraordinary resemblance to each other. When he got back to Brick Court, he lit a pipe and thought about a tale uniting these elements. The next morning he began to write *The Prisoner of Zenda;* he finished the first draft on 29 December.

At this point in his career, despite all his accomplishments and a reasonable amount of acclaim, Hawkins was depressed about his situation. He dis-

*Hawkins in the 1880s, as a student at Oxford*

liked the law more each year, but although his writing had yielded more income than in previous years, it offered no guarantees. In a diary entry dated 22 January 1894 he observes: "I begin the year absolutely *empty* as regards law (against which I am chafing more and more) and therefore money for the scribbling becomes more urgent."

In April 1894 *The Prisoner of Zenda* appeared. Its hero, Rudolf Rassendyll, the red-haired double of the king of Ruritania, assumes the throne when the king is imprisoned by his wicked half brother. Rassendyll is a successful and popular ruler, and he falls in love with Princess Flavia, who is expected to marry the king. Hawkins guessed that it was the combination of royalty and red hair which struck the popular fancy and made the novel an instant best-seller. "Its success," he wrote, "was quick and great."

Hawkins's life was transformed. Robert Louis Stevenson, in a letter found on Stevenson's writing table after his death, congratulated the author on his "very spirited and gallant little book," and the critic Walter Besant hailed Hawkins as the "new

Dumas of the nineteenth century." Based on the success of *The Prisoner of Zenda*, Hawkins employed a literary agent and, after much debate, took the "final plunge" of writing his farewell letters to the bar.

*The Prisoner of Zenda* brought Hawkins fortune as well as fame. No exact figures are available, but 7,000 copies had been sold by June 1894 and about 12,000 by November. In the United States 19,500 copies were sold by December. The novel's popularity created a demand for Hawkins's other works as well. Four different American publishers brought out *A Man of Mark* in 1895, and the previously unsuccessful *Father Stafford* was reprinted sixteen times between 1894 and 1919. *The Prisoner of Zenda* kept selling long after Hawkins's death. In 1934 the original publishers reported that the book was "still very much alive" and the American publisher had recorded sales of 260,000. Five editions of the novel are currently in print. In addition *The Prisoner of Zenda* was made into three silent movies (1912, 1915, 1922) and three sound versions (1937, 1952, 1979). Hawkins judged the 1912 version "interesting, queer, and slightly ridiculous." The best of the six is probably the 1937 version starring Ronald Coleman, Douglas Fairbanks Jr., and Madeleine Carroll. The novel has also been adapted for comic books and inspired a parody by Bret Harte, "Rupert the Resembler, by A-th-y H-pe" (1902), and two musicals, *Princess Flavia* (1925) and *Zenda* (1963).

Hawkins published three more novels in 1894. *The Dolly Dialogues* appeared as a book in September; its widespread popularity was obvious when it merited a parody in *Punch*. *The God in the Car*, Hawkins's most serious novel to that date, appeared the same month. Its protagonist, Willie Ruston, the organizer of the Omofaga Company in southern Africa, fascinates Maggie Dennison, the wife of the dull and decent Harry Dennison, who is Ruston's friend and a major investor. Hawkins's *The Indiscretion of the Duchess*, written for an 1894 Christmas annual, is sufficiently summed up by its subtitle: *Being a Story Concerning Two Ladies, a Nobleman, and a Necklace*.

By the end of 1894 more than one critic had identified "three Mr. Hopes": the Ruritanian romance writer of *The Prisoner of Zenda*, the serious and complex novelist of *The God in the Car*, and the happy trifler of *The Dolly Dialogues*. These three novels epitomize Hawkins's work. His novels are either swashbuckling romances set in "cardboard kingdoms" or more-serious studies of individuals who defy society's rules. Both types share the wit and mastery of dialogue of *The Dolly Dialogues*.

Despite his popularity, Hawkins did not rest. His daily routine was to leave Saint Bride's at 9:30 A.M. and walk to his two small rooms in Buckingham Street where he shared the neighborhood with "charities, companies, caretakers, and cats." He wrote until 1:00, stopped for lunch, and then resumed writing from 2:00 until 5:00. In early 1895 Hawkins finished *Rupert of Hentzau* (1898), the sequel to *The Prisoner of Zenda;* revised a collection of stories, *The Heart of Princess Osra* (1896), and a novel, *Phroso* (1896); and began a new novel, *Simon Dale* (1897). In October *The Chronicles of Count Antonio*, a historical romance about a medieval count, appeared to indifferent reviews. When he reread it in 1913, Hawkins described it as "a lot of *invention*, and a damned lot of 'Ands' and 'Nows' and 'Buts' – pseudo-Scriptural."

In the year 1896 two collections of Hawkins's short stories appeared, *Comedies of Courtship* and *The Heart of Princess Osra*. Each of the nine stories in the latter collection is set in Ruritania before *The Prisoner of Zenda* and describes one of the lovers of Prince Rudolf's sister. The *Manchester Guardian* praised its "happy blending of romantic ideals with modern humour and scepticism." By the end of 1896 Hawkins had earned more than five thousand pounds, but he began to feel discontented with the life of a writer. About this time he met Millicent, Duchess of Sutherland, and began a friendship that lasted until the end of his life. Their extensive correspondence, which echoes the wit of *The Dolly Dialogues*, catalogues Hawkins's "depressions and ascensions."

February 1897 marked the appearance of *Phroso*, the story of Lord Charles Wheatley, who purchases the Greek island Neopalia and whose life is saved by the beautiful Lady Euphrosyne (Phroso) when the natives rebel. The novel is full of sieges, secret passages, and smothered oaths. Years later Hawkins described it as "tosh." In May Hawkins gave a speech for the Royal Institution in which he argued that the essence of romance was that "emotion must be taken at high pitch." He claimed that romance expresses some of the deepest instincts of humanity in their clearest form: "It can give to love an ideal object, to ambition a boundless field, to courage a high occasion." At its best romance "can not only delight men, but can touch them to the very heart." In October Hawkins left on an American speaking tour, an invitation he had accepted "led by curiosity and the hope of gain" and looked forward to with "Horror, Fear, Laziness, Curiosity, Pleasure." He gave over seventy-five lectures between 18 October 1897 and 14 January 1898, travel-

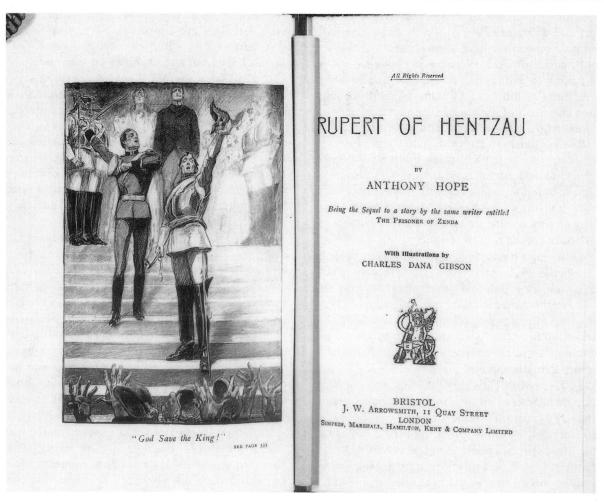

RUPERT OF HENTZAU

BY

ANTHONY HOPE

*Being the Sequel to a story by the same writer entitled*
THE PRISONER OF ZENDA

With Illustrations by
CHARLES DANA GIBSON

BRISTOL
J. W. ARROWSMITH, 11 QUAY STREET
LONDON
SIMPKIN, MARSHALL, HAMILTON, KENT & COMPANY LIMITED

*"God Save the King!"*
SEE PAGE 333

*Frontispiece and title page for Hawkins's sequel to his successful 1894 novel* The Prisoner of Zenda *(courtesy of the Lilly Library, Indiana University)*

ing from Montreal to Richmond and from New York to Minneapolis.

*Simon Dale,* an intricate historical romance featuring Charles II and Nell Gwyn, was published in February 1898 to moderately favorable reviews. *Rupert of Hentzau* came out in July and was an enormous success; by February 1899 it had sold thirty thousand copies in England and sixteen thousand in the United States. At the end of 1898, when Hawkins summed up his situation, he found himself "still in demand" but was experiencing increasing difficulty in inventing new stories. He had made eighty-four hundred pounds during the year and had invested much of it against the day when his popularity should fade.

The frequency of Hawkins's publication was declining. His only work published in 1899 was *The King's Mirror,* which he called "my best book." The introspective Augustin, king of an unnamed coun-

try, describes his lifelong inner conflict between his position and his self. The melancholy king never acts on the passions he feels and finds that "the acid of doubt bit into every axiom." He is a memorable figure and one in which Hawkins invested much of himself. Despite his slowing pace, Hawkins was still prospering. His annual summary notes that he had made "a lot of money": thirteen thousand pounds, of which four thousand came from plays.

Throughout his life Hawkins, who had wanted to be an actor, worked diligently if not always successfully for the stage. He wrote or collaborated on comedies, farces, melodramas, and adaptations of his novels. Hawkins included in his "short tally of dramatic success" Edward Rose's dramatization of his *The Prisoner of Zenda*; *The Adventure of Lady Ursula,* an eighteenth-century comedy which had, as he said in a letter to the duchess, "duels and a lady in boots and breeches and all the rest of it!"; *English*

*Nell,* a dramatization of *Simon Dale* written with Rose; and *Pilkerton's Peerage,* a political satire and Hawkins's only comedy in a modern setting.

Beyond his literary success, Hawkins was a public figure of some stature. He was prominent in the Authors' Club, and in January 1900 he was elected chairman of the Committee of the Society of Authors, which had been founded by Walter Besant in 1883. As chairman Hawkins acted vigorously in establishing the society's Pension Fund for Indigent but Meritorious Authors. Hawkins was also persuaded to stand as a candidate in Scotland pending the dissolution of Parliament, but in September 1900, the day before he was to go to Glasgow, a heart attack forced him to resign.

Hawkins's next novel, *Quisanté,* was published in October 1900. Its eponymous hero, loosely based on Disraeli, is a political adventurer or, as a reviewer for the *Spectator* called him, a "brilliant cad." This novel of psychological analysis centers on the relationship between Quisanté and Lady May Gaston, who is simultaneously repelled by Quisanté's vulgarity and attracted by his genius.

In December Hawkins gave up his rooms in Buckingham Street and took more elaborate ones in the Savoy Mansions. As he summed up 1900: "In money all right: £8,500 about (about £3,000 from plays, I think) – much less than last year, but much more than it will be and more than I need." He feared, however, that at the age of thirty-seven he was "becoming middle-aged rather early." Early in 1901 Hawkins suffered another heart attack; this time he was forced temporarily to stop writing and live on his means. He complained that the "bourgeoisdom of my ancestry is up in arms against any such thing." He was also unhappy for other reasons: he was ill, his father's health was failing, and he had never succeeded in finding a wife.

Hawkins's only work published in 1901 was *Tristram of Blent,* a study of legitimacy and an ancient peerage. Although reviews were mixed, the public liked the book, and it was both successful and remunerative. Afraid that his heart condition would cut short his life, Hawkins was writing less and spending more freely. He was pleased to learn in May 1902 that *Tristram of Blent* had already earned six thousand pounds. Still he was not really happy: "For myself much dining-out and fun. No work – no happiness – no content – life *in a knot.*"

*The Intrusions of Peggy* appeared in October 1902 to mediocre reviews and indifferent sales, although Peggy Ryle, who impulsively intrudes in the lives of her friends Trix Trevalla and Airey Newton, is perhaps Hawkins's most lovable heroine. As "A Susceptible Reviewer" wrote in *Punch:* "Where other heroines are concerned / I pay my homage quite discreetly, / But charming *Peggy Ryle* has turned / My head and captured me completely."

That same autumn Hawkins delivered a paper on "Realism in Fiction" to the Philosophical Society in Edinburgh. Romance and realism, he argued, lie not in what happens but in how people respond to the world and judge themselves. Romance seeks conquest and adventure, exhibiting a character's power and energy; realism minutely studies the environment of which the character may be a victim. Truth needs both of these "great and permanent tempers of the human mind."

Hawkins turned forty with "a bald head and a bad heart." On 10 February 1903 he sailed for the United States to visit friends and live for a few months as a New Yorker might. On his homeward voyage in April friends entrusted to his care Elizabeth "Betty" Sheldon, the daughter of Charles Henry Sheldon of New York, "a charming pretty girl of 18" whom he had met once or twice before. On 21 May he proposed to her and was accepted. They were married 1 July in Saint Bride's Church, and in September they moved from the rooms in Savoy Mansions to a house in Bedford Square.

Although Hawkins was relieved that he was able to break his long idleness by writing a few short stories, in 1903, for the first time since 1890, he published no new volume. The private happiness effected by his marriage was offset by "the slackening of the *brute strength* of imagination." He later identified the year as the "divide" in his life. Youth was gone, his manner of living changed, and he was less and less able to write.

Nevertheless, in 1904 Hawkins started and quickly finished *Sophy of Kravonia.* By spring he had also prepared for publication *Double Harness* (1904) and *A Servant of the Public* (1905), both of which he had been working on for some time. On 21 August a daughter was born to the Hawkinses, the first of their three children and their only daughter. They named her Millicent after the duchess of Sutherland.

*Double Harness* appeared in September to discouraging reviews. A study of six married couples whose fortunes affect the central couple, Grantley and Sibylla Imason, the novel preached comradeship and mutual forbearance. Though too melancholy to be widely popular, it was thought by many of Hawkins's friends to be his best work.

In an autumn 1904 address on "Modern Myths," given at Edinburgh's Philosophical Institution, Hawkins said that the true novelist was moved

*Dust jacket for Hawkins's novel about Sophy Grouch, an Essex
orphan who rises to the nobility and eventually becomes a queen
(courtesy of the Lilly Library, Indiana University)*

to write by "a curiosity, active and insatiable, for the study of human character." He was disappointed that modern novels were more inclined than their predecessors to philosophize and to use the exhibition of manners merely as a vehicle to convey the author's views: "The analysis and exhibition of human character tend to become a means towards the statement and illustration of a problem."

In 1905 Hawkins's *A Servant of the Public,* first conceived in 1896, was finally published. Its heroine, Ora Pinsent, whose husband is in the United States, feels free to exert her charms on any man who comes near. She is an actress, and the book reflects Hawkins's lifelong fascination with the stage. The novel sold briskly at first, but its popularity did not last. Although the *Times Literary Supplement* praised it for being "sad without being sour," many readers regretted that Hawkins had given them so much introspection and so little of the excitement of Ruritania.

*Sophy of Kravonia* (1905) gave these readers what they wanted. Hawkins called the novel "a haphazard venture"; it follows the fortunes of Sophy Grouch, an orphan from Essex, as she becomes in turn Mademoiselle de Gruche in Paris, Baroness Dobrava in Slavna, queen in the highlands of Volseni, and, almost certainly, Lady Dunstanbury of London in the end.

In February 1906 the death of his father contributed to Hawkins's growing despondency. He found himself struggling for ideas: he had written little new since finishing *Sophy of Kravonia* almost two years before, and he worried about a future lack of income. Much of his time was occupied with his growing family (his first son, Richard, had been born the previous November) and with reading books on philosophy, theology, and the history of religion. He was tempted to write on the problems of belief but did not because "the old instinct that that would be a sort of *treason* survives all rational argument."

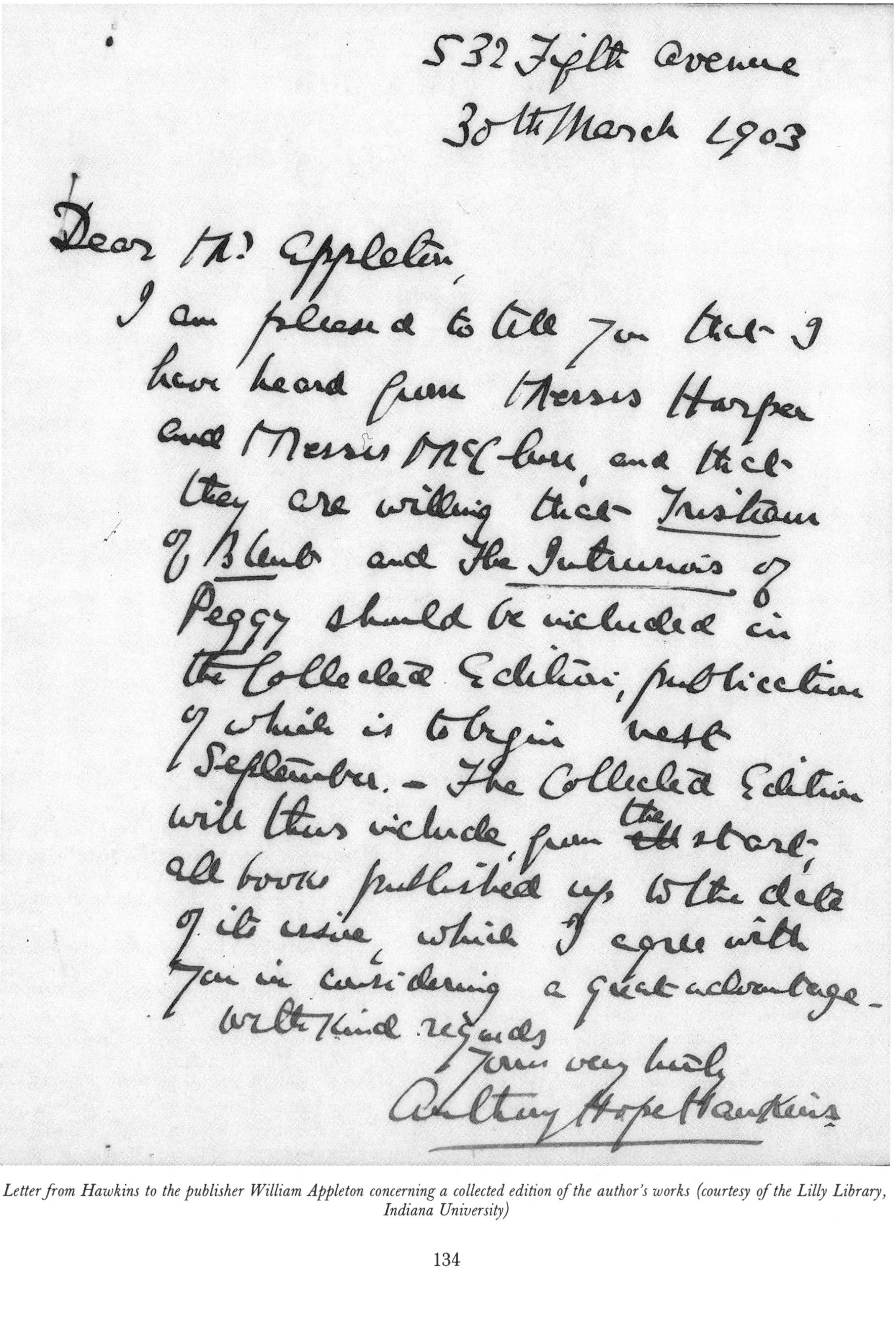

532 Fifth Avenue
30th March 1903

Dear Mr Appleton,

I am pleased to tell you that I have heard from Messrs Harper and Messrs McClure, and that they are willing that _Tristram of Blent_ and _The Intrusions of Peggy_ should be included in the Collected Edition, publication of which is to begin next September. — The Collected Edition will thus include, from the start, all books published up to the date of its issue, which I agree with you in considering a great advantage.

With kind regards
Yours very truly
Anthony Hope Hawkins

*Letter from Hawkins to the publisher William Appleton concerning a collected edition of the author's works (courtesy of the Lilly Library, Indiana University)*

Hawkins's depression lifted toward the end of 1906, and he was able to work again. The bishop of London, Dr. Mandell Creighton, had suggested that Hawkins write a novel based on Queen Elizabeth. The result was a "modernized miniature of the Great Queen," *The Great Miss Driver,* which he finished in March 1907 but which was not published until 1908. A collection of sixteen short stories, *Tales of Two People,* was published in 1907 to good reviews and solid sales. Hawkins was also reelected chairman of the Committee of the Society of Authors. Though concerned about the time this would demand, he reminded himself that "a little active row isn't a bad change in a mole-like life."

*The Great Miss Driver,* published in September 1908, echoes some recurring themes and techniques of Hawkins's fiction. Jenny Driver, like many of his heroines, is torn between two disparate lovers: Lord Fillingford, a well-mannered peer of little vitality; and Leonard Octon, a rough man of action. The story is told by one of Hawkins's bachelor observers, in this case Jenny's secretary. The novel sold few copies, and at the end of the year Hawkins noted that he had made less than thirty-five hundred pounds, his lowest income since before *The Prisoner of Zenda.* He felt that his career was coming to an end and was thankful for his miserliness during his prosperous days.

In April 1910 *Second String* was published to a civil reception but few sales. Its hero, Andy Hayes, was too tortoiselike to win over the public, while its villain, Harry Belfield, was too much a philanderer to please them. The book was an experiment in publishing, one of the earliest in the series of attractive two-shilling novels by Thomas Nelson and Sons. The comparative failure of *Second String* was balanced by the successful American sale of *Mrs. Maxon Protests* (1911), another tale of a rebel against society. Book rights for five years brought fifteen hundred guineas, and serial rights another one thousand pounds. Like all of Hawkins's novels, the strength of *Second String* lies in its dialogue, of which he was a master. In an address delivered to the English Association on 28 October 1909 and privately printed as *Dialogue,* Hawkins deplored the lifelessness of novels in which nobody says anything. The essence of dialogue, he argued, is "the meeting of minds in talk – the reciprocal exhibition of mind to mind." He believed that dialogue reveals characters' qualities and enables the novelist to maintain suspense. The crucial aptitude for writing good dialogue, he asserted, is the ability to fuse oneself with each of one's speakers, a process not of obliteration but of transformation.

Early in 1911 Hawkins's sister Joan Feiling died of heart failure. The year also proved unproductive for Hawkins. When he drew up his annual summation he recorded the first blank for twenty-two years. He had written nothing new, although *Mrs. Maxon Protests* had been published in September. The book was not successful, however, and reviewers were divided over the dilemma of Dick Dennehy, forbidden by his church to marry the divorced Winnie Maxon.

Hawkins did not publish another novel for three years. Fortunately his home life, especially his daughter Millicent, were sources of great interest and joy, and his past thrift meant that he was "not under compulsion to *earn* immediately." He resolved to write nothing unless it was good and produced a few short stories which satisfied him. As he turned fifty he was "worried at not working, and sad to recognize the limitations I can hardly hope now ever to pass," but he was also more accepting of his "place in the ranks" and "more free of spiritual terrors." His home was happy, but war was threatening his country.

World War I began in August 1914, and Hawkins immediately looked for useful work. In September he and twenty-five other authors were invited to help the government counteract German propaganda and influence opinion in neutral countries. The Editorial and Public Branch Department soon developed into the Ministry of Information. Hawkins wrote extensively during his years with the government, including *The New (German) Testament* (1914), which argued against German militarist theories; *The Fleet of Mercy* (1915), which appealed for the International Commission for Relief in Belgium; and *Impressions d'un touriste en France* (1915), which reminded the French that a third party would gain if they quarreled with England.

In 1915 Hawkins's *A Young Man's Year,* which had been finished before the war, appeared to generally favorable reviews but disappointing sales. The most autobiographical of his works, the novel relates the struggles of Arthur Lisle, a young barrister who is fascinated by his cousin's wife, Bernadette Lisle, and is tempted to abandon the bar for the theater.

Early in 1916 Hawkins's second son, David, was born. Hawkins worked long hours for the government, and financial worries forced him to give up the house in Bedford Square; in March 1917 the family moved to a smaller house in Gower Street. There was no time for writing fiction, but he did find time to read. After finishing several novels by Alexandre Dumas père, Hawkins wrote in his diary,

*Frontispiece and title page for Hawkins's autobiography*

"Is there really any other sort of novel worth writing? If ever I can write again (which I don't think) it shall be a *yarn,* and not why Mrs. Smith proposed to Mr. Brown." On 6 January 1918 Hawkins was knighted for his work with the Ministry of Information. In August *Captain Dieppe,* which had been published in New York in 1900, was published in England. The novel is a tale of love and honor in the vein of *The Indiscretion of the Duchess.*

After the war ended in November 1918, Hawkins discovered to his pleasure that with his new leisure came an idea for a new novel, *Beaumaroy Home from the Wars* (1919). Critics were generally favorable to the slight story of a former officer-companion of the mysterious Mr. Saffron who believes himself to be the former kaiser. In addition, thanks to *Captain Dieppe,* cheap reprints, and films of *The Prisoner of Zenda, Rupert of Hentzau,* and *Sophy of Kravonia,* Hawkins's finances were in better shape than they had been for years.

*Lucinda* (1920) tells the story of Lucinda Knyvett, who is loved by two men: the plausible rogue Arsenio Valdez and the placid gentleman Waldo Rillington. It received flattering reviews, and although Hawkins was satisfied with the novel, he saw no hope of a steady income from new books and was troubled by financial concerns despite his income from film rights and reprints. He suffered from the depression that had plagued him throughout his life and regretted that he was "anchored in no faith." On his sixtieth birthday he said of himself: "I still pine for fame, and fret for work, and love luxury and desire money."

Hawkins's last novel, *Little Tiger,* was published in July 1925. Its observer-commentator-narrator relates the story of a woman, Cora Dyke, who defies society to leave her husband for the man she loves and refuses the man who loves her. Reviewers agreed that Hawkins had lost neither his craft nor his gift of conversation. Hawkins's final book was an autobiography, *Memories and Notes* (1927), in which he struggled to include "a Self, as well as 'People I have met.' " He largely succeeded, though the work is reticent in certain areas. He drew little, for instance, on the diary he had kept since 1890, probably because he felt it was better

"to be damned for dullness rather than for indecorum."

In 1927 the Hawkinses left London for Surrey, to live permanently at Heath Farm, which they had purchased in 1915. With Richard's move to Paris to work for Price Waterhouse, Millicent's engagement to James Minoprio, and David's enrollment at Marlborough, the money from the Gower Street house was needed more than the space, much as Hawkins missed London and yearned for at least a burrow there.

Hawkins found it impossible to write any more fiction. Despite his fame and his financial success, he recognized that he had not achieved greatness. That failure was a permanent distress to him, for he thought greatness the only thing finally worth having: "But what is a man doing in the arts at all unless he is great?" The major events in Hawkins's remaining life were personal rather than professional: the birth of Millicent's daughter; the marriage of Richard to Carley Robinson, an American; and the deaths of Hawkins's brother Geoffrey and of his first cousin Kenneth Grahame, the author of *The Wind in the Willows* (1908). Hawkins himself was troubled by deafness, and his ulcerated throat proved to be cancerous.

Sir Anthony Hope Hawkins died at Heath Farm on 8 July 1933. Though he always feared he was a third-rate novelist, *The Prisoner of Zenda* stands indisputably in the first rank of romance. His most fitting epitaph is J. M. Barrie's tribute: "He made more people happy than any other author of our time."

### References:

Peter Keating, *The Haunted Study: A Social History of the English Novel 1875–1914* (London: Secker & Warburg, 1989);

Charles Mallet, *Anthony Hope and His Books: Being the Authorized Life of Sir Anthony Hope Hawkins* (London: Hutchinson, 1935);

S. Gorley Putt, "The Prisoner of *The Prisoner of Zenda:* Anthony Hope," in his *Scholars of the Heart: Essays in Criticism* (London: Faber & Faber, 1962), pp. 110–131;

Raymond P. Wallace, "Cardboard Kingdoms," *San Jose Studies*, 13 (September 1987): 23–34.

# W. H. Hudson

*(4 August 1841 – 18 August 1922)*

## George Woodcock

See also the Hudson entry in *DLB 98: Modern British Essayists, First Series.*

BOOKS: *The Purple Land that England Lost: Travels and Adventures in the Banda Oriental,* 2 volumes (London: Low, Marston, Searle & Rivington, 1885); revised as *The Purple Land* (London: Duckworth, 1904; New York: Illustrated Editions, 1904);

*A Crystal Age* (London: Unwin, 1887; revised, 1906; New York: Dutton, 1906);

*Argentine Ornithology,* 2 volumes, by Hudson and P. L. Sclater (London: Porter, 1888, 1889); revised as *Birds of La Plata,* 2 volumes, by Hudson (London: Dent / New York: Dutton, 1920);

*The Naturalist in La Plata* (London: Chapman & Hall, 1892; New York: Appleton, 1892);

*Fan: the Story of a Young Girl's Life,* 3 volumes, as Henry Harford (London: Chapman & Hall, 1892); 1 volume, by Hudson (London: Dent / New York: Dutton, 1923);

*Idle Days in Patagonia* (London: Chapman & Hall, 1893; New York: Appleton, n.d.);

*Birds in a Village* (London: Chapman & Hall, 1893; Philadelphia: Lippincott, 1893); revised and enlarged as *Birds in Town and Village* (London: Dent / New York: Dutton, 1919);

*Lost British Birds* (London: Chapman & Hall, 1894); enlarged as *Rare, Vanishing & Lost British Birds,* compiled by Linda Gardiner (London: Dent / New York: Dutton, 1923);

*British Birds* (London & New York: Longmans, Green, 1895);

*Birds in London* (London & New York: Longmans, Green, 1898);

*Nature in Downland* (London & New York: Longmans, Green, 1900);

*Birds and Man* (London & New York: Longmans, Green, 1901; revised edition, London: Duckworth, 1915; New York: Knopf, 1916);

*El Ombu* (London: Duckworth, 1902; enlarged edition, London & Toronto: Dent / New York: Dutton, 1923); published as *South American Sketches* (London: Duckworth, 1909); revised

*W. H. Hudson*

as *3 Tales of the Pampas* (New York: Knopf, 1916);

*Hampshire Days* (London & New York: Longmans, Green, 1903);

*Green Mansions: A Romance of the Tropical Forest* (London: Duckworth, 1904; New York: Putnam, 1904);

*A Little Boy Lost* (London: Duckworth, 1905; New York: Knopf, 1918);

*The Land's End* (London: Hutchinson, 1908; New York: Appleton, 1908);

*Afoot in England* (London: Hutchinson, 1909; New York: Knopf, 1922);

*A Shepherd's Life: Impressions of the South Wiltshire Downs* (London: Methuen, 1910; New York: Dutton, 1910);

*Adventures Among Birds* (London: Hutchinson, 1913; New York: Kennerley, 1915);

*Far Away and Long Ago* (London: Dent / New York: Dutton, 1918);

*The Book of a Naturalist* (London & New York: Hodder & Stoughton, 1919);

*Dead Man's Plack and An Old Thorn* (London: Dent / New York: Dutton, 1920);

*A Traveller in Little Things* (London: Dent, 1921; New York: Dutton, 1921);

*A Hind in Richmond Park* (London: Dent, 1922; New York: Dutton, 1923);

*Ralph Herne* (New York: Knopf, 1924).

**Editions:** *The Collected Works of W. H. Hudson,* 24 volumes (London: Dent / New York: Dutton, 1922–1923);

*A Hudson Anthology,* edited by Edward Garnett (London & Toronto: Dent / New York: Dutton, 1924);

*Tales of the Gauchos,* edited by Elizabeth Coatsworth (New York: Knopf, 1946);

*The Best of W. H. Hudson,* edited by Odell Shepard (New York: Dutton, 1949).

*Hudson, circa 1868*

It is not easy to categorize W. H. Hudson (as he preferred to be called). He was not primarily a fiction writer, yet his best known book, and perhaps his best book, was a novel, *Green Mansions: A Romance of the Tropical Forest* (1904), which has retained its place as a minor classic. Generically, it is related to the romance, with the preoccupation of that genre with the fantastic and marvelous. In this respect, it has affinities with other works that belong to the efflorescence of romance around the turn of the century (including writers such as Rider Haggard, H. G. Wells, Robert Louis Stevenson, Bram Stoker, and George Macdonald), as well as an obvious ancestry in the Romantic narratives of the late eighteenth and early nineteenth century. Yet Hudson also wrote as a naturalist, producing work of genuine scientific value, as well as more personal accounts of nature. He combined his observations of nature with an interest in the history of animals and plants (and rural customs) – for example, he notes the way animals disappear from the scene, including strains of domesticated animals. Hudson anticipates recent ecological writers such as Annie Dillard or Barry Lopez. Hudson also has claims as a travel writer, and his idiosyncratic wanderings yielded the

insights of an intelligent outsider, again anticipating the work of writers of our own time. He also produced an autobiographical study of unusual interest. His complex identity – he was both English and Argentine – no doubt underlies the complexity and many-sidedness of his work as a writer.

The life of W. H. Hudson was divided sharply into two unequal parts: the period of his boyhood and young manhood on the Argentinean pampas and the remaining five decades of his life, beginning on the day in 1874 when he stepped onto the ship at Buenos Aires that would take him to Southampton. Hudson never returned to the Argentine, as English people then called it, for the characteristic reason that he feared (rightly as it turned out) that the wildlife of the pampas would be greatly diminished by the great immigration of Italian peasants during this period.

William Henry Hudson was born in Argentina at Quilmes, not far from Buenos Aires, on 4 August 1841. His grandfather had been a Devonshire farmer who immigrated to New England,

THE

PURPLE LAND THAT ENGLAND
LOST.

TRAVELS AND ADVENTURES IN THE BANDA
ORIENTAL, SOUTH AMERICA.

BY

W. H. HUDSON.

VOL. I.

LONDON:
SAMPSON LOW, MARSTON, SEARLE, AND RIVINGTON,
CROWN BUILDINGS, 188, FLEET STREET.
1885.
[All rights reserved.]

*Title page for Hudson's first novel, published soon after his
arrival in England from Argentina (courtesy of the Lilly
Library, Indiana University)*

and his father immigrated in turn to the Argentinean pampas. An Argentinean citizen, Hudson was brought up to speak English as well as Spanish and was able to ride a horse bareback at a gallop by the time he was six. As an adolescent he would often wander over the great expanses of flat country, observing its wildlife. He also acquired a passionate interest in English books, and in *Afoot in England* (1909) he recalls his joy at discovering a second-hand bookshop in Buenos Aires that had books in English scattered in piles on the floor. Hudson served for a short time in the Argentinean army, and in his some of his books he describes the brutal discipline he suffered there. Even when he was an old man in England, his friend R. B. Cunninghame Grahame spoke of Hudson as "an old Gaucho, born on the plains, with the slow speech and silent ways of the plainsman."

Hudson first became fascinated with natural history when he was still a boy. He read Charles Darwin's books with great attention, and in later years his writing was greatly influenced by the fine narrative style of the great Victorian travelers, such as Darwin and H. W. Bates. Even at the end of his life Hudson described himself as a naturalist, specifically, a field naturalist concerned with the behavior of birds more than with their physical characteristics (though the effect of one on the other interested him greatly). Although he had little use for the scientist who spends his life in a laboratory or a museum, Hudson, like Bates and Alfred Russell Wallace before him, started his career as a naturalist by becoming a collector of South American birds for great museums, beginning with the Smithsonian Institute in 1866 and then the London Zoological Society in 1869. Later in his life Hudson's concern for endangered species led him to condemn such collecting if it included rare species.

Hudson's early years in England were poor and lonely and partly spoiled for him by the fact that he was largely forced to reside in London, the only place in which he could earn money from his pen. In 1876 he married Emily Wingrave, a failed singer who became a relatively unsuccessful proprietor of a series of boarding houses, ending with one in Bayswater, where Hudson spent his final years. He could never afford a country house like his friend Joseph Conrad. Hudson began to emerge as a writer in the 1880s and from then until his death lived what might be considered the life of a naturalist man of letters, writing narratives of rural expeditions, fictional works, and books of amateur ornithology; his *British Birds* (1895) was for many years the best field handbook for bird-watchers.

Though Hudson was austere and often remote in manner, he attracted a large circle of friends largely by the intensity of his love for wild nature and its creatures. When Hudson died Conrad said of him that "he was a nature-production himself and has some of its fascinating mysteriousness." Grahame was both Hudson's competitor as a writer on South America and his devoted friend. Edward Garnett was Hudson's editor and in fact virtually discovered him; their correspondence was extensive. Ford Madox Ford published his work in the prestigious *English Review,* and after Conrad died he pronounced their shared view of Hudson: "Our greatest admiration for a stylist in any language was given to W. H. Hudson of whom Conrad said that his writing was like the grass that the good God made to grow and when it was there you could not tell how it came." Among his younger friends were Morley Roberts and the poet Edward Thomas. Hudson was closer to Thomas than to most of his

*Edward Garnett, Hudson's editor. The two men carried on an*
*extensive correspondence throughout Hudson's career.*

other literary friends, and when Thomas died in 1917 as one of the victims of World War I, he mourned him like a son. Hudson in fact had no children of his own.

Hudson was a steady and prolific writer. His collected works, published after his death, filled twenty-four volumes but were by no means complete. In both his fiction and his nonfiction the author frequently drew on his observations and experiences in South America and in England. Hudson's imaginative territory in South America ranged from Venezuela, where he had not been, to his familiar pampas. In the English narratives he talked of travel in the southern counties, mainly the layer of them near the channel from Kent on the east to Cornwall on the west, though it must be said that Hudson, like a good Devonshire man, regarded the Cornish as in some way foreigners. He was especially attached to the downland countries, perhaps because their bare chalk hills reminded him of the bare lowlands of the pampas. He did not go north of the classic boundary between North Country and South

Country, the course of the Trent, nor west of the Severn into Wales and Welsh Marches.

Some of the books most characteristic of Hudson described his wanderings in the country; *Afoot in England* is a good example. He typically escaped from London into the countryside from one to three times each year, sometimes accompanied by his wife, until she became too ill to endure the rigors of their expeditions. His journeys were as little planned as possible, either in direction or time, for he always expected the unexpected and was often rewarded. In the earlier years he went on foot, and in later years he was mounted, not on a horse like his admired predecessor, William Cobbett, but on a bicycle. In old age Hudson continued his expeditions but made the concession of traveling by motorcar.

All of Hudson's books, whether of South America or southern England, reflect a view of the superiority of rural over urban life and stress the importance of what many of his contemporaries regarded as the lower orders of life and with those

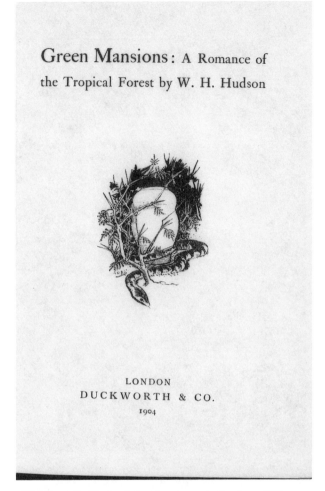

Green Mansions: A Romance of
the Tropical Forest by W. H. Hudson

LONDON
DUCKWORTH & CO.
1904

*Title page for Hudson's best-known work, the story of Rima, a
mysterious girl who lives in the jungles of Venezuela (courtesy
of the Lilly Library, Indiana University)*

human beings – like gaucho herders or downland shepherds – who live humbly and in close touch with the earth. His observations of birds were especially acute and more accurate than many professional scientists of his time liked to grant.

Hudson observed human beings with the same objective curiosity, adopting an attitude of compassionate pantheism somewhat akin to Buddhism in such works as *A Shepherd's Life: Impressions of the South Wiltshire Downs* (1910). This novel presents a kind of life as close to nature as is possible in an agrarian country, that of the man who lives in solitude with his sheep and learns of nature by observing and enduring it from day to day. In a way Hudson rediscovers the gaucho of the pampas in the man herding sheep on a windswept solitary down.

Yet at the same time there emerged from his experience a kind of nature mysticism, which develops into a nature aesthetic, evident in his description of the failure of poetic description in contrast with what nature offers directly: "Do we not see that words fail us as pigments do – that the effect is too coarse, since in describing it we put it before the mental eye as something distinctly visible, a thing of itself and separate. But it is not so in nature; the effect is something almost invisible and is yet part of all and makes all things – sky and sea and land – as insubstantial as itself." In a sense Hudson seems to belong to that school of outdoor writers who became evident after the trial of Oscar Wilde in 1896 and the collapse of the decadent movement of the 1890s. Yet there is little evidence in his writing of the beery heartiness of G. K. Chesterton or Hilaire Belloc. Hudson's work is more akin to such traditional English rural writers as Cobbett, Thomas, and Richard Jefferies.

At the same time, Hudson's work betrays a distinct stylistic echo of the 1890s, a whiff of aes-

thetic deliberation. Nothing could be more elementally earthy than Hudson's travel in the English countryside, yet when he returned to his house in London he seemed to feel constrained to write in the urbane manner of a man of letters, a style of which Ford would approve and that would inspire Vita Sackville West to write a remarkable tribute in a *Listener* essay (2 June 1938).

In regard to Hudson's fiction, it might be argued that he can hardly be regarded as a novelist in the generally accepted sense. He did not think of himself as primarily a novelist but rather as a naturalist, and in that role he was a pioneer, anticipating modern environmentalists in his concern for the protection of the wild birds. Nevertheless, the first book Hudson published after his arrival in England was his first novel, *The Purple Land that England Lost: Travels and Adventures in the Banda Oriental* (1885). Set in the 1840s in Hudson's native pampas, though he has transferred the scene across the Rio de la Plata to Uruguay, still often referred to locally as the Banda Oriental, the novel tells the story of revolution and civil war between two rival armies of gauchos. The narrative is direct but without subtlety, the characters are shallow and unmemorable, complications in human situations are avoided, and the book holds the reader's interest mainly through its vividly descriptive passages, some of them based on Hudson's brief service in the Argentinean army.

Hudson's next novel, *A Crystal Age* (1887), has often been described as utopian. Marie Louise Berneri in her *Journey Through Utopia* (1950) classes it more exactly as a "utopian romance" that makes "no pretence of giving a fool-proof plan for a perfect society" but describes "the kind of community in which the author would like to live." She quotes Hudson's preface to a 1906 reprint of the book, in which he states that books such as his novel, "however fantastic they may be, have for most of us a perennial mild interest, since they are born of a common feeling: a sense of dissatisfaction with the existing order of things, combined with a vague faith or hope in a better one to come." The lack of passion in this passage reflects a similar lack in *A Crystal Age,* in which men and women live sexless, siblinglike lives together.

A deep-rooted puritanism, or perhaps a desperate sexual incompetence, seems to lie at the heart of Hudson's writings. Even in his travel essays, his wife appears as a voiceless kind of burden, and in his novels, when sexual intercourse does take place, it is usually violent and harmful, especially to the women. This situation appears repeatedly in *El Ombu* (1902), a book which appeared as both *South*

*American Sketches* (1909) and *3 Tales of the Pampas* (1916), the last title perhaps the most faithfully describing the collection. One story, "El Ombu," is long enough to be described as a novella; Hudson claimed it had been told to him, for the most part, by an old gaucho. It is really a discontinuous narrative, with a gigantic old *ombu* tree and the house it overshadows as the uniting symbols, images evoking a theme of tragic destiny. The *ombu* tree is said to exert a malign influence on the lives of those it overhangs, and Hudson relates the sad histories of its victims. In the first, an old landowner of great pride and fury kills his favorite servant, flees the house, and goes mad waiting for a pardon in Montevideo. Next, a poor sheepherder who comes to live in the house is swept into the Argentinean army in one of its wars against the Indians. After being severely lashed by a sadistic general, he is brought home, where he dies on his doorstep. His son Bruno grows up dreaming of revenge and eventually makes an attempt on the life of the general, but he fails and is tied down for the vultures to eat. Meanwhile, the general goes mad, as does the girl Monica, who loves Bruno and is the last inhabitant of the house called *El Ombu* before it is torn to the ground. The other stories are similar combinations of the melodrama of existence in a violent land and vividly realistic descriptions of pampas life.

Hudson's most ambitious, most imaginative, and best-known work of fiction is *Green Mansions: A Romance of the Tropical Forest* (1904). It is set in the jungles of Venezuela, near the Orinoco, and relates the adventures of Abel, a wealthy and cultured young man whom the novel's narrator encounters in Georgetown, British Guiana. Abel, the narrator is informed, had to flee Caracas because he was engaged in a revolutionary plot. He escaped into wild territory and lived among Indian tribes. In a charmed woodland, which the Indians avoid and where all the animals are happy and tame, Abel hears a strange birdlike monologue that seems to be addressed to him, and eventually he sees the girl who utters it, Rima or Riolama, named after the place where her pregnant mother mysteriously appeared. The local people regard her as the daughter of an evil water spirit and avoid her part of the forest, explaining why the animals there show no fear of humans. In the hope of finding her people, Rima, Abel, and an old man who poses as her grandfather set out for Riolama, but they are unsuccessful and return separately to the enchanted woodland. During their absence, the Indians pluck up their courage and invade the territory. Rima is killed when her enemies burn down a tree where she has taken

*Page from the manuscript for Hudson's memoir* Far Away and Long Ago *(Sotheby's auction catalogue, sale number 5998, 30 April–1 May 1990)*

refuge. Abel finds her charred bones and flees with them through the jungles until he finally reaches Georgetown.

*Green Mansions* has often been interpreted as a symbolic tale of the natural world being victimized by human beings, and perhaps this idea fits in with the suspensions of disbelief that Hudson evidently expects his readers to make, as implied by his labeling the book a romance. The uninterrupted after-dinner tale that Abel tells the narrator – filling more than two hundred printed pages – produces a failure of verisimilitude not completely balanced by the realistic exactness with which Hudson, the old naturalist, describes both human beings and wild creatures. As for Rima, her presence is as shadowy as her past, which is never discovered on the abortive journey to Riolima. She is quite evidently meant to be, as W. J. Keith has remarked, "the natural spirit of the tropical forest," and in her immolation man's savagery to all natural things outside himself is exemplified.

One special characteristic of Rima is the resemblance of her early language to the speech of birds, and this kind of coalescence between the human and the avian is found elsewhere in Hudson's works. *Afoot in England* includes a collection of essays written during the early 1900s. One of them includes a description of the speech of certain children that may give a clue to the origin of Rima in Hudson's mind: "Their voices were well suited to their small brilliant forms; not loud though high-pitched and singularly musical and penetrating like the high clear notes, which have a human quality, of some of our songsters – the wallow, redstart, pied wagtail, whin-chat, and two or three others. Such pure and beautiful sounds are sometimes heard in human voices, chiefly in children, where they are talking and laughing in joyous excitement." Thus, the observation of a naturalist provides a characteristic of a romantic projection of nature in human form, and Hudson's two vocations seem to be united.

W. H. Hudson's major fiction is undoubtedly *Green Mansions,* which is a novel very much in the mode of the fantastic. It gives the impression of probing the limits of ordinary experience into another dimension of reality. *Green Mansions* grows out of the author's work as a naturalist, for his studies of nature are full of hints that reality is bigger and more complex than ordinary human commonsense can admit. In *A Hind in Richmond Park,* Hudson suggests that there is a form of extrasensory perception available to people – a suggestion paralleled in *Nature in Downland,* which posits another sense in addi-

tion to the standard five, a sense for beauty: this intuition finds fictional expression in the figure of Rima in *Green Mansions* and the mystic life of nature she symbolizes. Hudson was much prized in his own time as a stylist (most famously by his friend Joseph Conrad), but perhaps his greatest contribution is in the nature mysticism of his writing, a mode of perception which he found both in the Romantic poets that fascinated him – and in his own concrete experience as a traveler and naturalist.

**Letters:**

*Letters from W. H. Hudson, 1901–1922,* edited by Edward Garnett (New York: Dutton, 1923);

*Men, Books and Birds,* edited by Morley Roberts (London: Nash & Grayson, 1925);

*W. H. Hudson's Letters to R. B. Cunninghame-Grahame,* edited by Richard Curle (London: Golden Cockerel, 1941);

*Letters on the Ornithology of Buenos Ayres,* edited by David R. Dewar (Ithaca, N.Y.: Cornell University Press, 1951).

**Bibliographies:**

G. F. Wilson, *A Bibliography of the Writings of W. H. Hudson* (London: Bookman's Journal, 1922);

John R. Payne, *W. H. Hudson: A Bibliography* (Folkestone, Kent & Hamden, Conn.: Dawson/Archon, 1977).

**Biographies:**

Morley Roberts, *W. H. Hudson: A Portrait* (London: Dutton, 1924);

Harold Goddard, *W. H. Hudson: Bird-Man* (New York: Dutton, 1929);

Robert Hamilton, *W. H. Hudson: The Vision of Earth* (London: Dent, 1946);

Samuel J. Looker, ed., *William Henry Hudson: A Tribute* (Sussex: Aldridge, 1947);

Ruth Tomalin, *W. H. Hudson* (London: Withehby, 1954);

Herbert F. West, *For a Hudson Biographer* (Hanover, N.H.: Westhold, 1958);

Amy D. Ronner, *W. H. Hudson: The Man, the Novelist, the Naturalist* (AMS, 1986).

**References:**

Richard Aldington, "The Prose of W. H. Hudson," *Egoist,* 1 (15 May 1914): 186–187;

Arnold Bennett, "W. H. Hudson," in his *Books and Persons: Being Comments on a Past Epoch, 1908–1911* (New York: Doran, 1917), pp. 278–279;

Christopher Brown, "Hudson's Far Away and Long Ago: The Uses of the Past," *Research Studies,* 49 (December 1981): 221–230;

Walter de la Mare, "Naturalists," in his *Pleasures and Speculations* (London: Faber & Faber, 1940), pp. 47–65;

Marjory Stoneman Douglas, "W. H. Hudson: Monuments to His Green World," *Carrell,* 15 (1974): 1–16;

Hoxie N. Fairchild, "Rima's Mother," *PMLA,* 68 (June 1953): 357–370;

John T. Frederick, *William Henry Hudson* (New York: Twayne, 1972);

John Galsworthy, "Four More Novelists in Profile: An Address," in his *Candelabra: Selected Essays and Addresses* (New York: Scribners, 1933), pp. 249–269;

Edward Garnett, "W. H. Hudson: An Appreciation," *Academy and Literature,* 1572 (21 June 1902): 632–634;

R. B. Cunninghame Grahame, Introduction to Hudson's *Far Away and Long Ago* (London: Dent, 1951), pp. v–ix;

Ford Madox Hueffer, "W. H. Hudson: Some Reminiscences," *Little Review VIII,* 1 (May–June 1920): 1–12;

Merritt Y. Hughes, "A Great Skeptic: W. H. Hudson," *University of California Chronicle,* 26 (April 1924): 161–174;

Compton Mackenzie, "Great Individuals," in his *Literature in My Time* (Freeport, N.Y.: Books for Libraries Press, 1934), pp. 175–183;

H. J. Massingham, *Untrodden Ways* (New York: Dutton, 1933);

Massingham, "W. H. Hudson," in *The Post Victorians,* edited by W. R. Inge (London: Ivor, Nicholson & Watson, 1933): pp. 255–271;

John Moore, "The Eagle and the Caged Bird," in his *Country Men* (Freeport, N.Y.: Books for Libraries Press, 1935), pp. 170–190;

Lewis Mumford, *The Story of Utopias* (New York: Boni & Liveright, 1922), pp. 171–190;

Mervyn Nicholson, " 'What We See We Feel': The Imaginative World of W. H. Hudson," *University of Toronto Quarterly,* 47 (Summer 1978): 304–322;

John Rees, "A Reading of *The Purple Land,*" *Kansas Quarterly,* 14 (Spring 1982): 135–148;

Frank Swinnerton, "Travellers: R. B. Cunninghame, W. H. Hudson, Joseph Conrad, H. M. Tomlinson, Norman Douglas," in his *The Georgian Scene: A Literary Panorama* (New York: Farrar & Rinehart, 1934), pp. 131–167;

Edward Thomas, "W. H. Hudson," in his *A Literary Pilgrim in England* (New York: Dodd, Mead, 1917), pp. 190–199;

William York Tindall, "Myth and the Natural Man," in his *Forces in Modern British Literature 1885–1946* (New York: Knopf, 1947), pp. 360–386;

John Walker, " 'Home Thoughts from Abroad': W. H. Hudson's Argentine Fiction," *Canadian Review of Comparative Literature,* 10 (September 1983): 333–376;

Walker, "W. H. Hudson, Argentina, and the New England Tradition," *Hispania,* 69 (March 1986): 34–39;

A. C. Ward, "Travellers and Biographers," in his *Twentieth-Century Literature 1901–1940* (New York: Longmans, Green, 1940), pp. 222–244;

Leonard Woolf, "A Traveller in Little Things," in his *Essays on Literature, History, Politics, Etc.* (New York: Harcourt, Brace, 1927), pp. 72–80.

# Vernon Lee
## (Violet Paget)
### (14 October 1856 – 13 February 1935)

Patricia Thomas Srebrnik
*University of Calgary*

See also the Lee entry in *DLB 57: Victorian Prose Writers After 1867.*

BOOKS: *Studies of the Eighteenth Century in Italy* (London: Satchell, 1880; Chicago: McClurg, 1908);

*Belcaro: Being Essays on Sundry Aesthetical Questions* (London: Satchell, 1881);

*Ottilie: An Eighteenth-Century Idyl* (London: Unwin, 1883);

*The Prince of the Hundred Soups: A Puppet-Show in Narrative* (London: Unwin, 1883; New York: Lovell, 1886);

*The Countess of Albany* (London: Allen, 1884; Boston: Roberts, 1884);

*Euphorion: Being Studies of the Antique and the Mediaeval in the Renaissance,* 2 volumes (London: Unwin, 1884; Boston: Roberts, 1884); revised, 1 volume (London: Unwin, 1885);

*Miss Brown: A Novel,* 3 volumes (Edinburgh & London: Blackwood, 1884); 1 volume (New York: Harper, 1885);

*A Phantom Lover: A Fantastic Story* (Edinburgh: Blackwood, 1886; Boston: Roberts, 1886);

*Baldwin: Being Dialogues on Views and Aspirations* (London: Unwin, 1886; Boston: Roberts, 1886);

*Juvenilia: Being a Second Series of Essays on Sundry Aesthetical Questions,* 2 volumes (London: Unwin, 1887); 1 volume (Boston: Roberts, 1887);

*Hauntings: Fantastic Stories* (London: Heinemann, 1890; New York: Lovell, 1890);

*Vanitas. Polite Stories* (London: Heinemann, 1892; New York: Lovell, Coryell, 1892; enlarged edition, London: John Lane / New York: John Lane, 1911);

*Althea: A Second Book of Dialogues on Aspirations and Duties* (London: Osgood, McIlvaine, 1894);

*Renaissance Fancies and Studies: Being a Sequel to "Euphorion"* (London: Smith, Elder, 1895; New York: Putnam, 1896);

*Vernon Lee (Violet Paget)*

*Limbo and Other Essays* (London: Richards, 1897; enlarged edition, London: John Lane / New York: John Lane, 1908);

*Genius Loci: Notes on Places* (London: Richards, 1899; London: John Lane / New York: John Lane, 1908);

*Ariadne in Mantua: A Romance in Five Acts* (Oxford: Blackwell, 1903; Portland, Maine: Mosher, 1906);

*Penelope Brandling: A Tale of the Welsh Coast in the Eighteenth Century* (London: Unwin, 1903);

*Hortus Vitae: Essays on the Gardening of Life* (London: John Lane / New York: John Lane, 1904);

*Pope Jacynth and Other Fantastic Tales* (London: Richards, 1904; London: John Lane / New York: John Lane, 1907);

*The Enchanted Woods, and Other Essays on the Genius of Places* (London: John Lane / New York: John Lane, 1905);

*Sister Benevenuta and the Christ Child: An Eighteenth-Century Legend* (New York: Kennerley, 1905; London: Richards, 1906);

*The Spirit of Rome: Leaves from a Diary* (London: John Lane / New York: John Lane, 1906);

*The Sentimental Traveller: Notes on Places* (London: John Lane / New York: John Lane, 1908);

*Gospels of Anarchy and Other Contemporary Studies* (London & Leipzig: Unwin, 1908; New York: Brentano / London: Unwin, 1909);

*Laurus Nobilis: Chapters on Art and Life* (London: John Lane / New York: John Lane, 1909);

*Beauty and Ugliness and Other Studies in Psychological Aesthetics*, by Lee and Clementina Anstruther-Thomson (London: John Lane / New York: John Lane, 1912);

*Vital Lies: Studies of Some Varieties of Recent Obscurantism*, 2 volumes (London: John Lane / New York: John Lane / Toronto: Bell & Cockburn, 1912);

*The Beautiful: An Introduction to Psychological Aesthetics* (Cambridge: Cambridge University Press, 1913; New York: Putnam, 1913);

*The Tower of the Mirrors and Other Essays on the Spirit of Places* (London: John Lane / New York: John Lane / Toronto: Bell & Cockburn, 1914);

*Louis Norbert: A Two-Fold Romance* (London: John Lane / New York: John Lane, 1914);

*The Ballet of the Nations: A Present-day Morality* (London: Chatto & Windus, 1915; New York: Putnam, 1915);

*Peace with Honour: Controversial Notes on the Settlement* (London: Union of Democratic Control, 1915);

*Satan, The Waster: A Philosophic War Trilogy* (London: John Lane / New York: John Lane, 1920); republished, with a new preface by Lee (London: John Lane / New York: John Lane, 1930);

*The Handling of Words and Other Studies in Literary Psychology* (London: John Lane, 1923; New York: Dodd, Mead, 1923);

*The Golden Keys and Other Essays on the Genius Loci* (London: John Lane, 1925; New York: Dodd, Mead, 1925);

*Proteus or the Future of Intelligence* (London: Kegan Paul, Trench, Trubner / New York: Dutton, 1925);

*The Poet's Eye. Notes on Some Differences between Verse and Prose* (London: Hogarth Press, 1926);

*For Maurice: Five Unlikely Stories* (London: John Lane, Bodley Head, 1927);

*Music and its Lovers. An Empirical Study of Emotional and Imaginative Responses to Music* (London: Allen & Unwin, 1932; New York: Dutton, 1933).

PLAY PRODUCTION: *Ariadne in Mantua,* Gaiety Theatre, London, May 1916.

OTHER: *Tuscan Fairy Tales, Taken Down from the Mouths of the People*, edited anonymously by Lee (London: Satchell, 1880);

Clementina Anstruther-Thomson, *Art and Man: Essays and Fragments*, edited, with an introduction, by Lee (London: John Lane, 1924; New York, Dutton: 1924);

"J. S. S. In Memoriam," in *John Sargent,* by Evan Charteris (London: Heinemann, 1927), pp. 233–255.

The prolific author known as Vernon Lee occupies an unusual position in the intellectual history of the late nineteenth and early twentieth centuries. Had she been male, her extensive albeit undisciplined scholarship, her keen sense of aesthetic appreciation, and her passionate desire to reform society would surely have won her an enduring place in any list of Victorian men of letters. But "Vernon Lee" was in fact Violet Paget, and when her identity became known in the early 1880s, she was acclaimed not as the last of the Victorian sages but as the first of the new type of professional woman writer. Critics in the periodical press greeted her as "a powerful mind . . . an independent woman" of "gloriously lawless" opinions. Despite her intense fear of being influenced by others, Lee insisted that Walter Pater and Henry James served as her mentors. Her work was praised by Robert Browning, Olive Schreiner, Edith Wharton, Bernard Berenson, Bernard Shaw, H. G. Wells, Aldous Huxley, and Mario Praz. But not all of these admirers remained personal friends: although James was impressed by the "prodigious cerebration" of this "most astounding young female," he came eventually to believe that she was "as dangerous and uncanny as she is intelligent – which is saying a great deal."

Lee achieved this formidable reputation through her early researches into eighteenth-century Italian culture; her many essays on contemporary literature, society, and philosophy; her later trea-

tises on the psychology of aesthetic response; and the travel sketches for which she was best known by the wider reading public. Compared to her more than thirty volumes of nonfiction, Lee's fictional output seems slight: four novels and four volumes of short stories, including many tales of the supernatural. But in Lee's case there is good reason to blur the distinction between fiction and nonfiction, because the author used the techniques of fiction to write history, biography, and criticism. Many of her essays, for example, are in the form of dialogues, and her travel sketches often read like novels. In turn, much of Lee's fiction was inspired either by her historical research or by her response to contemporary developments in art and literature: Lee satirized the aesthetic movement in *Miss Brown: A Novel* (1884), and in the short story "Lady Tal" she takes aim at psychological novelists. Another recurring theme of Lee's works lies in their analysis of social structures and literary stereotypes that constrained many nineteenth-century women to lives of frustration, futility, and boredom.

Violet Paget was born on 14 October 1856 to British parents living near Boulogne, France. Her father, Henry Ferguson Paget, was an eccentric who declined even to take meals with his family. Matilda Paget was, according to her daughter in *The Handling of Words and Other Stories in Literary Psychology* (1923), a woman of "passionate and unmistakable individuality which recognized no law but its own." By an earlier marriage Matilda had a son, Eugene Lee-Hamilton, who achieved a slight reputation as a poet. Her efforts to prepare both of her children for literary careers were enhanced by the family's habit of moving constantly among Germany, Switzerland, France, and Italy. Violet Paget grew up fluent in four languages; she also acquired a thorough knowledge of European history, art, literature, and music. In the 1860s the Pagets met an American family, the Sargents. Violet was the same age as John Singer Sargent, the future portrait painter, who joined her in many explorations of Nice, Rome, and Bologna.

While still a teenager Paget published essays in Italian and Swiss periodicals. Her first publication in English, an essay entitled "Tuscan Peasant Plays," appeared in *Fraser's Magazine* in February 1877. Already she had become convinced that "no one reads a woman's writing on art, history, or aesthetics with anything but mitigated [*sic*] contempt," and so she began to use the Vernon Lee pseudonym both professionally and in her personal life. In the late 1870s Lee's essays on Italian music and drama began to appear in the leading English journals.

*Violet Paget with her half brother, Eugene Lee-Hamilton, in 1866*

When they were collected under the title *Studies of the Eighteenth Century in Italy* (1880), critics praised the author as "learned, subtle, imaginative, and eloquent" and remarked that "the severity of his studies and the patience of his research are evident at every step." They were astonished to learn that the author was not a seasoned male scholar, but a woman still in her early twenties.

*Studies of the Eighteenth Century in Italy* was soon followed by *Belcaro: Being Essays on Sundry Aesthetical Questions* (1881) and by *Euphorion: Being Studies of the Antique and the Mediaeval in the Renaissance* (1884), which was dedicated to Pater. In these early essays Lee argues that art should be valued solely for the type of pleasure it alone can give. But she warns that many of those who claim to believe in art for art's sake are actually in search of "sensuous stimulation . . . strange mixtures of beauty and nastiness . . . excitement which the responsibilities of society do not permit their obtaining, except in imaginative form."

By this time the Pagets were settled in Florence, where their home became a center for literary and intellectual discussion. James was a frequent visitor, although he regarded Matilda Paget as "grotesque" and Henry Ferguson Paget as "mysterious and sinister." Lee-Hamilton suffered from a psychosomatic paralysis that made him dependent on the ministrations of his mother and half sister. In a letter written in 1894 Lee explained that her family was "acutely neuropathic and hysterical" and that her own early years "were admirably calculated . . . to develop these characteristics." Many of Lee's friends believed that her emotional problems were the result of sexual repression: Irene Cooper Willis, who lived with Lee in the 1920s, asserted that although Lee was a lesbian, "she never faced up to sexual facts. . . . She had a whole series of passions for women, but they were all perfectly correct. Physical contact she shunned."

One of the earliest of these intense attachments was to Agnes Mary Robinson, an aspiring poet and novelist whose affluent parents were well known for their lavish literary soirees, and Lee visited England for the first time in 1881 as their guest. In a portrait painted that summer by Sargent, Lee is shown with short hair, in tailored clothing, eyes gleaming behind prominent spectacles. The portrait suggests her energetic, inquisitive, often tactless personality. Sargent introduced Lee to many Pre-Raphaelite painters and poets, including Edward Burne-Jones, William Morris, William Michael Rossetti, and Dante Gabriel Rossetti. At parties in the Robinson home she met Browning, Matthew Arnold, and Oscar Wilde. Mary Augusta Ward introduced her to Pater and his two sisters, who became close friends.

During Lee's visit to London she was attempting to interest editors and publishers in poems written by her brother, and in one of her works, a short novel titled *Ottilie: An Eighteenth-Century Idyl* (1883), which is set in Germany. It takes the form of a journal written by Ottilie's brother Christophe, who lives through the Sturm und Drang period and earns a slight reputation as an author. Neighbors, however, assume that Ottilie is the mastermind behind Christoph's literary productions, and in his journal Christoph confesses that in his youth he was callously indifferent to the happiness of his devoted sibling.

In her preface to the novel Lee indicates the connection between her historical studies and her fiction, including the stories of the supernatural that she began to write at about this time. She explains that an essayist possesses some of the same instincts as does a novelist and is tempted "to tell you some

adventures and thoughts and feelings" that he is perfectly persuaded "happened in the life and passed through the mind of the historical character." Indeed, the essayist is "haunted" by men and women "who have never existed, and who yet present him with a more complete notion of the reality of the men and women of those times than any real, contradictory, imperfectly seen creatures for whose existence history will vouch."

In 1883 authors and critics were already embroiled in a discussion of the art of fiction that was to become much more heated: they were debating whether fiction should emphasize plot or attempt detailed psychological analysis of characters. The latter method was frequently associated with James. Karl Hillebrand, the German critic to whom *Ottilie: An Eighteenth-Century Idyl* is dedicated, wrote to Lee praising the novel, precisely because the characters were not "psychologically analyzed or anatomically described, as is the fashion now a days . . . no moralizing intention is visible" – which may explain why other critics dismissed the book as slight.

Nevertheless Lee was apparently eager to attempt the new fashion deplored by Hillebrand. Her next published book was a biography, *The Countess of Albany* (1884), concerning the wife of Charles Edward Stuart, "the Young Pretender," who was also mistress of the Italian poet and nationalist, Count Vittorio Alfieri. The book was generally well received, but some critics were appalled to find that Lee drew upon her scholarly understanding of the social mores of eighteenth-century Italy to contextualize what they regarded as the sexual immorality of the countess. Lee's narrative is sympathetic to its subject, describing the countess's devotion to the study of art, music, and philosophy. Critics such as J. Arthur Blaikie in the *Academy* and Harriet Waters Preston in the *Atlantic Monthly* wondered if Lee felt intellectual kinship with the countess, and they deplored her attempts at what they described as morbid psychological analysis.

Objections to *The Countess of Albany* were soon overshadowed, however, by the controversy over Lee's three-volume novel, *Miss Brown,* an attack on the aesthetic movement. The topic was by no means original: in the early 1880s, aestheticism was satirized in many plays and novels, including Gilbert and Sullivan's *Patience* (1881) and James's *The Portrait of a Lady* (1881). But Lee's novel was unusually savage. Despite her close relationship with Pater and her belief that art should be valued only for the pleasure specific to it, Lee was horrified by what she regarded as the social irresponsibility and sexual prurience that some aesthetes attempted to camou-

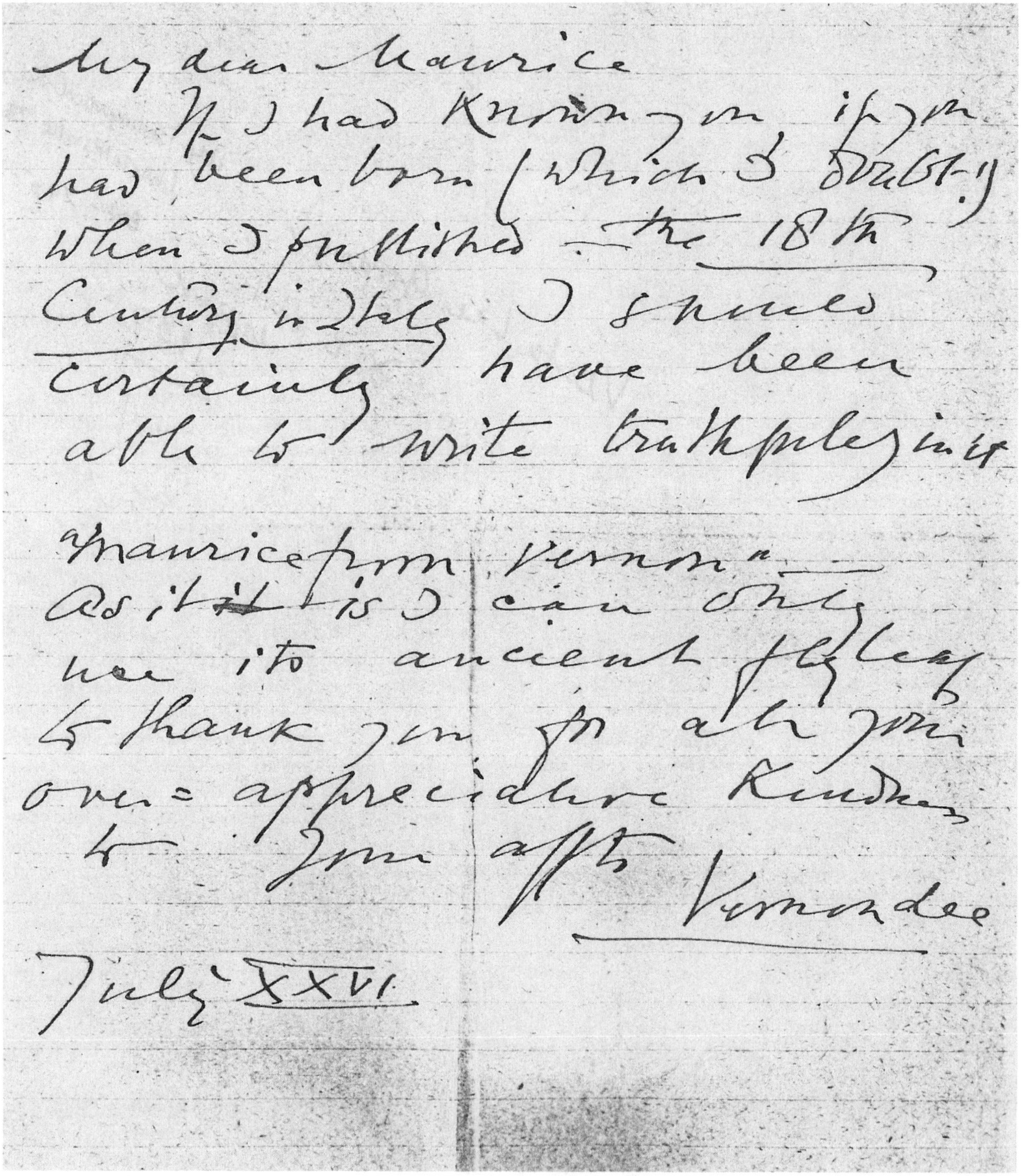

My dear Maurice

If I had Known you, if you
had been born (which I doubt-)
when I published the 18th
Century in Italy I should
certainly have been
able to write truthfuly in it

Maurice from Vernon
As it is I can only
use its ancient flyleaf
to thank you for all your
over = appreciative Kindness
to you affly
Vernon Lee

July XXVI

*Lee's inscription to Maurice Baring, laid into his copy of her first book,* Studies of the Eighteenth Century in Italy *(The Colbeck Collection, Special Collections Division, University of British Columbia Library)*

flage by a pseudodevotion to the study of beauty. As she worked on her novel, she decided to dedicate it to James, who was, as she explained in letters to her mother, "most paternal . . . most sweet and encouraging."

The novel's protagonist, Anne Brown, is a half-Scottish, half-Italian orphan. While working as a nursemaid for an English family, she meets Walter Hamlin, a wealthy aesthete who dabbles in painting and poetry. Intrigued by Anne's unconventional beauty, Walter offers to educate her at his own expense and establish her in London society; she will then decide whether they should marry. Over the protests of her cousin and guardian, a Scottish labor leader who clearly wishes to marry Anne, she accepts Hamlin's offer. But once in London, Anne is disgusted by Walter's friends and by the poor quality of his verses. She learns that Walter is sexually involved with his cousin, the pathetic and decadent Sacha. Although by this time Anne has seen through Walter's pretensions, she insists on marrying him in order to save him from Sacha.

Reviews of *Miss Brown* were mixed. Some critics, such as those in the *Contemporary Review,* the *Spectator,* and *The New York Times,* commended Lee for exposing "the falseness of the aesthetic ideal," while others insisted the aesthetic movement had become a stale joke. The *Pall Mall Gazette* admired Anne Brown's noble self-sacrifice, but Cosmo Monkhouse in the *Academy* condemned the plot as "immoral" and "very nasty." The only point on which virtually every critic agreed was that the book was entirely devoid of humor. As James explained in a letter to Lee, *Miss Brown* is marred by "a certain ferocity . . . you take the aesthetic business too seriously, too tragically, and above all with too great an implication of sexual motives." What made the novel most controversial, however, was the perception that many of the characters were thinly disguised portraits of people Lee knew personally, including Wilde; Dante Gabriel Rossetti; the painter Ford Madox Brown; and Brown's daughter Lucy, wife of William Michael Rossetti. May Morris, who had been educated by William Morris to become his wife, was so painfully embarrassed by the plot of *Miss Brown* that she and many of her friends ended all social relationships with Lee.

Lee seems to have been genuinely surprised by the hostile responses to *Miss Brown.* In her journal she undertook a painful analysis of her own character and motives, considering the possibility that she had attacked in others the same corruption and disease she feared in herself. Lee also reexamined her theories concerning the practice of fiction.

For example, in "A Dialogue on Novels" (1885; collected in *Baldwin: Being Dialogues on Views and Aspirations,* 1886), Lee condemned the type of novel she had attempted in *Miss Brown* by arguing that the novelist should eschew the "humourless morbidness," "prurient description," and "pessimistic misrepresentation" found in the novels of Emile Zola and his followers. She also spoke out against the detailed psychological analysis of characters in fiction, arguing that "it is not morally correct, any more than it is artistically correct, to see the microscopic and the hidden."

In the wake of the *Miss Brown* controversy, Lee abandoned realistic narratives of contemporary life. For several years the only fiction she produced were stories of the supernatural. Like *Ottilie: An Eighteenth-Century Idyl* and *The Countess of Albany,* the majority of Lee's supernatural stories are inspired by her researches in the history of art and music; many express the scholar's yearning to meet, see, and hear the historical figures she studies. It is difficult to know how fully Lee was aware of other recurring themes, such as the destructive power of female eroticism, that seem so evident to twentieth-century readers. But the stories certainly reflect the author's growing interest in pre-Freudian theories of the unconscious mind and the part it plays in artistic creation.

In "A Culture Ghost: or, Winthrop's Adventure" (1881), a young painter is haunted by the portrait of an eighteenth-century Italian composer holding the score to a piece of music that has since been lost. He locates the house where the composer was murdered, spends the night there, and is rewarded by a vision of the composer playing the score that appears in the painting. A few years later Lee drastically revised this story, transforming it into the far more sinister "A Wicked Voice," in which a nineteenth-century composer becomes obsessed with the story of Zaffirino, an eighteenth-century castrato whose voice, with its terrible beauty, kills any woman who listens to his singing. The narrator survives his encounter with Zaffirino but finds that he has lost his own artistic vision, lamenting "My head is filled with music . . . not my own."

*A Phantom Lover: A Fantastic Story* (1886) is atypical of Lee's supernatural fiction in that it is set primarily in Victorian England. The story begins when the narrator arrives to paint the portrait of Mrs. Oke, a beautiful woman married to her kindly but dull cousin. Mrs. Oke is obsessed by the painting of a female ancestor who reputedly, in the seventeenth century, assisted her husband in murdering her lover. The present Mrs. Oke torments her husband when she apparently conducts a romance

with the murdered lover's ghost. Perhaps because he has been driven to madness by his wife's rejection, Oke believes one evening that he sees the ghost. He shoots at the apparition, kills his wife instead, and then turns the gun on himself.

"Amour Dure" and "Dionea" describe women even more beautiful and sadistic than Mrs. Oke. Most of "Amour Dure" is in the form of a diary kept by Spiridion Trepka, a Polish-German historian who falls under the malevolent influence of Medea da Carpi. In 1592 Medea had been strangled for having caused the deaths of five of her lovers. Three hundred years later, at Medea's insistence, Trepka commits an act of vandalism against the statue of the duke who ordered her execution. The next morning Trepka is found stabbed, the last of Medea's victims. The possibility remains that the diary records not actual ghostly visitations but the hallucinations of a madman.

In "Faustus and Helena," contained in *Belcaro: Being Essays on Sundry Aesthetical Questions,* Lee remarks that the supernatural is that which has been banished by "official Christianity" and "men of science." Her story "Dionea" describes the resurgence of erotic forces once celebrated in the religious rites of pre-Christian civilizations. The title character is clearly meant to be associated with Dionea, mother of Aphrodite. As a child Dionea survives a shipwreck, is washed up on an Italian coast, and is placed in a convent. Although the adolescent girl has no lovers of her own, her presence seems to stimulate inappropriate erotic attachments. When a young painter comes to the village, accompanied by his pregnant wife, he asks Dionea to sit as his model. One morning the villagers realize that Dionea has disappeared. They find the painter's body at the foot of a cliff, and the mutilated body of his pregnant wife has been sacrificed on an ancient altar to Venus.

In 1890 four of these stories were collected and published as *Hauntings: Fantastic Stories.* Lee seems to have hoped that with this book she might achieve some degree of popular success: in 1891 she wrote to her mother that none of her previous books had sold as many as twelve hundred copies. Her hopes were dashed, however, when almost the entire Heinemann edition of *Hauntings* was destroyed in a warehouse fire. She sent one of the few surviving copies to James, and the recipient informed Lee, in his letter of thanks, that "the supernatural story . . . is not the *class* of fiction I myself most cherish. . . . But that only makes my enjoyment of your artistry more of a subjection."

Although Lee had acquiesced in James's criticism of *Miss Brown,* she came increasingly to resent

*Mary Robinson, Lee's traveling companion beginning about 1881. When Robinson announced her engagement to marry in 1887, Lee suffered a complete physical and emotional collapse.*

what James himself described, in a moment of candor, as his patronizing attitude toward her fiction. She may also have been offended by James's characterization of women in *The Bostonians* (1886) and in *The Princess Casamassima* (1886). Certainly the relationship between Olive Chancellor and Verena Tarrant in *The Bostonians* resembled Lee's friendship with Mary Robinson in many details, such as her determination that Robinson should remain single and dedicated, as Lee was dedicated, to her literary work. When Robinson suddenly married in 1887 Lee suffered a complete breakdown. Lee was more fortunate than James's character, Olive, who is left alone after Verena's marriage. Lee soon commenced a "new love, new life" with Clementina "Kit" Anstruther-Thomson.

In her 1895 essay "On Literary Construction" (collected in *The Handling of Words and Other Studies in Literary Psychology* ), Lee remarked that in the character of Olive Chancellor, James realized "the kind of temperament – the mode of feeling and being most organically detestable to him in all womankind." Lee referred to *The Princess Casamassima* in two stories that infuriated James when they were published in the volume *Vanitas. Polite Stories* (1892). In

these "sketches of frivolous women" Lee analyzes the social and economic forces that caused all but the most extraordinary of upper-class women to appear materialistic and socially callous. For example, Valentine Flodden, the heroine of "A Worldy Woman," is determined to remain single even though she has no money of her own. She asks Leonard Greenleaf, a graduate of Oxford who professes socialist ideas, to introduce her to women who live and work among the poor. But Leonard, who has read *The Princess Casamissima,* insists on believing that Val must be as deficient in "moral earnestness" as the heroine of James's novel. Ten years later Leonard meets Val again at a fashionable dinner party. Val explains that she has married a wealthy, vulgar man she can neither love nor respect because Leonard made her realize she was "locked . . . into the place into which I had been born."

"Lady Tal" is a witty satire on Lee's relationship with James at the time she was writing *Miss Brown.* Lady Tal resembles her creator in many ways: her first name is Violet, her home is in Italy, and her behavior is overbearing. Lady Tal is writing a novel that by its title, "Christina," recalls the heroine of *The Princess Casamassima.* When she meets Jervaise Marion, "a psychological novelist . . . a kind of Henry James, of a lesser magnitude," she bullies him into reading her manuscript. Although Marion can see that "Christina" is little more than "an unconscious, complete imitation" of the type of fiction he writes, he encourages Lady Tal to think that she can become the "George Eliot of fashionable life." But Lady Tal is shrewd enough to guess that Marion is studying her so that he may use her as a character in his own fiction. Lady Tal also realizes that "Christina," revised according to Marion's ideas, is "a hideous hash." But she decides she will publish the novel anyway, dedicating it to him. In the concluding scene Lady Tal suggests that she and Marion should collaborate on a fictionalized account of their own relationship; she seems also to be proposing marriage. The wary reader should remember, however, that Lady Tal is a character much given to sarcasm and irony.

Reviews of *Vanitas* praised the stories for their "searching analysis and skilled portrayal." Inevitably the critics remarked that Lee was indebted to James for her prose style and subject matter. It was perhaps equally inevitable that the volume ended her friendship with James, who wrote to his brother William that Lee's satire upon himself was a "particularly impudent and blackguardly sort of thing to do to a friend and one who has treated her with such particular consideration as I have. . . . She's a tiger-cat!"

Meanwhile Lee was immersing herself in a new research interest: the psychology of aesthetic response. She regarded Kit Anstruther-Thomson, who lived with the Pagets in Florence, as an equal partner in this work. Together, and in discussions with Berenson, they developed a theory of aesthetic empathy that Lee eventually applied to the study of music and literature. Still, the mid 1890s were difficult years. Lee's most faithful mentor, Pater, died in 1895. In 1896 Matilda Paget died, and Lee's brother, who had passed many years as an invalid, abruptly announced that he was sufficiently recovered to move out of the Paget home; two years later he married the novelist Annie E. Holdsworth. His actions embittered Lee, who had devoted much of her life to nursing him. In the midst of these events, Berenson accused Lee and Anstruther-Thomson of plagiarizing his ideas. Anstruther-Thomson suffered a nervous breakdown and decided to return to England. Although the two women remained friends, Lee was depressed by this conclusion to what she had regarded as an eternal love.

During these years Lee wrote several stories based on medieval and Renaissance legends; they were eventually collected in *Pope Jacynth and Other Fantastic Tales* (1904) and in *For Maurice: Five Unlikely Stories* (1927). The *Athenaeum* remarked that these exotic and decadent fictions were written in the style of Pater, "a style like enamels and mosaic in its sensuous and studious selection."

"Prince Alberic and the Snake Lady" (1896) was originally published in the *Yellow Book,* a periodical associated with the decadent movement. The story's protagonist, Prince Alberic, is a lonely orphan in seventeenth-century Italy. At the age of eleven he is befriended by a tame grass snake and by a lady who claims to be his godmother. From a passing tinker he hears the legend of Oriana, who is half snake, half woman. Oriana can be freed from her enchantment only when a prince of the Alberic line remains faithful to her for ten years. The present prince, recognizing the identity between Oriana, his so-called godmother, and the pet snake, is determined to break the spell. But when he refuses to enter into an arranged marriage, the snake is killed. Prince Alberic dies also, and in his room the servants find not the dead snake but the naked and mutilated body of a woman. Vineta Colby describes "Prince Alberic and the Snake Lady" as an allegory of the struggle of pure beauty and art against worldliness and carnality. Ruth Robbins interprets the story as an allegory of the defeat of feminine anarchy by the masculine forces of history.

"The Doll" (written in 1899 and published in *For Maurice: Five Unlikely Stories*) is narrated by a

*A sketch of Lee by John Singer Sargent (Ashmolean Museum, Oxford University)*

tourist in search of antiques. In an Italian palace she comes upon a life-size doll, the effigy of a young countess who died soon after her marriage. For a time the doll was idolized by her grieving husband, but after he remarried the doll was shut in a closet. The narrator conflates the doll with the dead wife when she speculates that the count made no attempt to understand the doll. In the concluding scene the narrator ends the doll's sorrows by sacrificing her on a giant funeral pyre. The story recalls a passage from Lee's 1902 essay on "The Economic Dependence of Women" (collected in *Gospels of Anarchy and Other Contemporary Studies,* 1908), in which the au-

thor analyzes her own mind to understand why she has "evaded and avoided" any conscious consideration of the struggle for female emancipation. Lee remarks in the essay that the relationship between a man and a woman is all too often that of "a human being playing with a doll."

Lee develops a more idealistic view of romantic love in *Ariadne in Mantua: A Romance in Five Acts* (1903), a drama. The main characters are Ferdinand, Duke of Mantua, and Diego, a prostitute who has been the duke's mistress, and who is disguised during most of the play as a male. In her preface to the published version of this work, Lee describes it as an

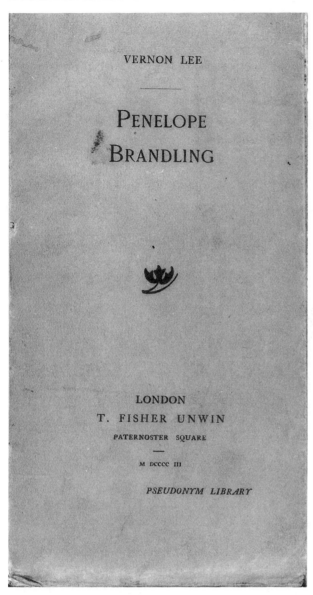

VERNON LEE

PENELOPE
BRANDLING

LONDON
T. FISHER UNWIN
PATERNOSTER SQUARE

M DCCCC III

*PSEUDONYM LIBRARY*

*Front wrapper for the paperbound edition of Lee's 1903
novel set on the Welsh coast (courtesy of the Lilly Library,
Indiana University)*

allegorical representation of the struggle between impulse and tradition (or duty), which she labels "the contending forces of history and life." *Ariadne in Mantua* was performed in London in 1916 and in Florence in 1934.

Lee's next novel, *Penelope Brandling: A Tale of the Welsh Coast in the Eighteenth Century* was published in 1903. The title character unwittingly marries into a family of wreckers and goes to live in their gloomy, mysterious house on the Welsh coast. Though it successfully invokes an atmospheric setting, the novel is unremarkable. The author's final novel, *Louis Norbert: A Two-Fold Romance* (1914), has been aptly described by Colby as a "scholarly detective story." It relates the story of a young archaeologist and a middle-aged Englishwoman who join forces to investigate the mysterious histories of two seventeenth-century figures: Artemesia, an Italian poetess, and Louis Norbert, who, it turns out, was probably a son of Louis XIV. The twentieth-century couple pursue their research in libraries and archives in England and on the Continent, explaining their discoveries in letters to each other. Lee manages to convey the excitement of historical research, although critics expressed more interest in Louis and Artemesia than in their twentieth-century counterparts.

In the years leading up to World War I, Lee continued her work on the psychology of aesthetic response. She published several collections of essays, including two volumes, *Gospels of Anarchy and other Contemporary Studies* and *Vital Lies: Studies of Some Varieties of Recent Obscurantism* (1912), that address contemporary social and philosophical problems. Lee also joined a desperate struggle to avert military conflict. She wrote *The Ballet of the Nations: A Present-day Morality* (1915), an allegorical shadow play that analyzes the psychological causes and effects of war. Lee's pacifist views made her many enemies but also many new friends, including Bertrand Russell, John Maynard Keynes, Lytton Strachey, and Lady Ottoline Morrell. Her contributions to the periodical press elicited a letter from Olive Schreiner, who wrote, "Can I tell you how splendid I think your articles on the war. You 'take away the shame of women from among us.'" In 1920 Lee added a prologue, epilogue, and explanatory notes to *The Ballet of the Nations: A Present-day Morality* and published the new work under the title *Satan, The Waster: A Philosophic War Trilogy* (1920). It was reviewed in the London *Nation* by Bernard Shaw, who proclaimed that Lee, "by sheer intellectual force, training, knowledge and character, kept her head when Europe was a mere lunatic asylum. . . . I take off my hat to the old guard of Victorian cosmopolitan intellectualism, and salute her as the noblest Briton of them all."

Lee did not publish any important new fiction in the last twenty years of her life, but she developed her ideas on the writing of fiction in *The Handling of Words and Other Studies in Literary Psychology*, in which she argues that the novel should be considered as a structure of devices used by the author to manipulate "the contents of the Reader's mind." She demonstrates her theories by analyzing passages from the work of such authors as Thomas Hardy, Eliot, Pater, and James.

Although Kenneth Graham suggests that Lee's essays on the novel deserve to be ranked alongside any similar piece by James, in the 1920s her intellec-

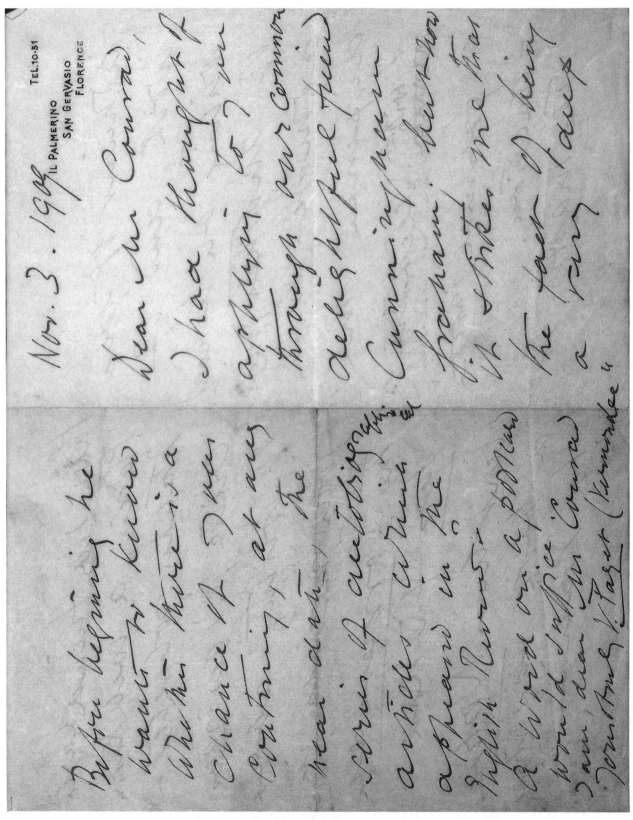

*Letter from Lee to Joseph Conrad mentioning their "common delightful friend," R. B. Cunninghame Graham (courtesy of the Lilly Library, Indiana University)*

tual reputation plummeted. To a younger generation her writing seemed unfashionably earnest and verbose. *The Poet's Eye. Notes on Some Differences between Verse and Prose* (1926) was published by Virginia and Leonard Woolf at Hogarth Press, but in her diary Woolf describes Lee's prose as "slack and untidy." As she took stock of her career, Lee grew increasingly despondent. In *The Handling of Words* she describes her early writings as the work of "an adulterated Ruskin, Pater, Michelet, Henry James." Shortly before her death on 13 February 1935, Lee told Willis that her lack of influence was due to her isolated social position as "an alien, having no ties, either of nation, blood, class or profession."

As "an independent woman" Lee certainly was at a professional disadvantage. But she underestimated both the quality of her writing and the extent of her influence. Ed Block Jr. has recently suggested that in letters and conversation Lee and Pater "were working simultaneously toward a similar form of short fiction." James also was probably more influenced by Lee's literary criticism and by her stories of the supernatural than he cared to admit after their friendship ended.

Lee's work has never been entirely forgotten. Her early essays on fiction have been included in modern collections of Victorian criticism; *The Handling of Words* has been reprinted in a paperback edition; her short stories have appeared in many anthologies; and *Miss Brown* has been republished in a facsimile edition. In recent years the stories of the supernatural have attracted the greatest amount of critical attention. Now scholars are beginning to revalue the stories of contemporary society and to reconsider the circumstances of Lee's life and career.

**Letters:**

*Vernon Lee's Letters,* edited by Irene Cooper Willis (London: Privately printed, 1937).

**Bibliographies:**

Phyllis F. Mannocchi, " 'Vernon Lee': A Reintroduction and Primary Bibliography," *English Literature in Transition 1880–1920,* 26, no. 4 (1983): 231–267;

Carl Markgraf, " 'Vernon Lee': A Commentary and An Annotated Bibliography of Writings About Her," *English Literature in Transition 1880–1920,* 26, no. 4 (1983): 268–312.

**Biography:**

Peter Gunn, *Vernon Lee: Violet Paget, 1856–1935* (London: Oxford University Press, 1964).

**References:**

Edwin F. Block, *Rituals of Dis-integration: Romance and Madness in the Victorian Psychomythic Tale* (New York: Garland, 1993): 61–88;

Carlo Caballero, " 'A Wicked Voice': On Vernon Lee, Wagner, and the Effects of Music," *Victorian Studies,* 35 (Summer 1992): 385–408;

Peter G. Christensen, "The Burden of History in Vernon Lee's Ghost Story 'Amour Dure,' " in *Studies in the Humanities,* 16 (1989): 33–43;

Vineta Colby, "The Puritan Aesthete: Vernon Lee," in her *The Singular Anomaly: Women Novelists of the Nineteenth Century* (New York: New York University Press, 1970), pp. 235–304;

Burdett Gardner, *The Lesbian Imagination (Victorian Style): A Psychological and Critical Study of "Vernon Lee"* (New York: Garland, 1987);

Kenneth Graham, *English Criticism of the Novel, 1865–1900* (Oxford: Clarendon Press, 1965);

Merete Licht, "Henry James's Portrait of a Lady: Vernon Lee in *The Princess Casamassima,*" in *A Literary Miscellany Presented to Eric Jacobsen,* edited by Graham D. Caie and Holger Norgaard (Copenhagen: University of Copenhagen, 1988), pp. 285–303;

Phyllis F. Mannocchi, "Vernon Lee and Kit Anstruther-Thomson: A Study of Love and Collaboration Between Romantic Friends," *Women's Studies,* 12 (1986): 129–148;

Harriet Waters Preston, "Vernon Lee," *Atlantic Monthly,* 55 (February 1885): 219–227;

Ruth Robbins, "Vernon Lee: Decadent Woman?," in *Fin de Siecle/Fin du Globe: Fears and Fantasies of the Late Nineteenth Century,* edited by John Stokes (New York: St. Martin's Press, 1992), pp. 139–161.

**Papers:**

Vernon Lee's literary executor, Irene Cooper Willis, divided the papers between Colby College in Waterville, Maine, and Somerville College, Cambridge University. Lee's correspondence with the publishing firm of T. Fisher Unwin is at the New York Public Library. Other correspondence is located at the Harry Ransom Humanities Research Center, University of Texas at Austin.

# Ada Leverson

*(10 October 1862 – 30 August 1933)*

## Margaret Crosland

BOOKS: *The Twelfth Hour* (London: Richards, 1907);

*Love's Shadow* (London: Richards, 1908);

*The Limit* (London: Richards, 1911; New York: Norton, 1951);

*Tenterhooks* (London: Richards, 1912);

*Bird of Paradise* (London: Richards, 1914; New York: Norton, 1952);

*Love at Second Sight* (London: Richards, 1916).

**Collection:** *The Little Ottleys* (London: MacGibbon & Kee, 1962; New York: Dial, 1982) – includes *Love's Shadow, Tenterhooks,* and *Love at Second Sight.*

OTHER: *Letters to the Sphinx from Oscar Wilde and Reminiscences of the Author,* with a biographical essay by Leverson (London: Duckworth, 1930).

Ada Leverson, who published her series of six novels during and soon after the Edwardian period, had virtually no competition from other women writers of the time. Her style of fiction was different from that of such contemporaries as Elizabeth von Arnim, Elinor Glyn, May Sinclair, Edith Wharton, or Willa Cather. Katherine Mansfield, who had come to London from New Zealand, published nothing before 1911, while slightly later came the deeply romantic, even sentimental fiction of Ethel M. Dell. It has to be said that Ada Leverson's fiction appeals particularly to women, although several male literary critics, including V. S. Pritchett, C. P. Snow, Anthony Powell, and Vernon Scannell, have given it the praise it deserves, especially during the last generation.

Ada Esther Leverson was born on 10 October 1862 into the world portrayed in her novels, that of fashionable London society at the close of the Victorian era. Her father, Samuel Beddington, the son of a wool merchant, made money as a broker of diamonds, pearls, and precious stones, while her mother, Zillah, née Simon, known for her beauty, was a gifted pianist, an amateur who played well enough to count the great Polish virtuoso pianist

Paderewski among her friends. Ada, who had three younger sisters and four younger brothers, was educated at home, as was usual at the time for a girl of her class.

However, this secure background did not satisfy the handsome, golden-haired, self-willed girl who at the age of nineteen insisted on marrying a man, Ernest Leverson, twelve years older than herself against the wishes of her parents. The marriage was not happy, and Ada soon discovered that Ernest's "ward," who was being educated in France, was in fact his illegitimate daughter. Leverson gambled heavily, usually without success, and was often bad tempered. Although Ada was attracted to the Irish Lord Desart, a minor novelist and a divorcé, and also to the novelist George Moore, she wished at all costs to avoid scandal and remained with her husband. Their son, George, died of meningitis at the age of four months. Ada was saved from deep unhappiness by her developing social life and the birth of her second child, her daughter, Violet, born in 1892 in Paris. In 1923 this young woman married a widower of fifty-eight and became the mother of Francis Wyndham, the British writer.

In 1902, however, the Leversons separated, for Ernest had made such disastrous speculations that his fortune disappeared, and he decided to immigrate to Canada. His wife was forced to move to a smaller house and was grateful that she was able to earn a little money through writing. Her first stories and sketches had been published in 1892 and 1893 in the periodicals *St. Stephen's Review* and *Black and White,* while she was also soon able to contribute to *Punch,* then a popular weekly magazine. There have been differing accounts of how and when she met the writer who influenced her the most, Oscar Wilde. Possibly it was through her clever parody of his long poem *The Sphinx* (1894) – she called her poem *The Minx* (1894) – or they may have been introduced to each other earlier. Their friendship was close, and through Wilde, Leverson met all the fashionable figures of the day, including the illustrator Aubrey Beardsley and the painter Walter Sickert, who made a portrait drawing of her in pastel.

*Ada Leverson*

Much of Leverson's early writing shows her appreciation of Wilde. The unpublished "An Afternoon Party" (1893), for example, brings together at an imaginary tea table Lady Windermere (from Wilde's play) and two other, markedly different women: the biblical Salome and Nora, the heroine of Henrik Ibsen's *A Doll's House* (1879). Leverson affected not to understand the nature of the criminal charges brought against Wilde in the mid 1890s but did all she could to help him, hiding him in her house, often in the children's nursery. His trials and imprisonment in no way changed the nature of their friendship; Leverson was the first to greet him when he was released from prison, and she was deeply upset by his death in 1900.

During 1895 and 1896 she had published two stories in the *Yellow Book,* the illustrated quarterly that appeared between 1884 and 1897. One of them, titled "Suggestion," concerns a young man whose adolescent rebellion takes the form of intervention in his widowed father's possible marriage plans. It has the teasing, lighthearted atmosphere characteristic of Leverson's novels and, beneath the surface, an understanding of complicated sexual and family relationships which are characteristic of everything she wrote.

Leverson claimed that she disliked writing her novels – in fact, she dictated them from her bed –

and no doubt she preferred the opportunities for conversation offered by the social occasions she so much enjoyed, for she had become famous in society for her wit and satiric approach to life. However, she transferred her experience of social life into her writing, remembering how she had lived as a girl in the 1880s and 1890s. *The Twelfth Hour* was published in 1907 and *Love's Shadow* the following year.

The principal characters in *The Twelfth Hour* could be described in late–twentieth century terms as some of London's "beautiful people." The heroine, Felicity Chetwode, is about twenty-five, witty, and a blonde beauty. She has been married for one year to the wealthy but unappreciative Lord Chetwode. He is often away from home, either at the races or buying antiques, and his wife becomes so lonely that she decides to make him jealous. She tries to develop a flirtation with a young man named Bertie Wilson, who is attractive but uninteresting; although Felicity feels sorry for him, he is "lonely and unhappy," like her.

Her husband is not much inclined to feel jealous, for he does not like scenes. Leverson includes in the episode a brilliant description of Lord Chetwode and his forbears: "His voice and manner had the soft unobtrusive gentleness that comes to those whose ancestry for long years have dared and com-

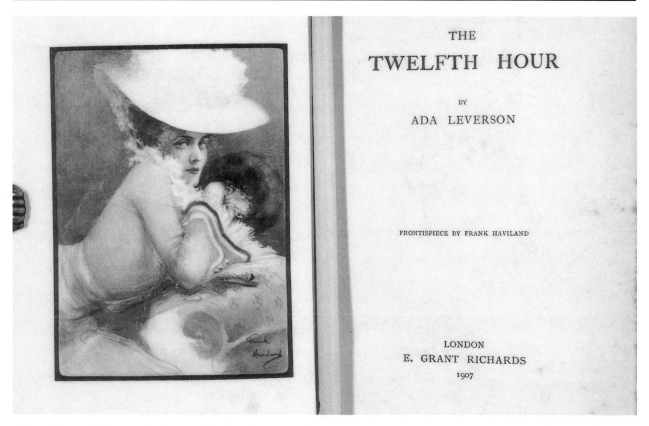

THE

# TWELFTH HOUR

BY

ADA LEVERSON

FRONTISPIECE BY FRANK HAVILAND

LONDON
E. GRANT RICHARDS
1907

*Frontispiece and title page for Leverson's first novel, the story of the marital problems of Lord Chetwode and his wife, Felicity (courtesy of the Lilly Library, Indiana University)*

manded. In time, when there's nothing to fight for, the dash naturally dies out." After Felicity discovers a portrait of a mysterious woman among her husband's possessions, her sixteen-year-old brother, Savile, an Eton schoolboy, takes her part, and after his intervention Chetwode tells his wife that the woman is of no importance to him. The story ends with the reconciliation of the husband and wife.

The novel includes a subplot and various characters who are not always directly involved in the story but allow their creator to write the amusing descriptions that characterize her work: for example, Mrs. Ogilvie, who had changed her name from Lucy to Vera "on the ground that it was 'more Russian.' There seemed no special object in this, as she had married a Scotchman." There is also the unforgettable Aunt William, who spent much time doing Berlin wool work, which she hated, "but did so partly from tradition and partly from a "contrary" disposition; because other people didn't like it, and even because she didn't like it herself."

Leverson's preoccupation with the problems of marriage and unresponsive husbands was no doubt based on her domestic situation and those of

various friends. Although she hints that these problems are depressing, this first novel is essentially entertaining and contains portraits of people she knew, including the minor novelist Robert Hichens (author of *The Green Carnation,* anonymously published in 1894), who appears as F. G. Rivers, "a wonderfully clever novelist." The *Daily Mail* noticed these recognizable portraits. Hichens reviewed the book favorably in the *Westminster Gazette* and hoped that Ada Leverson would one day write something more serious.

Valentia, the heroine of Leverson's next novel, *Love's Shadow,* thinks that she escapes from her unutterably boring husband by conducting a secret, virtually harmless romance with her cousin Harry. When he eventually reveals himself as selfish and mercenary, Valentia finally comes to understand the secret strength of her husband, Romer, and realizes he loves her. *Love's Shadow* became better known after it was collected with *Tenterhooks* (1912) and *Love at Second Sight* (1916) into a trilogy entitled *The Little Ottleys,* published in 1962 with a perceptive introduction by the novelist Colin MacInnes, the son of another novelist, Angela

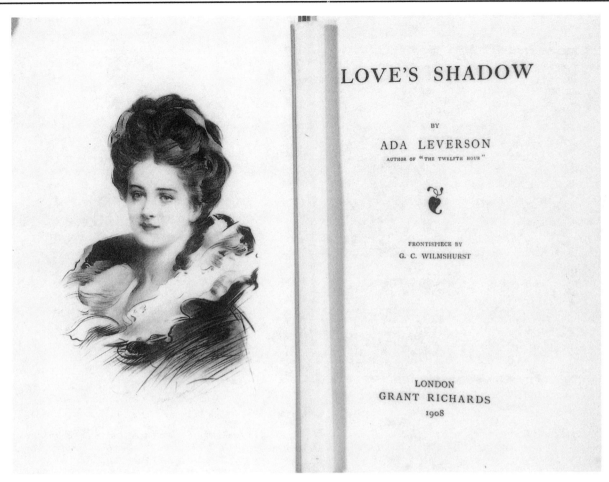

*Frontispiece and title page for Leverson's second novel, in which a married woman becomes involved in a secret romance with her cousin (courtesy of the Lilly Library, Indiana University)*

Thirkell. Edith and Bruce Ottley, who appear in all three novels, were no doubt based to some extent on Ada and Ernest Leverson, although they were both obviously exaggerated: Bruce is the most irritating, humorless, and selfish husband in the world; Edith is forgiving to a superhuman extent. The reader applauds everything she does, and after Bruce's departure with the treacherous and ridiculous Madame Frabelle the reader can only be delighted that the forgiving Edith is destined to find happiness through "love at second sight."

Julie Speedie, Leverson's biographer, believes that this second novel is one of the author's best. A reviewer in the *Spectator* wrote of it that Edith's "behaviour . . . in most trying circumstances would be hard to credit were it not for the unquestioned fact that intelligent women do very often suffer foolish husbands gladly." Edith's creator, unfortunately, did not find "love at second sight," for she refused to divorce her husband. She was for a time at least said to be in love with her publisher, Grant

Richards, who was a married man and did not respond.

Leverson was admired by such different people as Max Beerbohm, W. Somerset Maugham, and V. S. Pritchett. She has been seen by later critics, such as Sally Beauman, as a distant descendant of Jane Austen, sensitive to the hidden motives of behavior, ready to laugh at vanity, understanding of married couples, parents, and children, yet seemingly little preoccupied with all that was going on in the world outside. Leverson wrote about the society she knew, and if she did not feel capable of writing about international affairs, she still noticed every minute detail of what was happening in her own world. *Bird of Paradise* (1914) proves that the author was not limited to lighthearted social chat and examines seriously the problem of jealousy. The novel was praised by the *Daily Telegraph,* where the reviewer wrote that the author's "glamour never covers emptiness, but is a sparkle from the heart of things." *Punch* indicated that the plot was not pro-

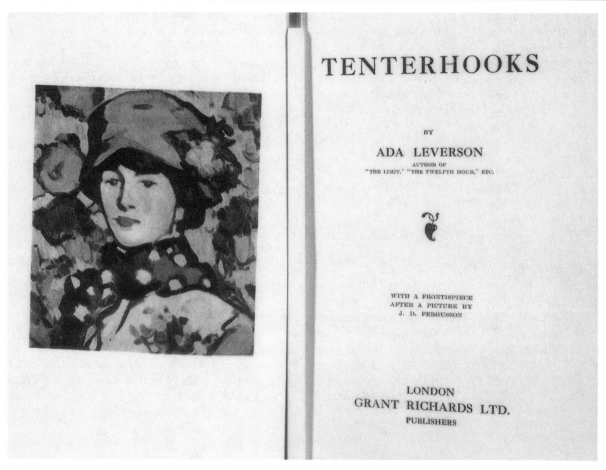

*Frontispiece for Leverson's 1912 novel, which was eventually collected in a single volume with* Love's Shadow *(1908) and* Love at Second Sight *(1916) as a trilogy titled* The Little Ottleys *(1962) (courtesy of the Lilly Library, Indiana University)*

found but praised the character drawing and the light, "most airy" dialogue.

In *The Limit* (1911) the theme of all Leverson's fiction is clear: the endless problems of marriage, for marriage was still seen as the only lifestyle for women of the upper middle class and the aristocracy. If men could be married and free, women could only be married and far from free, subject to their husbands' will. Their only empires were the drawing room, the nursery, and the kitchen, where their plans as manager and mother were carried out by their domestic staffs. The married woman retained, of course, the important role of hostess, and social life at the time among the upper classes was highly organized and always based on a set of firm rules.

Leverson never took up any obvious literary or social attitude, and if other novelists wrote about the suffragettes and women's rights, she was concerned to write about women in the discovery of their true selves and in their relationship to men. She was a feminist in her belief that a woman

should be certain of her own personality, for she felt that once that was understood other aspects of independence would surely follow. She was aware that a few women did not want to marry and would thus live as lonely spinsters; she was also aware that rich young men, especially artists such as Edith Ottley's friend Vincy, would take advantage of the working girls who posed as models and hoped in vain for something more.

These themes, which are discussed in her novels in brief but telling incidents, never intrude on the plots, and they make it clear that Leverson's work deserves to be regarded as much more than a group of period novels. Admittedly the decorative detail she includes, descriptions of every type of dress, of hairstyles, and even of interiors, such as an onyx-paved bathroom floor, probably tell the present-day reader more about the late Victorian and the Edwardian periods than any carefully planned exhibition could do. However, these details form only the background to her work; it is the married couples, the occasional eccentrics, and most of

all the women, including a few of the spinsters, groups whose emotional problems are not resolved at the end of the twentieth century, who remain in the memory.

After publishing her last novel, *Love at Second Sight,* the "Sphinx" wrote no more fiction. The previous year she had written the preface to an American book about astrology, *Whom You Should Marry* (1915). In 1930 a valuable reminder of her late friend, *Letters to the Sphinx from Oscar Wilde and Reminiscences of the Author,* with Leverson contributing the "reminiscences," was published. T. S. Eliot had included one piece from this collection, "The Last First Night," in the *Criterion* in 1926. Leverson also worked on a play titled "The Triflers," but she never completed it.

In the autumn of 1919 Leverson had met the gifted trio Edith, Osbert, and Sacheverell Sitwell, although none of them had yet published a best-known work. Osbert, who had in fact had a glimpse of Ada earlier when he was a schoolboy, became a close friend and often invited Ada to travel with him and members of his circle to Italy. Often, too, she stayed with the Sitwell family at their famous country house, Renishaw, in Derbyshire. Although

she had become deaf, she retained her elegance and wit and her interest in people until the end of her life. She died on 30 August 1933 at the age of seventy, having developed pneumonia on her return from one of the trips to Italy that she enjoyed so much.

**Biography:**

Julie Speedie, *Wonderful Sphinx, The Biography of Ada Leverson* (London: Virago, 1993).

**References:**

Sally Beauman, Introduction to Leverson's *The Little Ottleys* (London: Virago, 1982);

Colin MacInnes, Introduction to Leverson's *The Little Ottleys* (London: MacGibbon & Kee, 1962);

Osbert Sitwell, *Noble Essences* (London: Macmillan, 1950);

Francis Wyndham, "Ada Leverson," in *The Theatre of Embarrassment* (London: Chatto & Windus, 1991);

Violet Wyndham, *The Sphinx and Her Circle: A Biographical Sketch of Ada Leverson, 1862–1933* (London: Deutsch, 1963).

# E. V. Lucas

*(11 June 1868 – 26 June 1938)*

George Allan Cate
*University of Maryland*

See also the Lucas entries in *DLB 98: Modern British Essayists, First Series,* and *DLB 149: Late Nineteenth- and Early Twentieth-Century British Biographers.*

BOOKS: *Sparks from a Flint: Odd Rhymes for Odd Times,* as E. V. L. (London: Howe, 1891);

*Songs of the Bat* (London: W. P. Griffith, 1892);

*Bernard Barton and His Friends* (London: Richards, 1897);

*The Flamp, The Ameliorator, and The Schoolboy's Apprentice* (London: Richards, 1897);

*All the World Over,* by Lucas and Edith Farmiloe (London: Richards, 1898);

*Willow and Leather: A Book of Praise* (Bristol: Arrowsmith / London: Simpkin, Marshall, Hamilton, Kent, 1898);

*The Book of Shops* (London: Richards, 1899);

*What Shall We Do Now? A Book of Suggestions for Children's Games and Enjoyment,* by Lucas and Elizabeth Lucas (London: Richards, 1900; New York: Stokes, 1901);

*Four and Twenty Toilers* (London: Dalton, 1900);

*Domesticities: A Little Book of Household Impressions* (London: Smith, Elder, 1900);

*The Visit to London* (London: Methuen, 1902);

*Wisdom While You Wait,* by Lucas and Charles Larcom Graves (London: Privately printed, 1902; New York & London: Inside-Britt, 1903);

*England Day by Day,* by Lucas and Graves (London: Methuen, 1903);

*Highways and Byways in Sussex* (London & New York: Macmillan, 1904; revised, 1935); published in 3 volumes as *West Sussex, Mid-Sussex,* and *East Sussex* (London: Macmillan, 1937);

*The Life of Charles Lamb,* 2 volumes (London: Methuen, 1905; New York & London: Putnam, 1905; revised, London: Methuen, 1921);

*A Wanderer in Holland* (London: Methuen, 1905; New York: Macmillan, 1905);

*Listener's Lure: An Oblique Narration* (London: Methuen, 1906); published as *Listener's Lure: A*

*Kensington Comedy* (New York & London: Macmillan, 1906);

*Change for a Halfpenny,* by Lucas and Graves (London: Rivers, 1906);

*A Wanderer in London* (London: Methuen, 1906; New York: Macmillan / London: Methuen, 1906);

*Signs of the Times,* by Lucas and Graves (London: Rivers, 1906);

*Fireside and Sunshine* (London: Methuen, 1906; New York: Dutton, 1907);

*Character and Comedy* (London: Methuen, 1907; New York: Macmillan, 1907);

*The Doll Doctor* (London: G. Alleri, 1907);

*A Swan and Her Friends* (London: Methuen, 1907);

*Hustled History,* by Lucas and Graves (London: Pitman, 1908);

*Over Bemerton's: An Easy-Going Chronicle* (London: Methuen, 1908; New York: Macmillan, 1908);

*Anne's Terrible Good Nature, and Other Stories for Children* (London: Chatto & Windus, 1908; New York: Macmillan, 1908);

*If: A Nightmare in the Conditional Mood,* by Lucas and Graves (London: Pitman, 1908);

*A Wanderer in Paris* (London: Methuen, 1909; New York: Macmillan, 1909);

*One Day and Another* (London: Methuen, 1909; New York: Macmillan, 1909);

*Farthest From the Truth,* by Lucas and Graves (London: Pitman, 1909);

*Mr. Ingleside* (London: Methuen, 1910; New York: Macmillan, 1910);

*The Slow Coach* (London: Gardener, Darton, 1910; New York: Macmillan, 1910);

*What a Life!,* by Lucas and George Morrow (London: Methuen, 1911);

*Old Lamps for New* (London: Methuen, 1911; New York: Macmillan, 1911);

*A Little of Everything* (London: Methuen, 1912; New York, Macmillan, 1912);

*London Lavender* (London: Methuen, 1912; New York: Macmillan, 1912);

*E. V. Lucas in 1931 (photograph by Howard Coster)*

*A Wanderer in Florence* (London: Methuen, 1912; New York: Macmillan, 1912);

*The British School: An Anecdotal Guide to the British Painters and Paintings in the National Gallery* (London: Methuen, 1913); published as *British Pictures and Their Painters: An Anecdotal Guide to the British Section of the National Gallery* (New York: Macmillan, 1913);

*Harvest Home* (London: Methuen, 1913; New York: Macmillan, 1913);

*Loiterer's Harvest* (London: Methuen, 1913; New York: Macmillan, 1913);

*All the Papers,* by Lucas and Graves (London & New York: Pitman, 1914);

*Landmarks* (London: Methuen, 1914; New York: Macmillan, 1914);

*A Wanderer in Venice* (London: Methuen, 1914; New York: Macmillan, 1914);

*Cloud and Silver* (London: Methuen, 1916; New York: Doran, 1916);

*Variety Lane* (London: Methuen, 1916);

*London Revisited* (London: Methuen, 1916); published as *More Wanderings in London* (New York: Doran, 1916);

*The Vermillion Box* (London: Methuen, 1916; New York: Doran, 1916);

*Outposts of Mercy: The Record of a Visit in November and December, 1916, to the Various Units of the British Red Cross in Italy* (London: Methuen, 1917);

*A Boswell of Beghdad, with Diversions* (London: Methuen, 1917; New York: Doran, 1917);

*'Twixt Eagle and Dove* (London: Methuen, 1918);

*Quoth the Raven: An Unofficial History of the War,* by Lucas and Morrow (London: Methuen, 1919);

*Mixed Vintages, A Blend of Essays Old and New* (London: Methuen, 1919);

*The Phantom Journal, and Other Essays and Diversions* (London: Methuen, 1919);

*David Williams, Founder of the Royal Literary Fund* (London: Murray, 1920);

*Adventures and Enthusiasms* (New York: Doran, 1920);

*Specially Selected* (London: Methuen, 1920);

*Verena in the Midst* (London: Methuen, 1920; New York: Doran, 1920);

*Roving East and Roving West* (London: Methuen, 1921; New York: Doran, 1921);

*Rose and Rose* (London: Methuen, 1921; New York: Doran, 1921);

*Urbanites* (London: Methuen, 1921);

*Edwin Austin Abbey, Royal Academician: The Record of His Life and Work,* 2 volumes (London: Methuen, 1921; London: Methuen / New York: Scribners, 1921);

*Vermeer of Delft* (London: Methuen, 1922);

*Genevra's Money* (London: Methuen, 1922; New York: Doran, 1923);

*Giving and Receiving: Essays and Fantasies* (London: Methuen, 1922; New York: Doran, 1922);

*You Know What People Are* (London: Methuen, 1922; New York: Doran, 1922);

*Advisory Ben: A Story* (London: Methuen, 1923; New York: Doran, 1924);

*Luck of the Year: Essays, Fantasies, and Stories* (London: Methuen, 1923; New York: Doran, 1923);

*Encounters and Diversions* (London: Methuen, 1924);

*The Same Star: A Comedy in Three Acts* (London: Methuen, 1924);

*A Wanderer Among Pictures: A Companion to the Galleries of Europe* (London: Methuen, 1924; New York: Doran, 1924);

*Chardin and Vigee-Lebrun* (London: Methuen, 1924; London: Methuen / New York: Doran, 1924);

*John Constable, The Painter* (London: Halton & Smith, 1924; London: Halton & Smith / New York: Minton, Balch, 1924);

*Michael Angelo* (London: Methuen, 1924; New York: Doran, 1924);

*Rembrandt* (London: Methuen, 1924);

*Introducing London* (London: Methuen, 1925; London: Methuen / New York: Doran, 1925);

*Zigzags in France, and Various Essays* (London: Methuen, 1925);

*Playtime & Company: A Book For Children* (London: Methuen, 1925; New York: Doran, 1925);

*Frans Hals* (London: Methuen, 1926; New York: Doran, 1926);

*Giorgione* (London: Methuen, 1926; London: Methuen / New York: Doran, 1926);

*Leonardo da Vinci* (London: Methuen, 1926; London: Methuen / New York: Doran, 1926);

*Van Dyck* (London: Methuen, 1926; London: Methuen / New York: Doran, 1926);

*Velasquez* (London: Methuen, 1926; London: Methuen / New York: Doran, 1926);

*Selected Essays of E. V. Lucas,* edited by E. A. Wodehouse (London: Methuen, 1926);

*A Wanderer in Rome* (London: Methuen, 1926; New York: Doran, 1926);

*Events and Embroideries* (London: Methuen, 1926; New York: Doran, 1927);

*A Cat Book* (London: Chatto & Windus, 1926; New York & London: Harper, 1927);

*A Fronded Isle, and Other Essays* (London: Methuen, 1927; Garden City, N.Y.: Doubleday, Doran, 1928);

*The More I See of Men: Stray Essays on Dogs* (London: Methuen, 1927);

*Introducing Paris* (London: Methuen, 1928);

*Out of a Clear Sky: Essays and Fantasies About Birds* (London: Methuen, 1928);

*A Rover I Would Be: Essays and Fantasies* (London: Methuen, 1928; New York: Dutton, 1928);

*The Colvins and Their Friends* (London: Methuen, 1928; New York: Scribners, 1928);

*Mr. Punch's County Songs* (London: Methuen, 1928);

*Vermeer the Magical* (London: Methuen, 1929; New York: Doubleday, Doran, 1929);

*Windfall's Eve: An Entertainment* (London: Methuen, 1929; Philadelphia: Lippincott, 1930);

*Turning Things Over: Essays and Fantasies* (London: Methuen, 1929; New York: Dutton, 1929);

*If Dogs Could Write: A Second Canine Miscellany* (London: Methuen, 1930; Philadelphia: Lippincott, 1930);

*Down the Sky: An Entertainment* (London: Methuen, 1930; Philadelphia: Lippincott, 1930);

*Traveller's Luck: Essays and Fantasies* (London: Methuen, 1930; Philadelphia: Lippincott, 1931);

*"And Such Small Deer"* (London: Methuen, 1930; Philadelphia: Lippincott, 1931);

*The Pekinese National Anthem* (London: Methuen, 1930);

*French Leaves* (London: Methuen, 1931; Philadelphia: Lippincott, 1931);

*Visibility Good: Essays and Excursions* (London: Methuen, 1931; Philadelphia: Lippincott, 1931);

*The Barber's Clock: A Conversation Piece* (London: Methuen, 1931; Philadelphia: Lippincott, 1931);

*No-Nose at the Show* (London: Methuen, 1931);

*At the Sign of the Dove* (London: Methuen, 1932);

*Lemon Verbena and Other Essays* (London: Methuen, 1932; Philadelphia: Lippincott, 1932);

*The Day of the Dog* (London: Methuen, 1932);

*Reading, Writing, and Remembering* (London: Methuen, 1932; New York & London: Harper, 1932);

*Audrey, Elizabeth, and E. V. Lucas, 1904*

*English Leaves* (London: Methuen, 1933; Philadelphia: Lippincott, 1933);

*Saunterer's Rewards* (London: Methuen, 1933; Philadelphia: Lippincott, 1934);

*At The Shrine of St. Charles: Stray Papers on Lamb Brought Together for the Centenary of His Death in 1834* (London: Methuen, 1934; New York: Dutton, 1934);

*Pleasure Trove* (London: Methuen, 1935; Philadelphia: Lippincott, 1935);

*The Old Contemporaries* (London: Methuen, 1935; New York: Harper, 1935);

*Only the Other Day* (London: Methuen, 1936; Philadelphia: Lippincott, 1937);

*London Afresh* (London: Methuen, 1936; Philadelphia & London: Lippincott, 1937);

*All of a Piece: New Essays* (London: Methuen, 1937; Philadelphia & New York: Lippincott, 1937);

*As the Bee Sucks,* edited by Ernest H. Shepard (London: Methuen, 1937);

*Adventures and Misgivings* (London: Methuen, 1938).

**Editions:** *Cricket All His Life,* edited by Rupert Hart-Davis (London: Hart-Davis, 1950);

*Selected Essays of E. V. Lucas,* edited by H. N. Wethered (London: Methuen, 1954).

OTHER: *A Book of Verses for Children,* edited by Lucas (London: Richards, 1897);

*Charles Lamb and the Lloyds,* edited by Lucas (London: Smith, Elder, 1898; Philadelphia: Lippincott, 1899);

*The Open Road: A Little Book for Wayfarers,* edited by Lucas (London: Richards, 1899; New York: Holt, 1901);

Charles Lamb, *The Essays of Elia,* introduction by Lucas (London: Methuen, 1902);

*The Works of Charles and Mary Lamb,* 7 volumes, edited by Lucas (London: Methuen, 1903–1905; New York: Putnam, 1903–1905);

*The Friendly Town: A Little Book for the Urbane,* edited by Lucas (London: Methuen, 1905; New York: Holt, 1906);

*Another Book of Verses for Children,* edited by Lucas (London: Gardner, Darton, 1907; New York: Macmillan, 1907);

*The Gentlest Art: A Choice of Letters by Entertaining Hands,* edited by Lucas (London: Methuen, 1907; New York: Macmillan, 1907);

*The Hambledon Men,* edited by Lucas (London: Frowde, 1907);

*Her Infinite Variety: A Feminine Portrait Gallery,* edited by Lucas (London: Methuen, 1908); pub-

lished as *The Ladies' Pageant* (New York: Macmillan, 1908);

*Runaways and Castaways,* edited by Lucas (London: Gardner, Darton, 1908);

*William Cowper's Letters: A Selection,* edited by Lucas (London & New York: Frowde, 1908);

*The Second Post: A Companion to the Gentlest Art,* edited by Lucas (London: Methuen, 1910; New York: Macmillan, 1910);

*Remember Louvain! A Little Book of Liberty and War,* edited by Lucas (London: Methuen, 1914);

*The Joy of Life: An Anthology of Lyrics Drawn Chiefly From the Works of Living Poets,* edited by Lucas (London: Methuen, 1927);

*Post-Bag Diversions,* edited by Lucas (London: Methuen, 1934; New York & London: Harper, 1934);

*The Letters of Charles Lamb, To Which Are Added Those of His Sister Mary Lamb,* 3 volumes, edited by Lucas (London: Dent/Methuen, 1935; New Haven: Yale University Press, 1935).

For nearly fifty years E. V. Lucas was one of the most accomplished and respected literary men in London. As an author of books, a journalist, an editor, a bookman, and a publisher's reader, he knew nearly all of the leading English writers of his time, including H. G. Wells, John Galsworthy, J. M. Barrie, and Bernard Shaw; and Joseph Conrad was his next-door neighbor for several years. Blessed with a facile pen and strong professional discipline, Lucas wrote more than one hundred books, including collections of essays, children's books, novels, biographies, travel books, art books, anthologies, editions of letters, and satires in both prose and poetry. Although Lucas received his greatest praise and fame for his essays – he is considered one of the six best practitioners of that form in England in the first half of the twentieth century – he also produced thirteen novels that deserve to be remembered and studied.

Edward Verrall Lucas was born on 11 June 1868 near London, in Eltham in the county of Kent. Before Lucas was one year old, he and his family moved to Brighton in Sussex, where he made his home until he was twenty-three. The most recent generations of his ancestors were country yeomen and tradesmen who belonged to the Society of Friends, as did his parents, Jane Drewett Lucas and Alfred Lucas. Lucas's father was in the insurance business and was, in his son's later opinion, a selfish and strict man who was a despicable example of "piety without works." It was deep love for his mother that kept Lucas in attendance at Quaker ser-

MR. INGLESIDE

BY

E. V. LUCAS

METHUEN & CO. LTD.
36 ESSEX STREET W.C.
LONDON

*Title page for Lucas's novel about a reclusive fifty-one-year-old man (courtesy of the Lilly Library, Indiana University)*

vices until he was in his twenties; after that he lost all religious beliefs. A shy and lonely child who greatly loved to read, Lucas was sent to and withdrawn from nine different schools by his father, who invariably quibbled over costs; and at age sixteen he was apprenticed for a five-year term to a bookseller in Brighton. He next worked for two years as a reporter for the local *Sussex Daily News,* and in 1892 he went to London after a kindly uncle gave him money to attend lectures at University College (though he was not officially enrolled in a degree program). Lucas became the quintessential London man from that point on. He befriended W. P. Ker and Arnold Bennett, as well as Wells and Conrad.

He joined the staff of and was first published in the *Globe* newspaper in 1893. In that same year he was given a commission by the Quakers to write a book on a friend of Charles Lamb, *Bernard Barton and His Friends* (1897). In 1896 he joined the staff of

the prestigious weekly journal the *Academy;* he also worked for the publisher Grant Richards as an editor and reader. He soon bought a house in the Kent countryside, and in 1897 he married Elizabeth Gertrude Griffin, the daughter of an American couple living in London. The Lucases' daughter, Audrey, was born in 1898. After twenty years of a seemingly happy marriage, the couple separated permanently at the end of World War I. Lucas, who by that time had established himself as a writer of high quality and variety, settled into book-lined bachelor flats in London, where he died on 26 June 1938.

Early in his career Lucas met and befriended Charles Lamb, and from the older writer Lucas learned to use a consistent persona in all of his writing; in fact, he adapted Lamb's persona to his own use. In a passage from his autobiographical novel *Landmarks* (1914), the central character of the book, at a time when he is still a young, fledgling author, receives this advice from an older friend: "The subject needn't be interesting. It's the author who has got to be interesting." Following this advice, Lucas created a personality on the printed page and engaged his readers with it throughout his career. His works present a man of mild, kindly sentiment; tasteful and winsomely epicurean in his love of old books, old wine, old friends, old times; easygoing and tolerant, yet sharply observant; having just money enough to supply with delicious strain his meager and lovably eccentric, fastidious middle-class needs for comfort, culture, and companions. His prose style is clear, tasteful, and pleasantly light in touch, creating the charming atmosphere that Lucas always sought to convey; in his last work of fiction, *The Barber's Clock: A Conversation Piece* (1931), he repeats his lifelong view that art exists "not as a mirror of life . . . but as some compensation for it: an anodyne."

His thirteen novels, like his essays, aim to create a lightness of being to make life endurable. In keeping with his creative strategy, he called them not novels but "entertainments" and constructed them all in such a way that, in Arthur St. John Adcock's words, "the essayist and the novelist work in collaborating." They are, in effect, deliberately slight romances, with slender plots that exist only to provide occasion for clever dialogue, description, and the characters who make up Lucas's world: a good-hearted mixture of genteel gentlemen and ladies and colorful lower-placed persons who attend them. His novels always revolve around a middle-aged, avuncular narrator or central character who somehow befriends everyone and whose voice is the chief conveyer of essaylike commentary. All se-

rious ideas and conflict are avoided or diminished so that the anodyne may smooth and deaden the crumple and crunch of life's complications. It is a world which is strangely but effectively of a piece with the literary world of the earlier nineteenth century – of not only Lamb, but also the Charles Dickens of *Pickwick* or the Jane Austen of Mr. Bennet.

Lucas's first novel, *Listener's Lure* (1906), subtitled "An Oblique Narration" in its British edition and "A Kensington Comedy" in its American edition, is an epistolary novel that has the feel of a drawing-room comedy. It concerns the relation between a "middle-aged" (as he calls himself) thirty-seven-year-old scholarly bachelor named Lynn Harberton and a charming young woman in her early twenties, Miss Edith Graham, Harberton's ward, who has also just finished a three-year stint as his assistant in the completed task of editing the works of Boswell. Acting out of what he thinks is his due concern for his ward, Harberton arranges for the placement of Edith in comfortable lodgings among friends in London, where Edith encounters a host of colorful London acquaintances of all generations and sexes, who write letters to each other and to Harberton. The reader is introduced to a hilarious assortment of young men who, one after another, propose marriage to the obviously superior Edith. When Edith eventually accepts the proposal of a sophisticated, slightly older man named Royce, Harberton is surprised to find himself unhappy at the news and realizes that he has loved Edith all the time. The sad situation is relieved smoothly when Edith realizes that she loves Harberton after all and breaks her engagement to Royce (who takes the loss philosophically, as civilized men should in such romances).

The book's humor is light and good-natured. It springs mostly from the letters of the absurd young friends and suitors of Edith, such as the wealthy Oxford student Algernon Damp, who fusses desperately about changing his last name to attract a bride; or Dennis Albourne, a woeful, money-hungry young poet who tries to woo Edith through "culture." There are also Mrs. Pink, a dotty benefactress of dotty causes; her estranged but equally odd husband the Reverend Wilberforce Pink; the self-exiled Wordsworth Harberton; and many others whose names suggest the nature of the book's fun and who collectively present an amusing but biting picture of upper-middle-class vacuity, set against the sanity of Harberton and Edith.

Lucas's next novel, *Over Bemerton's: An Easy-Going Chronicle* (1908) has a different aura about it and is perhaps his most Lamb-like effort of fiction.

*Participants in a 1913 cricket match at Downe House, Sussex. Bottom row: Percy Lucas, Audrey Lucas, T. Wrigley, Charles Tennyson, Willie Winter; middle row: A. A. Milne, Maurice Hewlett, J. M. Barrie, George Morrow, E. V. Lucas, Walter Frith; top row: George Davies, T. L. Gilmour, Will Meredith, G. Meredith Jr., Denis Mackail, Harry Graham, and Dr. Goffe*

It was published not long after Lucas's *The Life of Charles Lamb* (1905), and the influence shows. Lucas is much more the gentle humorist in this novel, creating a quiet "freemasonry of laughter" that consists of a circle of middle-aged bachelors and widowers – all "quiet and learned gentlemen" – who are joined by Mr. Kent Falconer, the central character, a fifty-five-year-old bachelor who has returned to London after thirty years in Brazil and who moves into quiet rooms over a secondhand bookshop named Bemerton's. Falconer describes himself as having "nothing to do" and as a man who is "out . . . for no other purpose than to occupy a stall in the theatre of life and watch the play." His old friends are of the same state and persuasion; and since they are all also articulate and voluble, their visits provide occasions for many talks on many subjects. There are miniessays, for instance, on a Chinese biographical dictionary; on the "quaint and learned gentlemen of the seventeenth century"; on flowers and gardening; on the history of cricket, with a good description of the great W. G. Grace (Lucas was a lifelong fanatic about the game); and, thanks to the quirky Mr. Trist, on "the art of life."

In this novel Lucas creates a world whose essential theme is wistful regret for change and the ageless nature of the small pleasures of the mind and heart. But there is another world placed against it throughout the book: the world of contemporary London and its music halls and motor cars, which is the world of Falconer's stepniece Naomi Wynne and her young friends, and, more interestingly, of Naomi's sister Drusilla, who is arrested for participating in a suffragette demonstration, much to the sympathetic confusion and embarrassment of the men, both old and young. Both worlds are brought together, rather awkwardly, at the end of the book, when Lucas arranges to have Naomi and Kent Falconer marry, in a somewhat pallid and overcivilized love match that rather woodenly brings about a kind of forced closure to the basically peripatetic structure of the plot.

The open nature of this tale is continued in another "entertainment," *London Lavender* (1912), so named because it continues the married lives of Kent and Naomi Falconer to the point at which a daughter, whom they name Lavender, is born to them at the end of the book. On the way to this birth, Lucas provides visits to varied people and

# THE VERMILION BOX

BY

## E. V. LUCAS

METHUEN & CO. LTD.
36 ESSEX STREET W.C.
LONDON
*Colonial Library*

*Title page for Lucas's 1916 comic war novel (courtesy of the Lilly Library, Indiana University)*

and Ingleside's best old friends have either died or moved away, and the novel ends with its protagonist wandering down a London street, depressed and lonelier than ever, thinking "with renewed longing" of one of his oldest friends, now irretrievably absent.

*Landmarks* was written when Lucas was forty-six and is strongly autobiographical. A bildungsroman structured around the whimsical idea that "it is curious how many things happen to us, often at the time apparently momentous . . . which do not count; . . . curious how lasting can be the effect of what seem to be trivial occurrences and experiences," *Landmark* is more serious than Lucas's previous work. The novel traces the stages of moral and intellectual growth of his protagonist, Rudd Sergison, from the age of seven through his late twenties. Lucas is deft in his presentations of the gradual loss of idealistic impressions in the young man. He relates with mellow sadness how reality presses upon Rudd as he grows past medical school into journalism and book publishing, experiencing the "lost divinity" of his father, the sense of the "trumpery" of everything, the compromises one must confront, and, in an episode in which the protagonist accompanies a wealthy American to Paris, a strong insight into the "prison" of money. But, along with these tough lessons, Rudd also learns a "new sense of style" and a love for the things that Montmartre represents. Eventually he meets Helen Brooks, whom he marries at about the same time that his first book is published.

Published in the midst of the Great War years, *The Vermillion Box* (1916) is a comedic war novel, intended, as Lucas says in the preface, to "throw some light on social England under the war." The title refers to the red pillar postbox used throughout England and alludes to the novel's epistolary form. Beneath the warm humor in *The Vermillion Box* lies a serious and accurate montage portrait of public opinion and feelings during the war years, based on the author's experiences. Lucas, too old to serve in the army and a pacifist at heart, nevertheless worked hard in France, along with his wife Elizabeth, on behalf of French children who had been hurt or displaced during the war. When he returned to England in 1916, Lucas worked for the Red Cross until the war's end, and in 1917 he published a book, *Outposts of Mercy: The Record of a Visit in November and December, 1916, to the Various Units of the British Red Cross in Italy,* about that organization's valuable work at the front lines. In *The Vermillion Box,* through exchanges of letters centered around the sensible, middle-aged protagonist, Richard Havens,

places, with each chapter turned into a vignette of encounter with a different personality, place, or attitude, forming a living London kaleidoscope, offered with kindly intent and effect.

The effect of *Mr. Ingleside* (1910), however, is not so kindly and pleasant. The novel employs the same kind of wandering structure and a similar central character – a reclusive fifty-one-year-old man – but the tone in this book is darker, and the ending is bleak. As the book opens, Mr. Ingleside has been quietly living in his apartment in London. Although he had amicably separated from his wife and his two daughters many years previously, one morning, in a "new sense of loneliness," Ingleside selfishly sends for his teenaged daughter Ann to leave school and come to live with him, to soothe the "tiny ache in his heart." Throughout the book occur the expected episodes involving Ingleside's circle of friends, as well as the efforts of both daughters (Ingleside becomes a widower by midbook) to find occupations of their own and/or husbands. By the last chapter the two daughters have gone their own way

the reader encounters the boy eager to enlist to serve his country, the sensitive young man who becomes an officer and grows into sobering heroism, the dodging young men who draw salaries for war-related committee work, the old man who does nothing but write pessimistic and outraged letters to the newspapers about spies and administrative ineptitude, the pampered lady whose version of "economising for the war effort" is to cut the wages of her servants, the formerly idle young woman who finds existential focus and self-maturation in war work, and many others, handled by Lucas with an effectively deceptive lightness of touch that allows the reader to understand and forgive all.

The book's less-effective sequel, *Verena In The Midst* (1920), carries the Richard Havens character (and some others) through the postwar year of 1919 and again uses the epistolary method of narration. What emerges from the exchanges of letters from people surrounding the bedridden Verena Raby, "the centre of this epistolary circle" and an old friend of Richard's, is a picture of a society in the midst of a "period of ferment and unrest," in which bewildered people search for their places in a world that will never again be the same – a world, remarks the sad, conservative, aging Richard Havens, of such new phenomena as short skirts, silk stockings, jazz, cigarettes, spiritualist seances, general cynicism, intensified war between labor and capitalism, and the deep need for real leaders. Such critiques lurk beneath the flurry of gossipy social life seen in the letters of various younger relatives and friends writing to "Aunt Verena" for news and advice about love problems and a funny assortment of personal entanglements.

Lucas's next novel, *Rose and Rose* (1921), is a return to the mild, rather inconsequential "entertainment" of his earlier years, but the work is peculiar and even a bit daring for its usually prudent author. Probably based upon a real incident in the life of the author Edward FitzGerald, it is narrated by a bachelor physician, Dr. Julius Greville, who in his early thirties is suddenly given a neighbor's five-year-old daughter, named Rose, to raise as his own. Despite the moral outrage of Rose's aunt, the grim Mrs. Stratton, Greville succeeds in his charge, and Rose grows up and marries the pleasant, respectable, and solicitous Eustace Holt, by whom she has a daughter, also named Rose. But the older Rose becomes unhappy, runs away with an old childhood friend named Ronnie Fergusson, and leaves her five-year-old daughter to be raised by Dr. Greville, still a bachelor and now in his late fifties. He ac-

*Caricature of Lucas by Max Beerbohm (from Beerbohm's* Things Old and New, *1923)*

cepts the challenge of surrogate fatherhood once again and raises the younger Rose, who goes to London at age eighteen to study painting, with the reluctant financial support of her father Eustace. The novel ends smoothly when the older Rose, now a rich widow, returns to London, reconciles with her daughter, and takes a home in London for herself and Dr. Greville, now seventy years old.

The novel is unusual not only in the way that it deals sympathetically with the problem of single-male-parent adoption but also in the way in which it deals sympathetically with the elder Rose's abandonment of her husband and child. Her marriage is seen not in sensationalistic terms but as an example of essential incompatibility between husband and wife; and the narrator, perhaps following the lead of George Meredith's *Modern Love* (1862), sees that the blame is mixed and maintains friendly relations with both parents for the good of their daughter. The younger Rose, in fact, appears as a character in

Lucas's next novel, *Genevra's Money* (1922), where she is living in Paris with a young British man who is a fellow artist, occasioning a discussion of contemporary French art — one of the few points of interest in a rather lackluster book.

Indeed, there is a general drop in the quality of Lucas's novels beginning with *Genevra's Money*. Throughout the 1920s and 1930s, Lucas lived the life of a busy and affable *bon vivant,* producing books on a wide variety of subjects, continuing to write for and edit *Punch,* traveling widely, and acting first as director and then as chairman of the board of the Methuen publishing company. His fiction during these years has little to recommend it.

*Advisory Ben: A Story* (1923) is about a capable, independent young woman named Benita Stavely, who creates "The Beck and Call," a business designed to give professional advice on domestic problems to families in the London area. Her clients and their various difficulties give Lucas a chance to fashion another humorous picture of genteel London life, this time of the 1920s.

Lucas's last three "entertainments" — *Windfall's Eve: An Entertainment* (1929), *Down the Sky: An Entertainment* (1930), and *The Barber's Clock: A Conversation Piece* — form a trilogy devoted to the presentation and praise of a character named Mrs. Jenny Candover. The narrator of the three books is a retired British Museum official in his early sixties named Richard, who has formed a close and mutually devoted friendship with Jenny, who is about ten years younger than he. Jenny is introduced in *Windfall's Eve,* when Richard consults her about the problem of what to do with a six-figure sum that he has just won as a prize in the "Calcutta Sweeps." Although she is married to a man named Jack, she has long been amicably separated from him, and she now lives an independent, honest, classless, and unconventional life. As Richard, reminiscent of Kent Falconer, admiringly says, "The world was, to her, a comedy, which she watched from the best seats." Jenny and Richard travel all over England and Europe together, encountering new people and places.

In *Down the Sky* the pair make a trip to Ceylon, allowing Lucas to write a descriptive essay on that country. Although Jack dies in the novel, Richard and Jenny never marry, though she tries to coax the reluctant Richard toward that idea. The last book in the trilogy, *The Barber's Clock,* is a slender work that can barely be called fiction. It consists entirely of a conversation between Jenny and Richard, in which Jenny feeds topical questions to him and he indulges in an old man's essaylike chapters of reminiscences. "And what do you think of life, Richard?"

Jenny asks in the last chapter. Richard's answer, obviously Lucas's final summation of things, is that he has been very fortunate, but "all the time I've been conscious of the other things, the petty things and the ugly things; and I can't forget the way we're being hurried to the tomb, the rapidity with which decay sets in and the stupidity and blindness of chance. No, not a well-managed world, and I shall be quite willing to leave it when my time comes."

The novels of E. V. Lucas never sold well: none went into a second edition. Lucas was fully aware of his lack of the necessary creative imagination or ideological heat and so chose to stay within small and simple fictional aims. Having made his way as a master of light prose in his essays before he tried his hand at fiction, Lucas safely continued to provide what he felt his readers expected of him — an entertaining encounter with people, offered by an amiable and familiar authorial persona. Lucas's adoption of that mask meant that he could always be relied upon; but it also meant that his fiction was somewhat predictable, showing no development in technique, thematic range, or purpose. Even by the 1930s the author had come to be regarded as outmoded — representative of a pleasantly fastidious, unpolitical, leisurely sensitivity that belonged in the sadly unrecoverable Edwardian ambience and not to the churning wars and suffering of that later age. Modern-day readers may also find Lucas irrelevant, but dated as his novels are, they retain a deceptively reflective quality that provides both a good view of a lost time and a sly commentary upon that time, achieved quietly through relentlessly sharp, detailed observation. Furthermore, his prose exhibits a mastery of style that will always appeal to anyone who loves words. Obsolete though the prevailing temperament of his novels may seem to be — with its detached, unhurried enjoyment of beauties, pleasures, and people for their own sake, to give meaning to the moments as they pass toward the grave — such an attitude will always exist in some ageless portion of the human mind, if only as a pale ideal.

**References:**

Arthur St. John Adcock, "E. V. Lucas," in his *The Glory That Was Grub Street* (London: Low, Marston, 1928), pp. 191–201;

James Agate, *Ego 3* (London: Harrap, 1938), pp. 388–389;

George Leonard Barnett, "A Critical Analysis of the Lucas Edition of Lamb's Letters," *Modern Language Quarterly,* 9 (September 1948): 303–314;

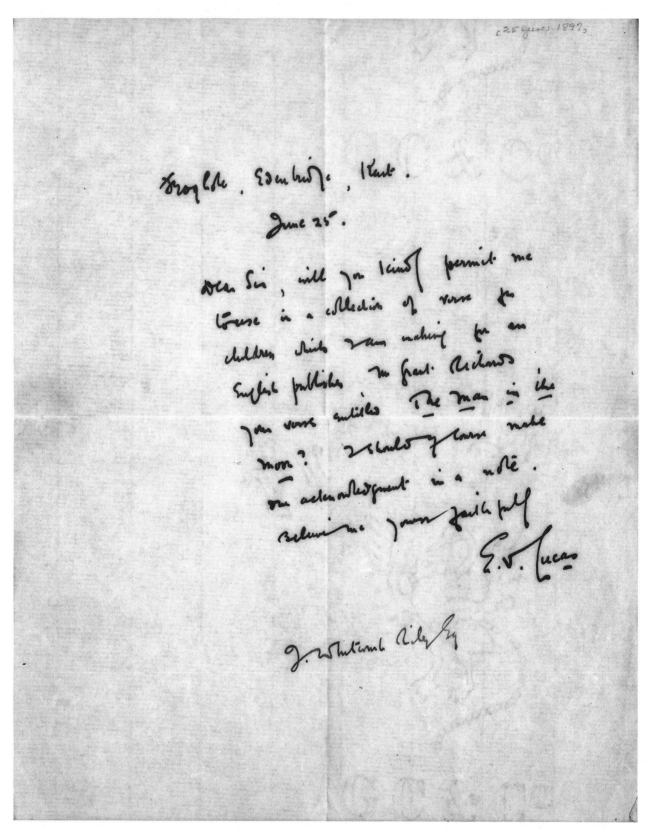

*Letter from Lucas to James Whitcomb Riley asking Riley's permission to use one of his verses for an anthology to be published by Grant Richards*
*(courtesy of the Lilly Library, Indiana University)*

Arnold Bennett, "Chesterton and Lucas," in his *Books and Persons* (London: Chatto & Windus, 1917), pp. 150–154;

Visranath Chatterjee, "E. V. Lucas: Prince of Essayists," *Calcutta Review,* new series 3 (April–June 1972): 315–320;

John Farrar and others: *E. V. Lucas: Appreciations* (New York: Doran, 1925);

Edmund Gosse, "The Essays of Mr. Lucas," in his *Books on the Table* (London: Heinemann, 1921), pp. 103–110;

Audrey Lucas, *E. V. Lucas: A Portrait* (London: Methuen, 1939);

Christopher Morley, "E. V. Lucas (1868–1938)," in his *The Ironing Board* (Garden City, N.Y.: Doubleday, 1949; London: Faber & Faber, 1950), pp. 166–167;

Grant Overton, "That Literary Wanderer, E. V. Lucas," in his *Cargoes For Crusoes* (New York: Appleton, 1924), pp. 212–231;

Claude A. Prance, "Edward Verrall Lucas," *Charles Lamb Bulletin,* new series 8 (October 1974): 157–162;

R. G. G. Price, *A History of Punch* (London: Collins, 1957);

Duant Schneider, "The Lucas Edition of Lamb's Letters: Corrections and Notes," *Notes and Queries,* 219 (May 1974): 171–174;

Frank Swinnerton, "E. V. Lucas," in his *Figures in the Foreground: Literary Reminiscences, 1917–40* (London: Hutchinson, 1963), pp. 82–88;

Swinnerton, "Literary Men," in his *The Georgian Scene: A Literary Panorama* (New York: Farrar & Rinehart, 1934), pp. 231–251;

A. B. Walkley, " 'E. V.' and Proust," in his *More Prejudice* (London: Heinemann, 1923), pp. 52–56;

Arthur Waugh, "Mr. E. V. Lucas," in his *Tradition and Change* (London: Chapman & Hall, 1919), pp. 292–298.

**Papers:**

The Harry Ransom Humanities Research Center, University of Texas at Austin, has the largest collection of E. V. Lucas' manuscripts. Other Lucas manuscripts and letters, including his letters to Grant Richards and Arnold Bennett, are at the Butler Library of Columbia University in New York City. The British Library, London, has Lucas's correspondence with the Macmillan Publishing Company; the Bodleian Library, Oxford, has his correspondence with Bertram Dobell. Some letters from Lucas to John Galsworthy are at the University of Birmingham, and letters from Lucas to Sir Edward Elgar are in the Hereford and Worcester County Archives, Worcester, England.

# Lucas Malet
## (Mary St. Leger Kingsley Harrison)
### (4 June 1852 – 27 October 1931)

Patricia Thomas Srebrnik
*University of Calgary*

BOOKS: *Mrs. Lorimer, a Sketch in Black and White* (2 volumes, London: Macmillan, 1882; 1 volume, New York: Appleton, 1883);

*Colonel Enderby's Wife: A Novel* (3 volumes, London: Kegan Paul, 1885; 1 volume, New York: Appleton, 1885);

*A Counsel of Perfection* (London: Kegan Paul, 1888; New York: Appleton, 1888);

*Little Peter: A Christmas Morality for Children of Any Age* (London: Kegan Paul, 1888; New York: Appleton, 1888);

*The Wages of Sin: A Novel* (3 volumes, London: Swan Sonnenschein, 1891; 1 volume, New York: Fenno, 1890);

*The Carissima: A Modern Grotesque* (London: Methuen, 1896; Chicago: Stone, 1896);

*The Gateless Barrier* (London: Methuen, 1900; New York: Dodd, Mead, 1900);

*The History of Sir Richard Calmady: A Romance* (London: Methuen, 1901; New York: Dodd, Mead, 1901);

*The Far Horizon* (London: Hutchinson, 1906; New York: Dodd, Mead, 1907);

*The Score* (London: John Murray, 1909; New York: Dutton, 1909);

*The Golden Galleon* (London and New York: Hodder & Stoughton, 1910; New York: Doran, 1910);

*Adrian Savage: A Novel* (London: Hutchinson, 1911; New York: Harper, 1911);

*The Tutor's Story: An Unpublished Novel by Charles Kingsley. Revised and Completed by His Daughter, Lucas Malet* (London: Smith, Elder, 1916; New York: Dodd, Mead, 1916);

*Damaris: A Novel* (London: Hutchinson, 1916; New York: Dodd, Mead, 1916);

*Deadham Hard: A Romance* (London: Methuen, 1919; New York: Dodd, Mead, 1919);

*The Tall Villa: A Novel* (London: Collins, 1920; New York: Doran, 1919);

*Da Silva's Widow, and Other Stories* (London: Hutchinson, 1922; New York: Dodd, Mead, 1922);

*The Survivors* (London: Cassell, 1923; New York: Dodd, Mead, 1923);

*The Dogs of Want* (London: Hutchinson, 1924; New York: Dodd, Mead, 1925);

*The Private Life of Mr. Justice Syme: A Novel . . . Completed by Gabrielle Vallings* (London: Hutchinson, 1932).

OTHER: William Harrison, *Clovelly Sermons,* preface by Malet (London: Methuen, 1898), vii-xi.

SELECTED PERIODICAL PUBLICATIONS –
UNCOLLECTED: "The Youngest of the Saints," *Fortnightly Review,* new series 38 (September 1885): 395–412;

"The Other Side of the Moon," *Fortnightly Review,* new series 39 (May 1886): 615–632;

"The Progress of Women in Literature," *Universal Review,* 2 (October 1888): 295–301;

"The Threatened Re-Subjection of Woman," *Fortnightly Review,* new series 77 (May 1905): 806–819;

"A Conversion," *World Fiction* (August 1922): 64–76.

From the 1880s through the early 1900s Lucas Malet, the pseudonym of Mary St. Leger Kingsley Harrison, was regarded as a major literary figure whose reputation was certain to survive the test of time. In bookshops and in circulating libraries, the reading public clamored for Malet's latest novel; demand was particularly great for *The Wages of Sin: A Novel* (1891) and *The History of Sir Richard Calmady: A Romance* (1901). At the same time, those professional critics who constituted the literary establishment were alarmed by Malet's powerful treatment of such "morbid" themes as illicit sexuality, physical defor-

*Lucas Malet (Mary St. Leger Kingsley Harrison)*

mity, emotional sadism, self-sacrificing masochism, the misogyny of English middle-class culture, and the reality of the supernatural. Critics agonized over how much latitude should be allowed a woman writer and struggled to assign Malet to a recognizably "English" tradition of fiction. In the 1880s Malet's fiction was compared to that of George Eliot, while in the 1890s it was grouped with the works of the "New Women" novelists, despite Malet's bitter denunciations of "the *feministes*." After her conversion to Catholicism in 1902, Malet's increasingly elaborate prose style prompted some critics to compare her to George Meredith and Henry James. Malet insisted that she was more influenced by Honoré de Balzac and Emile Zola than by any English author.

The fascination of the reading public and the bewilderment of the critics were intensified by Malet's true identity: she was the daughter of Charles Kingsley, the Anglican clergyman closely identified with "Christian socialism" and "muscular Christianity." In his sermons, essays, and novels, Kingsley attacked the pernicious influence of Catholicism, celebrated the history and culture of Protestant England, and extolled the spiritual salvation to be achieved by heterosexual love between husband and wife. Mary St. Leger Kingsley, born on 4

June 1852, was the third of four children born to Charles and Frances Kingsley. Malet was a niece of the novelist Henry Kingsley and a first cousin to Mary Henrietta Kingsley, who became widely known as an intrepid lady traveler for her journeys in West Africa.

In interviews granted to several periodicals during the 1890s, Malet recalled her lonely childhood at the rectory in Eversley, Hampshire. Although her father had many illustrious visitors, Mary had no friends her own age, and Frances Kingsley considered herself too much an invalid to take her daughters into society. Malet was not allowed to read novels, but she read extensively in theology, philosophy, and science, developing a particular interest in religious heresies, magic, and the black arts. She also demonstrated a talent for painting, and she attended the Slade School of Fine Art, where she studied under Sir Edward Poynter. Her father did not believe in careers for women, however, and at his urging Mary became engaged to Kingsley's former curate, William Harrison, who was thirteen years her senior and a canon at Westminster. They were married in July 1876.

Mary's first novel, *Mrs. Lorimer, a Sketch in Black and White,* appeared in 1882. The pen name she devised for herself served as an implicit rebuke to those critics who assumed she was indebted to

her father for her literary talent: Lucas was the maiden name of her paternal grandmother, and Malet was the name of the grandmother's unmarried aunt. Soon after the novel appeared, William Harrison was appointed to the living of Clovelly, North Devon, where Charles Kingsley's father had been rector. The Harrisons had no children, and Mary was unhappy in her father's boyhood home. She blamed the climate for her poor health and began to spend winters abroad, usually in Italy or Switzerland. The money she earned from writing novels and essays was used to pay for these trips.

In her essays Malet expresses opinions markedly different from those of her father. In "The Youngest of the Saints," for example, Malet dryly remarks that "the genius of Protestantism must obviously be somewhat of the battering-ram," and she alludes to "the charmed and glorified, the rich and magical atmosphere of Catholic thought" in "The Other Side of the Moon." In "The Progress of Women in Literature," Malet attacks "the Squaw and Toy superstition" that relegates women either to servitude or to folly. She urges women to become greater writers, not by imitating that "inferior being . . . the average Englishman" but by exercising "our high and daring temper."

Yet in her first three novels, Malet depicts women who must learn humility and self-renunciation. The heroine of *Mrs. Lorimer, a Sketch in Black and White* (1882) is a young, childless widow. Through flashbacks the reader learns that *Mrs. Lorimer* married her husband in order to escape the isolated vicarage where she spent a lonely childhood. When the husband developed a fatal illness, she was so horrified by his suffering that she withdrew from him emotionally. Now, unable to find any purpose in life, she yearns for the type of "real friendship" that men enjoy with each other. When she attempts a platonic relationship with a friend of her late husband's, however, the friend is so unnerved that he persuades himself he is in love and must propose marriage. Mrs. Lorimer then decides to eschew "mere temporal happiness" and devotes herself instead to charitable work. She dies from a fever she contracts while nursing the poor. The narrator of *Mrs. Lorimer, a Sketch in Black and White* denies that he is either a moralist or a preacher; nonetheless, he praises Mrs. Lorimer's "martyrdom," comparing her to a medieval saint.

Jessie Enderby, the protagonist of *Colonel Enderby's Wife: A Novel* (1885), is another self-centered woman who does not love the older man she has married. When the colonel's health begins to fail, Jessie is unable to treat him with even minimal sym-

pathy. Instead, by insisting he dance with her at a ball, she hastens his final heart attack.

The narrator of *Colonel Enderby's Wife: A Novel* is said to be a "social historian" whose business is "to observe faithfully, and then set down his observations." In another passage the narrator compares himself to a scientist wielding a scalpel in "the moral dissecting-room," and he advances harsh criticisms concerning British men, British marriages, and British literature. He remarks that "the ordinary Anglo-Saxon is a very quiet and domestic sort of animal, who requires a wife" and asserts that since an Englishman has "a curious necessity for the backing up of his own inclination with . . . Divine approval" he has "exalted marriage to the very highest place in the catalogue of good works." The narrator also observes that "the respectable Englishman entrenches himself behind his open Bible, and flings a text – almost any one will do – in your inquiring face" and concludes that, in order to convey these "British sentiments," there has evolved "a whole literature of fiction and biography [that] may be briefly described as the apotheosis of suburban villas, solid worth, and side whiskers."

*Colonel Enderby's Wife: A Novel* also includes evidence of Malet's growing interest in Catholicism. One of the characters is told by a priest that the Roman Church alone "has had the glorious audacity to look at human nature as it really is. . . . She treats the diseases of the soul as modern science treats those of the body; she is always experimenting, acquiring new facts, recognizing fresh manifestations of eternal law."

In Malet's third novel, *A Counsel of Perfection* (1888), the heroine, Lydia Casteen, refuses a proposal from the man she loves so that she may continue to assist her father, a famous scholar. Dr. Casteen is oblivious to the needs of his daughter, but her suitor, a writer of shallow society verses named Antony Hammond, is so unworthy of her that, as the narrator remarks, it is doubtful that she would have been happy had she married him.

Reviewers pointed out that Lydia and her father bore a remarkably close resemblance to the characters of Dorothea and Mr. Casaubon in George Eliot's *Middlemarch* (1872). Despite this criticism, however, Malet's early novels were on the whole well received: the author was commended for her narrative power, for her gentle, ironic humor, and above all, for her subtle, detailed analysis of character.

Malet lost the goodwill of many critics, however, when she published the novel that made her one of the best-known writers of the decade. *The*

*Wages of Sin: A Novel* (1891) is the story of James Colthurst, a painter who rebels against the Calvinistic creed of his minister father because that creed rejects "the artistic and intellectual inheritance bequeathed to us by centuries of human imagination." The public does not appreciate Colthurst's "honest and fearless" style of painting; some go so far as to accuse him of "a love of actual physical deformity and a relish of horror for mere horror's sake." The narrator, however, defends Colthurst, remarking, "he invariably, as far as I could see, rejected that which was unnatural or unsavoury, unless the presentation of it formed so essential a part of his subject that to omit it was to spoil the point of the story."

Depressed by his failure to win public recognition, Colthurst drifts into a sexual liaison with his model, Jenny, whose father is another fanatical Calvinist. Jenny gives birth to a daughter, and Colthurst promises to marry her. His sense of obligation turns to disgust when, during a trip to Paris, Colthurst falls ill, and Jenny becomes a prostitute to earn money for his food. Colthurst finally achieves success with a painting entitled "The Road to Ruin"; Jenny was the model for the work, which shows a woman beckoning a man to follow her. Although Colthurst continues to support Jenny, he becomes engaged to Mary Crookenden, who is beautiful, wealthy, and virtuous. Mortally ill with consumption, Jenny appeals directly to the unsuspecting Mary, who tries to make amends by nursing the sick woman. Chastened by Mary's example, Colthurst vows to devote the rest of his life to his daughter and his art. As he leaves Jenny's deathbed, however, Colthurst is killed in a struggle with Jenny's father.

Within weeks of its publication *The Wages of Sin* was being hailed as "the book of the season," according to C. E. Oldham, who reviewed it in the *Newbery House Magazine*. The *Scotsman* described the novel as "undoubtedly the greatest work of art this already successful author has yet produced . . . one of the boldest, most realistic . . . sketches of a . . . human soul, that the whole range of our fiction contains."

Some critics were disturbed, however, by the book's frank portrayal of an illicit sexual relationship. They were also dismayed by the possibility that Malet might share the religious and aesthetic views of her painter-hero. In the opening paragraph of an eighteen-page review for the *Contemporary Review* entitled "Morality in Fiction" (1891), Malcolm MacColl objects to the novel's "morbid craving after what is abnormal," to its presentation of "Zolaism in its ugliest developments," and protests that it

"sneer[s] at the British *bourgeoisie*." MacColl argues that Colthurst was wrong to rebel against religious constraints upon art and literature. The review concludes with the warning that "we may have too much of the pathology of evil," leading to "a morbid and bastard realism."

Malet sent a copy of *The Wages of Sin* to Thomas Hardy, who in a letter dated 26 February 1892 praised her as "one of the few authors of the other sex who are not afraid of logical consequences." After calling on Malet in early April 1892, Hardy described her as "a striking woman: full, slightly voluptuous mouth, red lips, black hair and eyes: and most likeable."

Critics who shared MacColl's reservations were even more disturbed by Malet's next novel, *The Carissima: A Modern Grotesque* (1896). The story of Constantine Leversedge is told to the narrator by his acquaintance Antony Hammond, the rejected suitor who first appeared in *A Counsel of Perfection*. Hammond explains that, while traveling in southern Africa, Constantine had a gruesome experience: he came upon the remains of a caravan stranded in the desert. All the people were dead, but a dog had survived by sucking the blood from a baby's corpse. Leversedge shot at the dog but managed only to sever the rope by which it was tied. Since then he has been haunted by the dog's ghost. Back in England, he marries Charlotte Perry, referred to by her vulgar, middle-class parents as "the Carissima." Although Leversedge idealizes Charlotte, this "modern young woman" is in fact shallow, heartless, and materialistic. Charlotte attempts to drive Leversedge insane by claiming to see the dog that haunts him. But it is not until she confesses her game that Leversedge commits suicide, leaving her in possession of all his property.

Malet anticipated her critics by having Antony Hammond explain in the novel's epilogue that it is not the function of art to contribute to happiness. Rather, art should fix the mind upon extremes that lie outside ordinary experience by describing, for example, the experiences of criminals or saints. Like religion, which is said to be art in a higher manifestation, it breathes fresh air through the stagnant atmosphere of the commonplace, thereby keeping ideals alive. Certainly Hammond seems inspired by the story he has just told. The majority of critics, however, were unpersuaded: although they again praised Malet for her power and originality, many found the book too painful to read.

William Harrison died in April 1897. Malet had been living apart from her husband for the greater part of each year; she spent the winter of

1894–1895, for example, in India with her sister Rose. In 1898 Malet edited a collection of Harrison's *Clovelly Sermons,* and in the preface to this volume she remarks that Harrison's Evangelical faith lacked "philosophical breadth . . . and daring spiritual experiment." Within a few years of her husband's death, Malet adopted her second cousin, Lilian Mary Vallings, who became the author's constant companion. Malet was described by those who met her at about this time as a tall, handsome woman and a brilliant conversationalist.

Malet's next novel, *The Gateless Barrier* (1900), concerns a young Englishman whose pretty American wife cares for nothing but society. Laurence returns to England to visit his dying uncle, and in a sealed-off room of the family estate he meets a beautiful ghost named Agnes. She apparently died of grief when her lover, one of Laurence's ancestors, was killed in a naval battle. There are hints that Agnes may have been held captive by her guardian, another of Laurence's ancestors, who wanted to marry her and who may have assaulted her sexually. Laurence comes to believe that he is the reincarnation of Agnes's lover. But in his desire to consummate their relationship, Laurence behaves more in the style of Agnes's guardian: he tries to drag Agnes back into this life by forcing her to eat. Agnes escapes to await Laurence in the spiritual world. Only then are her physical remains discovered, entombed in the walls of the sealed room. Some reviewers recognized this complex and subtle story as one of Malet's finest efforts, but others claimed to find it merely baffling or boring.

Throughout the 1890s Malet had been at work on the most controversial novel of her career: *The History of Sir Richard Calmady: A Romance.* It turns upon what the Victorians delicately referred to as "sexual inversion," that is, a reversal of the gender roles conventionally assigned on the basis of male or female anatomy. In fulfillment of a centuries-old family curse, Sir Richard is born grotesquely deformed, with his feet embedded in his knees. Unable to participate in the public, physically aggressive world of men, Richard is confined to the domestic realm of women. Richard becomes engaged to a young, naive girl from a noble family, but she humiliates him by eloping with another man, and Richard undertakes a sexually scandalous "rake's progress" across Europe. Even in debauchery, however, Richard must assume the passive role: he is "ravished" by his cousin, the sinister but beautiful Helen de Vallorbes, who is sexually aroused by his deformity. Helen's virginal counterpart within the novel is another cousin of Richard's, the boyish

THE HISTORY OF
SIR RICHARD CALMADY

A ROMANCE

BY

LUCAS MALET

METHUEN & CO.
36 ESSEX STREET W.C.
LONDON
1901

*Title page for Malet's novel about a deformed man and his "rake's progress" across Europe (courtesy of the Lilly Library, Indiana University)*

Honoria Quentin, who wears tailored jackets and excels at such masculine activities as shooting, fishing, billiards, and riding. She plans to embrace celibacy and use her wealth "to espouse the cause of womanhood at large." When Honoria meets Richard, she is physically repelled by him, but she feels a sense of "knight-errancy" in regard to "all feminine as against all masculine creatures." This "chivalry" finally compels her to propose marriage to Richard.

In "A Novelist of the 'Nineties" (1932) Janet Hogarth Courtney suggests that Malet delayed publication of this novel because she was waiting out "the decadent Beardsley 'Yellow-Book' period, followed by the violent revulsion of 1895 after the Oscar Wilde scandal." However, in an interview published in the *Windsor Magazine* in 1899, Malet hints at the direction her thought was taking: she asserts that fate had erred in making her a woman rather than a man and that nature had "jumbled things up altogether" by distributing "male and fe-

male characteristics at random" among the individual members of her family.

In any case *The History of Sir Richard Calmady: A Romance* triggered extreme responses. Malet received hundreds of letters of abuse; she also received letters from the physically handicapped thanking her for her sympathetic understanding of their problems. Some critics pronounced the novel an undeniable masterpiece; others, especially those who had always deplored what they regarded as Malet's unhealthy obsession with the grotesque and macabre, denounced the book as unsavory, gruesome, and repulsive. Nearly every critic found it necessary to comment on Malet's gender and parentage: some denied that the novel was in any sense "woman's work"; others asserted that Richard's romantic adventures would have offended Charles Kingsley, with his notions of "muscular Christianity."

The controversy still persisted in 1902, when Malet and Vallings were received into the Roman Catholic Church. In an interview with William Archer, Malet explained the connection between her religious beliefs and her aesthetic values, arguing that the "unphilosophic . . . Puritanism" of English culture is "inimical to art" because it "insists on our wearing, or pretending to wear, blinkers." The typical English novelist is thus unable to portray life as a whole. Catholicism, in contrast, fosters the "magnificent breadth of outlook and freedom of utterance" to be found, for example, in the work of Balzac.

Malet's opinions seemed to become more constricted after her conversion. In "The Threatened Re-Subjection of Women," an essay published in 1905, the author insists that the majority of women should devote themselves to home and family. She acknowledges that her arguments are based upon the teachings of "the great mother church of Christendom, despoiled, penalised, scoffed at in England as obscurantist during close on four centuries."

*The Far Horizon* (1906) continues to develop Malet's critique of English culture. Dominic Iglesias, the half-Irish, half-Spanish hero of the novel, is a dignified, elderly bachelor who grew up in London and who is retiring from his monotonous job as a bank clerk. Dominic has had little contact with the Catholic faith of his ancestors. His few friends pride themselves on being respectable, middle-class members of the Church of England. In fact, they are vulgar, bigoted, and unimaginative: they are alarmed when Dominic develops a platonic friendship with the actress Poppy St. John, and they feel obliged to break with Dominic entirely when he finds the spir-

itual peace he has sought all his life by rejoining the Catholic Church.

*The Far Horizon* received many favorable reviews. Critics noted its poignant characterization of Dominic, its evocative descriptions of London streets and neighborhoods, and its witty satire upon middle-class prejudices. But many reviewers objected to the idealized depiction of Poppy and to her implausible friendship with Dominic. Other critics were angered by what they termed Malet's "contemptuous" attitude toward English Protestantism.

The title character of *Adrian Savage: A Novel* (1911) is young, handsome, wealthy, and charming. Although his father was English, Adrian was born and raised in France as a Catholic. He explains to his Parisian friends that Englishmen "crave to exercise power" over their female relatives; as a result, English women are "snubbed, depressed, depreciated, grumbled at, scolded, made to think meanly of [themselves]." When Adrian visits England to serve as the executor of a cousin's estate, he meets a particularly pathetic example of this type of abuse: his cousin's daughter, Joanna, is plain in appearance and so lacking in sophistication that when Adrian treats her with European courtesy and compassion she assumes he must be in love with her. Inevitably, after Adrian returns to France, Joanna begins to realize her error. In her desperation to ascertain the truth, Joanna undergoes a psychic, out-of-body experience: she projects her soul into the body of a prostitute who follows Adrian through the streets of Paris, until she learns from his own lips that he can never desire her. Even critics who resented Malet's criticism of the typical English male were impressed by her painful, penetrating analysis of the miserable Joanna.

During the war and for a few years after the war ended, Malet and Vallings lived primarily in England. In 1916 Vallings published a novel, *Bindweed;* in 1918 she published *Tumult: A Romance.* Although reviews were discouraging, Vallings wrote ten more novels in the 1920s and 1930s, several of them advocating socialism. She also studied to be a singer and appeared in several operatic productions at the "Old Vic" Theatre. By this time Malet was experiencing severe financial difficulties. Her novels were not selling as well as they had in the 1890s, and the copyrights to her father's work, which Malet and her sister Rose had inherited, were also generating far less income. Perhaps Malet hoped to stimulate renewed interest in her father's writings when she decided to complete *The Tutor's Story* (1916), an unfinished manuscript found in his papers. She was not successful, however; the reviewer

*Page from the Methuen stock ledger with an entry for Malet's* The History of Sir Richard Calmady
*(courtesy of the Lilly Library, Indiana University)*

for the *Bookman* dismissed the work as "a survival of an almost forgotten fashion in literature."

Critics were beginning to hint the same thing about Malet's novels. Drawing on memories of her trip to India in 1894–1895, Malet wrote *Damaris: A Novel* (1916), a sentimental tale of Anglo-Indian society; the title character is a five-year-old child. The same characters reappear in *Deadham Hard: A Romance* (1919). Damaris is now eighteen, and she and her father have returned to England, where Damaris meets her illegitimate half-brother. The protagonist has a governess who models herself consciously but ineffectually on the title character Jane Eyre from Charlotte Brontë's novel (1847). Malet may have been recalling her own youth when she described Damaris as an omnivorous reader who discovers, when she assists her father in writing a book, that she wants to become an author herself. Damaris was characterized by the *Dial* as "a mid-Victorian heroine."

The plot of Malet's next novel, *The Tall Villa: A Novel* (1920), recalls that of *The Gateless Barrier*. Frances Copley is unhappily married. While her husband is in South America on a business venture, she lives in a house she has inherited from her mother. There Frances encounters the ghost of a kinsman who killed himself over an unhappy love affair. To assist the ghost in escaping from his earthly purgatory, Frances endures great physical suffering, and, at what is to be their last meeting, she decides to accompany him to the world beyond. Critics were divided over the merits of the book. Even those who admired the characterization of Frances suggested that the dialogue was stilted. Others ridiculed the plot; the *Boston Transcript,* for example, objected that "to review the volume rightly one needs a ouija board."

In its review of Malet's *The Survivors* (1923), the *Times Literary Supplement* refers to the author as "a voice from the past" and recalls "the time when she was a leader of the shocking and subversive newer novelists, back in the '80s or '90s – which are all one to us now." Many critics were repelled by the story of Sybella Aylwin, who is motivated partly by vanity and partly by a half-sadistic obsession with pain to run a hospital for wounded soldiers. They regarded as macabre the scene in which Sybella insists that an unnecessary operation be performed on the young soldier with whom she has fallen in love.

*The Dogs of Want* (1924) was the last novel by Malet to be published in her lifetime. Its protagonist, Barbara Heritage, is employed as a companion to the thoroughly unattractive Marie Louise Syme, who stands to inherit the fortune of her father, Sir

Robert Syme. Sir Robert wants Marie Louise to marry Denison Fisher, the penniless son of an old friend, but Denison and Barbara are attracted to each other. Morbidly afraid of poverty, Denison proceeds with his courtship of Marie Louise, however, and in a conclusion that some critics deemed unduly cynical, Barbara guarantees her own financial security by marrying Sir Robert. Malet began work on a sequel, *The Private Life of Mr. Justice Syme: A Novel . . . Completed by Gabrielle Vallings,* that was published in 1932.

In 1924 Malet and Vallings moved to Montreux, Switzerland. At the Hotel Byron, they became members of a literary coterie that included Romain Rolland, Robert Hichens, and Cyril McNeile (better known as "Sapper"). The playwright Louis N. Parker collaborated with Vallings in preparing a dramatization of *The History of Sir Richard Calmady: A Romance.* Malet was disappointed, however, in her hope that the play might be produced in New York.

By the late 1920s Malet was seriously ill with cancer and so deeply in debt that she could not always pay her hotel bills. In 1930 she was awarded a civil list pension. Despite the fact that Malet owed the British government several hundred pounds in back taxes, she and Vallings returned from the Continent to live in Tenby, South Wales, where Malet died on 27 October 1931.

Newspaper headlines throughout England, Scotland, and Wales commemorated Malet as an important novelist. She was also praised for her well-constructed plots, her sense of comedy, her skill in depicting "the well-bred social scene," and for "a certain strange intensity in portraying wildness and despair." The London *Times* proclaimed that "in the literary history of the last quarter of the nineteenth and the first quarter of the twentieth century Lucas Malet can hardly be denied a secure place."

In the late twentieth century, however, Malet has largely been forgotten, partly because neither her prose style nor her themes appeal to modern readers and partly because her work is difficult to categorize. Unlike Mrs. Humphrey Ward or Mrs. Margaret Oliphant, Malet cannot be said to express the dominant values and assumptions of her time. Nor has she benefited from the renewed interest in secular Victorian feminism that has led to the rediscovery of such authors as Olive Schreiner and "Sarah Grand." Yet Lucas Malet deserves to be remembered, not only as the author of several fine novels but also for her persistent and highly origi-

nal probing of the religious, aesthetic, and sexual ideologies of late Victorian England.

**Interviews:**

Frederick Dolman, " 'Lucas Malet' At Home. A Chat with the Daughter of Charles Kingsley," *Young Woman,* 4 (February 1896): 145–149;

Laura Alex Smith, "Western Women of Note. Lucas Malet (Mrs. Harrison)," *Western Weekly News,* 29 January 1898;

Mary Angela Dickens, "A Talk with 'Lucas Malet,' " *Windsor Magazine,* 10 (October 1899): 522–524;

Frances Whiting Halsey, "Lucas Malet," in *Women Authors of Our Day In Their Homes. Personal Descriptions and Interviews* (New York: Pott, 1903), pp. 65–72;

William Archer, "Conversation XI. With Mrs. Mary St. Leger Harrison (Lucas Malet)," in *Real Conversations* (London: Heinemann, 1904), pp. 216–234;

Dorothy Foster Gilman, "An Afternoon with Switzerland with Lucas Malet," *Boston Evening Transcript,* 6 June 1925, part 6, p. 1.

**References:**

Florence Bell, "Sir Richard Calmady," *Fortnightly Review,* new series 70 (November 1901): 894–901;

Janet Courtney, "Lucas Malet's Novels," *Fortnightly Review,* new series 71 (March 1902): 532–540;

Courtney, "A Novelist of the 'Nineties," *Fortnightly Review,* new series 131 (February 1932): 230–241;

" 'Lucas Malet': A Novelist of Character," *Times,* 29 October 1931, 14d;

Malcolm MacColl, "Morality in Fiction," *Contemporary Review,* 60 (August 1891): 234–252;

Patricia Thomas Srebrnik, "The Re-Subjection of 'Lucas Malet': Charles Kingsley's Daughter and the Response to Muscular Christianity," in *Muscular Christianity: Embodying the Victorian Age,* edited by Donald E. Hall (Cambridge: University of Cambridge Press, 1994): 194–214.

**Papers:**

Gabrielle Vallings destroyed many of Lucas Malet's papers; she bequeathed the remainder, which includes correspondence between Frances Grenfell Kingsley, Rose Kingsley, William Harrison, and the publishing firm of Methuen, to her niece, Mrs. Angela Covey-Crump. The Macmillan archives at the British Library include letters from Malet and Rose Kingsley, as well as Malet's applications to the Royal Literary Fund. Other correspondence is located at the Harry Ransom Humanities Research Center, University of Texas at Austin.

# John Masefield

*(1 June 1878 – 12 May 1967)*

Stephen R. Whited
*Piedmont College*

See also the Masefield entries in *DLB 10: Modern British Dramatists, 1900–1945;* and *DLB 19: British Poets, 1880–1914.*

BOOKS: *Salt-Water Ballads* (London: Richards, 1902; New York: Macmillan, 1913);

*Ballads* (London: Elkin Mathews, 1903);

*A Mainsail Haul* (London: Elkin Mathews, 1905; enlarged edition, London: Elkin Mathews, 1913; New York: Macmillan, 1913);

*Sea Life in Nelson's Time* (London: Methuen, 1905);

*On the Spanish Main* (London: Methuen, 1906);

*A Tarpaulin Muster* (London: Richards, 1907; New York: Dodge, 1908);

*Captain Margaret: A Romance* (London: Richards, 1908; Philadelphia: Lippincott, 1909);

*Multitude and Solitude* (London: Richards, 1909; New York: Kennerley, 1910);

*The Tragedy of Nan and Other Plays* (New York: Kennerley, 1909; London: Richards, 1909);

*The Tragedy of Pompey the Great* (London: Sidgwick & Jackson, 1910; New York: Macmillan, 1910);

*Ballads and Poems* (London: Elkin Mathews, 1910);

*Martin Hyde: The Duke's Messenger* (Boston: Little, Brown, 1910; London: Wells, Gardner, Darton, 1910);

*A Book of Discoveries* (London: Wells, Gardner, Darton, 1910; New York: Stokes, 1910);

*Lost Endeavour* (London: Nelson, 1910; New York: Macmillan, 1917);

*My Faith in Woman Suffrage* (London: Woman's Press, 1910);

*The Street of To-Day* (London: Dent, 1911; New York: Dutton, 1911);

*Jim Davis* (London: Wells Gardner, Darton, 1911; New York: Stokes, 1912);

*The Street of Today* (London: Dent, 1911; New York: Dutton, 1911);

*William Shakespeare* (London: Williams & Norgate, 1911; New York: Holt, 1911);

*The Everlasting Mercy* (London: Sidgwick & Jackson, 1911; Portland, Maine: Smith & Sale, 1911);

*John Masefield*

*Jim Davis* (London: Wells, Gardner & Darton, 1911; New York: Stokes, 1912);

*The Everlasting Mercy and The Widow in the Bye Street* (New York: Macmillan, 1912);

*The Widow in the Bye Street* (London: Sidgwick & Jackson, 1912);

*The Story of a Round-House and Other Poems* (New York: Macmillan, 1912);

*The Daffodil Fields* (New York: Macmillan, 1913; London: Heinemann, 1913);

*Dauber: a Poem* (London: Heinemann, 1913);

*Philip the King and Other Poems* (London: Heinemann, 1914; New York: Macmillan, 1914);

*Job M. Synge: A Few Personal Recollections, With Biographical Notes* (Churchtown, Dundrum: Cuala Press, 1915; New York: Macmillan, 1915);

*The Faithful: A Tragedy in Three Acts* (London: Heinemann, 1915; New York: Macmillan, 1915);

*Good Friday and Other Poems* (New York: Macmillan, 1916);

*Sonnets* (New York: Macmillan, 1916);

*Good Friday: A Play in Verse* (Letchworth: Garden City Press, 1916);

*Sonnets and Poems* (Letchworth: Garden City Press, 1916);

*The Locked Chest; The Sweeps of Ninety-Eight* (Letchworth: Garden City Press, 1916; New York: Macmillan, 1916);

*Gallipoli* (London: Heinemann, 1916; New York: Macmillan, 1916);

*Lollingdon Downs and Other Poems* (New York: Macmillan, 1917); republished as *Lollingdon Downs and Other Poems, With Sonnets* (London: Heinemann, 1917);

*The Old Front Line* (London: Heinemann, 1917; New York: Macmillan, 1917); republished as *The Old Front Line, or, the Beginning of the Battle of the Somme* (London: Heinemann, 1917);

*Rosas* (New York: Macmillan, 1918);

*The War and the Future* (New York: Macmillan, 1918);

*Collected Poems and Plays,* 2 volumes (New York: Macmillan, 1918);

*A Poem and Two Plays* (London: Heinemann, 1918);

*St. George and the Dragon* (London: Heinemann, 1919);

*The Battle of the Somme* (London: Heinemann, 1919);

*Reynard the Fox: or, The Ghost Heath Run* (New York: Macmillan, 1919; London: Heinemann, 1919);

*Enslaved and Other Poems* (London: Heinemann, 1920; New York: Macmillan, 1920);

*Right Royal* (New York: Heinemann, 1920; London: Heinemann, 1920);

*King Cole* (London: Heinemann, 1921; New York: Macmillan, 1921);

*The Dream* (London: Heinemann, 1922; New York: Macmillan, 1922);

*Melloney Holtspur* (London: Heinemann, 1922; New York: Macmillan, 1922);

*King Cole and Other Poems* (London: Heinemann, 1923); republished as *King Cole, The Dream, and Other Poems* (New York: Macmillan, 1923);

*The Taking of Helen* (London: Heinemann, 1923; New York: Macmillan, 1923);

*A King's Daughter: A Tragedy in Verse* (New York: Macmillan, 1923; London: Heinemann, 1923);

*The Collected Poems of John Masefield,* 2 volumes (London: Heinemann, 1923);

*Recent Prose* (London: Heinemann, 1924; revised, 1932; New York: Macmillan, 1933);

*Sard Harker* (London: Heinemann, 1924; New York: Macmillan, 1924);

*The Trial of Jesus* (London: Heinemann, 1925);

*Collected Works,* 4 volumes (New York: Macmillan, 1925);

*Odtaa* (New York: Macmillan, 1926; London: Heinemann, 1926);

*Tristan and Isolt: A Play in Verse* (London: Heinemann, 1927; New York: Macmillan, 1927);

*The Midnight Folk* (London: Heinemann, 1927; New York: Macmillan, 1927);

*The Coming of Christ* (New York: Macmillan, 1928; London: Heinemann, 1928);

*Midsummer Night and other tales in Verse* (London: Heinemann, 1928; New York: Macmillan, 1928);

*Easter: a Play for Singers* (New York: Macmillan, 1929; London: Heinemann, 1929);

*The Hawbucks* (London: Heinemann, 1929; New York: Macmillan, 1929);

*The Wanderer of Liverpool* (London: Heinemann, 1930; New York: Macmillan, 1930);

*Poetry Essays* (London: Heinemann, 1931);

*Minnie Maylow's Story and Other Tales and Scenes* (London: Heinemann, 1931; New York: Macmillan, 1931);

*A Tale of Troy* (London: Heinemann, 1932; New York: Macmillan, 1932);

*The End and Beginning* (London: Heinemann, 1933; New York: Macmillan, 1933);

*The Bird of Dawning* (London: Heinemann, 1933; New York: Macmillan, 1933);

*The Taking of the Gry* (London: Heinemann, 1934; New York: Macmillan, 1934);

*The Box of Delights; or When the Wolves Were Running* (London: Heinemann, 1935; New York: Macmillan, 1935);

*Victorious Troy; or, The Hurrying Angel* (London: Heinemann, 1935; New York: Macmillan, 1935);

*Plays,* 2 volumes (London: Heinemann, 1936);

*A Letter from Pontus and Other Verse* (London: Heinemann, 1936; New York: Macmillan, 1936);

*Eggs and Baker* (London: Heinemann, 1936; New York: Macmillan, 1936);

*The Square Peg: or The Gun Fella* (London: Heinemann, 1937; New York: Macmillan, 1937);

*John Masefield in his HMS* Conway *cadet uniform, with his sister, Nora. The telescope was a prize Masefield won in an essay contest.*

*Dead Ned* (New York: Macmillan, 1938; London: Heinemann, 1938);

*Some Verses to Some Germans* (London: Heinemann, 1939; New York: Macmillan, 1939);

*Live and Kicking Ned* (London: Heinemann, 1939; New York: Macmillan, 1939);

*Basilissa: A Tale of the Empress Theodora* (London: Heinemann, 1940; New York: Macmillan, 1940);

*Some Memories of W. B. Yeats* (New York: Macmillan, 1940);

*In the Mill* (London: Heinemann, 1941; New York: Macmillan, 1941);

*Conquer: A Tale of the Nika Rebellion in Byzantium* (London: Heinemann, 1941; New York: Macmillan, 1941);

*The Nine Days Wonder* (London: Heinemann, 1941; New York: Macmillan, 1941);

*Guatama the Enlightened and Other Verse* (London: Heinemann, 1941; New York: Macmillan, 1941);

*A Generation Risen,* by Masefield and Edward Seago (London: Collins, 1942);

*Natalie Maisie and Pavilastukay: Two Tales in Verse* (London: Heinemann, 1942; New York: Macmillan, 1944);

*Wonderings: Between One and Six Years* (London: Heinemann, 1943; New York: Macmillan, 1943);

*New Chum* (London: Heinemann, 1944; New York: Macmillan, 1945);

*Thanks Before Going* (London: Heinemann, 1946); enlarged as *Thanks Before Going with Other Gratitude for Old Delight including A Macbeth Production and Various Papers Not Before Printed* (London: Heinemann, 1947; New York: Macmillan, 1947);

*A Book of Pooth Sorts* (London: Heinemann, 1947);

*Badon Parchments* (London: Heinemann, 1947);

*A Play of St. George* (London: Heinemann, 1948; New York: Macmillan, 1948);

*On the Hill* (London: Heinemann, 1949; New York: Macmillan, 1949);

*St. Katherine of Ledbury and Other Ledbury Poems* (London: Macmillan, 1951);

*So Long to Learn: Chapters of an Autobiography* (London: Heinemann, 1952; New York: Macmillan, 1952);

*The Bluebells and Other Verse* (London: Heinemann, 1961; New York: Macmillan, 1961);

*Old Raiger and Other Verse* (London: Heinemann, 1964; New York: Macmillan, 1965);

*In Glad Thanksgiving* (London: Heinemann, 1966; New York: Macmillan, 1967);

*Grace before Ploughing: Fragments of Autobiography* (London: Heinemann, 1966; New York: Macmillan, 1966).

John Masefield is perhaps best known as the poet laureate of England from 1930 until his death in 1967, and his long career as a minor novelist falls under the shadow of his enormously popular poetry. In recent years readers and critics have ignored Masefield's novels, which is unfortunate because his fiction offers an antidote to currently fashionable pessimism and nihilism. In *Grace Before Ploughing: Fragments of Autobiography* (1966) Masefield claims that early in life he was certain "of spiritual powers ever ready to help bright human endeavour; the certainty that the individual life follows a law from of old, the law of his being, and must obey that law with all that is good in him, and achieve

what is good in him, or fail." His twenty-one novels reflect this certainty through the repetition of several important themes: the promotion of an intellectual purity and simplicity, an unswerving faith in the preserving power of art, and a belief in the good heart's capacity for endurance. Nostalgic for a heroic past, Masefield champions the traditional virtues and exposes the hypocrisy of twentieth-century pessimism, for he proposes to reclaim "a perception of the Life of the Universe," and he asserts that "Great art cannot and will not appear in generations or nations careless of the finer kinds of intellect, and therefore not attuned to the spirit of the Universe, which is all splendour and beauty."

John Edward Masefield was born on 1 June 1878 to Caroline and Edward Masefield. In his autobiography Masefield refers to his early life at the "Knapp" in Ledbury as a "Paradise," and, as Constance Babington Smith points out in her 1978 biography of the author, the child's Ledbury experiences were set in the magnificent fields and meadows of Herefordshire, with the Malvern Hills to the east, commercial traffic on the canal, and the literary magic of the nearby Welsh border. Masefield's doting mother encouraged the boy to memorize poems, and a comfortable Victorian respectability was provided by his father's work as a solicitor in the family law firm.

As a young child, Masefield discovered an imaginative ability, which he recalls in *So Long to Learn* (1952) as a major Wordsworthian epiphany: "one wonderful day, when I was little more than five years old, as I stood looking north, over a clump of honeysuckle in flower, I entered that greater life; and that life entered into me with a delight that I can never forget. I found suddenly that I could imagine imaginary beings complete in every detail, with every faculty and possession, and that these imaginations did what I wished for my delight, with an incredible perfection, in a rightness not of this world."

However, Masefield's childhood paradise was cruelly lost. When he was six years old, his mother died of complications attributed to pneumonia after the birth of his sister Norah. Masefield never recovered emotionally from the effects of her death; only the power of his imagination consoled him. His poetry, plays, and fiction refer frequently to the civilizing virtues embodied by a woman's nurturing, maternal influence. The following year, both of his grandparents died, and the family learned that their wealth and social standing had been lost because of the paternal grandfather's poor management. Masefield's father sank into depression, leaving the

*Dust jacket for Masefield's novel in which a young nobleman is forced to help conspirators against the king (courtesy of the Lilly Library, Indiana University)*

children in the care of a "hated" governess and Edward's eldest brother, William, and his wife Kate. Aunt Kate, a stern and practical woman who disapproved of the dreamy child's proclivity for stories and poems, presided over the affairs of the priory after the death of Masefield's father in 1891. Although no friend to Caroline, she took over the guardianship of the children. During these years Masefield found comfort during the summers, which he spent with his godmother, Ann Hanford-Flood, at Woollas Hall. Her influence on Masefield was profound.

Memories of good times at Woollas Hall surface in the novels *The Midnight Folk* (1927) and *The Box of Delights* (1935). These two books written for children are perhaps the most representative of Masefield's colorful imagination and didactic bent, for they possess vitality and inspire a narrative expectation unlike anything in his other novels. The protagonist in both is "young master Kay Harker," an ancestor of Sard Harker, the title character of an-

*Dust jacket for Masefield's 1924 novel, in which the title character faces a series of adventures with the aid of dream knowledge and magic (courtesy of the Lilly Library, Indiana University)*

other of Masefield's novels. In a fine example of stream of consciousness, the narrator moves freely and seamlessly in and out of Kay's imagination as the boy escapes the tedium of Latin lessons, solves criminal mysteries, regains the lost honor and treasure of his ancestors, foils the plots of evil priests and magicians, and saves the life of his beloved guardian, Miss Caroline Louisa, who loved Kay's mother and comes to care for him at the conclusion of *The Midnight Folk*. The sheer pleasure to be derived through fantasy and childhood imagination that is presented in these novels can be explained by what Masefield calls in *So Long to Learn* a desire for the "re-establishment of the idea of holiness, of the brightness that endures, of the truth that blesses, of the peace that burns away all self," a desire for "the finer kind of intellect," which he developed early in life to escape loneliness and neglect.

As he grew, he says in *So Long to Learn,* "Stories of some kind were going on in my head whenever I was alone; three or four main stories (none about myself) going from incident to incident and climate to climate." Despite such imaginative gifts, Masefield's earliest educational experiences were terrible. The unhappy boy attempted suicide at one point by eating laurel leaves, but he failed. He also attempted to run away but was caught by a policeman and received a flogging upon his return. Although his school life improved at Warwick School, his aunt decided the thirteen-year-old Masefield must learn a trade, and he was sent to the schoolship HMS *Conway* in autumn 1891, where he received the anachronistic training of sailing vessels and acquired his lifelong love of sailing ships and seafaring.

In his autobiographical account of the *Conway* years, *New Chum* (1944), Masefield describes an ordered life full of work, discipline, insecurity, hero worship, and awe for the beauty of the ships. He made friends with an older boy, H. B. Meiklejohn, by telling ghost stories, and he was distraught when Meiklejohn received his orders and departed. *New Chum* also describes Masefield's discovery of "the getting of tranquility," a hedge against his feelings of abandonment and loneliness: "I read a page of some thoughtful prose, then, shutting my eyes, I repeated to myself a couple of poems, and then sang to myself with a mental voice, one, two, three or even four songs. Usually, before I reached the fourth, I had attained a mental quiet, in which I could sort out the experiences of the day, annul its trouble as illusion and see its good as jolly." Masefield finished his course of study and received his orders to sail on the *Gilcruix* of the White Star Line. His experience was unhappy, for he was plagued with seasickness. He apparently suffered some kind of breakdown on the trip out and was discharged in August 1894 for illness. He spent time in a British hospital at Valparaiso and had worked his way back to Ledbury by the end of October. His aunt merely expressed disappointment that he "failed to stick it," and although Masefield had made up his mind to pursue a career in writing, he returned to the sea at her insistence. Subsequently, in New York, he deserted to spend time working at various odd jobs, finally settling at a mill in Yonkers.

Masefield's account of these days in America, *In the Mill* (1941), portrays a young man desperate to become a writer. He spent his money on books and read widely from the living writers of America, France, Russia, and England. In *So Long to Learn*

Masefield mentions reading the short fiction of the American magazines and discovering the joys of Sir Thomas Malory, the *Mabinogion,* Geoffrey Chaucer, John Milton, and Gabriel Dante Rossetti. After two years at the mill, Masefield decided London was the place for a budding, self-taught writer, and he returned home.

In 1899 he discovered the poetry of W. B. Yeats, and over the next two years his prospects increased thanks to his close association with Jack Yeats, W. B. Yeats, Lady Gregory, John Millington Synge, Arthur Symons, Laurence Binyon, and Harley Granville-Barker. With such impressive influences in poetry, theater, and folklore, Masefield published over the next ten years two novels, three books of poetry, several plays, and such lengthy historical essays as *Sea Life in Nelson's Time* (1905) and *On the Spanish Main* (1906). He had also edited a two-volume edition of *Dampier's Voyages, The Poems of Robert Herrick,* the *Lyrics of Ben Jonson, Beaumont and Fletcher,* and many reviews and essays.

Masefield identified 1911 as the year in which he seriously began to write, a view that neglects much important early short fiction, some of which is collected in *A Mainsail Haul* (1905) and *A Tarpaulin Muster* (1907). The year 1901 more accurately marks the beginning of his furious and exhausting career as a freelance writer, and Smith notes that in that year he sent W. B. Yeats a sea story ("a tale of piracy") for critique, but it never attained publication. Things progressed quickly. On 23 July 1903 Masefield married Constance de la Cherois Crommelin. With growing responsibility, Masefield adopted an extraordinary writing schedule. By 1904 he could complain to Yeats, "I cannot write prose all day, and verses when the prose is done. I have written 160,000 words (the length of two novels) this year." Nevertheless, his poems, ghost stories, tall tales, essays, and book reviews appeared in the *Tatler,* the *Speaker/Nation,* the *Pall Mall Magazine,* the *Daily News,* the *Manchester Guardian,* and the *Gentleman's Magazine.* Masefield's productivity was the result of his belief that the best way to hone his skills as a writer was to write frequently and "against the clock," that is, with firm deadlines.

Masefield's production of novels can be divided into two phases that fall between his interest in poetics. His first novels, *Captain Margaret: A Romance* (1908), *Multitude and Solitude* (1909), *Lost Endeavour* (1910), *Martin Hyde: The Duke's Messenger* (1910), *The Street of Today* (1911), and *Jim Davis* (1911), were written for the popular media. His best novels, however, were published in a second phase of production, after his experiences in

*Dust jacket for one of Masefield's most acclaimed novels, the story of a young man who finds himself in charge of a small crew of shipwreck survivors (courtesy of the Lilly Library, Indiana University)*

World War I. While he wrote several historical accounts of the war, including *Gallipoli* (1916), *The Old Front Line* (1917), and *The Battle of the Somme* (1919), his experience seems to have done more to confirm his moral sentiments than to fragment them, for he continued to set his fiction in the past, where heroes held strong against a more manageable adversary than mechanized war. The best of these novels, *Sard Harker* (1924), *The Bird of Dawning* (1933), *The Taking of the Gry* (1934), *Victorious Troy; or, The Hurrying Angel* (1935), *Dead Ned* (1938), and *Live and Kicking Ned* (1939), are in many ways typical of competently written popular fiction of the period, but they mark an improvement in Masefield's use of dialogue and in his conception of characterization.

While these novels offer amusing diversion with their poetic language and adventurous plots, they also provide insight into the mind of an important poet whose devotion to narrative, glory, duty,

and hope presents a curious anomaly when considered alongside the pessimism of the modernist experiments going on around him. For one so well connected with the literary world, Masefield seemed singularly untouched by the noisy manifestos emanating from the Continent.

Masefield's first group of novels can be characterized by a passage from a 1903 letter to his wife, in which the author tells of his desire to write "a simple story . . . in white clean verse as wholesome as wheat, telling of man and his sorrows and all the joy of earth, and the beauty of friendship and gentle love, and all the strength and passion of noble angers." The plots of his early novels, adult versions of *The Midnight Folk,* reflect an attachment to childhood experiences with the sea; with imagined smugglers and kidnappers; with the adventurous novels of Tobias Smollett, Robert Louis Stevenson, and Frederick Marryat; and with popular Victorian sentiments.

In *Captain Margaret* Masefield offers a view of chivalric love. Charles Margaret, owner of the *Broken Heart,* sets out to found an English colony and to check Spanish oppression of the Indians on the Spanish Main. On board is his former sweetheart, Olivia, who has made an unfortunate marriage to the blackguard Tom Stukeley. After many adventures the colony fails, Tom's treachery is exposed, and Charles is comforted by Olivia, who offers the book's theme: "There is no dishonour, Charles. You failed. The only glory is failure. All artists fail. But one sees what they saw. You see that in their failure." While character development seldom rises beyond allegorical types and dialogue is generally contrived and stylized (perhaps in the style of the popular theater of the day), the novel's ideas are forcefully expressed in the psychology of its characters and the author's concern for moral fiber and endurance.

Other weighty personal concerns make appearances in Masefield's early fiction. *Multitude and Solitude,* for example, explores a London playwright's struggles against failure and his altruistic longing to help mankind by aiding the search for a cure for "sleeping sickness" (malaria), an interest Masefield had vowed years earlier to pursue for the sake of suffering sailors. In *Martin Hyde: The Duke's Messenger* a young nobleman is forced to help conspirators against the king, but the love of a beautiful woman saves him from the dire consequences of a failed rebellion. In *Lost Endeavour* Masefield presents a kidnapping, a utopian scheme, and pirates, offering what Muriel Spark calls a "feeling of a deeper order than is to be found in much of Mr.

Masefield's later, more detached, more purely entertaining fiction." Since previous novels have a conspicuous lack of believable female characters, it is curious that he attempts in *The Street of Today* a cautionary tale about the decadence of the city and the dangers of marriage between a dreamy idealist and a stylishly neurotic woman. In *Jim Davis* the author recounts the adventures of a young boy kidnapped by smugglers and the boy's relentless desire to find his way home.

Although Masefield's novels improved in quality and conception after the war, psychological needs define their subjects, for their characters are troubled souls who seek their place in the world, "orphans" who pursue comfort against indifference and who demand the just triumph of a deserved reward. Masefield's world is not determined or fated; one discovers one's destiny through responsible action. The title character of *Sard Harker,* for example, begins as a sardonic young man but matures through a series of adventures by meeting his destiny with grace and hope. He succeeds with the help of dream knowledge and magic and of bravery and heroism on the high seas. He shoulders his burden in every possible setting – deserts, jungles, snowy mountains – and for his endurance he is rewarded with the companionship of an ideal woman.

While many of Masefield's later novels make interesting use of exotic settings and heroic male characters, the author never creates a fully realized female character, perhaps explained by his lifelong romantic view of women as representative of nurturing, humane goodness. This view led to many interesting relationships between Masefield and older women. Because he had lost his mother in childhood, Masefield's marriage to Constance Crommelin, eleven years his senior, was viewed by many of his friends as worrisome, but the marriage was by all accounts successful. His godmother, Miss Flood, had been a close friend of his mother and was an important confidant during Masefield's childhood and his apprenticeship years in London, guiding his views on matters of art and learning. She appeared to satisfy intellectual needs his sisters, Ethel and Norah, could not meet, despite the affection the siblings shared for one another. In 1910 Masefield met the fifty-year-old American expatriate actress and author Elizabeth Robins, a friend of Henry James, and developed a "mother/son" relationship with her that inspired a correspondence hidden from his wife.

Masefield's interest in woman suffrage, inspired by Robins, was based on sentiments less about equality than about the perfectibility of the

world through women's better nature. In *The Hawbucks* (1929), for example, Masefield offers the taming of a romantic and adventurous young second son, George Childrey, whose life is finally ordered by the right girl. In his childish way, Childrey desires the "porcelain" qualities of a girl named Carrie but matures to appreciate the "earthenware" solidity of Margaret, a distinction that expresses Masefield's regard for simplicity, authenticity, practicality, and independence. Nevertheless, the female characters of this and other late novels provide foils for the plot and little else of interest. Masefield writes most comfortably about the "manly virtues."

One of his best novels, *The Bird of Dawning*, has no women and little talk of them. Cyril "Cruiser" Trewsbury, twenty-two years old, finds himself suddenly in charge of a small crew of shipwreck survivors from the *Black Gauntlet* who recover a drifting, abandoned clipper ship, *The Bird of Dawning*, and miraculously win a China tea-trade race. The young man exhibits courage, humility, integrity, duty, and honor during his trials, and he is duly rewarded for his enduring hope. But for "Cruiser" the "real" life is not about reward and comfort. He says to a mate that the "real" exists "when you've got nothing except just your bare life and you're up against destiny or death. When you're up against your Fortune, whether it goes for you or against you." That experience is reward enough for "few people get anything real into their lives."

This theme is also advanced in *The Taking of the Gry,* in which two distant cousins discover each other during revolutionary times in the Spanish Main. The *Gry,* a ship with a horsehead figurehead, is filled with armament necessary for the success of the Nationalist Party resistance. Young cadet Charles Tarlton is on his way up in the shipping company that employs him, but after discovering the aims of his heroic cousin, he finds himself piloting the *Gry* through a narrow, treacherous channel last used by Sir Francis Drake in another daring escape. Curiously, the value of the cause is never questioned by Tarlton, and he says later, "What struck me most at that instant [stealing the *Gry*] was the beauty of the singing of a liberty party in some boat not now visible near the landing stairs. They had a couple of flutes with them playing the Evening Hymn to which men sang. The flute music came like a blessing to us: it made the hymn one of the most lovely things I have heard." Although Tarlton exhibits poise and concentration while under great pressure, his importance as an example of Masefield's values is expressed in Tarlton's spiri-

*Masefield and T. S. Eliot looking at William Caxton's edition of Chaucer*

tual awareness of the "real" value of life. In the greatest moments of stress, Tarlton can observe beauty. Similarly, in *Victorious Troy*, Dick Pomfret, an eighteen-year-old senior apprentice, makes use of his training and three years at sea to save the *Hurrying Angel* after she loses her foremast and mainmast in a cyclone. He returns to a hero's welcome for the "Boy-Captain" given by Sir Theopompous Harker, chairman of the Harker and Harker shipping firm, and, incidentally, guardian to Kay Harker of *The Midnight Folk*. The theme, of course, is always hope for the best and endure all adversity.

Among Masefield's last novels, which Spark judges his best prose work, the author expands on his themes to examine larger social and political issues. In *Dead Ned* and *Live and Kicking Ned,* Ned Mansell, fresh out of a medical apprenticeship, is falsely accused of murder, tried, convicted, and hanged. Ned is miraculously revived by his father's friends and escapes by ship to Africa, where adventure leads him to discover a lost white race in the interior, to mediate the grievances of a war, to fight the slave trade, and to recover his dead mother's portrait. Ultimately exonerated and married, he discovers, thanks to the digging of his dog, a hidden treasure. Unlike Marlow in Joseph Conrad's "Heart of Darkness" (1899), Ned's African experiences lead him to fulfill his destiny and free him of all his hatred for the pretense and hypocrisy of his own people.

In other novels Masefield attacks the cruelty of foxhunting, the narrowness of provincial life in

the English countryside, and the "barbarism" of capital punishment. *Eggs and Baker* (1936) relates the social conscience of one of Ned's progeny, a poor baker named Robert Frampton Mansell, who – in a fit of indignation over the unjust death sentence brought against a mentally deficient employee – pelts the judge with an egg that is not quite hard-boiled and thus goes to prison. Family enmities are finally dissolved by this stand for human dignity, and Mansell eventually finds his fortunes improved.

In *The Square Peg: or The Gun Fella* (1937) Frampton Mansell, Robert Frampton's grandson, is a wealthy manufacturer of guns who, after the death of his fiancée, decides to build a bird sanctuary and housing development in the middle of a hunting ground. Mansell's plans for the development of his property and his distaste for foxhunting put him at odds with the local gentry, but his stand for dignity and principle results in the development of a garden city, a theater of ballet, a national forest and wildlife sanctuary with world-famous bronze statuary, and a new wife. According to Smith these stories mirrored Masefield's new interest in ballet and his unhappiness with his Pinbury Park neighbors, whose hunting dogs had killed his cats.

During World War II Masefield published two historical novels reflecting his interest in Byzantium: *Basilissa: A Tale of the Empress Theodora* (1940) and *Conquer: A Tale of the Nika Rebellion in Byzantium* (1941). They present idealized impressions of the rise of Christianity and an enlightened monarchy under the rule of Theodora and Justinian I, again common people who rise to greatness. Along with the memoir *In the Mill*, the historical account *The Nine Days Wonder* (1941), and the poems in *A Generation Risen* (1942), the Byzantium novels celebrate courage and sacrifice for ideals. They were meant to offer much-needed comfort to readers worried over the threat of Nazi invasion and probably helped Masefield deal with his fear for his beloved son Lewis, who while serving in Africa with the RAMC was killed in 1942.

Masefield's final novel, *Badon Parchments* (1947), claims to be eyewitness accounts and historical documents sent to Justinian and Theodora to report the success of Christian forces against the heathen at Badon. An interesting experiment, the book is an allegorical allusion to England's recent defeat of the Nazis and is informed by the author's recurrent thematic messages of endurance and hope.

In his long poem "Dauber" (1913), an account of a lonely young seaman who wishes only to paint the beauty of the sailing clippers, Masefield offers an illustration of the artist-hero who "had done with fear – / Fronted the worst and looked it in the face." Masefield told Muriel Spark that "Dauber" relates how "the artist is compelled to obey an inner law of his being, no matter if disaster or death results." This description also offers an apt epigraph for this man and his inspiring, if not always inspired, novels. Constance died in 1960, but Masefield continued writing poetry every day and earning many accolades. He died on 12 May 1967.

Recent work in ethical criticism may renew academic interest in Masefield's work, since his artistic claims are manifestly didactic; current fashion for political activism in literary pursuits may even stir critics to examine Masefield's novels of manner. However, readers outside the academy have kept his work in print, which suggests that the ethos presented by such novels is not as far removed from contemporary life as some critics claim. Moreover, because readers' demands for sea tales continue, scholars interested in ethical criticism or popular culture might benefit by reviewing Masefield's work, which aims to delight readers while also instructing them in matters of virtue and courage.

**Bibliography:**

Geoffrey Handley-Taylor, *John Masefield, O.M.: The Queen's Poet Laureate, A Bibliography and Eighty-First Birthday Tribute* (London: Crambrook Tower, 1960).

**Biography:**

Constance Babington Smith, *John Masefield: A Life* (New York: Macmillan, 1978).

**References:**

Fraser B. Drew, *John Masefield's England: A Study of National Themes in His Work* (Rutherford, N.J.: Fairleigh Dickinson University Press, 1973);

Corliss Lamont, *Remembering John Masefield* (Rutherford, N.J.: Fairleigh Dickinson University Press, 1971);

Muriel Spark, *John Masefield* (London: Nevill, 1953);

Sanford Sternlicht, *John Masefield* (Boston: Twayne, 1977).

# William McFee

*(15 June 1881 – 2 July 1966)*

Paul A. Love
*Gettysburg College*

BOOKS: *Letters from an Ocean Tramp* (London: Cassell, 1908); revised as *An Ocean Tramp* (New York: Doubleday, Page, 1921; revised again, 1927);

*Aliens* (London: Arnold, 1914; New York: Longmans, Green, 1914; revised edition, New York: Doubleday, Page, 1918);

*Casuals of the Sea* (London: Secker, 1916; New York: Doubleday, Page, 1916);

*A Port Said Miscellany* (Boston: Atlantic Monthly Press, 1918);

*Captain Macedoine's Daughter* (New York: Doubleday, Page, 1920; London: Secker, 1921);

*A Six-Hour Shift* (New York: Doubleday, Page, 1920);

*Harbours of Memory* (New York: Doubleday, Page, 1921; London: Heinemann, 1921);

*An Engineer's Notebook: Essays on Life and Letters* (New York: Shay, 1921);

*Command* (New York: Doubleday, Page, 1922; London: Secker, 1922);

*Race* (New York: Doubleday, Page, 1924; London: Secker, 1924);

*Swallowing the Anchor* (New York: Doubleday, Page, 1925; London: Heinemann, 1925);

*Sunlight in New Granada* (New York: Doubleday, Page, 1925; London: Heinemann, 1925);

*The Life of Sir Martin Frobisher* (New York: Harper, 1928; London: Bodley Head, 1928);

*Pilgrims of Adversity* (New York: Doubleday, Doran, 1928; London: Heinemann, 1928);

*Sailors of Fortune* (New York: Doubleday, Doran, 1929; London: Heinemann, 1930);

*North of Suez* (New York: Doubleday, Doran, 1930; London: Heinemann, 1930);

*Born to Be Hanged* (Gaylordsville: Slide Mountain Press, 1930);

*The Harbourmaster* (New York: Doubleday, Doran, 1932; London: Heinemann, 1932);

*No Castle in Spain* (New York: Doubleday, Doran, 1933);

*William McFee*

*The Reflections of Marsyas* (Gaylordsville: Slide Mountain Press, 1933);

*More Harbours of Memory* (New York: Doubleday, Doran, 1934);

*The Beachcomber* (New York: Doubleday, Doran, 1935);

*Sailor's Wisdom* (London: Cape, 1935);

*Sailor's Bane* (Philadelphia: Rittenhouse, 1936);

*Derelicts* (New York: Doubleday, Doran, 1938);

*Watch Below* (New York: Random House, 1940);

*Spenlove in Arcady* (New York: Random House, 1941);

*Ship to Shore* (New York: Random House, 1944; London: Faber & Faber, 1946);

*In the First Watch* (New York: Random House, 1946;
London: Faber & Faber, 1947);
*Family Trouble* (New York: Random House, 1949);
*The Law of the Sea* (Philadelphia: Lippincott, 1950;
London: Faber & Faber, 1951);
*The Adopted* (London: Faber & Faber, 1952).

OTHER: Milton Raison, *Spindrift*, introduction by
McFee (New York: Doran, 1922);
Joseph Conrad, *Lord Jim*, introduction by McFee
(New York: Doubleday, Page, 1922);
Arthur Mason, *Ocean Echoes*, introduction by McFee
(New York: Holt, 1923);
Margery Allingham, *Black 'erchief Dick*, introduction
by McFee (New York: Doubleday, Page,
1923);
Y, *Odyssey of a Torpedoed Transport*, introduction by
McFee (Boston: Houghton Mifflin, 1923);
*Iron Men and Wooden Ships*, edited by Frank Shay, in-
troduction by McFee (New York: Doubleday,
Page, 1924);
Joseph Conrad, *Almayer's Folly*, introduction by
McFee (New York: Doubleday, Page, 1925);
W. H. Hudson, *The Purple Land*, introduction by
McFee (New York: Modern Library, 1926);
Henry Justin Smith, *Innocents Aloft and Other Souvenirs
of Days in France*, preface by McFee (Chicago:
Covici, 1927);
Michael Scott, *Tom Cringle's Log*, introduction by
McFee (New York: Dodd, Mead, 1927);
*The Life and Times of Aloyius Horn*, volume 2, intro-
duction by McFee (New York: Simon & Schus-
ter, 1928);
*A Cruise of the Seven Seas*, introduction by McFee
(New York: International Mercantile Marine,
1928);
Joseph Conrad, *Youth* (Educational Edition), intro-
duction by McFee (New York: Doubleday,
Doran, 1929);
Herman Melville, *Moby Dick*, introduction by
McFee, illustrated by Anton Otto Fischer
(Philadelphia & Chicago: Winston, 1931);
John Tinkham Babb, *A Bibliography of the Writings of
William McFee*, with introduction and notes on
each major entry by McFee (New York: Dou-
bleday, Doran, 1931);
David Stanley Livingstone, *Full and By*, introduction
by McFee (New York: Dodge, 1936);
*World's Great Tales of the Sea*, edited, with introduc-
tion and notes, by McFee (Cleveland & New
York: World, 1944);
*Great Sea Stories of Modern Times*, edited, with intro-
duction by McFee (New York: McBride,
1953).

William McFee's accomplishments as a writer
sprang from the same character traits that led him
to make seagoing his career — an adventurous and
romantic spirit, an insatiable curiosity about the
world and his fellow man, and a need to tell stories
about what he found. He speaks in what seemed to
his many readers a new voice, unembellished and
unladen with literary artifice. His subject is the
human condition, but because of the settings for his
stories and the occupations of his characters his
tales are exotic as well as universal. McFee breaks
no new literary ground, but his stories were popular
with a wide range of readers during most of his
writing life. His popularity can be attributed, in part
at least, to the clarity with which he views the people and the world he describes and to the detached
irony of the narrators he employs. McFee is one of
the few novelists of the period who was able to balance two disparate careers — as a seagoing engineering officer and as a prolific writer of fiction — and to
achieve success in each.

William McFee was born on 15 June 1881 on
the three-masted, square-rigged ship, *Erin's Isle*,
which was homeward bound from India and within
sight of the English coast. His father, John Henry
McFee — a sea captain, as his father had been before
him — had designed, built, and owned *Erin's Isle*.
McFee's father was of Irish descent, while his
mother, who often accompanied her husband on his
voyages, was born in Nova Scotia. After McFee's
birth, the family settled in New Southgate, a suburb
in North London and the setting for the author's
first successful novel, *Casuals of the Sea* (1916).
McFee was educated at several local schools, completing his formal education at East Anglian School,
Bury Saint Edmunds, Suffolk, a public school for
the sons of the middle class where McFee discovered his talent for storytelling by regaling his class-
mates after lights-out with embellished versions of
his own wide reading.

Following school McFee, at age sixteen, was
apprenticed for three years to the engineering firm
of McMuirland's at Aldersgate in London at a cost
to his family of one hundred pounds per annum.
Thus prepared for employment, McFee spent some
time working at a water pumping station at Tring
before joining a firm of Yorkshire engineers in their
London office. It was during this time that McFee
became acquainted with artists and writers living in
Chelsea and pursued his passionate interests in
Rudyard Kipling and socialism, as odd as that combination may seem. McFee had become a voracious
and eclectic reader and spent much of his free time
in the British Museum reading room, when he was

*The dust jacket for the American edition of* Pilgrims of Adversity *(1928) providing a McFee collector's guide.*

not attending evening classes at the Northampton Institute, where he also lectured occasionally. It was also at this time that he became a close friend of Arthur Elder, the artist, who was to figure in his later literary career.

In 1905 at age twenty-four McFee, through the influence of a ship-owning uncle, went to sea as a junior engineer, leaving behind forever the stuffy office and engineering position he felt to be a dead end (and possibly also leaving behind a failed love affair). His first ship was the *Rotherfield,* a tramp steamer calling at African, Asian, and Mediterranean ports, the latter a part of the world that McFee would return to during World War I and which was to inspire much of his writing in the future. From these early voyages as junior engineer, the author developed the material for his first published book, *Letters from an Ocean Tramp* (1908), published by Cassell and Company in a small edition of fewer than one thousand copies. Long after McFee had made a name for himself as an author, a second edition, slightly revised, was published in 1927.

*Letters from an Ocean Tramp,* although not a novel, is an early example of McFee's interests,

writing ability, and erudition. His interests, as they would be throughout his career, are focused on character rather than action, and he brings his people to life through careful and sympathetic observation, detached and ironic, with a great deal of philosophical commentary of the commonsense variety. He states in *Aliens* (1914), "It is for humanity I live, for them I work, and their praise is my reward. I am, in a way, in love with humanity. All the time I want *people*. They are the only thing that matters." His great theme then and later is, as he calls it, "the ineluctable problem of human folly."

In his first attempt to reach the reading public, McFee is not shy about displaying his wide reading. There are allusions to John Ruskin, Walter Pater, Friedrich Nietzsche, Heinrich Heine, Nicolas Boileau, Pierre-Augustin Caron Beaumarchais, George Borrow, Robert Browning, and many others, a pedantic tendency the author would subdue in later books. *Letters from an Ocean Tramp* is essentially what its title implies, a series of epistolary sketches about the tramp steamers of the day and the men who sailed in them. There is no plot to the book, and the only unifying device is the author's

voice, which is often too self-consciously literary for his subject but which is also vigorous, intelligent, unsentimental, and self-assured. There was little critical attention paid to the book on its first publication, but somewhat more notice was taken in its later incarnation when McFee was better known.

With the completed but as yet unpublished *Letters from an Ocean Tramp* under his arm, McFee returned to London to take the Board of Trade examination for engineer, which he passed in 1907 with a score of 98 percent, afterward shipping on the *Burrsfield* for Savannah, Georgia, as third engineer. During the time he was in London preparing for his examination McFee began to write what was to be his best-known novel, *Casuals of the Sea* (1916), which would take him nearly five years to complete and even longer to sell to a publisher.

In the meantime McFee's second published book and first published novel, *Aliens,* appeared. It was written during a year's respite from the sea in 1912–1913, while McFee was living with his friends from his early Chelsea days – Arthur Elder, the artist, and his wife in Nutley, New Jersey, thinly disguised in the novel as Netley Heights – and while he was trying to find a publisher for the completed *Casuals of the Sea. Aliens* is frankly autobiographical, as McFee later acknowledged, and centers on an English writer living with an English artist couple in Netley Heights. Neighbors to this ménage à trois are a handsome Italian woman, Mrs. Rosa Carville; her two sons, Giuseppe Mazzini and Benvenuto Cellini; and her seaman husband. The Carvilles, especially Rosa, are as alien to this new American environment as are the narrator and his artist friends. An actively employed seaman, Mr. Carville is rarely at home and then only on brief visits between voyages. His character, revealed to his neighbors as he tells them the story of his life, as a rather stolid, hardworking, and essentially decent man is well developed and is in sharp contrast to that of his brother, who is almost his complete moral opposite, a ravening, brilliant, and womanizing "go-getter" who from early youth preys upon his brother's good nature and respectability to get what he wants and whose behavior finally drives Carville to leave his safe, respectable job ashore to go to sea as an engineer, meet and marry the Italian orphan Rosa, and move to America.

The novel is narrated in the first person by the English writer and is highly discursive, as are many of McFee's novels, but the most interesting part of the book is devoted to Carville's narration of his own life. His story reflects McFee's own life and experiences. McFee had not yet created his garrulous

alter ego, Mr. Spenlove, as the narrator of his tales, but even without that equivalent to Joseph Conrad's Marlow, *Aliens* was compared by reviewers to Conrad's works, mainly on the basis of Mr. Carville's seagoing experiences. *Aliens* was first published in England in 1914, but McFee completely revised the novel during his wartime duty in the Mediterranean; the new edition was published in 1918 and received more respectful attention from reviewers because of the popular reception of *Casuals of the Sea.*

*Casuals of the Sea* established McFee in the eyes of the critics and the public as a serious novelist deserving of attention, a reputation he would retain for the rest of his career. James Huneker, the learned, influential, and acerbic American music and literature critic, writing in *The New York Times* on 20 August 1916, said that *Casuals of the Sea* "reeks with actuality, for the author's sincerity is a form of his talent . . . he does not write for a popular audience nor does he despise the public. But he insists on telling his tale in his own fashion. . . . It is my notion that Flaubert is his major god; indeed, he has been compared with the great Frenchman . . . also with Dickens, Zola, Conrad, and William De Morgan." Christopher Morley, the poet, novelist, playwright, and critic, after reading *Casuals of the Sea,* also became a McFee champion, so much so that when his son was born a year later his friends suggested naming the child "Casuals." H. L. Mencken praised McFee's early work as well. Such attentions presage a curious phenomenon that would last throughout McFee's writing career: he would receive more serious critical attention in the United States than he would in his native land, although he remained a quintessential English novelist.

*Casuals of the Sea* is an ambitious novel covering several generations of a poor working-class family, the Gooderiches, in and around London. Most of the novel focuses on the children of the laborer, Herbert, and his wife, Mary. McFee divides the novel into three books. The first, "The Suburb," deals with the aimless struggles and chaotic life of the family as the three children, Minnie, Bert, and Hannibal, are growing up in a grim North London suburb. The second book, "The City," follows Minnie, after the death of her father, as she breaks away from the constrictions of poverty for a life of sin and excitement as mistress to a succession of well-to-do men, a life that ultimately leads to a respectable marriage and material comfort. The third book, "The Sea," is the story of the youngest Gooderich, Hannibal, known as Hanny, who drifts into a life at sea and finds in that life, through

McFee's brilliantly evoked details, both his manhood and some satisfaction for his inarticulate yearnings. The Gooderichs' story is told in the third person by an omniscient narrator who takes the liberty of interjecting commentary from time to time on such subjects as the newly fashionable electric lighting, theosophy, advertising, class distinctions both ashore and afloat, and the demimonde, of which Minnie Gooderich is a part until she marries a sea captain and settles into middle-class respectability.

There is no question that the third part of the novel is among the best fiction that McFee wrote. Although the plot creaks and the ending is overly contrived, the characterization of Hannibal Gooderich is masterful. The reader's sympathy is deeply engaged by the boy's struggle to find a place for himself in the world, by his yearnings for a life of his own where he can spread his wings and be somebody. His shipping out on a tramp steamer and finding a measure of happiness in traveling the world as a part of the crew whose work, though menial, is essential, his meeting the girl he will later marry, and his growth into manhood are the stuff that McFee shapes into this gripping episode.

When McFee left his friends the Elders in 1913, he still had not found a publisher for either *Casuals of the Sea* or *Aliens,* but he had acquired a United States chief engineer's license and found work with the United Fruit Company. He was serving in that company's *SS Cartago* when the war broke out in Europe. He returned to England in October 1914 to offer his services to the war effort.

After being refused by the army McFee found employment as engineering officer on British transports in the Mediterranean service and later received an appointment as sublieutenant in the British navy. He was to become thoroughly familiar with that part of the world during the next four or five years, especially the ports of the Levant, such as Saloniki, Smyrna, Port Said, and Alexandria. These ports and their people would become major ingredients in his writing during the war and afterward. By this time *Aliens* had been published, but its author was dissatisfied with the novel and began working on the second version. In addition to McFee's wartime duties amid the dangers of the eastern Mediterranean, he not only struggled with the rewriting of *Aliens* but also found time to write a series of articles for *Land and Water,* a London magazine, which brilliantly picture the wartime Mediterranean naval forces.

In *Captain Macedoine's Daughter* (1920) and *Command* (1922), both set in the eastern Mediterranean,

*Dust jacket for McFee's novel set in Port Said, Egypt, during World War I (courtesy of the Lilly Library, Indiana University)*

McFee begins to elaborate upon a theme obliquely introduced in *Aliens* – the contrasting civilizations of the East and the West. Rosa of *Aliens* is the first of a series of remarkable women characters nurtured in mysterious, exotic locales and circumstances who come into contact with complacent, stolid, and unimaginative Englishmen – with results that are always dramatic and often tragic.

In *Captain Macedoine's Daughter* the reader is introduced to the intriguing Artemisia Macedoine, "half schoolgirl and half adventuress," who gives Mr. Spenlove, McFee's narrator, the impression of "a young person who has chanced upon some astounding revelation, and who was pre-occupied with both past and future more than the immediate present." The setting of the narration is aboard a British warship, lying off the island of Ipsilon somewhere in the Aegean Archipelago. The place reminds Spenlove, the ship's chief engineer, of events several years previous, when he had served on a

tramp steamer that had brought Artemisia, as acting maid to the captain's wife and small child, to Ipsilon to join her father. He then begins to relate the story of Artemisia and himself to a group of fellow officers.

Artemisia is the attractive half-caste daughter of Macedoine, facetiously known as "Captain" because of his aloofness and claims of an exalted lineage, who had served as a steward years before in a ship in which Spenlove was engineer. As the story opens, Artemisia is aboard Spenlove's ship on her way to join her father at a tiny coaling port in the Aegean where he is employed in a menial job and is hatching grandiose schemes to make his fortune. Spenlove tries to befriend Artemisia, who, although she had captivated the officers of the ship on the way to her destination, feels herself to be friendless and hopeless, and, as Spenlove discovers, she is also pregnant. The main line of the novel traces the development of Spenlove's interest in Artemisia from his early objective curiosity about her and his avuncular concern for her unhappiness to his deeper and more intimate feelings for her.

The narrative technique of having Spenlove relate to an attentive audience events that had happened years before is new to McFee in *Captain Macedoine's Daughter* but would be used by the author in many of his subsequent novels. In this first novel the narrator is the central character as well, but in later novels his position is more that of a detached observer who relates the stories of other people, his own role subordinate and tangential.

*Captain Macedoine's Daughter* is the most Jamesian of McFee's novels – that is, the interest resides in the subtle psychological relationship between Artemisia and Spenlove as it unfolds over several years while Artemisia is living a materially comfortable life as mistress to a rich Middle Eastern businessman. Out of this relationship with Artemisia, and the contrast between Occidental and Eastern civilizations and philosophies, Spenlove draws his insights about human nature and the mystery of love.

McFee dedicated *Captain Macedoine's Daughter* to "Pauline." During his war years in the eastern Mediterranean he had met Pauline Khondoff, a Bulgarian refugee, whom he married in 1920 and from whom he was divorced in 1932. This period of his first marriage is believed to have inspired his *Harbourmaster* (1932).

McFee set his next novel, *Command,* in the same general area as *Captain Macedoine's Daughter,* the waters of the eastern Mediterranean, and the spy-ridden port of Saloniki (the present-day Salonika, an Aegean port in northern Greece). The novel's plot unfolds during World War I as Allied ships plied the submarine-infested waters between once quiet, out-of-the-way ports now crowded with refugees, adventurers, and ambitious officeholders.

The central character, Reginald Spokesley, is a vaguely dissatisfied mate on one of the rust buckets engaged in this wartime traffic. Although he believes he deserves better than his present position, his fecklessness results only in feeble rebellion as he goes about his duties. War has a way of radically changing what seems to be one's destiny, however. McFee explores this truth in following Spokesley's adventures after both responsibility and romance are suddenly thrust upon him.

The responsibility comes directly from the sinking of Spokesley's ship and the loss of its captain and most of the other officers. Spokesley is saved from the general disaster, however, and, because he has master's papers, he is given a command of his own. The romance is provided by Evanthia Solaris, a refugee from the Balkans. She is the companion to an English woman who is married to a local Greek businessman engaged in various subrosa activities. Evanthia is a self-centered, exotic, and strong-willed survivor who tempts Spokesley to abandon his English respectability (and his English fiancée waiting at home) to save her from a life of exile and poverty. Spokesley's efforts on her behalf risk his future career as well as his newly discovered sense of responsibility. But his efforts to save Evanthia are to no avail; she abandons him at the end for a seemingly more certain savior.

*Command* presents many well-rounded minor characters realistically portrayed. The settings evoke the heady excitement of front-line wartime ports where the ordinary rules of society are suspended and characters change or revert to more primitive states. The backdrop to the novel's main plot provides the atmosphere that makes this one of McFee's most interesting and readable books.

In *Captain Macedoine's Daughter* and *Command* McFee treated his wartime and prewartime experiences in the eastern Mediterranean. Between the publication of these two novels, he wrote *A Six-Hour Shift* (1920), a series of nonfiction sketches about his duties as a refrigeration engineer, which was first published in serial form by the *Atlantic Monthly* in 1917. Also published in the *Atlantic Monthly* (March 1918) was a short story titled *A Port Said Miscellany,* which was separately published in 1918. McFee revised his 1908 *Letters from an Ocean Tramp* as *An Ocean Tramp* (1921). In the same year both *Harbours of*

*Memory* (1921), a collection of fourteen pieces previously published in periodicals, and *An Engineer's Notebook: Essays on Life and Letters* (1921), a collection of shorter pieces on various topics, including several on writing and criticism, were also published.

Following his wartime service in the Mediterranean, McFee had returned to the United Fruit Company. He quickly rose in his profession to chief engineer in that company's passenger liners in service between New York, Cuba, and mainland Latin America. During this time McFee began to think about leaving the sea to become a full-time writer, which he did in 1924.

In McFee's next novel, *Race* (1924), he returns to the setting of the first parts of *Casuals of the Sea,* a dreary London suburb, but, unlike the earlier novel, the setting does not turn to ships or the sea. *Race* is essentially a landlocked social novel that examines the lives of a large group of neighbors of differing social and economic standings whose interactions provide the interest. Among the crowded cast of characters, four become the focus of attention: Hazel and Lena, two of the seven daughters of the poor but respectable Heath family; Francis Striker, the son of a rich wine merchant, who returns home from Germany; and his French schoolmate, Louis Chaillu who comes home with him. The development of these young people and their ambitions form the central interest of the novel, and by the end of the book they are on the verge of successful futures. Hazel has gotten an offer from a publisher for one of her stories, Lena has bolted to London from a stultifying life of drudgery to become an artist's model, and Francis with his friend Louis are off to South America to build a railway. The reader can imagine that Hazel will become a successful writer, that Louis will return from South America to claim her as his wife, and that Francis will become one of England's successful empire builders.

Structurally, *Race* is not one of McFee's most successful novels. For one thing, the cast of characters is much too large and although McFee imbues his main characters and many of the minor ones with distinctive and arresting personalities, their stories never take coherent shape. In addition, McFee never fully develops the theme of racial differences among his characters, which at first seems his purpose and is suggested by the novel's title. McFee recognized the work's failings: in his introduction to the entry for *Race* in John Tinkham Babb's 1931 bibliography, McFee says: "*Race* is not one of my pet children" and goes on to explain that the novel was the first book of his purely literary life after he had left the sea. He blames the novel's

defects partly on his having failed to cut out a portion of what he had intended to be a much longer work and partly on his having finished it too hastily. Despite its defects, however, *Race* was reviewed favorably both in the United States and in England.

After *Race* was published, the author celebrated his decision to settle ashore with the publication of *Swallowing the Anchor* (1925), the title being a seaman's phrase for quitting the sea. McFee's lengthy subtitle for the book is revealing: "Being a Revised and Enlarged Collection of Notes Made by an Engineer in the Merchant Service Who Secured Leave of Absence from His Ship to Investigate and Report upon the Alleged Superiority of Life Ashore." But the title and subtitle promise more than is provided within the book. Only in his introduction does McFee touch upon his reasons for choosing the United States as his future home or on the considerations that went into his decision to leave the sea. The remainder of the book is made up of previously published essays, book reviews, and other miscellaneous pieces.

Soon after *Swallowing the Anchor* McFee's *Sunlight in New Granada* (1925) was published, his first attempt at literary travel writing. This book consists of a series of individual sketches based mainly in Colombia. The book had only a small printing and received very little notice, favorable or otherwise, although it is an excellent example of McFee's powers of observation and sympathetic imagination.

McFee's next full-length book was a biography, another new departure for him, proving that he was determined to make a success of being a full-time writer. *The Life of Sir Martin Frobisher* (1928) was commissioned by *Harper's Magazine* for London's Bodley Head Golden Hind Series. McFee spent several weeks at the British Museum digging up material and more than one year absorbing the details of the Elizabethan sea dog's life and times. While he was at work on Frobisher's life, McFee also began writing another novel, *North of Suez* (1930).

The two decades following World War I were McFee's most productive in a very busy writing life. There was hardly a book brought out that dealt even tangentially with the sea for which McFee was not asked to write a preface, an introduction, or a review. All the while he kept producing his own novels as well. He also found time to participate in the mildly bohemian literary life of Greenwich Village, which reminded him of his London days in Chelsea.

In the same year that his biography of Frobisher was published, McFee's next novel came

THE
HARBOUR-
MASTER

≈

WILLIAM McFEE

*Dust jacket for McFee's 1932 novel, which was compared by contemporary reviewers to the works of Joseph Conrad (courtesy of the Lilly Library, Indiana University)*

out: *Pilgrims of Adversity* (1928). Of this novel McFee writes in Babb's bibliography:

> This was formulated at first as a sort of sequel to *Race*. . . . I was influenced by *Nostromo,* of course. Anyone who has read that vast work will always think of it when he writes of Latin America.
>
> I suppose I shall always be floundering about trying to portray the men I know best, lower middle-class Englishmen. Here the idea was to depict a friendship. Friendships in books often seem to me hollow because they evade the curious semi-sexual nature of friendship. I have tried to bring this to the surface.

*Pilgrims of Adversity* unfolds against a revolutionary background in Central America. James Wishart, on the rebound after being jilted by a woman, joins the crew of the *Candleshoe* as third engineer. Just before the dilapidated ship sails for Havana, Wishart meets an actress, Winifred, who falls in love with him. Then, once he has arrived in Havana, he meets the exotic revolutionary Yolanda with whom he becomes enamored and who gets him involved with a developing revolution in the fictitious Costaruga. Yolanda is later killed, and at the end of the novel Wishart is reunited with Winifred.

As in many of McFee's novels, the subplots and the minor characters provide much of the interest. The captain of the *Candleshoe,* Millerton, is a testy skinflint who keeps the crew on short rations. He has been secretly briefed by the owners to turn over the ship to one of the revolutionary factions in Costaruga as part of a complicated arrangement from which the owners hope to profit. Millerton's opposite in the engine room is the chief engineer, Mr. Barker, who argues constantly with the captain over the sorry state of the engine room equipment, which frequently breaks down, and over the food upon which the crew must subsist. Adding to the captain's animosity toward the chief engineer is the presence of Humphries, the second engineer. Barker protects Humphries, who is a silent, efficient worker but almost always drunk, by refusing to sail without him, knowing that the captain would never be able to find another chief to sail in such a wreck. It is the friendship between Barker and Humphries to which McFee alludes in the quotation above. These characters and others among the revolutionaries ashore are well drawn as part of the turmoil and intrigue of the civil war and help to make *Pilgrims of Adversity* one of McFee's most interesting novels.

McFee followed the novel with a collection of short stories, *Sailors of Fortune* (1929), all of which had appeared earlier in popular magazines such as *Redbook.* In the following year *North of Suez* was published. It takes place in Port Said, Egypt, during World War I, thus returning McFee to the scenes of his wartime experiences. The story is a convoluted struggle between passion and duty played out in the person of Stephan, a desk-bound British navy officer. Rumford is at odds with his wife, his allies, his government, and his native subordinates yet is determined to stick to them and to do his job. In the midst of news about the far-off war and the local chicanery involving the police and his duties, Rumford becomes intrigued with a flamboyant local woman. The novel ends with Rumford's fiery death during a quixotic attempt to prevent a disaster in the crowded Port Said harbor. McFee accurately described the book as "a combination of absolutely authentic local colour and pure invention." More than earlier novels, *North of Suez* is a concentrated study

of one man's character amidst the stress of wartime duty.

Almost every reviewer called McFee's next novel, *The Harbourmaster,* Conradian, but the resemblance to Conrad's works is merely superficial. Chief Engineer Spenlove is not Conrad's Marlow, and the novel is much more diffuse than anything in Conrad's works. Spenlove relates to a group of passengers the story of his good friends, Captain Fraley, harbormaster of Puerto Balboa, and his wife Francine, both of whom had just died, he as a suicide after the death of his wife. The novel relates much of Captain Fraley's seagoing life before he meets "the woman he sought, the woman who afterwards came up, out of the Aegean Sea into his arms." Francine is not rescued from the sea until well into the story, but this romantic episode results in Fraley's leaving the sea and settling in New York with Francine. Their story is related by Spenlove with careful attention to the characters and backgrounds of the major actors as well as a large cast of memorable minor actors.

The contrast between the setting of Spenlove's two-day yarn-spinning to a group of casual listeners aboard a cruise ship and the grim backgrounds of Fraley and Francine and their stormy life together gives the novel a melancholic atmosphere and an occasional power. The year 1932 was also when McFee and his foreign wife finally divorced. He was later to marry again, this time happily, to Dorothy North, an American and fellow writer.

With McFee's next two novels, *The Beachcomber* (1935) and *Derelicts* (1938), the author reaches the final elaboration of Spenlove's role as a narrator of and psychological commentator on "the ineluctable problem of human folly." In both of these novels Spenlove tells the story of English seafarers and their alienation from the ordinary lives of people living ashore. In *The Beachcomber* his subject is a former sea captain, whose many love affairs have culminated in his passion for the mysterious Athalie Rhys. In *The Derelicts* Spenlove recounts the story of Captain Remson, an English gentleman thwarted by life and circumstances who begins a new life in the tropics.

These two novels represent the final flowering of McFee's talents as a storyteller, and each of them was praised by critics and reviewers (with no mention of Conrad). McFee had finally been recognized for his own distinctive gifts, which can be summarized as an ability to create in brief strokes memorable minor characters, an unwavering ironic detachment coupled with an underlying sympathy, and a deep philosophical understanding of the vagaries of circumstances and character. McFee seems to have more in common with Charles Dickens, Somerset Maugham, and Anatole France than with Conrad, despite the similarities of their nautical callings.

These novels were not the last McFee was to write; there would be three additional ones during and after World War II: *Ship to Shore* (1944), *Family Trouble* (1949), and *The Adopted* (1952). Despite their many felicities, these three works were a falling-off from McFee's best work into a less serious, less deeply felt, and more entertaining mode. His reviewing continued, as did his incidental writing for magazines. He was now a respected writer and member of a settled community of friends living a quiet life ashore.

William McFee died at his home in New Milford, Connecticut, on 2 July 1966, at the age of eighty-five, having outlived his second wife by twelve years. His obituaries both in the United States and in England were fulsome in their praise of his life as a seagoing engineer and his work as a writer. Since his death his books have fallen out of favor and out of print, and McFee has received little posthumous critical attention. Actually the decline in his popularity began, as did that of many other writers, after World War II. The world of passenger liners and the tramp steamers was gone, as was the leisure of prewar days. The exotic locales McFee used so effectively were no longer exotic but had become familiar because of the war. McFee's books remain entertaining, however, and the passage of time has made them seem exotic again.

# Viola Meynell

*(15 October 1885 – 27 October 1956)*

Raymond N. MacKenzie
*University of Saint Thomas*

BOOKS: *Martha Vine: A Love Story of Simple Life,* anonymous (London: Herbert & Daniel, 1910);

*Cross-in-Hand Farm* (London: Herbert & Daniel, 1911);

*Lot Barrow* (London: Secker, 1913);

*Modern Lovers* (London: Badger, 1914; Boston: Gorham, 1914);

*Columbine* (London: Secker, 1915; New York: Putnam, 1915);

*Narcissus* (London: Secker, 1916; New York: Putnam, 1916);

*Julian Grenfell* (London: Burns & Oates, 1917);

*Second Marriage* (London: Secker, 1918; New York: Doran, 1919);

*Verses* (London: Secker, 1919);

*Antonia* (London: Secker, 1921);

*Young Mrs. Cruse* (London: Arnold, 1924; New York: Harcourt, Brace, 1925);

*A Girl Adoring* (London: Arnold, 1927; New York: Dutton, 1928);

*Alice Meynell: A Memoir* (London: Cape, 1929; New York: Scribners, 1929);

*The Frozen Ocean and Other Poems* (London: Secker, 1930);

*Follow Thy Fair Sun* (London: Cape, 1935); revised as *Lovers* (London: Richards, 1944);

*Kissing the Rod and Other Stories* (London: Cape, 1937);

*First Love and Other Stories* (London: Cape, 1947);

*Ophelia* (London: James Barrie, 1951);

*Francis Thompson and Wilfrid Meynell: A Memoir* (London: Hollis & Carter, 1952);

*Louise and Other Stories* (London: James Barrie, 1954);

*Collected Stories* (London: Reinhardt, 1957).

OTHER: *Eyes of Youth: A Book of Verse,* edited by Meynell (London: Herbert & Daniel, 1910);

*George Eliot,* edited by Meynell (London: Herbert & Daniel, 1913);

George Eliot, *Romola,* edited by Meynell (London: Oxford University Press, 1922);

*Love Poems of John Donne,* edited by Meynell (London: Nonesuch Press, 1923);

*Viola Meynell*

Herman Melville, *Moby Dick: or the Whale,* edited by Meynell (London: Oxford University Press, 1925);

*The Poet's Walk: A Nature Anthology,* edited by Meynell (London: Cape, 1936);

Sydney Carlyle Cockerell and others, *Friends of A Lifetime: Letters to Sydney Carlyle Cockerell,* edited by Meynell (London: Cape, 1940);

*An Anthology of Nature Poetry,* edited by Meynell (London: Cape, 1941);

*Letters of J. M. Barrie,* edited by Meynell (London: Davies, 1942; New York: Scribners, 1947);

Sydney Carlyle Cockerell and others, *The Best of Friends: Further Letters to Sydney Carlyle Cockerell,*

edited by Meynell (London: Hart-Davis, 1956).

SELECTED PERIODICAL PUBLICATIONS –
UNCOLLECTED: "Alice Meynell: A Personal Note," *Dublin Review,* 220 (Autumn 1947): 13–19;
"Alice Meynell: An Incident in Her Reading Life," *Renascence,* 5 (Spring 1953): 111–113.

Although Viola Meynell is best remembered as the author of two books of memoirs about her parents, she was also an accomplished novelist and short-story writer. Her novels are usually realistic psychological studies that gradually lead her characters up to a moral or spiritual epiphany. Events in her novels subtly suggest the interpenetration of the divine and the everyday, a theme that gives her work a surprisingly powerful impact.

Viola Mary Gertrude Meynell was born in London on 15 October 1885. She was the third daughter and the fifth of eight children born to Wilfrid and Alice Meynell, and she grew up in a home dominated by writing – her mother was a poet and essayist, and her father was a journalist and editor. In her 1929 memoir of her mother, Meynell recalls the children playing below the table on which the parents worked, producing their own newspaper while the adults worked frantically to meet their constant deadlines. Both her parents were Catholic converts, and their religion informed their work and daily lives. Meynell was given a Catholic education at the Convent of Our Lady of Sion in London. Several of her siblings did some writing, but only Viola produced a significant body of literary work.

The Meynells enjoyed many literary friendships, and the house was frequently visited by many of the great writers of the day, such as George Meredith, Coventry Patmore, and Francis Thompson. Thompson had a special relationship with the family, as Wilfrid had rescued him from a deepening solitude and despair; for a time he became a fixture in the Meynell home, and he wrote one of his most charming poems, "The Making of Viola," to celebrate his favorite Meynell daughter. His poem "To Stars" also concerns Viola, written after an accident she had as a little girl. Leaning too far over a balcony, she fell to the floor below and was feared to be seriously hurt; Thompson's poem is a fervent prayer that she might recover.

Thompson, like Patmore and Meredith, became infatuated with Viola's mother, Alice; Wilfrid Meynell seems to have handled all these admirers with impressive patience. Viola grew up observing the almost universal admiration lavished on her beautiful and successful mother and no doubt tried to model herself on Alice. She drew closer to her mother in every way: when Alice was away, it was Viola who most frequently wrote to her, and it was Viola who could best imitate (to the family's delight) Alice's walk and manner. When, as a child, she would injure herself, her first concern was always to let her mother know it was not serious. When a formal banquet was given for Alice in 1906 at the Lyceum Club, Viola accompanied her mother. Viola was the member of the family who most enjoyed her mother's fame, and she determined to follow her mother's literary lead. She began writing poetry and fiction while still living at home, and her parents, especially her mother, always took a strong interest in her work.

Meynell's first three novels have fairly similar settings and characters. The first – *Martha Vine: A Love Story of Simple Life* (1910) – was published anonymously; her brother Francis later said that Viola decided on anonymity out of humility: she did not want her novel to attract more notice than it was due simply because she was the famous Alice Meynell's daughter. *Martha Vine,* like many of Meynell's later works, intermixes love and spirituality, as the main character, Martha, is deterred from a spiritual quest by falling in love with Rupert Graham. When he marries her sister, Martha is devastated, only gradually arising out of her state by a slowly developing new love for Stephen Flint. The story of emotional resurrection and salvation in love is more richly developed in Meynell's later works, but *Martha Vine* nonetheless received strong reviews: the *Observer* said it approached genius, and Wilfrid Scawen Blunt and Alfred Noyes (both family friends) had kind words for it also.

Some contemporary reviewers saw the influence of Thomas Hardy in *Martha Vine.* That influence is even more marked in Meynell's next novel, *Cross-in-Hand Farm* (1911), with its brooding landscape and its characters drawn from village life, who are never fully aware of the forces governing them. Like many of the author's later works, this novel involves a love triangle, and it suffuses the subject of love with an intensity drawn from religious allusion and diction. Dorcas Lilliot – vain, shallow, amoral – is contrasted with the serious, spiritual Jane Haffenden. Both are in love with Evan Davidstow, the village's altruistic young lawyer, but Dorcas is engaged to him. Though Dorcas's true character is gradually revealed to Evan, he is too scrupulous to consider trying to break off the engagement, and it appears that he and Jane will

have to give up their unspoken love for each other in the name of a higher moral duty. The impasse is broken by an aunt, who, like a deus ex machina, convinces Dorcas to go away with her, leaving the two deserving lovers to each other.

Although the novel's plot is weak, both Jane and Dorcas are richly drawn, interesting characters. Jane's spirituality is not empty piety, for she experiences anguish, brooding on the topics of sin and mortality, and the reader comes to share her sense of moral dilemma. The story gains interest and an atmosphere of significance through Meynell's use of religious diction and motifs which are seamlessly knit into the work. *Cross-in-Hand Farm* was published with two illustrations by Charles Stabb, a young painter to whom Meynell was briefly engaged. Though Stabb planned to convert to Catholicism, and though he was well liked by her parents, Meynell broke off the engagement out of concerns over their financial future.

The best of these early novels is *Lot Barrow* (1913), which goes even further in its naturalism, for most of its characters are self-serving and imperceptive – some are almost brutish. The work is rich in irony, both in plot and theme. Charlotte "Lot" Barrow, a young woman who is severely limited intellectually and morally, comes to stay as a live-in servant with the Childs, ignorant and uncouth farmers. Their chief boarder is Mr. Bravery, a young writer who is developing a stoic philosophy of indifference, though he is having trouble finding a publisher for his exposition of it. He shows kindness to Lot, and in her dark existence he takes on heroic stature; in order to demonstrate her love for him, she fiercely adopts his philosophy. Touched by her feeling, he rashly promises to marry her if she ever finds herself too sad to go on.

Mrs. Child tells Bravery about Lot's unsavory past: her lover in her home village had killed himself when he discovered her infidelity. Bravery is horrified by the story and even more so when Lot confirms it, preaching back at him his philosophy of indifference. The episode reveals to Bravery the falseness of his philosophy and its inadequacy as a response to human misery. His life begins to change, and he becomes engaged to a visiting friend. She utterly rejects Bravery's philosophy and espouses a contrary ethos of sympathy, saying that we are meant to feel and to grieve at the sight of suffering in this life. Her attitude is the key to the book and to the attitude Meynell wants her reader to take, as opposed to the inarticulate, unheroic suffering of Lot.

Thus, Bravery's life and his spiritual state improve greatly (even his new writing is better, and a

book of his essays on nature quickly finds a publisher), while Lot drifts more deeply into unhappiness and contends with the crude attentions of Humphrey, the Childs' loutish son. At the story's end, when Mr. Child dies, even Humphrey leaves, seizing his chance for freedom at last. Lot and Mrs. Child, who have hated and distrusted each other from the outset, are left together. Bravery provides them with a small house to soothe his mild guilt over his treatment of Lot; it becomes known in the neighborhood as Memory Cottage.

*Lot Barrow* excels in characterization; Meynell is fully in command of her authorial voice in this novel, laying bare her characters without commentary or intrusion. The novel's greatest strength, perhaps, is that Meynell makes these limited, self-deceptive characters sympathetic and demands that the reader take a wider view than the characters. Since Thomas Hardy's success with such characters, and with the example of Continental naturalists like Emile Zola, the novel of primitive, sensual rural people had a considerable vogue in England during the first two decades of the twentieth century. One of its best-selling exemplars was Sheila Kaye-Smith's *Sussex Gorse* (1916). The genre was brilliantly satirized in 1932 by Stella Gibbon's *Cold Comfort Farm*. Meynell's early novels are not as melodramatic or formulaic as Kaye-Smith's, but they do participate in the genre's characteristics.

*Lot Barrow* was widely reviewed and highly praised. Most reviewers were reminded of Hardy, and many thought the book the equal of any of his. The Meynell family watched the reviews carefully, and when the *Manchester Guardian* was especially enthusiastic, Wilfrid Meynell sent a copy to his wife. She wrote back that it was "without exception the most intelligent review I have ever read. It fills me with happiness that Viola's meanings have found such a reader."

With *Lot Barrow* Meynell had established herself as a novelist, and her next novel, *Modern Lovers* (1914), is one of her finest works. She leaves behind the rural naturalism of her first works and extends her range to include comedy – both broad and subtle – and to include characters from different social strata.

*Modern Lovers* presents many scenes with the Rutherglen family, who are reminiscent of the Bennets in Jane Austen's *Pride and Prejudice* (1813). Mrs. Rutherglen is petty, vain, and stupid; that she is no worse, one concludes, is due only to the limitations imposed on her by her age and appearance: on several occasions she flirts embarrassingly with an itinerant tradesman so as to bolster her self-image. Mr. Rutherglen is a cold, cruel tyrant; his family despo-

tism "imposes deceit" on the others: they learn to lie in order to deal with him. Effie's elder sister Millie combines her mother's vanity with her father's tyranny, which motivates her marriage to the timid and hapless Harry Adams. Meynell presents these characters' dark sides comically, however.

The word *modern* in *Modern Lovers* refers to the triangle that develops between Effie Rutherglen and the two men she loves: Oliver Bligh (with whom she has lived in sin before the novel's opening, when she was a schoolteacher in another town) and Clive Maxwell, young, handsome, well connected, and both socially and morally superior to Bligh. Effie's dilemma, as she comes to understand, is a moral one: to whom does she owe allegiance and with whom is it right to continue? Love in Meynell's novels is never separate from moral duty; when lovers depart from duty, misery ensues. She would have been familiar with this theme from her mother's work, especially in Alice Meynell's well-known poem "Renouncement." The theme is Victorian, but Viola Meynell's work insists on its validity in the twentieth century as well.

The two men in the love triangle are divers, and the story leads up to a climactic diving meet. Along the way, diving – falling off a cliff into thin air – evolves into a metaphor for life, for the sheer uncertainty and fragility of human existence. The metaphor helps move the story up out of the realm of the purely comic and onto a plane of greater significance. The final third of the story develops into a more serious tale of sin, repentance, and redemption. Meynell again employs religious diction and imagery suggestively – including a confession scene in which a character works through her sense of guilt – endowing the love story with a greater significance.

*Modern Lovers* was reprinted several times, and it is certainly one of Meynell's most successful books. It also develops more complex themes than Meynell's earlier work, as in its treatment of gender issues. Her female characters tend to adore men, wanting nothing more than to serve and to please, and the men are amiably dull-witted. Clive, for example, is a quite decent fellow, but he really wants nothing more out of life than to go on charming and being universally applauded. The satire is subtle and effective – though not all contemporary readers got the point.

In 1911 Wilfrid Meynell purchased eighty acres and a large old house near the village of Greatham, Sussex, and the family began spending much of their time there. In 1914 he converted an old cattle shed on the property into a cottage for Viola; with humorous pretension, he named it Shed Hall, a name Viola always disliked. The Meynell

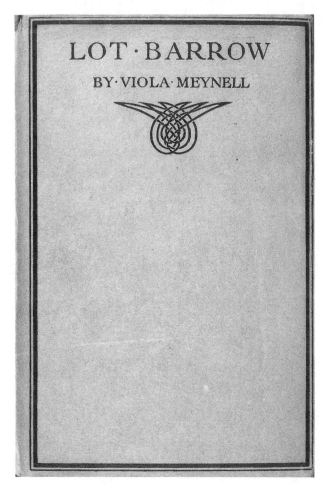

Cover for the book that established Meynell's reputation as a novelist. Many reviewers compared Lot Barrow *to the works of Thomas Hardy (courtesy of the Lilly Library, Indiana University).*

family continued to thrive on guests and visitors in both London and Sussex. D. H. Lawrence was a new friend of Viola's; she and her friends Eleanor Farjeon and Ivy Low had read his *Sons and Lovers* (1913) and were enthusiastic about the intense, unconventional young author. Lawrence borrowed Viola's Greatham cottage from 21 January 1915 to the end of July, living there with his wife Frieda while working on his novel *The Rainbow* (1915). The Lawrences quarreled frequently while at Greatham, and it was evident that Frieda was uncomfortable there, but Lawrence tried to make himself agreeable. He painted designs on the cookware, gave language lessons to one of Viola's nieces, and let Viola help type the manuscript of his novel.

The friendship was not to last long, however. In October 1915 Lawrence published a short story, "England, My England," which depicted the Meynell family – only slightly disguised – as twisted

and deeply unhealthy. Lawrence took the liberty of fictionalizing some painful family memories – including the accident that lamed Viola's young niece, Sylvia Lucas, which his story blames on her father, Percy Lucas (though he was in fact in Italy when the accident occurred). The situation worsened when Percy Lucas was killed in action in France in 1916. The deeply offended Meynell family considered that Lawrence's story blackened memories of Lucas, and Viola's friendship with Lawrence was never reestablished. Another important relationship in the early war years was with Maitland Radford, a young doctor who treated the wounded in France. Radford read the drafts of her novels and introduced her to the work of Anton Chekhov, Pierre Loti, and Fyodor Dostoevsky. In 1915 he proposed marriage to her, but she declined.

Meynell's next novel, *Columbine* (1915), was praised by reviewers, several commenting on her growing stature as a novelist. The work has some impressive points, including a challenging Augustinian view of human nature, but it is marred by structural weaknesses, the most frustrating of which is the dropping of a major character (Alison Parish) midway through. The story concerns Dixon Parish, a young writer who lives with his parents. Dixon's family is middle class and on the rise, but he falls in love with the vulgar and insecure Lily Peak (who later renames herself Lily Lestrange), a would-be actress and dancer. Dixon is attracted to her because of her helplessness. As he admits later in the book, "I need to be responsible for some one weaker than myself. I want to save some one from sin and folly. There can never be anything fine about me, but if I could have done that I would have been something." Again, Meynell places love within the context of moral duty.

Lily's self-expression is often ludicrous: during an awkward visit with the Dixons, she opines, "I think people always like to do the things they're fond of doing." But Lily is vulgar in more ways than one, as Meynell gradually reveals hard corners of the character, little ways in which she preys upon others for sympathy and support, but which are either not apparent to Dixon or are ignored by him. Dixon's family, uncomfortable with Lily, try to steer him toward the father's hardworking secretary, Jennifer Watts, and slowly but surely he begins to become attracted to her. He wavers between the two women but eventually returns to Lily. Jennifer, who has fallen deeply in love with Dixon, suffers greatly; she dies from pneumonia a year or so after the breakup.

As in most of Meynell's novels, the primary interest of *Columbine* resides not in the plot but in the analysis of motivation, the subtleties and ambiguities of intention, and the moments of self-revelation and self-deception along the way. *Columbine* also includes beautiful descriptions of nature, a point several reviewers praised highly. It also includes some ambitious and tantalizing religious symbolism, working up to its climactic scenes in a garden that clearly allude to Eden. Sin is an important theme: through the developing anxieties of Jennifer, Meynell explores an Augustinian view of human nature as sadly corrupted. Ultimately, Dixon realizes that his choice between Lily and Jennifer is a choice between "two faces of God"; while struggling to reach his decision, he labors in the garden, pulling up weeds. Meynell makes the meaning of the scene explicit: "He had never had the knowledge of himself which would enable him to guide himself with understanding. So even now he did not deal straight with himself, but through a symbol. He cleaned the earth, and he was clean himself." Jennifer's suffering is finally understood as a kind of gift, a purification – a view of suffering often articulated in the Catholic intellectual tradition – and finally she comes to be grateful for it. *Columbine,* then, is about sacrifice and suffering, which turn out to be more real and more important than love itself.

Meynell's next novel, *Narcissus* (1916), is longer and more ambitious than anything she had done before. It tells the story of two brothers, Victor and Jimmy Carmichael, as they grow from children to men. As the story covers considerable time, historical background becomes important, which is unusual in Meynell's work. A growing city, London gradually encroaches upon the Carmichaels' suburban home, and the empty field the boys used to play in becomes the site for a train station. Trains and the advent of the automobile figure in the background, and arguably the advent of modernism is reflected in some of the characters. The delightful, if not quite chaste, Edie Cumming and the handsome wastrel Clifford Rendel, who drinks too much, drives too fast in his bright red car, and thinks too little of his future, anticipate Lost Generation types from the succeeding decade, and their lifestyles are much like those of characters in the works of Ernest Hemingway or F. Scott Fitzgerald.

The two Carmichaels live alone with their widowed mother. Victor, the elder brother, is hasty and quick to anger, liable to overstate and overread other people and himself. Jimmy is quieter and grows to hate and fear emotional outbursts (such as those of his brother), and eventually he avoids emotional expression of any kind. The brothers complement each other as two halves of one picture. Each

receives an inheritance of two hundred pounds a year, so they do not have to work, but they nevertheless feel a moral obligation to do something with themselves. Jimmy succeeds, while Victor flounders, struggling with his mercurial nature. His intense response to life often leads him into trouble, and as he grows older he becomes involved with "low" girls, including prostitutes.

The novel is relatively frank in its treatment of sexuality – sometimes surprisingly so. The intense physicality in a game of mixed hockey played by the young people of the neighborhood serves as an outlet for and sublimation of their sexuality. There is frankness also in Victor's taking on Edie Cumming as a mistress. Edie is a fallen creature of infinite good humor, given to slangy verbal tics like exclaiming "Mother! Help!" in the middle of a sentence, and always referring to people as "a friend of mine that I know." Victor tires of her and falls in love with her friend Imogen, who becomes a central figure in the story, as Jimmy ultimately falls in love with her as well. Imogen finally chooses him over Victor, and her choice provides the novel's denouement. Jimmy's torment lies in having to experience real love, the kind of disruptive, uncertain, frightening emotion that he has always struggled to avoid.

*Narcissus* also includes a spiritual layer. The title refers to a habit of living without thinking of the higher life, of being obsessed with one's own reflection. Imogen is explicitly depicted this way, but she is bothered by her tendency toward what she calls "temptation," and she struggles to come to terms with a lifestyle that seems to allow everything, even though she knows that such behavior is not desirable. Meynell uses Imogen – just as she had used Jennifer in *Columbine* – to get at her theological theme concerning people who have confused love for the created world with love for the Creator. Religious symbolism also comes into play, most interestingly with a trinity-like family called the Jenners; and *Narcissus*, like *Columbine*, leads up to its climax in a garden.

Although Meynell's novels avoid the gravest topic of the day, the ongoing war with Germany, the author voiced her concerns over the situation outside of her fiction. She wrote an essay on the life and heroic death of the soldier Julian Grenfell for the *Dublin Review* that was reprinted as a separate pamphlet in 1917, and it is best seen as part of the home-front effort to maintain morale and idealize the British fighting man. She also did volunteer work, as did many middle-class women of the era, working as a typist, for example, with the Women's Emergency Corps. That her fiction does not reflect

any of these wartime realities is not unusual: the great majority of contemporary novelists avoided the topic of the war; apparently the reading public wanted their fiction to provide an escape from such grim realities.

Meynell's next novel, *Second Marriage* (1918), takes her theme of the intermixing of love and spirituality to new heights. Here she returns to a rural setting, this time England's fen country, which is brilliantly evoked by the novel. The strangeness of the landscape creates an atmosphere of mystery that helps Meynell introduce her vision of a benign and intervening providence.

The plot concerns the Glimour family, whose farm is on the edge of Skirth Fen. It introduces a set of characters and conflicts that seem to suggest a traditional rural love story; then a ghostly storm blows through the fen: "Through the night, pools brimmed, creeping things sought shelter, and stones that had long lain quiet turned in their bed." Seemingly brought by the storm, the eldest Glimour daughter, Ismay, returns home in mourning after the sudden death of her young husband. Although clearly a flesh-and-blood human, Ismay is described in otherworldly imagery, and there are hints that she should be viewed as mythical, a healing earth-mother figure.

She soon falls in love with a relation, Arnold Glimour, a young Promethean engineer obsessed with achieving greatness. He is so wrapped up in his vision for a fen-clearing steam pump that he can think of nothing else and only scarcely notices the growing love of the beautiful young widow. Ismay's love torments her, and she explains to Maurice, a minor character who briefly plays the role of an observer and confidant, her inner sense of what is happening: her husband, she is convinced, loved her so passionately that he died of torment when she could not return his love in kind. Now, through her love for Arnold, she feels pain akin to that which killed her husband, who, Ismay claims, is always present and knows everything. Maurice later speculates that there is a symmetry in life controlling people's destinies, in this case causing Ismay to love as she was loved. He comes to believe in what Meynell in an 1889 essay called "a perpetual rhythm of life."

Arnold is too good a man not to see Ismay for what she is (in fact he refers to her in reverential terms as one who will see God, and even as the image of God), and the two are eventually married. Along the way, though, the novel is enriched by deft social satire involving some locals who believe Ismay has inherited a fortune from her husband (she did not) and by a subplot concerning Arnold

*The Meynells at Palace Court: Madeline, Everard, Viola, Alice, Wilfrid, Olivia, and Francis (collection of Sir Francis Meynell)*

Glimour's spiritual rebirth, which involves the physical recovery of his crippled younger brother.

*Second Marriage* is arguably one of Meynell's best novels – rich in incident and imagery and suggestive in themes but also focused and taut. While the novel's title suggests its outcome, this advance knowledge lends the whole story a mythic overtone, greatly aided by the mysterious fen country setting and imagery suggesting a gently guiding providence.

After 1918 Meynell entered a creative dry spell, producing only a brief volume of *Verses* (1919) and no fiction until *Antonia* (1921), which, despite some interesting moments, is her weakest novel. It employs the same themes – the intermingling of the spiritual with a human love story – but less successfully. The dialogue often becomes melodramatic, and some of the characters' intense sufferings are unconvincing. There is virtually no humor and little natural description; in fact, only part of the book seems to take place in England. The story concerns a set of wealthy deracinated Europeans who flit from country to country, from hotel to mansion, and from London to Paris. Antonia is the daughter of Count Oscar Borch. Early in the story she is on

the brink of marriage to a decent but unspectacular young man when two far more attractive men – Captain Brooke and Prince Mitrany – enter the picture. Later, she has an extended affair with Brooke, and they become engaged, although she secretly loves Mitrany. On the eve of her wedding, however, Mitrany arrives, and she runs away with him. During several anguished days in the country Mitrany treats her as his confessor, going over all the guilts of his past. He tells her that she has "been moved" (by an outside force) to love him because he is so great a sinner and that "you are one of the great ones of the world, you can bear anything." The story ends with the two of them planning to be married, sinner and confessor-redeemer having found each other.

*Antonia* includes a few good Meynell touches in addition to the awkward religious layering. But it also involves structural problems with neglected minor characters and subplots; the design of the book is baffling. Critics did not know quite what to make of it; for example, the reviewer for the *London Mercury* referred to its puzzling air of unreality.

On 28 February 1922 Meynell married John Dallyn, a farmer who also lived in the Sussex neigh-

borhood of Greatham. Dallyn was neither a writer nor part of the Meynell literary circle – nor was he a Catholic. Meynell and Dallyn had one child, Jacob, born in January 1923, but their marriage was not happy. Beginning in 1929 they led mostly separate lives, and they separated permanently in 1934. Meanwhile, Alice Meynell had died on 27 November 1922, an event which deeply affected Viola. Shortly after her mother's death, Meynell began gathering materials for a biographical work, *Alice Meynell: A Memoir* (1929). It is an outstanding example of biographical writing: the prose is polished, and incidents and characters are brought to life brilliantly and memorably; the book is full of feeling without becoming sentimental. It was widely praised by reviewers and has been often reprinted.

During this period Meynell began to strike out on some new literary paths. She published her first collection of short stories, *Young Mrs. Cruse* (1924), demonstrating her considerable command of the genre. Her stories are wide-ranging in subject matter and scope, but most of them are marked by close psychological analysis of her characters. Many of them bring a character up to an epiphanic moment – like young Mrs. Cruse, the newlywed who comes perilously close to realizing she is not happy in her "perfect" marriage. Among Meynell's later stories, "The Brownings" should be singled out for its craft and insight into the sometimes guileful, manipulative nature of love. "Louise," one of her longest stories, likewise traces devious mental pathways, this time within the mind of an invalid who cannot be sure of her lover; its tragic ending is darkened by irony, as Louise's friends ascribe utterly wrong reasons to actions that caused her death. If some of Meynell's novels, such as *Columbine* and *Antonia*, suffer from structural flaws, her short stories are nearly always polished and strictly focused; many reviewers said her true genius was with the story rather than the novel.

Six years passed between *Antonia* and Meynell's next novel, *A Girl Adoring* (1927). It is relatively slight in incident and seems rather like a long short story in its lack of plot complication and its use of irony as a focusing device, its emphases falling on character development and on psychological analysis, on depictions of shades of feeling and motive. The novel did in fact grow out of a short story, which was published in 1954 as "At the Rendez-vous." The story concerns three children of the deceased Sir Philip Vanderleyden: Gilda, the daughter with the guilty love affair in her past; Morely, the eldest son, gradually revealed to be utterly self-serving and a petty tyrant; and the youngest, Claire, the title character.

Claire goes to live with Morely and his wife, Laura (a sensible and sympathetic character). Claire senses unhappiness below the surface and feels constantly as if she must do something about it; she even comes to feel her presence is necessary to ensure Morely and Laura's continued marriage. Tragedy lies in the family's past – another brother, Raymond, had committed suicide, leaving Gilda with deep guilt (he had sent for her before his death, but she had not gone, choosing to make an assignation with her married lover instead); and Morely and Laura had lost a child, a three-year-old who had been sickly from birth.

This somber subject matter is subsumed within an ironic worldview. For example, when Raymond's wife, Louise, shows up some years after the suicide, Gilda and Claire worry over how miserable she must have been; Louise has sent a telegram about feeling "like a broken toy that life has cast aside," a "battered, tear-stained creature," but this is mere rhetoric, and in fact she soon sets her cap for any available men in the neighborhood, including the one with whom Claire is in love. The novel frequently punctures the overly dramatic and tragic in a way that recalls Jane Austen; sometimes there are vivid echoes of Austen's style: "Anyone who watched the two men standing together would have been so immediately won by Morely's looks to admire and like him that it would have been only slowly and unwillingly that they would have perceived that Mr. Corbett had the advantage in good sense and simplicity."

The story comes to focus on young Claire's developing love for Richard Hague, a young farmer who has recently bought land neighboring Morely's. The path of their love runs rather crookedly due to some misunderstandings and to Hague's insensitivity – as is the case with many of Meynell's male characters. At one point he convinces himself that Claire does not love him; this conviction allows him to fall quickly out of love himself, and when Louise shows up and goes after Hague, more difficulty ensues. Claire fades into the narrative background during the latter chapters, Meynell becoming uncharacteristically silent about the character's feelings and reactions, until a crisis in the final chapter reveals Claire's pain to Hague, and he chooses her once and for all.

Structurally, *A Girl Adoring* is intriguing, seeming to circle around its subject before finally getting there. Its prose style is unlike Meynell's earlier work, marked by an abundance of elaborated, reflective similes that distance us from the action. It is one of Meynell's least theological novels, and while

it is a highly satisfying story, many readers feel it lacks the intensity of her earlier work. Still, the book received high praise from many sources, including Louise Bogan, who saw in it a brilliant depiction of "the ravaging torture inherent in early and untutored love."

Meynell published relatively little over the next several years. Her biography of her mother appeared, followed in the next year by a thin volume of poems titled *The Frozen Ocean and Other Poems* (1930). Poetry had been her mother's preferred genre, and these two publications might be viewed as Meynell's attempt to move back into the security of her family and to redefine who she was as a writer. The poems in *The Frozen Ocean and Other Poems* are formal, written in what would now be called a Georgian vein; her brother Francis thought she was a better poet than their mother, but few readers would agree. Meynell's poetry is much more limited than her mother's, but at its best it is haunting and evocative, creating subtle shades of feeling that resist definition. It is often beautiful, if minor, poetry.

Meynell produced no new fiction until *Follow Thy Fair Sun* (1935). In her later years she called this her favorite novel, and in fact she thought enough of it to give it a complete revision, republishing it as *Lovers* (1944). With this novel the author returns to her Catholic worldview, and her theology of love, duty, and the purifying value of suffering creates a powerful framework for her story, which concerns the star-crossed love between Mary Sheldon and Dennis Gower. The pain each undergoes is explicable only by viewing their story as one of sin, penance, and redemption rather than one of simple lovesickness; indeed, this identification with penance is made explicit as the book progresses. Thus, the ordeals undergone by these well-off and cultured young people are the agonies of coming into full spiritual being.

The novel's interest lies less in its incidents than in the characters' psychological states, which Meynell renders in minute detail. Mary Sheldon is recently widowed (recalling the situation of Ismay in *Second Marriage*). While married she had met and fallen in love with Dennis Gower, but nothing more than declarations passed between them then. After a significant interval has passed after the funeral of Mary's husband, however, they can at last be together. Mary gradually comes to love Dennis with an intensity that he cannot match (again recalling a motif from *Second Marriage*), and he withdraws from her more and more, sending her into a slow, agonizing period leading to a near breakdown. She sees

that he does not feel little trials like their daily separations the way she does and that he exhibits "the incredible immunity of one who no longer loves."

One night Mary goes out with the intention of suicide. She walks on a frozen lake where a village boy had recently broken through the ice and drowned: "She was exalted with the only happiness she had known for years, the comradeship of the defeated, the triumph of suffering that is whole and perfect." But the ice does not crack: she walks off into a road, into the path of an oncoming car. To avoid her, the driver veers off, running into a tree. The driver, who dies, turns out to have been her half-brother, Godfrey. Mary suffers a mental breakdown and begins a slow recovery: she ends up in a little village in Kent, where, at the hands of a nurturing older woman — a mother figure, perhaps recalling Alice Meynell — she regains her mental and spiritual strength, which means giving up her destructive love for Dennis.

Dennis meanwhile begins to see his role in Mary's suffering and comes to see the situation in religious terms: he recognizes that he has "betrayed Mary, and in some ways possibly denied the very existence of God in his life." As Dennis begins a descent into his own spiritual agony, Mary becomes a whole person, strong and capable and assertive. The two exchange roles now, as Dennis goes through a long penitential period. The book ends ambiguously: a scientist friend of Gower's comes and takes him on an expedition to Africa (it was in Africa that Mary and Dennis had first met), and after he leaves Mary yearns so deeply for his return that there is a suggestion that the cycle will begin again.

The strengths of *Follow Thy Fair Sun* are in its painstaking descriptions of the gradual psychological disintegrations of Mary and Dennis and in its rich cast of minor characters, such as the beautiful young Ianthe, who nearly manages to seduce Gower and who experiences tragedy when a car wreck kills her little brother. She seems to function as an inverse mirror image of Mary — shallow, heartless, self-obsessed — and the duplication of the plot device of a car wreck killing her brother underlines the connection. After the car accident, Ianthe fades from the story. There are wise women in the novel also, such as Eleanor Vaisey and Mary's old friend the Baroness Üxküll; they each provide Mary with perspective and emotional help, and they are each well-delineated characters. The novel's title is that of a song by the Elizabethan poet Thomas Campion that suggests the hopelessness and the inevitable inequality of love, and the work as a whole suggests

that for Meynell the state of being in love was a metaphor for a spiritual quest, for the movement through sin, penance, and redemption.

Her 1944 revision, *Lovers*, tightens things up and makes the religious theme less explicit. Meynell changed the ending, removing all its ambiguity and providing Mary and Dennis with a hopeful future. The novel may be structurally improved by the revision, but most readers will prefer the more stark, more challenging original.

Meynell's final novel was *Ophelia* (1951), another story about a love triangle, but with a twist: both mother and daughter are in love with the same young man, and he ends up choosing the mother. The novel orchestrates scenes, themes, and motifs from many of Meynell's earlier novels one last time. Twenty-eight-year-old Richard Landor meets nineteen-year-old Rosalind Weldon on a train, and a mutual attraction grows between them. Eventually, she brings him home to meet her stepmother, Mrs. Angela Weldon, who is highly protective because Rosalind's father had abandoned them eleven years previously. A sense of abandonment has dominated her thinking and feeling ever since, making her highly suspicious of men and of love relationships, but she gradually comes to accept Richard as a possible son-in-law.

While Angela is slowly thawing toward him, however, he is falling in love with her. As in many Meynell novels, the psychological process of falling in love is subtly and effectively described. When Richard finally declares his feelings, she realizes she feels the same — and yet, since her evolving thought processes have not been described as have Richard's, she simply seems to come into line, as if a man's declaring himself has brought about her assent. The two begin a semiclandestine affair, trying to keep things from Rosalind, who is away at school. As Angela and Richard carry on their affair, they scandalize some of the local villagers, and Meynell again employs some deft and witty satire in describing their growing indignation.

At Rosalind's school a crisis arises when it appears the headmistress's dog is lost and that it may have fallen through the ice on a pond. The headmistress becomes extremely distraught, and as the evening progresses the entire school reaches a near panic state. Finally, a policeman arrives, bringing in the unhurt dog at the same time that a visitor for Rosalind is announced: it is her father, Mark, whom she has not seen in eleven years. This combination of crisis and arrival of a major figure recalls the characters in *Second Marriage* and *Modern Lovers*. The self-centered prodigal father has come to de-

*Dust jacket for Meynell's last novel, in which a mother and daughter fall in love with the same man (courtesy of the Lilly Library, Indiana University)*

mand that Rosalind take care of him without even notifying her stepmother; he moves into her apartment near the school. Over the following weeks the burden of her new responsibility drains Rosalind even further. Religious imagery and diction come into play as Mark feels the need to make a full confession to his daughter, a narrative of his life and sins. He admits that he was unfaithful to Angela and had traveled to South Africa with his young lover. There, he was again unfaithful, and the young lover shot herself (a scene reminiscent of Lot's past in *Lot Barrow*).

Rosalind finally sends news to Angela of her father's arrival. Meanwhile, Angela's relationship with Richard has been degenerating because of his growing jealousy: like the lovers in *Follow Thy Fair Sun*, he becomes miserable because her love for him is not all-consuming, and he begins to bully her and torment himself over it. He is obsessed with the idea of Angela's first marriage, an obsession that grows into an unhealthy insistence that at every turn she repudiate her husband and demonstrate that she

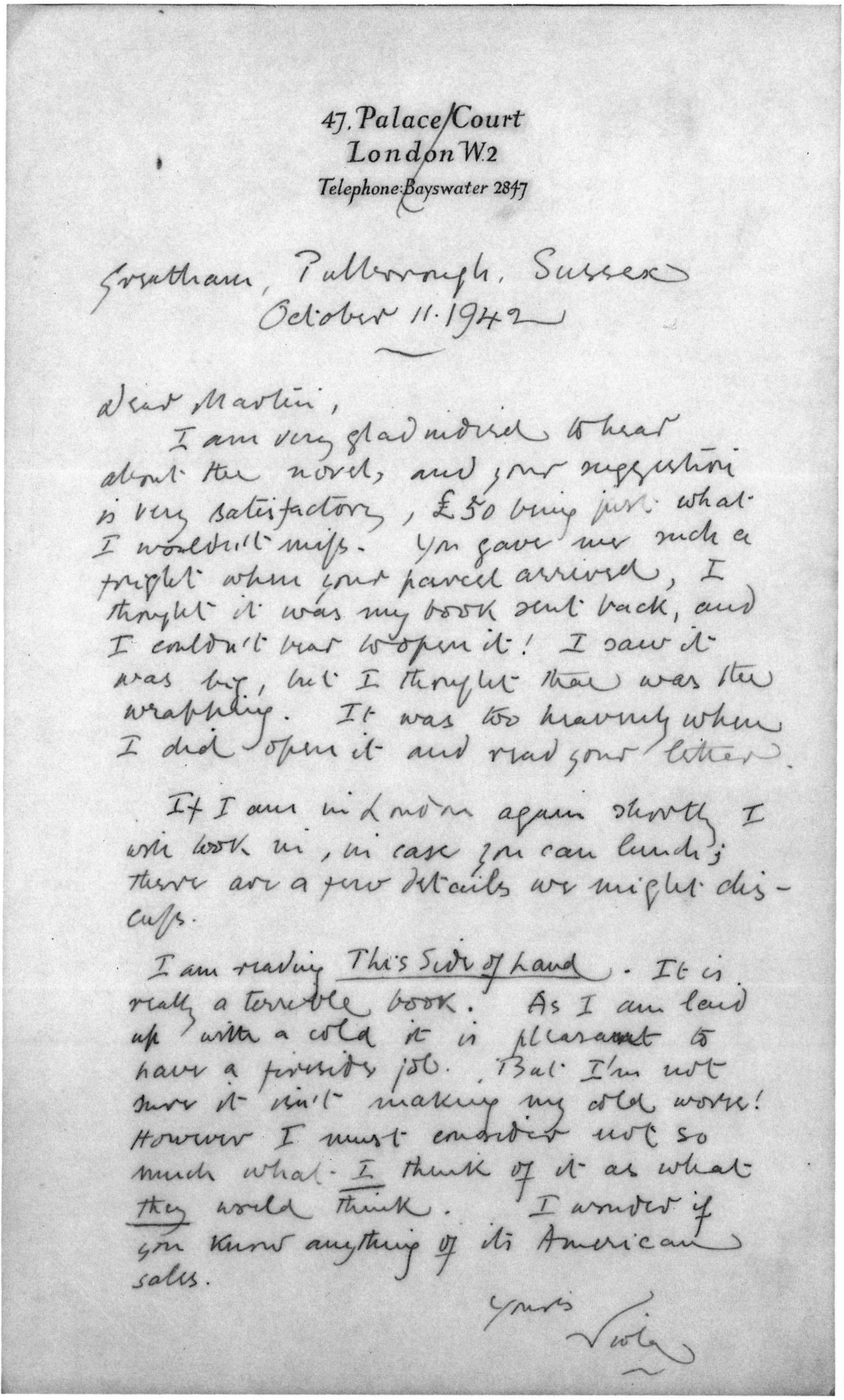

47, Palace Court
London W.2
*Telephone: Bayswater 2847*

Greatham, Pulborough, Sussex
October 11. 1942

Dear Martin,

I am very glad indeed to hear
about the novel, and your suggestion
is very satisfactory, £50 being just what
I wouldn't miss. You gave me such a
fright when your parcel arrived, I
thought it was my book sent back, and
I couldn't bear to open it! I saw it
was big, but I thought that was the
wrapping. It was too heavenly when
I did open it and read your letter.

If I am in London again shortly I
will look in, in case you can lunch;
there are a few details we might discuss.

I am reading *This Side of Land*. It is
really a terrible book. As I am laid
up with a cold it is pleasant to
have a fireside job. But I'm not
sure it isn't making my cold worse!
However I must consider not so
much what *I* think of it as what
*they* would think. I wonder if
you know anything of its American
sales.

yours
Viola

*Letter from Meynell to the publisher Martin Secker (coutesy of the Lilly Library, Indiana University)*

214

never really loved him. This emotional warfare is wearing Angela down when the letter from Rosalind reaches her. In a climactic scene on a London street, she breaks off with Richard and goes to help her daughter with Mark: love with Richard is incongruent with duty to the man who is still her husband. She then agrees to join Mark on his return to South Africa, where he has left behind property and possessions, but the weakened, sickly man dies in a hotel before they can get started. In the final scene Angela proclaims that she will continue the journey to Africa without him. Her strength and full emotional maturity do not require a man for validation.

It is implied that Richard will recover, because his love had been sinful, as was Angela's for him. Rosalind's recovery is also suggested: she is last described at the wedding of a friend, enjoying the normalcy of it and the normalcy of some young men's attentions to her. The emotional and spiritual canker has been rooted out for all of the characters.

*Ophelia* is more closely tied to time and place than many of Meynell's novels; there are frequent references to postwar Europe and some references to wartime experience. But in the main the events are timeless, in no way dependent on their setting or era. The book received some high praise, but neither it nor any of Meynell's novels ever reached a wide and appreciative audience. In her final years the author produced another excellent biographical work, *Francis Thompson and Wilfrid Meynell: A Memoir* (1952), which almost rivals her memoir of her mother, and she turned her attention to the short story once again. She also edited two volumes of letters relating to her old friend Sydney Carlyle Cockerell. Later, Hugh Whitemore wrote *The Best of Friends* (1988), a play based on these letters that was also adapted for television by the BBC. In 1955–1956 Meynell sold several stories to *The New Yorker*, and she finished working on her *Collected Stories* just a few days before her death.

During these years Meynell struggled with a debilitating form of motor neuron disease, which took her life on 27 October 1956. A relative's tribute in the London *Times* refers to Meynell's graciousness, her unfailing good humor, and her presence at the center of the family circle at Greatham up until the end. Her obituarist in the *Tablet* refers to Meynell's sense of humor and regrets that more of this side of the author did not inform her novels. To those who knew her, the intense moral seriousness of her fiction may have seemed to be contradicted by the woman, who was cheerful, sympathetic, and easy to talk to and confide in. Yet per-

haps these traits show that she deeply understood the truth she dramatized in her novels – that in honoring each other, as her characters learn, we honor God.

**Biography:**
June Badeni, *The Slender Tree: A Life of Alice Meynell* (Padstow, Cornwall: Tabb House, 1981).

**References:**
Wilfrid Blunt, *Cockerell: Sydney Carlyle Cockerell, Friend of Ruskin and William Morris and Director of the Fitzwilliam Museum, Cambridge* (London: Hamish Hamilton, 1964);

Brigid M. Boardman, *Between Heaven and Charing Cross: The Life of Francis Thompson* (New Haven: Yale University Press, 1988);

Louise Bogan, "Viola Meynell," *Literary Opinion in America,* edited by M. D. Zabel (New York: Harper, 1937): 390–396;

Terence L. Connolly, *Francis Thompson, In His Paths: A Visit to Persons and Places Associated with the Poet* (Milwaukee: Bruce, 1944);

Emile Delavenay, *D. H. Lawrence: The Man and His Work, The Formative Years: 1885–1919*, translated by Katherine M. Delavenay (Carbondale: Southern Illinois University Press, 1972): 431–433;

Annabel Farjeon, *Morning Has Broken: A Biography of Eleanor Farjeon* (London: Julia MacRae, 1986);

Eleanor Farjeon, *Edward Thomas: The Last Four Years* (London: Oxford University Press, 1958);

Gerald Gould, *The English Novel of Today* (London: John Castle, 1924);

R. Brimley Johnson, *Some Contemporary Novelists (Women)* (London: Parsons, 1920);

C. E. Maguire, "Another Meynell," *Renascence,* 11 (Summer 1959): 175–184;

Sir Francis Meynell, *My Lives* (London: Bodley Head, 1971);

Harry T. Moore, *The Priest of Love: A Life of D. H. Lawrence* (New York: Farrar, Straus & Giroux, 1974);

Thomas Vargish, *The Providential Aesthetic in Victorian Fiction* (Charlottesville: University of Virginia Press, 1985).

**Papers:**
There is no major collection of Viola Meynell's letters and manuscripts, but small groups of letters and individual manuscripts can be found at several libraries, including those of Boston College, Oxford University, and Cambridge University.

# E. Nesbit

## (15 August 1858 – 4 May 1924)

### Judith Barisonzi
#### University of Wisconsin Center – Fond du Lac

See also the Nesbit entry in *DLB 141: British Children's Writers, 1880–1914.*

BOOKS: *Fading Light: Verses by E. Nesbit* (London & New York: Hagelberg, n.d.);

*Apple Pie* (N.p., n.d.);

*Miss Mischief* (London: Nister / New York: Dutton, n.d.);

*Fairies* (London: Tuck, n.d.);

*The Prophet's Mantle,* by Nesbit and Hubert Bland, as Fabian Bland (London: Drane, 1885; Chicago: Clarke, 1889);

*Lays and Legends* (London: Longmans, Green, 1886);

*The Lily and the Cross* (London: Griffith, Farran, 1887; New York: Dutton, 1887);

*The Star of Bethlehem* (London: Nister, 1887; New York: Dutton, 1887);

*All Round the Year,* by Nesbit and Caris Brooke (London: Von Portheim, 1888);

*The Better Part, and Other Poems* (London: Drane, 1888);

*Easter-tide: Poems by E. Nesbit and Caris Brooke* (London: Drane, 1888; New York: Dutton, 1888);

*Landscape and Song* (London: Drane, 1888; New York: Dutton, 1888);

*The Message of the Dove* (London: Drane, 1888; New York: Dutton, n.d.);

*Leaves of Life* (London: Longmans, Green, 1888);

*Corals and Sea Songs* (London: Nister, 1889; New York: Dutton, 1889);

*Songs of Two Seasons* (London: Tuck, 1890);

*The Voyage of Columbus: Discovery of America* (London: Tuck, 1891);

*Sweet Lavender* (London: Nister, 1892; New York: Dutton, 1892);

*Lays and Legends: Second Series* (London & New York: Longmans, Green, 1892);

*Grim Tales* (London: Innes, 1893);

*Something Wrong* (London: Innes, 1893);

*The Butler in Bohemia,* by Nesbit and Oswald Barron (London: Drane, 1894);

*The Marden Mystery* (Chicago: Clarke, 1894);

*Pussy Tales* (London: Ward, 1895);

*Doggy Tales* (London: Ward, 1895);

*Rose Leaves* (London: Nister, 1895);

*A Pomander of Verse* (London: John Lane, 1895; Chicago: McLurg, 1895);

*Holly and Mistletoe: A Book of Christmas Verse by E. Nesbit, Norman Gale and Richard Le Gallienne* (London: Ward, 1895);

*As Happy as a King* (London: Ward, 1896);

*In Homespun* (London: John Lane, 1896; Boston: Roberts, 1896);

*The Children's Shakespeare,* edited by Edric Vredenburg (London: Tuck, 1897; Philadelphia: Altemus, 1900);

*Romeo and Juliet, and Other Stories* (London: Tuck, 1897);

*Royal Children of English History* (London: Tuck, 1897);

*Dog Tales, and Other Tales,* by Nesbit, A. Guest, and Emily R. Watson, edited by Vredenburg (London: Tuck, 1898);

*A Book of Dogs: Being a Discourse on Dogs, with Many Tales and Wonders Gathered by E. Nesbit* (London: Dent, 1898; New York: Dutton, 1898);

*Songs of Love and Empire* (Westminster: Constable, 1898);

*Pussy and Doggy Tales* (London: Dent, 1899; New York: Dutton, 1900);

*The Story of the Treasure Seekers: Being the Adventures of the Bastable Children in Search of a Fortune* (London: Unwin, 1899; New York: Stokes, 1899);

*The Secret of Kyriels* (London: Hurst & Blackett, 1899; Philadelphia: Lippincott, 1899);

*The Book of Dragons* (London & New York: Harper, 1900);

*Nine Unlikely Tales for Children* (London: Unwin, 1901; New York: Dutton, 1901);

*The Wouldbegoods: Being the Further Adventures of the Treasure Seekers* (London: Unwin, 1901; New York & London: Harper, 1901);

*To Wish You Every Joy* (London: Tuck, 1901);

*Thirteen Ways Home* (London: Treherne, 1901);

*E. Nesbit, circa 1887*

*The Revolt of the Toys, and What Comes of Quarrelling* (London: Nister, 1902; New York: Dutton, 1902);

*Five Children and It* (London: Unwin, 1902; New York: Dodd, Mead, 1905);

*The Red House: A Novel* (London: Methuen, 1902; New York & London: Harper, 1902);

*The Rainbow Queen, and Other Stories* (London: Tuck, 1903);

*Playtime Stories* (London: Tuck, 1903);

*The Literary Sense* (London: Methuen, 1903; New York: Macmillan, 1903);

*Cat Tales,* by Nesbit and Rosamund Bland (London: Nister, 1904; New York: Dutton, 1904);

*The Phoenix and the Carpet* (London: Newnes, 1904; New York: Macmillan, 1904);

*The New Treasure Seekers* (London: Unwin, 1904; New York: Stokes, 1904);

*The Story of the Five Rebellious Dolls* (London: Nister, 1904; New York: Dutton, 1904);

*Pug Peter* (Leeds & London: Cooke, 1905);

*Oswald Bastable and Others* (London: Wells, Gardner, 1905);

*The Rainbow and the Rose* (London: Longmans, Green, 1905);

*The Railway Children* (London: Wells, Gardner, 1906; New York & London: Macmillan, 1906);

*The Story of the Amulet* (London: Unwin, 1906; New York: Dutton, 1907);

*The Incomplete Amorist* (London: Constable, 1906; New York: Doubleday, Page, 1906);

*Man and Maid* (London: Unwin, 1906);

*The Enchanted Castle* (London: Unwin, 1907; New York & London: Harper, 1908);

*Twenty Beautiful Stories from Shakespeare: A Home Study Course, Being a Choice Collection from the World's Greatest Classic Writer, William Shakespeare, Retold by E. Nesbit,* edited by E. T. Roe (Chicago: Jenkins, 1907);

*The Old Nursery Stories* (London: Frowde/Hodder & Stoughton, 1908);

*The House of Arden: A Story for Children* (London: Unwin, 1908; New York: Dutton, 1909);

*Jesus in London* (London: Fifield, 1908);

*Ballads and Lyrics of Socialism, 1883–1908* (London: Fifield, 1908);

*Harding's Luck* (London: Hodder & Stoughton, 1909; New York: Stokes, 1910);

*These Little Ones* (London: George Allen, 1909);

*Daphne in Fitzroy Street* (London: George Allen, 1909; New York: Doubleday, Page, 1909);

*Nesbit's husband, Hubert Bland. The couple were among the founding members of the socialist Fabian Society and collaborated on several works published under the pseudonym of Fabian Bland.*

*Salome and the Head: A Modern Melodrama* (London: Rivers, 1909); republished as *The House with No Address* (New York: Doubleday, Page, 1909; London: Newnes, 1914);

*Cinderella: A Play with Twelve Songs to Popular Airs* (London: Sidgwick & Jackson, 1909);

*Garden Poems* (London & Glasgow: Collins, 1909);

*The Magic City* (London: Macmillan, 1910);

*Children's Stories from English History,* by Nesbit and Doris Ashley (London: Tuck, 1910);

*Children's Stories from Shakespeare* (London: Tuck, 1910; Philadelphia: McKay, n.d.);

*Fear* (London: Paul, 1910);

*The Wonderful Garden, or the Three C's* (London: Macmillan, 1911; New York: McCann, 1935);

*Ballads and Verses of the Spiritual Life* (London: Matthews, 1911);

*Dormant* (London: Methuen, 1911); republished as *Rose Royal* (New York: Dodd, Mead, 1912);

*The Magic World* (London & New York: Macmillan, 1912);

*Wet Magic* (London: Laurie, 1913; New York: McCann, 1937);

*Wings and the Child: Or, the Building of Magic Cities* (London & New York: Hodder & Stoughton, 1913);

*The Incredible Honeymoon* (New York & London: Harper, 1916);

*The New World Literary Series, Book Two,* edited by Henry Cecil Wyld (London & Glasgow: Collins, 1921);

*The Lark* (London: Hutchinson, 1922);

*Many Voices: Poems* (London: Hutchinson, 1922);

*To the Adventurous* (London: Hutchinson, 1923);

*Five of Us — and Madeline* (London: Unwin, 1925; New York: Adelphi, 1926);

*The Complete History of the Bastable Family* (London: Benn, 1928);

*Long Ago When I Was Young* (London: Whiting & Wheaton, 1966; New York: Watts, 1966).

PLAY PRODUCTIONS: *Cinderella,* Deptford Board School, December 1892;

*A Family Novelette,* by Nesbit and Oswald Barron, New Cross, February 1894;

*Sleeping Beauty,* Deptford Board School, December 1895;

*Aladdin,* Deptford Board School, December 1896;

*The King's Highway,* by Nesbit and Dorothea Deakin, Woolwich, Freemasons' Hall, 13 May 1905;

*The Philandrist, or the Lady Fortune-Teller,* by Nesbit and Deakin, Woolwich, Freemasons' Hall, 13 May 1905;

*The Magician's Heart,* London, Saint George's Hall, 14 January 1907;

*Unexceptionable References,* London, Royalty Theatre, Autumn 1912.

OTHER: *Spring Songs and Sketches; Summer Songs and Sketches; Autumn Songs and Sketches; Winter Songs and Sketches; Morning Songs and Sketches; Noon Songs and Sketches; Eventide Songs and Sketches; Night Songs and Sketches,* 8 volumes, selected and arranged by Nesbit and Robert Ellice Mack (London: Griffith, Farran, 1886–1887; New York: Dutton, 1886–1887);

*River Sketches* (London: Von Portheim, 1887; New York: Dutton, 1887);

*The Time of Roses* (London: Drane, 1888) – includes poem by Nesbit;

*By Land and Sea,* selected by Nesbit (London: Drane, 1888);

*Autumn Leaves,* selected and arranged by Nesbit (London: Drane, 1888; New York: Dutton, 1888);

*Winter Snow,* selected and arranged by Nesbit (London: Drane, 1888; New York: Dutton, 1888);

*Lilies and Heartsease: Songs and Sketches; Falling Leaves: Songs and Sketches,* 2 volumes, arranged by Nesbit and Mack (London: Griffith, Farran, Okeden & Welsh, 1888; New York: Dutton, 1888);

*Daisy Days* (London: Griffith, Farran, Okeden & Welsh, 1888) – includes poems by Nesbit;

*Evergreen from the Poet's Corner,* selected by Mack (London: Nister, 1889; New York: Dutton, 1889) – includes two poems by Nesbit;

*The Lilies Round the Cross,* by Nesbit and Helen J. Wood (London: Nister, 1889; New York: Dutton, 1889);

*Life's Sunny Side* (London: Nister, 1890; New York: Dutton, 1890) – includes poems by Nesbit;

"The Excursion," in *Told by the Fireside* (London: Griffith, Farran, Okeden & Welsh, 1890);

*Songs of Scotland,* selected by Nesbit (London: Nister, 1890; New York: Dutton, 1890);

"Finding a Sister," in *Twice Four* (London: Griffith, Farran, Browne, 1891);

*The Poets and the Poetry of the Century. Vol. 8, Robert Bridges and Contemporary Poets,* edited by Alfred H. Miles (London: Hutchinson, 1891) – includes eleven poems by Nesbit;

"Allie's House-Keeping," in *Story upon Story, and Every Word True* (London: Tuck, 1892; New York: Publishers' Union, 1896);

*Flowers I Bring and Songs I Sing* (London: Tuck, 1893) – includes seven poems by Nesbit, as E. Bland;

*Our Friends and All About Them* (London: Tuck, 1893) – includes poems and three stories by Nesbit: "The Self Respecting Pussies"; "Down at Grannie's"; "Mabel's Pussy";

*Listen Long and Listen Well* (London: Tuck, 1893) – includes two stories by Nesbit, "Midsummer Day" and "The Oak Panel";

"Ella's Adventure," in *Sunny Tales for Snowy Days,* edited by Vredenburg (London: Tuck, 1893);

*Told by the Sunbeams and Me,* edited by Vredenburg (London: Tuck, 1893) – includes two stories by Nesbit, "Dorothy's Birthday" and "Being Bandits";

"The Babe in the Wood, or What Happened at Kitty's Party," in *What Really Happened* (London: Tuck, 1893);

*We've Tales to Tell* (London: Tuck, 1893) – includes two stories by Nesbit, "How Jack Came to Tea" and "A Crooked Tail";

*Hours in Many Lands,* edited by Vredenburg (London: Tuck, 1894) – includes two stories by Nesbit, "The Little Heroine" and "Effie's Birthday";

"Lonely Mabel," in *Tales That Are True for Brown Eyes and Blue,* edited by Vredenburg (London: Tuck, 1894);

"Mother's Present," in *Tales to Delight from Morning till Night,* edited by Vredenburg (London: Tuck, 1894);

"More Haste, Less Speed," in *Fur and Feathers, Tales for All Weathers* (London: Tuck, 1894), pp. 15–19;

"Hot Pies," in *All But One, Told by the Flowers,* edited by Vredenburg (London: Tuck, 1894);

*The Girls' Own Birthday Book,* selected and arranged by Nesbit (London: Drane, 1894);

"The Glordy John," in *Tick Tock: Tales of the Clock* (London: Tuck, 1895);

"The Rainbow Queen," in *Stories in a Shell* (London: Tuck, 1895);

"Linda and the Prince," in *Treasures from Storyland,* edited by Vredenburg (London: Tuck, 1895);

"A House of Her Own," in *Friends in Fable: A Book of Animal Stories,* edited by Vredenburg (London: Tuck, 1895);

"Finding a Sister," in *Dulcie's Lantern, and Other Stories* (London: Tuck, 1895);

*Poets' Whispers: A Birthday Book,* selected and arranged, with an introductory poem, by Nesbit (London: Drane, 1895);

*Dinna Forget* (London: Nister, 1897; New York: Dutton, 1897) – includes two poems by Nesbit and G. Clifton Bingham;

*Tales Told in the Twilight* (London: Nister, 1897; New York: Dutton, 1897) – includes twenty stories by Nesbit;

*The Children's Bookcase,* volumes 1–5, 7 edited by Nesbit (London: Frowde/Hodder & Stoughton, 1908–1911);

"The Fairy Godmother," in *Days of Delight,* edited by Vredenburg (London: Tuck, 1910);

*Our New Story Book* (London: Nister, 1913; New York: Dutton, 1913) – includes two stories by Nesbit, "Our Black Cat" and "The Likeness";

*Battle Songs,* selected by Nesbit (London: M. Goschen, 1914);

Hubert Bland, *Essays,* edited by Nesbit as E. Nesbit-Bland (London: M. Goschen, 1914).

SELECTED PERIODICAL PUBLICATIONS – UNCOLLECTED:

FICTION

"The Social Cobweb," by Nesbit and Hubert Bland, as B., *Weekly Dispatch* (6 January–23 March 1884);

THE STORY OF THE TREASURE SEEKERS

BEING·THE ADVENTURES·OF·THE BASTABLE·CHILDREN IN·SEARCH·OF A·FORTUNE

E·NESBIT

WITH PICTURES BY GORDON BROWNE & LEWIS BAUMER

*Cover for the 1899 novel that introduced the Bastable children, who reappeared in two more of Nesbit's novels for children,* Wouldbegoods *(1901) and* The New Treasure Seekers *(1904)*

"The Hour Before Day," by Nesbit and Hubert Bland, as Fabian Bland, *Weekly Dispatch* (20 September–4 October 1885);

"Something Wrong," by Nesbit and Bland, as Fabian Bland, *Weekly Dispatch* (28 March–4 July 1886);

"The Criminal," *Neolith,* no. 1 (November 1907): 17–22;

"In the Queen's Garden," *Neolith,* no. 4 (August 1908): 1–11;

"The Doll's House," *Children's Annual 1920* (1920).

NONFICTION

"When I Was a Girl," *John O'London's Weekly* (15 November 1919).

Edith Nesbit Bland, often considered the originator of the juvenile fantasy novel, discovered her vocation as a children's writer late and reluctantly. Disappointed by the reception of her lyric poetry, she found the ideal outlet for her wit and exuber-

ance in a succession of humorous and imaginative novels for children, published under the name E. Nesbit, that have influenced many other writers and are still discovered with pleasure by both children and adults. Her novels for adults were less well received in her lifetime and have been nearly forgotten since her death, but although marred by the banalities of romantic convention, they nonetheless reveal the combination of realism and fantasy that marks Nesbit's best work for children.

Nesbit's unhappy childhood is reflected only indirectly in her novels, in which she re-creates her life as she wished it to have been. The youngest of six children, Edith Nesbit was born on 15 August 1858 in Kennington, South London. Her father, John Collins Nesbit, head of an agricultural college, died when she was four years old, and she spent her childhood at a series of boarding schools she hated, alternating with a bewildering routine of European travel, while her mother, Sarah Green Nesbit, and older stepsister, Sarah Green, devoted themselves to restoring the health of Edith's tubercular sister, Mary. The brightest memories of Nesbit's early life were the carefree, unsupervised summers spent roaming the French or English countryside with her two brothers, Henry and Alfred. From these childhood experiences stemmed her hatred for formal schooling and her conviction that children need freedom to engage in adventurous, imaginative play, beliefs that underlie her adult nostalgia for childhood.

A moody, fearful, imaginative child, Nesbit began writing poetry at an early age and idolized Christina Rossetti, having an indirect acquaintance with the pre-Raphaelite circle through Mary's fiancé, the poet Philip Bourke Marston. After Mary's death in 1871, however, the fortunes of the Nesbit family gradually declined. As she grew up, Nesbit began to publish a small amount of poetry and to engage in rebellious, unconventional behavior. She entered into a relationship with Hubert Bland, a young socialist and aspiring businessman, whom she married on 22 April 1880, when she was already seven months pregnant. Their marriage, apparently a reluctant one on Bland's part, began under unfavorable conditions: Bland became seriously ill, and his business failed. Nesbit was forced to support her husband and children – Paul, born in 1880; Iris, in 1881; and Fabian, in 1885 – by designing greeting cards and writing short stories for magazines.

Despite financial insecurity and constant work, Nesbit and Bland enjoyed a bohemian lifestyle, participating in the cultural and political life

of London in the 1880s. They became founding members of the Fabian Society in 1884 and through the group formed close friendships with George Bernard Shaw and H. G. Wells. Nesbit's active involvement in the Fabians was short-lived, although Bland, who became a prominent socialist journalist, was a member of the Executive Committee and treasurer of the organization until 1908.

While Nesbit and her husband pursued their separate careers as writers, they also collaborated on short stories and novels, which they published under the pen name of Fabian Bland. Their first collaborative novel, *The Prophet's Mantle* (1885), was based on their acquaintance with Russian political émigrés living in London, combining this political background with a conventional romance plot. Their second attempt, *Something Wrong* (1893), also about contemporary political movements, was serialized by the *Weekly Dispatch* in 1886 but never published as a book (Nesbit later used the title for a volume of stories).

Despite the close intellectual relationship of the couple, their marriage was strained by Bland's constant, almost compulsive infidelity. Nesbit undertook to bring up as her own the two children (Rosamund and John) that Bland fathered with her close companion, Alice Hoatson, who lived with the family – an unconventional arrangement carefully hidden from friends and associates. Nesbit responded to this uncomfortable situation by forming close sexual and literary relationships not only with friends such as Shaw but also with a series of young male admirers, several of whom, particularly Oswald Barron and Noel Griffith, greatly influenced her work.

Writing was for Nesbit always a financial necessity she approached with some reluctance. Between 1886 and 1898 she published twenty volumes of minor though well-regarded poetry, many sentimental short stories and poems for children, romance and horror stories for adults, several plays that were performed but not published, and other ephemeral writings and collaborations. Her first novel, *The Marden Mystery,* was apparently published in Chicago in 1894, but no record of it remains.

Her next attempt, *The Secret of Kyriels* (1899), an elaborate Gothic romance set near Dymchurch, her favorite vacation area, deals obliquely with her feelings of rage and victimization in her marriage through its plot of female imprisonment, loosely derived from Charlotte Brontë's *Jane Eyre* (1847). The novel's protagonist, Esther, is based on Nesbit, although another part of the author's personality is revealed in the less desirable Bertha, and the name

"Edith" is given to Esther's mother, a madwoman locked up in an invisible inner courtyard. *The Secret of Kyriels* fails to rise above the conventions of its genre, however. Nesbit had trouble finding a publisher for this book, and after its publication its sales were not promising.

In the same year, at the age of forty, Nesbit started on another, more productive direction in her career with the publication of her first children's novel, *The Story of the Treasure Seekers* (1899), which had already appeared as a magazine serial in *Windsor* and *Pall Mall,* both adult magazines. Nesbit's new direction apparently resulted from a reawakening of her memories of childhood experiences, occasioned by her friendship with Oswald Barron and a commission for a series of reminiscences, published as "My School Days" in the *Girl's Own Paper* in 1896–1897.

While bearing some resemblance to earlier writing for children by authors of the "Golden Age" such as Mrs. Molesworth and Kenneth Grahame, *The Story of the Treasure Seekers* was quite different from the moralizing juvenile books favored at the time. Nesbit's novel depicts realistic children quarreling, misbehaving, and getting embroiled in humorous misadventures. Her style also differed from conventional children's novels, for the book was written in contemporary diction, with a liberal use of slang. Contributing to the appeal of *The Story of the Treasure Seekers* is the ostensibly anonymous juvenile narrator, Oswald Bastable, Nesbit's most memorable character, who is thoroughly realistic, convincingly childlike, and highly intelligent. This narrative viewpoint, unusual in a juvenile book, allowed Nesbit to write from a child's perspective while exploiting Oswald's limitations of vision, particularly his unquestioning class and gender superiority. Using a thin plot line, in which a family of six middle-class children, loosely based on the author and her siblings, falls on hard times but finally succeeds in restoring their family fortunes, Nesbit concentrates on character and humorous situation. Reception of this novel was gratifying. Although some reviewers objected that she offered no moral lessons, *The Story of the Treasure Seekers* was widely praised by readers. Andrew Lang, who reviewed the book for *Longman's Magazine,* praised the work as ideal for both adults and children, and it was reissued almost annually for many years.

Nesbit followed the success of *The Story of the Treasure Seekers* with another book about the Bastables, *The Wouldbegoods: Being the Further Adventures of the Treasure Seekers* (1901), which also appeared serially in adult magazines before being pub-

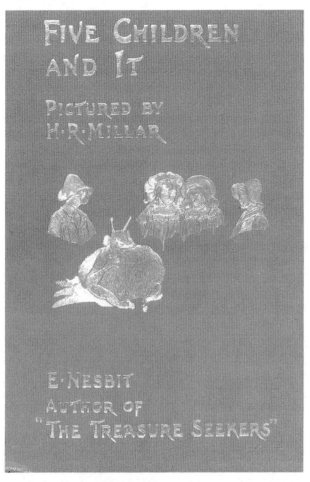

*Cover for the novel in which Nesbit mocks belief in the supernatural (courtesy of the Lilly Library, Indiana University)*

writer and her ambivalent attitude toward her "liberated" role as chief family breadwinner. Reprinted three times in as many months, the novel sold well for several years.

*The Red House* includes several scenes involving the Bastable children that are retold, with identical events but from a child's perspective, in *The New Treasure Seekers* (1904), in many ways the least appealing of the Bastable books, weak in plot and inconsistent in time. This book had less success with readers, but it presents delightful adventures in which the children again try to "do good" with the usual disastrous results; it also moves into new territory for Nesbit, with a satiric adult perspective that raises serious questions about poverty and social class.

After *The New Treasure Seekers,* Nesbit abandoned the Bastables, perhaps sensing that she had exhausted the possibilities of Oswald's limited perspective and the framework of humorous, realistic adventure. She had already started a new series of books, serialized in *The Strand* and imaginatively illustrated by H. R. Millar, featuring a different family (based on her five children), which is introduced to fantasy adventures by the chance acquisition of various mythical animals. In *Five Children and It* (1902) Nesbit creates a Psammead, or Sand-Fairy, who grants wishes that involve traveling to distant lands as well as adventures at home. It reappears in *The Story of the Amulet* (1906), while in *The Phoenix and the Carpet* (1904) Nesbit uses a traditional mythological figure.

The children in these books – Anthea, Robert, Cyril, Jane, and the Lamb – are not strongly individualized; instead, the memorable characters are the Psammead and the Phoenix, who are vain, selfish, and ill-tempered. Like adults, they can dispense seemingly magical largesse but resent being bothered by children and need to be propitiated and flattered; at the same time, they are lovable though eccentric friends. Each has a distinctive personality, but both criticize the children's lack of intelligence and culture and their moral weaknesses, allowing Nesbit to write from a juvenile viewpoint while maintaining the perspective of a mature adult.

These three books, like the Bastable novels, have an episodic structure. In *Five Children and It* and *The Phoenix and the Carpet,* the children's magic powers clash incongruously with everyday adult reality. The magic, always limited by the internal logic of an arbitrary set of rules, repeatedly leaves the children stranded in awkward predicaments in the adult world. The underlying moral lesson of all three fantasy books is that imaginative escape from

lished as a juvenile book. The sequel is also narrated by Oswald and employs the same formula of a minimal romantic plot, episodic structure, humorous adventures, and realistic juvenile characters. The children form a club to "do good," a device that enables Nesbit to ridicule conventional religious morality, as the children's well-intentioned efforts run aground on the realities of England's class society.

Similar to her children's books in its structure and humor is *The Red House* (1902), Nesbit's best-received adult novel. A lighthearted romance about a young couple, Chloe and Len, who restore an ancient, decayed homestead, the book was obviously based on Nesbit's experiences in restoring Well Hall in Eltham, where she and her family lived for many years, although the author omits the disastrous events of a stillbirth and the death of her teenage son Fabian in 1900, providing instead a happy ending. Behind its humorous surface, *The Red House* also reveals Nesbit's doubts about her ability as a

the real world, although exciting, is potentially dangerous and ultimately unsatisfying; happiness is found not in fulfillment of wishes for unlimited wealth or great beauty but in the warmth of family love. The children's final wish is that their invalid mother be restored to them, and, once this is granted, they have no more to desire. This serious moral perspective, however, does not interfere with the reader's enjoyment of the adventures or of the delightful fantasy animals.

*The Story of the Amulet,* the final book in this fantasy group, was the most thoroughly researched of Nesbit's fiction. She worked on the novel for at least three years with the assistance of Dr. Wallis Budge of the British Museum, who became Nesbit's close friend. The work examines the possibilities of social organization, from primitive prehistory to a utopian future influenced by H. G. Wells's *A Modern Utopia* (1905), as the children protagonists travel through time to find the missing half of an ancient Egyptian amulet, restore its power, and finally win their hearts' desire. The scene shifts among locales as diverse as ancient Egypt and Babylonia, mythical Atlantis, and Caesar's Gaul, but the novel never becomes a didactic lesson in history or anthropology. Infused with the poetic impressionism of Nesbit's depictions of past cultures and the mysterious sense of moving in and out of time, it is simultaneously grounded in reality by the five children. This most wide-ranging of Nesbit's books inspired C. S. Lewis to comment in *Surprised by Joy* (1955) that, "It first opened my eyes to antiquity, the 'dark backward and abysm of time,' " and provides an early example of serious social criticism in children's literature, using both past and future as touchstones to expose injustice in the present.

Although influenced by the earlier fantasies of Charles Kingsley and George MacDonald, Nesbit's novels for children were distinctive in that they are less allegorical and more specifically directed toward children. They also resemble the contemporary adult fantasies of F. Anstey but reveal greater depth of social vision. *The Story of the Amulet* bears obvious similarities to Rudyard Kipling's *Puck of Pook's Hill* (1906), but the influence appears to have been mutual, with both writers admiring each other. Although Nesbit's fantasy books sold less well than the Bastable adventures, they have proved of enduring interest to later writers and readers.

At the same time that she was writing *The Story of the Amulet,* Nesbit was also composing what has proved her most frequently reprinted and dramatized work of juvenile fiction, *The Railway Children* (1906), a realistic adventure story involving a fam-

ily of three children – Peter, Phyllis, and the fearless, caring, and lovable Roberta. In this book Nesbit creates a female character who appealingly combines the masculine and feminine traits presented stereotypically in the earlier Bastable novels. *The Railway Children* includes some social critique, with its themes of unjust imprisonment and escape and its treatment of the plight of Russian émigrés. The children's father has been falsely accused of spying, and their mother must support the family by writing, as Nesbit herself did, until the children heroically prevent a railway accident, indirectly leading to the exoneration of their father. The absent father, hardworking mother, English village setting, and economic decline of the family all reflect Nesbit's own experiences, making this book, despite criticism of its sentimentality, a popular depiction of family life.

In the same year Nesbit also published a novel for adults titled *The Incomplete Amorist* (1906), in which she deals indirectly with her experience of sexuality and marriage. Betty, the independent heroine, is a wishful projection of Nesbit. She runs away from a repressive stepfather to become an art student in Paris, is attracted to a heartless philanderer named Eustace Vernon (who resembles Hubert Bland), and in the end (unlike Nesbit) makes an eminently suitable marriage. The author's evocation of a youthful, bohemian existence, descriptions of the French countryside, and satiric humor are the best features of this novel. With its evasive treatment of its sexual subject it made little impression in England, but the book met with some success in the United States, where it was serialized in the *Saturday Evening Post.*

Given the usual absence of psychological complication in Nesbit's fiction, her next novel, *The Enchanted Castle* (1907), provides a somewhat unexpected departure as the only one of her children's books to deal at length with the author's inner fears. The novel portrays inanimate objects that come to life, such as statues of mythological figures and hollow dinosaur images, humans that turn to stone, and a set of imaginary beings called the Ugly Wuglies, who are made up only of clothing but act like real adults. These nightmare creations terrify the children protagonists of the story, but Nesbit also uses them to satirize the empty life of the upper middle class. As in her other fantasies, all problems are resolved through a romantic reunion of lovers and repudiation of magical powers. The complicated but perfectly resolved plot of this book, the beauty of its language, and the Platonic vision of universal harmony at its end have made *The Enchanted Castle* a favorite of many critics.

The concept of time travel and the social critique that Nesbit began to develop in the historical

*Cover for the novel in which Nesbit introduced the Psammead, or Sand-Fairy, who grants the wishes of the five child protagonists (courtesy of the Lilly Library, Indiana University)*

settings of *The Story of the Amulet* and the concern with poverty and contemporary problems evident in *The Railway Children* are combined in her most complicated pair of children's novels, *The House of Arden: A Story for Children* (1908) and *Harding's Luck* (1909), in which Nesbit drew on her fascination with English history to present the story of the interlocking lives of three children — Dicky Harding, a crippled orphan from the slums of London; and Elfrida and Edred Arden, a sister and brother seeking the return of their lost father and fallen family fortunes. The three children travel through time on intersecting paths, with the reign of James I given the most emphasis. Although seemingly an odd choice for a socialist, the Jacobean era is depicted by Nesbit as an idyllic time when natural beauty was untouched by industrial squalor and the country was ruled by a benevolent, paternalistic upper class. Her Catholicism, to which she and her husband had converted in the early 1900s, also influenced her historical sympathies for this period.

The moral virtues stressed in these two books are love and abnegation. Dicky sacrifices his desire to return to the past, where he is not crippled, out of loyalty to Mr. Beale, a tramp whom he mistakenly perceives as befriending him when he is actually being exploited as a criminal accomplice. By his sacrifice, he effects Beale's moral reformation. Ultimately, Dicky gives up his true status as heir to the Arden fortune in the interests of the Arden relatives he has come to love. Meanwhile, Edred pursues his quest to become "wise and good," overcoming his childish ignorance and lack of confidence, becoming a fit partner for his intelligent and fearless older sister.

The Arden books reveal Nesbit's yearning for an idealized, rural English past, but their treatment of the contemporary evils of poverty and inequality, as well as their concern with enduring problems of moral choice, give them intellectual depth. These serious themes, combined with an intricate fantasy of time travel and a new magic animal (the Mouldiwarp, a white mole who speaks in Sussex dialect and performs white magic), make these books complex but rewarding.

In the same year that Nesbit completed the Arden books she also published two adult novels, both of which also stress the virtue of giving oneself unconditionally for a loved one, as Nesbit no doubt felt she had done for her husband. *Daphne in Fitzroy Street* (1909) is based on her relationship with George Bernard Shaw, who appears as Mr. Henry, an artist to whom Daphne is passionately attracted. Along with the romance plot are poorly integrated sections based on Nesbit's experiences at a French convent school and her friendship with Russian émigrés. Strong-willed and independent, Daphne runs away from her conventional, narrow-minded family and lives in a bohemian style, supporting herself and a little sister as an artist's model. In this wish-fulfillment plot, Daphne finally wins Henry, who realizes that love is more important than art.

The same message appears in *Salome and the Head: A Modern Melodrama* (1909), where the orphaned Sandra becomes Sylvia, an idolized dancer. She becomes entrapped in a rebellious, youthful marriage to a scoundrel, but she is loved by a crippled musician, who sacrifices himself for her by murdering her sinister husband and then shooting himself. Although the novel's plot is unconvincing, the heroine's self-sufficiency and independence in rejecting an additional morally unfit suitor are of interest, as is Nesbit's evocative creation of a hidden retreat in which Sandra lives a secret life. Like Henry, Sandra comes to understand that love means self-sacrifice and gives up her art for marriage to a man who is redeemed from a misspent youth by his pure, self-sacrificing love for her. De-

spite their deeply personal themes, neither novel enjoyed much success.

The years 1908–1909 marked a turning point in Nesbit's career. Her serious moral and social concerns had overpowered the humorous depiction of family life and the lighthearted fantasy that had made her children's books so widely loved. Although she did not stop writing novels of high quality, Nesbit's appeal to the public declined. Her later juvenile books, each with a different family of children, continue to raise important issues combined with fantasy adventures in charming but by now somewhat stereotyped patterns. *The Magic City* (1910) is based on Nesbit's interest in constructing elaborate structures out of children's blocks and common household objects, the type of imaginative play she believed vital for children. The orphaned Philip constructs such a city, which of course comes to life, becoming the scene of many adventures through which he must not only reconcile himself to the marriage of his beloved older sister but also come to accept and admire a new stepsister, Lucy. Modern critics object to *The Magic City* because of its unfriendly satire of the suffragettes, but it also portrays Lucy as at least the equal of Philip, and often, to his embarrassment, his superior. The value of creativity and self-sacrifice and the ugliness of modern industrial society are thematic concerns of this book.

*The Wonderful Garden, or the Three C's* (1911) bases its magic on traditional flower symbolism, while making fun of a belief in the supernatural, for the young protagonists of the story insist on a magical interpretation of events that have natural, logical explanations. Here again the result of the "magic" spells is a reunion with absent parents, who in this case are in India.

Some of the enchantment of *The Wonderful Garden* is also felt in *Dormant* (1911), often considered Nesbit's finest adult novel. In showing magic (identified, for adult readers, with occult science) overcoming time and death, it is the closest to her children's fantasy books. Anthony Drelincourt, a young scientist, inherits an old estate, where he finds a secret inner room containing a young woman, apparently in an enchanted sleep, with whom he falls in love. Although their efforts to achieve eternal life are finally condemned as unnatural, the book is filled with the yearning to escape from material reality to a hidden, timeless realm. The book's final words, expressing faith in the eternal existence of love and ideals, were read at Nesbit's burial service.

After *Dormant*, Nesbit wrote one more children's novel, *Wet Magic* (1913), which takes place in

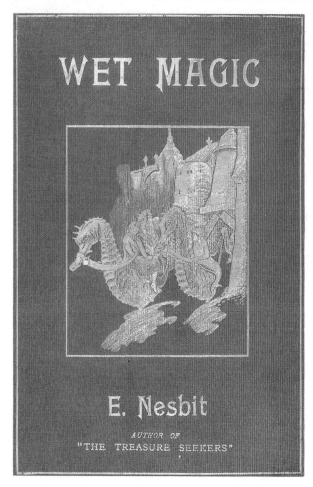

Cover for Nesbit's final novel for children, set in an undersea realm (courtesy of the Lilly Library, Indiana University)

an underwater realm that five children, after rescuing a mermaid from human cruelty, are taken to visit. By carelessly touching the sky, they expose the kingdom to danger, starting a war that threatens to end the underwater civilization but then cleverly restore peace. Written during the political tensions leading to World War I, the book is a plea for international harmony and the acceptance of differences between people.

Nesbit's last years were marred by a deep depression following the death of her husband in 1914 and a descent into poverty as the sales of her books and her ability to write declined. She found comfort in religion and immersed herself in studying Baconian ciphers, an enthusiasm that wasted her money but stimulated her imagination by appealing to her sense of a hidden, deeper reality. This preoccupation appears in *The Incredible Honeymoon* (1916), a lighthearted romance with little plot; the book takes the reader on a tour through Nesbit's favorite scenic

and historic places. On a serious level, it also reveals Nesbit's ambivalence toward marriage, which the adventurous, independent heroine, Katherine, pretends to reject, and shows her concern with poverty and inequality. The book raises the question of how individuals can use their wealth to advance social justice and suggests paternalistic utopian solutions. *The Incredible Honeymoon* did not appeal to English readers; it was first published in the United States and did not appear in England until 1921.

Meanwhile, Nesbit's life took a happier turn with a second marriage to a socialist sea captain, Thomas Terry Tucker, on 20 February 1917, but she wrote little more before her death on 4 May 1924 at Jesson Saint Mary's near Dymchurch. Her last novel, *The Lark* (1922), a romance based on the financial problems of her later years, obviously draws once again on *Jane Eyre* in characterization and situation. The book features two independent young heroines, Jane Quested and Lucilla Craye, who try to earn a living by selling flowers and running a boarding house, but it also shows a poignant awareness of the unhappiness of an aging woman.

Although Nesbit's reputation was at its lowest point in the early 1920s, interest in her books grew after her death. Her poetry and adult fiction have been largely forgotten, but her enduring legacy has been her children's novels, admired for their unique combination of fantasy and realism. The social attitudes they depict are conservative, middle-class, and traditional, but the subtlety of Nesbit's irony may hide the fact that she is just as likely to be satirizing these attitudes as endorsing them. Her greatest ambivalence appears in matters of gender. Nesbit's heroines, both children and adults, are stronger in character than their male counterparts, but their fate is inevitably marriage and submission; and her usual choice of a male narrator, as well as her sexually anonymous pseudonym, reveal her doubts about female independence and assertion. Unsympathetic to women's suffrage and married to a man whose views on gender issues were deeply reactionary, Nesbit appears to have difficulty reconciling her internalized social stereotype of women as inherently maternal and emotional with the reality of her own independent personality and career.

Many aspects of Nesbit's portrayal of Victorian and Edwardian society are deeply personal. Her dislike for school and absorption in books are obvious in her juvenile novels, often considered the most "bookish" in children's literature. The family structure in her novels is also derived from her personal experience, and the frequent search for an absent parent, usually the father, is clearly based on

Nesbit's early loss of her father and her relationship with a preoccupied mother. The constant interplay between fantasy and reality reflects the author's divided sense of self: the imaginative child coexisting with the mature, adult self. Perhaps for this reason no sharp demarcation is possible between the concerns of her juvenile and her adult novels. Both deal with themes of imprisonment and escape, with deep feelings of loss, and with the attraction of a temporary retreat from reality and time, and both endorse the values of family, self-sacrifice, and love.

Moral and political concerns are also important in Nesbit's fiction. Although she portrays self-righteous reformers as narrow-minded and unfeeling, she esteems personal charity to relieve poverty and injustice when it arises from a generous spirit. Nesbit's books clearly reveal her socialist beliefs, with her attacks on poverty and industrialism balanced by a utopian vision of a just society. Nesbit disliked schools but recognized education as the critical agency for creating moral attitudes that would eventually eliminate social inequity. *Wings and the Child: Or, the Building of Magic Cities* (1913), addressed to parents and teachers, presents ideas on education reform similar to those of Froebel and A. S. Neill. Nesbit attacks public schools that "instruct rather than educate" and urges respect for children's individuality, creativity, and moral seriousness.

Nesbit died regretting her reputation as a writer for children rather than as a poet, but later generations have appreciated the talent she undervalued. Writers like C. S. Lewis, who took from Nesbit, among other borrowings, the idea of a magic wardrobe opening into a hidden land; or Edward Eager, who openly borrows from her novels in his own children's fantasies; or Noel Streatfeild, whose realistic family relationships owe a deep debt to Nesbit, all learned their craft from her. She was also a favorite author of writers as diverse as "Clemence Dane," Noel Coward, and E. M. Forster. Her adult novels have never attracted the same interest, but they are clearly products of the same vision; and it is chiefly their sexual reticence, lack of psychological complexity, and departures from realistic narrative that have made them less popular. Nesbit's books generally lack convincing plots, often falling into mere variations of a simple episodic adventure formula and relying on stock romantic situations. Strong characters are few, and character development is often lacking. Against these weaknesses, however, must be weighed Nesbit's strong but not intrusive moral sense, her skill in manipulating the dual perspective of both

adult and child to create narratives that appeal to both mature and juvenile readers, and her ability to dramatize her belief in the importance of the imagination in creating a better world.

**Biographies:**

Noel Streatfeild, *Magic and the Magician: E. Nesbit and Her Children's Books* (London: Ernest Benn, 1958);

Anthea Bell, *E. Nesbit* (New York: H. Z. Walck, 1964);

Doris Langley Moore, *E. Nesbit: a Biography,* revised edition (Philadelphia: Chilton, 1966);

Julia Briggs, *A Woman of Passion: The Life of E. Nesbit* (New York: Meredith Press, 1987).

**References:**

Marcus Crouch, *Treasure Seekers and Borrowers: Children's Books in Britain 1900–1960* (London: Library Association, 1962);

Mary Croxson, "The Emancipated Child in the Novels of E. Nesbit," *Signal,* 14 (May 1974): 51–64;

Roger Lancelyn Green, *Tellers of Tales: Children's Books and Authors from 1800 to 1968,* revised edition (London: Kaye & Ward, 1969): 206–215;

Reva Pollack Greenburg, *Fabian Couples, Feminist Issues* (New York: Garland, 1987): 163–273;

Colin N. Manlove, "Fantasy as Witty Conceit: E. Nesbit," *Mosaic,* no. 10 (Winter 1977): 109–130;

Stephen Prickett, *Victorian Fantasy* (Brighton: Harvester, 1979): 209–233;

Margaret and Michael Rustin, *Narratives of Love and Loss* (London: Verso, 1987): 59–82;

Barbara Smith, "The Expression of Social Values in the Writing of E. Nesbit," *MLAA Children's Literature,* 3 (1974): 153–164;

John Stephens, *Language and Ideology in Children's Fiction* (London and New York: Longmans, 1992): 125–132.

**Papers:**

No complete collection of E. Nesbit's papers exists. Her working notes, drafts, and manuscript of *The Magic City* are in the Greenwich Public Library. The Fabian Papers at Nuffield College also contain material on Nesbit.

# George Oliver Onions

*(13 November 1872 – 9 April 1961)*

Leonard R. N. Ashley
*Brooklyn College of the City University of New York*

BOOKS: *The Compleat Bachelor* (London: John Murray, 1900; New York: Stokes, [1901]);

*Tales from a Far Riding* (London: John Murray, 1902);

*The Odd-Job Man* (London: John Murray, 1903);

*The Drakestone* (London: Hurst & Blackett, 1906);

*Back o' the Moon* (London: Hurst & Blackett, 1906);

*Admiral Eddy* (London: John Murray, 1907);

*Pedlar's Pack* (London: Eveleigh Nash, 1908);

*Draw in Your Stool* (London: Mills & Boon, 1909);

*Little Devil Doubt* (London: John Murray, 1909);

*The Exception* (London: Methuen, 1910);

*Widdershins* (London: Secker, 1911); published as *The First Book of Ghost Stories: Widdershins* (New York: Dover, 1978);

*Good Boy Seldom* (London: Methuen, 1911);

*In Accordance with the Evidence* (London: Secker, 1912; Boston: J. W. Luce, [1913]; New York: Doran, 1913);

*The Debit Account* (London: Secker, 1913; Boston: Luce, 1913);

*The Story of Louie* (London: Secker, 1913; New York: Doran, 1914);

*The Two Kisses* (London: Methuen, 1913; New York: Doran, 1913);

*A Crooked Mile* (London: Methuen, 1914; New York: Doran, 1914);

*Gray Youth* (New York: Doran, 1914);

*Mushroom Town* (London: Hodder & Stoughton, 1915 [1914]; New York: Doran, [1914]);

*The New Moon* (London: Hodder & Stoughton, [1918]);

*A Case in Camera* (Bristol: Arrowsmith, [1920]; New York: Macmillan, 1921);

*The Tower of Oblivion* (London: Hodder & Stoughton, [1921]; New York: Macmillan, 1921);

*Peace in Our Time* (London: Chapman & Hall, [1923]);

*Ghosts in Daylight* (London: Chapman & Hall, 1924);

*The Spite of Heaven* (London: Chapman & Hall, 1925; New York: Doran, [1926]);

*Whom God Hath Sundered* (London: Secker, 1925; New York: Doran, [1926]);

*Cut Flowers* (London: Chapman & Hall, 1927);

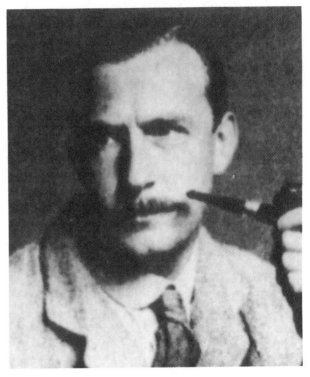

*George Oliver Onions*

*The Painted Face* (London: Heinemann, 1929);

*The Open Secret* (London: Heinemann, 1930; Boston & New York: Houghton Mifflin, 1930);

*A Certain Man* (London: Heinemann, 1930);

*Catalan Circus* (London: Nicholson & Watson, 1934);

*The Collected Ghost Stories of Oliver Onions* (London: Nicholson & Watson, 1935);

*The Hand of Kornelius Voyt* (London: Hamilton, 1939);

*The Italian Chest* (London: Secker, 1939);

*Cockcrow; or, Anybody's England* (London: Hamilton, 1940);

*The Blood Eagle* (London: Bale & Staples, [1941]);

*The Story of Ragged Robyn* (London: Secker, 1945);

*Poor Man's Tapestry* (London: M. Joseph, 1946);

*Arras of Youth* (London: M. Joseph, 1949);

*A Penny for the Harp* (London: M. Joseph, 1952);

*Bells Rung Backwards* (London & New York: Staples, 1953);

*A Shilling to Spend* (London: M. Joseph, 1965).

Oliver Onions changed his name to George Oliver in 1918 but always signed his original surname to his popular short stories and novels. His wife was the popular romantic novelist Berta Ruck; she was born in India under the Raj in 1878 and died in England one century later. Onions and his wife each adapted their copious literary productions to satisfy the changing tastes of the public. As novelists, both published frequently and built up popular followings for their fiction; in time, they also overcame critical objections to prolific publication. Theirs was an age when the inexpensive book brought comfort to the lonely, entertainment to the idle, and information to the curious. Popular authors such as Onions and Ruck built up loyal readerships and needed only the occasional hit to maintain their careers.

Born 13 November 1872 in the manufacturing town of Bradford, Oliver Onions grew up with an unusual interest in art. He studied in London and Paris and tried his hand at posters and book designing, but such work paid poorly. Soon he turned to writing for periodicals, and eventually he expanded to novels. In later years Onions designed the dust jackets for his own books – they suggest that his dropping art for a writing career was not altogether a bad move. In both his illustrations and his writing Onions stayed close to current fashion.

In the art department of Amalgamated Press, which published several periodicals, Onions began writing *The Compleat Bachelor* (1900), which Frank Swinnerton describes as "a collection of chats in the manner of *The Dolly Dialogues,* but it did not achieve the lightness of the original." *The Compleat Bachelor* and any model it had have both been forgotten. Onions followed with various short stories for magazines, many of which were later collected in book form as *Tales from a Far Riding* (1902), *Back o' the Moon* (1906), *Admiral Eddy* (1907), *Widdershins* (1911), *Ghosts in Daylight* (1924), *The Painted Face* (1929), *The Collected Ghost Stories of Oliver Onions* (1935), *The Italian Chest* (1939), and *Bells Rung Backwards* (1953). His gloomy tales of the supernatural were popular, and his work was included in *Best Short Stories of 1929,* and in Lady Asquith's anthology of *New Stories of Murder and Mystery* (1927), as well as being popular in the magazines of his day.

It was on his novels, however, that Onions's reputation was chiefly built. Of the books Onions published in the 1910s, the most notable are probably his collection of Yorkshire stories in *Tales from a*

Dust jacket for Onions's novel set in a small Welsh seacoast resort (courtesy of the Lilly Library, Indiana University)

*Far Riding* and the superior *Widdershins.* His reputation was established, however, by the trilogy of *In Accordance with the Evidence* (1912), *The Debit Account* (1913), and *The Story of Louie* (1913). With these novels Onions became a writer from whom the public expected fine work. He was not always consistent, but he hit high points with *The Story of Ragged Robyn* (1945) and *Poor Man's Tapestry* (1946), and he followed the success of the latter with the only slightly less satisfactory *Arras of Youth* (1949). Surveying contemporary fiction in 1934, Swinnerton praised Onions's "autobiographical studies of ambitious young men" – *Little Devil Doubt* (1909), *Good Boy Seldom* (1911), and *In Accordance with the Evidence* – but complained that most of Onions's works "curiously lack momentum; one reads them with respect for their veracity, but one is conscious that the author is not a natural creator of illusion."

Swinnerton is one of the few useful contemporary commentators on Onions. Most of the reviewers of his day reacted more to the so-called sordid aspects of his realism than to the author's work per se, and many reviewers seem to have been prompted to praise Onions more for his industry or

*Dust jacket for Onions's 1925 novel that presents two novelists as its main characters (courtesy of the Lilly Library, Indiana University)*

the public he was building by his frequent novels than for his own merit as a writer.

Emerging from the obscurity of periodicals at about the time that H. G. Wells's *The First Men in the Moon* (1901), Henry James's *The Sacred Fount* (1901), and Rudyard Kipling's *Kim* (1901) were being published, Onions faced major problems in making a name for himself as a novelist of fancy, of psychology, or of adventure. *The Compleat Bachelor* showed that he had creative possibilities, and later in *Little Devil Doubt* he explored the possibilities of muckraking satire. He kept experimenting, trying to find a niche in vaguely poetic or detailed realistic novels — in the latter his experience in the graphic arts stands him in good stead — and writing short stories of ghosts and misty moors. Eventually Onions wrote several historical novels, which entertained a generation too young to remember the author's earliest successes.

Among Onions's early books, the one written with the most artistry was *The Exception* (1910). The

2 July 1911 review in *The New York Times* praised the book's "many passages of intense emotion," but in England the *Spectator* condemned the work as unpleasant and "exceedingly painful." This reaction was principally over the novel's Jewish villain and the prominence of that nasty blackmailer threatening the novel's protagonist, Berice Beckwith, with her past. Before her marriage she had had an affair with a man, and although this man has died, she does not want her husband to find out about the affair. Faced with this unsavory situation, the *Spectator* critic thought that Onions had better return to his earlier, harmless "poetic fancy."

Out of a short-story idea Onions crafted a clever, if no more comforting, fiction in the first novel of a realistic trilogy. *In Accordance with the Evidence* is the sordid story of a young man named Jeffries, a poor, struggling stenographer in a tacky business college. He decides to better his prospects by murdering a rival, Archie Merridew, and marrying the rival's girl, Evie Soames. Jeffries gets away with his crimes, and as the terrible tale of murder ends, the narrator grimly observes: "Nobody had paid yet. Nobody ever will." Swinnerton writes that *In Accordance with the Evidence* "is not a pretty book; the manner of it is even common and gritty, as such a theme demands that it should be; but it is like no other book, and it bears re-reading after its denouement has lost all surprise. It has, that is to say, a permanent quality," though he advises the reader to skip the rest of the trilogy.

The 13 April 1913 review of the novel in *The New York Times* accused Onions of "dealing in dirt and plague, sores and misery" and called for "normal and healthy subjects." The reading public, on the whole, was more positive in its reaction. Hailed as a realist, especially by Americans, Onions parlayed the fame of *In Accordance with the Evidence* into *The Debit Account* and *The Story of Louie*.

*The Debit Account* (1913) continues *In Accordance with the Evidence* and describes Jeffries' marriage to Evie Soames. Guilt about the past assails him, and Archie Meridew, whom he greatly wronged, haunts him. One of Jeffries' associates at the business school where he works figures out what Jeffries did to Meridew. In fact, the reader is left to make several important deductions.

*The Story of Louie* presents a spiritual or psychological biography of the girl in love with Jeffries, the murderer who made the first volume of the trilogy so captivating. The *Independent* (16 March 1914) praised the book as an "arresting romance built around an unmoral woman," while the *Nation* (12 February 1914) censured it as a neat but unfortunate "framework of

repellant fact." British reviewers were shocked, but Americans, more used to violence and vice in their popular fiction, liked the book; the *Boston Transcript* (21 January 1914) declared *The Story of Louie* a cautionary tale, a serious "study of an intellectual temperament."

Following two minor novels, *The Two Kisses* (1913) and *A Crooked Mile* (1914) – published in one volume as *Gray Youth* (1914) – was Onions's *Mushroom Town* (1915), set in a small Welsh seacoast resort. The English have begun to frequent an area that was originally developed for the tourist trade by the father of John Willie Garden, the novel's protagonist. As the story begins, the resort has mushroomed into a busy, if rather bland, place – bustling, but soulless. Although some love is provided by John Willie, who is enamored of Ynys Lovell, a local lass, but who returns in the end to the more respectable June Lacey, the chief appeal of the novel is not in its characters but in its minutely detailed descriptions of the environment. There is little substance in *Mushroom Town* beyond the scenery, however, and the minute details of setting are ultimately less interesting than well-developed characters and plot.

Onions's best characters have complex consciences, even though in this respect his work could never challenge that of Henry James, Arnold Bennett, or Virginia Woolf. When his characters are "flat" (to employ E. M. Forster's terminology), Onions often resorts to describing scenery or complicating the plot. His incomplete characterizations cannot be excused as puppets presenting the ideas of the writer, for Onions is not a writer of ideas. He cannot be counted upon for much more than occasional propaganda, and he is at his best when he relaxes into ingenious, sentimental, or exciting story lines.

The varying quality of Onions's work can be seen in an examination of four of his novels, *A Case in Camera* (1920), *The Tower of Oblivion* (1921), *The Spite of Heaven* (1925), and *The Open Secret* (1930), all written during the time in which Onions was most consistently well received by the book-buying public. *A Case in Camera* begins with "the killing, on a May morning of the year 1919, of one young man by another who claimed, and still claims, to have been his friend." The novel is not strictly a mystery, as the details of the crime and its motivation are secondary to the psychological effect of both the homicide and the process of detection on a dozen leading characters. Although the reader may guess the novel's outcome, interest in the narration is maintained through its psychological analyses.

*The Tower of Oblivion* involves the forty-five-year-old novelist Derwent Rose, who travels back

*Onions in middle age (Hulton-Deutsch Collection)*

in time to revisit his life when he was eighteen, at which point he falls desperately in love. The fantasy quickly becomes less plausible, and the narration is marred by overdetailed presentations of character and an increasingly creaky plot. The novel attempts to combine the fantastic with the factual, and its plot often seems contrived. In addition, the book seems overlong, as is also true of *A Case in Camera*. *The Spite of Heaven* presents two novelists as characters. One, the narrator, is a bit of a bore and the other sort of a cad. The Ardriss marriage is on the rocks, and the complacent husband and the straying, artistic wife are subjected to various complications by Onions, but in the long run they fail either to entertain or to instruct the reader. Despite the faddishness of its Roaring Twenties theme, the reader has trouble caring what happens to any of these people.

Feminists may object to the way Mrs. Ardriss is treated in the story and to Onions's habit of portraying women in his novels as dangerous when not merely silly. In *The Story of Louie* Jeffries experiences trouble because Louie falls in love with him, and a similar pattern surfaces in *The Open Secret,* in which Bettine Frühling, a spy, draws Halsey Vibart into difficulties not of his own making. In the same

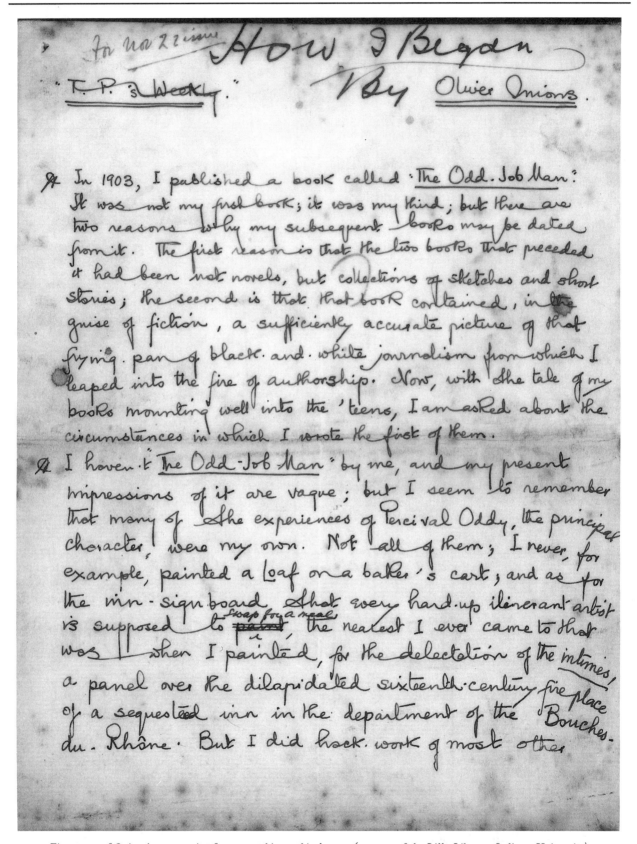

for nov 22 issue How I Began

"T. P.'s Weekly." By Oliver Onions.

In 1903, I published a book called 'The Odd-Job Man'. It was not my first book; it was my third; but there are two reasons why my subsequent books may be dated from it. The first reason is that the two books that preceded it had been not novels, but collections of sketches and short stories; the second is that that book contained, in the guise of fiction, a sufficiently accurate picture of that frying-pan of black-and-white journalism from which I leaped into the fire of authorship. Now, with the tale of my books mounting well into the 'teens, I am asked about the circumstances in which I wrote the first of them.

I haven't 'The Odd-Job Man' by me, and my present impressions of it are vague; but I seem to remember that many of the experiences of Percival Oddy, the principal character, were my own. Not all of them; I never, for example, painted a loaf on a baker's cart; and as for the inn-signboard that every hard-up itinerant artist is supposed to soap for a meal, the nearest I ever came to that was when I painted, for the delectation of the intimes, a panel over the dilapidated sixteenth-century fire-place of a sequested inn in the department of the Bouches-du-Rhône. But I did hack-work of most other

*First page of Onions's manuscript for an autobiographical essay (courtesy of the Lilly Library, Indiana University)*

novel a man named Clarry Moss falls for a laundress, Lottie Smith, and their relationship comes to no good. The novel's action is rushed, messy, even baffling. Despite successful moments the novel remains unrealized, confusing more than compelling.

Years later Onions found new readers and better organization in the likes of *The Story of Ragged Robyn* and *Poor Man's Tapestry*. The first of these is set in seventeenth-century England, and the second, for which the author won the James Tait Black Memorial Prize, takes place during the Wars of the Roses. Both are times of unrest; this perks up the action. In both novels Onions reveals his sincere love for his country and its traditions, historical or legendary. Most of all, he has mastered prolix detail and has improved his sense of narrative pace: he can keep the reader turning the pages even of long books.

These later novels are free from pedestrian realism and from the modern, superficial heroines of Onions's earlier work. They are also less preachy than some of his earlier novels, an element that had been singled out for criticism by J. B. Priestley in his review of Onions's *Peace in Our Time* (1923) for the *London Mercury,* in which he remarked, "the tale, which is very slight, is constantly held up by the author's remarks on all manner of topical subjects; and while a very useful book might have been written on the problem of the ex-officer, Mr. Onions has not done it because his young men are not typical specimens of the ex-officer in general, but only of a certain type to be found in West End bars."

The "topical" always engaged Onions because he was convinced that his readers were interested in it. Constantly seeking, rather than consistently exhibiting, a style, he might present it for public acceptance with or without "ideas," with a realistic or a fantastic plot, as a slice of life or a venture into the supernatural, with eccentric or stereotypical characters, or with the comfortingly sentimental or the downright bizarre.

He experienced dry spells, but he kept writing; and although readers could never be certain what his next novel would be, the author could be counted on for collections of effective ghost stories. In fact, with more stories such as those in *Widdershins* he might have equaled Algernon Blackwood, and occasionally he did so. Most feel, however, that Onions's ghost stories, while well written and still deserving of an audience, simply have not earned him a place among the masters of supernatural fiction.

It was characteristic of Onions as a popular writer to experiment and not to confine himself to one market, nor did he strive for a career-spanning collection of stories, content as he was to leave a shelf of novels and other works. With dogged determination and usually with some success, he tried many variations. Striving for popular success kept Onions from dropping into mannerism and self-parody (the fate of some of his betters in his time, even Ernest Hemingway), but it produced only the occasional triumph and the eventually evanescent effect.

Berta Ruck, like her husband, was industrious and occasionally popular. She lived one hundred years and wrote more than fifty novels. Onions wrote less and is the better remembered. Born in 1872, the year that Anthony Trollope published *The Eustache Diamonds* and Thomas Hardy *Under the Greenwood Tree,* Onions died on 9 April 1961, in the year that Graham Greene published *A Burnt-Out Case* and Iris Murdoch *A Severed Head.* Onions was lucky to have inherited a cultivated reading public and to have occasionally earned their approbation, as his "competition" included the likes of Joseph Conrad, John Galsworthy, James Joyce, Virginia Woolf, and D. H. Lawrence, all of whom were actively interpreting life in lasting literature.

When the Great War began, Onions had already established himself as promising. Although his experiments with realism shocked some contemporary critics with its treatment of unpleasant social conditions, few present-day readers would be so affected. Today readers might say that if there is any fault to be found with the realism of Onions, it is not that it is ignoble or ugly but that the author does not go far enough – he does not dig out the whole unpleasant truth.

The reviewer for *Atlantic* who in 1914 hailed Onions as "not only the cleverest" but also "the most advanced of the younger English novelists" could not have foreseen that a writing style that was regarded earlier in this century as probing would eventually be considered pedestrian. Onions's work includes some excellent short stories in the supernatural vein and some adequate novels in the realistic vein, but present-day readers and literary historians generally ignore the latter.

## Bibliography:

John Gawsworth (Terence Ian Fytton Armstrong), *Ten Contemporaries: Notes Towards Their Definitive Bibliographies* (London: Joiner & Steele, 1933).

## References:

Frank Swinnerton, *The Georgian Scene* (New York: Farrar & Rinehart, 1934);

Sir Hugh Walpole, *Joseph Conrad* (New York: Holt, 1916).

# Eden Phillpotts

*(4 November 1862 – 29 December 1960)*

James Y. Dayananda
*Lock Haven University*

See also the Phillpotts entry in *DLB 10: Modern British Dramatists, 1900–1945; DLB 70: British Mystery Writers, 1860–1919;* and *DLB 135: British Short-Fiction Writers, 1880–1914: The Realist Tradition.*

BOOKS: *My Adventure in the Flying Scotsman: A Romance of London and North-Western Railway Shares* (London: Hogg, 1888);

*The End of Life* (Bristol: Arrowsmith / London: Simpkin, Marshall, Hamilton, Kent, 1891);

*Folly and Fresh Air* (London: Trischler, 1891; New York: Harper, 1892; revised edition, London: Hurst & Blackett, 1899);

*A Tiger's Cub* (Bristol: Arrowsmith / London: Simpkin, Marshall, Hamilton, Kent, 1892);

*In Sugar-Cane Land* (London: McClure / Simpkin, Marshall, Hamilton, Kent, 1893);

*Summer Clouds and Other Stories* (London, Paris & New York: Tuck, 1893);

*Some Every-Day Folks* (3 volumes, London: Osgood, McIlvaine, 1894; 1 volume, New York: Harper, 1895);

*A Deal with the Devil* (London: Bliss, Sands & Foster, 1895; New York: Warne, 1917);

*A Breezy Morning* (London & New York: French, 1895);

*The Prude's Progress,* by Phillpotts and Jerome K. Jerome (London: Chatto & Windus, 1895);

*Down Dartmoor Way* (London: Osgood, McIlvaine, 1896);

*My Laughing Philosopher* (London: Innes, 1896);

*Lying Prophets* (London: Innes, 1897; New York: Stokes, 1898);

*Children of the Mist* (London: Innes, 1898; New York & London: Putnam, 1899);

*Loup-Garou!* (London: Sands, 1899);

*A Golden Wedding,* by Phillpotts and Charles Groves (London & New York: French, 1899);

*The Human Boy* (London: Methuen, 1899; New York & London: Harper, 1900);

*A Pair of Knickerbockers* (New York & London: French, 1900);

*Eden Phillpotts (Hulton-Deutsch Collection)*

*Sons of the Morning* (London: Methuen, 1900; New York & London: Putnam, 1900);

*The Good Red Earth* (Bristol: Arrowsmith / London: Simpkin, Marshall, Hamilton, Kent, 1901; New York: Doubleday, Page, 1901); published as *Johnny Fortnight* (Bristol: Arrowsmith, 1904; revised, 1920);

*The Striking Hours* (London: Methuen, 1901; New York: Stokes, 1901);

*Fancy Free* (London: Methuen, 1901);

*The River* (London: Methuen, 1902; New York: Stokes, 1902);

*The Transit of the Red Dragon and Other Tales* (Bristol: Arrowsmith / London: Simpkin, Marshall, Hamilton, Kent, 1903);

*The Golden Fetich* (London: Harper, 1903; New York: Dodd, Mead, 1903);

*My Devon Year* (London: Methuen, 1903; New York: Macmillan, 1903);

*The American Prisoner* (London: Methuen, 1904; New York & London: Macmillan, 1904);

*The Farm of the Dagger* (London: Newnes, 1904; New York: Dodd, Mead, 1904);

*The Secret Woman* (London: Methuen, 1905; New York & London: Macmillan, 1905);

*Knock at a Venture* (London: Methuen, 1905; New York & London: Macmillan, 1905);

*Up-Along and Down-Along* (London: Methuen, 1905);

*The Portreeve* (London: Methuen, 1906; New York: Macmillan, 1906);

*The Unlucky Number* (London: Newnes, 1906);

*My Garden* (London: Newnes / New York: Scribners, 1906);

*The Poacher's Wife* (London: Methuen, 1906); published as *Daniel Sweetland* (New York & London: Authors & Newspapers Association, 1906);

*Doubloons,* by Phillpotts and Arnold Bennett (New York: McClure, Phillips, 1906); published as *The Sinews of War* (London: Laurie, 1906);

*The Whirlwind* (London: Chapman & Hall, 1907; New York: McClure, Phillips, 1907);

*The Folk Afield* (London: Methuen, 1907; New York & London: Putnam, 1907);

*The Mother* (London: Ward, Lock, 1908); published as *The Mother of the Man* (New York: Dodd, Mead, 1908);

*The Statue,* by Phillpotts and Bennett (London, Paris, New York, Toronto & Melbourne: Cassell, 1908; New York: Moffat, Yard, 1908);

*The Human Boy Again* (London: Chapman & Hall, 1908);

*The Virgin in Judgment* (London, Paris, New York, Toronto & Melbourne: Cassell, 1908; New York: Moffat, Yard, 1908);

*The Three Brothers* (London: Hutchinson, 1909; New York: Macmillan, 1909);

*The Fun of the Fair* (London: John Murray, 1909);

*The Haven* (London: John Murray, 1909; New York: John Lane, 1909);

*The Thief of Virtue* (London: John Murray, 1910; New York: John Lane, 1910);

*Tales of the Tenements* (London: John Murray, 1910; New York: John Lane, 1910);

*The Flint Heart: A Fairy Story* (London: Smith, Elder, 1910; New York: Dutton, 1910; revised edition, London: Chapman & Dodd, 1922);

*A Fight to a Finish* (London: Cassell, 1911);

*Wild Fruit* (London & New York: John Lane, 1911);

*Demeter's Daughter* (London: Methuen, 1911; New York: John Lane, 1911);

*The Beacon* (London: Unwin, 1911; New York: John Lane, 1911);

*Dance of the Months* (London & Glasgow: Gowans & Gray, 1911);

*The Secret Woman: A Play in Five Acts* (London: Duckworth, 1912; New York: Brentano's, 1914; revised, London: Duckworth, 1935);

*The Forest on the Hill* (London: John Murray, 1912; New York: John Lane, 1912; revised edition, London: Newnes, 1914); published as *The Forest* (London: Macmillan, 1927);

*The Iscariot* (London: John Murray, 1912; New York: John Lane, 1912);

*The Three Knaves* (London: Macmillan, 1912);

*From the Angle of Seventeen* (London: John Murray, 1912; Boston: Little, Brown, 1914);

*The Lovers: A Romance* (London, Melbourne & Toronto: Ward, Lock, 1912; Chicago & New York: Rand, McNally, 1912);

*Curtain Raisers* (London: Duckworth, 1912; New York: Brentano's, 1914);

*Widecombe Fair* (London: John Murray, 1913; Boston: Little, Brown, 1913);

*The Old Time Before Them* (London: John Murray, 1913); revised as *Told at "The Plume"* (London: Hurst & Blackett, 1921);

*The Joy of Youth: A Comedy* (London: Chapman & Hall, 1913; Boston: Little, Brown, 1913);

*The Shadow* (London: Duckworth, 1913; New York: Brentano's, 1914);

*The Mother: A Play in Four Acts* (London: Duckworth, 1913; New York: Brentano's, 1914);

*The Master of Merripit* (London, Melbourne & Toronto: Ward, Lock, 1914);

*The Judge's Chair* (London: John Murray, 1914);

*Faith Tresilion* (New York: Macmillan, 1914; London, Melbourne & Toronto: Ward, Lock, 1916);

*Brunel's Tower* (London: Heinemann, 1915; New York: Macmillan, 1915);

*My Shrubs* (London & New York: John Lane, 1915);

*The Angel in the House,* by Phillpotts and Basil Macdonald Hastings (London & New York: French, 1915);

*Old Delabole* (London: Heinemann, 1915; New York: Macmillan, 1915);

*The Human Boy and the War* (London: Methuen, 1916; New York: Macmillan, 1916);

*The Green Alleys* (London: Heinemann, 1916; New York: Macmillan, 1916);

*"Delight"* (London: Palmer & Hayward, 1916);

# Children of the Mist

A NOVEL

By

Eden Phillpotts

Author of " Down Dartmoor Way," " Some Everyday Folks,"
" My Laughing Philosopher," " Lying Prophets,"
etc.

London

A. D. Innes & Company

Limited

1898

*Title page for the first novel in Phillpotts's successful Dartmoor Cycle (courtesy of the Lilly Library, Indiana University)*

*The Girl and the Faun* (London: Palmer & Hayward, 1916; Philadelphia: Lippincott / London: Palmer & Hayward, 1917);

*The Farmer's Wife: A Play in Three Acts* (London: Duckworth / New York: Brentano's, 1916);

*The Nursery (Banks of Colne)* (London: Heinemann, 1917); published as *The Banks of Colne* (New York: Macmillan, 1917);

*Plain Song 1914–1916* (London: Heinemann, 1917; New York: Macmillan, 1917);

*The Chronicles of St. Tid* (London: Skeffington, 1917; New York: Macmillan, 1918);

*The Spinners* (London: Heinemann, 1918; New York: Macmillan, 1918);

*A Shadow Passes* (London: Palmer & Hayward, 1918; New York: Macmillan, 1919);

*Storm in a Teacup* (London: Heinemann, 1919; New York: Macmillan, 1919);

*St. George and the Dragons: A Comedy in Three Acts* (London: Duckworth, 1919);

*Evander* (London: Richards, 1919; New York: Macmillan, 1919);

*Miser's Money* (London: Heinemann, 1920; New York: Macmillan, 1920);

*As the Wind Blows* (London: Elkin Mathews / New York: Macmillan, 1920);

*A West Country Pilgrimage* (London: Parsons, 1920; New York: Macmillan, 1920);

*Orphan Dinah* (London: Heinemann, 1920; New York: Macmillan, 1921);

*The Bronze Venus* (London: Richards, 1921);

*Eudocia: A Comedy Royal* (London: Heinemann, 1921; New York: Macmillan, 1921);

*A Dish of Apples* (London & New York: Hodder & Stoughton, 1921);

*The Grey Room* (New York: Macmillan, 1921; London: Hurst & Blackett, 1922);

*Pan and the Twins* (London: Richards, 1922; New York: Macmillan, 1922);

*Pixies' Plot* (London: Richards, 1922);

*Number 87,* as Harrington Hext (London: Butterworth, 1922; New York: Macmillan, 1922);

*The Red Redmaynes* (New York: Macmillan, 1922; London: Hutchinson, 1923);

*Black, White, and Brindled* (London: Richards, 1923; New York: Macmillan, 1923);

*Children of Men* (London: Heinemann, 1923; New York: Macmillan, 1923);

*The Market-Money: A Play in One Act* (London & Glasgow: Gowans & Gray / Boston: Phillips, 1923); republished in *Three Short Plays* (London: Duckworth, 1928);

*The Lavender Dragon* (London: Richards, 1923; New York: Macmillan, 1923);

*Cherry-Stones* (London: Richards, 1923; New York: Macmillan, 1924);

*The Things at Their Heels,* as Harrington Hext (London: Butterworth, 1923; New York: Macmillan, 1923);

*"Cheat-the-Boys"* (London: Heinemann, 1924; New York: Macmillan, 1924);

*A Human Boy's Diary* (London: Heinemann, 1924; New York: Macmillan, 1924);

*Thoughts in Prose and Verse* (London: Watts, 1924);

*Bed Rock: A Comedy in Three Acts,* by Phillpotts and Hastings (London: "The Stage," 1924);

*Redcliff* (London: Hutchinson, 1924; New York: Macmillan, 1924);

*The Treasures of Typhon* (London: Richards, 1924; New York: Macmillan, 1925);

*A Harvesting* (London: Richards, 1924);

*Who Killed Diana?,* as Harrington Hext (London: Butterworth, 1924); published as *Who Killed Cock Robin?* (New York: Macmillan, 1924);

*A Comedy Royal* (London: Laurie, 1925; revised edition, London: Duckworth, 1932);

*Devonshire Cream: A Comedy in Three Acts* (London: Duckworth, 1925; New York: Macmillan, 1925);

*A Voice from the Dark* (London: Hutchinson, 1925; New York: Macmillan, 1925);

*Up Hill, Down Dale* (London: Hutchinson, 1925; New York: Macmillan, 1925);

*George Westover* (London: Hutchinson, 1925; New York: Macmillan, 1925);

*The Monster,* as Harrington Hext (New York: Macmillan, 1925);

*Circé's Island and The Girl and the Faun* (London: Richards, 1926; New York: Macmillan, 1926);

*The Marylebone Miser* (London: Hutchinson, 1926); republished as *Jig-Saw* (New York: Macmillan, 1926);

*Peacock House and Other Mysteries* (London: Hutchinson, 1926; New York: Macmillan, 1927);

*The Augustan Books of Modern Poetry: Eden Phillpotts,* edited by Edward Thompson (London: Benn, 1926);

*The Miniature* (London: Watts, 1926; New York: Macmillan, 1927);

*A Cornish Droll* (London: Hutchinson, 1926; New York: Macmillan, 1928);

*Yellow Sands: A Comedy in Three Acts,* by Phillpotts and Adelaide Eden Phillpotts (London: Duckworth, 1926; New York: French, 1927);

*Brother Man* (London: Richards, 1926);

*The Blue Comet: A Comedy in Three Acts* (London: Duckworth, 1927);

*The Jury* (London: Hutchinson, 1927; New York: Macmillan, 1927);

*It Happened Like That* (London: Hutchinson, 1927; New York: Macmillan, 1928);

*Arachne* (London: Faber & Gwyer, 1927; New York: Macmillan, 1928);

*The Ring Fence* (London: Hutchinson, 1928; New York: Macmillan, 1928);

*Brother Beast* (London: Secker, 1928);

*Three Short Plays* (London: Duckworth, 1928);

*Goodwill* (London: Watts, 1928);

*The Runaways: A Comedy in Three Acts* (London: Duckworth, 1928);

*Tryphena* (London: Hutchinson, 1929; New York: Macmillan, 1929);

*The Torch* (London: Hutchinson, 1929; New York: Macmillan, 1929);

*A Hundred Sonnets* (London: Benn, 1929);

*Buy a Broom: A Comedy in Three Acts* (London: Duckworth, 1929);

*The Apes* (London: Faber & Faber, 1929; New York: Macmillan, 1929);

*The Three Maidens* (London: Hutchinson, 1930; New York: Smith, 1930);

*A Hundred Lyrics* (London: Benn, 1930; New York: Smith, 1930);

*Alcyone (A Fairy Story)* (London: Benn, 1930);

*Cherry Gambol* (London: Hutchinson, 1930);

*Jane's Legacy: A Folk Play in Three Acts* (London: Duckworth, 1931; London & New York: French, 1932);

*"Found Drowned"* (London: Hutchinson, 1931; New York: Macmillan, 1931);

*Essays in Little* (London: Hutchinson, 1931);

*Stormbury* (London: Hutchinson, 1931; New York: Macmillan, 1932);

*The Broom Squires* (London: Benn, 1932; New York: Macmillan, 1932);

*Becoming* (London: Benn, 1932);

*A Clue from the Stars* (London: Hutchinson, 1932; New York: Macmillan, 1932);

*Bred in the Bone* (London: Hutchinson, 1932; New York: Macmillan, 1932);

*The Good Old Days: A Comedy in Three Acts,* by Phillpotts and Adelaide Eden Phillpotts (London: Duckworth, 1932; New York: French, 1932);

*They Could Do No Other* (London: Hutchinson, 1932; New York: Macmillan, 1933);

*The Captain's Curio* (London: Hutchinson, 1933; New York: Macmillan, 1933);

*Mr. Digweed and Mr. Lumb* (London: Hutchinson, 1933; New York: Macmillan, 1934);

*Witch's Cauldron* (London: Hutchinson, 1933; New York: Macmillan, 1933);

*A Shadow Passes* (London: Hutchinson, 1933; New York: Macmillan, 1934);

*A Cup of Happiness: A Comedy in Three Acts* (London: Duckworth, 1933);

*Nancy Owlett* (London, Paris & New York: Tuck, 1933; New York: Macmillan, 1933);

*Song of a Sailor Man: Narrative Poem* (London: Benn, 1933; New York: Macmillan, 1934);

*A Year with Bisshe-Bantam* (London & Glasgow: Blackie, 1934);

*Minions of the Moon* (London: Hutchinson, 1934; New York: Macmillan, 1935);

*The Oldest Inhabitant: A Comedy* (London: Hutchinson, 1934; New York: Macmillan, 1934);

*Portrait of a Gentleman* (London: Hutchinson, 1934);

*Ned of the Caribees* (London: Hutchinson, 1935);

*Sonnets from Nature* (London: Watts, 1935);

*The Wife of Elias* (London: Hutchinson, 1935; New York: Dutton, 1937);

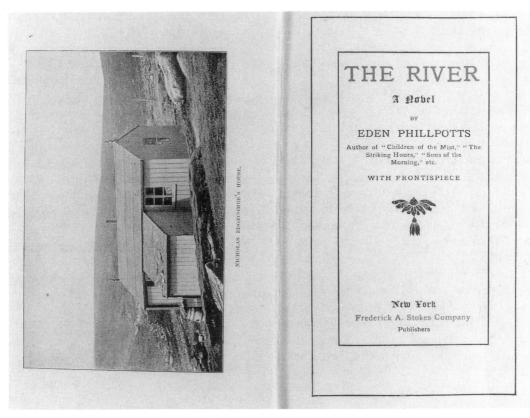

*Frontispiece and title page for the American edition of Phillpotts's 1902 novel in the Dartmoor Cycle*

*Physician, Heal Thyself* (London: Hutchinson, 1935); published as *The Anniversary Murder* (New York: Dutton, 1936);

*Once Upon A Time* (London: Hutchinson, 1935);

*A Close Call* (London: Hutchinson, 1936; New York: Macmillan, 1936);

*The Owl of Athene* (London: Hutchinson, 1936);

*The White Camel* (London: Country Life, 1936; New York: Dutton, 1938);

*Wood-Nymph* (London: Hutchinson, 1936; New York: Dutton, 1937);

*Farce in Three Acts* (London: Hutchinson, 1937);

*A Dartmoor Village* (London: Watts, 1937);

*Lycanthrope: The Mystery of Sir William Wolf* (London: Butterworth, 1937; New York: Macmillan, 1938); published as *The Mystery of Sir William Wolf* (London: Butterworth, 1938);

*Portrait of a Scoundrel* (London: John Murray, 1938; New York: Macmillan, 1938);

*Dark Horses* (London: John Murray, 1938);

*Golden Island* (London: M. Joseph, 1938);

*Saurus* (London: John Murray, 1938);

*Monkshood* (London: Methuen, 1939; New York: Macmillan, 1939);

*Tabletop* (New York: Macmillan, 1939);

*Thorn in Her Flesh* (London: John Murray, 1939);

*Awake Deborah!* (London: Methuen, 1940; New York: Macmillan, 1941);

*Chorus of Clowns* (London: Methuen, 1940);

*A Mixed Grill* (London: Watts, 1940);

*Goldcross* (London: Methuen, 1940);

*A Deed Without a Name* (London & Melbourne: Hutchinson, 1941; New York: Macmillan, 1942);

*Ghostwater* (London: Methuen, 1941; New York: Macmillan, 1941);

*Pilgrims of the Night* (London: Hutchinson, 1942);

*Miniatures* (London: Watts, 1942);

*Flower of the Gods* (London & New York: Hutchinson, 1942; New York: Macmillan, 1943);

*A Museum Piece* (London & New York: Hutchinson, 1943);

*At the 'Bus-Stop: A Duologue for Two Women* (London: French, 1943);

*They Were Seven* (London & New York: Hutchinson, 1944; New York: Macmillan, 1945);

*The Changeling* (London & New York: Hutchinson, 1944);

*The Drums of Dombali* (London & New York: Hutchinson, 1945);

*Quartet* (London & New York: Hutchinson, 1946);

*There Was an Old Woman* (London & New York: Hutchinson, 1947);

*Fall of the House of Heron* (London & New York: Hutchinson, 1948);

*The Enchanted Wood* (London: Watts, 1948);

*Address Unknown* (London & New York: Hutchinson, 1949);

*Dilemma* (London: Hutchinson, 1949);

*The Waters of Walla* (London & New York: Hutchinson, 1950);

*The Orange Orchard,* by Phillpotts and Nancy Price (London: French, 1951);

*Through a Glass Darkly* (London & New York: Hutchinson, 1951);

*From the Angle of 88* (London & New York: Hutchinson, 1951);

*George and Georgina* (London & New York: Hutchinson, 1952);

*The Hidden Hand* (London: Hutchinson, 1952);

*His Brother's Keeper* (London: Hutchinson, 1953);

*One Thing and Another* (London: Hutchinson, 1954);

*The Widow Garland* (London: Hutchinson, 1955);

*Connie Woodland* (London: Hutchinson, 1956);

*Giglet Market* (London: Methuen, 1957);

*There Was an Old Man* (London: Hutchinson, 1959).

PLAY PRODUCTIONS: *The Policeman,* by Phillpotts and Walter Helmore, Ealing, Lyric Hall, 12 January 1887;

*A Platonic Attachment,* Ealing, Lyric Hall, 20 February 1889;

*A Breezy Morning,* Leeds, Grand Theatre, 27 April 1889;

*The Councillor's Wife,* New York, Empire Theatre, 6 November 1892; revised as *The Prude's Progress,* by Phillpotts and Jerome K. Jerome, Cambridge, Theatre Royal, 16 May 1895;

*Allendale,* by Phillpotts and G. B. Burgin, London, Strand Theatre, 14 February 1893;

*The MacHaggis,* by Phillpotts and Jerome, Peterborough, Theatre Royal, 22 February 1897;

*For Love of Prim,* London, Court Theatre, 24 January 1899;

*A Pair of Knickerbockers,* London, St. George's Hall, 26 December 1899;

*A Golden Wedding,* by Phillpotts and Charles Graves, London, Playhouse Theatre, 22 February 1908;

*The Carrier Pigeon,* Glasgow, Royal Theatre, 7 April 1913;

*Hiatus,* Manchester, Gaiety Theatre, 22 September 1913;

*The Shadow,* Manchester, Gaiety Theatre, 6 October 1913;

*The Mother,* Liverpool, Playhouse, 22 October 1913;

*The Point of View,* London, St. George's Hall, 18 November 1913;

*The Angel in the House,* by Phillpotts and Basil MacDonald Hastings, London, Savoy Theatre, 3 June 1915;

*Bedrock,* Manchester, Gaiety Theatre, 16 October 1916;

*The Farmer's Wife,* by Phillpotts and Adelaide Eden Phillpotts, Birmingham, Repertory Theatre, 11 November 1916;

*St. George and the Dragons,* Birmingham, Repertory Theatre, 30 March 1918;

*The Secret Woman,* Birmingham, Repertory Theatre, 14 October 1922;

*Devonshire Cream,* by Phillpotts and Adelaide Eden Phillpotts, Birmingham, Repertory Theatre, 6 December 1924;

*Jane's Legacy,* Birmingham, Repertory Theatre, 24 October 1925;

*The Blue Comet,* Birmingham, Repertory Theatre, 11 September 1926;

*Yellow Sands,* by Phillpotts and Adelaide Eden Phillpotts, London, Haymarket Theatre, 3 November 1926;

*The Purple Bedroom,* London, Colosseum, 27 December 1926;

*Something to Talk About,* London, Colosseum, 17 January 1927;

*My Lady's Mill,* by Phillpotts and Adelaide Eden Phillpotts, London, Lyric Theatre, 2 July 1928;

*The Runaways,* Birmingham, Repertory Theatre, 1 September 1928;

*The Market-Money,* Liverpool, Playhouse, 5 June 1929;

*The Good Old Days,* by Phillpotts and Adelaide Eden Phillpotts, Birmingham, Repertory Theatre, December 1931;

*A Cup of Happiness,* London, Royalty Theatre, 24 December 1932;

*The Orange Orchard,* by Phillpotts and Nancy Price, London, New Lindsay Theatre, 12 April 1950.

The literary career of Eden Phillpotts lasted for more than seventy-five years, linking the Victorian era with the modern period. Though Phillpotts wrote an average of three books per year during his professional life, for a total of more than 225 volumes, the quantity of his work is not its only distinguishing feature. His range of literary effort, spanning the gamut of expression, is also striking. Phillpotts tried his hand at almost every form, including novels (ninety-five, including eighteen Dart-

moor novels); plays (forty-five); short stories (twenty-three volumes); verse (twenty-two volumes); children's stories and fairy tales (twenty-eight volumes, including the Human Boy series); detective stories and mysteries (nineteen volumes); and miscellaneous prose – essays, travel, and memoirs (three volumes). Not even the prodigious efforts of his Victorian predecessors come close to his output of novels: Charles Dickens, for example, wrote fifteen and Anthony Trollope, forty-seven.

Eden Phillpotts was born on 4 November 1862 at Mount Abu in India, the son of Henry Phillpotts, an officer in the Indian Army, and Adelaide Matilda Sophia Waters Phillpotts. When Captain Phillpotts died in 1865, Eden's mother took him and his two brothers to England. He spent his early boyhood with his widowed mother at Dawlish, Devon, and was educated at Mannamead School, Plymouth (later incorporated with Plymouth College).

At seventeen, Phillpotts left school, went to London, and became a clerk at Sun Fire Company, an insurance firm, where he worked from 1879 to 1889. For two years, after office hours, he studied acting at a school of dramatic art, but he decided that he was not suited for acting and turned to writing instead. Night after night he worked laboriously on the writer's craft, while working during the day at the insurance company.

His first book, *My Adventure in the Flying Scotsman: A Romance of London and North-Western Railway Shares,* was published in 1888; it was a story of stolen railroad stocks that may have been written as an advertisement for the London and North-Western Railway. Before long Phillpotts was earning four hundred pounds a year with his writing. In 1890 he left the insurance company to become an assistant editor of *Black and White,* a weekly periodical. Since it only required his presence for three days each week, the job gave him leisure to pursue his own writing as well as a chance to practice writing for deadlines. In 1899 Phillpotts decided to devote all his energy to his own writing and gave up the editorial job. He also left London to settle in his beloved Devon, first at Torquay, where he lived from 1889 to 1929, and later at Broadclyst near Exeter, where he lived from 1929 until his death. Both places are not far from Dartmoor, the setting or scene for most of his fiction. He never returned to London, not even to see his own successful plays.

In 1892 he married Emily Topham. They had a daughter, Adelaide (born 23 April 1896), who became an author, and a son, Henry (born January 1895). After Emily's death in 1928, Phillpotts was married again, in 1929, to Lucy Robina Joyce Webb.

Phillpotts had a rather unusual relationship with Adelaide, especially during the period of his first marriage. Father and daughter collaborated often on writing projects and are joint authors of *Yellow Sands: A Comedy in Three Acts* (1926), *The Good Old Days: A Comedy in Three Acts* (1932), and the play *My Lady's Mill* (1928). They dedicated books to each other and wrote sonnets to each other. Adelaide Phillpotts established a successful career on her own, as well, with thirty-four books to her credit, including works of fiction, poetry, drama, and autobiography. She claimed that her relationship with her father extended beyond literary collaboration to incest and to extreme jealousy and cruelty on his part, as when he cut her off after her marriage to Nicholas Ross in 1951.

In his literary career, Phillpotts exhibited many of the obsessional symptoms and traits of character of the world's great creators such as Dickens, Jonathan Swift, and Henrik Ibsen: extreme orderliness, regularity of habits, and meticulousness. He was scrupulous about recording the money he earned and the number of words he produced every day. His desk diary of 1899, for instance, records details of his work day by day from January to December. At the end he has the following summary of his literary output for the year 1899:

**Analysis of the Year's Work**
1 Play in 4 Acts
2 Draft of Novel 134,500 words of finished copy
46,000 words
1 Short Story
53 General Articles
2 Reviews
11 Poems
10 My Devon Year Book Papers –

---

Total number of words 460,000
Average, 1250 words per day
78 holidays when I wrote nothing
Therefore average number of words to
working days or writing days about 1600
Words written: January 55,000 (highest)
March 26,000 ( lowest)

His letters and diaries also describe his typical workday, which began at 7:30 A.M.: he wrote letters in the morning, worked at his serious writing from 10:30 A.M. to 1:00 P.M., did gardening in the afternoon, returned to his desk in the evening, and went to bed at about 11:00 P.M.

Phillpotts wrote all his books and letters by hand on plain white paper with a steel pen, often

THE SECRET WOMAN

BY

EDEN PHILLPOTTS

WITH A FRONTISPIECE

METHUEN & CO.
36 ESSEX STREET W.C.
LONDON

*Frontispiece and title page for Phillpotts's story of a woman who murders her adulterous husband and then hides her crime (courtesy of the Lilly Library, Indiana University)*

dipping it into an inkwell. A secretary typed his manuscript for the publisher. When Phillpotts could not write with his right hand because of gout he trained himself to write with his left hand. His 290-page manuscript of *Lycanthrope: The Mystery of Sir William Wolf* (1937), now at the Humanities Research Center, Austin, Texas, was written entirely with his left hand.

Phillpotts was not always at his desk with his pen in hand, however. He made frequent trips into every nook and corner of Dartmoor, making notes on local flora and fauna and talking to rustics during his daily walks.

Phillpotts's name is almost synonymous with Dartmoor. His best-known works are the eighteen novels and two collections of short stories that make up his "Dartmoor Cycle," and the author described his connection to the area with the phrase, "Here was my playground when a child, my workshop as a man." What Emily Brontë did for the

Yorkshire moors, Dickens for London, and Thomas Hardy for Dorset, Phillpotts did for Dartmoor. On Phillpotts's choice of this locale as the setting for his novels, the authors R. D. Blackmore and Hardy had perhaps some influence. Blackmore's *Christowell* (1881) is set in Dartmoor, and in 1898 Phillpotts dedicated his first novel in the Dartmoor Cycle, *Children of the Mist,* to Blackmore. On 26 April 1904 at the dedication of the memorial window to Blackmore in Exeter Cathedral, Phillpotts said, "It was not true to say that Blackmore was the author of many good books and one great one. He enriched the language with many great works, works inspired by his own wealth of head and heart."

Hardy, on the other hand, had already put Dorset, next door to Dartmoor, his 'Wessex,' on the literary map of England and had emerged as the classic novelist of the English countryside and country people. Phillpotts admired Hardy's novels, dedicated one of his own to him, and corresponded with

him regularly. Between 1898 and 1923, Phillpotts "annexed" Dartmoor as his own literary territory.

Of Dartmoor and Phillpotts, Arnold Bennett says in his introduction to the Widecombe edition of the Dartmoor novels: "It is unlike, even spectacularly unlike, any other district in Great Britain. . . . It is an undulating moor with high smooth slopes, morasses, bogs – and the stony peaks. The landscapes are beautiful, majestic, and intimidating. . . . What a district for a novelist – compact, complete, withdrawn, exceptional, traditional, impressive, and racy!"

Each book of Phillpotts's Dartmoor Cycle focuses on a specific part of the moor and describes it faithfully and in detail. *Children of the Mist* is set in Chagford, *The River* (1902) in West Dart and Two Bridges, *The Secret Woman* (1905) in Belstone, and *The Thief of Virtue* (1910) in East Dart and Postbridge. A reader could visit Dartmoor with any one of these books in hand and see how closely Phillpotts's words match the actual place.

Phillpotts's Dartmoor in these novels is a picture of southwest England's rural way of life, of peasants, their country speech, and customs. Few English novelists have been more minutely specific about their settings, and no other English writer has depicted more persistently and comprehensively the physical qualities, both natural and manmade, of Dartmoor.

Although not all the eighteen novels, even the revised ones, present the author at his best, many critics – as did Phillpotts himself – regard the Dartmoor novels as the crown of his achievement. *The River* and *The Secret Woman* are among his best works, and Phillpotts considered *The Thief of Virtue* the best of the Dartmoor Cycle. The excellence of these novels lies in their convincing dialogue in West Country dialect, their believable plots, their facility for dramatizing the undramatic, and the author's sympathy for his characters and faithfulness in describing their setting. Two dominating elements of the Dartmoor novels – topography and the rural experience – had the greatest appeal to readers. In fact, Phillpotts's novels promoted tourism in the West Country and attracted thousands of visitors each year. The three best novels of the cycle all start with topographical essays of several pages describing flowers, rivers, tors, and clouds before their protagonists are introduced, and lengthy essays on topography are interspersed throughout the novels. Modern readers who want to get on with the story may find these elaborate sections as obstacles to the narrative – unlike Hardy, Phillpotts does not subordinate topographical descriptions to the narrative as a whole – and perhaps this is one of the reasons he has failed to attract much serious critical attention outside the West Country.

The rural experience, the second dominant element of the Dartmoor Cycle, is informed by the "cult of the primitive," the appeal of the country life in contrast with the industrialized town life. The cycle portrays the lives of local rustics, living in villages and hamlets, as being removed from the tensions and pressures of town life and as being closer to nature. This country life tends to be identified with the "natural" and "unspoiled" life of a lower class of rustics rather than the "artificial" and "corrupt" life of the urban middle class. The novels have farmers and farm-related workers as their main characters, and villages as their settings. Timothy Oldreive and Nicholas Edgecombe live in West Dart and Two Bridges, Anthony Redvers and Joseph Westway in Belstone, and Philip Ouldsbroom and Quinton Crymes in Postbridge. Phillpotts celebrates the simplicity of their lives, often romanticizing aspects of them from his townsman's point of view.

The Dartmoor Cycle novels typically relate triangular love stories of two women and one man, or vice versa. *The River* is the story of Nicholas Edgecombe's difficult choice between Hannah Bradridge and Mary Merle. Nicholas is deserted by his bride, Hannah, on the day of his wedding. She elopes with Timothy Oldrieve, his rival, who later is drowned. *The Secret Woman* is the tragic tale of Ann Redvers, who caught her husband in adultery, murdered him in a fit of anger, and kept the murder a secret. The jury rules that Anthony Redvers died accidentally. The other woman's identity (Salome Westaway) is not revealed until the novel's end. Phillpotts later published a controversial play with the same title (1912). Phillpotts writes with economy and psychological penetration about Anne's intense agony while carrying her tremendous secret. *The Thief of Virtue* is also a tragic story, with Philip Ouldsbroom as its hero who is deceived by his wife Unity Crymes and disappointed by the son he fondly imagines his own. These novels also reveal Phillpotts's keen ear for Devon dialect with the fresh and lively dialogue of the farmers, their wives, daughters, and sons.

Contemporary reviewer L. A. G. Strong praises the Dartmoor Cycle: "An achievement without parallel in our time, the Dartmoor Cycle ensures [Phillpotts] at the least a local immortality. No student of the regional novel will be able to neglect him. No one interested in English dialects will be allowed to miss the most accurate transcription of

*Dust jacket for Phillpotts's 1930 detective novel*

Devon, in spirit and letter, that has ever been set on paper." Glen Cavaliero, on the other hand, in his *The Rural Tradition in the English Novel 1900–1939* (1977) does not think highly of the cycle: "For all their faithfully recorded speech and landscapes, the Dartmoor Novels are essentially bookish creations born of the English rustic myth, ultimately means of escape rather than of illumination."

Not all of Phillpotts's novels are set in Dartmoor, however. He also wrote a series of nine "industrial" novels with several industries as their subject matter and with settings outside Dartmoor: *Lying Prophets* (1897), about fishing in Cornwall; *The Haven* (1909), on fishing at Brixham; *Brunel's Tower* (1915), on the pottery industry in Devon; *Old Delabole* (1915), concerning slate quarries in Cornwall; *The Green Alleys* (1916), on the hop industry in Kent; *The Nursery (Banks of Colne)* (1917), concerning horticulture and oyster fishing in Essex; *The Spinners*

(1918), about spinning in Dorset; *Storm in a Teacup* (1919), about papermaking in Devon; and *"Cheat-the-Boys"* (1924), concerning apple orchards in Devon. These novels are a unique blend of fact and fiction and are clearly the result of patient research.

Phillpotts also claims a place in literary history as one of the influential writers who made detective fiction "respectable" literature. His skill as a novelist is evident in his detective fiction as clearly as in his Dartmoor novels. His first novel – *The End of Life* (1891) – was a detective novel, and in *Queen's Quorum* (1969), Ellery Queen selects Phillpotts's *My Adventure in the Flying Scotsmen* as one of 106 most important detective stories ever written. Although Phillpotts regarded his detective fiction as minor work, he managed to produce nineteen books in this genre, many of them worthwhile. Many fans of detective fiction regard *The Grey Room* (1921) as Phillpotts's best mystery, with its device of a bed

*Phillpotts in later years (Hulton-Deutsch Collection)*

that emits poisonous fumes when warmed by a body. Jacques Barzun regards Phillpotts's *"Found Drowned"* (1931) and *The Red Redmaynes* (1922) as classic detective novels.

Phillpotts often took time off from serious fiction to write children's books. He wrote fairy stories, fables, and schoolboy tales, primarily to amuse himself. Many of Phillpotts's fantasy stories present the author's interpretations of classical figures, such as Athene, Bacchus, Apollo, Pan, Epicurus, Eros, Circe, and Odysseus, but the author also employs other subject matter, as in *The White Camel* (1936), which is set in the deserts of the Middle East. Phillpotts's realistic stories of schoolboys at a private school are collectively known as the "Human Boy Series" and were collected in several volumes.

Twenty-three years after his death, the task of critical evaluation of Phillpotts's more than 225 works still remains. Phillpotts, as his letters reveal, dismissed a great deal of his writing as "chaff," as short-term potboiling material. Contemporary critics underestimated Phillpotts and ignored his works, and most of his books have now sunk from sight even though he was once a best-selling author.

There is little reason, however, to doubt that a few of Phillpotts's novels, stories, and plays will continue to be read. His main achievement lies in putting Dartmoor on the literary map of England with a topographer's accuracy. He is the foremost spokesman of that region in English literature. *The River, The Secret Woman, The Red Redmaynes,* and the Human Boy series belong to the summit of his oeuvre. The loving care and meticulous eye with which Phillpotts describes Dartmoor and its atmosphere and his power to create a sense of place and make it as real as his own living room give Eden Phillpotts the claim to be regarded as a serious writer.

No one will claim that Phillpotts ranks among the masters of prose, poetry, or drama of the Victorian or modern period. He is not in the class of Dickens, Hardy, George Eliot, or Anthony Trollope. He is, however, one of the ablest minor writers of the period. Phillpotts represents the classic case of someone whose quantity of production obscured the quality of his work. He is the opposite of Jane Austen and Franz Kafka, who allowed publication of only a small selection of high quality from their writings. Phillpotts's vast and uneven canon strikingly conveys that he was a writer with a compelling passion for words and work but that he went on producing and publishing page after page, day

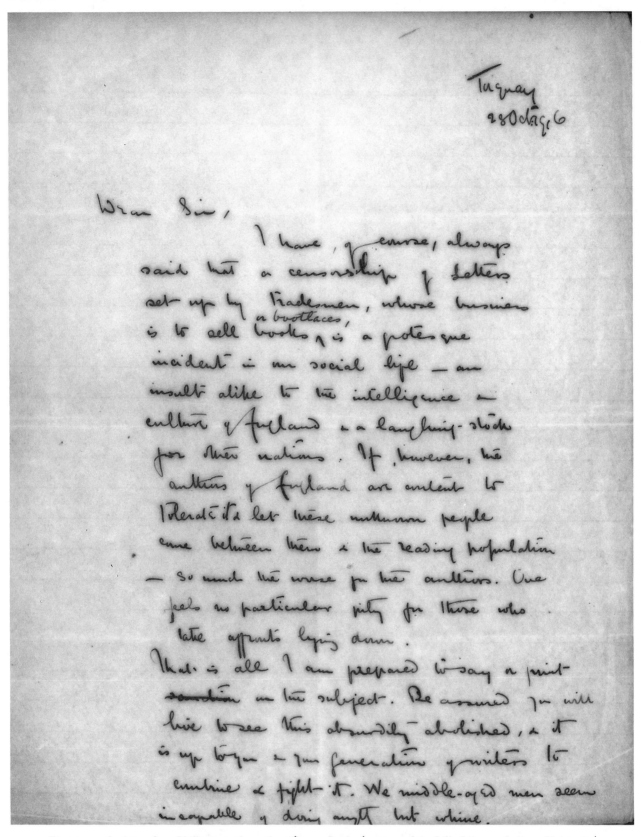

*First page of a letter from Phillpotts to the author Thomas Burke (courtesy of the Lilly Library, Indiana University)*

after day, without regard to consistency of its quality.

**Letters:**

*Eden Phillpotts (1862–1960): Selected Letters,* edited by James Y. Dayananda (New York: University Press, 1984).

**Bibliography:**

Percival Hinton, *Eden Phillpotts: A Bibliography of First Editions* (Birmingham: Greville Worthington, 1931).

**References:**

Richard C. Carpenter, "Eden Phillpotts," in *Twentieth Century Crime and Mystery Writers* (New York: St. Martin's Press, 1980);

Glen Cavaliero, *The Rural Tradition in the English Novel 1900–1939* (London: Macmillan, 1977);

Kenneth F. Day, *Eden Phillpotts on Dartmoor* (London: David & Charles, 1981);

C. S. Evans, *Phillpotts and the Epic of Dartmoor* (London: Bookman, 1916);

Waveney Girvan, *Phillpotts: An Assessment and a Tribute* (London: Hutchinson, 1953);

C. W. Meadowcroft, *The Place of Phillpotts in English Peasant Drama* (Philadelphia: University of Pennsylvania Press, 1924);

Thomas Moult, "Eden Phillpotts," in *Dictionary of National Biography, 1951–1960* (London: Oxford University Press, 1971);

Ellery Queen, *Queen's Quorum: A History of the Detective-Crime Short Story as Revealed in the 106 Most Important Books Published in This Field Since 1845,* new edition, with supplements through 1967 (New York: Biblio & Tannen, 1969);

Adelaide Phillpotts Ross, *Reverie: An Autobiography* (London: Hale, 1981);

George Brandon Saul, "Phillpotts's Use of Classic Subject Matter: A Selective Consideration," *Modern British Literature,* 2 (1977): 30–43;

Anthony Storr, *The Dynamics of Creation* (London: Secker & Warburg, 1972);

R. Z. Temple, "Phillpotts, Eden," in *A Library of Literary Criticism: Modern British Literature,* volume 2 (New York: Ungar, 1966), pp. 423–426;

C. Timms, *The Humanity of Phillpotts* (London: Quart & Holborn Review, 1951).

**Papers:**

The major collections of Eden Phillpotts's correspondence and manuscripts are at the Humanities Research Center, University of Texas at Austin; at the Harold B. Lee Library, Brigham Young University, Provo, Utah; and at the Research Library, University of California, Los Angeles.

# Arthur Thomas Quiller-Couch

*(21 November 1863 – 12 May 1944)*

## Michael Douglas Smith

See also the Quiller-Couch essay in *DLB 135: British Short-Fiction Writers, 1880–1914: The Realist Tradition.*

BOOKS: *Athens: A Poem* (Bodmin, U.K.: Lidell, 1881);

*Dead Man's Rock: A Romance* (London & New York: Cassell, 1887);

*The Astonishing History of Troy Town* (London: Cassell, 1888; New York: Cassell, 1890);

*The Splendid Spur* (London & New York: Cassell, 1888);

*The Blue Pavilions* (London & New York: Cassell, 1891);

*Noughts and Crosses: Stories, Studies, and Sketches* (London: Cassell, 1891; New York: Scribners, 1898);

*I Saw Three Ships, and Other Winter's Tales* (London & New York: Cassell, 1892);

*The Warwickshire Avon* (London & New York: Osgood, McIlvaine, 1892);

*Green Bays: Verses and Parodies* (London: Methuen, 1893; enlarged edition, London: Milford, 1930);

*The Delectable Duchy: Stories, Studies, and Sketches* (London: Cassell, 1893; New York & London: Macmillan, 1893);

*Wandering Heath: Stories, Studies, and Sketches* (London: Cassell, 1895; New York: Scribners, 1895);

*Ia: A Love Story* (New York: Scribners, 1895); published as *Ia* (London: Cassell, 1896);

*Poems and Ballads* (London: Methuen, 1896);

*Adventures in Criticism* (London: Cassell, 1896; New York: Scribners, 1896);

*The Ship of Stars* (London: Cassell, 1899; New York: Scribners, 1899);

*Old Fires and Profitable Ghosts: A Book of Stories* (London: Cassell, 1900; New York: Scribners, 1900);

*The Laird's Luck and Other Fireside Tales* (London: Cassell, 1901; New York: Scribners, 1901);

*Arthur Quiller Couch ("Q"), circa 1894*

*The White Wolf and Other Fireside Tales* (London: Methuen, 1902; New York: Scribners, 1902);

*The Westcotes* (London: Simpkin, Marshall, Hamilton, Kent, 1902; Philadelphia: Coates, 1902);

*The Adventures of Harry Revel* (London: Cassell, 1903; New York: Scribners, 1903);

*Hetty Wesley* (London & New York: Harper, 1903);

*Two Sides of the Face: Midwinter Tales* (London: Simpkin, Marshall, Hamilton, Kent, 1903; New York: Scribners, 1903);

*Fort Amity* (London: Murray, 1904; New York: Scribners, 1904);

*Shining Ferry* (London: Hodder & Stoughton, 1905; New York: Scribners, 1905);

*The Mayor of Troy* (New York: Scribners, 1905; London: Methuen, 1906);

*Shakespeare's Christmas and Other Stories* (London: Smith, Elder, 1905; New York: Longmans, Green, 1905);

*Sir John Constantine* (New York: Scribners, 1905; London: Smith, Elder, 1906);

*From a Cornish Window* (London: Bell, 1906; New York: Dutton, 1906);

*Poison Island* (New York: Scribners, 1906; London: Murray, 1907);

*Major Vigoureux* (London: Methuen, 1907; New York: Scribners, 1907);

*Merry-Garden and Other Stories* (London: Methuen, 1907; Leipzig: Tauchnitz, 1907);

*True Tilda* (Bristol: Arrowsmith, 1909; New York: Scribners, 1909);

*Lady Good-for-Nothing* (London & New York: T. Nelson, 1910);

*Corporal Sam and Other Stories* (London: Smith, Elder, 1910);

*The Roll Call of Honour: A New Book of Golden Deeds* (London & New York: T. Nelson, 1911);

*Brother Copas* (Bristol: Arrowsmith, 1911; New York: Scribners, 1911);

*Hocken and Hunken, A Tale of Troy* (Edinburgh: Blackwood, 1912; New York: Appleton, 1913);

*The Vigil of Venus and Other Poems* (London: Methuen, 1912);

*News from the Duchy* (Bristol: Arrowsmith, 1913; London: Bell, 1913);

*Nicky-Nan, Reservist* (Edinburgh & London: Blackwood, 1915; New York: Appleton, 1915);

*On the Art of Writing: Lectures Delivered in the University of Cambridge, 1913–1914* (Cambridge: Cambridge University Press, 1916; New York: Putnam, 1916);

*Mortallone and Aunt Trinidad, Tales of the Spanish Main* (Bristol: Arrowsmith, 1917);

*Memoir of Arthur John Butler* (London: Smith, Elder, 1917);

*Notes on Shakespeare's Workmanship* (New York: Holt, 1917); published as *Shakespeare's Workmanship* (London: Unwin, 1918);

*Foe-Farrell* (London: Collins, 1918; New York: Macmillan, 1918);

*Studies in Literature, 1918–1930,* 3 volumes (Cambridge: Cambridge University Press, 1918–1929; New York: Putnam, 1918–1930);

*On the Art of Reading* (Cambridge: Cambridge University Press, 1920; New York & London: Putnam, 1920);

*A Lecture on Lectures: Introductory Volume* (London: Leonard & Virginia Woolf, 1923; New York: Harcourt, 1923);

*Charles Dickens and Other Victorians* (Cambridge: Cambridge University Press, 1925; New York & London: Putnam, 1925);

*The Age of Chaucer* (London: Dent, 1926; New York: AMS, 1970);

*Paternity in Shakespeare: Annual Shakespeare Lecture to the British Academy* (London: Milford, 1932; New York: Haskell House, n.d.);

*The Poet as Citizen, and Other Papers* (Cambridge: Cambridge University Press, 1934; New York: Macmillan, 1935);

*Cambridge Lectures* (London: Dent, 1943; New York: Dutton, 1943).

**Editions and Collections:** *Poetry,* edited by Mary Stratton (London: Batsford, 1914; New York: Dutton, 1914);

*Selected Stories by "Q"* (London: Dent, 1921; New York: Dutton, 1921);

*The Duchy Edition of Tales and Romances by Q ,* 30 volumes (London & Toronto: Dent, 1928–1929; New York: Dutton, 1928–1929);

*Poems* (London: Oxford University Press, 1929);

*Memories & Opinions: An Unfinished Autobiography of Q ,* edited, with an introduction, by S. C. Roberts (Cambridge: Cambridge University Press, 1944; New York: Macmillan, 1945);

*A Q Anthology,* edited by Frederick Brittain (London: Dent, 1948).

OTHER: *The World of Adventure: A Collection of Stirring and Moving Accidents,* 3 volumes, edited by Quiller-Couch (London: Cassell, 1889–1891);

*The Golden Pomp, A Procession of English Lyrics from Surrey to Shirley,* edited by Quiller-Couch (London: Methuen, 1895);

*Fairy Tales Far and Near,* retold by Quiller-Couch (London & New York: Stokes, 1895);

*The Story of the Sea,* 2 volumes, edited by Quiller-Couch (London: Cassell, 1895–1896);

*English Sonnets,* edited by Quiller-Couch (London: Chapman & Hall, 1897; enlarged edition, London: Chapman & Hall, 1935; New York: Crowell, 1936);

*Historical Tales from Shakespeare,* edited by Quiller-Couch (London: Arnold, 1899; New York, Scribners, 1900);

*The Oxford Book of English Verse, 1250–1900,* edited by Quiller-Couch (Oxford & New York: Clarendon, 1900; revised edition published as *The Oxford Book of English Verse, 1250–1918* (Oxford & New York: Clarendon Press, 1939);

*The Pilgrim's Way: A Little Scrip of Good Counsel for
    Travellers,* edited by Quiller-Couch (London:
    Seeley, 1906; New York: Dutton, 1907);
*Select English Classics,* 33 volumes, edited by Quiller-
    Couch (Oxford: Clarendon, 1908–1912);
*The Sleeping Beauty and Other Fairy Tales from the Old
    French,* retold by Quiller-Couch (London &
    New York: Hodder & Stoughton, 1910);
*The Oxford Book of Ballads,* edited by Quiller-Couch
    (Oxford: Clarendon, 1910);
*The Oxford Book of Victorian Verse,* edited by Quiller-
    Couch (Oxford: Clarendon, 1912);
*In Powder & Crinoline: Old Fairy Tales Retold,* edited by
    Quiller-Couch (London: Hodder & Stough-
    ton, 1913); published as *The Twelve Dancing
    Princesses and Other Fairy Tales Retold* (New
    York: Doran, 1923);
*The Cambridge Editions of the Works of Shakespeare: The
    Comedies,* edited with introductions by Quiller-
    Couch and J. Dover Wilson (Cambridge:
    Cambridge University Press, 1921–1931; New
    York: Macmillan, 1921–1966);
*A Bible Anthology,* edited by Quiller-Couch (London:
    Dent, 1922; New York: Dutton, 1922);
*The Oxford Book of English Prose,* edited by Quiller-
    Couch (Oxford: Clarendon, 1925);
*Felicities of Thomas Traherne,* edited by Quiller-Couch
    (London: P. J. & A. E. Dobell, 1934).

At the end of the nineteenth century, Arthur
Quiller-Couch was a prominent man of letters, one
of a group of literary, often scholarly, journalists
whose work filled the pages of the better magazines
with short stories, book reviews, and causeries. As
assistant editor of the liberal weekly *The Speaker,*
published by Cassell from 1890 to 1899, "Q.," as he
usually signed his works, met and worked with
many of the major writers of the period, including
Oscar Wilde, George Moore, J. M. Barrie, Lord
Acton, William Butler Yeats, William Watson, and
Henry James. Cassell also published Q's first novels
and provided a steady stream of commissions, some
for hackwork and some for creative work. Q wrote
twenty-one published novels and left one unfinished
at the time of his death. Thirteen of the novels dealt
in some way with Cornwall and its people: sometimes tangentially, often humorously, but always
with affection. The nine others ranged over time,
events, and style without the common thread of
place.

One facet of Q as a novelist, therefore, is as
the great chronicler of Cornwall and the Cornish, a
position further reinforced by his scores of short
stories. His is a restricted window, however, for Q

*Cover for Q's 1887 adventure novel, strongly influenced by
the work of Robert Louis Stevenson (courtesy of the Lilly
Library, Indiana University)*

disliked the brooding, dark side of humanity and
wrote little of it. Another facet is as the adventurist:
Q's most popular novels were rousing tales of daring exploits in foreign lands. These are the most
perishable of Q's novels, and unlike Robert Louis
Stevenson's works, which influenced them, they
have had little to offer succeeding generations. A
third facet is as an explorer of human character,
both male and female; Q was particularly adept at
depicting a woman in distress.

The eldest of five children, Arthur Thomas
Quiller-Couch (pronounced "Cooch") was born in
Bodmin, Cornwall, on 21 November 1863. His father, Thomas Quiller Couch, was a doctor, descended from generations of Cornishmen from the
fishing village of Polperro. His mother, Mary Ford
Quiller Couch, was from Devonshire, near Newton
Abbot. Q's father was an amateur painter and naturalist, as well as a writer on Cornish antiquities and
folklore, and his grandfather, Jonathan Couch,

wrote a major treatise on ichthyology, *The History of British Fishes* (1836).

When Q came of age, he went to Newton Abbot College, staying with his mother's parents for the first two of his seven years there. Financial difficulties at home induced him to try for a scholarship at one of the bigger public schools, and he was successful in the examination for Clifton College, Bristol. Established in 1862, Clifton College had grown to nearly seven hundred boys when Q entered the school in 1880. In his first year he won the school prize for an original English poem on a set theme – Athens. His principal competitor was Henry Newbolt, who became a lifelong friend. In 1882 Q went to Trinity College, Oxford, where he was befriended by Charles Cannan, a fellow of the college and a future secretary of the university press. In 1885 Cannan accepted the editorship of *The Oxford Magazine* with the understanding that Q would lend a hand. Some of Q's finest poems and parodies were written for this journal, and it was here that he began signing his works with the initial "Q." A second-class degree dashed his hopes of a fellowship, and a financial reverse for his grandfather thrust him into the position of supporting his mother and four brothers and sisters. At this time he impetuously asked Louisa Amelia Hicks, who lived in the little Cornish port of Fowey, to marry him. She accepted, but the ceremony had to wait until his finances were in better shape.

In 1886, before taking up a one-year lectureship at Trinity College, Q earned money during the summer vacation by tutoring the son of Lord Leconfields at Petworth, Sussex. While at Petworth Q started *Dead Man's Rock* (1887), his first novel. It was completed at Oxford and accepted by Cassell in May 1887. This was the beginning of a long association with Cassell, which immediately contracted with Q for another novel.

*Dead Man's Rock* is an adventure story, strongly influenced by Stevenson (whose works were also published by Cassell), and it sold fairly well. The next year Fowey (pronounced "Foy") and its inhabitants were comically portrayed in Q's *The Astonishing History of Troy Town* (1888), and this was followed by *The Splendid Spur* (1888), another adventure tale in the Stevensonian style, this time of the English Civil War. Both books sold well (*The Splendid Spur* remained popular for decades, and an Arabic translation by one of Q's students did very well in 1939) and enabled the author to pay off his father's debts and to marry Louisa on 22 August 1889. By this time Q had moved to London, where he mostly wrote freelance articles for Cassell.

In 1890 Q began writing for *The Speaker* and assisting its editor, Thomas Wemyss Reid. This periodical published articles on politics, literature, and the arts; its political slant was liberal and tilted to the more radical side of the movement. There Q met many notable artists and began his lifelong friendship with J. M. Barrie. Throughout the year and into 1891, Q wrote constantly – a weekly story or causerie for *The Speaker,* various stories for other magazines, and a draft of his fourth novel. He had added responsibilities by this time: a son, Bevil Bryan, was born in Fowey in October 1890. The first and finest of Q's twelve short-story collections, *Noughts and Crosses: Stories, Studies, and Sketches,* appeared in 1891. Most of the stories were from *The Speaker,* and they drew heavily on Cornish legends and superstition. *The Blue Pavilions* (1891) was also published and was another adventure tale, though this time none of the action takes place in Cornwall. It is set in the time of William III and traces the friendship of two English captains during the latter part of the seventeenth century.

The pace of work caught up with Q in the autumn of 1891, and he suffered a nervous breakdown. His doctor's prescription was to leave the city and live by the sea, advice the writer was happy to take. In early 1892, having agreed to continue to write for *The Speaker* wherever he lived, Q joined his family in Fowey. The house he bought there, The Haven, remained his home until his death fifty-two years later.

Q's health gradually returned, and by the fall of 1893 he was completely recovered. He continued his work for *The Speaker* and resumed his other writing. Q collected more of his magazine articles in *I Saw Three Ships, and Other Winter's Tales* (1892). That same year Q and the painter Alfred Parsons jointly produced their impressions of a trip down the river Avon in *The Warwickshire Avon* (1892).

During the following seven years, Q wrote or edited fifteen major works. A second collection of stories, mostly from *The Speaker* and about Cornwall, appeared as *The Delectable Duchy: Stories, Studies, and Sketches* (1893). The title was so popular that it became a synonym for Cornwall. Less well received was his *Green Bays: Verses and Parodies* (1893), a compilation of light verse and college parodies. A letter from the future poet laureate Robert Bridges in January 1893 began a lifelong friendship, mostly conducted through the mails, but with occasional visits at Oxford or London, and once Fowey.

Then came another collection of tales, again mostly from magazines other than *The Speaker,* titled *Wandering Heath: Stories, Studies, and Sketches* (1895).

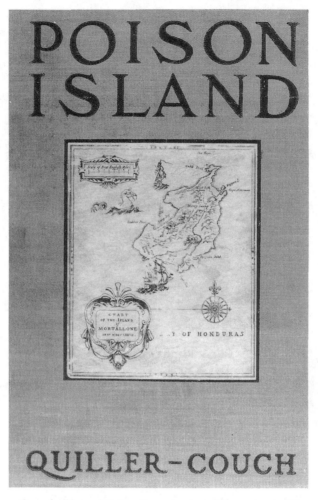

*Cover for Q's novel that combines adventure with comedy, something that, according to Q, Stevenson "had just failed to do" in* The Wreckers *(1892)*

His first poetical anthology, *The Golden Pomp, a Procession of English Lyrics from Surrey to Shirley* (1895), was well received. *Ia: A Love Story* (1895), the sad story of a young Cornish girl who falls in love with a rogue of a higher class, came out and sold poorly. In 1896 Q was also asked to finish Stevenson's novel *St. Ives* (1898). The last six chapters – nearly a quarter of the 312 pages – were written by Q and were highly praised. Q's material is so well integrated and so imitative of Stevenson's style that few can tell where Q begins and Stevenson ends. In the meantime Q's collection titled *Adventures in Criticism* (1896) was published. It shows a wide range of reading from Laurence Sterne, whose work Q defended, to Sir Walter Scott, Emile Zola, Björnstjerne Björnson, Henrik Ibsen, and George Moore.

Q returned to character study in his novel *The Ship of Stars* (1899). Much autobiographical material

is in this story of a Cornishman who goes to Oxford, has to leave when his father dies (Q barely escaped this fate), and then makes his way successfully without a degree. With its excellent style and superb characterization, *The Ship of Stars* is one of Q's best novels.

That same year Q tried to emulate Charles and Mary Lamb by recounting in modern prose the history plays of Shakespeare, but his *Historical Tales from Shakespeare* (1899) never caught the public's fancy. A short book of light verse, *A Fowey Garland,* also came out at this time.

In the spring of 1899 Q met Kenneth Grahame, and they quickly became friends. Grahame liked Fowey so much that he and his fiancée were married there the following summer, and during the three Sundays that the wedding banns were called in Fowey Church, Grahame stayed at The Haven. Fowey made a covert appearance in Grahame's

*The Haven, Q's home in the Cornish port of Fowey*

*Wind in the Willows* when the Sea Rat describes "the little grey sea town that clings along one steep side of the harbour."

Another collection of Q's tales, *Old Fires and Profitable Ghosts: A Book of Stories* (1900) largely concerned mysteries and the netherworld. As he was preparing this volume for publication, Q was also furiously readying his second anthology of poetry, *The Oxford Book of English Verse, 1250–1900* (1900), for the university press. His friend Cannan, at this time secretary of the Clarendon Press, had asked Q to do the book, and the result was the finest anthology of verse published to that time. It took some time to gain acceptance, but by 1912 its popularity was so great that *The Oxford Magazine* could jest that "no civilized person in Great Britain, the Dominions, or the United States is married" without receiving a copy of the book. When Q revised and expanded it in 1939, the anthology had gone through twenty editions. Neither Q nor Cannan suspected that the *Oxford Book of English Verse* would be the progenitor of scores of Oxford anthologies. Q himself added to the list with *The Oxford Book of Ballads* (1910), *The Oxford Book of Victorian Verse* (1912), and *The Oxford Book of English Prose* (1925).

Between 1900 and his return to academia in 1912, Q wrote or edited twenty volumes of fiction, thirteen of which were novels. He also published a book of poems, *The Vigil of Venus and Other Poems* (1912), edited *Pervigilum Veneris* (1911) for the Oxford Plain Text series, edited a variety of children's books and a series of great English writers, and wrote introductions to works by others. He turned out scores of short stories in *The Laird's Luck and Other Fireside Tales* (1901), *The White Wolf and Other Fireside Tales* (1902), *Two Sides of the Face: Midwinter Tales* (1903), *Shakespeare's Christmas and Other Stories* (1905), *Merry-Garden and Other Stories* (1907), and *Corporal Sam and Other Stories* (1910).

In three of the novels of this period, Q returned to the study of women. *The Westcotes* (1902) sympathetically deals with the story of an unattractive, middle-aged woman who loves a much younger man. *Hetty Wesley* (1903) combines actual documents with a fictional narrative to tell the unhappy story of Hetty and her famous family, including her brothers John and Charles. Despite denunciations in the Methodist press, *Hetty Wesley* was very popular, sold well, and ranks with *The Ship of Stars* as Q's finest effort. In *Lady Good-for-Nothing* (1910) Q again

turned to the theme of a maltreated woman. This novel was based on a true story set in New England: the loves and adventures of Sir Henry Frankland, collector of Boston Port; and Agnes Surriage, daughter of a poor fisherman.

The action in Q's *The Adventures of Harry Revel* (1903) ranges from Plymouth in 1813 to Spain during the Peninsular War. Several of the characters in this book return in *Poison Island* (1906), a novel Q described as an attempt to do what Stevenson "had just failed to do in *The Wreckers,*" that is, to combine adventure with comedy. *Fort Amity* (1904), set in Canada during the Seven Years' War, essays the effect war has on a young officer and presents sympathetically the suffering caused by the condition now commonly termed shell shock.

Two novels of the period renew Q's chronicles of life in Fowey: *Shining Ferry* (1905) is based on the author's work to establish an elementary school system in Cornwall, and *Hocken and Hunken, A Tale of Troy* (1912) is a comedy that centers on the yearly regatta in Fowey harbor. Q turned to another part of Cornwall, the Scilly Isles, for *Major Vigoureux* (1907), which exhibits the political sentiments behind a contemporary Liberal Party slogan, "Land for the People."

Q claimed another of his novels from this period, *Sir John Constantine* (1905), as his favorite work. Strongly influenced by Q's admiration for Miguel de Cervantes, the book relates the adventures of a Cornish knight in Corsica during the eighteenth-century struggle for independence. The hero reflects much of Q's personality in his nobility of mind and concern for the weak and oppressed. Also written at this time was *The Mayor of Troy* (1905), a humorous novel that relates the downfall of the pompous mayor who, captured during the Napoleonic Wars by the French, returns to Troy after many adventures only to find that he had not been missed.

In *True Tilda* (1909) Q tells the story of two children who get lost and make their way down the Warwickshire Avon to the sea. Along the way they helped everyone they asked for help. Two years later Q incorporated much of his political and philosophical beliefs in *Brother Copas* (1911), which is set in an almshouse and depicts the petty feuds within that institution. It is uncharacteristically scornful, probably reflecting Q's reaction to the demise of Liberal hopes and his concern for a future over which German power was already casting a pall. The title character serves as a mouthpiece for Q's political opinions: patriotic, Liberal, distrustful of

German critics of English literature, and conscious of national failings.

In addition to the quantity and variety of his literary work, Q managed to maintain a full social and public life in Fowey and Cornwall. A strong supporter of the Liberal Party, Q worked tirelessly for improvements in Cornish education (serving on the county educational committee for thirty years), served as a justice of the peace, and held several local offices. His popularity in the county was only briefly diminished by his courageous opposition to the Boer War in the early 1900s, though nationally it cost him sales and caused him financial hardship. His ultimate reward for faithful service to the party, though a surprise to Q when it came, was knighthood in 1910.

In 1912 Q was appointed the second King Edward VII Professor of English Literature at the University of Cambridge, replacing the noted classicist Arthur Woolgar Verrall. His duties at the university soon precluded his fiction writing, and he completed only two novels and two collections of short stories afterward. A third novel, *Castle Dor,* left unfinished at his death, was completed by Daphne du Maurier in 1961.

Q's appointment to the position was controversial: most members of the university knew him only as a novelist, but he proved a popular lecturer and indefatigable proponent of a school of English literature. His inaugural lecture was a great success and showed how deeply he had absorbed the classics. His critics must have been surprised when he opened with words about Plato's "The Laws" and moved to Cardinal Newman, Lucian, Cervantes, Samuel Johnson, Thomas à Kempis, Thomas Carlyle, and others before closing with homage to the French critic Charles-Augustin Sainte-Beuve. In this beginning, Q set forth principals by which he would approach literary studies. First, he said that a work of genius should be studied with the intention of understanding "just what the author's mind intended." This meant to Q principally the study of an author's works and only secondarily the perusal of scholarly commentators, though some early writers required a guide from the beginning. He also stressed that the study of "style" would not degenerate into mere dilettantism, because of the search for the concrete intention and the avoiding of general definitions and theories that would likely prove inadequate in explaining the achievement of genius. His main argument was that "Literature is an Art," not an exact science with exact definitions, "the success of which depends on personal persuasiveness, on the author's skill to give as on ours to receive." Q also

*Q in uniform as the commodore of the Royal Fowey Yacht Club*

emphasized that English was a living language: thus, it must be practiced and "kept alive, supple, active in all honourable use."

These early lectures were usually presented to a packed lecture room, and their publication in 1916 in *On the Art of Writing* expanded Q's audience. For the next fifteen years Q's collections of lectures and essays sold well throughout the English-speaking world, and many were translated into French and German.

During the First World War Q published two novels: *Nicky-Nan, Reservist* (1915) records the effect of the war's beginning on an English village through the story of a penurious naval reservist; *Foe-Farrell* (1918) warns the English not to let their zeal in prosecuting the war turn them into the enemy. This tale relates the story of two men who wreck each others' lives, and in the end the victim, through his hate, has "exchanged nature[s]" with his enemy, whom he has killed. The novel's epigraph, a quotation from Marcus Aurelius, sums up the story's moral: "The best kind of revenge is not to become like him." The last of Q's novels to be completed, *Foe-Farrell* received little favor from critics but was popular with the public.

Q expended much effort at this time in the campaign to establish a school of English at Cambridge. Allied with H. F. Stewart, a fellow of Saint Johns and later Trinity, and H. M. Chadwick, professor of Anglo-Saxon, Q argued for an English Tripos examination separate from the Medieval and Modern Languages Tripos, which meant philology and Anglo-Saxon would be optional and replaceable by literary criticism and comparative literature. Despite some opposition inside the university and outside by the English Association, the three allies carried the day in the late spring of 1917.

Soon thereafter, however, Q's personal world crumbled when his son Bevil died on 6 February 1919 while serving with the Allied occupation forces in Germany. Q never completely recovered from this tragedy. For a time he considered resigning his professorship but decided to stay and throw himself into his work.

In the first years of the 1920s Q began editing The King's Treasuries of Literature, a series of text-

books for the publisher J. M. Dent that would grow to more than 250 volumes in Q's lifetime. For Cambridge University Press, Q joined Professor Dover Wilson in editing Shakespeare's plays. He provided the introductions to the fourteen comedies before withdrawing from the project in 1931. The university press also enlisted Q to work with two colleagues, Alexander Nairne and T. R. Glover, to produce three biblical anthologies: *The Children's Bible* and *The Little Children's Bible* appeared in 1924, and *The Cambridge Shorter Bible* came out four years later. Q also continued his *Studies in Literature* (three series: 1918, 1922, 1929), which presented a selection of his lectures and articles. A separate volume of lectures was collected in *Charles Dickens and Other Victorians* (1925). In the mid 1920s Q began to develop serious eye trouble and feared he would become blind, but by 1927 the problem had passed. The next year Dent began publishing a thirty-volume collected edition of his work with new introductions by the author.

Modifying the Tripos continued to occupy Q during the 1920s. His major contribution was a paper on English moralists that was adopted as a requirement in 1928. During this period he continued to serve on Cornwall's Educational Committee, gave lectures around the country, especially in Oxford, delivered addresses to the Village Drama Society, and attended many clubs, meetings, and dining societies.

In the 1930s Q published a final volume of collected lectures and essays, titled *The Poet as Citizen, and Other Papers* (1934), and he revised and expanded *The Oxford Book of English Verse* (1939). He also began his memoirs, *Memories and Opinions* (1944), and returned to his draft of *Castle Dor*. Both would be finished by others.

Q died on 12 May 1944, several weeks after he fell stepping out of the way of a military vehicle. The shock weakened his resistance, and he succumbed to cancer of the mouth, a condition brought about by a lifetime of smoking. Q was the quintessential storyteller and at his best in the short story. As a novelist he was ahead of his time in describing shell shock and notable for his defense of women, as well as choosing many of his chivalrous heroes from the poorer classes. He believed in the nobility of the human race and did not equate money or high social status with virtue. His chronicles of life in Cornwall at the turn of the century are unsurpassed, but his adventure tales and more serious works are largely forgotten. Partly this neglect is the result of changing tastes, but more fundamentally it reflects Q's inability to deal adequately with the darker human emotions or portray more than superficial evil. But the revamped school system in Cornwall; the English School at Cambridge; and a cultural guidepost of the twentieth century, *The Oxford Book of English Verse,* remain as his legacy.

**Biographies:**

F. Brittain, *Arthur Quiller-Couch. A Biographical Study of Q* (Cambridge: Cambridge University Press, 1947);

A. L. Rowse, *Quiller Couch. A Portrait of "Q"* (London: Methuen, 1988).

**Papers:**

Trinity College, Oxford, has created a "Q" archive that includes manuscripts, letters, and various materials such as photographs and book reviews. The family retains most of Q's letters that are basically personal. In the National Library of Scotland are several dozen letters between Q and Professor John Dover Wilson concerning their collaborative Shakespeare edition. Other major holdings of Q's correspondence are in the possession of Jesus College, Cambridge; Cambridge University Library; Harry Ransom Humanities Research Center, University of Texas at Austin; Princeton University Library; the British Library; the Beinecke Rare Book and Manuscript Library, Yale University; and the archives at Oxford University Press.

# Forrest Reid

*(24 June 1875 – 4 January 1947)*

George J. Johnson

BOOKS: *The Kingdom of Twilight* (London: Unwin, 1904);

*The Garden God: A Tale of Two Boys* (London: Nutt, 1905);

*The Bracknels: A Family Chronicle* (London: Arnold, 1911);

*Following Darkness* (London: Arnold, 1912);

*The Gentle Lover: A Comedy of Middle Age* (London: Arnold, 1913);

*W. B. Yeats: A Critical Study* (London: Secker, 1915; New York: Dodd, Mead, 1915);

*At the Door of the Gate* (London: Arnold, 1915; Boston & New York: Houghton Mifflin, 1916);

*The Spring Song* (London: Arnold, 1916; Boston & New York: Houghton Mifflin, 1917);

*A Garden by the Sea. Stories and Sketches* (Dublin: Talbot Press, 1918; London: Unwin, 1918);

*Pirates of the Spring* (Dublin: Talbot Press, 1919; London: Unwin, 1919; Boston & New York: Houghton Mifflin, 1920);

*Pender Among the Residents* (London: Collins, 1922; Boston & New York: Houghton Mifflin, 1923);

*Apostate* (London: Constable, 1926; Boston & New York: Houghton Mifflin, 1926);

*Demophon: A Traveller's Tale* (London: Collins, 1927);

*Illustrators of the Sixties* (London: Faber & Gwyer, 1928); published as *Illustrators of the Eighteen Sixties: An Illustrated Survey of the Work of 58 British Artists* (New York: Dover, 1975);

*Walter De La Mare: A Critical Study* (London: Faber & Faber, 1929; New York: Holt, [1929]);

*Uncle Stephen* (London: Faber & Faber, 1931; revised, 1945);

*Brian Westby* (London: Faber & Faber / Toronto: Ryerson, 1934);

*The Retreat; or, the Machinations of Henry* (London: Faber & Faber / Toronto: Ryerson, 1936);

*Peter Waring* (London: Faber & Faber / Toronto: Ryerson, 1937);

*Private Road* (London: Faber & Faber / Toronto: Ryerson, 1940; New York: AMS Press, 1978);

*Forrest Reid in December 1907*

*Retrospective Adventures* (London: Faber & Faber / Toronto: Ryerson, 1941);

*Notes and Impressions* (Newcastle: Mourne, 1942);

*Young Tom; or, Very Mixed Company* (London: Faber & Faber, 1944);

*The Milk of Paradise. Some Thoughts on Poetry* (London: Faber & Faber, 1946);

*Denis Bracknel* (London: Faber & Faber, 1947);

*Tom Barber* (New York: Pantheon, 1955) – includes *Young Tom, The Retreat,* and *Uncle Stephen.*

OTHER: "Modern Irish Prose: the Novel," in *The Voice of Ireland,* edited by W. G. Fitzgerald (Dublin: Heywood, 1923), pp. 481–484;

*Poems from the Greek Anthology,* translated by Reid (London: Faber & Faber, 1943).

SELECTED PERIODICAL PUBLICATIONS –
UNCOLLECTED:
FICTION
"Pan's Pupil," *Ulad,* 1 (May 1905): 17–19;
"The Visitors," *Living Age* (6 December 1919): 604–607;
"Orange Peel," *Nation and Atheneum* (30 April 1921): 168–169.
POETRY
"The Earth Cry," *Northern Whig* (24 July 1905);
"By the Nursery Fire," *Irishman* (15 January 1916).
NONFICTION
"The Exhibition of Pictures at the Royal Hibernian Academy, Dublin," *Ulad,* 1 (February 1905): 20–23;
"Ernest Dowson," *Monthly Review* (June 1905): 107–113;
"Emily Bronte," *Northern Whig* (2 June 1906);
"The Novels of George Moore," *Westminster Review* (August 1909): 200–208;
"The Exhibition of Pictures in the Free Library, Belfast," *Northern Whig* (4 August 1911);
"Modern Picture Galleries: a Lecture," *Evening Telegraph* (Belfast) (27 and 29 November 1911);
"The Boy in Fiction," *Morning Post* (9 September 1912);
"Henry James," *Irishman* (15 March 1916): 3–4;
"The Poetical Works of Lionel Johnson," *Irishman* (15 March 1916): 15;
"Poems Pleasant and Unpleasant," *Irish Statesman* (6 March 1920);
"British Literature," *Times of Brazil* (15 June 1920);
"The Ulster Players," *Times* (5 December 1922);
"Some Recent Painters," *Times* (5 December 1922);
"Hopes for Ulster Literature," *Ulster Review* (January 1925);
"The Poetry of the Rose," *Rose Annual* (1929): 124–127;
"Charles Keene, Illustrator," *Printed Collectors Quarterly* (January 1930): 23–47;
"Criticism and Reviewing," *Current Literature* (February 1932);
"The Artist and the World Today," *Bookman* (May 1934): 93;
"Childhood and Children," *Listener* (8 May 1935);
"Wizard of Fonthill," *Listener* (10 March 1937);
"Fiction," *Spectator* (28 May 1937–8 September 1939);
"Written with Second Thoughts," *Readers' News,* no. 17 (January 1939): 2–3.

As an Ulsterman who was averse to both oriental mysticism and the formal interest in psychical research espoused by many contemporary English writers, Forrest Reid may appear out of place in a volume on British novelists. Early in his career, however, Reid broke from the Irish Literary Revival's tradition and spurned the Northern Irish Ulster Renaissance. Indeed, in *Cavalcade of the English Novel* (1954), the American critic Edward Wagenknecht labels Reid "one of the outstanding individualists among contemporary British novelists." His lack of popularity can be explained, too, by the narrow range of his subjects; by the controversial relationships depicted, especially following Oscar Wilde's trial in 1895 and Britain's Censorship Bill (1928) forbidding writing about "non-normal" behavior; by what E. M. Forster called Reid's inability "to pull wires or advertise himself"; and by his persistence in remaining, unknown, in Belfast despite attempts, notably by Walter de la Mare, to resettle him in England. Lastly, his rejection of the more-organized approaches to the paranormal did not mean that he eschewed this area altogether: he felt that "the spiritual world offers far more opportunity for conscious artistry than the world of everyday reality"; he also established his values through the use of fantasy. Mary C. Bryan attributed the author's approach to his Celtic racial inheritance, which gave him "a Celt's feeling for mystery, the remote, and the distant; for the supernatural in the natural; for the psychic states of feeling; and, of course, for dreams."

Forrest Reid was born on 24 June 1875. His Irish father, Robert Reid, came from a well-established middle-class Presbyterian family, but Forrest was equally proud that his mother, Frances Parr Reid, could trace her English lineage to the eleventh century; consequently, Robert Reid's overnight loss of his Liverpool shipping business compounded the religious and social differences already existing between himself and the aristocratic Church of Ireland, as well as his wife and her family, who already considered Robert socially inferior. When he returned to Belfast, Reid's father was reduced to managing Anderson's felt works. Adelaide, the eldest Reid child and one of three girls, was fourteen years older than Forrest; while Charlie, the youngest of his three brothers, was four years older. Reid never felt close to his seemingly indifferent mother; his father, who died when Forrest was five, he barely remembered.

His father's death caused even more straitened circumstances, necessitating a move to a smaller house and probably the loss of Reid's only adult

*Andrew Rutherford, whom Reid met in the 1890s, when both boys served as apprentices to a tea and sugar merchant. For Reid their friendship embodied the Hellenic ideal, and he referred to Rutherford as his first love.*

provider of security and companionship: the family nurse, Emma Holmes, who had encouraged his imagination and love of animals by helping him "feed" the stone lions at the local botanic gardens; during Emma's Sunday Scripture reading he was allowed to play at her feet or to create marvelous dream landscapes. Shortly after his father's death, Emma left abruptly, waking Forrest to announce her departure. Separation from the only religious person with whom he felt comfortable led the boy to rebel even more strongly against the restrictive atmosphere of Sunday and the orthodoxy of the Church of Ireland; the weekly battles culminated in Reid's refusal to attend church following his confirmation.

Emma's departure also meant that, during the interval before his formal education began at Miss Hardy's Prep School, the reluctant Reid was taught by his resentful sister Adelaide. In September 1888

he entered the Royal Belfast Academical Institution, but he did not devote much of his energy to his studies there. Reid did, however, gain access to the classics and the imaginative work of writers such as Edgar Allan Poe; at age eleven he wrote his first "novel," "Tom Vere"; and, most important, he became conscious of an internal private life dominated by "paganism, the Greek view of nature, [and] the adoration of youth," which was as real as his external schoolboy life. Following graduation in 1891, Reid's dream life gradually disappeared and he became more depressed at not finding employment; he even attempted suicide.

Early in 1893 Reid was apprenticed to Henry Musgrave, a tea and sugar merchant. Because the work was routine, Reid found himself with spare time, which he spent studying Greek in a den that he constructed in the warehouse attic. During this time Reid also discovered the ideal Socratic relationship with Andrew Rutherford, a fellow apprentice, with whom Reid shared his most intimate thoughts in a journal he had composed during the development of their friendship; Reid felt that his giving Andrew the journal to read on 1 February 1896 marked his transition from boyhood to manhood and his first love. Reid never fully relinquished his boyhood, however, and his writing, largely autobiographical, deals mainly with childhood and adolescence as he tried to recapture the happiness of life with Emma and compensate for the loss of human affection from his mother and, later, Rutherford.

Despite his mother's lack of maternal affection, Reid joined her in moving to a smaller house, where they lived together until her death in 1901. In the interval he developed an interest in opera and broadened his study of Greek culture, especially the lesser gods, Pan and Hermes, thus completing his rejection of Christianity. His mother's death provided Reid with funds, and Rutherford coached him to pass the examinations to enter Christ's College, Cambridge, in October 1905, but Reid's age (thirty), his broad reading background and established tastes, and his having already written two novels contributed to his feeling that Cambridge offered him little.

Reid's first two novels, *The Kingdom of Twilight* (1904) and *The Garden God: A Tale of Two Boys* (1905), demonstrate the early influences on his technique and introduced his major themes. Forty years after the publication of the first novel, Reid admitted that its "pretentious title points to [Gabriel] D'Annunzio, the opening sentence is pure Henry James. I detest this book." Nevertheless, from James

and Walter Pater, Reid learned the value of diction, syntax, and overall structure, although twenty years later he was inspired to align his style more closely to the Hellenic ideal found in the clarity of Anatole France.

Reid's first two novels also introduce his significant themes, which focus on youth, nature, and fantasy or the supernatural. Reid's obsession with boyhood and youth allowed him to compensate for his own childhood unhappiness by creating characters and situations he could control and alter at will. In seeking the Hellenic ideals of beauty, goodness, and truth, most of Reid's fictional boys, innocent but precocious, seek either the friendship of a peer, as Reid had with Rutherford, or that of a teacher, as the students of Socrates had done. This tendency has led to assumptions that Reid was homosexual, but Brian Taylor refutes this claim, suggesting instead that, "If there can be such a thing as a puritanical pederast, Forrest Reid was that person."

From the ancient Greeks Reid also gained support for his feeling of kinship with nature, which extended beyond the writing of descriptive passages to an animism that, coupled with his humanism, dominated his view of life. It showed itself most clearly in his treatment of animals, and particularly dogs, likely the consequence of a stern mother who forbade him to have a pet, or a nurse who assisted him in feeding the stone lions, or even his own need for constant and unquestioning affection.

Dogs in Reid's novels often have the ability to speak to their young masters, thus developing Reid's third typical theme, variously labeled supranormal, supernatural, or fantasy. As strange dreams or visions, the fantastic element in Reid's novels either creates an unreal atmosphere or serves as the basis for plot. This use of dreams was natural for a writer who as a child created his own private, heavenly dream world, who as an adolescent saw "dream landscapes, the sadness of beauty, the dream playmate, and . . . the disturbing figure of destiny," and who as an adult envisaged novels in dreams. To the charge that he was an escapist Reid responded that his work was "what *I* should call the literature of imagination for the escape is only from the impermanent into the permanent."

Reid was dissatisfied with *The Kingdom of Twilight* even before its publication. He apologized to Rutherford, to whom the book was dedicated, complained about the appearance of the bound volumes, and attempted to destroy any copy he could obtain by fair or foul means. In the novel Willie Trevelyan sets the pattern for Reid heroes: he is imaginative, sensitive, and unusual. Resembling Reid,

*Reid with E. M. Forster; the two men met in 1911 and remained friends until Reid's death in 1947*

Willie rebels against the strict religion of his father, the Reverend Arthur Trevelyan, creates his own imaginary world, enters the tea business, and extends his affections toward his friend Nick Grayson; unlike Reid, however, he has the love of a cousin, Eva.

Beginning with Willie's unexplained return from an English boarding school, the first part of the novel presents ordinary incidents involving the protagonist and observations about him by family and friends. The second and least successful part of the work depicts his search for good while beset by obstacles, including the "strangely beautiful" Mrs. Hester Urquhart. The final section leaps ahead nine years, recounts the events occurring in the interval, and continues with Willie's solitary return to Ireland, following the death of his son, Prospero. There he works on his autobiography, and Eva joins him. Reid's immature and imitative style fails in dealing with adult characters and situations.

Reid also disliked his second novel, which he labeled a "false start." Originally titled "The River," after the Lagan River in Dublin, it was revised and

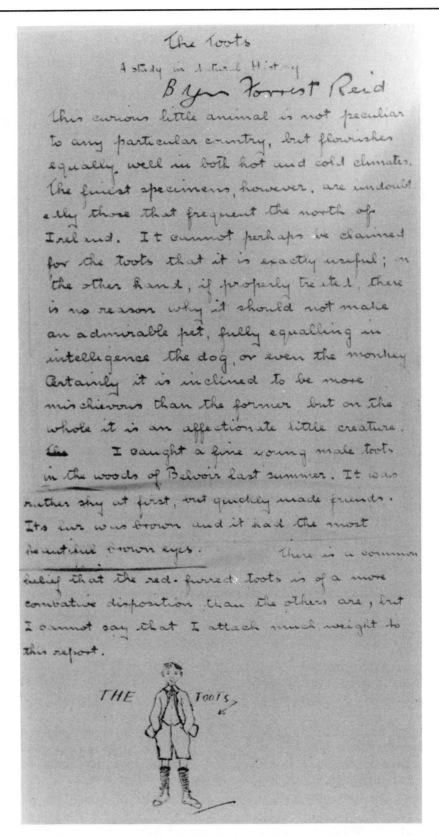

*Page from the first issue (1917) of* Kenneth's Magazine, *which Reid produced in collaboration with twelve-year-old Kenneth Hamilton and exists only in manuscript. The page includes the beginning of a story by Reid that humorously recounts their early friendship, with a drawing by the author (from Brian Taylor,* The Green Avenue, *1980).*

issued as *The Garden God: A Tale of Two Boys* six years later, just one month after Reid entered Cambridge in October 1905. This novel also features a maturing young boy, but in this case Graham Iddesleigh's story is told from his perspective as an adult, musing on his school days and particularly on the summer visit of Harold Brocklehurst, who had become, for the motherless Graham, the living embodiment of an imaginary playmate in a beautiful dream world inhabited by gods and goddesses. Following an idyllic day, sensuously described by Reid and including a somewhat erotic pagan ritual, Harold sacrifices his life for Graham. After seeing Harold later in a vision, Graham spends thirty years with only melancholy remembrances. Reid was devastated by the reception of the book, especially by the furious response of Henry James, to whom it was dedicated. What Reid saw as the fictitious depiction of a platonic friendship, James saw as perverse; the outcome was the termination of their friendship.

In 1908, following his graduation from Cambridge and a summer tour of Europe, Reid returned to Ireland where he met young Denis "Skinny" Bracknel, the inspiration for his next novel, which Reid outlined that same evening. Originally intended as a lyrical romance titled "The Moon Story," it emerged three years later as a realistic novel, *The Bracknels: A Family Chronicle* (1911). In the interval Reid moved to his first nonfamily residence, which he shared with one of Rutherford's brothers, a twin, Rev. James Rutherford; he acquired dogs; and, in his search for spiritual values, he rejected psychical experiences and eastern mysticism in favor of his own paganism.

This latter belief influenced Reid's creation of another sensitive outsider as the protagonist of *The Bracknels*. Fifteen-year-old Denis Bracknel is the youngest member of a family dominated by an unpleasant father — other family members include a weak mother; a brother, Alfred; and two sisters, May and Amy. Denis's isolation is somewhat mitigated by a new tutor, Hubert Rusk, who, although sympathetic, is mystified when he observes Denis late one night in a secret grove performing a pagan ritual to the moon. Denis relates his father's sudden death to one of his own recurring dreams, and as a result he hangs himself. While the reviewer for *Nation* (9 December 1911) criticized the book because it was neither fully moon-worshiping fantasy nor completely realistic, he praised its descriptions of the Lagan valley and its treatment of the friendship theme and found it to be "a good example of a somber work of art, which braces and fortifies the spiri-

tual life by its very refusal to ignore things 'unpleasant.' "

During this period Reid met both Walter de la Mare and E. M. Forster, with whom he formed close personal and literary ties; within four months of their meeting Forster had agreed to having Reid's *Following Darkness* (1912) dedicated to him. The adult narrator of this novel, Owen Gill, presents a fragment of an autobiography by a schoolboy friend, Peter Waring, a dreamy, sensitive adolescent at the "dawn of obscure sex instincts." Peter shares a joyless house in Newcastle, County Down, with his father, David, who is a schoolmaster. The young man escapes frequently to Derryaghy House and his benefactor, Mrs. Carroll. There he meets Mrs. Carroll's niece Katherine, who becomes his first love, and her strange but talented nephew Gerald. From this pleasant summer experience Peter moves to Belfast, shares a shabby room with his cousin George, who has a "licentious imagination," and meets the intellectual Owen Gill. The following summer brings a changed Katherine and Peter's final confession to his surrogate mother, Mrs. Carroll, that he has been "following darkness," that is, he had given in to the power of evil. Forster was pleased to be connected with the novel; an American psychologist and authority on adolescence, G. Stanley Hall, commended its understanding of the psychology of youth, and, while *The Times Literary Supplement* criticized the book for not achieving "its own intention," the review concluded that "*Following Darkness* is not a book that will be easily forgotten."

Reid's writing of book reviews for the *Manchester Guardian* and the *Irish Statesman,* combined with James Rutherford's income, provided for their needs, as well as two trips to the Continent. Rutherford suggested the title for Reid's next novel, *The Gentle Lover: A Comedy of Middle Age* (1913). Although Reid did not like this title, it probably helped the book's sales, which were much better than those of his previous two novels. *The Gentle Lover* features adult characters and is the only one of Reid's novels to be set in Europe. It depicts the attraction of a middle-aged, gentle, Irish artist, Bennet Allingham, to the Grimshaw children, Brian and Sylvie. Through them he meets their mother, Lucy, the sister of Sophy Kilronan, a former close friend. Allingham's growing affection for Sylvie is countered by her love for the celibate Anglican priest, Mr. Halvard. While Allingham's attempt to resolve the situation fails, he is changed by the experience and looks for happiness elsewhere. In this work Reid was writing about relationships beyond his

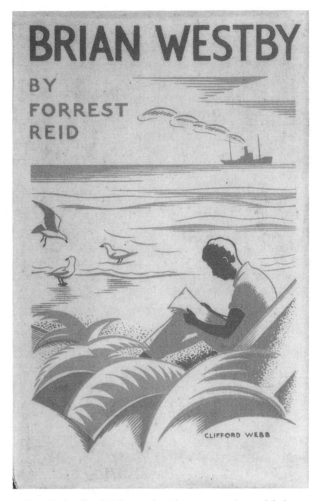

*Dust jacket for Reid's novel with a protagonist modeled on Stephen Gilbert, who would become the author's literary executor (courtesy of the Lilly Library, Indiana University)*

own experience; consequently, the *Times* reviewer claimed that "The plot is too slight for a story of this length and its *denouement* disappointing." Even Reid's friends found problems with the book: Theodore Bartholomew found it uncharacteristic of Reid, and Forster saw its action as inconsistent with its atmosphere.

Originally entitled "Three Women," the title the author preferred, Reid's next novel was published as *At the Door of the Gate* (1915). While it provides his only picture of Belfast working-class life, the story draws its themes from the biblical hound of heaven (depicted in P. 139:7–10); and the three Moerae (or Parcae), the Greek goddesses of fate. Furthermore, the plot uses the Cain and Abel story, with the younger, sensitive, and imaginative Richard Seawright developing an intense jealousy of his handsome but dissolute and fawning brother, Martin, who is favored by their widowed, working-class

mother. Adding to his troubles, Richard is in love with his mother's ward, Grace Mallow, although he is married to a shallow woman named Rose. Subsequent events lead to a violent fraternal confrontation, after which Richard finds himself cleansed and in harmony with the spirit of the earth. The credibility of the book's treatment of adult relationships was questioned by contemporary reviewers, and de la Mare, to whom the novel was dedicated, was not enthusiastic, although he did aid in having it published in the United States. Reviewers praised Reid's handling of the novel's themes, however, as well as his depictions of the two younger women and his descriptions of nature.

The title of Reid's seventh novel, *The Spring Song* (1916), is taken from an Italian aria and identifies the flute song heard by the thirteen-year-old hero, Griffith "Grif" Weston. Along with two brothers, two sisters, and one brother's friend from

school, Palmer Dorset, Grif is spending a carefree summer in the country with a generally congenial group of adults. Reid uses the myth of Orpheus and Pan to emphasize the mental turmoil in the mind of the sensitive and fragile Grif as he comes under the influence of the disturbed church organist, Dr. Bradley. When Grif becomes more ensnared and physically ill, Palmer and the local doctor investigate, with tragic consequences. Bradley commits suicide and Grif dies from the shock of discovering the truth behind Bradley's lies. Critics were generally positive, complimenting the novel's artistry and its characterizations of children, especially the younger ones, but expressed doubts about the book's mass appeal, doubts which proved well founded.

In the year 1916 James Rutherford married, and Reid, already devastated by this change, had to move to an industrial section of Belfast. In the summer his anguish was alleviated by a friendship he formed with twelve-year-old Kenneth Hamilton. They collaborated on *Kenneth's Magazine,* "published" irregularly between 1917 and 1919, with only one copy per issue. This relationship helped Reid through his grief in 1917, when Willie Rutherford, James's twin brother, was killed in France, a casualty of the war, and James departed to serve as a stretcher bearer.

Reid's perception of the male adolescent psyche is probably most clearly established in his *Pirates of the Spring* (1919), a psychological study of four schoolboys and their shifting relationships. Osborne School, patterned after the Royal Belfast Academical Institute, brings the group together, but most of the action occurs in the surrounding countryside or at Belvoir Park, the wealthy home of the central character, Beach Traill. He and the impoverished but brilliant scholarship student Evan Hayes develop a boyish infatuation that displaced Beach's relationship with Miles Oulton; intellectual differences then cause a transfer of Beach's friendship to the more direct and somewhat ruthless Palmer Dorset, a character who had appeared in Reid's previous novel. These changes occur amid schoolboy escapades, with adults as onlookers. *The New York Times* (28 March 1920) called the novel "a study handled delicately and sympathetically, with much subtlety and many deft touches of humour." The (London) *Times* also praised the book, claiming, "the boys are boys and not merely the mouthpieces of ideas."

In 1920 Hamilton joined the merchant service and corresponded with Reid as he traveled. Meanwhile, Reid published his next novel, *Pender Among the Residents* (1922). Patterned after de la Mare, middle-aged Rex Pender, a World War I veteran, has inherited Ramoan from his grandfather, Edward Kilmartin. The "residents" include a cousin, Nellie Burton, busy promoting Pender's marriage to her daughter, Norah; the neighbors, especially George Best, Norah's lover; and the ghosts of Pender's ancestors, whose pictures and letters lead Pender to become the unseen witness to an illicit romance of his great-aunt, Roxana Kilmartin, and to the murder of her husband's spy. Criticism was divided, with The (London) *Times* wondering why the fantasy was included with the country comedy or vice versa and *The New York Times* proclaiming that "there is no one writing today who exceeds [Reid] in the ability to deal effectively, persuasively with occult themes."

Four years passed before Reid's next novel was published. In the interval he moved to a semi-detached house subsidized by the local council, where he would remain until his death. *Apostate* (1926), written at the publisher's suggestion, is a spiritual autobiography depicting Reid's life to the time that he showed his diary to Andrew Rutherford at age seventeen. During the writing of his next novel, an unopened letter to Hamilton was returned to Reid from Australia marked "deceased." The heartbroken Reid later learned that Kenneth had traveled into the bush alone, never to be seen again.

*Demophon: A Traveller's Tale* (1927) is a mythological rendering of *Apostate,* with Reid being represented by the child Demophon, who is separated from Demeter, the life-giving force (nurse Emma Holmes), as she is attempting to immortalize him. The story follows the odyssey of Demophon as he travels to the mountains of Thessaly and back, in the process acquiring a humanistic education from the sages and a friend, Hermes, the idealized dream-child companion of *Apostate,* from whom he is then separated. Demophon's education teaches him that he is one with nature and that happiness lies within himself; while learning, he must reject physical desire, a death cult, and sexual temptation. The novel's conclusion brings reunion with the ideal friend, Hermes. The reviewer for the (London) *Times* found this resolution disappointing, but other critics praised the book's mythological scholarship, its believable, adolescent point of view, and its clear, simple style.

By December 1928 Reid had started "My Uncle's a Magician"; later he considered calling it "Music to the Wind"; it was finally published as *Uncle Stephen* (1931). During this period, in addition to book reviews and short articles, Reid published

*Reid's home at Knock, on the outskirts of Belfast, where he lived from 1924
until his death*

two nonfiction books: one an authoritative and well-documented study of illustrators of the 1860s, based on illustrations Reid had collected over the course of thirty-eight years; the other a critical study of the works of de la Mare, a difficult task since the two men consulted each other regularly on works in progress and de la Mare accommodated Reid on his annual trips to croquet tournaments in England. In April 1930 de la Mare invited Reid to be a fellow of the Royal Society of Literature.

Reid claimed that the basic idea and much of the earlier version of *Uncle Stephen* came from dreams. The novel opens with fifteen-year-old Tom Barber musing at his father's funeral. Soon thereafter, a sympathetic stepsister, Jane, aids his flight to his sixty-three-year-old great-uncle Stephen Collet, an eccentric recluse who keeps a fragmented statue of Hermes in his room and divines Tom's arrival. While Stephen starts the practical process of adoption, Tom visits and journeys with Philip Coombe, really a young version of Uncle Stephen. At the end Stephen is planning a trip to Europe to initiate Tom into the Greek way of life. In addition to time and the supernatural, the novel touches on personal themes of a boy's search for a father and a childless man's search for a son. The (London) *Times* (29 Oc-

tober 1931) complimented Reid on his balance of reality and fantasy, his mingling of "the experience of age . . . [and] youth's wonder," and his ability to "bring us for a while into a fairer world of marvelous intuitions."

While writing *Uncle Stephen,* Reid met nineteen-year-old Stephen Gilbert, who, besides eventually becoming Reid's literary executor, established a relationship with the older Reid that became a model for the realistic *Brian Westby* (1934), which the (London) *Times* called "a kind of postlude to *Apostate.*" In the novel middle-aged Martin Linton, a successful novelist but a failed husband, is recovering from a serious illness. Drawn to a young schoolboy whom he discovers reading one of his earliest novels, Linton learns that the boy, Brian Westby, is trying to write; furthermore, Brian is actually a son born to Linton's wife after their acrimonious divorce. The father-son friendship develops through their shared choice of career, but Brian must ultimately make a choice between the assistance his father offers and the love he has always known from his embittered, narrow mother. The book's ending in which Brian fails to meet Martin and opts to remain with his mother, was suggested by Gilbert and was not the one Reid would have chosen. Labeled by

*Dust jacket for Reid's 1936 novel that depicts the dreams,*
*fantasies, and activities of an imaginative, sensitive boy*
*protagonist (courtesy of the Lilly Library,*
*Indiana University)*

many critics as one of Reid's best works in its technique, *Brian Westby* uses interior monologues by both major characters, in addition to skillful narration, description, and dialogue.

In 1934 Reid exhibited the first signs of an unidentified chronic illness. He also met and acquired the lifelong friendship of a future M.P., Knox Cunningham. In the same year Reid's fame led to his receiving an honorary doctorate from Queen's University, Dublin, his portrait having been hung in a Belfast gallery one year earlier.

While written after *Uncle Stephen* and being complete in itself, *The Retreat; or, the Machinations of Henry* (1936) again depicts the dreams, fantasies, and activities of imaginative, sensitive Tom Barber. In this novel he is thirteen years old, in the last summer of childhood. Dedicated to Cunningham and intended for Emma Holmes, *The Retreat* developed from a dream, a visit to a London graveyard with Forster, a bonfire built with Desmond Montgomery, and a holiday with Stephen Gilbert; many of its characters were based on people Reid knew. After he has a horrifying dream that ends happily, Tom proceeds to school, where he converses with his scientific friend Pascoe and hears his music teacher comment on his changing voice, the first intimation of the "retreat" from youth. The second part of the novel describes an idyllic holiday replete with natural beauty, Pascoe, another dream, and new acquaintances, especially an angel named Gamelyn, whose appearances mark stages in the development of Tom's soul. The book's third section concerns

Tom's return to ordinary school life. Edwin Muir commended the novel's originality and skill of execution, while Russell Burlingham called it characteristic of Reid's "mystical awareness of the natural world [that] made him correspondingly sensitive to the whole range of ordinary natural impressions."

During a 1937 summer holiday, Reid helped Stephen Gilbert start his first novel, only to be angered later by Gilbert's intention to become engaged: Reid was a possessive friend. Meanwhile, at his publisher's suggestion and against Forster's advice, Reid completed a revision of *Following Darkness* (retitled *Peter Waring* [1937]), which he claimed was completely rewritten, to avoid the biblical implications of its original. Owen Gill is eliminated as the book's narrator and replaced by Peter, returning to Mrs. Carroll's after twenty years and imaginatively reminiscing about his boyhood. The story remains basically the same, however, with a slightly altered ending, in which Peter's confession to Mrs. McCarroll is replaced with his admission that their relationship has been beneficial to him. The major differences lie in Reid's refinement of technique – rather than including references to Platonic philosophy, for example, Reid now has the Platonic search for goodness, beauty, and truth take place through Peter – and, influenced by Anatole France, a clarity and directness of style. Again the book received good reviews but experienced poor sales.

In 1938 and 1939 Reid wrote the less-imaginative second part of his autobiography, *Private Road* (1940). The beginning of World War II brought the loss of his book-reviewing income because of difficulties with mail from England and the "double loss" of Stephen, who left for active service overseas and married on his return in 1945. On a more pleasant note for Reid was the dedication to him of Gilbert's first novel, *The Landslide* (1943), for which Reid had provided the title.

Written forty years after his first, Reid's last original novel, *Young Tom; or, Very Mixed Company* (1944), completed a trilogy of Tom Barber novels written in reverse, as it presents Tom at age eleven. Without a structured plot, the novel explores the innocent Tom's pleasant summer world, as the protagonist rambles outdoors; converses with the three neighborhood dogs Barker, Roger, and Pincher; swims with his adolescent friend James-Arthur; and builds an aquarium with his school friend, Pascoe. Part 2 destroys this pleasant existence when the local parson's son, Max, deliberately shoots Tom's pet squirrel, Edward, and Tom reacts to this evil by disposing of Max's gun. Rather than apologize as his father would have him do, Tom flees to his sym-

pathetic grandmother; she and his mother resolve the issue. Mixed with these real events are Tom's dreams, both sinister and pleasant, and his mystical encounters with Ralph Seaforth, a boy memorialized in a church window. The (London) *Times* (17 June 1944) criticized the book, claiming that its events tend "to lack other than private significance." Mary Bryan, however, praises the novel for its characterizations, especially of Tom, its rhythmic but conversational language, and its use of the small and personal events of Tom's life to relate to universal issues. *Young Tom; or, Very Mixed Company* also won the James Black Tait Memorial Prize for the best work of fiction published in 1944.

Reid's routine in his later years included writing in the morning, walking or visiting in the afternoon, and writing, reading, or playing records in the evening. Interspersed with these activities were visits from aspiring young writers, cricketers, or stamp collectors, along with games of bridge or croquet. In September 1945 Reid started to revise *The Bracknels,* although he had been under a doctor's care since March. Ironically, he spent part of the fall of 1946 resting in a Belfast clinic, funded by the Musgrave family, his first employers. On his release in October he journeyed to Warrenpoint to stay with James Rutherford's widow. Intending to return to Belfast on 6 January to arrange future care, Forrest Reid died on 4 January 1947 and was buried in Belfast three days later, his gravestone reading simply, "Forrest Reid, 1875–1947."

*Denis Bracknel* (1947) was published in September. Reid had claimed that it was "practically a new book," referring to the work's style and focus. Stylistically it is the culmination of his movement toward a more direct and simple form of expression. In it the Bracknel family story has been subordinated: Denis's moon worship and the steps leading to his demise are emphasized; Rusk's inability to comprehend Denis's condition is more clearly presented; and the ending of *The Bracknels* has been replaced by Reid's original ending, the gruesome discovery by Rusk and Dr. Birch of Denis's body hanging in the grove where he had conducted his moon worship. While the reviewer for the (London) *Times* (25 October 1947) claimed that *Denis Bracknel* differed less from its predecessor than *Peter Waring* did from *Following Darkness,* he concluded, "It is fitting that . . . Forrest Reid was able to take up again such a characteristic theme and to expose afresh the light bare beauty of an early love."

Following Reid's death, a prize was donated in his memory at the Royal Belfast Academical Institu-

tion. A memorial project, featuring addresses by Forster, de la Mare, and Gilbert, was planned in 1952, culminating in the unveiling of a plaque at his last residence. Another exhibition of his work planned for the centenary of his birth actually occurred a year later. In 1955 in the United States *Young Tom, The Retreat,* and *Uncle Stephen* were collected as *Tom Barber,* with an introduction by E. M. Forster. A review in *The New York Times* (9 October 1955) praised Reid's "complete seriousness" in dealing with his central character.

Over the four decades of his writing career Reid improved his style and literary technique; however, Reid recognized the narrowness of his subject matter as the result of his arrested development. While Forster interprets this focus as a means of "making all the surrounding landscape intelligible," Peter Coveney condemns it as a form of "emotional constriction," which makes Reid blind to the rest of human experience. Certainly, Reid "died disappointed that he had not received the recognition he deserved," as Brian Taylor phrases it; however, the press was generally receptive to his work, even if the public was less so. Perhaps with changing sexual mores, greater awareness of the psychological development of youth, and more general interest in forms of consciousness and psychic phenomena the modern reader would be more receptive to Reid's work.

**References:**

Sam Hanna Bell, ed., *The Arts in Ulster* (London: Harrap, 1951), pp. 111–116;

John Boyd, "The Achievement of Forrest Reid," *Dublin Magazine* (July–September 1945): 18–24;

Boyd, "Forrest Reid: An Introduction to his Work," *Irish Writing* (Cork) (April 1948): 72–77;

Mary C. Bryan, *Forrest Reid* (Boston: Twayne, 1976);

George Buchanan, "The Novels of Forrest Reid," *Dublin Magazine,* 27 (January–March 1952): 23–32;

Russell Burlingham, *Forrest Reid: A Portrait and a Study* (London: Faber & Faber, 1953);

James N. Cahalan, *The Irish Novel: A Critical History* (Boston: Twayne, 1988), pp. 213–216;

Peter Coveney, *Poor Monkey: the Child in Literature* (Rockliff, 1957), pp. 192–228;

E. M. Forster, "Forrest Reid," in his *Abinger Harvest* (London: Arnold, 1936), pp. 75–80;

J. W. Foster, *Forces and Themes in Ulster Fiction* (Gill & Macmillan, 1974), pp. 189–221;

Morris Fraser, *The Death of Narcissus* (Martin, Secker & Warburg, 1976), pp. 105–136;

J. Hill, *The Protestant Imagination in Northern Ireland* (Belfast: Blackstaff, 1985): 79–98;

R. Liddell, *Some Principles of Fiction* (London: Cape, 1953), pp. 123–158;

P. S. O'Hegarty, "About Ulster Novelists," *The Bell,* 4 (July 1942): 289–297;

V. S. Pritchett, "Forrest Reid: Escaping from Belfast," in his *Lasting Impressions: Selected Essays* (London: Chatto & Windus, 1990), pp. 111–115;

Pritchett, *Midnight Oil* (London: Chatto & Windus, 1971);

S. Gorley Putt, "Pan in Ulster," in his *Scholars of the Heart: Essays in Criticism* (London: Faber & Faber, 1962), pp. 43–48;

Brian Taylor, "Forrest Reid, a Neglected Ulster Writer," *Canadian Journal of Irish Studies,* 4 (1978): 33–40;

Taylor, "Forrest Reid and *Kenneth's Magazine,*" *Irish Booklore,* 3, no. 2 (1976): 104–113;

Taylor, "Forrest Reid and the Literature of Nostalgia," *Irish Studies,* 45 (Winter 1976): 291–296;

Taylor, *The Green Avenue: the Life and Writings of Forrest Reid, 1875–1947* (Cambridge: Cambridge University Press, 1980);

Taylor, "Private Road: Memory and Escape in the Fiction of Forrest Reid," *Eire-Ireland,* 14 (1979): 122–126;

Taylor, "A Strangely Familiar Scene: a Note on Landscape and Locality in Forrest Reid," *Irish University Review,* 7, no. 2 (1977): 213–218;

*Threshold* (Belfast), no. 28 (Spring 1977).

# M. P. Shiel

*(21 July 1865 – 14 February 1947)*

C. J. Keep
*Queen's University*

BOOKS: *Prince Zaleski* (London: John Lane, 1895;
    Boston: Roberts, 1895);
*The Rajah's Sapphire* (London: Ward Lock, 1896);
*Shapes in the Fire* (London: John Lane, 1896; Boston:
    Roberts, 1896);
*The Yellow Danger* (London: Richards, 1898; New
    York: Fenno, 1899);
*Contraband of War* (London: Richards, 1899; revised
    edition, London: Pearson, 1914; Ridgewood,
    N.J.: Gregg Press, 1968);
*Cold Steel* (London: Richards, 1899; New York:
    Brentano's, 1900; revised edition, London:
    Gollancz, 1929; New York: Vanguard, 1929);
*The Man-Stealers* (London: Hutchinson, 1900; Phila-
    delphia: Lippincott, 1900; revised edition,
    London: Hutchinson, 1927);
*The Lord of the Sea* (London: Richards, 1901; New
    York: Stokes, 1901; revised edition, New
    York: Knopf, 1924; London: Gollancz, 1929);
*The Purple Cloud* (London: Chatto & Windus, 1901;
    revised edition, London: Gollancz, 1929; New
    York: Vanguard, 1930);
*The Weird O' It* (London: Richards, 1902);
*Unto the Third Generation* (London: Chatto &
    Windus, 1903);
*The Evil That Men Do* (London: Ward Lock, 1904);
*The Lost Viol* (New York: Clode, 1905; London:
    Ward Lock, 1908);
*The Yellow Wave* (London: Ward Lock, 1905);
*The Last Miracle* (London: Laurie, 1906; revised edi-
    tion, London: Gollancz, 1929);
*The White Wedding* (London: Laurie, 1908);
*The Isle of Lies* (London: Laurie, 1909);
*This Knot of Life* (London: Laurie, 1909);
*The Pale Ape and Other Pulses* (London: Laurie, 1911);
*The Dragon* (London: Richards, 1913; New York:
    Clode, 1914); revised as *The Yellow Peril* (Lon-
    don: Gollancz, 1929);
*Children of the Wind* (London: Richards, 1923; New
    York: Knopf, 1923);
*How the Old Woman Got Home* (London: Richards,
    1927; New York: Vanguard, 1928);

*M. P. Shiel (photograph by Elliott and Fry)*

*Here Comes the Lady* (London: Richards, 1928);
*Dr. Krasinki's Secret* (New York: Vanguard, 1929;
    London: Jarrolds, 1930);
*The Black Box* (New York: Vanguard, 1930; Lon-
    don: Richards, 1931);
*Say Au R'Voir But Not Goodbye* (London: Benn,
    1933);
*This Above All* (New York: Vanguard, 1933); pub-
    lished as *Above All Else* (London: Cole,
    1943);

*The Invisible Voices* (London: Richards, 1935; New
    York: Vanguard, 1936);
*Richard's Shilling Selections from Edwardian Poets —
    M. P. Shiel* (London: Richards, 1936);
*The Young Men Are Coming!* (London: Allen &
    Unwin, 1937; New York: Vanguard, 1937).
**Editions:** *The Best Short Stories of M. P. Shiel* (London: Gollancz, 1948);
*Science, Life and Literature* (London: Williams &
    Norgate, 1950);
*Xélucha and Others* (Sauk City, Wis.: Arkham, 1975);
*The New King* (Cleveland, Ohio: Morse, 1980);
*The Works of M. P. Shiel,* 4 volumes, edited by A.
    Reynolds Morse (Cleveland, Ohio: Morse,
    1980).

M. P. Shiel's first book, *Prince Zaleski* (1895),
opens with a short story called "The S. S." It is a
mystery concerning a series of apparent suicides
which are revealed to be murders perpetrated by
the "Spartan Society," a group dedicated to the
elimination of genetic weaklings. With its almost
uncanny foreshadowing of a group known by the
same initials five decades later, the story illustrates
much of what makes Shiel so fascinating yet so difficult to read today. On the one hand, there is the
dark, at times even baroque, prose draping the decadent posturings of the narrative's exotic detective,
Prince Zaleski. This is a Holmesian mystery as it
might be imagined by J. K. Huysmans or Edgar
Allan Poe, but Shiel's prose style is unique: long,
rhythmic sentences replete with strange, startling
words tumbled together from every possible literary
resource. On the other hand, there is the frightening
sense that the author does not wholly disapprove of
the eugenic scheme hatched by the society. Shiel's
work, with an alarming consistency, endorses a variety of Nietzschean faith in the overman that sends
alarms ringing in the modern reader. To read Shiel
today is to struggle with the fact that people of his
evident skill and intelligence once harbored the
same theories that contributed to the Holocaust.
Shiel, in short, represents much of that which modern readers would rather forget, and it is thus
hardly surprising that, despite his abilities as a storyteller and a prose stylist, he too has been largely
forgotten.

Matthew Phipps Shiel was born on 21 July
1865, in the town of Plymouth on the island of
Montserrat in the British West Indies. He was the
only son of Matthew Dowdy Shiell (M. P. later
dropped the second "l"), a shipowner and storekeeper of Irish descent, and Priscilla Ann Blake
Shiell, a native of the island who appears to have

Cover for Shiel's 1898 novel, which describes an invasion of Europe by
"yellow hordes" led by Dr. Yen How. Though racist by today's
standards, the book was praised by contemporary reviewers and
went through several printings (courtesy of the Lilly
Library, Indiana University).

been at least partially descended from slaves. Shiel's
father may have been a businessman by occupation,
but he was a clergyman by vocation. A Methodist
lay preacher, his fire-and-brimstone sermons, liberally punctuated with quotations from the prophets
of the Old Testament, set the tone for the Shiell
household. Shiell lorded over his family like a biblical patriarch, cowing his children with his booming
voice and prophecies of the end of the world.
Though Shiel would spend much of his later life fulminating against the obfuscations of religion, the
voices of Daniel and Ezekiel echo throughout the
dithyrambic stresses and the apocalyptic clamor of
his writing, lasting testaments to the force of his
father's presence.

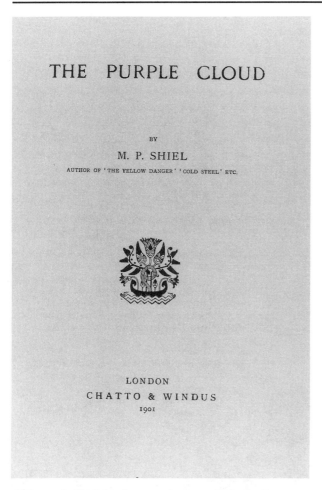

THE PURPLE CLOUD

BY

M. P. SHIEL

AUTHOR OF 'THE YELLOW DANGER' 'COLD STEEL' ETC.

LONDON
CHATTO & WINDUS
1901

*Title page for Shiel's best-known work, an apocalyptic scientific romance*

Shiel was preceded by eight or nine sisters (the number varies from account to account). The answer to his father's prayers for a son, Shiel was pampered by the women in his family, who treated him like a little king. He soon developed the self-confidence and egotism that were to be among the hallmarks of his character; he treated his siblings, as he would later treat all women, with a casual disdain. Shiel spent his youth roaming the verdant hills of Montserrat, developing close friendships among the West Indian boys. His literary inclinations began to show at an early age: at twelve he wrote a novel; the following year he published a newspaper, each copy of which he reproduced by hand for his seven "subscribers"; and at fifteen he had a serial appearing in a local newspaper.

Shiel's inflated sense of self can be traced to a remarkable event: on his fifteenth birthday his father, who claimed descent from the Irish kings, named his son "King of Redonda," a tiny, uninhabited island some twelve miles to the north of Montserrat. With a small fleet of ships witnessing the

event from the harbor, the Reverend Hugh Semper, a Methodist minister from Antigua, placed a crown on the boy's black curling hair. This coronation left a lasting impression on Shiel. Though the British government annexed the island not long after, Shiel persisted in styling himself the King of Redonda. In later life he fashioned Redonda into a literary kingdom, appointing the executor of his literary estate, the poet John Gawsworth, as successor to the crown. Gawsworth, in turn, took to granting phantom peerages to various friends and admirers of Shiel and, when his own fortunes turned sour, to selling the crown to various contenders for a modest price. The legend of Redonda has unfortunately survived Shiel, too often deflecting interest from his novels and stories and casting a somewhat ludicrous light on his literary achievements.

Details of Shiel's education are confused, as are all the details of his biography, by the author's habit of letting his imagination play on every aspect of life, including himself. His autobiographical essay, "About Myself," published in the 17 August 1901 *Candid Friend,* concludes with these words of caution: "[this] '*self*' I know is a fancy, has no reality, being a succession of little selves connected by a thread of memory, and only One is real: to know which thing is weal, I think." It is likely that he attended school in England between 1877 and 1880. In 1881 Shiel was enrolled at Harrison College in Bridgetown, Barbados, one of the most reputable colleges in the islands, and, as such, a fit place for the newly crowned "king." But his subsequent education is far from certain. He claimed to have received a B.A. from King's College and studied medicine at Saint Bartholomew's. Records show that he did in fact matriculate at the University of London while still at Harrison College. In 1885 Shiel traveled to London, but there is no record of his having taken any degree examinations either at the University of London or at King's College, though it appears that he received some training in languages from a college affiliated with the latter. His memory of having attended Saint Bartholomew's seems to rest wholly on his having witnessed a single eye operation there.

Shiel fell upon hard times after arriving in London. His father's business and health both took turns for the worse, and his father died of a stroke in 1888, leaving no money. The West Indian émigré thus had to eke out a living as a boarding-school teacher in various posts in and about Devonshire. In December of 1889 Shiel had his first story published in England. Titled "The Doctor's Bee," it won a twenty-shilling prize and appeared in

the magazine *Rare Bits*. Shiel apparently felt that this was a good omen; he moved to London and began working in various capacities for the penny-weekly and six-penny magazines that were beginning to flourish in the wake of the success of the *Strand*. Shiel's ability with languages – he claimed competence in half a dozen – stood him in good stead through the early 1890s. Not only did he do translation work for the *Strand,* but he was also appointed an interpreter to the International Congress of Hygiene and Demography. By 1893 he had come to the attention of the publisher and journalist W. T. Stead, and the two men collaborated on a story for Stead's new venture, the *Daily Paper*. The paper failed after a single issue, but the story was subsequently revised and published as *The Rajah's Sapphire* (1896), in which Shiel credited Stead with providing him the plot viva voce.

In the meantime Shiel turned to another project, a series of stories featuring an occult detective, Prince Zaleski. His timing was opportune: by 1893 Arthur Conan Doyle had begun to think of his popular fictional hero as a hindrance to his literary career and had sent Sherlock Holmes to his apparent doom. Zaleski was one of the more remarkable of the scores of sleuths that sought to fill the gap. Much indebted to Poe's Dupin, Zaleski is a self-exiled Russian who has renounced the world and retired to the seclusion of a "vast palace of the older world." He lives in quiet contemplation of the arcane with his giant Negro servant, Ham. Shiel himself poses as the Watson figure, bringing the detective the bare facts of mysteries that have baffled the police but that Zaleski, through his superior intellect and enormous erudition, quickly solves.

These stories were collected as *Prince Zaleski* (1895), which was published by John Lane, the man behind the notorious organ of fin de siècle decadent thought, *The Yellow Book*. It was thus an auspicious debut for an otherwise unknown writer and helped propel Shiel into the limelight. The book received favorable reviews, and its author began to be sought out by the social set of London's bohemian underground. In the next years he became acquainted with Oscar Wilde, Robert Louis Stevenson, and Pierre Louÿs and could count among his friends Arthur Machen, Edgar Jepson, and Ernest Dowson. His relationship with Louis Tracy, a popular writer of adventure stories, had the greatest impact on his early career, however.

After following up *Prince Zaleski* with another series of Edgar Allan Poe–like diversions called *Shapes in the Fire* (1896), Shiel was persuaded by Tracy to try his hand at a "future war" tale. The

vogue for stories envisioning an invasion of Britain by a foreign army had begun in 1871, when George Tomkyns Chesney capitalized on the panic following the defeat of France in the Franco-Prussian War with a little pamphlet entitled "The Battle of Dorking." Thereafter every event in foreign affairs that portended armed conflict was met with a barrage of tales demanding greater attention to Britain's home defenses. Tracy had cashed in on the public taste for such tales with a veritable paean to the might of the Anglo-Saxon race called *The Final War* (1896). In return for Shiel's help in writing several of the serial installments of his novel *The American Emperor* (1897), Tracy secured for his friend a commission for a future-war novel of his own. The result was *The Yellow Danger* (1898). Originally serialized as "The Empress of the Earth" in *Short Stories* (5 February 1898–18 June 1898), it describes the invasion of Europe by the "yellow hordes" under the leadership of the "evil genius" of Dr. Yen How. The Asians are foiled in their attempt to invade England, however, by the superhuman endeavors of Midshipman John Hardy. After towing naval transports laden with ten million Chinese and Japanese soldiers into the maelstrom, where all drown, Hardy then conceives of a plan for eradicating the oriental forces now occupying Europe. He injects several thousand Asian prisoners with cholera and releases the infected men among their compatriots. This action turns the tide in favor of the Europeans, and the world is made ready for a new order.

While displaying the unevenness typical of serial writing (in which the author must provide a series of partially discrete installments over many weeks), *The Yellow Danger* includes the basic plot elements of much of Shiel's later fiction. The main dramatic conflict derives from the contest between two overmen, superidealized heroes who are both the antithesis and the double of one another. While xenophobically dwelling on the "dark and hideous instincts of the Chinese race," the text suggests a certain admiration for Yen How: when the Chinese ruler captures Hardy, the two men carry on a philosophical discussion that demonstrates not only their intellectual superiority over the common lot but also their mutual admiration for one another. Critic Paul Spencer singles out Shiel's refusal to polarize his characters into simple "good" and "bad" stereotypes as crucial to the "dialectical quality" of his work. Although the characterization of Yen How is racist, according to Spencer "something in Shiel has pulled him back from the Final Solution."

*The Yellow Danger* clearly struck a chord in the jingoistic imagination of the fin de siècle British

*Shiel's home, L'Abri, in Horsham, Sussex*

reading public. The *Bookman* proclaimed, "Mr. Shiel is a marvelous man. His audacity is splendid. He relates the history of Armageddon. He slaughters not regiments, but races; he blows up not ships, but fleets. He harrows our very souls with prophecies of horror." The novel went through several printings, including an American and a Colonial edition, and was even quoted at length in the House of Commons by Lord Roberts during a debate on the defense budget. Its success, however, seems to have lured Shiel away from the literary market to which *Prince Zaleski* and *Shapes in the Fire* belonged and toward the more immediate rewards of sensationalist serial novels. He would later return to the "yellow peril" theme several times, as in *The Yellow Wave* (1905) and *The Dragon* (1913; revised as *The Yellow Peril,* 1929).

Shiel led a peripatetic life, keeping just ahead of a succession of rent-seeking landlords in London and occasionally escaping to the Continent. In 1898, while visiting Paris, he met and subsequently married a sixteen-year-old girl named Carolina Garcia Gomez. According to Shiel, his new wife did not care for London, and so the couple began to commute between the English and French capitals. In his 1907 memoir, *Bohemia in London,* Arthur Ransome recalls visiting the Shiels in their cramped Bloomsbury apartment and provides some insight into the fury with which the author churned out his

serials during those years: "always the room was in the same [dishevelled] condition, the child howling, the wife pretty, as untidy as ever, the great man unwashed but working. How he could work! Sheet after sheet used to drop from his desk. Sometimes when I called upon him he would be in the middle of a chapter, and then he would ask me to sit down and smoke, while his pen whirled imperturbably to the end." The child Ransome mentions was one of two that Carolina bore before her death in 1902. Shiel seems to have been no more disturbed by his wife's death than by her living presence; Ransome records a visit some years after the one described above during which Shiel casually informed his guest, "my wife is dying in Dublin this week. Pass the toast."

By the turn of the century, Shiel's powers were at their zenith. He contributed several serials to *Pearson's Weekly,* including *Contraband of War* (1899), a tale of the Spanish-American War, and a pair of historical romances, *Cold Steel* (1899) and *The Man-Stealers* (1900). These were followed by his two best-known works, *The Lord of the Sea* (1901) and *The Purple Cloud* (1901). Conceived as part of a trilogy with the later and weaker *The Last Miracle* (1906), these novels are supposedly Shiel's transcriptions of the diaries of a woman who can see into the future.

*The Lord of the Sea* takes place during a period of violent anti-Semitism: fleeing the pogroms on the

*Dust jacket for Shiel's 1927 mystery novel (courtesy of the Lilly Library, Indiana University)*

Continent, large numbers of Jews immigrate to England. One of these is the usurious financier Baruch Frankl, who uses his money to accumulate large plots of land in England; he requires his tenants to wear uniforms. The overman of this tale is a young farmer named Richard Hogarth, who becomes involved with Frankl's daughter, Rebekah. Hogarth and Frankl quarrel, and the latter has the Englishman framed for murder. While in prison Hogarth ponders the inequities of society and, through his reading of Henry George, concludes that the British system of land tenure is at the heart of the nation's ills. Hogarth escapes and recovers a cache of diamonds from a fallen meteorite. With his new wealth, the former farmer builds a series of giant floating fortresses, the strategic positioning of which effectively gives him control of the seaways. The navies of the world prove no match for Hogarth, and he is able to use his power to coerce Britain into

giving up its system of permanent landownership. Seeking revenge against Frankl, Hogarth, now regent of Britain, institutes sweeping prohibitions on the Jews in Britain. In compensation, he purchases Palestine from Turkey and allows them to return to their homeland. His reign as "King Richard, Lord of the Sea," however, is short-lived: British commandos overthrow the sea forts, and Hogarth, who is revealed to be a Jew, is forced to leave England. He travels to Palestine, where he marries Rebekah (Frankl has been killed earlier) and leads the Jews as their messiah.

*The Lord of the Sea* has proved to be one of Shiel's most enduring and most controversial works. It went through several printings in its first year of release and has been republished several times. More recently, it has come under attack by Sam Moskowitz for its anti-Semitism; in his *Explorers of the Infinite* (1963) Moskowitz compares it to

Adolf Hitler's *Mein Kampf* (1924) and suggests that Shiel's work could have served as an inspiration to Hitler. In subsequent studies of Shiel's work Moskowitz traces the author's attitude toward the Jews to his secret shame concerning his mother's descent. In "The Dark Plots of One Shiel" (1980) the critic asserts that Shiel's anti-Semitism served to distract attention from his ancestry and to "solidify the fact that he was one with the whites, voicing opinions, in spades, like those of many around him, against the Jews." Moskowitz is correct in pointing out the ways in which *The Lord of the Sea* capitalizes on the widespread anti-Semitism of the day: Frankl is a distillation of the worst stereotypes of the Jewish character, from Shylock to Fagin. But, as in *The Yellow Danger,* there is a certain doubleness to Shiel's rendering of the racial other that, if it does not justify the text's racism, at least increases its complexity. Hogarth, the British overman, is himself a Jew, and the novel strives to portray the rebuilding of the Jewish state as emblematic of the evolution of humankind toward a higher perfection.

Shiel's fascination with the dualistic nature of the overman found its most effective vehicle in the apocalyptic mise-en-scène of *The Purple Cloud.* Originally serialized in the *Royal Magazine* (January 1901–June 1901), it concerns a doctor named Adam Jeffson who is haunted by two voices, one white and the other black, which struggle not only for possession of his soul but also for the universe itself. Jeffson – his name a contraction of the words *Jehovah's Son* – is compelled by his fiancée to join an expedition to the North Pole, despite the warnings of a preacher who claims that it is God's will that no human ever set foot there. The black voice, however, gains the upper hand, and Jeffson's polar ambitions are compromised by several murders for which he is at least partly responsible. Jeffson reaches the pole alone (the rest of the expedition having perished in the cold) and makes his way back to the flagship. Upon returning to civilization, the doctor discovers that the preacher's prophecy has come true: a vast cloud of hydrocyanic gas, unleashed by a volcanic explosion on the day of Jeffson's triumph, has drifted across the earth; Jeffson is thus the last man in the world. The novel is thus cast as a rewriting of Genesis: Jeffson's fall is precipitated by the ambitions of a woman who tempts him to transgress a divine edict. The punishment for this is not simply expulsion into the wilds of history but the end of history itself.

Returning to London, Jeffson falls prey to a strange madness. Dressing himself as an oriental potentate, he effectively combines the forces of East and West polarized in *The Yellow Danger* and allows himself to act out the overman's grandest fantasies of power: carefully setting explosive charges all about the capital, Jeffson burns it to the ground in a fiery orgy of pent-up libidinal energy: "Near three in the morning I reached the climax of my wicked sweets, my drunken eyelids closing in a luxury of pleasure, and my lips lay stretched in a smile that drivelled; a feeling of dear peace, of power without bound, consoled me." The burning of the city is thus cast as a kind of virginal sacrifice on the altar of Jeffson's newfound masculinity, a sacrifice which provides not only the consummation of the deferred marriage to Clodagh but of the end of history as embodied by the capital of its greatest nation.

Jeffson wanders the world, burning one great city after another in a vain attempt to satisfy his pyromaniacal desires. Seventeen years pass, some of which are occupied in the building of a great palace of gold, before his solipsism is disturbed by the appearance of a woman. Trapped in an oubliette in Istanbul, she has lived her life in perfect innocence of the outside world until one of Jeffson's conflagrations allows her to escape. The last man is repulsed by her maternal desire to re-create the race of humans. "No, not a good race, that small infantry that called itself Man," he argues, enumerating the species' many faults and vowing, "Never through me shall it sprout and fester afresh." He spurns her entreaties, at one point going so far as to shoot her, but the white forces foil his attacks. The woman, who names herself Leda after Jeffson vetoes Eve, finally succeeds in winning the man's trust: the two are married and the novel ends with the prospect of the race renewed.

*The Purple Cloud* is Shiel's most respected work, earning the admiration of writers as diverse as H. G. Wells, Carl Van Vechten, Arnold Bennett, J. M. Barrie, Arthur Machen, L. P. Hartley, and Raymond Chandler. In his survey of horror literature, H. P. Lovecraft claims that Shiel's descriptions of Jeffson's wanderings through the ruined cities of the world "are delivered with a skill and artistry falling little short of actual majesty." After the novel's initial serialization, it was published in a moderately successful hardcover edition, translated into several languages, and adapted as a motion picture, *The World, The Flesh and the Devil* (1958). Regularly reprinted, the novel has become an acknowledged classic and has guaranteed its author a place in the history of science fiction and fantasy literature.

The melodramatic adventures Shiel published in the wake of *The Purple Cloud* and *The Lord of the*

*Page from the manuscript of Shiel's final work,* Jesus, *which he described as "a (truer) translation of Luke, with my criticisms." Though the work was apparently finished before Shiel's death, the complete manuscript has not been discovered (collection of John Gawsworth; from* The Works of M. P. Shiel, *1948).*

*Sea* suffer precisely in that the quotidian world of the present offered him little room for the expansiveness of his imagination. Almost entirely neglected today, works such as *The Weird O' It* (1902), *Unto the Third Generation* (1903), and *The Evil That Men Do* (1904) are nonetheless crucial to an understanding of Shiel's evolving philosophy. In *The Weird O' It* Shiel propounds a social Darwinism that emphasizes humanity's ability to evolve to a higher moral plane through the assiduous exercise of its mental faculties. Key to this evolutionary development is abstinence, self-denial, and vigorous physical exercise. His model is Jesus, "who was not born a man, but an overman." Shiel's overman, however, is distinct from that of Nietzsche: "He wants man to crush out the weak, as the brutes and Romans have done, and become overmen; but since man comes between the brutes and overman, therefore overman must be less like the brutes than man is: how, then, can man evolve into overman by copying those very brutes and brutish Empires built on the sands, that couldn't last a day? Can Satan cast out Satan? Can the brute eliminate the brute?" Shiel, like Prince Zaleski, believed society requires renovation in order to pull itself out of its moral turpitude but placed his faith in scientists and intellectuals as the agents of this evolution. As Brian Stableford asserts in his *Scientific Romance in Britain 1890–1950* (1985), "Shiel is a moral collectivist who insists that overmen must not think of themselves, but of the whole race, and must be ever ready to suffer and sacrifice themselves for the common good."

Shiel continued his prodigious output through the first decade of the twentieth century, usually producing at least one new title each year under his own name, as well as collaborating with Louis Tracy on adventure novels published under the pseudonym of Gordon Holmes. The outbreak of World War I, however, brought an end to the first phase of his literary career. He published nothing between 1913 and 1923, working in the Censor's Office during the war and spending the latter part of it in Italy. In 1918 Shiel married again, this time to a divorcée named Lydia Gerald Newson. Aside from these scant facts, however, little is known of Shiel's activities during these years.

Indeed, it is likely that Shiel might have disappeared from the literary map entirely had it not been for his "rediscovery" by the publisher Victor Gollancz in 1929. Shiel had taken up the pen again in 1923, writing the South African adventure (and one of his own favorites) *Children of the Wind*. He also had some success in America with the mystery

*How the Old Woman Got Home* (1927), but it was Gollancz's decision to reissue five of Shiel's early novels (*The Purple Cloud, The Lord of the Sea, Cold Steel, The Last Miracle,* and *The Yellow Peril*) that brought the author back to prominence for a time. Several of the titles from this latter phase are noteworthy: *How the Old Woman Got Home* contains lengthy philosophical asides that explicate Shiel's "political system"; *This Above All* (1933) is a compelling rewrite of the Wandering Jew myth, featuring an immortal Lazarus; and *The Invisible Voices* (1935) collects some of the author's best short stories. Most notable, however, is the last book that Shiel saw through to press in his lifetime, *The Young Men Are Coming!* (1937).

Though he was seventy-two years old by the time it was published, Shiel's last novel shows little diminution of his imaginative powers. No doubt influenced by the science fiction then appearing in the pulp magazines, the story concerns an aging scientist named Dr. Warwick who is kidnapped by a flying saucer and taken to the first moon of Jupiter. Here he debates the theory of relativity with a Cosmic Egg, an alien intelligence of peculiarly Shielian beliefs. The Egg gives Warwick a youth potion, which transforms him on his return to Earth into a vigorous leader of a group called the Young Men. Warwick and his followers seek to overthrow the fascistic government of Britain and depose Christianity in favor of Science. As civil war rages, the plot culminates in a struggle between the scientist and a preacher, a struggle that might be said to mirror the chief tensions in the author's life. The two men call on their gods to raise a great storm, but only the scientist, with the aid of the Egg, is successful. With a bleak irony that is typical of Shiel's narrative endings, the earth is largely destroyed by the ensuing cataclysms.

Shiel's later life was spent in poverty and loneliness. He was separated from his second wife in 1929, and only the timely intervention of Gawsworth, who secured the aging writer a pension through the Civil List in 1938, kept him from utter destitution. He retired to a cottage outside of Horsham, Sussex, where he kept up his strenuous daily physical exercises and worked on his translation of the Gospels. In 1942 he wrote, "Now for three years I have been doing a book called *Jesus* — a (truer) translation of Luke, with my criticisms, in which is some detective work, proving, for example, that the Apostle Paul was the Lazarus who in his anti-Sadducee craze for resurrection stayed for four days in a tomb." The text for this book was apparently completed before Shiel's death in 1947, but

only portions of the manuscript have been found among Shiel's papers.

The meager critical interest that Shiel has received in recent decades has been divided into two camps. The first, exemplified by A. Reynolds Morse's four-volume amateur collection, *The Works of M. P. Shiel* (1980), seeks to lionize the author as a master stylist. Morse writes: "I personally regard M. P. Shiel as one of the greatest writers ever to use the English language. I attend time's slow integration of the superlatives I feel he deserves with all the impatience of prophecy, for I have been deeply conscious of the radiant glow of his inextinguishable genius." The second group, exemplified by Moskowitz, tends to play down Shiel's mastery of language in order to foreground his anti-Semitism, misogyny, and racism. Both camps make valid points: there is little denying Shiel's abilities as a stylist of great imagination or his often callous, sometimes reprehensible disregard for anyone other than white male scientists. Separating the one aspect of Shiel from the other, however, has the effect of occluding his work's context in the social and political movements of his time. As Brian Aldiss writes in his *Trillion Year Spree* (1988): "Shiel's brain seems to have encompassed many of the ideas swilling about in the Europe of his day: socialism, evolution, new messiahs, conquests, Schopenhauer, industrialism, the yellow peril, revolutions, orgies of blood, overpopulation, Nietzscheism, spiritualism, eugenics, insanity, disease, miscegenation, and 'the biology of war' – in short, all the ingredients that go to make life in the West such a heady experience." Only when readers cease to consider Shiel as either a genius or a monster and come to perceive the ways in which his texts take up and transform the dominant ideological currents of their age will they be able to appreciate the enormous complexity and cultural richness of Shiel's work. To read Shiel today is to review the ideas that propelled the West into modernism.

**References:**

Brian Aldiss, *Trillion Year Spree* (London: Paladin, 1988), pp. 181–182;

H. P. Lovecraft, *Supernatural Horror in Literature* (New York: Dover, 1973), pp. 77–78;

A. Reynolds Morse, Introduction to *The Works of M. P. Shiel, Volume III,* edited by Morse (Cleveland, Ohio: Morse, 1980), pp. 481–486;

Sam Moskowitz, "The Dark Plots of One Shiel," in *Shiel in Diverse Hands,* edited by Morse (Cleveland, Ohio: Morse, 1980), pp. 57–66;

Moskowitz, *Explorers of the Infinite* (Cleveland, Ohio: World, 1963), pp. 142–156;

Arthur Ransome, *Bohemia in London* (London: Chapman & Hall, 1907), pp. 247–256;

Paul Spencer, "Shiel versus Shiel," in *Shiel in Diverse Hands,* edited by Morse (Cleveland, Ohio: Morse, 1980), pp. 23–30;

Brian Stableford, *Scientific Romance in Britain 1890–1950* (London: Fourth Estate, 1985), pp. 75–84, 175–178;

Gary K. Wolfe, "Shiel, M(atthew) P(hipps)," in *Twentieth-Century Science-Fiction Writers,* edited by Curtis C. Smith (New York: St. Martin's Press, 1987), pp. 488–489.

**Papers:**
A large holding of M. P. Shiel's papers is located at the Harry Ransom Humanities Research Center, University of Texas at Austin.

# H. de Vere Stacpoole

*(9 April 1863 – 12 April 1951)*

Edward A. Malone
*University of Missouri at Rolla*

BOOKS: *The Intended: A Novel* (London: Bentley, 1894);

*Pierrot! A Story* (London: John Lane / Philadelphia: Altemus, 1896);

*Death, the Knight, and the Lady: A Ghost Story* (London & New York: John Lane, 1897);

*The Rapin* (London: Heinemann, 1899; New York: Holt, 1899); republished as *Toto: A Parisian Sketch* (London: Heinemann, 1910);

*The Doctor: A Study from Life* (London: Unwin, 1899);

*Pierrette* (London & New York: John Lane, 1899); enlarged as *Poppyland* (London & New York: John Lane, 1914);

*The Bourgeois* (London: Unwin, 1901; New York: Brentano, 1910);

*The Lady-Killer* (London: Unwin, 1902);

*Fanny Lambert: A Novel* (London: Unwin, 1906; New York: Fenno, 1910);

*The Golden Astrolabe,* by Stacpoole and W. A. Bryce (London: Gardner, 1906);

*The Meddler: A Novel of Sorts,* by Stacpoole and Bryce (London: Rivers, 1907);

*The Crimson Azaleas: A Novel* (London: Unwin, 1907; New York: McClure, 1908);

*The Blue Lagoon: A Romance* (London: Unwin, 1908; Philadelphia: Lippincott, 1908);

*The Cottage on the Fells* (London: Laurie, 1908); published as *Murder on the Fell* (London: Allied Newspapers, 1937);

*Patsy: A Story* (London: Unwin, 1908; New York: McClure, 1908);

*The Reavers: A Tale of Wild Adventure on the Moors of Lorne,* by Stacpoole and Bryce (London: SPCK, 1908);

*The Man Without a Head,* as Tyler De Saix (New York: Moffat, Yard, 1908);

*The Vulture's Prey,* as Tyler De Saix (London: Unwin, 1909); republished, as Stacpoole (London: Unwin, 1918);

*Garryowen: The Romance of a Race-Horse* (London: Unwin, 1909; New York: Duffield, 1909);

*The Pools of Silence* (London: Unwin, 1909; New York: Doubleday, Page, 1909);

*The Drums of War* (London: John Murray, 1910; New York: Duffield, 1910);

*Poems and Ballads* (London: John Murray, 1910; New York: Duffield, 1910);

*The Cruise of the "Kingfisher": A Tale of Deep-Sea Adventure* (London: Gardner, 1910; New York: Duffield, 1911);

*The Ship of Coral: A Tropical Romance* (London: Hutchinson, 1911; New York: Duffield, 1911);

*The Order of Release* (London: Hutchinson, 1912);

*The Street of the Flute-Player: A Romance* (London: John Murray, 1912; New York: Duffield, 1912);

*Molly Beamish* (New York: Duffield, 1913; London: Benn, 1933);

*Bird Cay* (London: Gardner, Darton, 1913);

*The Children of the Sea: A Romance* (London: Hutchinson, 1913; New York: Duffield, 1913);

*Words of "England Expects"* (London: Curwen, 1914);

*Father O'Flynn* (London: Hutchinson, 1914);

*The New Optimism* (London & New York: John Lane, 1914);

*Monsieur de Rochefort: A Romance of Old Paris* (London: Hutchinson, 1914); published as *The Presentation* (New York: John Lane, 1914);

*The Blue Horizon: Romance from the Tropics and the Sea* (London: Hutchinson, 1915);

*The North Sea, and Other Poems* (London: Hutchinson, 1915);

*The Pearl Fishers* (London: Hutchinson, 1915; New York: John Lane, 1915);

*The Red Days, Being the Diary of a Prussian Officer in France and Belgium During the Autumn and Early Winter of 1914* (London: Pearson, 1915);

*The Reef of Stars: A Romance of the Tropics* (London: Hutchinson, 1916); published as *The Gold Trail: A Romance of the South Seas* (New York: John Lane, 1916);

*Corporal Jacques of the Foreign Legion* (London: Hutchinson, 1916);

*François Villon: His Life and Times, 1431–1463* (London: Hutchinson, 1916; New York: Putnam, 1916);

*In Blue Waters* (London: Hutchinson, 1917);

*Sea Plunder* (New York: John Lane, 1917);

*The Starlit Garden: A Romance of the South* (London: Hutchinson, 1917); published as *The Ghost Girl* (New York & London: John Lane, 1918);

*The Willow Tree: The Romance of a Japanese Garden* (London: Hodder & Stoughton, 1918);

*The Man Who Lost Himself* (London: Hutchinson, 1918; New York: John Lane, 1918);

*The Beach of Dreams: A Story of the True World* (London: Hutchinson, 1919; New York: John Lane, 1919);

*Under Blue Skies* (London: Hutchinson, 1919);

*A Man of the Islands* (London: Hutchinson, 1920);

*Uncle Simon,* with Margaret Stacpoole (London: Hutchinson, 1920); published as *The Man Who Found Himself (Uncle Simon)* (New York: John Lane, 1920);

*Satan: A Story of the Bahamas* (London: Hutchinson, 1921; New York: McBride, 1921);

*Men, Women, and Beasts* (London: Hutchinson, 1922);

*Vanderdecken: The Story of a Man* (New York: Mc-Bride, 1922; London: Hutchinson, 1923);

*The Garden of God* (London: Hutchinson, 1923; New York: Dodd, Mead, 1923);

*Golden Ballast* (London: Hutchinson, 1924; New York: Dodd, Mead, 1924);

*Ocean Tramps* (London: Hutchinson, 1924);

*The House of Crimson Shadows: A Romance* (London: Hutchinson, 1925; Boston: Small, Maynard, 1926);

*The Gates of Morning* (London: Hutchinson, 1925; New York: Dodd, Mead, 1925);

*The City in the Sea* (London: Hutchinson, 1925; New York: Doran, 1925);

*Stories East and West: Tales of Men and Women* (London: Hutchinson, 1926);

*The Mystery of Uncle Bollard* (London: Cassell, 1927; Garden City, N.Y.: Doubleday, Doran, 1928);

*Goblin Market: A Romance of To-Day Telling How Anthony Harrop, a Respectable Citizen, Met in with the Goblin Folk, How He Attended Their Market, What He Bought There and How It Served Him* (London: Cassell, 1927; New York: Doran, 1927);

*Tropic Love* (London: Readers Library, 1928);

*Roxanne* (London: Cassell, 1928); published as *The Return of Spring: A Romance* (Garden City, N.Y.: Doubleday, Doran, 1928);

*Eileen of the Trees* (London: Cassell, 1929; Garden City, N.Y.: Doubleday, Doran, 1929);

*The Girl of the Golden Reef: A Romance of the Blue Lagoon* (London: Hutchinson, 1929);

*The Tales of Mynheer Amayat* (London: Newnes, 1930);

*The Chank Shell: A Tropical Romance of Love and Treasure* (London: Hutchinson, 1930); published as *The Island of Lost Women* (New York: Sears, 1930);

*Pacific Gold* (London: Collins, 1931; New York: Sears, 1931);

*Love on the Adriatic* (London: Benn, 1932);

*The Lost Caravan* (London: Collins, 1932; New York: Sears, 1932);

*Mandarin Gardens* (London: Hutchinson, 1933);

*The Naked Soul: The Story of a Modern Knight* (London: Collins, 1933);

*The Blue Lagoon Omnibus* (London: Hutchinson, 1933);

*The Vengeance of Mynheer Van Lok, and Other Stories* (London: Hutchinson, 1934);

*The Longshore Girl: A Romance* (London: Hutchinson, 1935);

*Green Coral* (London: Hutchinson, 1935);

Cover for Stacpoole's second novel, concerning a French boy's relationship with a patricidal doppelgänger (courtesy of the Lilly Library, Indiana University)

*The Sunstone* (London: Hutchinson, 1936);

*In a Bonchurch Garden* (London: Hutchinson, 1937);

*Ginger Adams* (London: Hutchinson, 1937);

*High-Yaller* (London: Hutchinson, 1938);

*Old Sailors Never Lie, and Other Tales of Land and Sea, By One of Them* (London: Hutchinson, 1938);

*Due East of Friday* (London: Hutchinson, 1939);

*An American at Oxford* (London: Hutchinson, 1941);

*Men and Mice, 1863–1942* (London & New York: Hutchinson, 1942);

*Ivan Ivanovich* (London: Hutchinson, 1943);

*The Doctor's Love Story and That Kid* (London: Todd, 1943);

*The Killing of Mynheer Katz, and the Story of O Toyo* (London: Todd, 1943);

*Oxford Goes to War: A Novel* (London & New York: Hutchinson, 1943);

*The Lost Diana, and the Lost Feather* (London: Hodgson, 1944);

*More Men and Mice* (London & New York: Hutchinson, 1945);

*Harley Street: A Novel* (London & New York: Hutchinson, 1946);

*The Story of My Village* (London & New York: Hutchinson, 1947);

*The Man in Armour* (London & New York: Hutchinson, 1949);

*The Land of Little Horses* (London & New York: Hutchinson, 1949).

OTHER: *The Poems of François Villon,* translated, with an introductory essay, by Stacpoole (London: Hutchinson, 1913; New York: John Lane, 1914);

*Sappho: A New Rendering,* translated by Stacpoole (London: Hutchinson, 1920);

Untitled essay, in *My Religion* (London: Hutchinson, 1925; New York: Appleton, 1926), pp. 77–82;

William Diapea, *Cannibal Jack: The True Autobiography of a White Man in the South Seas,* foreword by Stacpoole (London: Faber, 1928; New York: Putnam, 1928), pp. v–viii;

*The Book of François Villon,* translated by Algernon Charles Swinburne and others, introduction by Stacpoole (Boston: International Pocket Library, 1931), pp. 5–13.

Between 1894 and 1949 H. de Vere Stacpoole published more than sixty novels, fifteen collections of stories, three volumes of original verse, two volumes of translations, two autobiographies, a literary biography, and a philosophical treatise. Though extremely prolific, often relying on hackneyed formulas, he managed to distinguish himself with several original novels, including *The Pools of Silence* (1909), *The Street of the Flute-Player: A Romance* (1912), and *Goblin Market* (1927). He is best remembered for *The Blue Lagoon: A Romance* (1908), his most successful novel. His neoromantic fiction is characterized by exotic settings, vivid topography, hints of the supernatural, gender reversals, treasure hunts, and doppelgängers. His significance lies in the size and diversity of his corpus, the immense popularity he enjoyed during his life, his descriptive powers, and his contributions to the romance genre.

Born on 9 April 1863 in Kingstown, Ireland, Henry de Vere Stacpoole grew up in a household dominated by his mother and three older sisters. William C. Stacpoole, a doctor of divinity from Trinity College and headmaster of Kingstown school, died some time before his son's eighth birthday, leaving the responsibility of supporting the family to his Canadian-born wife, Charlotte Au-

gusta Mountjoy Stacpoole. At a young age Charlotte had been led out of the Canadian backwoods by her widowed mother and taken to Ireland, where their relatives lived. This experience had strengthened her character and prepared her for single parenthood. She cared passionately for her children and was perhaps overly protective of Henry. As a child Stacpoole suffered from severe respiratory problems, misdiagnosed as chronic bronchitis by his physician, who in the winter of 1871 advised that the boy be taken to southern France for his health. With her entire family in tow, Charlotte made the long journey from Kingstown to London to Paris — where signs of the Franco-Prussian War were still evident — settling at last in Nice at the Hôtel des Iles Britannique. Nice was like paradise to Henry, who marveled at the city's affluence and beauty as he played in the warm sun.

After several more excursions to the Continent, Stacpoole was sent to Portarlington, a bleak boarding school more than one hundred miles from Kingstown. In contrast to his sisters, the Portarlington boys were noisy and uncouth. In his autobiography, *Men and Mice, 1863–1942* (1942), Stacpoole recounts how they abused him mentally and physically, making him feel like "a little Arthur in a cage of baboons." One night he escaped through an adjacent girls' school and returned to Kingstown, only to be betrayed by his family and dragged back to school by his eldest sister. When his family moved to London, Stacpoole was taken out of Portarlington and enrolled at Malvern College, a progressive school with refined students and plenty of air and sunshine. The young man thoroughly enjoyed his new surroundings, which he associated with the description of Malvern Hills in Elizabeth Barrett Browning's *Aurora Leigh* (1857): "Keepers of Piers Plowman's visions / Through the sunshine and the snow." This environment encouraged his interest in literature and writing.

The idyll ended, however, when he began his medical training. At his mother's prodding, Stacpoole entered the medical school at St. George's Hospital. On his way to and from classes, he had to pass through a park frequented by perambulating nursemaids, and he became romantically involved with one of them. When his mother discovered their affair, she insisted that he transfer to University College, and he complied. More interested in literature than in corpses, Stacpoole began to neglect his studies and miss classes, especially the required dissections. Finally, the dean of the medical school confronted him, and their argument drove Stacpoole to St. Mary's Hospital, where he com-

pleted his medical training and qualified L.S.A. in 1891. At some point after this date, Stacpoole made several sea voyages into the tropics (at least once as a doctor aboard a cable-mending ship), collecting information for future stories.

Stacpoole's literary career, which he describes in his autobiography as being "more like a Malay fishing prahu than an honest to God English literary vessel," began inauspiciously with the publication of *The Intended* (1894), a tragic novel about two look-alikes, one rich, the other poor, who switch places on a whim. Though well plotted, it was a failure, both commercially and artistically, mainly because Stacpoole had failed to develop the humor in the situation. Bewildered by the novel's lack of success, Stacpoole consulted his friendly muse, Pearl Craigie, alias John Oliver Hobbes, who suggested a comic rather than tragic treatment. Years later, Stacpoole took her advice and retold the story in *The Man Who Lost Himself* (1918), a commercially successful comic novel about a down-and-out American who impersonates his wealthy look-alike in England. Yvan Noé dramatized the story in French as *Monsieur Le Comte* (1933). A film version of *The Man Who Lost Himself* was made in 1941.

Set in France during the Franco-Prussian War, Stacpoole's second novel, *Pierrot! A Story* (1896), recounts a French boy's eerie relationship with a patricidal doppelgänger. It was the first volume in Pierrot's Library, a Bodley Head series published by John Lane. Aubrey Beardsley designed the front and back covers, front and back endpapers, title page, and spine for the series — six illustrations in all. While the novel was still in press, Stacpoole moved to Oxford to practice medicine, and Lane soon brought him a copy of the novel, along with clippings of press notices, all of them favorable. Lane's enthusiasm for the book and the rave reviews encouraged Stacpoole. "I have only once experienced the full feeling of success — it was just then," he admitted years later. The feeling did not last long. Despite its artistic merits *Pierrot! A Story* was a commercial failure. It was at this point, perhaps, that Stacpoole began to view literary success only in terms of sales figures and numbers of editions.

The weak sales of *Pierrot! A Story* probably caused the publication of Stacpoole's third novel to be delayed; it was originally planned as another volume in Pierrot's Library but was eventually published separately, without Beardsley's illustrations. A strange tale of reincarnation, cross-dressing, and uxoricide, *Death, the Knight, and the Lady: A Ghost Story* (1897) purports to be the deathbed confession

THE LAGOONER

*Cartoon from* Punch *depicting Stacpoole and alluding to his best-known novel,* The Blue Lagoon *(1908)*

of Beatrice Sinclair, who is both a reincarnated murderer (male) and a descendant of the murder victim (female). She falls in love with Gerald Wilder, a man disguised as a woman who is both a reincarnated murder victim (female) and the descendant of the murderer (male). This confusing though clever plot probes the psychology of sexual identity, family feuding, and revenge. Despite its originality, the novel met with "Public Indifference" (Stacpoole's term), as did *The Rapin* (1899), a novel about an art student in Paris. The latter was republished more successfully as *Toto: A Parisian Sketch* (1910).

During the summer of 1898 Stacpoole lived in Somerset, where he temporarily took over the medical practice of an ailing country doctor. So peaceful were his days that he had time to write *The Doctor: A Study from Life* (1899), a novel about an old-fashioned physician practicing medicine in rural England. "It is the best book I have written," Stacpoole declared more than forty years later. He could also

say, in retrospect, that the book's weak sales were a disguised blessing, "for I hadn't ballast on board in those days to stand up to the gale of success, which means incidentally money." He would be spared the gale of success for nine more years, during which he published seven books, including a collection of children's stories and two collaborative novels with his friend William Alexander Bryce.

In 1907 two events occurred that altered the course of Stacpoole's life: he wrote *The Blue Lagoon,* and he got married. Unable to sleep one night, he found himself thinking about and envying the caveman, who in his primitiveness was able to marvel at such commonplace phenomena as sunsets and thunderstorms. Civilized, technological man had unveiled these mysteries with his telescopes and weather balloons, so that they were no longer "nameless wonders" to be feared and contemplated. As a doctor, Stacpoole had witnessed countless births and deaths, and these events no longer

seemed miraculous to him. He conceived the idea of two children growing up alone on an island and experiencing storms, death, and birth in almost complete ignorance and innocence. The next morning, he started writing *The Blue Lagoon*. The exercise was therapeutic because he was able to experience the wonders of life and death vicariously through his characters.

*The Blue Lagoon* is the story of two cousins, Dicky and Emmeline Lestrange, who are shipwrecked and stranded on a remote island with a beautiful lagoon. As children, they are cared for by Paddy Button, a portly sailor who drinks himself to death after only two and a half years in paradise. Frightened and confused by the man's gruesome corpse, the children flee to another part of Palm Tree Island. Over a period of five years, they grow up and eventually fall in love. Sex and birth are as mysterious to them as death, but they manage to copulate instinctively and conceive a child. The birth is especially remarkable: fifteen-year-old Emmeline, alone in the jungle, loses consciousness and awakes to find a baby boy on the ground near her. Naming the boy Hannah (an example of Stacpoole's penchant for gender reversals), the Lestranges live in familial bliss until they are unexpectedly expelled from their tropical Eden.

The parallels between *The Blue Lagoon* and the biblical story of Adam and Eve are obvious and intentional, but Stacpoole was also influenced by Lewis Carroll's *Alice's Adventures in Wonderland* (1865), which he invokes in a passage describing the castaways' approach to Palm Tree Island:

> One could see the water swirling round the coral piers, for the tide was flooding into the lagoon; it had seized the little dinghy and was bearing it along far swifter than the sculls could have driven it. Seagulls screamed about them, the boat rocked and swayed. Dick shouted with excitement, and Emmeline shut her eyes *tight*.
>
> Then, as though a door had been swiftly and silently closed, the sound of the surf became suddenly less. The boat floated on an even keel; Emmeline opened her eyes and found herself in Wonderland.

This direct reference to Carroll's work prepares the reader for the many parallels that follow. When their respective adventures begin, both girls are about the same age, Alice seven and a half, Emmeline exactly eight. Just as Alice joins a tea party in Wonderland, Emmeline plays with her tiny tea set on the beach after they land. Emmeline's former pet, like the Cheshire Cat, "had stripes on it and a white chest, and rings all down its tail" and died

"showing its teeth." Whereas Alice looks for a poison label on a bottle that says "Drink Me," Emmeline innocently tries to eat the "never-wake-up-berries" and receives a stern rebuke and a warning about poison from Paddy Button. "The Poetry of Learning" chapter echoes Alice's dialogue with the caterpillar. Like the wily creature smoking a hookah, Paddy smokes a pipe and shouts "Hurroo!" as the children teach him to write his name in the sand. The children lose "all count of the flight of time," just as the Mad Hatter does. Whereas Alice grows nine feet taller, Dick sprouts "two inches taller" and Emmeline "twice as plump." Like the baby in Carroll's "Pig and Pepper," Hannah sneezes at the first sight of Dicky. The novel is artfully littered with references to wonder, curiosity, and strangeness – all evidence of Stacpoole's conscious effort to invoke and honor his Victorian predecessor.

Stacpoole presented *The Blue Lagoon* to the publisher T. Fisher Unwin in September 1907 and went to Cumberland to assist another ailing doctor in his practice. Every day from Eden Vue in Langwathby, Stacpoole wrote to his fiancée, Margaret Robson (or Maggie, as he called her), and waited anxiously for their wedding day. On 17 December 1907 the couple were married, and for a wedding gift Unwin sent them a copy of Edward John Hardy's *How to Be Happy Though Married* (1885), a book which Stacpoole later said he had never had to read. The newlyweds spent their honeymoon at Stebbing Park, a friend's country house in Essex, about three miles from the village of Stebbing. There Stacpoole stumbled upon Rose Cottage and said, "Thou art mine!" The cottage would serve as the couple's home for many years.

Published in January 1908, *The Blue Lagoon* was an immediate success, both with reviewers and the public. The novel was reprinted more than twenty times in the next twelve years and remained popular in other forms for more than eighty years. Norman MacOwen and Charlton Mann adapted the novel for the stage, and their play ran for 263 performances in London from 28 August 1920 to 16 April 1921. Motion-picture versions of the novel were made in 1923, 1949, and 1980. Stacpoole wrote two successful sequels: *The Garden of God* (1923) and *The Gates of Morning* (1925). These three books and two others were collected in *The Blue Lagoon Omnibus* (1933). *The Garden of God* was filmed as *Return to the Blue Lagoon* in 1991.

Over the next two years Stacpoole published seven novels, including *The Pools of Silence*, a bleak tale about an American doctor who joins a hunting

# THE STREET OF
# THE FLUTE-PLAYER

### A ROMANCE

BY H. DE VERE STACPOOLE

YEAR: *The year of the first production of " The Frogs "*
TIME: *The grape harvest*

LONDON
JOHN MURRAY, ALBEMARLE STREET, W.
1912

*Title page for Stacpoole's novel set in Athens in 405 B.C., the year of the first performance of Aristophanes'* The Frogs *(courtesy of the Lilly Library, Indiana University)*

expedition to the Congo and witnesses the atrocities under Belgian rule. The idea for the story was suggested by E. D. Morel, head of the Congo Reform Society, who told Stacpoole horrifying stories about the Congo. Primarily a political novel, *The Pools of Silence* elicited strong reactions from readers, who were both impressed by Stacpoole's powers of description and appalled by his graphic depictions of violence. His topographical descriptions are occasionally sublime and inspiring:

> Here, in the very depths of the hopeless jungle, as if laid out and forgotten by some ancient god, lie the Silent Pools of Matabayo and the parklike lands that hold them. Like a beautiful song in some tragic and gloomy opera, a regret of the God Who created the hopeless forest, sheltered by the great n'sambya trees, they lie; pools of shadowy and tranquil water, broken by reflections of branches and mirroring spear-grass ten feet high and fanlike fern fronds.
>
> All was motionless and silent as a stereoscopic picture; the rocketing palms bursting into sprays of emer-

ald green, the n'sambyas with their trumpet-like yellow blossoms, the fern fronds reduplicating themselves in the water's glass, all and each lent their motionless beauty to the completion of the perfect picture.

Yet the beauty of these landscapes is often shattered by discordant scenes of violence and cruelty:

> A semicircle of blood on the ground marked her gyrations. Once she almost gained her feet, but a blow in the face sent her down again. She put her hands to her poor face, and the rhinoceros-whips caught her on the hands, breaking them. She flung herself on her back and they beat her on the stomach, cutting through the walls of the abdomen till the intestines protruded. She flung herself on her face and they cut into her back with the whips till her ribs were bare and the fat bulged through the long slashes in the skin.

The horrors, of course, served a rhetorical purpose: Stacpoole wanted to shock and outrage his readers, inciting them to action. His presentation was at least partly successful because it prompted Sir Arthur Conan Doyle to call a meeting at St. James's Hall to discuss the atrocities, which included the rape, torture, and murder of Congolese.

Between 1910 and 1914 Stacpoole published nine novels, including *The Street of the Flute-Player: A Romance,* a tale set in ancient Athens in the year of the first performance of Aristophanes' *The Frogs* (405 B.C.). In this story of a wealthy Athenian's forbidden love for a young Persian woman, Stacpoole superimposes the death of Socrates on the tragedy of Romeo and Juliet. He manages to create an attractive, though somewhat implausible, portrait of ancient Athens, especially in the novel's first section, before the narrative becomes overly preoccupied with plot. The reader is shown the Agora, Athens's crowded marketplace, from the point of view of a young harbor boy, Pheidon, who serves as the temporary purse carrier of the wealthy Athenian Diomed. As they walk from booth to booth conducting their daily business, they encounter a fishmonger, a barber, a banker, and others who represent the diverse population of Athens. In the background, city children croak like frogs in imitation of Aristophanes's chorus. A man recites Homer in a loud voice, while a nearby fountain weeps "like some city-chained Naiad." These emotional images, influenced by classical literature, communicate the wit and charm of the earlier age.

Socrates and Aristophanes have minor roles in the plot and are humanized by their placement in unexpected settings. For example, in the bedroom of a prostitute, Diomed meets Socrates, who had apparently come to the brothel in search of a woman's

wisdom and counsel. Ironically, Socrates avoids a dialogue with Diomed on the nature of woman and slinks away. At one of Diomed's parties, Aristophanes participates in a drunken "symposium" with the other guests. The reader is told that the protagonist, Diomed, is "the mental brother of Aristophanes" and an admirer of Socrates. In fact, his emulation of Socrates has earned him the animosity of his fellow Athenians, who grumble, "Socrates shews men their folly by sense, Diomed by nonsense." They eventually conspire against Diomed on the pretext that he has committed blasphemy against the state. In the end he shares Socrates's fate, consuming a draught of hemlock. Nitetis, the woman he loves, and his faithful servant Xanthias (a common name for servants in Aristophanes' plays) also commit suicide. This tragic ending is clumsily foreshadowed by the appearance of a blackbird at the celebration of the grape harvest, the mention of a virgin's spartan tomb, and the figure of a ghostly flute player, also a suicide, who wanders the streets late at night, playing sullen music.

This novel, like Stacpoole's other books following *The Blue Lagoon,* was commercially successful, earning the writer handsome royalties. He could afford to rent a winter cottage in Ventnor, Isle of Wight, where he worked in his garden and entertained occasional guests. On one of Lane's visits, the two friends philosophized about the future of mankind, and Stacpoole later turned their discussion into a book, which Lane published. *The New Optimism* (1914) is, in part, a Socratic dialogue between a despairing young woman and an older man. Like Socrates' students, the young woman always asks the right questions, never seriously challenges the older man's answers, and accepts his facile conclusion – in this case, that there is hope for mankind. Stacpoole was criticized publicly for his naiveté and pomposity. H. G. Wells sent a copy of his *First and Last Things* (1908) with the inscription "think *harder*."

Not to be discouraged, Stacpoole continued to write prolifically, publishing eighteen more books before 1922, including another volume of original verse, a biography of François Villon, and several collections of stories. *The Red Days* (1915), a thin volume with a long subtitle, purports to be the authentic war diary of a young Prussian military man in 1914, but it is probably a work of fiction by Stacpoole. *The Starlit Garden: A Romance of the South* (1917), titled "The Dead Lovers" in manuscript, is a novel about an Irish teenager's romance with her American guardian in South Carolina and her psychic relationship with a doppelgänger from the past.

*The Willow Tree: The Romance of a Japanese Garden* (1918), set in Japan, is the novel version of the successful stage play by Benrimo and Harrison Rhodes. *The Beach of Dreams: A Story of the True World* (1919), titled "The Sea Lion" in manuscript, tells the story of a wealthy flapper shipwrecked on a desolate island with two libidinous sailors, later joined by a virtuous sailor.

One of Stacpoole's neighbors in Ventnor was Arthur S. Way, the translator of Homer and Virgil and the author of *The Sons of the Violet-Crowned* (1929), a work erroneously attributed to Stacpoole. Way inspired Stacpoole to publish *Sappho: A New Rendering* (1920), a collection of verse translations from Greek. That same year, in collaboration with his wife, Stacpoole published *Uncle Simon* (1920) and then went to work on *Satan: A Story of the Bahamas* (1921).

*Satan* is arguably Stacpoole's best treasure-hunt novel. Satan Tyler, twenty-nine, and his sister Jude, fifteen, both Americans, team up with Bobby Ratcliffe, an Englishman, in search of sunken treasure. The title, though criticized by reviewers for being misleading, accurately represents the novel's concern with the morality of Satan Tyler and the efficacy of romance in embellishing evil. Named Satan because he had a demoniac yell as a baby, the young scavenger and con artist manipulates people through his wile and rhetoric; yet he is an attractive figure, appealing to readers in the way that murderous pirates appeal to children, who don eye patches and brandish plastic swords in emulation of villainy. Sailing in such paradoxically lovely settings as Lone Reef and Cormorant Cay, Satan is a static character, an embodiment of romance itself.

Ratcliffe and Jude, however, are dynamic characters and undergo opposite transformations in the course of the narrative. A member of the idle rich, Ratcliffe degenerates morally because of his association with the Tylers. His name becomes "Rat" through diminution. When he descends into a cave to check on the Tylers' hidden cache, Jude refuses to pull him out until he curses. Unwittingly he says "Damn!" twice, and his degeneration accelerates, reaching its nadir when he participates in the looting of an abandoned yacht and corroborates Satan's lie to a British naval officer. Meanwhile, Jude, who has convinced herself that " 'Girls is trash' " and vows to dress and act like a boy, experiences a regeneration and maturation. When Ratcliffe joins the crew of the *Sarah Tyler,* she perks up noticeably and grudgingly begins to accept her gender. She also becomes more honest. In the end the lovers marry and light out for a honeymoon in the islands.

*Stacpoole in later years*

This popular novel inspired two motion-picture adaptations: *Satan's Sister* (1925) and *The Truth about Spring* (1965).

During World War I Stacpoole moved from Ventnor to Astle House, Castle Hedingham, where he lived for a short time under the shadows and roar of zeppelins. Around 1922, when he was almost sixty, he moved to Cliff Dene in Bonchurch, next to the cemetery where Algernon Charles Swinburne had been buried, and lived there for the rest of his life.

His twenty-four books, mostly novels, published between 1922 and 1934 are largely formulaic in plot and distinguishable only by title. Most of them are treasure-hunt tales involving a man and woman who inevitably fall in love. A few of these novels are memorable for their atypical settings. For example, *The Lost Caravan* (1932) is set in Sarajevo, Ragusa, and northern Africa. During this period Stacpoole also wrote several detective novels and stories. Set in San Francisco and the South Seas, *The Mystery of Uncle Bollard* (1927) recounts the hunt for the murderers of a man who had devised a method for breeding pearls. *The Tales of Mynheer Amayat*

(1930) is a collection of fourteen detective stories, including "The Story of O Toyo," all of them about Mynheer Amayat of the Tayas Detective Agency. *Mandarin Gardens* (1933), set in Java, follows the exploits of a police commissioner who falls in love with a beautiful amnesiac and shields her from a murder investigation.

Stacpoole's most impressive work from this period is *Goblin Market,* which takes its title from the poem by Christina Rossetti. Bored with his existence and no longer in love with his wife, Anthony Harrop wanders almost accidentally into a nightclub one evening and meets a sixteen-year-old girl, who turns out to be ill and also a prostitute. He escorts her to her apartment, calls a doctor, pays her bills, and embarks upon a chaste friendship with the girl. His wife, Selina, sympathizes with him as he struggles to recapture his lost youth and experience the romance he never had in life. *Goblin Market* is both a novel of social protest and a sensitive psychological study of a man's midlife crisis. Stacpoole uses Rossetti's poem as a metaphor for London, where young women are pushed into lives of prostitution by powerful social and economic forces. Although he risks his social position by helping the girl, Harrop dives headlong into their relationship and grows as a person, rising above his society and redeeming himself. The girl fills the voids in his life: his longing to be a father, his yearning for romance, and his quest for purpose. Her ghostly doppelgänger even accompanies him when they are physically apart. Unlike many of Stacpoole's novels, which have exotic settings, unusual plots, and effusive styles, *Goblin Market* achieves its effect through understatement and a simple plot.

In 1934 Stacpoole's wife died. Four years later he married her sister, Florence, whom he regarded as "one of the noblest women in the world." These events did little to affect his productivity. Between 1935 and 1940 he published eight books, including five novels and a collection of poems. During the summer of 1941, as the war in Europe raged on, the seventy-eight-year-old Stacpoole was busy correcting the proofs of his *An American at Oxford* (1941), a novel about a young Virginian's romance with a female undergraduate at Oxford, and writing *Men and Mice,* his first autobiography, in which he mentions his meetings with Doyle, James M. Barrie, Anatole France, and Haile Selassie, among others. Long, disjointed reminiscences are punctuated by frequent comments on the war in progress. Its sequel, *More Men and Mice* (1945), is even more discursive, frequently straying from the author's life to report the news of the day.

Of the eight books published between 1943 and 1947, *The Story of My Village* (1947) is the most remarkable. In this allegorical novel set in postwar England, a Jewish engraver, Amiel Lazaroff, and his wife, Eva Braile, wait in terror as an epidemic corneitis creeps toward England and eventually their farm, depriving most men, some women, but no children of their sight. Obviously inspired by Wells's "The Country of the Blind" (1904), *The Story of My Village* examines the sight bias of modern society, suggesting that human beings were better off in simpler times, before the proliferation of technology and especially before the atomic bomb. The novel is brimming with postwar angst. As it does in most of Stacpoole's later fiction, autobiography plays an important role in *The Story of My Village,* providing settings, names, and important dates. Amiel and Eva live at Rose Cottage in Essex, for example, and one of their neighbors is Wells.

Stacpoole's last published novels were *The Man in Armour* (1949), a romance about a young Italian diplomat sent to Germany to spy on a baroness, and *The Land of Little Horses* (1949), an exotic tale about a young married couple, both scientists, who travel to Patagonia to investigate the origin of horses. The author's later years were spent in protest against the dumping of oil at sea. He was the founder of the Penguin Club, an organization dedicated to the study and protection of sea birds, and a frequent contributor of letters to newspapers. His last letter to the London *Times* was published on 15 September 1950. On 12 April 1951, at the age of eighty-eight, Stacpoole died in Shanklin, Isle of Wight. His funeral was attended by a small group, including the poet Alfred Noyes, who in the *British Medical Journal* (21 April 1951) remembered his friend as "an imaginative writer" who "knew that the special function of art was the revelation of beauty."

**References:**

Ashley Gibson, "Dr. H. de Vere Stacpoole," *Bookman* (May 1908): 48–49;

Louis J. McQuilland, "H. de Vere Stacpoole," *Bookman* (June 1921): 126–128.

**Papers:**

The Harry Ransom Humanities Research Center at the University of Texas at Austin houses an important collection of H. de Vere Stacpoole's papers, including part of an unpublished novel by Tyler De Saix, three unpublished plays, and letters to Stacpoole from Arthur Conan Doyle, James M. Barrie, and J. B. Priestley. The following institutions hold manuscripts and/or letters by Stacpoole: the University of Bristol, the University Library of Manchester, the British Library, the Royal Literary Fund, the University of Reading, the Brotherton Library, the Garrick Club, the Glasgow District Libraries, the Bodleian Library, the West Sussex Record Office, the New York Public Library, and the University of Kansas.

# Flora Annie Steel

## (2 April 1847 – 12 April 1929)

### Rebecca J. Sutcliffe
#### Simon Fraser University

BOOKS: *From the Five Rivers* (London: Heinemann, 1893);

*Miss Stuart's Legacy* (New York & London: Macmillan, 1893);

*The Flower of Forgiveness and Other Stories,* 2 volumes (London: Macmillan, 1894);

*The Potter's Thumb* (New York: Harper, 1894; London: Heinemann, 1898);

*Tales of the Punjab Told by the People* (New York & London: Macmillan, 1894);

*Music Hath Charms* (New York & London: Macmillan, 1895);

*Red Rowans* (New York & London: Macmillan, 1895);

*The Swimmers* (New York & London: Macmillan, 1895);

*On the Face of the Waters* (London: Nelson, [1896]; Rahway, N.J.: Mershon, 1896);

*In the Permanent Way* (New York & London: Macmillan, 1897); published as *In the Permanent Way and Other Stories* (London: Heinemann, 1898);

*In the Tideway* (New York & London: Macmillan, 1897);

*The Hosts of the Lord* (London: Heinemann, 1900; Toronto: Copp, Clark, 1900);

*Voices in the Night* (London: Heinemann, 1900); published as *Voices in the Night, a Chronicle of Fantasia* (New York & London: Macmillan, 1900);

*In the Guardianship of God* (London: Heinemann; New York: Macmillan, 1903);

*A Book of Mortals: Being a Record of the Good Deeds and Good Qualities of What Humanity Is Pleased To Call the Lower Animals. Collected by a Fellow Mortal* (London: Heinemann, 1905);

*A Sovereign Remedy* (London: Heinemann, 1906; New York: Trow, 1906);

*India Through the Ages; A Popular and Picturesque History of Hindustan* (New York: Dutton, 1908; London: Routledge, 1909);

*A Prince of Dreamers* (London: Heinemann, 1908; New York: Doubleday, 1909);

*The Gift of the Gods* (London: Heinemann, 1911);

*King-Errant* (London: Heinemann, 1912; New York: Stokes, 1912);

*The Adventures of Akbar* (London: Heinemann, 1913);

*The Mercy of the Lord* (London: Heinemann, 1914; New York: Doran, 1914);

*Dramatic History of India* (Bombay: Cooper, 1917);

*Marmaduke* (London: Heinemann, 1917; New York: Stokes, 1917);

*Mistress of Men* (London: Lane, 1917; New York: Stokes, 1917);

*English Fairy Tales. Retold by F. A. Steel* (London: Macmillan, 1918);

*A Tale of Indian Heroes; Being the Stories of the Mahabharata of the Ramayana* (London: Hutcheon, 1923; New York: Stokes, 1923);

*Tales of the Tides, and Other Stories* (London: Heinemann, 1923);

*The Law of the Threshold* (London: Heinemann, 1924; New York: Macmillan, 1924);

*The Builder* (London: Lane, 1928);

*The Curse of Eve* (London: Lane, 1929);

*The Garden of Fidelity: Being the Autobiography of Flora Annie Steel, 1847–1929* (London: Macmillan, 1929);

*Indian Scene, Collected Short Stories of Flora Annie Steel* (London: Arnold, 1933).

OTHER: *Wide-awake Stories. A Collection of Tales Told by Little Children between Sunset and Sunrise, in the Panjab and Kashmir,* by Steel and Richard C. Temple (Bombay: Education Society, 1884);

*The Complete Indian Housekeeper & Cook; Giving the Duties of Mistress and Servants, the General Management of the House and Practical Recipes for Cooking in All Its Branches,* by Steel and Grace Gardiner (London: Heinemann, 1898);

Mortimer Menpes, *India,* text by Steel (London: Black, 1916).

With characteristic forthrightness, Flora Annie Webster Steel begins her autobiography, *The*

*Flora Annie Steel (photograph by Swaine)*

*Garden of Fidelity* (1929), with the words "Of course I was born; everyone is." She then proceeds to detail for her reader the far more interesting facts of her conception. The event involved an "autocratic mother-in-law, an equally autocratic husband, and an heiress wife who ought to have had control over her own money." Flora was the result of what was apparently an uneasy truce between her parents after her father's "voluntary cessation of marital relations" apparently succeeded in subduing her heiress mother. Whether or not her parents' sex life had anything to do with what Flora terms her "inborn dislike to the sensual side of life" is difficult to say. Far more certain is the influence this story and the Webster domestic scene had on her writing. Although Flora Steel is and was known best as one of

the more prolific female novelists of British India, her work as a whole presents the question of women's sexual, economic, and moral powers and whether they can find expression under the social and legal constraints placed upon it.

Born in Harrow, England, on 2 April 1847 to Scottish parliamentary agent George Webster and his wife (born Margaret Isabella MacCallum), Flora Annie Webster moved in 1856 with her family to Scotland because of her father's bankruptcy. In *Delusions and Discoveries: Studies on India in the British Imagination* (1972), Benita Parry describes the Webster family as "solidly middle class," of a group which "traditionally sent its sons to serve in India," and she sees this background as having given Flora the "assured self-righteousness," immodesty, and indi-

viduality for which she was known all her life. In the autobiography, which has become the chief primary source for our information about Steel, the author records an early life of theatricals, visits, and parties, at one of which she met her future husband, Henry Steel. Following the family's financial crisis, the house the Websters came to occupy in Scotland was not large but could comfortably accommodate the family's eleven children and a modest household staff. Situated in the country, it apparently afforded the aptly named Flora early opportunities to cultivate that acute and fond observation of nature that later found detailed expression in her novels.

Nevertheless, the circumstances of Steel's birth seem to have affected her all her life and marred her middle-class family's apparent "solidity." She was much younger than her female siblings, and it was not deemed feasible for the family to engage a governess just for one girl. So while the money that her father had bullied from her mother could cover the cost of sending the Webster boys away to school at Harrow, Flora had to content herself with a family library of novels and medical textbooks sent home by a relative in Jamaica. By her own account she read voraciously and had briefly considered becoming a doctor. She must have realized, however, that her self-education and gender precluded this. On 31 December 1867 she married Henry Steel, whom she baldly states she did not love. The couple had been married less than twenty-four hours when they took ship for India.

The novels and short stories Steel began writing on her return from the Indian subcontinent in 1889 are mostly based on her experiences there, although *Red Rowans* (1895) and *The Gift of the Gods* (1911) are set in the Scotland of her youth. Steel's husband was appointed district officer of Kasur (a region of the Punjab, now in Pakistan), and the Steels spent most of their time there, although they were moved to other official posts, sometimes at a moment's notice, over the course of their residency. In many ways Flora was an atypical memsahib. She traveled extensively with her husband, cutting her hair short and wearing breeches to accommodate herself to hot weather and horseback. She was intensely interested in Indian customs and languages. She learned to speak Punjabi in order to gain an intimate knowledge of history and folklore, publishing while still in India a pamphlet on Indian handicrafts. Far from experiencing the lethargy which affected most Englishwomen in India, Steel found the country an invigorating outlet for energies she had been unable to express at home. After suffering through what may have been an abortion or a still-

birth in 1869, followed by the birth of her daughter, Mabel, on 10 December 1870, Steel traveled to Scotland on home leave in 1872. As was the custom for Anglo-Indian mothers, she left her daughter with relatives and returned to Kasur, where she immediately set out on an energetic course of "reform." She was an outspoken critic of what she saw as waste, inefficiency, and cruelty in government and elsewhere. She was no cultural relativist, and as she toured, taught, or doctored, she was frequently appalled by the position of women in India. What Steel thought of as slavery inspired her to set up schools for girls that replaced Euclid with hygiene on their curriculum, to become in 1884 the first female "Inspectress of Schools" in India, to investigate employment options for women in the then male-dominated Indian embroidery industry, and to oppose Indian independence on the grounds that, with half its population "imprisoned" in poverty or the *zenana,* India's electorate was as yet imperfect.

With the obvious exception of Queen Victoria, women had little or no official role in the running of the British Empire. Because of their position somewhere between oppressor and oppressed, women who lived and wrote under imperialism make particularly interesting studies of subjectivity in this period, and Steel was one such woman. A popular writer in her day, her light has since dimmed under the overshadowing fame of her near contemporary, Rudyard Kipling. Her life and work reflect her contradictory position in India: she was an ardent, paternalistic, and often racist supporter of the idea of empire, yet she vehemently criticized its practice on the subcontinent and was until the final years of her life an outspoken defender of women's rights.

Since the nature of most of her writing was retrospective, Steel wrote between housekeeping duties at her Scottish shooting lodge or in her London home, either from memory, from journals she kept while in India, or from research. Steel even claimed that some of her early stories were dictated verbatim by one Nathaniel James Craddock, an engine driver on the Indian railroad who appeared at her side to have his stories translated into print. Two of her early works, *From the Five Rivers* (1893) and *The Potter's Thumb* (1894), were the means of Steel's initiating a close friendship with the publisher William Heinemann, whose house was to issue many more of her short stories and novels. In order to gather material for this novel, Flora returned to India in 1894 without Henry. In Kasur and Delhi she lived among the townspeople on a rooftop dwelling, which she took great pride in furnishing and keep-

ing without a servant. She maintains that she was one of the first people to be given unlimited access to the huge archive of the mutiny, or rebellion, at Delhi. She was permitted to remove it to her lodgings and in her autobiography typically notes the sense of power over the past this gave her, since she could have altered or burned at her discretion parts of this priceless Western account of history (leading her reader to wonder if, in fact, she did).

Flora's version of the rebellion, the result of several weeks of poring over dusty notes and dispatches, is a rather uneven romance. It tells the story of two Englishwomen, the matronly Kate Erlton, and the risqué Alice Gissing, their government spy-protector, the wayward soldier Jim Douglas, and his widowed Indian servant, Tara Devi. By delineating the romantic and financial entanglements of her characters – Kate Erlton becomes attracted to Jim Douglas when she tries to bribe him to ignore the questionable gambling of her husband, who spends his earnings on his mistress Alice Gissing – Steel builds an atmosphere of intrigue, greed, and decadence in the chapters leading up to the first outbreak of hostilities. What is now known as the Indian Rebellion, or the First War of Independence, began in Bengal in 1857 when a regiment of Sepoy cavalry refused for religious reasons to use British-issue gun cartridges, which had been smeared with animal grease. Steel uses this incident, and the violence that then spread to other parts of India, as a way to put her female characters in need of rescue. Alice Gissing dies beautifully and heroically, while Kate Erlton is hidden by Tara Devi on a Delhi rooftop during the siege of that city (Steel bases this episode on an actual incident) and is finally saved partly by her own innate goodness and partly by the aid of a persistent Jim Douglas. The story moves along at a dramatic pace and is fairly suspenseful, except when it becomes bogged down in lengthy narratives of battle strategy or when it adheres too strictly to the actual time line of historical events.

Steel was determined that her account should be definitive and therefore rigidly accurate. One of her aims in writing *On the Face of the Waters* was to reduce the fear and distrust that had existed between Indians and the English since the mutiny and before. According to Rebecca Saunders in her article "Gender, Colonialism, and Exile: Flora Annie Steel and Sara Jeannette Duncan in India" (1989), Steel succeeds only in the first half of the novel in giving her readers what she hoped was a "fair and unbiased" picture of the conduct of both sides in the conflict. It is in the early chapters that Steel is (for

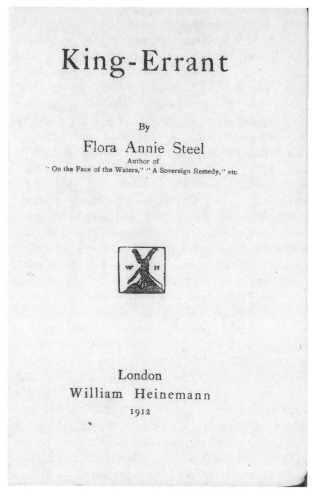

*Title page for one of Steel's novels on the Moghul dynasty, featuring the warrior emperor Babar (courtesy of the Lilly Library, Indiana University)*

the time perhaps shockingly) critical of English behavior. Yet the criticism here (and in her autobiographical accounts of her many disagreements with government) is tempered by its tone and intent. To Steel the events leading up to the rebellion happened because the British were not conducting themselves along the lines of honor and moral purity to which they, as Englishmen and Englishwomen, were bound by pride in their race. It was not that Steel thought the British should not be in India; to the contrary, she viewed India as Britain's special destiny and charge and thought that the English, by their conduct, were not fulfilling their obligations. She comments throughout her autobiography on the niggardliness and inefficiency of a bureaucracy that she felt lowered British prestige in the eyes of Indians. To this extent, then, she was critical of her compatriots' behavior but only insofar as it undermined Britain's hold on the subcontinent. The criti-

cisms of the rebellion that appear in the first few chapters of her novel, although on occasion quite virulent, are nevertheless undermined by the last few chapters, where Steel seems to take prurient delight in describing the forms of revenge the English took against India's native population for the outrages the rebels supposedly committed.

According to Saunders, one of Steel's achievements in her novel of the rebellion was to create a new type of female character in Anglo-Indian fiction. Alice Gissing is a "frank woman . . . described with frankness." She would not be acceptable in English society, and, although she is barely admitted to the social world of Anglo-India, she chooses to remain independent of it. She is undaunted by what was for other English people the "beastly" Indian climate and its "hideous" customs, and, as Saunders notes, she does not participate in the English "cult of home." Saunders views Alice Gissing as Steel's attempt to work through India's meaning to British women: it could represent simultaneously immense freedom and stifling restraint. Steel had experimented earlier with such concepts in *The Potter's Thumb* in the characters of Gwen Boynton and Rose Tweedie. This novel, about corruption involving irrigation and racing (two English-controlled sources of revenue) also follows Gwen, Rose, and a Eurasian woman named Azizan as they struggle with one of the chief reasons for European women's presence in India: marriage. Although some married women went out to India to find independence, many single women, including Steel's daughter, Mabel, went there because the chances of finding a husband were better there than in England, where women outnumbered men. The Alice Gissings of Steel's novels vacillate between masculine and feminine norms of behavior in their attempts to navigate the traditions and possibilities of frontier society.

The penchant for historical accuracy demonstrated in *On the Face of the Waters* and the reasons behind it reassert themselves in a series of novels Steel wrote on the Mogul dynasty. *A Prince of Dreamers* (1908), *King-errant* (1912), *Mistress of Men* (1917), and *The Builder* (1928) follow the fortunes and failures of four successive emperors of India and are based, as Steel sometimes quite self-consciously asserts, on the rulers' memoirs and poetry. Steel seems to have shared her compatriots' romanticized conception of the period of Mogul rule as a time of grandeur, prosperity, and civilization along Western lines for the subcontinent before it lapsed into the perceived squalor, anarchy, and sloth that the British sought to cure. In Steel's view the British were a better, stronger reincarnation of the Mogul

dynasty. In *King-errant* she tells the life of the warrior emperor Babar, superimposed with images and language from English sporting life: as a boy, Babar's experience "taught him that if you fought fair you failed at times, but in the end you came out top-dog in the general scrimmage of claims and clans." Steel is careful to detail Babar's lineage and to point out that these "paler" invaders from "North and West" are descended from Genghis Khan, as were the British monarchs. As Steel chronicles Babar's relentless campaign to attack, annex, and subdue the various principalities of India, she pauses to remark of this precursor to British conquerors, "He would seize all; but he would remain a kindly gentleman." When Babar finally conquers India, he is faced with cholera, intense heat, scarcity of provisions, and growing hostility between his own people and the native population they have conquered. One of his advisers counsels "the wisdom of doing as all the past conquerors of India had done; that is leaving so soon as the treasures had been divided," but Steel writes that Babar "meant, with all the strength of his vivid vitality, to found a dynasty; he meant that his son and his son's sons should inherit what he had won for them," the implication for her English readers being that true rulers do not give in to India's hardships or temptations as other Western nations had seemed to do.

Neither do their women, and one of the most interesting of the quartet of Mogul novels from this perspective is *Mistress of Men*. Ostensibly a life of the "complete lover," the emperor Jahanghir, it is actually an exploration of one of the main themes of Steel's life and work: what strong women can make of marriage to passive men. *Mistress of Men* is dedicated not to Jahanghir but to his influential wife, Mihr-un-Nissa (later Nurjahan), a "Great Woman who in turns was Queen 'O Woman, Light of the Home, Light of the World." *Mistress of Men* is unique in telling the whole life of a woman, where most romances or novels of the Victorian period ended women's lives either at marriage or in picturesque death from childbearing. In stark contrast to the standard opinions of her time, Steel regarded the years following menopause as being the most productive for women. She began her own writing career in her late forties. Of setting out to do research for *On the Face of the Waters,* she writes in her autobiography, "I was nearing the great climacteric for most women, and I was beginning to feel — not any diminution of energy, any failure physical or mental; but the exact contrary," and continues, "I doubt, in fact, if in all my youth I had ever felt so much alive as the day in the autumn of 1894 when I

set sail, alone, for India." This energy is transferred in the novel to Nurjahan, who comes into her fullest power in her fifties.

The varieties of power Indian women could exercise was a fascinating subject for Steel, and the study of Nurjahan reflects this interest. During her stay in 1894 in her husband's former station of Kasur, she inquired into the relations between the sexes and was sensitive in her later comments to what she saw as the imperatives of religious duty that caused women to find ingenious ways to manipulate their own destinies. She was allowed behind the restriction of purdah to do "an immense amount of doctoring . . . having very often as many as fifty patients a day" and comments on the special privileges and powers widows seem to have held in their own societies. She disapproved of the practice of purdah, since she thought that the justification of it as protection of women as special beings in their own right was really just an excuse for its real motive, the segregation from prostitutes of good breeder stock. Steel tried to communicate her horror at the treatment of women in India to her English readers through Nurjahan. As an infant the future empress is abandoned in the desert, as was frequently the practice when pregnancy resulted in a female child, and is found by a retainer of the court who decides to keep her after he notices the "pluck" the infant displays. Through her cunning and her beauty, and with the help of a lucky charm, Nurjahan makes an advantageous marriage, is widowed, and eventually marries the emperor, whom she inspires to conquest and protects from court intrigues. Nevertheless, Nurjahan is always aware of her precarious position as a female member of court. Ruminating on her future after her lucky charm is lost, Nurjahan recalls that the charm "had been something outside herself, and life had taught her that her only safety lay in self-reliance; that she, and she only made or marred her fate." Yet she also realizes that her beauty, and men's responses to it, puts her in a double bind: "What had she gained in the past?" she thinks. "Power, it is true; but power gained not so much by talent as by beauty. She felt cribbed, cabined, confined by it; She felt that she could not be true to herself." In the end Nurjahan is defeated by the treachery of detractors who feel threatened by the specter of a woman holding the reins of power. With the story of Nurjahan, Steel brought before her English readers the specter of the late empress of England and India, Queen Victoria, a woman who ruled a world where women were not thought fit to venture alone outside their own doors.

Steel in 1897 (photograph by Elliott & Fry, Ltd.)

*Mistress of Men* represents one of Steel's stronger forays into the realm of women's rights in fiction. In her later years she kept up her active and energetic life. She acted as secretary to a committee organized to give a jubilee dinner at which prominent women would ask their favorite prominent man to dinner; she ran a small business selling embroidered scarves to benefit the secluded, impoverished retainer-widows of Delhi; and, near the end of her life, demonstrating the strength of age, she sailed to Jamaica with her nephew to claim hereditary rights over a family plantation that had lapsed into the hands of its overseer. She also spent hours in the reading room of the British Museum, studying books on human sexuality, a subject that became uppermost in her mind after years of writing romances. Her final novel, based on these researches, seems to backtrack on her earlier support of the women's movement, however.

With the telling title *The Curse of Eve* (1929), Steel's last novel, set in post–World War I England, tells the story of the Graham siblings, George, Eve,

and Alan. Alan, a doctor, becomes obsessed by a prostitute/dancer named Lil, whom he meets while he is tending her dying mother. His sister, Eve, is equally obsessed with the fiancé of her best friend, Margie. Margie is heiress to her ancestral seat and wants to keep the estate in the family by marrying her impoverished but handsome cousin from India. On his arrival in England, however, he is mesmerized by Eve, who eventually marries him after Margie is killed in an accident. An aging society woman believes that the third Graham, George, intends to marry her, but instead he proposes to the woman's daughter after a rather unsightly contest between the two women. Much sadness and mayhem follows these entanglements, and blame for the whole must be laid, according to Steel, at the feet of "Woman," the supreme temptress who repeats her original sin in every contact with the male sex. Curiously, *The Curse of Eve* begins positively as a diatribe against overpopulation and the misery that follows from women having too many children, but Steel concludes that women's oversexed nature is responsible for the situation. Her cure for overpopulation is longer skirts and celibacy.

In addition to such untenable conclusions, Steel's racist pronouncements must also be considered in any assessment of her work. Her novels are in this respect products of their time, as were those of Kipling or Mark Twain. Parry has commented on Steel's conception of Indians as suffering from "curious resignation," "placidity," "impassive acquiescence," a total disregard for time of day, "lawlessness," and "ferocious passions." Such thinking furthered the imperialist project in India and elsewhere, since the success of the project depended on a perception of Anglo-Saxon superiority. Steel's favorite word for India was "unfathomable," although she felt peculiarly called upon to fathom it for her English audience. She was fond of stereotyping, and few groups escaped: her books are peopled with excitable drunken Irish and Scots; cool, reserved English; and unscrupulous, money-hungry Jews.

Yet Steel should be recognized for her adeptness at creating a sense of the sometimes beautiful, sometimes ugly, often painful or ironic contrasts and contradictions that constitute a life spent negotiating a sense of self in unfamiliar territory. As one of the first to use literature to attack one of the most sacred myths of the Raj, the mutiny of 1857, she paved the way for more stringent and comprehensive criticisms of imperialism, such as Joseph Conrad's "Heart of Darkness" (1902) and E. M.

Forster's *A Passage to India* (1924). Steel was also a powerful stylist. A passage from *The Curse of Eve*, in which the author describes the observations of one of her characters as he paces the streets of London, illustrates Steel's powerful talent for rhythmic, evocative description:

> The fresh fallen snow still lay unsullied on the roofs, and showed like edgings of swansdown on the cornices and window frames; but it had quite gone from the streets. And the pavement lay bare and mottled with mud by the passage of much humanity. It was blistered as if with smallpox, he thought. Yes, humanity could sully most things, even the pure snow from heaven. The shops were all gay with preparations for coming Christmas, and the carcasses of fat animals, slain for the festival, hung decorated with holly and mistletoe in the butchers' shops. Just six o'clock on a Saturday night! So the workmen's wives were thronging to make their purchases for the week end; but it was not only provision shops which attracted their attention. The drapery shops made them stop for a minute or two, and round some, where wax mannequins stood petrified at their own superexcellence of attire, crowds gathered, melted away and gathered again.

Flora Steel's novels have much to tell the present-day reader about how Englishwomen presented themselves in their lives and in their writing and the often equivocal roles they had to play in sustaining or undermining the economic, social, and moral underpinnings of the British Empire; for that reason, if none other, they should be read.

**References:**
Benita Parry, *Delusions and Discoveries: Studies on India in the British Imagination, 1880–1930* (Berkeley: University of California Press, 1972), pp. 100–130;
Daya Patwardhan, *A Star of India: Flora Annie Steel, Her Works and Times* (Bombay, 1963);
Nancy L. Paxton, "Complicity and Resistance in the Writings of Flora Annie Steel and Annie Besant," in *Western Women and Imperialism,* edited by Napur Chaudhuri and Margaret Strobel (Bloomington: Indiana University Press, 1992), pp. 156–176;
Violet Powell, *Flora Annie Steel, Novelist of India* (London: Heinemann, 1981);
Rebecca Saunders, "Gender, Colonialism, and Exile: Flora Annie Steel and Sara Jeannette Duncan in India," in *Women's Writing in Exile,* edited by Mary Lynn Broe and Angela Ingram (Chapel Hill: University of North Carolina Press, 1989), pp. 363–394.

# James Stephens

*(9 February 1880 or 2 February 1882 – 26 December 1950)*

Kiernan Ryan
*University of Cambridge*

See also the Stephens entry in *DLB 19: British Poets, 1880–1914.*

BOOKS: *Insurrections* (Dublin: Maunsel, 1909; New York: Macmillan, 1909);

*The Charwoman's Daughter* (London: Macmillan, 1912); published as *Mary, Mary* (Boston: Small, Maynard, 1912);

*The Hill of Vision* (New York: Macmillan, 1912; Dublin: Maunsel, 1912; revised edition, London: Macmillan, 1922);

*The Crock of Gold* (London: Macmillan, 1912; New York: Macmillan, 1913);

*Here Are Ladies* (London & New York: Macmillan, 1913);

*Five New Poems* (London: Flying Fame Chapbooks, 1913);

*The Demi-Gods* (London & New York: Macmillan, 1914);

*Songs from the Clay* (London & New York: Macmillan, 1915);

*The Adventures of Seumas Beg/The Rocky Road to Dublin* (London & New York: Macmillan, 1915);

*Green Branches* (Dublin & London: Maunsel, 1916; New York: Macmillan, 1916);

*The Insurrection in Dublin* (Dublin & London: Maunsel, 1916; New York: Macmillan, 1916);

*Hunger: A Dublin Story,* as James Esse (Dublin: Candles Press, 1918);

*Reincarnations* (London & New York: Macmillan, 1918);

*Irish Fairy Tales* (London & New York: Macmillan, 1920);

*Arthur Griffith: Journalist and Statesman* (Dublin: Wilson, Hartnell, 1922);

*Deirdre* (London & New York: Macmillan, 1923);

*Little Things* (Freelands, Ky.: W. M. Hill, 1924);

*In the Land of Youth* (London & New York: Macmillan, 1924);

*A Poetry Recital* (New York: Macmillan, 1925; revised and enlarged edition, New York & London: Macmillan, 1926);

*James Stephens. The photograph shows the author in the National Library in Dublin and is inscribed to the book collector John Quinn (Anderson Galleries, Sale 1806, 11–13 February 1924).*

*A Poetry Recital* (London: Macmillan, 1925);

*Collected Poems* (London & New York: Macmillan, 1926);

*Etched in Moonlight* (London & New York: Macmillan, 1928);

*On Prose and Verse* (New York: Bowling Green Press, 1928);

*Julia Elizabeth: A Comedy in One Act* (New York: Crosby Gaige, 1929);

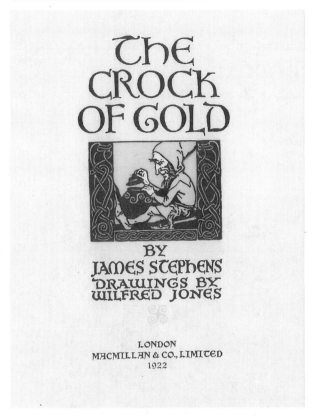

*Title page for the illustrated edition of Stephens's first novel (courtesy of the Lilly Library, Indiana University)*

*The Optimist* (Gaylordsville, Conn.: Slide Mountain, 1929);

*The Outcast* (London: Faber & Faber, 1929);

*Theme and Variations* (New York: Fountain Press, 1930);

*How St. Patrick Saves the Irish* (N.p.: Privately printed, 1931);

*Strict Joy* (London & New York: Macmillan, 1931);

*Stars Do Not Make a Noise* (Los Angeles: Deux Magots Press, 1931);

*Kings and the Moon* (London & New York: Macmillan, 1938);

*James Stephens: A Selection,* edited by Lloyd Frankenberg (London: Macmillan, 1962); published as *A James Stephens Reader* (New York: Macmillan, 1962);

*James, Seumas and Jacques: Unpublished Writings by James Stephens,* edited by Frankenberg (London & New York: Macmillan, 1964);

*Desire and Other Stories,* selected and introduced by Augustine Martin (Dublin: Poolbeg, 1980).

James Stephens was the most beguiling and enigmatic of the writers who contributed to the Irish literary revival during the early decades of the twentieth century. His reputation now rests almost entirely on *The Crock of Gold* (1912), but at the height of his powers he created a remarkable body of poetry and fiction, which won him acclaim in his own lifetime and which is long overdue for reappraisal. To William Butler Yeats, AE (George Russell), and George Moore, the lions of Ireland's literary renaissance, Stephens's originality and distinction were beyond dispute; James Joyce, who at first perceived in Stephens "my rival, the latest Irish genius," later became his fast friend and admirer, entrusting him with the completion of *Finnegans Wake* (1939) in the event of his proving unequal to the task. Stephens's prestige as a writer was threatened only by his prowess as a conversationalist and raconteur, which secured his canonization with AE and Stephen MacKenna as one of the three legendary giants of Dublin talk. Although the novelist's muse deserted him in later years, his loquacity and wit never did, and the twilight of his career found him filling American lecture halls and bewitching radio audiences with his readings and reminiscences.

Stephens's charismatic appeal was enhanced by his odd physique and the mystery of his origins. His diminutive stature (he was barely five feet tall), large head, gnomish features, and melancholy gaze doomed him to celebrity as the leprechaun of Irish literature. But as Oliver St. John Gogarty recalled, "His lack of inches gave him one advantage. He could cast off the conventions which bound ordinary people and become a gleeman, the most lyrical spirit of his time." Stephens himself was far from reluctant to cultivate an image that captivated readers and listeners alike. Indeed he looked, to quote Augustine Martin, "as if he had somehow invented himself," and in a sense that is just what he did, shrouding his parentage and early years in a haze of speculation that subsequent scholarship has done little to dispel.

The exact date of his birth is uncertain. James Stephens claimed he had been born, to parents he would not or could not name, somewhere in County Dublin on the same day as Joyce, 2 February 1882. But a persuasive case has been made for his having been born in the city of Dublin two years earlier, on 9 February 1880, to Francis Stephens, a van man, and his wife, Charlotte Collins. Nor can the possibility be excluded that Stephens was a foundling whose time and place of birth he himself did not know and that James Stephens was a name he assumed or acquired. The fact that he published or acted under five other names as well (Stephen James, James Esse, Samuel James, Seumas James,

and Shemus Beg) lends weight to this thesis, suggesting a rootlessness of identity that might explain his lifelong obsession with reincarnation and metamorphosis. There is, however, no firm proof in which to anchor any of these theories, and the puzzle remains unsolved.

Stephens was equally secretive about his childhood years and early youth. Probability points to his being the James Stephens registered as a boarder from his sixth to his sixteenth year at the Meath Protestant Industrial School for impoverished or homeless boys. Whatever the truth is, Stephens preferred to spin more colorful yarns about this period of his life. Dublin lapped up his tales of working as a circus acrobat and clown, tramping the roads of Ireland like a gypsy, sleeping rough in parks and fighting a swan for a scrap of bread, and being saved from near starvation by a tenderhearted whore. His compulsion to mythologize his life, to invent an appropriate past for himself, does little to alleviate the task of the biographer, but it speaks volumes about the wellsprings of Stephens's creativity. His habitual response to queries about the facts was "My life began when I started writing." The one sure circumstance of his boyhood is that he knew what it meant to be ravenous, for hunger haunted his imagination, just as malnutrition blighted his health, for the rest of his life: "I have been a hungry man," he wrote to Lewis Chase, "many, many times."

Stephens's biography begins to materialize only in 1896, when he is known to have been employed as a junior clerk in the office of a Dublin solicitor. For the next sixteen years he languished in the purgatory of countless similar posts. What he learned from this experience he would later sum up in one sentence: "I would sooner be a corpse than a clerk." Nevertheless it was during these years that he surfaced as a writer. By 1907 he had established himself as a regular contributor of essays, poems, and stories to Arthur Griffith's newspaper *Sinn Féin*. AE spotted his talent, took the fledgling author under his wing, and ushered him into the literary salons of Dublin. It was AE who introduced Stephens to the theosophical doctrines that enthralled the architects of the revival and which fostered in his protégé an enduring absorption in oriental philosophy. But he also encouraged Stephens to attend political meetings of *Sinn Féin* and Gaelic League classes to help forge the cultural revolution upon which the political liberation of the nation depended.

About this time Stephens set up house with Millicent Kavanagh, or "Cynthia" as he rechristened her, a married woman recently estranged from her husband. Stephens introduced Cynthia to his friends as his wife and raised her baby daughter, Iris, as his own child. (They eventually married in 1919 after the death of Cynthia's husband.) Cynthia gave birth to Stephens's son, James Naoise, in 1909. The same year saw the publication of Stephens's first book of poetry, *Insurrections* (1909), which signaled the arrival of an energetic new voice in Irish letters. The weakness for pastoral lyrics and metaphysical musing that would eviscerate his subsequent verse is already apparent in this volume, but the unbridled tirades of furious and demented figures, the sinister sketches of Dublin's backstreets by night, and the book's apprehension of life as a "frenzied fight for food" are startlingly vivid.

In 1910 Stephens's first novel was serialized as *Mary, A Story* in the *Irish Review,* a new journal which he had helped to launch. The year 1911 saw the production of his play *The Marriage of Julia Elizabeth* by the Theatre of Ireland, a company with which Stephens had occasionally acted. But it was the following year which was to prove his annus mirabilis and change his life forever, for the critical and financial success of *The Charwoman's Daughter* (1912), *The Crock of Gold,* and his second volume of poems, *The Hill of Vision* (1912), allowed Stephens to abandon his clerical drudgery and concentrate entirely on his writing.

Stephens held that the author's true biography, his inner psychological life, was to be sought in his works rather than in the contingencies of his daily existence. For this most secretive of men each book harbored two tales, the one consciously written for the reader and the coded confession that "the writer has not been able to keep out of his pages." In his essay "The Novelist and Final Utterance" (1924) Stephens states: "In every book it is the author that is the real subject. The story he is telling is his own choice. And in considering it we are investigating one true aspect of the author in his desire-nature." Stephens's own "desire-nature" is already plainly visible in his first novel, *The Charwoman's Daughter,* where the squalid realities glimpsed in the verse of *Insurrections* are transmuted into a fairy-tale finale whose implausibility only intensifies its fragile charm.

The book's psychological penetration and complexity of mood marked it from the outset as the work of a singular talent. Its golden-haired heroine, Mary Makebelieve, lives with her mother in a dingy room at the top of a Dublin tenement. Mrs. Makebelieve toils as a domestic in wealthier abodes, leaving her daughter free to stroll through the parks

*A letter from Stephens to his stepdaughter, Iris, in which he discusses Walter Scott, George Eliot, and popular fiction (private collection; from* Letters of James Stephens, *edited by Richard J. Finneran, 1974)*

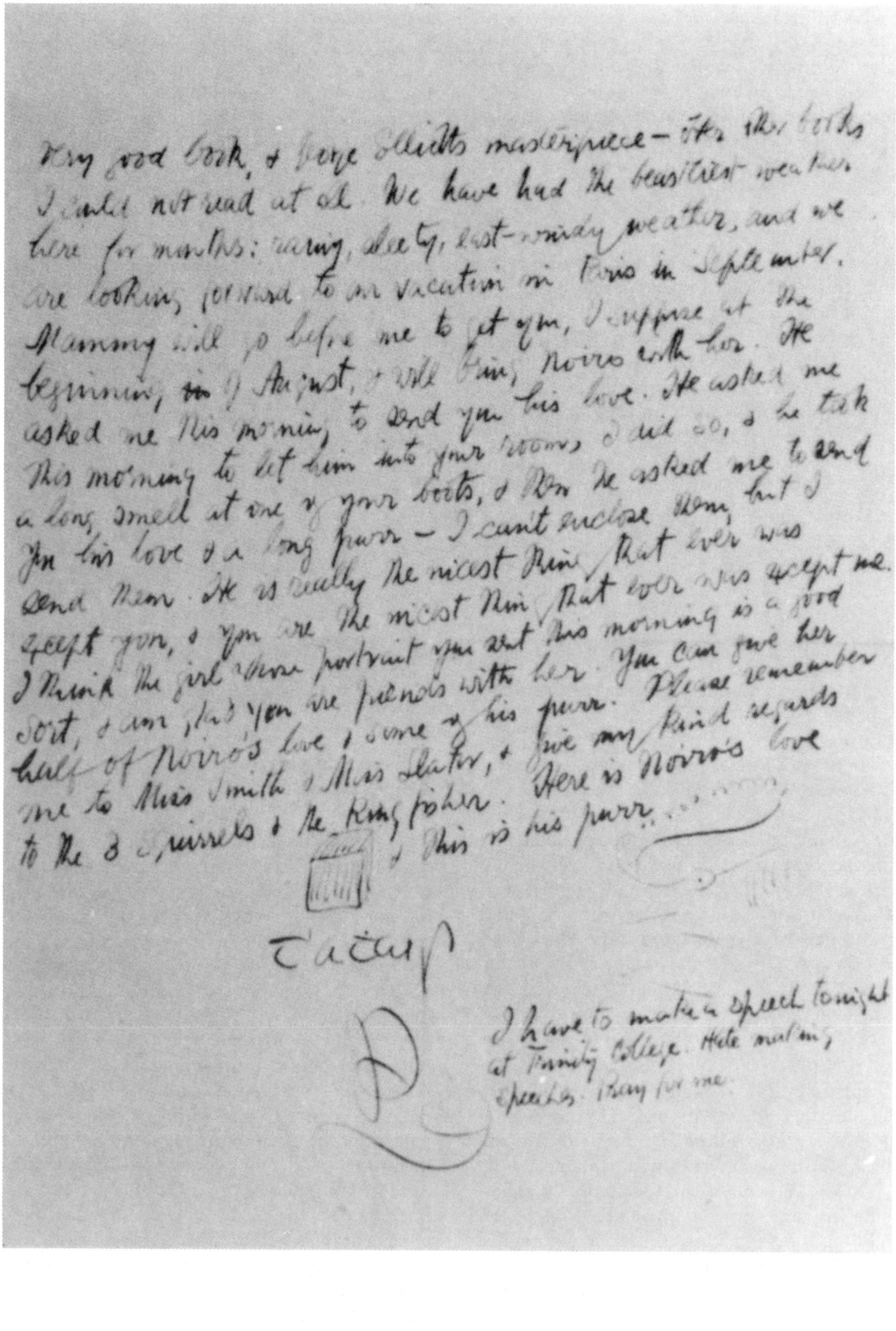

very good book, & George Elliott's masterpiece — Her other books
I could not read at all. We have had the beastliest weather
here for months: raining, sleety, east-windy weather, and we
are looking forward to our vacation in Paris in September.
Mammy will go before me to get you, I suppose at the
beginning of August, & will bring Noirro with her. He
asked me this morning to send you his love. He asked me
this morning to let him into your rooms I did so, & he took
a long, smell at one of your boots, & then he asked me to send
you his love & a long purr — I can't enclose them, but I
send them. He is really the nicest thing that ever was
except you, & you are the nicest thing that ever was except me.
I think the girl whose portrait you sent this morning is a good
sort, & am glad you are friends with her. You can give her
half of Noirro's love & some of his purr. Please remember
me to Miss Smith & Miss Slater, & give my kind regards
to the 3 squirrels & the Kingfisher. Here is Noirro's love

[drawing] & this is his purr ............

Tacup

[signature]

I have to make a speech tonight
at Trinity College. Hate making
speeches. Pray for me.

and streets of the city, dreaming of the glamorous lover who will transport her to a world of wealth and elegance, to "that Somewhere which is the country of Romance." What she actually encounters is the huge, forbidding figure of the policeman, a recurrent object of fascinated loathing in Stephens's work. Mary is mesmerized by his brute masculinity and the strange promise of violence in his hands. What follows is a tale of innocence disillusioned, as Mary discovers the shallow, predatory motives of her admirer, whose love is unmasked as raw greed: "he wanted to eat her up and go away with her bones sticking out of his mouth as the horns of a deer protrude from the jaws of an anaconda." But the ogre is finally banished, the tenement princess finds truer love in a famished young clerk who dreams of an emancipated Ireland and a socialist utopia, and a rich uncle's legacy from America delivers the Makebelieves safely into the realm of wish fulfilment.

Stephens claimed that he modeled Mary on Cynthia and found the charwoman's character within himself. Nor need one look further than the author for the blueprint of the indigent, idealistic clerk who wrests Mary's heart from the oppressive incarnation of the law. The book's success derives in large part from Stephens's ability to immerse himself in the mentality of his protagonists. A work of art, in his view, fails only "when the artist cannot will to be his matter, and, so, cannot will his matter to be . . . to fuse self and not-self, is the privilege, and is the first and the last duty, of an artist." But *The Charwoman's Daughter* is distinguished also by its eagerness to embrace divergent attitudes and effects. Poignant yearnings slide into wry comedy, stark pathos reposes beside aphoristic wisdom, and cool rage at the misery of the destitute consorts with unembittered celebrations of sheer kindness and the resilience of the imagination. "*The Charwoman's Daughter*," wrote the reviewer in the *Nation* of 13 April 1912, "is rich in atmospheric freshness, in its cunning, cumulative appeal to our sense of common humanity, to our faith, our courage and our love."

Stephens's gift for juggling ostensibly incompatible tones and emotions led Frank O'Connor, in *A Short History of Irish Literature* (1967), to applaud him as the Irish writer with "the most agile mind," to see in him "a sort of literary acrobat, doing hair-raising swoops up in the roof of the tent." Though his adventures as a circus tumbler were in all likelihood apocryphal, it is true that Stephens had once been an accomplished gymnast whose team won the Irish Shield in 1901 and that

he had delighted in demonstrating his agility in public to his friends.

The same passion to defy gravity, to dazzle the witness with virtuoso displays of balancing and buoyancy, finds displaced satisfaction in his career as a writer graced with lightness of being, and nowhere in his fiction is the performance more exhilarating than in *The Crock of Gold*. With this incomparable comic idyll Stephens vaulted out of the Dublin slums into an Irish Arcadia. The story revolves around the quests of two characters: the Philosopher, who dwells in the dark wood with the Thin Woman and their children Seumas and Brigid Beg, and the exquisitely beautiful shepherdess Caitilin Ni Murrachu, the epitome of ripe virginity on the brink of sexual initiation. The Philosopher, whose solemn eccentricity accounts for much of the book's hilarity, is at first entombed in his own arid abstractions. Caitilin, on the other hand, is consumed by a frustrated yearning whose nature she cannot yet identify. Both characters find their sensuous delight in life and love released by encounters with the Greek god Pan and the Celtic god Angus Óg. In the tangled course of events the Philosopher is wrongly blamed by the leprechauns of Gort na Cloca Mora for the theft of their crock of gold, and he is arrested and sentenced to death for a murder that never took place. The grim account of his incarceration threatens to plunge the book into despair, but the fairy host led by Angus Óg and Caitilin marches upon the city, frees the Philosopher from prison, and inaugurates the liberation of the whole land from the tyranny of commercial calculation and repressive morality.

"In this book," Stephens explained, "there is only one character – Man – Pan is his sensual nature, Caitilin his emotional nature, the Philosopher his intellect at play, Angus Óg his intellect spiritualised, the policemen his conventions and logics, the leprecauns his elemental side, the children his innocence, and the idea is not too rigidly carried out, but that is how I conceived the story." On one level the novel is a prophetic Blakean allegory about the fragmentation of the human faculties and their triumphant reintegration. On another plane it is the dream Stephens shared with Yeats and AE of the ancient pagan gods returning to herald a new dispensation. "We could wish for Ireland," wrote AE in the *Irish Homestead* of 12 October 1912, "the ecstatic finale of the 'Crock of Gold' and the conquest of its heart by a nobler Eros." As Stephens stressed, however, there is nothing schematic about the novel's elaboration of its vision. Around the vatic fable frolic slapstick and sublime nonsense, sly iro-

*The* Aonach Tailteann *festival in Dublin (August 1924). Standing are G. K. Chesterton, Stephens, and Lennox Robinson; seated are W. B. Yeats, Sir Compton MacKenzie, Augustus John, and Sir Edward Lutyens.*

nies and uproarious farce, which redeem the work's rapt prefigurings from solemnity and turn the tale into a carnival of absurdities, a bubbling primal stream of gaiety. AE described *The Crock of Gold* in a letter to John Quinn as "the great literary success of the year 1912," and the following year it was awarded the Polignac Prize. In his speech to the Royal Society of Literature at the award ceremony, Yeats hailed *The Crock of Gold* as "a beautiful, wise, wayward phantasy . . . a phantasy that plays with all things, that reverences everything and reverences nothing, an audacious laughter, a whimsical pity." He proclaimed the novel to be proof that Dublin had "begun to live with deeper life."

In May 1913 Stephens moved to Paris, where he completed and published *Here Are Ladies* (1913) and his third novel, *The Demi-Gods* (1914), which he wrote in a Montparnasse café. The short stories in *Here Are Ladies* return to contemporary urban reality to brood over dead or dying marriages. The war between the sexes is a constant preoccupation of Stephens's work, but these tales of love turned to boredom, revulsion, and betrayal harbor, like their most memorable character, "a kind of masked ferocity" unrivaled in his fiction. In "A Glass of Beer" a widower sits in a Paris café savoring his hatred of his deceased wife and still nursing a fantasy of butchering her: "He had caressed it, rehearsed it, relished it, and jerked her head back, and hacked, and listened to her entreaties bubbling through blood!" His gaze lingers on the repulsive yet irresistible mouths of passing women: "Ragged lips that had been chewed by every mad dog in the world. What lips there were everywhere! Bright scarlet splashes in dead-white faces. Thin red gashes that suggested rat-traps instead of kisses." It is important to set Stephens in this vein alongside the creator of *The Charwoman's Daughter* and *The Crock of Gold,* with their radiant, inviolable heroines and serene faith in the redemptive might of love and laughter, for the contrast exposes what the novels had to suppress: a gut impulse to regard life as a vicious, unremitting struggle between eaters and eaten, tormentors and victims, affording the reader at best what Stephens describes in *The Hill of Vision* as "a chuckle in the void."

*The Demi-Gods* blends the miraculous and the mundane with as little sense of discord as *The Crock of Gold.* Three angels alight on Irish soil one night, share a meal with the tinker Patsy MacCann and his daughter Mary, and decide to tag along with their vagabond hosts. The picaresque narrative tracks

them south from Donegal through Connemara and Kerry and then back up to Donegal, improvising bizarre encounters and extravagant yarns along the way. A vague romantic plotline is discernible beyond the intricate prevarications of the prose: by the end of the novel the violent breach between Patsy and his volatile lover Eileen Ni Cooley has been healed, and two of the angels have flown off, leaving one handsome young demigod behind to enjoy mortal love and a footloose life with Mary MacCann. To reduce the book to its plot, however, would be to miss the point of its freewheeling, digressive technique.

The picaresque form suits Stephens's mischievous, nomadic soul perfectly, unshackling it from novelistic conventions and moral codes. His tinkers dwell beyond the social pale, knuckling under to no man's creed, scorning the customs and obligations of organized communities. Patsy survives through his ingenuity in giving conformity the slip, in staying one step ahead of its clutches: "Laws were for other people, but they were not for him; he crawled under or vaulted across these ethical barriers, and they troubled him no more than as he had to bend or climb a little to avoid them." In a letter dated 1911 to Lord Dunsany, Stephens had proclaimed under the abiding influence of William Blake: "I only know of one morality and that is Energy. I call every *thing* or *thought* that acquiesces or sits down Vice & I call everything that disobeys, and refuses, and breaks, 'Virtue' & again I call Force Virtue & Energy Vice and the latter seems to me the better of the two. . . . A city would travel as long a distance on Blasphemy & Laughter as on Prayer and Fasting and be much better to live in."

The impact of the war on Paris and the need for a stable income drove Stephens home to Dublin in August 1915 to take up the post of registrar of the National Gallery of Ireland, an office he held for the next ten years. In letters Stephens announced his intention to explore on his return "the passionate, varied story that Ireland is and has been," to express through his art "a consciousness of Ireland in all its dimensions." If his art needed a prompt from reality, it did not have long to wait. On his way back from lunch to the National Gallery on Easter Monday in 1916 Stephens came across a barricade being thrown up by rebel troops, watched as a civilian was shot before his eyes, and realized he was witnessing a heroically botched attempt to cast off the British yoke. The eyewitness account he wrote of the rising, *The Insurrection in Dublin* (1916), is recognized as a classic piece of reportage, which conveys with dramatic immediacy how it felt to be caught up in that bewildering week of momentous violence.

The events of 1916 and their turbulent aftermath, as the nation stumbled toward civil war, hardened Stephens's resolution to devote himself to the resurrection of his nation's ancient culture. His most significant work thereafter took the form of acts of imaginative translation designed to reclaim the native Irish literature for a modern, English-speaking readership. The first fruit of these labors was *Reincarnations* (1918), a collection of poems adapted from the works of Gaelic poets of the seventeenth and eighteenth centuries. The book enabled him to serve the political needs of the present by assuming the voices of his poetic forebears. In David O'Bruadair, especially, Stephens found a kindred spirit, as his postscript to *Reincarnations* makes clear: "O'Bruadair lets out of him an unending, rebellious bawl which would be the most desolating utterance ever made by man if it was not also the most gleeful." The collection restored to Stephens's verse the colloquial masculine vigor evident in *Insurrections* and only fitfully glimpsed thereafter. It also blazed a trail for the mythological prose redactions that were to absorb his last great burst of creative energy over the next six years.

The first of these works was *Irish Fairy Tales* (1920), ten superbly crafted stories of heroic adventure, enchantment, and metamorphosis. Stephens's obsession with reincarnation and shape-shifting, themes predictably congenial to one so anxious to bury his past and reinvent himself, spurred him in this book to some of his finest writing. "The Story of Tuan Mac Cairill" in particular, which chronicles the hero's transmigration from man to stag to hawk to salmon, Stephens rightly regarded as "a colossal and terrific, and unsurpassable, top-hole story." The description of the salmon's sensations as it is netted and torn from its element offers a powerful example of his genius for total empathy with other creatures: "I was in air, and it was as though I was in fire. The air pressed on me like a fiery mountain. It beat on my scales and scorched them. It rushed down my throat and scalded me. It weighed on me and squeezed me, so that my eyes felt as though they must burst from my head, my head as though it would leap from my body, and my body as though it would swell and expand and fly in a thousand pieces."

For his last two novels Stephens drew on the saga cycle known as the *Táin Bó Cuailnge* (The Cattle Raid of Cooley). He thought the first of them "the best thing I have done – It is the first book (complete in itself) of a story in five volumes to be

*Stephens during one of his BBC broadcasts, circa 1937*

called the 'Tain Bo,' and although it is as old as time, it will be as modern as tomorrow's newspaper." The book was *Deirdre* (1923), Stephens's stirring version of a tragic tale about which AE, Yeats, and John Millington Synge had already written plays. The story, an Irish variant of the Tristram and Isolde legend of doomed young love, tells of how Deirdre's refusal to wed King Conachúr of Ulster leads, through the treachery of the outraged monarch, to the slaying of her lover, Naoise, and to her own grief-stricken demise. Stephens transmutes his material with admirable dexterity: epic narration can afford to be abrupt and depthless in its rendering of incident, but the novel requires explanations, an unfolding rationale for what happens. To this end Stephens compresses, expands, or splices his sources, filling in contexts and filling out characters, scripting convincing dialogue and spicing the narrative with enough restrained comedy to humanize the heroic protagonists without deflating them. The psychological portrait of Conachúr in thrall to his brooding jealousy and vindictive pride is especially compelling.

The second novel in the *Táin Bó Cuailnge* sequence, *In the Land of Youth* (1924), elegantly intertwines four tales. It opens with the adventures of

Nera, whose acceptance of a gruesome challenge on Halloween strands him in the land of the fairies. Nera's story frames Queen Maeve's tale of the mysterious maiden who captured the heart of Angus Óg in a vision. Maeve's story in turn secretes a Rabelaisian fable told by Bove the magician about two herds of swine: the one prodigiously gluttonous, the other starved to the bone. And the novel concludes with Maeve's tale of how Etain, wife of Eochaid Airem, king of Ireland, was lured back to Tir na n-Og (the Land of Youth) by her fairy husband, King Midir. Stephens found his latest heroine irresistible: "Mary Pickford is seconded as the World's Sweetheart. I have her licked to a frazzle with Etain. By George, that's a real girl and she's nicer than pie. She'll make a whole male generation mad that they didn't live two thousand years ago."

*In the Land of Youth* invited Stephens to commute with his characters between the sublunary kingdom of humanity and the ethereal empire of the immortal. It released him into an imaginary universe in which the self was forever changing and one world invariably turned out to enclose another. The elaborate narrative braidings and embeddings of the book articulate these dizzying involutions of existence in which he loved to lose himself. Recy-

cling the old Irish sagas enabled Stephens to keep the sophisticated art of oral narration alive within the novel, but it also preserved a pristine era of lost simplicities. While some novelists of the day settled for urban realism and others plunged into the vortex of textual experiment, Stephens chose to sing in prose of love, magic, and war, of figures commanded by one fierce, pure passion in an epoch blissfully uncontaminated by modernity.

*In the Land of Youth* was the last novel Stephens published. What made him abandon his five-volume version of the *Táin Bó Cuailnge* after the first two books remains unclear. Although *Deirdre* was awarded the medal for fiction at the *Aonach Tailteann* festival, the novels were not a commercial success, perhaps because the brutalities and privations of the civil war left the Irish public little appetite for heroic legends. Stephens's departure from Ireland with his family to take up permanent residence in London in 1925 may have played some part in uprooting him from his native sources of inspiration. Close friends like AE and Gogarty were dismayed at their loss of what the latter hailed in a valedictory poem as "half of Erin's energy," and Stephens badly missed his Dublin haunts and conversations. Nevertheless, he made new friends in London, where he attended the literary gatherings of Lady Ottoline Morrell, as well as in America, which he visited annually from 1925 to 1935 to give readings and to relax at the Kentucky home of his patron W. T. H. Howe.

Stephens produced little new or memorable work after moving to England. His last important book, *Etched in Moonlight* (1928), collects stories published several years earlier, most notably the harrowing tale "Hunger," which had appeared in 1918 under the pseudonym James Esse. The story chronicles a slum family's relentless slide from unemployment to poverty to begging, starvation, and death. It is Stephens's most unflinching confrontation with the demon that gnawed at his imagination all his life, just as it had gnawed at his empty belly as a boy. The other stories in the volume, which pursue the consequences of desire, guilt, and subjection to their pitiless destination, afford no relief from the spectacle of human cruelty and folly. It is thus not surprising to find the poet of *Strict Joy* (1931) and *Kings and the Moon* (1938) striving to slough off the earthbound nature of his kind and glorify the extinction of being in the nirvana of nothingness. The poetry inevitably expires beneath the burden of formulating what lies by definition beyond

words, and the once ceaseless stream of Stephens's verse dried up altogether during the last decade of his life.

A fresh career as a broadcaster for the BBC had swung open for him just before the war, however, and until his death he enjoyed renewed celebrity for indulging his greatest gift on the radio: mulling over his favorite poems, reciting his own verse, and sharing his memories of Joyce, Yeats, Moore, and AE. He was awarded a British Civil List pension in 1942. In 1947 he received a grant from the Royal Bounty Fund to enable him to travel to Dublin to be awarded an honorary degree from Trinity College. He passed his final years plagued by poor health, feeling increasingly marooned in an alien postwar world. He gave his last broadcast on 11 June 1950, and, fittingly, it spun one final sunlit myth around the childhood days whose reality he took with him to the grave. He died in London on Saint Stephen's Day, 26 December 1950.

Throughout his life as a writer James Stephens was driven by two kinds of hunger. One was the terrible physical craving that he both feared and revered as the appetite for life in its most ravenous guise; the other was an insatiable desire for spiritual satisfaction in a transfigured world. In a letter to John Drinkwater dated 1917 Stephens declared: "I believe that everything the best mind of humanity really wishes for, and formulates the wish, must come to pass. So I look on certain abstract words such as 'love,' 'honour,' 'spirit' as prophetic words, having no concrete existence now, but to be forged in the future by the desire which has sounded them. Poems, too, are to me prophesies, and there will be a gay old world sometime." Yet this perspective repeatedly mutates into its Darwinian twin: the reduction of existence to a devouring gullet. The two kinds of hunger are indivisible in Stephens. The transfiguring movement of vital desire and the ruthless imperative to kill and consume are one: "We eat death," he concluded in one of his last broadcasts. "Life lives on death."

None of his contemporaries summed up the vision of James Stephens more shrewdly than Stephen MacKenna in a biographical note he wrote on his friend in 1923: "Novel, story, hero-tale, poem, the pages sing and shine: caprice and tenderness, subtle generosities underlain by painful brutalities, extraordinary force with a winning innocence: it is seeing power like that of a savage, a song and dance as of a child, the loving tolerance of a mystic discerning in all things, noble or trifling or ugly, always some trace of some god."

**Letters:**

*Letters of James Stephens,* edited by Richard J. Finneran (London & New York: Macmillan, 1974).

**Bibliographies:**

Birgit Bramsbäck, *James Stephens: A Literary and Bibliographical Study,* Upsala Irish Studies, 4 (1959): 55–199;

Richard J. Finneran, "Appendix B: Printed Writings by James Stephens," in *Letters of James Stephens,* edited by Finneran (London & New York: Macmillan, 1974), pp. 420–458;

Werner Huber, *James Stephens' Frühe Romane* (Frankfurt & Bern: Peter Lang, 1982), pp. 257–291.

**Biography:**

Hilary Pyle, *James Stephens: His Work and an Account of His Life* (London: Routledge & Kegan Paul, 1965; New York: Barnes & Noble, 1965).

**References:**

Padraic Colum, "James Stephens as a Prose Artist," in *James Stephens: A Selection,* edited by Lloyd Frankenberg (London: Macmillan, 1962), pp. ix–xix;

Colum and others, *On James Stephens* (Folcroft, Pa.: Folcroft Library, 1973);

Barton R. Friedman, "Returning to Ireland's Fountains: Nationalism and James Stephens," *Arizona Quarterly,* 22 (Autumn 1966): 232–252;

George Evon Hatvary, "Re-reading 'The Crock of Gold,'" *Irish Writing* (March 1953): 57–65;

*Journal of Irish Literature,* special issue on Stephens, 4, edited by Richard J. Finneran and Patricia McFate (September 1975);

Augustine Martin, *James Stephens: A Critical Study* (Dublin: Gill & Macmillan, 1977);

Patricia McFate, *The Writings of James Stephens: Variations on a Theme of Love* (London: Macmillan, 1979);

Vivian Mercier, "James Stephens: His Version of Pastoral," *Irish Writing* (March 1951): 48–57;

George Brandon Saul, *Stephens, Yeats, and Other Irish Concerns* (New York: New York Public Library, 1954);

Saul, "Withdrawn in Gold," *Arizona Quarterly,* 9 (Summer 1953): 115–131.

**Papers:**

The principal repositories of James Stephens's manuscripts and correspondence are the Berg Collection in the New York Public Library, the Beinecke Rare Book and Manuscript Library at Yale, and the Houghton Library at Harvard. Scripts of Stephens's radio broadcasts are held in the BBC archives in London.

# Katharine Tynan
*(23 January 1861 – 2 April 1931)*

## Katherine Sutherland
*University College of the Cariboo*

BOOKS: *Louise de la Vallière and Other Poems* (London: Kegan Paul, 1885);

*Shamrocks* (London: Kegan Paul, 1887);

*Ballads and Lyrics* (London: Kegan Paul, 1891);

*A Nun (Mother Xaviera Fallon)* (London: Kegan Paul, 1891);

*Irish Love-Songs* (London: Unwin, 1892);

*A Cluster of Nuts: Being Sketches Among My Own People* (London: Lawrence & Bullen, 1894);

*Cuckoo Songs* (London: Elkin Mathews, 1894);

*The Land of Mist and Mountain: Short Stories* (London: Unwin, 1895);

*Miracle Plays* (London: Bodley Head, 1895);

*The Way of a Maid* (New York: Dodd, Mead, 1895);

*An Isle in the Water* (London: Elkin Mathews, 1896);

*A Lover's Breast-Knot* (London: Elkin Mathews, 1896);

*Oh, What a Plague is Love* (London: Black, 1896);

*The Wind in the Trees* (London: Richards, 1898);

*The Dear Irish Girl* (London: Smith, Elder, 1899);

*She Walks in Beauty* (London: Smith, Elder, 1899);

*A Daughter of the Fields* (London: Smith, Elder, 1900);

*The Queen's Page* (New York: Benziger, 1900);

*Poems* (London: Lawerence & Bullen, 1901);

*That Sweet Enemy* (Philadelphia: Lippincott, 1901);

*A Union of Hearts* (London: J. Nisbet, 1901);

*A Girl of Galway* (London: Blackie, 1902);

*The Golden Lily* (New York: Benziger, 1902);

*The Great Captain* (New York: Benziger, 1902);

*The Handsome Quaker and Other Stories* (London: Bullen, 1902);

*A King's Woman* (London: Hurst & Blackett, 1902);

*Love of Sisters* (London: Smith, Elder, 1902);

*A Red, Red Rose* (London: Eveleigh Nash, 1903);

*The French Wife* (London: F. V. White, 1904);

*A Daughter of Kings* (New York: Benziger, 1905);

*Dick Pentreath* (London: Smith, Elder, 1905);

*For the White Rose* (New York: Benziger, 1905);

*Innocencies* (London: Bullen, 1905);

*Julia* (Chicago: McClurg, 1905);

*Katharine Tynan*

*The Luck of the Fairfaxes* (London: Collins, Clear Type Press, 1905);

*The Adventures of Alicia* (London: F. V. White, 1906);

*The Yellow Domino and Other Stories* (London: F. V. White, 1906);

*Her Ladyship* (London: Smith, Elder, 1907);

*A Little Book of Twenty-four Carols* (Portland, Maine: Mosher, 1907);

*The Story of Baron* (Chicago: McClurg, 1907);

*The Story of Our Lord for Children* (Dublin: Sealy, Bryers, 1907);

*Twenty-one Poems* (Dundrum: Dun Emer Press, 1907);

*The Lost Angel* (Philadelphia: Lippincott, 1908);

*The House of the Crickets* (London: Smith, Elder, 1908);

*The Book of Flowers*, by Tynan and Frances Maitland (London: Smith, Elder, 1909);

*Cousins and Others: Tales* (London: T. Werner Laurie, 1909);

*Her Mother's Daughter* (London: Smith, Elder, 1909);

*Ireland* (London: Black, 1909);

*A Little Book for John O'Mahony's Friends* (Portland, Maine: Mosher, 1909);

*Mary Gray* (London: Cassell, 1909);

*Peggy the Daughter* (London: Cassell, 1909);

*Three Fair Maids* (London: Blackie, 1909);

*Betty Carew* (London: Smith, Elder, 1910);

*Freda* (New York: Cassell, 1910);

*Paradise Farm* (New York: Duffield, 1911);

*Princess Katharine* (New York: Duffield, 1911);

*New Poems* (London: Sidgwick & Jackson, 1911);

*The Story of Cecilia* (New York: Benziger, 1911);

*Honey, My Honey* (London: Smith, Elder, 1912);

*Rose of the Garden* (London: Constable, 1912; Indianapolis: Bobbs-Merrill, 1913);

*A Midsummer Rose* (London: Smith, Elder, 1913);

*A Mésalliance* (New York: Duffield, 1913);

*Miss Pratt of Paradise Farm* (London: Smith, Elder, 1913);

*Twenty-Five Years: Reminiscences* (London: Smith, Elder, 1913);

*The Wild Harp* (London: Sidgwick & Jackson, 1913);

*Irish Poems* (New York: Benziger, 1914);

*John Bulteel's Daughters* (London: Smith, Elder, 1914);

*A Little Radiant Girl* (London: Blackie & Son, 1914);

*Countrymen All: A Collection of Tales* (London: Maunsel, 1915);

*The Curse of Castle Eagle* (New York: Duffield, 1915);

*The Flower of Peace* (New York: Scribners, 1915);

*Flower of Youth* (London: Sidgwick & Jackson, 1915);

*Since I First Saw Your Face* (London: Hutchinson, 1915);

*The House of the Foxes* (London: Smith, Elder, 1915);

*The Holy War* (London: Sidgwick & Jackson, 1916);

*John-A-Dreams* (London: Smith, Elder, 1916);

*Lord Edward* (London: Smith, Elder, 1916);

*Margery Dawe* (London: Blackie & Sons, 1916);

*The Middle Years* (London: Constable, 1916);

*The Web of Fraulein* (London: Hodder & Stoughton, 1916);

*Kit* (London: Smith, Elder, 1917);

*Late Songs* (London: Sidgwick & Jackson, 1917);

*Miss Mary* (London: John Murray, 1917);

*The Rattlesnake* (London: Ward, Lock, 1917);

*Herb O'Grace* (London: Sidgwick & Jackson, 1918);

*Miss Gascoigne* (London: John Murray, 1918);

*My Love's But a Lassie* (London: Ward, Lock, 1918);

*Love of Brothers* (London: Constable, 1919);

*The Man From Australia* (London: Collins, 1919);

*The Years of the Shadow* (Boston: Houghton Mifflin, 1919);

*The House* (London: Collins, 1920);

*Denys the Dreamer* (New York: Benziger, 1921);

*Sally Victrix* (London: Collins, 1921);

*The Second Wife* (London: John Murray, 1921);

*The Wandering Years* (Boston: Houghton Mifflin, 1922);

*Evensong* (Oxford: Blackwell, 1922);

*White Ladies* (London: E. Nash & Grayson, 1922);

*Mary Beaudesert, V.S.* (London: Collins, 1923);

*Pat, the Adventurer* (London: Ward, Lock, 1923);

*They Loved Greatly* (London: Nash & Grayson, 1923);

*The Golden Rose* (London: Nash & Grayson, 1924);

*The House of Doom* (London: Nash & Grayson, 1924);

*Memories* (London: Nash & Grayson, 1924);

*Wives* (London: Hurst-Blackett, 1924);

*Life in the Occupied Area* (London: Hutchinson, 1925);

*Miss Phipps* (London: Ward, Lock, 1925);

*The Moated Grange* (London: Collins, 1925);

*The Briar Bush Maid* (London: Ward, Lock, 1926);

*The Heiress of Wyke* (London: Ward, Lock, 1926);

*The Infatuation of Peter* (London: Collins, 1926);

*The Face in the Picture* (London: Ward, Lock, 1927);

*The Respectable Lady* (London: Cassell, 1927);

*Twilight Songs* (New York: Appleton, 1927);

*Haroun of London* (London: Collins, 1927);

*The Wild Adventure* (London: Ward, Lock, 1927);

*Castle Perilous* (London: Ward, Lock, 1928);

*The House in the Forest* (London: Ward, Lock, 1928);

*Lover of Women* (London: Collins, 1928);

*A Fine Gentleman* (London: Ward, Lock, 1929);

*The Most Charming Family* (London: Ward, Lock, 1929);

*The River* (London: Collins, 1929);

*The Rich Man* (London: Collins, 1929);

*The Admirable Simmons* (London: Ward, Lock, 1930);

*Collected Poems* (London: Macmillan, 1930);

*Grayson's Girl* (London: Collins, 1930);

*The Playground* (London: Ward, Lock, 1930);

*A Lonely Maid* (London: Ward, Lock, 1931);

*Delia's Orchard* (London: Ward, Lock, 1931);

*The Forbidden Way* (London: Collins, 1931);

*The Other Man* (London: Ward, Lock, 1932);

*The Pitiful Lady* (London: Ward, Lock, 1932);

*Connor's Wood,* revised and completed by P. Hinkson (London: Collins, 1933);

*An International Marriage* (London: Ward, Lock, 1933);

*The House of Dreams* (London: Ward, Lock, 1934);

*A Lad was Born* (London: Collins, 1934);

*Poems,* edited by Monk Gibbon (Dublin: Allen Figgis, 1963);

*Her Father's Daughter* (New York: Benziger, n.d.).


Katharine Tynan's importance to English literature is difficult to assess. Her tastes were as varied as her writing was prolific. During her career of more than fifty years, she wrote as many as seven books in one year, and, not surprisingly, not all of her works can be described as masterpieces. Her first book of poetry, *Louise de la Vallière and Other Poems* (1885), was regarded by many critics as an important work, and, as Anne Connerton Fallon writes, it "was both a financial and social success. It took the reviewers by storm in a way that the modern reader can hardly understand . . . she was considered in Ireland the most promising young poet of her generation." Tynan was an important figure in the Irish Renaissance as well as a close friend of W. B. Yeats, who was also involved in the Irish literary revival. It is often suggested, however, that she did not fulfill the promise of her early work, turning instead to the production of a steady stream of pulp fiction, written in whatever style was popular at the time. While it may be true that she sacrificed quality for quantity in her work – her memoirs extend over no less than six lengthy tomes – it should be noted that her writing sustained her less financially successful husband and their children. Although not always carefully wrought, Tynan's books are generally entertaining and engrossing.

Katharine Tynan was born 23 January 1861 in Dublin to Andrew and Elizabeth Tynan; she was their fourth daughter and one of eleven children. The family moved to Whitehall, Clondalkin, County Dublin, in 1868, and in 1871 Tynan left to attend boarding school at the Dominican Siena Convent for three years, returning home in 1874 at fourteen as her father's companion. Tynan was close to her father, and he is mentioned frequently in her autobiographical works, while her invalid mother and her siblings are scarcely mentioned. Indeed, she writes poignantly in her memoirs of her grief at the death of her father and barely mentions the death of her husband, Henry Albert Hinkson, in 1919.

As a young woman, Tynan was given a room in the house by her father to use as a study for her writing; he decorated it for her, and she continued over the years before her marriage to choose carefully items worthy to be kept in this room. Such rooms figure quite often in her novels as gifts to young women, and the room clearly came to symbolize an intellectual haven for Tynan, presaging by more than forty years Virginia Woolf's notorious comment that "a woman must have money and a room of her own if she is to write fiction." For Tynan writing was a form of social liberation as well, allowing her both freedom of action and many intimate male friends otherwise forbidden a woman of her time.

In the late 1860s Tynan suffered for two years from ulcerated eyes, probably due to the measles. This illness left her with poor eyesight and also resulted in her being kept in a darkened room for many months without being allowed to read. The experience had a profound impact on the author and perhaps helps to explain her love of beautiful things. Tynan has been criticized for her fascination with clothes, interior decoration, and fine foods and wines; it has been argued that it was in order to satisfy her craving for finery that she wrote so much, sacrificing literary integrity for material trifles. Her taste for these things is discernible in the detailed descriptions of them in her novels. In the novel *Honey, My Honey* (1912), for instance, the character Mrs. Bellair is described as "more extravagant than she had any business to be as the wife of a plain country gentleman of moderate fortune," but this authorial rebuke is followed by three descriptions of Mrs. Bellair's wardrobe of "beautiful things, muslins and chiffons as fine as cobweb, delicate laces, furs, lovely evening wraps, fans, feathers, and what not." Mrs. Bellair is callous enough to comment that she will have "some of [her] finest things made into little garments for the babies of the poor," as she has too many to wear herself, adding "Why shouldn't they have lovely things even at an age when they can hardly appreciate them?" This insensitivity is contrasted with Honey's lack of interest in the trousseau which Mrs. Bellair is selecting for her, Mrs. Bellair taking "more interest in the pretty things than the prospective bride." Mrs. Bellair is also contrasted here with "Madame Louise of France who, at the Carmelites, chose to do kitchen work and had no plainer garments to do it in, before her habit was made, than a straight, simple gown of rose-coloured silk" and with the young Babette, who, on the next page, selects "a short-waisted frock of white satin, the sleeves and the

24

# Chapter III
## The New Estate

Mary took the news of her great promotion in an unthankful spirit—

"Lady Anne is very kind," she said tearfully. "But I don't want to stay with her. I could ill bear to stay anywhere but in Wistaria Terrace. It is absurd that you should say you have given your consent Papa. How could you possibly have consented on the house — could not get on without me? You know it would not. Why, even for a day things would be all topsy-turvy without me."

"And so you have not gone to school?" the father answered with an accent of reproach. "You have been weighed down with responsibilities + cares that you ought to have been free of for years to come. You have even been stunted in your growth as Lady Anne said. It is time things were altered. I did not know how I was so blind. We ought to be grateful to the accident that has opened a door to us."

When he had gone Lady Anne came + comforted Mary. There was a deal of kindness in the old lady's heart.

"You shall help them," she said. "Dear me, how much help you will be able to give them! Imagine beginning with a salary, although fifteen! You are to lend things to me, Mary. I have sent help to your stepmother, an excellent woman, Mrs Davies, whom I have known for many years. She is very capable. I will tell her that she must remain with your stepmother. It is amazing that one really capable

*Page from Tynan's manuscript for her 1909 novel* Mary Gray *(courtesy of the Lilly Library, Indiana University)*

fichu embroidered with roses, roses on the shoes instead of shoe buckles, a wreath of roses in the hair." (Roses or rose color, when associated with clothing in Tynan's work, tend to symbolize female goodness.) At one point, after a lengthy description of eighteenth-century clothing in *Rose of the Garden* (1912), the narrator intrudes to comment: "I have felt obliged to quote Sally on the fashion at such length, because it shows her very woman; perhaps, too, because such things must be of interest to the feminine mind." While this suggests a stereotypical view of female interests, it also addresses itself to a female reading audience, implying the narrator's relative lack of interest in the male mind.

Tynan's attitude toward material things is an excellent example of the paradoxical nature of her worldview. Somehow Tynan managed to be deeply interested in social and political issues, writing about them often, while simultaneously presenting herself as extremely superficial. This contrast has made her a difficult historical figure for critics to assess. For example, Tynan joined the Ladies Land League, led by Anna Parnell (sister of Charles Parnell), describing it in one of her memoirs, *Twenty-Five Years: Reminiscences* (1913), as "the expression of the Nationalist spirit in Ireland." However, she admits later in the same book, "my interest in the Land League was not a sincere one." Thus, she is regarded by some critics, such as Fallon, as something of a political trifler. Marilyn Gaddis Rose is kinder in her assessment of Tynan, noting rather cryptically that "Hers was the feminism of a devout Catholic" and arguing that although Tynan's social and political commentaries tend not to be particularly sophisticated, "as to the effects of the system, whatever it is, on children and women, she is alert, responsive, and aggressive." Nonetheless, even Rose's recuperative feminist arguments that Tynan "is a woman writer who sees herself and expresses herself in terms of women's roles" and that "In her journalism, she is quite explicit that a man's world is not the best of all possible worlds for a woman" seem equivocal.

In the analysis of a historical figure, it is only reasonable to refrain from applying current social and political attitudes to the past without considerable caution. Tynan is perhaps best described as a woman of her time, and in this context she may be seen as a more socially and politically radical figure than she would be by today's standards. First, she wrote in order to maintain her family when such activities were hardly the female norm; she often wrote from a female perspective, outlining the gender barriers that fettered women. While it seems true that she wrote partly to please her father and friends, as Rose suggests, it is also true that the ideal woman of the period is socially constructed precisely to please men; in this context it is more remarkable that Tynan's female protagonists are frequently less compliant than the stereotypical female heroine of even today's romantic novels.

In her own life, Tynan exhibited great strength of character in many ways: for example, notes Fallon, "Her attitude of courage and optimism in regard to her eyesight is characteristic of the way in which Tynan approached the many challenges which her life presented her." Although Fallon somewhat disdainfully comments that "the fame and social importance which [Tynan's] role as a successful writer brought to her were substantially more important than her art," it seems only fair to add that this fame and social importance might be seductive because they represented rare power for a woman of this period. While feminist critics might wish that Tynan had spoken more glowingly about her mother rather than her father, her mother was unfortunately often more preoccupied with her role as invalid than her role as mother, and, when in the latter role, she tended to be puritanical, forbidding her daughter dances, theater, and novels. Rose goes so far as to criticize Tynan's "lack of intellect," but the author's commitment to the Irish Renaissance movement and her friendships with Yeats, Douglas Hyde, AE (George Russell), Alice Meynell, Anna Parnell, and Christina Rossetti suggest a woman of considerable intellectual interest.

Tynan can be most justly criticized, perhaps, regarding her attitudes toward race and class. Though she often expresses sympathy in her work for the plight of the poor, Tynan's work propounds a system of charity and noblesse oblige as the solution to poverty. Her novel *Haroun of London* (1927) consists essentially of a series of anecdotes in which a wealthy benefactor gives to the poor, who are not only grateful but also acknowledge the nobility of the gesture. Her ideas about race and ethnicity are perhaps least palatable. Tynan does not question the superiority of the white, English-speaking person over all others, revealing anti-Semitic and xenophobic tendencies in her work. For instance, in *The Infatuation of Peter* (1926) the narrator notes that France smells bad because "The French nose is not sensitive to smells" and also comments that "They are hard, the French bourgeoisie." Critical distaste for these aspects of Tynan's work should not, however, overshadow the acknowledgment of her more advanced portrayal of women and of Irish nationalism.

Tynan's interest in Irish nationalism, perhaps not very consistently expressed through her political activities, emerges most evidently in her involvement with the Irish Revival, or Irish Renaissance. These terms are used interchangeably to describe the renewed interest in nationalism and culture that occurred in Ireland between the last quarter of the nineteenth century and the 1920s. In literature the revival was signaled by the translation and use of Irish folklore in Irish writing, the publication of Irish histories, and the establishment by Yeats in 1899 of the Irish Literary Theatre, which later became the Abbey Theatre. Rose asserts somewhat uncharitably that Tynan's role in the movement was that of "a briefly associated minor talent." The comment seems unjustified in light of Tynan's involvement in projects such as the preparation of the second edition of the four-volume *Cabinet of Irish Literature* (1902). Furthermore, in the "Preface to the Second Edition" the reader is given a sense of the strength of character which Tynan was capable of asserting:

> The first editor's scheme had included a good many names which seemed to the present editor to belong rather to other forms of energy than literature. She has followed her own judgement in excluding a good many of the early inclusions, which is not to say so much that she dissents from the first admirable editor's judgement, as that her sympathies necessarily are narrower. Some orators are gone because she thought that the fire had died out of the speeches with the passing of the man; and that it was a poor service to represent an illustrious name by many pages of dulness.

In the introduction to Tynan's *Collected Poems* (1930), fellow Irish Renaissance poet AE writes that Tynan "was the earliest singer in that awakening of our imagination which has been spoken of as the Irish Renaissance." Of her poetry, AE admits that "No one can be always on peaks of intensity. We, all of us, vacillate between our surfaces and our depths, from verse which makes itself lustrous and decorative with external colour or symbol to verse which embodies profundity of feeling," but he also points out with considerable enthusiasm that Tynan "had something which is rather rarer among poets than most people imagine, a natural gift for song." This latter comment is apt; though Tynan's poetry does not always inspire hyperbole in the critic, it cannot be denied that she had a faculty for the ballad and long poem, evident in one of her best-known works, "The Children of Lir," which is based on the Irish folktale "The Fate of the Children of Lir."

In her collection of poems titled *Ballads and Lyrics,* published in 1891, Tynan makes clear her nationalist poetical agenda:

> in my book there will be found
> No gleanings from a foreign ground
> If such you seek, go buy, go buy
> Of some more travelled folk than I.
> Kind Master Critic, say not, please,
> Since here she warns expectant eyes
> That homely is her merchandise!

Her poems allude frequently to Irish folklore; they also feature themes of nature, love, mother/child relations, and Catholic religion. Fallon notes that Tynan often uses Saint Francis of Assisi in her poems, as an example of "that saint who most completely embodie[s] the Christian precept of love in action." In her most famous poem, "Sheeps and Lambs," the animals of the title are the central metaphor, referring to the Lamb of God. In a poem like "The Fairy Foster Mother," the poet combines favorite elements, weaving Irish folklore with images of nature and themes of both romantic love and mother/child love. In the poem a mother dies giving birth to her son, and because she cannot nurse her own child or comfort her grieving husband, she instead nurses a fairy child. The poem is simple and even sentimental, but in its simplicity there is a certain beauty.

Tynan also wrote a large body of patriotic war poetry during World War I, again suggesting a puzzling, if not inconsistent, view of the world. It seems strange that a woman who writes sentimentally of mothers and children could also write forcefully in favor of those same children fighting in a war that was vehemently opposed by many Irish nationalists. Rose rightly points out that although World War I became increasingly unpopular in Ireland, Tynan's poetry treats the deaths of young Irishmen in the war as "holy sacrifices." This attitude is made more intriguing by the fact that both of Tynan's sons were called up for duty, and both were wounded and for some time missing in action – yet the author's belief in the necessity of their service never publicly wavered.

One of the plot elements of Tynan's novel *The Golden Rose* (1924) involves the separation of the protagonist, Carmel, and her lover when the latter leaves to fight in World War I. Carmel is the daughter of Dr. Reilly. When his first wife dies, he remarries and has another daughter and five sons, four of whom leave to fight in the war, where one is killed. The locals deeply disapprove of Dr. Reilly for allowing his sons to fight in the "English war," and he

*Dust jacket for a posthumously published novel by Tynan (courtesy of the Lilly Library, Indiana University)*

is voted out of his practice largely because he supports the war. He becomes an alcoholic as a result, but he is nonetheless portrayed as a victim of the misguided beliefs of his neighbors. The narrator clearly approves of the young men who fight, denouncing the "cynicism which saw nothing in the war for [young men] but a slaughterhouse." Several of the characters also regard the "Irish Rebellion" as a betrayal of the soldiers in the "continental" war. The elaboration of these views on war brings this novel as far into the sphere of realism as Tynan's work ever gets, yet these messages are reinforced by the primary plot in the novel, which involves the love story of Carmel and Beau, who is injured and missing in action for much of the book. His return is that of a hero wronged, and Carmel's constancy in his absence is evidently noble: they are rewarded with a happy marriage in the end.

Despite her fervent support of the war, Tynan's war poems are not without some very dark images; they are as likely to consist of a lament for the loss of young men, particularly as it affects their

mothers, as they are to consist of patriotic calls to arms. For example, in "The Broken Soldier" Tynan sentimentalizes the fine soul of a maimed soldier, showing him to be much nobler than other men: "Whole men and comely, they fret at little things / The soul of him's singing like a thrush in the grass." However, she does not spare her reader the grisly details of his injuries, writing in the first two lines, "The broken soldier sings and whistles day to dark; / He's but a remnant of a man, maimed and half-blind," and later on, "One hand is but a stump and his face a pitted mask." Even in a religious war poem, where Tynan suggests that a dead soldier will certainly find a place in heaven, images of death and grief are not exactly benign. Though the poem compares the young man to Christ and implies that he will be resurrected, there is a sense of underlying grief that this resurrection will be heavenly only, not earthly, and that his mother will never see him again in her lifetime.

While Tynan is most admired for her early poetry, the bulk of her work consists of prose. She also wrote children's books, autobiographies, and even *The Book of Flowers* (1909), which was written with Frances Maitland and presents a typical mixture of sentiment mixed with wit, evident in the book's introduction: "We offer this book made for our own pleasure with the hope that the reading of it may bring pleasure to other flower-lovers. It makes no pretense at all to completeness or to scientific knowledge or accuracy. It is as though one walked in a garden or the fields and picked at random a flower here and a flower there, tying them loosely in a bunch." The volume also contains many references to folk remedies, associating it in a sense with Tynan's nationalistic Irish poetry.

The bulk of Tynan's work, however, consists of 105 novels, which may be grouped essentially into three periods, each characterized by a specific genre: romantic, Gothic, and realistic. It might be argued that all of her novels are romantic – even the realistic ones, which tend to culminate with happy marriages. However, she does begin in these later novels, written after her husband's death in 1919, to make overt social and political comments. Tynan is best known, however, for the romantic novels with which she began her prose writing career, beginning with *The Way of a Maid* (1895).

In a frequently quoted passage Fallon summarizes Tynan's plot formula, in which a "young, inexperienced poor girl from a noble line in declining circumstances or an old family line which has suffered because of religious reasons" falls in love with "a young, refined, often wealthy, and high born

young man." Complications, usually minor, occur on the way to a happy marriage. It is usually in the secondary plots, which tend also to be love stories, where more eccentric characters appear and Tynan deviates from formula and stereotypes. One example of such a novel is *Three Fair Maids* (1909), in which a mother and her three daughters, formerly of much better circumstances, are forced to take boarders into their home in order to supplement their income. The youngest of the daughters, Delia, marries a rich lord, who has recently returned to the neighborhood; Elizabeth, the eldest daughter, tricks a rich but alienated great uncle into boarding with the family without revealing who they are. He is angry with the dead father of the girls for marrying their mother, whom he believes to be his social inferior. In the end he is so enamored of the family that they become his heirs again. Typically, the novel emphasizes the moral imperative of not looking down on the poor – so long as they are of noble lineage and especially if there is some pecuniary advantage involved in the reconciliation between rich and poor. As in many of her novels, Tynan uses dialect to indicate the speech of the poor or uneducated, a literary technique that implies class distinctions.

The most interesting character of the three sisters is Joan, the protagonist and narrator. Her love interest in the novel is a guest who comes to stay and who is already engaged to another woman whom, of course, he does not really love but feels obligated to. He and Joan are finally able to make a happy marriage in the end, but not until there has been lengthy but private lamentation on the part of Joan, all of which proves her constancy to her lover. Perhaps the most interesting figure in the novel is Miss Trescott, a peripheral and eccentric character who also boards with the family. She discreetly but forcefully introduces the subject of socialism into several conversations. She is also unmarried and makes it clear that this fate is chosen and is in no way unpleasant for her. Temperance figures as a theme in the novel as well, which may be associated with Miss Trescott, as first-wave feminism and various forms of social purity, such as temperance, were related or even part of the same social movements in Britain and North America at the turn of the century. One character in the novel, an alcoholic, calls his rum bottle "the enemy" and actually shoots it. It can be argued that there is an undercurrent of early feminist thought in this novel, evident not only in its references to socialism and temperance, but also in its main plot, in which Elizabeth finds a way to support the whole family through her own ideas and organizational abilities.

The last line of the novel also suggests some intriguing ideas that move beyond the romance formula. Of the many romantic engagements that occur at the conclusion, Joan states, "That makes six weddings. If it occurred in a novel instead of in real life, people would say that it was rather stretching the possibilities." The irony in this statement is more than merely amusing: it also constitutes a metafictional statement about novelistic realism, suggesting as it does that too much prosaic design is suspect to the reader or critic. However, recalling that Tynan was deeply religious, the reader is left to wonder whether or not design and reward for decent moral conduct might not be legitimate parts of some constructions of "real life."

Tynan's use of romantic formulas takes several forms. Her collection of short stories, *The Lost Angel* (1908), for example, uses the same basic plots repeatedly. Many of the stories involve the regaining of lost estates through lucky marriages, though it is always made very clear, as in the novels, that merely to marry for money is a highly dubious activity – one must also be genuinely in love with the wealthy person. Another recurring motif is the punishment in one form or another of those who look down on the poor – specifically, the gentry who have, through ill fortune, become poor. (It remains acceptable to look down on the poor who have always been poor.) In these stories the heroines tend to be described as childlike, their most admirable attributes being innocence and softness. In Tynan's novels the heroines tend to be much stronger characters. Indeed, in another form of romance, the historical romance, the author draws a sympathetic portrait of a married woman who has an affair.

*Rose of the Garden* (1912) tells the story of Lady Sarah Lennox, a famous eighteenth-century beauty who is courted by the Prince of Wales but jilted when he marries for the interests of the state. She, meanwhile, is secretly in love with her cousin. He, in turn, is in love with an Italian woman who is abused by her husband. Lady Sarah marries another man but eventually has an affair and runs away with her cousin. Though her husband ultimately is willing to take her back, she refuses and lives for many years in a state of celibacy, from which she is finally released by a happy marriage and several children.

This fictionalized account of Lady Sarah's life follows the romance formula in several ways – her retrieved constancy is rewarded in the end, for example – but it also deviates from this formula in interesting ways. First, it is partly an epistolary novel, consisting largely of letters between Lady Sarah and

her cousin Lady Sue. Thus, there is considerable development of these female characters from their own points of view. Lady Sarah is shown at one point to be reading Fanny Burney, and while the reading of Burney in this period might not imply the intellectual cachet that it does today, it might suggest the literary influence for the use of letters in the novel. Second, Tynan, who could be very censorious, is clearly sympathetic toward Lady Sarah, perhaps because the details of her story are fact rather than fiction: in the latter case the author would ultimately be more responsible, and it was extremely important to Tynan not to offend her audience. Finally, the novel also contains traces of the Gothic, another genre with which Tynan began to experiment around the turn of the century.

Never afraid to venture into new water, Tynan wrote several novels which included Gothic elements. In *A Girl of Galway* (1902) the protagonist is left in Britain with her grandfather, a nasty figure, while her mother joins Bertha's father in India. The grandfather has disowned his son's family because he does not approve of Bertha's mother, a poor governess. Bertha, like many Tynan heroines, is a spirited young woman, and she likes to read; her mother's parting gifts include a selection of Alfred, Lord Tennyson; Dante Gabriel Rossetti; William Wordsworth; Robert Browning; Coventry Patmore; and Mrs. Meynell – all authors favored by Tynan.

The novel relates a long, digressive tale of the estate of Corofin, which is owned by the grandfather. It is covered with a dark, forbidding forest, and, according to family legend, anyone who cuts down the trees there will die a grisly death. Early in the novel, Bertha is saved from certain death by Hugh Roper, the love interest, when she falls into quicksand in the evil forest. Bertha, Hugh, and Hugh's father, once they have met, continually outdo one another with generosity to the neglected tenants on the grandfather's estate. Meanwhile, there are mysterious dragging noises in the attic at night, which turn out in the end to be caused by the theft of estate goods by the grandfather's evil assistant, Mr. Bulger, who is also responsible for convincing him to cut down and sell the forest. The result is a terrible storm, which causes the estate to burn to the ground, killing the grandfather and Mr. Bulger. In the end everyone left alive reconciles and is happy. Though the novel is full of clichés and predictable ends, it is nonetheless difficult to put down. It includes all of Tynan's usual romantic details – a fortune lost and regained, a love story which does not always run smoothly, and generosity to the poor – but these details are enmeshed in Gothic elements.

*The Rattlesnake* (1917) is perhaps Tynan's best-known Gothic. The story begins with a sea voyage, in which the protagonist Delicia meets the love interest, Laurence Brooke. Brooke is possibly most interesting in the degree to which he reveals Tynan's racist attitudes: at one point he regards another man with distaste, focusing on his "nigger eyes," and then mentally chastises himself, thinking "Poor Edwards! He was a good chap – a white man, not a nigger." At any rate, the ship is wrecked, Delicia washes up on shore, and the love of her life is apparently drowned.

Coincidentally, Delicia's evil stepfather, who has abandoned her, runs an insane asylum that is virtually next door to the place where Delicia is convalescing. He captures Delicia and keeps her prisoner there. There is only one patient in the asylum, a lovely young woman named Verena, and a maid who envies her. The subsequent story revolves around the maid's attempts to kill Verena. In the end the stepfather kills himself, because he always loved Delicia's mother; the mother returns to save her daughter; Verena's lost lover returns, rescuing her from madness; and Delicia's lost lover also returns, rescuing her from an endlessly silly plot. The madhouse is burned down by the murderous maid, who dies in the flames. This novel, though popular, is not one of Tynan's better efforts, the only really interesting element being the symbolic cloistering of women, which may be seen as a metaphor for their social impotence. Such a reading is complicated, however, by the transformation of the stepfather from simply evil into a rather sympathetic spurned lover. It seems almost a relief to turn to Tynan's later realistic work.

After 1919 Tynan turned more often to realism. *The Infatuation of Peter* (1926), for example, tells the story of a young man who, like many young men, returns from the war with both emotional and physical injuries. Peter seeks a rest cure in France, in a hostel run by M. and Mme. Patourel, the latter an attractive, vain, and controlling woman. Peter falls in love with Mme. Patourel; she is contrasted with Peter's own mother, who is engaged in a symbolic battle for Peter's love with the Frenchwoman. Xenophobia pervades the novel: the French are associated with decadence, Mme. Patourel at one point giving Peter a "decadent" book. Another Englishman staying at the hostel with Peter also falls under the spell of Mme. Patourel: this character, Simon Agar, calls her a witch who enchanted, or "bewitched," him, and he tries to save Peter from

the same fate. In the end Peter returns to England, the two men marry suitable Englishwomen, and all is well.

Despite its simplistic plot, this novel is one of Tynan's more psychologically complex works. Its central love triangle is essentially between two mother figures struggling over the love of a son. It is made more intriguing by the obviously sexual attraction that Peter feels for Mme. Patourel, who is clearly associated with Peter's mother when he dreams of her "healing hands," which then turn into his mother's hands. Peter's mother is uncomfortable with any overt signs of Peter's sexuality: she is horrified when, on a trip home at Christmas, she discovers both his decadent book and the newly elaborate toilette he performs. She also feels that he has become a neurotic hypochondriac, all of these things signs of his becoming French, and the word in this novel becomes synonymous with *sexual*. However, Peter's love for his mother is not disturbing, as is his love for Mme. Patourel. Although Peter's mother is clearly a model for a lover, she is a healthy, unaffected English model, in contrast with the French. In other words the novel implies that a wholesome filial sexual desire for the mother is not only acceptable but even admirable so long as it is veiled, while a more obvious lust for the mother by the son is scandalous.

A better-known example of Tynan's realistic novels is *Haroun of London,* the story of a mysterious benefactor who splits his life between two towns and two names (Mr. Smith and Mr. Pratt), giving away his money to the poor. Once again, the poor are expected not only to express gratitude but also to acknowledge the noble character of the benefactor. The novel essentially consists of a series of anecdotes describing acts of financial charity. There is also an element of psychological interest, however, which involves the splitting of the character of Smith/Pratt. While there is ultimately no satisfactory explanation for his double life, the suggestion is that Smith/Pratt wishes symbolically to sever himself from his past. Nevertheless, he remains a riddle at the center of the text, and appropriately there are several events in the novel that can only be described as magic. What remains most interesting about the book is its ultimately inexplicable nature.

Perhaps, in the end, this is what continues to intrigue the reader of Katharine Tynan, for she is herself finally a paradox. Capable of profound insight and tremendous literary ability, her views and her work seem nonetheless often disappointingly flawed. Perhaps the key to her character may be found in her own description of Yeats, in *Twenty-Five Years: Reminiscences.* It is less than flattering, concluding "I feel that hitherto my references to W. B. Yeats have been somewhat in the direction of poking fun at him; and I hope that my readers have understood that the fun was affectionate, and that I am never for a moment without a deeply felt admiration and even reverence for his genius." The reader has the sense of an author of strong opinions and ideas, not always charitable, but an author who, in the end, does not want to hurt anyone.

**References:**

Anne Connerton Fallon, *Katharine Tynan* (Boston: Twayne, 1979);

Sandra M. Gilbert and Sandra Gubar, *The Madwoman in the Attic* (New Haven: Yale University Press, 1979);

Ellen Moers, *Literary Women: The Great Writers* (New York: Anchor, 1977);

Marilyn Gaddis Rose, *Katharine Tynan* (London: Bucknell University Press, 1974);

Elaine Showalter, *A Literature of Their Own: British Women Novelists From Brontë to Lessing* (Princeton: Princeton University Press, 1977);

Janet Todd, *Feminist Literary History* (New York: Routledge, 1988).

# Charles Williams

*(20 September 1886 – 15 May 1945)*

## David Llewellyn Dodds

See also the Williams entry in *DLB 100: Modern British Essayists, Second Series.*

BOOKS: *The Silver Stair* (London: Herbert & Daniel, 1912);

*Poems of Conformity* (London: Oxford University Press, 1917);

*Divorce* (London: Oxford University Press, 1920);

*Windows of Night* (London: Oxford University Press, [1925]);

*An Urbanity* (London: Privately printed, 1926);

*The Masque of the Manuscript* (London: Privately printed, 1927);

*A Myth of Shakespeare* (London: Oxford University Press, 1928);

*The Masque of Perusal* (London: Privately printed, 1929);

*Poetry at Present* (Oxford: Clarendon Press, 1930);

*War in Heaven* (London: Gollancz, 1930; New York: Pellegrini & Cudahy, 1949);

*Heroes and Kings* (London: Sylvan, [1930–1931]);

*Many Dimensions* (London: Gollancz, 1931; New York: Pellegrini & Cudahy, 1949);

*Three Plays* (London: Oxford University Press, 1931);

*The Place of the Lion* (London: Gollancz, 1931; New York: Norton, 1932);

*The Greater Trumps* (London: Gollancz, 1932; New York: Pellegrini & Cudahy, 1950);

*The English Poetic Mind* (Oxford: Clarendon Press, 1932);

*Shadows of Ecstasy* (London: Gollancz, 1933; New York: Pellegrini & Cudahy, 1950);

*Bacon* (London: Barker, 1933; New York: Harper, 1934);

*Reason and Beauty in the Poetic Mind* (Oxford: Clarendon Press, 1933);

*James I* (London: Barker, 1934; New York: Roy, 1953);

*Rochester* (London: Barker, 1935);

*Thomas Cranmer of Canterbury* (London: Oxford University Press, 1936);

*Cranmer of Canterbury: Acting Edition* (Canterbury: H. J. Goulden, 1936);

*Charles Williams*

*Queen Elizabeth* (London: Duckworth, 1936);

*Descent into Hell* (London: Faber & Faber, 1937);

*Stories of Great Names* (London: Oxford University Press, 1937);

*Henry VII* (London: Barker, 1937);

*He Came Down from Heaven* (London: Heinemann, 1938; Grand Rapids, Mich.: Eerdmans, 1984);

*Taliessin through Logres* (London: Oxford University Press, 1938);

*The Descent of the Dove: A Short History of the Holy Spirit in the Church* (London: Longmans, 1939; New York: Oxford University Press, 1939);

316

*Judgement at Chelmsford* (London: Oxford University Press, 1939);

*Witchcraft* (London: Faber & Faber, 1941; Cleveland: World, 1959);

*Religion and Love in Dante: The Theology of Romantic Love* (London: Dacre Press, 1941);

*The Way of Exchange* (London: James Clarke, 1941);

*The Forgiveness of Sins* (London: Bles, 1942; Grand Rapids, Mich.: Eerdmans, 1984);

*The Figure of Beatrice* (London: Faber & Faber, 1943; New York: Noonday Press, 1961);

*The Region of the Summer Stars* (London: Editions Poetry London, 1944);

*All Hallows' Eve* (London: Faber & Faber, 1945; New York: Pellegrini & Cudahy, 1948);

*The House of the Octopus* (London: Edinburgh House Press, 1945);

*Flecker of Dean Close* (London: Canterbury Press, 1946);

*Seed of Adam and Other Plays* (London: Oxford University Press, 1948);

*Arthurian Torso: Containing the Posthumous Fragment of the Figure of Arthur by Charles Williams and a Commentary on the Arthurian Poems of Charles Williams by C. S. Lewis* (London: Oxford University Press, 1948);

*The Image of the City and Other Essays*, edited, with a critical introduction, by Anne Ridler (London: Oxford University Press, 1958);

*Collected Plays* (London: Oxford University Press, 1963);

*Outlines of Romantic Theology*, edited and introduced by Alice Mary Hadfield (Grand Rapids, Mich.: Eerdmans, 1990);

*Charles Williams*, edited and introduced by David Llewellyn Dodds (Woodbridge, Suffolk & Rochester, N.Y.: Boydell & Brewer, 1991).

OTHER: Michal Williams, *Christian Symbolism,* in collaboration with Williams (London: Talbot, 1919);

*Poems of Home and Overseas,* compiled by Williams and V. H. Collins (Oxford: Clarendon Press, 1921);

*A Book of Longer Modern Verse,* selected by Edward A. Parker, with notes by Williams (Oxford: Clarendon Press, 1926);

*A Book of Victorian Narrative Verse,* edited by Williams (Oxford: Clarendon Press, 1927);

*The Oxford Book of Regency Verse,* edited by Humphrey Milford and Williams (Oxford: Clarendon Press, 1928);

Gerard Manley Hopkins, *Poems,* second edition, edited by Robert Bridges, with an appendix of additional poems and introduction by Williams (London: Oxford University Press, 1931);

*A Short Life of Shakespeare with Sources,* abridged by Williams from Edmund Chambers, *William Shakespeare: A Study of Facts and Problems* (London: Oxford University Press, 1933);

Robert Browning, *The Ring and the Book,* retold by Williams (London: Oxford University Press, 1934);

*The New Book of English Verse,* edited by Williams (London: Gollancz, 1935);

*The Story of the Aeneid,* retold by Williams (London: Oxford University Press, 1936);

*The Passion of Christ,* edited by Williams (London: Oxford University Press, 1939);

*The English Poems of John Milton,* introduction by Williams (London: Oxford University Press, 1940);

Søren Kierkegaard, *The Present Age,* introduction by Williams (London: Oxford University Press, 1940);

*The New Christian Year,* selected by Williams (London: Oxford University Press, 1941);

*The Letters of Evelyn Underhill,* edited by Williams (London: Longmans, 1943);

Wilfrid Gibson, *Solway Ford and Other Poems,* selected by Williams (London: Faber & Faber, 1945).

SELECTED PERIODICAL PUBLICATIONS –
UNCOLLECTED: "Scene from a Mystery," *New Witness* (12 December 1919): 70–73;

"Et in Sempiternum Pereant," *London Mercury,* 33 (December 1935): 151–158;

"The Noises That Weren't There," *Mythlore,* 2 (Autumn 1970): 17–21; "Chapter II: The Voice of the Rat," *Mythlore,* 2 (Winter 1971): 17–23; "Third and Final Chapter of the Unfinished Manuscript," *Mythlore,* 2 (Winter 1972): 21–25;

"A Myth of Francis Bacon," *Charles Williams Society Newsletter,* 11 (Autumn 1978); 12 (Winter 1978); 14 (Summer 1979).

The headstone of Charles Walter Stansby Williams has the single word "Poet" at its center – with *"UNDER THE MERCY"* inscribed at the foot. Williams thought his poetry most important, and indeed *Taliessin through Logres* (1938) and *The Region of the Summer Stars* (1944), together with a few unfinished contributions to the cycle, constitute the great modern poem about the Holy Grail. His early poetry was admired by Alice Meynell (who arranged for the publication of his first volume), Robert

CHARLES WILLIAMS

# THE PLACE OF THE LION

## A NEW NOVEL

PRICE **3**s NETT

mundanus Ltd

VICTOR GOLLANCZ PUBLISHER

1931

*Wrapper for the paperbound edition of Williams's fourth novel, in which archetypal powers are symbolized by a lion and an eagle (courtesy of the Lilly Library, Indiana University)*

Bridges, and G. K. Chesterton and (to his surprise) gained him a 1924 Olympic diploma and bronze medal. *Thomas Cranmer of Canterbury* (1936) followed T. S. Eliot's *Murder in the Cathedral* (1935) as the Canterbury Festival play. But he was not solely a poet. *The Figure of Beatrice* (1943) encouraged Dorothy L. Sayers to undertake her study and translation of Dante. *James I* (1934), *The New Christian Year* (1941), and *Witchcraft* (1941), all much admired by Helen Gardner, together with *The Descent of the Dove: A Short History of the Holy Spirit in the Church* (1939) and *The New Book of English Verse* (1935) serve as further examples of the breadth of reading, put to use in fresh and challenging ways, of a scholar and critic who was largely an autodidact. Yet it is for his extraordinary novels, which brought him the admiration of Rebecca West and the friendship of both T. S. Eliot and C. S. Lewis, that Williams is best known.

Williams was born in London. His mother, Mary, had the amateur antiquarian writer J. C. Wall for a brother. His father, Walter, was employed as a foreign correspondence clerk but published poems and short stories in periodicals, including Charles Dickens's *Household Words*. In 1894, when Walter's firm failed and his eyesight was deteriorating, the family moved to Saint Albans, where Mary opened an art-supply shop. Charles Williams won scholarships to the Grammar School and in 1901 to University College, London, but still could not afford to complete his studies there. In 1904 he found work at a Methodist publishing office and bookroom and began attending lectures at the Working Men's College. When, in 1908, the bookroom closed, he got a job as a proofreader at the London office of the Oxford University Press on the recommendation of his friend Frederick Page, who worked there. Rising through the hierarchy, Williams remained an employee of the Oxford University Press until his death. Soon after Christmas 1907 Williams met and fell in love with Florence Conway, "by whom," as he later wrote in a dedication, he "began to study the doctrine of glory." He had always been emphatically Anglican (demanding to be taken to church at age three and a half), but he recalled later in a letter to Lewis Chase that he experienced, as an imaginative shock, a profound intellectual sense that "the relationship of romantic love *is* (not like, but *is*) the same thing as Christianity." On 12 April 1917 they married and settled in London. Later that year, on 21 September, Williams was received into the Fellowship of the Rosy Cross, the successor to (and in many ways continuation of ) the Independent and Rectified Rite of the Order of the Golden Dawn which A. E. Waite had established after taking over the Isis-Urania Temple in 1903.

Williams said that his father encouraged him to read everything, also noting that he "had a very strong feeling for the Jewish tradition" which "to some extent" he passed on to his son. Perhaps this predisposed Williams to his interest in the cabala, which was nourished both by Waite's *The Secret Doctrine in Israel* (1913) and by the rituals of the Fellowship of the Rosy Cross (FRC). Williams noted another early imaginative shock: the apprehension of "some sort of distinction of 'eternity' from 'everlastingness,' and the notion of eternity as being the same thing as the existence of God: not a quality of, but the being of, perfection." E. Nesbit's *The Story of the Amulet* (1906) – which Williams could not have read before he was around twenty – had a particular appeal in this context. Attention to timeless eter-

nity and its implications is always a feature of Williams's novels, though with varying degrees of explicitness. There are other works among Williams's early reading which are relevant to his own subsequent fiction, such as those by two members of Waite's Order of the Golden Dawn – Arthur Machen's "The Great God Pan" (1894) and the novels of Evelyn Underhill (for example, *The Column of Dust,* 1908) – as well as R. H. Benson's *The Necromancers* (1909) and G. K. Chesterton's *The Napoleon of Notting Hill* (1904). Reference to these can aid the attempt to assess Williams's achievement in his novels, with their unique combination of exuberance, humor, convincing supernatural effects, and metaphysical seriousness.

In 1922 a son, Michael, was born, and Charles Williams added the task of evening institute lecturer to his responsibilities. On 10 July 1925 Williams became an *adeptus exemptus,* in practice the top grade of the FRC. At about the same time, so he told Olive Willis in a letter that December, "It occurred to me as, returning from my last lecture, I finished the sensational novel that supported me, that *I* would write a sensational novel." He did, between 8 July and the end of August. He called it "the joke of my life, and I love it as such." By December it was titled "Adepts of Africa," altered from the exuberantly sensationalistic title "The Black Bastard" since the protagonist Nigel Considine "wasn't black, nor a bastard."

By 5 January 1926, his friend John Pellow noted, Williams was writing another novel, "about the Holy Graal and Black Magic," and had "a third in view." Faber and Faber was then considering *Outlines of Romantic Theology* (1990) for publication, and Pellow suggested offering all three novels to them "as a trilogy," which Williams thought a "magnificent idea." The second novel, a fantastic excursion into the murder-mystery genre, was titled "The Corpse" after one which appears in the first sentence, where the telephone "was ringing wildly, but without result, since there was no one in the room but the corpse." Apparently it had been finished and both it and "Adepts" offered to, and rejected by, Faber and Faber by the end of May 1926. By December, Williams had sent "Adepts" to Knopf, who also rejected it.

In 1929 Williams was almost ready to discard the manuscript of "The Corpse" when he was encouraged by a colleague to try submitting it to Victor Gollancz. Gollancz was enthusiastic, though he wanted an arresting title, suggestive of neither detection nor black magic nor the Graal. It appeared in early summer 1930 as *War in Heaven.* So pleased was Gollancz with it that he wanted another immediately. In June 1930 Williams told a friend that he had "one novel that needs lots of revision and another half-done." The former was "Adepts." Williams obviously had misgivings about it, warning Gollancz that it had been refused "by several publishers" and submitting his own list of suggested alterations with the manuscript. Gollancz had misgivings too, and the book was set aside, to be delivered, in a much-rewritten form, only on 28 July 1932. It was thereafter published in 1933 as his fifth novel – with the title *Shadows of Ecstasy.*

Williams's earliest novels present several probably insolvable mysteries. Enough references survive to show that *Shadows of Ecstasy* in its original form was significantly like the book as published, but nothing indicates in satisfactory detail what changes were made. Therefore, while it may be best to treat it as Williams's first novel, this can only be done with caution.

Neither is it clear how much *War in Heaven* was revised for publication. This question becomes important in the context of Pellow's reference on 5 January 1926 to Williams having a third novel "in view" and his well-received suggestion of treating them as a trilogy. Williams certainly did not wait until he had written a third novel to offer the first two to Faber and Faber. Perhaps Pellow's suggestion was simply a gimmick. *Shadows of Ecstasy* in its final form has no internal connections with *War in Heaven.* There are, however, statements in *War in Heaven* that point to a possible sequel, which Williams's second novel to be published, *Many Dimensions* (1931), in fact provides.

On 30 December 1925 Williams referred in a letter to his long poem (*Heroes and Kings,* 1930–1931), which includes a wonderful Stone of Solomon – as does *Many Dimensions.* Perhaps the third novel "in view" was already conceived of as forming a sequel to the second, with the Stone succeeding the Cup. Presumably, *Many Dimensions* was the novel only "half-done" in June 1930: it remained unfinished in September but was completed in time to appear by 15 January 1931. Even if it is related to the mysterious "third novel" of 1926, however, much of it could not have been written before 1927.

Williams, apparently in late summer 1926, fell in love with Phyllis Jones, a colleague fifteen years younger than himself. In a later "sketch of an *autobiography,*" he said their "great period" was from September 1926 to April 1927: "After that, everything went wrong – except, of course, the Holy Ghost." There, he also points to Chloe Burnett, "general intellectual factotum" to the chief justice, Lord

*Williams as a young man in St. Albans (photograph by Phyllis Jones)*

Williams's novels are, however, worlds away from that of his friend D. H. S. Nicholson, *The Marriage-Craft* (1924), which is almost entirely devoted to the discussion of the possible purposes of sex and marriage by a party including characters clearly based on Williams, Nicholson, and their clerical friend, Arthur Hugh Evelyn Lee (who appears as Henry, possibly the origin of this nickname which Williams always used for Lee). By contrast, Williams's novels well deserve the description "metaphysical thrillers."

*Shadows of Ecstasy* is nonetheless thematically related to Nicholson's book. It is concerned with the "ecstasy of vivid experience" – such as Philip's experience of Rosamund in his love for her, or Roger's of poetry, or Rosamund's of the Western-educated Zulu king, Inkamasi – all in the context of "the repression by which man had held down his more natural energies" and "the strong refusal which Europe had laid on capacities it had so long ruled that it had nearly forgotten their independent life." Williams provides a focus by means of two sensational actions. One is a sudden, united, spectacularly successful attempt by the peoples of Africa to free their "continent from the government and occupation of the white race," which includes demonstration air raids and troop landings in London. The other is a financial crisis following the suicide of a magnate who leaves everything to devout cousins – who immediately sell all the shares to raise money to rebuild the Temple in Jerusalem. The liberation of Africa is announced by the mysterious High Executive of the allies, in a proclamation made "in the First Year of the Second Evolution of Man" to mark the end of the "age of intellect" and the opening of paths to be followed not "by the old habits of reason but by profounder experiments of passion."

It gradually becomes clear that Nigel Considine, wealthy sponsor of a university lectureship on Ritual Transmutations of Energy, has succeeded in living two hundred years by the imaginative transmutation of "sex and love and desire" and of all intense experience, including pain, into power which he has used to make himself impervious to aging – and that he is the High Executive. Taught the beginning of the "work" by his father, then initiated into tribal mysteries as a boy, Considine, with an inner circle of adepts (including many in the European imperial administrations), has secretly gained power over all the royalties of Africa. He will free Africa to secure his own control, that the occult "schools" may survive and flourish, and some adept eventually attain not merely a longevity subject to accident and death but self-resurrection.

Arglay, in *Many Dimensions,* as a reflection of Jones, though "not very close."

There are indeed no simple translations of real people into characters in Williams's novels, though there are characters related to people, not least Williams himself. The term *characters,* however, is problematic. Williams said that in his late poetry "there are no *characters*" but "only functions and offices," generalizing this by adding that all his work was "in a way, abstract." Yet, in the novels, there are not only vivid particularizing details – such as those in *War in Heaven* which make Julian Davenant, the archdeacon, both a fencer and a reader of Julian of Norwich – there are often convincing treatments of the psychology of even minor characters. Yet again, his characters are abstract in the sense that, whatever their particularity or complexity, they serve to embody various responses to existence – no doubt indebted to different aspects of Williams's own experience, as well as to his ability to entertain diverse positions. Part of the pleasure of the novels derives from the varied perspectives confronting each other in conversations or arguments between characters.

Memorable episodes include one adept's nearly successful attempt to return from the dead, a visionary glimpse by Roger of what the achieved end might feel like, the delivery of the Christian Inkamasi through a Eucharist celebrated by the archbishop from "the sleep" which Considine has imposed on his will and consciousness, and (perceptively foreshadowing many later historical incidents) the self-immolation "for the Master of Death" of the troops after they have served their purpose in terrifying London. Many of the wild improbabilities of plot are handled with considerable deftness, though the novel remains less successful in this respect than the even wilder ones which follow.

It is, however, the most critically intriguing of Williams's novels on account of its apparent ambiguity. Roger, who significantly resembles Williams, becomes a follower of Considine, and though he flees after seeing Considine assassinated, the book ends with the possibility that he secretly awaits and hopes for his return from the dead. The Anglican priest Caithness has effectively connived at the killing. And there are only quiet suggestions that Considine's "gospel" is not merely ruthless but also insufficient – because it will not let man despair of himself and so find "that which cannot despair and is other than man"; and that the Christians he has killed may be joined "with something greater" than him "because it had known defeat." Yet those making the suggestions both act astonishingly – Inkamasi, believing he will never serve as king indeed, allowing Considine to kill him; Isabel, out of "the vast experience of love which she had undergone," willing for Roger what he chooses as "his necessity." Whatever one concludes, there are details of the methods of "transmutation" which can illuminate the magical rituals that Williams himself seems to have developed after leaving the FRC in 1927 and to have practiced to the end of his life.

Williams's Christian sympathies are much clearer in *War in Heaven,* despite hints of doctrinal and speculative peculiarities. In contrast to the global disruptions in *Shadows of Ecstasy,* there are finally no certain public traces of the great wonders and dangers here – though the Satanists had aspired to use the Holy Graal in a Mass of Death which would destroy "all intelligible experience" of earth and heaven.

Sir Giles Tumulty has, for his study *Historical Vestiges of Sacred Vessels in Folklore,* traced the Cup of the Last Supper to a small Hertfordshire church and aids Gregory Persimmons, his (retired) publisher, who is a Satanist, in its pursuit, since "to push or delay any devotee upon the path was entertainment

to a mind too swiftly bored." Williams makes the Graal into a kind of *figura rerum* (to borrow a term from *Cranmer*) or universal figure – together with Prester John, whose form "appears to come forth from the universe it expressed," and who mysteriously declares, "I am John and I am Galahad and I am Mary; I am the Bearer of the Holy One, the Graal, and the keeper of the Graal." They evoke responses by characters to existence, giving opportunities for those responses to intensify or change. In this way Williams can economically distinguish and explore such responses with greater clarity than in *Shadows of Ecstasy.* Thus, among the Satanists, Gregory desires "to give himself out, to be one with something that should submit to him and from which he should yet draw nourishment," and he is destructive to this end; Manasseh, further along the way, is more wholeheartedly destructive, giving up the attempt to destroy the Graal only because he becomes convinced it might be used "to blast the world for ever"; Dmitri will help either, "for possession and destruction are both evil and are one," but has himself reached a purer nihilism, believing that in the end "there is nothing, nothing but a passing, and in the midst of the passing a weariness that is you" – and consciously pursuing that end.

The archdeacon, Davenant, thinks that both his allies and the Satanists attach too much importance to the Graal – "a symbol less near Reality now than any chalice of consecrated wine." But, withdrawing into "that place" where the "cause of all action . . . disposed itself according to that Will which was its nature," Davenant finds himself directed to rescue the Graal once Gregory has stolen it. (The Graal itself seems similarly directed, shuddering forward from its bracket, so that they come together.) Yet Davenant has no hesitation in surrendering it again, on the chance that this may help to deliver Barbara (suffering from Gregory's administration of a magical ointment).

Pattison, whose corpse provides the mystery (eventually solved by Inspector Colquhoun – with some help from Prester John), does not encounter the Graal until late in the story. He had been in Gregory's power, then became a Christian, but fearfully returned to Gregory, who says of "the unhappy soul," "It was willing to die when I slew it, and in the shadows it waits still upon my command." Gregory attempts to use the Graal, "the circle of all souls," to wreck those of Pattison and Davenant "in each other for ever." Davenant, prior to the attempt, has felt "the power" to which he lives in obedience "withdrawing and abandoning him" – "he cried desperately to God and God did not hear

*Williams with William Butler Yeats, circa 1917 (Marion E. Wade Collection, Wheaton College, Wheaton, Ill.)*

him" – until, as the attempt proceeds, he is "driven beyond consciousness." But in the attempt the Graal's essence was touched, and it "awoke in its own triumphant and blinding power," with "he that was the Graal," Prester John, emerging to reveal to those "who sought the centre of the Graal" that which they seek and to bestow that which they are. Davenant sees Pattison's face "free and happy and adoring." This is one of many powerful presentations of inner or visionary experience, also including Gregory's attendance at "the Witches' Sabbath" and the Graal Mass which ends the book, where Davenant, like Sir Thomas Malory's Galahad, dies and "the Graal and its Lord" vanish.

Powerfully imagining the serenity and obedience of Davenant, Williams also allows Lionel, a character with many resemblances to himself, to say as almost his last word that he desires annihilation: "I have not asked for life, and I should be content to know that soon I should not be."

*War in Heaven* is, in effect, a persuasive fictional theodicy – enriched and troubled by the strange figure of Prester John (who says at one point "I am myself and I am He that sent me"). John, having announced that "This war is ended

and another follows quickly," and having told Giles Tumulty that "I and the heavens" will watch and laugh when Giles "shall scrabble in the universe as an ant against the smoothness of the inner side of the Graal," does not reappear as a character in *Many Dimensions*. Giles does and, watched by "curious and pitiless" eyes, finds "himself gathered, a living soul, into the centre of the Stone." Perhaps Williams is playing with the idea of Graal as Stone from Wolfram von Eschenbach's *Parzival* (circa 1200–1210), though the novel contains no explicit reference to the Graal. However, Waite's *Secret Doctrine in Israel* (1913) includes an account of the cubical stone *Schethiyâ*, inscribed with the Divine Name and cast by God into the abyss to form the basis, and be the central point of the world – presumably among Williams's major sources for the material he develops so brilliantly in *Many Dimensions*. And Waite there compares *Schethiyâ* to both Wolfram's Graal and the stone from Lucifer's crown, which he identifies with each other in another book known to Williams, *The Hidden Church of the Holy Graal* (1909). Whatever its intentional relationship to the Graal, Williams's Stone functions to disclose, evoke, and challenge responses to existence even more thor-

322

oughly, as well as more complexly, than his Cup. Hajji Ibrahim, of the Persian family whose members have been its guardians for a millennium, thinks the Stone is the First Matter "from which all things are made – spirits and material things." It is a rich *figura rerum,* enabling the fulfillment of such aspirations as almost instantaneous movement through space – and backward through time, entry into and influence upon another's consciousness, healing of diseases, even survival of death – easily, if often surprisingly. This almost incidentally occasions the science-fictional interest, in the form of a "very fine working out of the logical consequences of time-travel," which C. S. Lewis notes is one of the novel's elements. The Stone's public impact is a concern from the first page, and the dilemmas of possible use – beginning with that presented by "the least of [its] graces," the effective abolition of spatial distance – are also finely worked out. They are intensified by the fact that the Stone can be easily and infinitely divided without suffering any diminution, as can each of the types so produced.

Thus, competing desires to limit its ownership or use – whether in the interest of monopoly in transport, or of protecting transport workers' jobs, or of national power – or to use it only for healing, or simply to withdraw it again into protected seclusion are all unlikely to succeed. Among those with any real knowledge of the Stone, only two have no such decided aspirations to do something with it – the chief justice, Lord Arglay, and his secretary, Chloe. *Many Dimensions* is particularly concerned with them and their developments in relation to each other in response to the Stone.

Arglay, like Sir Bernard Travers in *Shadows of Ecstasy* (1933), embodies a skeptical, yet even-handed, rational approach to existence, seeing everything in the light of a "fastidious and ironical goodwill." But Travers has, for the most part, only to keep his head – his faith in the intellect. Not so Arglay. In *War in Heaven* Davenant says, "No one can possibly do more than decide what to believe." This is what Arglay and Chloe, unable to analyze satisfactorily why they are so concerned that the Stone not be used in certain ways, find that they must do. When Arglay asks Chloe if she believes in God, she replies, "I think I do when I look at the Stone." He proposes that he will, if she will, then urges her to "consider how you will follow this God that we have decided to believe in, who, it seems, may give wisdom through the Stone." There is a delicately worked out reciprocity in their relationship, whereby Arglay helps to enable Chloe to do things he himself could not do, and vice versa. A

crucial factor is Arglay's determination to help Pondon, who, imposed upon by his employer, Professor Palliser, and Tumulty, has used the Stone to travel backward in time and become trapped in a short but infinite loop – continually traveling back, whenever he again reaches the moment from which he departed. Arglay attempts "to offer Pondon a way of return" while "submitting the whole thing to whatever Power reposed in the Stone" with Chloe joining in the attempt. With a nice intricacy, though Chloe does not see him, Pondon sees her (as he thinks) in the lab and reenters the present because he would courteously and dutifully ask her if she were looking for Professor Palliser. Chloe, meanwhile, is undergoing a process of purgation and choosing – which prepares her for the solution of all the dilemmas by making herself a path for the restoration of the Types to the Stone and the Stone to itself through her, at the cost of her life.

Arglay turns up again in "Et in Sempiternum Pereant" (1935), the only short story Williams published. Rushing to help at a cottage which may be burning, he discovers a door to hell. He sees another going to it and, confronting "the reality of his hate" for Giles, which "he had felt and been pleased to feel," clutches without effect at the smoke of "his greedy loves and greedy hates – at the cloud of the sin of his life" until he thinks that "*now* was the only possible other fact, chance, act" and, "defying infinity," cries "*Now!*" This delivers him, so that he may desire "to make a ladder of himself" by which the other "might perhaps mount from the nature of the lost." But he sees no one, then, spurred by a "wail of multitudes of the lost," he runs, crying "Now is God: now is glory in God," to end, "breathless and shaken," by quoting the last line of Dante's *Inferno.* It was his final appearance – perhaps because Williams's wife did not like the character, for when, on 9 June 1940, Williams told her he had "a kind of yearning towards a novel," he added, "if I do think of anything, I will promise you that Lord Arglay shall NOT come in."

Williams's fourth novel, *The Place of the Lion,* appeared in September 1931. In it he develops a *figura rerum* at once diversified and integrated. The adept Berringer (with some resemblance to "the Adam" in Williams's retelling of the Fall in a later poem) is in his garden engaged in contemplating the "world of principles" when an escaped lioness springs on him – and she is assumed into the Power which is particularly her archetype, breaching the separation between worlds and admitting the Powers into this world to draw it progressively into that. Here is a danger which, once begun, does not im-

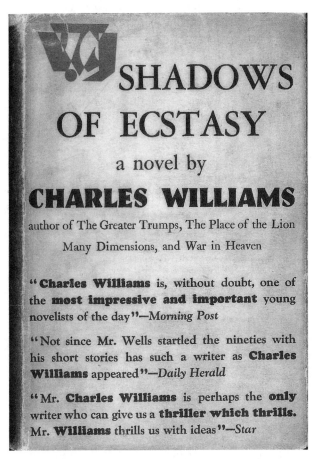

SHADOWS
OF ECSTASY
a novel by
**CHARLES WILLIAMS**
author of The Greater Trumps, The Place of the Lion
Many Dimensions, and War in Heaven

"**Charles Williams** is, without doubt, one of
the **most impressive and important** young
novelists of the day"—*Morning Post*

"Not since Mr. Wells startled the nineties with
his short stories has such a writer as **Charles
Williams** appeared"—*Daily Herald*

"Mr. **Charles Williams** is perhaps the **only**
writer who can give us a **thriller which thrills.**
Mr. **Williams** thrills us with ideas"—*Star*

*Dust jacket for Williams's 1933 book originally titled "Adepts"
(courtesy of the Lilly Library, Indiana University)*

mediately depend on any human agency, unlike those in the earlier novels. Yet both particular Powers, and their whole interrelated complex, challenge characters to respond and will affect them whether acknowledged or not – especially as, in different configurations, they are related to each person, who is in some sense "compact of powers." The butterfly collector, Mr. Tighe, passes into a satisfied inactivity after seeing a Power in the form of a glorious butterfly absorbing clouds of its phenomenal images. Two of Berringer's "study circle," Foster and Dora Wilmot, craving strength of different sorts, give themselves "to that Power which each of them best serves" and become ever more leonine or serpentine and less human. By contrast Quentin is driven wild by his fear that the Lion is hunting him, to be hunted at last by Foster. He does, however, make an effort to get Damaris Tighe to safety, because she is his friend Anthony's girl. This she denies and leaves him wriggling along a ditch. She is, however, miserable as a result, for, in her terms, "if her relations with Anthony had any truth at all,

then she was committed to at least such an amount of care for Anthony's wishes as he would have given to hers." Damaris is a scholarly, capable graduate student of classical philosophy and patristic and scholastic thought and a sensitive academic politician. Standing in for the comatose Berringer, she gives a paper arguing that the medieval angelic hierarchies represent "the last traces in a less philosophic age of the ideas which Plato taught his disciples existed in the spiritual world," saying, "We may not believe in them as actually existent – either ideas or angels" – before being interrupted by the manifestation of one of the Powers identified with both.

Anthony, acting mainly from his love of Damaris and Quentin, wants to find if anything can be done to resist this world "passing into that." He wishes that Damaris and he could "together find the right way" but thinks this futile and is first helped instead by Richardson – and the copy Berringer had lent him of Marcellus Victorinus's Latin version (1514) of a twelfth-century work by Alexander of Byzantion, *De Angelis*. Anthony has hoped "the authority which is in me over me shall be in me over them" but does not know how to accomplish this, though he has once been helped by seeing "some winged thing" high above – "the pure balance of that distant flight entered into him as if it had been salvation" – and, encountering the Lion, escaped when "he did not fight this awful opposition but poised himself within and above it." From Victorinus he learns that among the Powers is the Eagle: "this is he who knows both himself and the others, and is their own knowledge."

A marvelous visionary chapter follows. While seeking what he can discover at Berringer's, Anthony is challenged by the Eagle "to know himself as he was," with all his foolish and evil acts, and his denials and outrages of his "passionate desire for intellectual and spiritual truth and honesty." Anthony, enduring to know all this, finds himself "riding in the void," borne between gigantic wings, "under the protection of another of the great Ideas, that Wisdom which knew the rest and itself also." Damaris, however, encounters it as a rapacious pterodactyl, reeking of corruption, an image – in C. S. Lewis's words – of "the special sin of the abuse of intellect to which all my profession are liable," and of which she has been guilty. The horror of the confrontation makes her "unconscious of her work for the first time for years" and conscious of her need for others – and she calls for Anthony, who hears, comes, and helps to finish her conversion, subordinating "her to the complete realization of herself

and her past." She then goes, instead of Anthony, to find and help Quentin. Finally Anthony, in whom "the nature of Adam lived," trusting the Eagle to "show him how to serve," is led to call "the Ideas who are the Principles of everlasting creation" by "the names that were the Ideas," drawing them together into balance and bidding them to "pass back and close the breach."

About five months after the publication of *The Place of the Lion* in September 1931, Williams sent the manuscript of his fifth novel, *The Greater Trumps,* to Gollancz on 2 March 1932; the novel was published in April. Here Williams develops another complex, differentiated *figura rerum*. It is the original pack of tarot cards, together with a table upon which golden figures, corresponding to those on the cards, move continuously "as if to some complicated measure, and as if of their own volition."

It is possible that Richardson, the mystic of the negative way in Williams's fourth novel, may have some playful yet serious reference to his friend D. H. S. Nicholson. It seems impossible that Williams is not teasing their mutual friend, the occultist, vicar, and fanatically confirmed bachelor A. H. E. Lee, when, in *The Greater Trumps,* he gives the young lover the name "Henry Lee" and his grandfather the priestly name "Aaron Lee." Henry is a barrister, but both are preoccupied with seeking the knowledge and power which can result from recovering the original cards and bringing them together with the table to which they are the key.

In the tarot, whether cards or table, the suits are related to the four elements, and the Greater Trumps "are the meaning of all process and the measure of the everlasting dance." Williams, however, does not give the tarot exactly the same kind of unifying function as the Stone or the Powers have in the two preceding novels.

Henry discovers that Lothair Coningsby, the father of his fiancée, Nancy, has inherited a collection of playing cards, on the condition that he leave it to the British Museum, which includes the tarots. Henry and Aaron want to acquire the tarots but fear Coningsby would not part with them and "that violence breaks the knowledge of the cards." As a first step, they invite the Coningsbys to Aaron's country house for Christmas, and Henry gets Nancy to suggest bringing the tarots and to hint that Lothair might give them to Henry.

Aaron's sister, Joanna, once attempted to procreate a child "to be a Mighty One born within the measure" of "the dance" (something to which Henry also aspires). But her baby died at birth, and she went mad, ever after thinking she was the goddess Isis and seeking a phantasmagoric tangle of cards, child, and "the god," whether Osiris or Horus.

When Lothair refuses to part with the cards, Henry uses them to raise a snowstorm to kill him. Nancy interferes and some cards are blown away, releasing the storm to spread over the whole world and continue forever.

It is this disordering of the world and the tarot which variously challenges all the characters to respond. The tarot images also recur throughout the novel, often in striking visionary passages and in interplay with things in the world which quickens the imagination – particularly of Nancy (as well as the reader). The novel begins with a remark connected with the Trump, "The Falling Tower," as Williams develops the image – " 'perfect Babel,' Mr. Coningsby said peevishly" – and with family bickering, in which, however, Lothair's sister, Sybil, is not really involved. She has surrendered her will to "the working of that Fate which was Love" and grown from trying to enjoy to the realization "that there was no need for her to try or to enjoy: she had only to be still, and let that recognized Deity itself enjoy, as its omnipotent nature was."

Family relations, if always a feature of the earlier novels in one way or another, are a particular concern in *The Greater Trumps.* So is growth in love. Circumstances concerning the tarot – such as Henry's shift of attention from Nancy to the cards and his willingness to use her, the fact that only Sybil can see the figure of the Fool move on the table, the church service on Christmas morning, Henry's attempt to raise the storm and what follows – give opportunities for Sybil to contribute to the life of the family and to Nancy's growth in love. Nancy, encouraged by Sybil "to be life" between Henry and Lothair, approaches the table with the remaining cards, entering "into the secret dance," and "the warm hands of humanity in hers met the invasion and turned it." Sybil's hand completes the work of ending "the invasion of the Tarots." Joanna has tried to pierce Nancy's hand to let the god out, with Nancy not only enduring this but all the while trying to love Joanna " – wish her well – understand her – see her goodness." Joanna at last "thinks Nancy is her child." This puzzles Lothair, and Sybil explains, "She thought her child was Messias." When he asks, "And is Nancy Messias?" Sybil answers, "Near enough."

Victor Gollancz, writing to Williams on 5 March 1932 after reading the manuscript, was both enthusiastic (saying, "The snow storm is the very finest thing you have done") and of the opinion that "we shan't sell it – it is the most difficult of the lot." Less than five months later, Williams had sent him

*Dust jacket for Williams's 1945 novel set in the postwar future (courtesy of the Lilly Library, Indiana University)*

the revised version of his first novel, which appeared as *Shadows of Ecstasy* at the beginning of 1933.

Some mystery surrounds Williams's sixth novel, *Descent into Hell* (1937). Williams was writing it in August 1933: in *The Image of the City* Anne Ridler quotes a letter from him written then, which includes a passage occurring in chapter 6 of the published version. On 29 September 1936 Williams, writing to Ellis Roberts accepting the offer to do *He Came Down from Heaven* (1938), says that he is "struggling to reorganize a novel at the moment which is called *Descent into Hell*." He was still working on it at the end of October 1936.

At some point it was offered to Gollancz, who refused it. Thereafter, T. S. Eliot – who had been introduced by Lady Ottoline Morrell to *War in Heaven* and *The Place of the Lion* and then to Williams himself – took it for Faber and Faber, and it appeared in September 1937.

Glen Cavaliero, calling it Williams's best novel, says, "Outside of Williams's own work, *Descent into Hell* has no parallel in English fiction," particularly in the sense it gives of the interpenetration of the natural and supernatural. The complex *figurae rerum* of the last two novels are here succeeded by the production of a verse drama, a modern analogue of a Shakespearean tragicomedy by Peter Stanhope, which is essentially related to the novel's constant concern with the last things – death, judgment, hell, heaven. Williams shows more characters undergoing dynamic change than in any earlier novel, in complex interrelations. Margaret Anstruther, nearing death, uses what strength she has to continue to crawl toward the light up the mountain "that was she and others and all the world under her separate kind." But it is only through Stanhope's play that her orphaned granddaughter, Pauline, gets to know her – and learns more of their ancestor, John Struther, burned at the stake under Queen Mary. Pauline is isolated and oppressed by her fear of encountering her doppelgänger.

An unskilled workman, who after being fired hanged himself in a house he was helping to build, lingers, even though dead, where the historian Lawrence Wentworth now lives, neither aware of the other. Wentworth, who has a recurrent dream of descending a rope, "identified scholarship with himself, and asserted himself under the disguise of a defence of scholarship," while refusing to recognize this, or fully to admit his desire and need for Adela, or his distress at losing her. It is he who is on the descent into hell, increasingly preferring self-deception and illusion. This is figured in his absorption with "the true Adela who was apart and his," a succubus, both "drawn from his own recesses" and related to Lily Sammile, an old woman who offers soothing dreams, who is in fact Lilith "in one of her shapes." In the visionary chapter "Return to Eden" she says to Wentworth, "It's good for man to be alone," and he, agreeing, becomes a parody of Adam, who thinks "Eve had never told him he had made her, and so he wouldn't make her again." Turning away from "all otherness," he passes into "a living oblivion" and is "drawn, steadily, everlastingly, inward and down through the bottomless circles of the void."

Lily, however, fails to tempt Pauline with her promise, "You'll never have to do anything for others any more." For Pauline has confided in Stanhope and been convinced to try letting him bear her fear and distress for her, just as she might let someone relieve her of a physical burden.

*The Greater Trumps* includes a brief but striking substitutionary healing, with Sybil relieving a pain in Aaron's ankle by feeling it in her own. But *Descent into Hell* presents Williams's boldest exemplum of what he calls in one chapter title "The Doctrine of Substituted Love," connected both with his sharp awareness of the interdependence of all life and with his understanding of Christ's death as substitutionary.

Accepting Stanhope's offer, Pauline then encounters in Margaret's room not her double but the suicide. Margaret meets him with such love that he is freed to turn from his flight. Pauline is sent out to help him further, does so, and then finds that her "moment of goodwill" to him had opened to her "the place of the present and all the past." She encounters her ancestor, terrified on the eve of his execution. She wants to help but feels she "could never bear that fear." Behind her she hears her own voice say, "Give it to me": "this other had done what she desired, and yet not the other, but she, for it was she who had all her life carried a fear which was not hers but another's"; she "had lived without joy" that her ancestor "might die in joy, but when she lived she had not known and when she offered she had not guessed that the sacrificial victim had died before the sacrificial act was accomplished." Her double is known as her "manifested joy," her "beatitude," and thereafter she remembers her earlier life as if from her double's perspective: she has consciously begun to become the person she should be.

*Descent into Hell* was the last of Williams's novels written during the interwar period. At the declaration of war with Germany, the London branch of the Oxford University Press evacuated to Oxford, and Williams with them. He frequently traveled to London, where his wife had chosen to remain, and corresponded with her daily.

In March 1940 he received a depressing account of *Descent into Hell:* Faber and Faber had not yet recouped their advance in sales. Nevertheless, he was soon intending to write another novel, asking his wife, on 21 June, to think of a subject, adding, "let it be supernatural this time, because I am more certain there" — a hint of what may have become an enduring aspiration to write "a straightforward one" (something Williams's wife recalled as being among his plans for after the war). On 30 July he speculated to a friend about making this novel a kind of *Paradiso* as a logical successor to his last but doubted he could "do heaven": "An account of the Timeless in terms of time is bound to seem silly."

The bombing of London in September 1940 contributed to his thinking of a different subject. He sounded out Eliot, who liked it, and in January 1941 sent a synopsis to Faber and Faber. As he reported to a friend on 16 April 1941, it was the idea of the Devil trying to beget Antichrist "in the flesh and failing, and hence wars and tumults." At that time, he could not yet see his way, and he may not have actually written anything until after Eliot began pressing him for a novel in June 1943. He had begun in July with a haunted house, though unsure what the novel would be about, and told a friend on 23 July, "I push the sentences before me like bricks in a wheelbarrow" and that the "best thing so far is the title to the first chapter": " 'The Noises that were not there.' "

At least three draft versions of the beginning of this novel survive. The draft published in *Mythlore* (1970–1972) — with the erroneous suggestions that it was Williams's last novel and that the whole novel was titled "The Noises That Weren't There" — is apparently the latest draft. Set in the near future, after World War II, it clearly is concerned with a diabolic attempt at incarnation.

It was abandoned, apparently in September 1943; on 28 October Williams reported to a friend that C. S. Lewis "says of the opening of the new novel now that I have more in my little finger than all of them in their whole bodies" — which must have been said of the first chapter of *All Hallows' Eve* (1945): in its published form, among his finest pieces of writing.

Williams's last novel incorporates various elements from the abandoned draft. Unfortunately, it is not all on an equal level with its first chapter. Williams's own comments on it range from calling its prose "too undistinguished" to thinking it "lousy" and being "bitterly disappointed." But it was variously well received when it appeared in January 1945.

*All Hallows' Eve,* like the abandoned draft, is also set in the postwar future. In Simon Leclerc, Williams plays, even more than in Nigel Considine, with a figure who might be Antichrist. Like Considine, he has learned to direct power and lived since the eighteenth century. Unlike Considine, he is most interested in extending his personal domination — he would not only rule the world but extend his power "into the spiritual places." He has procreated his daughter, Betty, to this end, using her as "in some sense his substitute," sending her in trance into the other world and intending to establish her there permanently by "a compulsory dissolution of bonds between soul and body." Williams, dissatisfied, described him as "an unconvincing magician." Some details are less convincing than others, partic-

ularly those connected with Simon's production of two "images and actual copies of him, magically multiplied, flesh out of flesh"; with their careers as "a great religious philosopher in China, a great patriot preacher in Russia"; and with the likelihood that they "shall make a threefold World Leadership." Simon is defeated by two substitutions. Unknown to him, Betty's nurse baptized her. And, when he attempts to "divide without disuniting" Betty's body and soul, her dead friend, Lester, is present and puts herself at Betty's disposal. The dissolution begins to work on Lester in a different fashion, threatening to absorb her into "all that was not." But though she did not "in the least guess what was happening," she finds herself supported, "leaning back on something, some frame," and it seemed "her arms, flung out on each side held on to part of the frame, as along a beam of wood."

The novel begins with Lester and her friend Evelyn gradually discovering that they have been killed together in an accident. Williams then traces the process of their different responses to being dead, and particularly Lester's purgation and growth in love. As Eliot writes, "a study of these two figures will reveal his understanding of the depths and intricacies of human nature."

In Simon's creation of a single homuncula for Evelyn, who craves to "get back" – and for Lester, whom he would imprison – he appears as a convincing magician. Both Lester's willingness to descend into this magical body, on the chance she might help Evelyn so, and her renewed experience of physical sensation as a consequence, are movingly presented. And, as Anne Ridler writes of Lester and her husband, Richard, "Williams never went farther in his perception of human relationships, or wrote anything more poignant, than his description of these two lovers parted by death."

When Williams wrote to a friend on 5 July 1944, reporting Eliot's approval of *All Hallows' Eve* (which he had finished writing by mid May), he went on to say that another novel – "also about death – moves vaguely in my head: this time with some idea of touching on the Eucharist." But he died on 15 May 1945 without having started one.

Anne Ridler, agreeing with the suggestion that Williams looked on his novels as entertainments, adds that he never made a "distinction between literature and entertainment, either in his own reading or in what he wrote." One can see an emblem of this in a poem in *Windows of Night* (1925) beginning "I saw Shakespeare / In a Tube station," a youngish Shakespeare with "the notes for *The Merchant*" in his pocket – and "Sax Rohmer's best novel under his arm." This disregard has its risks, whether one thinks of the reader who wants sensational entertainment without any dimensions of seriousness or depth, or of the critic who is more likely to compare Williams unfavorably with Henry James than favorably with Sax Rohmer. Yet it is also part of the appeal of Williams's novels. Their literary inadequacies do not, in any case, outweigh their virtues. Both Eliot and Lewis point to one of the greatest of these, in similar terms. Eliot says that "Williams is telling us about a world of experience known to him," not merely persuading, but communicating "this experience he has had." And Lewis is quite sure "that he is describing something he knows which I should not have known unless he had described it; and something that matters." With their success in conveying such a sense, Williams's novels can be expected to continue to attract and challenge new readers.

**Letters:**

*Letters to Lalage: The Letters of Charles Williams to Lois Lang-Sims* (Kent, Ohio: Kent State University Press, 1989).

**Bibliographies:**

Lawrence R. Dawson, "A Checklist of Reviews by Charles Williams," *Papers of the Bibliographical Society of America,* 55 (April/June 1961): 100–117;

Lois Glenn, *Charles W. S. Williams: A Checklist* (Kent, Ohio: Kent State University Press, 1975).

**Biographies:**

Alice Mary Hadfield, *An Introduction to Charles Williams* (London: Hale, 1959);

Humphrey Carpenter, *The Inklings* (London: Allen & Unwin, 1978);

Alice Mary Hadfield, *Charles Williams: An Exploration of His Life and Work* (New York: Oxford University Press, 1983).

**References:**

Glen Cavaliero, *Charles Williams: Poet of Theology* (London: Macmillan / Grand Rapids, Mich.: Eerdmans, 1983);

Jan Curtis, "Charles Williams: His Reputation in the English-speaking World from 1917–1985," *Inklings-Jahrbuch,* 9 (1991): 127–164;

David Llewellyn Dodds, "An Introduction to the Unpublished Williams," *Charles Williams Newsletter,* 69 (Spring 1993): 7–22;

Dodds, "Magic in the Myths of J. R. R. Tolkien and Charles Williams," *Inklings-Jahrbuch,* 10 (1992): 37–55;

T. S. Eliot, "Introduction," in Williams's *All Hallows' Eve* (New York: Pellegrini & Cudahy, 1948), pp. ix–xviii;

R. A. Gilbert, *A. E. Waite: Magician of Many Parts* (Wellingborough: Thorson, 1987);

Gilbert, *The Golden Dawn: Twilight of the Magicians* (Wellingborough: Aquarian, 1983);

John Heath-Stubbs, *Charles Williams* (London: Longmans, 1955);

Kerryl Lynne Henderson, "Charles Williams: The Early Poetry," *Charles Williams Society Newsletter,* 64 (Winter 1991): 4–27;

Thomas T. Howard, *The Novels of Charles Williams* (New York: Oxford University Press, 1983);

Charles Huttar, "Charles Williams's Christmas Novel: *The Greater Trumps,*" *Seven: An Anglo-American Literary Review,* 4 (1983): 68–83;

Gisbert Kranz, ed., "Proceedings of the International Charles Williams Symposium," *Inklings-Jahrbuch,* 5 (1987): 59–296;

C. S. Lewis, "The Novels of Charles Williams," in his *On Stories,* edited by Walter Hooper (New York: Harcourt Brace Jovanovich, 1982), pp. 21–27;

Colin Manlove, *Christian Fantasy: From 1200 to the Present* (London: Macmillan, 1992);

Stephen Medcalf, "Living with Impossibility," *Times Literary Supplement* (21 October 1983): 1150;

Mary McDermott Shideler, *The Theology of Romantic Love: A Study in the Writing of Charles Williams* (New York: Harper, 1962);

Agnes Sibley, *Charles Williams* (Boston: Twayne, 1982).

**Papers:**

The largest collection of Williams's papers is in the Marion E. Wade Center, Wheaton College, Wheaton, Illinois. The second major collection is in the Bodleian Library, Oxford, England (with a considerable number of papers currently under restriction). The archives of the Oxford University Press (in Oxford) and of Victor Gollancz also include some papers. Many of Williams's papers are still in the hands of friends of his or their descendants. There are also some papers in the collections of the Harry Ransom Humanities Research Center, University of Texas at Austin, the Houghton Library, Harvard University, and the Charles Williams Society in Kings College Library, University of London.

# Percival Christopher Wren

*(1885 – 22 November 1941)*

Eric Thompson
*Université du Québec à Chicoutimi*

BOOKS: *The Indian Teacher's Guide to the Theory and Practice of Mental, Moral, and Physical Education* (Bombay: Longmans, Green, 1910);

*Indian School Organization, Management, Discipline, Tone, and Equipment, Being the Indian Headmaster's Guide* (Bombay: Longmans, Green, 1911);

*The "Direct" Teaching of English in Indian Schools* (Bombay: Longmans, Green, 1911);

*Dew and Mildew: Semi-Detached Stories from Karabad, India* (London: Longmans, Green, 1912); published as *Dew and Mildew: A Loose-Knit Tale of Hindustan* (New York: Stokes, 1927);

*Chemistry and First Aid for Standard VII,* by Wren and H. E. H. Pratt (Bombay: Longmans Green, 1913);

*Father Gregory; or, Lures and Failures: A Tale of Hindustan* (London: Longmans, Green, 1913; New York: Stokes, 1926);

*Physics and Mechanics,* by Wren and N. B. Macmillan (Bombay: Longmans, Green, 1914);

*Snake and Sword* (London: Longmans, Green, 1914); published as *The Snake and the Sword* (New York: Stokes, 1923);

*The Wages of Virtue* (London: John Murray, 1916; New York: Stokes, 1917);

*Driftwood Spars* (London: Longmans, Green, 1916; New York: Stokes, 1927);

*Stepsons of France* (London: John Murray, 1917; New York: Stokes, 1917);

*The Young Stagers, Being Further Faites and Gestes of the Junior Curlton Club of Karabad, India . . .* (London: Longmans, Green, 1917; New York: Stokes, 1926);

*Cupid in Africa; or, The Making of Bertram in Love and War – A Character Study* (London: Cranton, 1920);

*With the Prince Through Canada, New Zealand, and Australia* (Bombay: Athenaeum Press, 1922);

*Beau Geste* (London: John Murray, 1924; New York: Stokes, 1925);

*P. C. Wren (*Illustrated London News *Picture Library)*

*Beau Sabreur* (London: John Murray, 1926; New York: Stokes, 1926);

*Beau Ideal* (London: John Murray, 1928; New York: Stokes, 1928);

*Good Gestes: Stories of Beau Geste, His Brothers, and Certain of Their Comrades in the French Foreign Legion* (London: John Murray, 1929; New York: Stokes, 1929);

*Soldiers of Misfortune: The Story of Otto Belleme* (London: John Murray, 1929; New York: Stokes, 1929);

*Mysterious Waye: The Story of "The Unsetting Sun"* (London: John Murray, 1930; New York: Stokes, 1930);

*The Mammon of Righteousness: The Story of Coxe and the Box* (London: John Murray, 1930); published as *Mammon* (New York: Stokes, 1930);

*Sowing Glory: The Memoirs of "Mary Ambree," The English Woman-Legionary* (London: John Murray, 1931; New York: Stokes, 1931);

*Valiant Dust* (London: John Murray, 1932; New York: Stokes, 1932);

*Action and Passion* (London: John Murray, 1933; New York: Stokes, 1933);

*Flawed Blades: Tales from the Foreign Legion* (London: John Murray, 1933; New York: Stokes, 1933);

*Beggars' Horses* (London: John Murray, 1934); published as *The Dark Woman* (Philadelphia: Macrae Smith, 1943);

*Port o' Missing Men: Strange Tale of the Stranger Regiment* (London: John Murray, 1934; Philadelphia: Macrae Smith, 1943);

*Sinbad the Soldier* (London: John Murray, 1935; Boston: Houghton Mifflin, 1935);

*Explosion* (London: John Murray, 1935);

*Spanish Maine* (London: John Murray, 1935); published as *The Desert Heritage* (Boston: Houghton Mifflin, 1935);

*Fort in the Jungle: The Extraordinary Adventures of Sinbad Dysart in Tonkin* (London: John Murray, 1936; Boston: Houghton Mifflin, 1936);

*Bubble Reputation* (London: John Murray, 1936); published as *The Cortenay Treasure* (Boston: Houghton Mifflin, 1936);

*The Man of a Ghost* (London: John Murray, 1937); published as *The Spur of Pride* (Boston: Houghton Mifflin, 1937);

*Worth Wile* (London: John Murray, 1937); published as *To the Hilt* (Boston: Houghton Mifflin, 1937);

*Cardboard Castle* (London: John Murray, 1938; Boston: Houghton Mifflin, 1938);

*Rough Shooting: True Tales and Strange Stories* (London: John Murray, 1938; Philadelphia: Macrae Smith, 1944);

*Paper Prison* (London: John Murray, 1939); published as *The Man the Devil Didn't Want* (Philadelphia: Macrae Smith, 1940);

*The Disappearance of General Jason* (London: John Murray, 1940);

*Two Feet from Heaven* (London: John Murray, 1940; Philadelphia: Macrae Smith, 1941);

*Odd – But Even So: Stories Stranger Than Fiction* (London: John Murray, 1941; Philadelphia: Macrae Smith, 1942);

*The Uniform of Glory* (London: John Murray, 1941);

*The Hunting of Henri* (London: Vallancey, 1944);

*Dust jacket for the American edition of Wren's best-known work*

*Stories of the Foreign Legion* (London: John Murray, 1947);

*Dead Men's Boots and Other Tales from the Foreign Legion* (London: Gryphon, 1949).

OTHER: *The World and India, Adapted for Use in Indian Schools,* edited by Wren (Calcutta: Oxford University Press, 1905);

Sir Walter Scott, *Ivanhoe,* edited and simplified by Wren (London: Frowde, 1912);

*Longmans' Science Series for Indian High Schools,* 11 volumes, edited by Wren (Bombay: Longmans, Green, 1913–1914);

Ernest F. Row, *Work, Wealth, and Wages,* revised by Wren (Bombay: Cooper, 1950);

*First Lessons in English Grammar* (Bombay: Cooper, 1961);

Jonathan Swift, *Gulliver's Travels,* edited and simplified by Wren (Calcutta: Oxford University Press, 1963).

Percival Christopher Wren is chiefly remembered as the author of *Beau Geste* (1924). A child of

the Victorian era, he grew up in an atmosphere of privilege and with a strong sense of noblesse oblige. This commitment of service to the less fortunate, and especially those of Great Britain, is a constant theme in his books and is perhaps the best way to appreciate his sincere, if limited, writing talent.

Born in Devonshire in 1885 (the exact date of his birth is not recorded in any standard source), Percival Christopher Wren was a collateral descendant of the renowned seventeenth-century architect Sir Christopher Wren. More noteworthy is the fact that the house in which he was born was the model for the home of Amyas Leigh, the hero of Charles Kingsley's enormously influential romance of muscular Christianity, *Westward Ho!* (1855). The young Wren was idealistic about British history and highly patriotic, and, like many adolescents of his time, his imagination was stirred by the yarns of empire-building romancers like Frederick Marryat, R. M. Ballantyne, G. A. Henty, and H. Rider Haggard. The long-kept Pax Britannica, broken intermittently by British defeats which were propagandized into victories, reached a climax during the Boer War. The realities of modern warfare could no longer be ignored, but the sentiments surrounding Great Britain's mission in the world were all the more fiercely held. Still familiar are the following lines from "Vitaï Lampada," the most famous poem by Sir Henry Newbolt, a turn-of-the-century imperialist:

> The sand of the desert is sodden red –
> Red with the wreck of a square that broke; –
> The Gatling's jammed and the Colonel dead,
> And the regiment blind with dust and smoke.
> The river of death has brimmed his banks,
> And England's far, and Honour a name,
> But the voice of a schoolboy rallies the ranks:
> "Play up! play up! and play the game!"

In this poem is what Patrick Howarth calls "Newbolt Man" in the "voice of a schoolboy." Exhorting the troops to greater efforts in the timeless cheerleading phrase of the cricketer, the boy reminds them of their duty to defend their country's traditions of honor and fair play. He is the idealized product of Britain's public schools: no scholar, he is a dedicated sportsman; shy with women other than his mother or sisters, he is a chivalrous suitor; most of all, he is a manly gentleman of the upper classes, who loves his country and would serve her well.

There was, according to this philosophy, something more important than winning, and that was to live honorably. This was the code Wren embraced in his readings, and it accorded with his personality; certainly it is the dominant theme of his books. Later in life, responding to a questionnaire sent to him by Q. D. Leavis, Wren replied that he wrote for readers of the "cleanly-minded, virile, outdoor sort," with whom he clearly identified. Wren did not regard himself as a professional novelist, much less a "long-haired literary cove," and he concluded that his faithful publisher, Sir John Murray, and others like him had "somehow strayed into the muddy paths of commerce, and somehow contrived to remain sportsmen and gentlemen and jolly good business men as well." This must be ingenuous, but it nevertheless expresses another part of the Newboltian code: the idea of doing something well, in an amateur way, for its own sake. Wren's heroes try to conform to these values, long after they ceased to be fashionable.

Like those heroes, Wren grew up in an atmosphere of privilege. After graduating with an M.A. from Oxford, he finished his education by traveling the world for five years, working his way as "sailor, navvy, tramp, schoolmaster, journalist, farm laborer, explorer, hunter, and costermonger in the slums." Next he enlisted as a trooper in the British cavalry, moving on to further service with the French Foreign Legion. Then for ten years he worked in India for the Bombay government as assistant director of education and physical culture before returning to the military. During World War I he fought with the Indian army in East Africa, rising to the rank of major. Invalided to England in 1917, he settled in London, married, and had one son. Wren's lust for adventure was not entirely assuaged, for he did attempt to join the Moroccan secret service in 1926 but was turned down because of poor health. The last fifteen years of his life were spent in semirustication, looking much like Colonel Blimp: tall, monocle wearing, mustachioed, and pipe smoking.

But appearances were deceiving. Wren was, in fact, living a prolific existence as an author of short stories and novels. Every year during the late 1920s and 1930s he presented Murray with a new manuscript, largely based on his adventures. His fiction falls into two camps, in terms of setting: those tales which take place abroad and those which are located in the English countryside. Best known, of course, were his legionnaire stories, but other of his novels are set in India or the Far East, as well as sub-Saharan Africa, and feature the adventures of both heroic and antiheroic soldiers. Of his domestic novels, a dominant trait is a too respectful treatment of the wealthy or aristocratic, itself a notable aspect of popular fiction of the time. Both kinds of fiction

*Frontispiece and title page for a reprint promoting the 1926 motion picture of Wren's popular novel*

make use of the detective story and Freudian psychological tale then in vogue, but they eschew any experimental or modernist storytelling technique. In the sense that he knew what his audience wanted and stuck closely to the proven formulas of romance, Wren was a professional novelist but not a literary writer.

He had begun his career writing nonfiction in India – school texts and instructional manuals. His first attempts at fiction came with the collection of short stories *Dew and Mildew: Semi-Detached Stories from Karabad, India* (1912) and the novel *Father Gregory; or, Lures and Failures: A Tale of Hindustan* (1913), based on his Indian experience. Both books show the influence of Rudyard Kipling, especially the former, which introduces members of the Junior Curlton Club of Karabad with an authentic feeling for mess life among young subalterns. Another book which belongs to this period, *Driftwood Spars* (1916), tackles a problem not generally discussed in the polite society of British India: miscegenation. The hero is the son of a Scottish mother and a

Pathan father, and his duality of temperament is seen as a distinct aid in helping him out of bad scrapes.

Wren's first novel about the Foreign Legion, *The Wages of Virtue,* also appeared in 1916 although it was written three years earlier. It begins in East Africa before moving on to French colonial territory to the north. The plot is conventional, a love triangle in which Sir Montague Merline joins the legion when he learns his erstwhile friend and safari companion, Lord Huntingten, is having an affair with his wife. Enlisting under the name John Bull – which rapidly is Frenchified to Jean Boule – he is surprised to meet the son of his rival, Reginald Rupert, also a new recruit. The two men are drawn to each other because of nationality and a common sense of purpose, perhaps one of the first examples of Wren's exploration of male bonding in quest of lost honor. In a revealing passage Reginald's (and Sir Montague's) "fears" are succinctly stated: "What he loathed and feared was Modern Society life, and in fact all civilized life as it had presented itself to

his eyes – with its incredibly false standards, values and ideals, its shoddy shams and vulgar pretences, its fat indulgences, slothfulness and folly."

Joining the legion is not an escape, rather an assertion of determination to rid the world of some of that sinfulness. Ironically, it is the unwashed, uncivilized, and undifferentiated hordes against whom the legion is pitted who are the victims of this noble rebellion. It is obvious that Wren shares Reginald's indignation and his purblind attitude to non-British people.

Despite the not uncommon attitudes about race, *The Wages of Virtue* does have some strengths. Wren is in command of his material, expressing legionary lore in a multitude of vernaculars, spoken and acted by a convincing cast of ruffians. He is thereby able to catch popular attention with something new, yet in an accessible format, and to whet the reader's appetite for more of the same.

However, it was eight years before he achieved his major success, *Beau Geste,* the unrelated but companion volume to *The Wages of Virtue.* Two books of short fiction, *Stepsons of France* and *The Young Stagers,* each published in 1917, are important chronologically because they continue to develop the character of Jean Boule and his mates and to introduce the characters of the young Gestes. But why *Beau Geste* became such a popular success is a mystery. Perhaps it was a matter of timing: perhaps, in 1924, a society wearied by the suffering of World War I and the dashed hopes of the peace was once more ready to accept the heroism of soldiers in a positive mood. (Five years later it would have been much too late, for then the antiwar spate of fiction and memoirs dominated publishing on both sides of the Atlantic.) But perhaps, too, the British public was ready once again for a book such as A. E. W. Mason's *The Four Feathers* (1902), in which a young man's conquest of his fear turns out to be an act of the finest bravery. *Beau Geste* closely resembles Mason's novel as an essay in youthful honor, and together both books deserve a high place of excellence among modern adventure novels.

If readers in 1924 recognized the novel's lasting value, their standards were not those of the late twentieth century. Margery Fisher cautions on the point:

> Certainly the theme of honour in an adventure story has to be accepted in an historical context and if possible with a determined suspension of disbelief. How many of the popular novels of the past evoke derision rather than appreciation if we read them in too literal a spirit. We have to think ourselves back into a social system and culture very different from our own if we are to respond, in the way P. C. Wren required, to the improbable events and exalted sentiments of the three Geste brothers who, to serve their adored aunt and their fraternal obligations, vanished into the Foreign Legion, taking upon themselves the imputation of having stolen the blue diamond which she had long ago sold and replaced by a fake for the sake of her extravagant husband. How cruel, to present-day ears, sounds her final comment on the misguided heroism of the brothers – "a beau geste indeed."

As shrewd as these remarks are, though, Fisher belies her premise about suspension of disbelief and is altogether *too* literal in her interpretation. The case could be made that she misses the point about Michael Geste's commitment to honor. Moreover, the boys fight for a cause they believe in and grow into manhood in the process.

In choosing to tell the story from two points of view, Major de Beaujolais's partial and externalized account as well as John Geste's full and personalized narrative, Wren is taking liberties that scrupulous craftsmen would not. But the major's version effectively frames John's, giving it a credibility it might have lacked otherwise. John, finally, is the sole survivor of the tragedy at Fort Zinderneuf and its aftermath. It is his fate, and duty, to be the messenger of Michael's letter which explains the theft of the Blue Water diamond and the tragic experience of the boys in the desert. John is the youngest and smallest of the Gestes; Michael and Digby are twins, but Michael, known as Beau, is the natural leader. When he decides to wear the badge of dishonor to atone for Digby's theft, the stage is set for John joining them in the legion. John has no choice: "Should I follow my brothers' lead, asking nothing better than to do as they did, and win their approval? . . . It would be so like me." Fisher is quite right to point out the "improbable" nature of romance, and Wren's handling of plot and character here is a good illustration of the difference between fictional realism and romance. He does not ask the reader to question the motives of the boys, rather to understand them as boys. They have been a little band all their lives, thrilling to the magic names of French North African regiments – Spahis, Zouaves, Chasseurs – and to "tales of hot life and brave death, of battle and of bivouac" with the legion. What is more natural than that they stick together, through thick and thin, following their zeal for adventure?

The centerpiece of the action is the events at the fort – the hard life under the tyranny of Sergeant-Major Lejaune and the doomed defense when the Tuaregs attack. Wren leads up to this climax by tell-

ing us of the boys training in Marseilles, route marches under the Algerian sun, barracks life amid a score of different nationalities, and the increasing antagonism between the Gestes and Lejaune. Captain Renouf's suicide foreshadows the horrors to come, as does incipient madness among the men brought on by sunstroke, monotony, and fear. But Lejaune proves himself to be an effective, if unloved, leader when he puts down a mutiny and organizes the defense. His tactical skill is shown in the events of the final battle at the fort:

> not all those who lined the walls of Zinderneuf were beyond scathe by Arab bullets. Now and then there would be a cry, an oath, a gurgling grunt or cough, and a man would stagger back and fall, or die where he crouched, a bullet through his brain.
>
> And, in every case, Lejaune would prop and pose and arrange the body, dead or dying, in the embrasure whence it had fallen, and to the distant Arab eyes it must have seemed that the number of the defenders was undiminished.
>
> As the morning wore on, Lejaune took a rifle, and, crouching beside each dead man in turn, fired several shots from each embrasure, adding to the illusion that the dead were alive. . . .
>
> Later still, he set one man to each wall to do the same thing . . .[.]

But the *ruse de guerre* cannot work for long as the garrison dwindles; John himself shoots Lejaune when he discovers him trying to rob papers from Michael as he dies. Only Digby and John are left to make their escape after the attack, and for a year they wander as "Ishmaelites" until Digby is killed deep in the heart of the Sahara. Now stripped of his brothers' companionship, John feels that "the essential *me* was dead too." But the experience has turned John into a man.

Wren's success in wrapping his serious theme in a well-told, suspenseful action story was never repeated. *Beau Sabreur* (1926) and *Beau Ideal* (1928) attempted to create a "Geste series" by expanding on the life and personality of Major de Beaujolais, but they were mainly picaresques of incident without strong themes. *Soldiers of Misfortune: The Story of Otto Belleme* (1929) was another legion story. Some reviewers praised its insight into boxing technique and lore – drawing on Wren's experience as a boxer when he was young. (In later books Wren drew on his knowledge of the law and the penal system gained from his experience as a justice of the peace, and he also made occasional use of his expertise in fencing and card games to good effect.) He added other titles to his legion canon in the 1930s, including the Sinbad Dysart series, such as *Action*

*Dust jacket for the third novel in the Geste series (courtesy of the Lilly Library, Indiana University)*

*and Passion* (1933) and *Fort in the Jungle: The Extraordinary Adventures of Sinbad Dysart in Tonkin* (1936). Meant to capitalize on his *Beau Geste* fame – which was enhanced by the 1926 silent film and the 1939 sound version – these books tended to be more swashbuckling than serious in intent.

Among his domestic novels, four works seem particularly interesting: *The Mammon of Righteousness: The Story of Coxe and the Box* (1930), *Bubble Reputation* (1936), *Cardboard Castle* (1938), and *Paper Prison* (1939). One thing they share are oxymoronic titles, which suggest a link between something fragile and something solid. The titles point to Wren's increasing usage of abnormal psychology as a means for characterization in his later fiction, as compared to the relatively old-fashioned one-dimensional portraiture of his legion tales. Perhaps it is useful to know, too, that his favorite authors were William Makepeace Thackeray, Robert Louis Stevenson, H. G. Wells, Joseph Conrad, and John Galsworthy, all strong storytellers with acute perceptions into human nature. What is most striking about Wren's tales set in England, how-

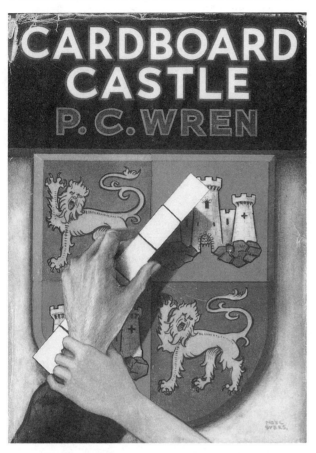

*Dust jacket for one of Wren's domestic novels, in which a tutor becomes romantically involved with his pupil's mother (courtesy of the Lilly Library, Indiana University)*

ever, is the weakness, or passivity, of the leading male characters, contrasted to the strong-willed (or sometimes just dangerously unpredictable) female figures.

*The Mammon of Righteousness* is the most dramatic illustration of these oxymoronic and contrasting features. Algernon Coxe is mother dominated, and since childhood it "had been scared, had been branded and had been burnt into him the belief that to 'fall' as Adam fell was not only blackest Sin — but a thing utterly foul, horrible, degrading, dirty and beastly beyond description." He is the indiscreet offspring of an adulterous affair which the mother, Minerva, has sought to conceal but which, in the concluding pages, is revealed just in time to save Coxe from the gallows. Wren's portrayal of the mother is an astounding tour de force, for her obsessive will is effectively highlighted by the calm rationality of the doctor who seeks to rid the young man of her influence. Symbolism is used adroitly to show Coxe's repressed manhood, both in the dream he has of a "box" and in the use of an actual box in

which is found the corpse of Coxe's sweetheart, who commits suicide when he is forced to spurn her in favor of his mother's choice of bride. Obviously, the plot is convoluted, sensational, and even preposterous. But the reader is also made aware of Wren's belief that women, in some circumstances, are the stronger sex.

The second of this group of novels, *Bubble Reputation,* has a more standard mystery format. Set on a country estate, Cortenay Old Hall, the novel tells of the search for a legendary chest of jewels reputedly hidden on the grounds of the estate. This time the weak hero, Bump Cortenay, must contend with a slick thief and master of disguise so that despite "the hardness of the times" and "the growing difficulty of carrying on" he can safeguard the family heritage. Significantly, he is assisted by his girlfriend, Honor, who is as pure as her name suggests, and by a former convict servant, Rodd, who proves to be as stalwart as his name connotes. In the event the young hero and heroine are ineffectual as the servant defeats the thief — and dies in the process. But, although the mystery is solved, no actual fortune is found; instead, Bump's legacy is an understanding of his ancestor's admonition — paraphrasing Jaques's lines in William Shakespeare's *As You Like It* — not to go seeking "the bubble reputation in the cannon's mouth," in short, not to confuse material wealth with love or honor.

The plot of *Bubble Reputation* is developed through many complications, but *Cardboard Castle* is quite straightforward. The young hero, Henry Waring, is engaged as tutor to the scion of Calderton House and thereby becomes romantically involved with the boy's mother and thus involved in her fight to ward off the suit of her first, never-divorced husband. Once again, the fragile ghosts of the past threaten to destroy the solid structure of present-day happiness. Henry Waring proves no match for the wily villain, the suave lady-killer Captain Montague Ferring-Chevigny, who does, after all, have a just claim on Lady Calderton's wealth (if not her heart) despite his long absence. She had remarried, believing him dead; now, with her second husband out of the country, she is in danger of being declared a bigamist and socially ruined.

Wren does a workmanlike job with this melodramatic situation. His characterization of the villain is especially good, and his method of dispatching him in the final chapters is in the best traditions of contrived storytelling. Throughout the book Henry plays a game of Cavalier and Roundhead with his young charge, Anthony — a game in which the boy pretends to be King Charles I, while his

tutor plays Oliver Cromwell; each dresses appropriately, and they have an earnest swordfight through the halls and staircases of the old manor. Just when the villain appears to be attacking his mother at a ball, young Anthony comes to the rescue and forces Ferring-Chevigny into a "death by misadventure" by tumbling down a hidden staircase and breaking his neck. Henry does the honorable thing and does not press his attentions on the vulnerable lady.

*Paper Prison* is a novel in the form of a three-part narrative in which the lives and personal reflections of twin brothers and the woman they love are presented. It is a work which can be placed with the legion books because of some parallels with *Beau Geste,* but it is also a psychological mystery with links to the English tales. The main plot revolves around the cowardice of Luke Tuyler; there is no doubt he was shell-shocked and temporarily blinded during a bombing attack in World War I, but his subsequent successful pretense of permanent blindness allowed him to be discharged honorably, to win the hand of the fair Rosanne, and to inherit a fortune. All of this is learned, accidentally, by Mark, Luke's brother, in an unguarded moment. Mark's is the first version of these events, and he is full of conflicting emotions concerning his brother and the ways of the world, as a result. Nevertheless, when Luke's happiness is threatened by a blackmailer privy to his secret, Mark kills the man without remorse. His notion of honor is somewhat comparable to that of the Gestes, albeit not something the world easily understands. Besides this personal drama, Mark tells of his experiences fighting with the legion and with the British army on the western front.

Luke's narrative follows. It is an apologia *pro vita sua,* compared to the confessional genre Mark uses. Luke has always regarded himself as superior to his brother in intelligence and gifted with visionary powers. Yet he acknowledges that Mark was always willing to lie to protect him from punishment, and thus from an early age it was Mark who "began the undermining of my character." Further, he reveals that Mark was also a deserter during the war but that they escaped punishment in the heat of battle. Thus, the reader gains a different perspective on Mark, and on Luke, reinforcing the axiom that human truth is always partial. Later the novel details how Luke faked blindness, apparently fooling the foremost ophthalmologists of his time. (Incidentally, since we know that Wren was ill in his last years, it is interesting to note his use of medical and psychological jargon in this section of the novel.) Finally, Luke is afraid to "put off my protective coloring": "I could not emerge, and face life again. . . . I could not leave my limelit stage and walk off into the cold dark wings and ordinary every-day existence; descend from my pedestal; cease to be the center of attraction and attention."

But Wren cannot leave Luke unpunished. At the same time that Mark is defending the family honor, Luke discovers he really *is* blind. From this it is legitimate to conclude that whereas good authors achieve ironic effects, bad ones rely on coincidence.

About the third narrative, Rosanne's, little need be said. The novel tells of her background and of her love for both men – loving Luke for his weakness and Mark for his strength of character. She discovers Luke's deception but decides to keep this to herself to shield him from Mark's anger. Unwittingly, then, she provokes Mark's murder of the blackmailer and contributes to the onset of Luke's real blindness. All ends happily – or, poetically, at least – when Luke is killed by a train and Mark and Rosanne are united. But, aside from the inveterate plot twists, *Paper Prison* is an absorbing tale.

It is easy to understand why Wren is so little known today; he began his career too late, being more suited to the Edwardian than the Georgian popular market, and like all commercial romancers he wrote much too quickly and thoughtlessly. It is easy to see missed opportunities in even his best work, times when, with a little care, he might have created more-plausible scenes; as for his poorer tales, they are neither better nor worse than thousands of others of the same ilk. He understood adolescent boys well, and his portraits of the rank and file of men are convincing. But he is usually not on safe ground with women, being given to treating them as either china dolls or harridans. He was also much too fond of sensational effects, usually the surest route to oblivion in the writing trade. Still, *Beau Geste* is notable as a late imperial novel and a fine example of the use of honor as a theme.

**References:**

Margery Fisher, *The Bright Face of Danger: An Exploration of the Adventure Story* (London: Hodder & Stoughton, 1986);

William C. Frierson, *The English Novel in Transition, 1885–1940* (New York: Cooper, 1965);

Patrick Howarth, *Play Up and Play the Game: The Heroes of Popular Fiction* (London: Eyre Methuen, 1973);

Q. D. Leavis, *Fiction and the Reading Public* (London: Chatto & Windus, 1968);

Colin Watson, *Snobbery With Violence: Crime Stories & Their Audience* (London: Eyre & Spottiswoode, 1971).

# Dornford Yates
# (Cecil William Mercer)
*(7 August 1885 – 5 March 1960)*

C. Gordon-Craig
*University of Alberta*

See also the Yates entry in *DLB 77: British Mystery Writers, 1920–1939.*

BOOKS: *The Brother of Daphne* (London: Ward, Lock, 1914);

*The Courts of Idleness* (London: Ward, Lock, 1920);

*Berry and Co.* (London: Ward, Lock, 1920; New York: Minton, Balch, 1928);

*Anthony Lyveden* (London: Ward, Lock, 1921); published with *Valerie French* as *Summer Fruit* (New York: Minton, Balch, 1929);

*Jonah and Co.* (London: Ward, Lock, 1922; New York: Minton, Balch, 1927);

*Valerie French* (London: Ward, Lock, 1923); published with *Anthony Lyveden* as *Summer Fruit* (New York: Minton, Balch, 1929);

*And Five Were Foolish* (London: Ward, Lock, 1924);

*As Other Men Are* (London: Ward, Lock, 1925);

*The Stolen March* (London: Ward, Lock, 1926; New York: Minton, Balch, 1933);

*Blind Corner* (London: Hodder & Stoughton, 1927; New York: Minton, Balch, 1927);

*Perishable Goods* (London: Hodder & Stoughton, 1928; New York: Minton, Balch, 1928);

*Maiden Stakes* (London: Ward, Lock, 1928);

*Blood Royal* (London: Hodder & Stoughton, 1929; New York: Minton, Balch, 1930);

*Fire Below* (London: Hodder & Stoughton, 1930); published as *By Royal Command* (New York: Minton, Balch, 1931);

*Adèle & Co.* (London: Hodder & Stoughton, 1931; New York: Minton, Balch, 1931);

*Safe Custody* (London: Hodder & Stoughton, 1932; New York: Minton, Balch, 1932);

*Storm Music* (London: Hodder & Stoughton, 1934; New York: Minton, Balch, 1934);

*She Fell Among Thieves* (London: Hodder & Stoughton, 1935; New York: Minton, Balch, 1935);

*And Berry Came Too* (London: Ward, Lock, 1936; New York: Minton, Balch, 1936);

*Dornford Yates (Cecil William Mercer)*

*She Painted Her Face* (London: Ward, Lock, 1937; New York: Putnam, 1937);

*This Publican* (London: Ward, Lock, 1938): published as *The Devil in Satin* (Garden City, N.Y.: Doubleday, Doran, 1938);

*Gale Warning* (London: Ward, Lock, 1939; New York: Putnam, 1940);

*Shoal Water* (London: Ward, Lock, 1940; New York: Putnam, 1941);

*Period Stuff* (London: Ward, Lock, 1942);

*An Eye for a Tooth* (London: Ward, Lock, 1943; New York: Putnam, 1944);

*The House That Berry Built* (London: Ward, Lock, 1945; New York: Putnam, 1945);

*Red in the Morning* (London: Ward, Lock, 1946); published as *Were Death Denied* (New York: Putnam, 1946);

*The Berry Scene* (London: Ward, Lock, 1947; New York: Putnam, 1948);

*Cost Price* (London: Ward, Lock, 1949); published as *The Laughing Bacchante* (New York: Putnam, 1949);

*Lower Than Vermin* (London: Ward, Lock, 1950);

*As Berry and I Were Saying* (London: Ward, Lock, 1952);

*Ne'er-Do-Well* (London: Ward, Lock, 1954);

*Wife Apparent* (London: Ward, Lock, 1956);

*B-Berry and I Look Back* (London: Ward, Lock, 1958).

PLAY PRODUCTION: *Eastward Ho,* by Yates and Oscar Asche, London, Alhambra, 9 September 1919.

OTHER: Charles William Stamper, *What I Know,* ghostwritten by Yates (London: Mills & Boon, 1913); published as *King Edward as I Knew Him* (New York: Dodd, Mead, 1913).

A best-selling author of popular fiction, Cecil William Mercer, who wrote using the assumed name of Dornford Yates, produced thirty-four volumes in all. His tales of Berry and the Pleydell family are amusing pieces evoking traditional values of the English scene, while the gentleman heroes of his romances who traveled through Europe thwarting villains appeal to the devotees of adventures in the vein of John Buchan, Sapper (Herman Cyril McNeile), and, later, Leslie Charteris.

A stylish writer who took his craft seriously, Mercer lived by his pen after abandoning a legal career, aiming his work at an audience that wanted lighter entertainment and engrossing escapist fantasy. As such, his works are largely formulaic and self-imitating. Most of his books, if not dated in their details, have an old-fashioned flavor that, despite charm and appeal, has placed a certain distance between them and the contemporary reader.

Cecil William Mercer was born at Wellesley House, Walmer, Kent, on 7 August 1885, the only child of Cecil John Mercer, a solicitor, and his wife, Helen Wall. Hector Hugh Munro, better known under his pseudonym of Saki, was Mercer's first

cousin, and it may be his example that Mercer was following when he took up a career as a writer. From Munro, too, Mercer probably adopted the idea of using a pen name, Dornford Yates, which he derived from the maiden names of both his grandmothers.

After initial schooling at a local preparatory school, Saint Clare, Mercer was accepted at Harrow, which he attended for four years as a home boarder and where he developed an appreciation for the use and precision of English as a language. During this period he formed his hero worship for Winston Churchill, who lectured at Harrow after the Boer War. Churchill, as an Old Harrovian, represented all that Mercer adored: he was an aristocrat, a symbol of the English, a great writer, a soldier, and a statesman. Harrow was Mercer's first real acquaintance with the society and attitudes of the English upper class as it existed before 1914, during that fabulous Edwardian period that was so soon to pass into memory. The Edwardian aristocracy was to remain fixed in his mind as an Arcadian ideal, both for the setting in which he wished to see himself and as the basis for his fictional heroes.

Mercer's family was not wealthy and must have made sacrifices to allow him to be at such a prestigious English public school. Without brothers or sisters, Mercer would have been conscious of his parents' hopes and expectations for his success and was probably under considerable pressure to gain a university entrance scholarship, though this was not to come his way.

Mercer was admitted as a member of University College, Oxford, in 1904 and set himself to read for the standard three-year undergraduate course in law. At barely nineteen years of age, however, he reveled in his newfound independence from his family and soon found his niche in the Oxford University Dramatic Society (OUDS), the intellectual but liberal-minded milieu he craved. From an ordinary member he advanced first to the position of secretary and then to president of the OUDS. In the persona of Boy Pleydell, Mercer recounts in his fictionalized memoir, *As Berry and I Were Saying* (1952), the opportunities he had to make the acquaintance of such luminaries as Herbert Beerbohm Tree; Arthur Bourchier; Henry B. Irving, the son of the great actor; and Compton Mackenzie. He also mentions having "to look after" Rudyard Kipling, which was probably on the occasion of the latter's receiving an honorary degree from Oxford University in 1907.

Mercer threw himself fully into the life of the theater, productions at Oxford, visits to stage per-

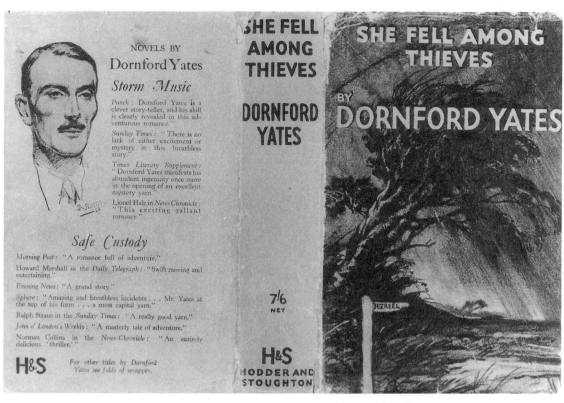

*Dust jacket for one of Yates's popular adventure novels featuring Richard Chandos and Jonathan Mansell*

formances in London, and, of course, the many social occasions in which he was involved as president of the OUDS. Inevitably these took their toll, and it is not entirely surprising that he graduated with a Third Class Honours degree.

This poor academic showing could have ended Mercer's aim to become a barrister, but his father used his professional connections, and Mercer was accepted as a pupil by H. G. Muskett, an eminent solicitor to the London police. This unorthodox professional route culminated in Mercer's being called to the bar as a member of the Inner Temple in 1909 and then becoming pupil to Travers Humphreys, a highly regarded specialist in criminal law. Mercer valued the experiences this association was to provide, one of the most memorable being when, as junior prosecuting counsel to Humphreys, he was brought into the spotlight of the sensational trial for murder of Dr. H. H. Crippen, a case that attracted enormous attention and interest at the time. Mercer later was to give a detailed account of the case in *As Berry and I Were Saying.* When his pupilage was completed, Mercer moved into a respected law chambers, which gave him access to civil law work in addition to his criminal cases.

Plunged into the heart of London Police Court work, the Central Criminal Court, and the Southeastern circuit, Mercer gained an unusual perspective on the most exotic ranges of society, and these experiences provided him with the diversity of character, the insight into human life, and the raw drama for the plots of his stories.

Mercer, under his chosen pen name of Dornford Yates, had already tried his hand at writing, his first article being accepted by the prestigious *Punch* magazine in 1910. When he found his legal practice to be insufficiently rewarding financially, Mercer cast around for a means to supplement his income, and his initial literary success inspired him to turn to short stories. Concentrating on the monthly magazines, a well-paying market, Mercer looked to the *Windsor Magazine,* a journal begun in January 1895 by the publishing house of Ward, Lock, a firm specializing in general fiction and which was later to publish all but eight of Yates's works.

Ward, Lock had not been slow to notice the opportunities for publishers provided by the popularity of train travel and had profited by the issue of a successful series of guidebooks. With the *Windsor Magazine* the intention was to provide entertaining reading material aimed especially at what the pub-

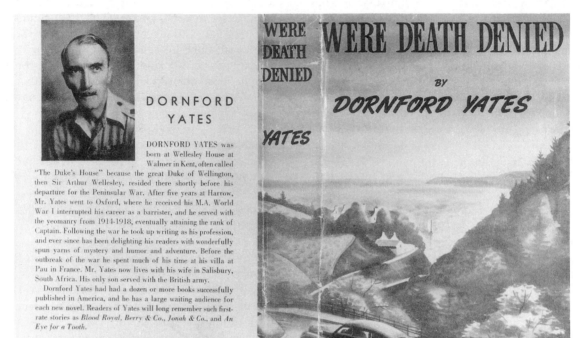

DORNFORD YATES

DORNFORD YATES was born at Wellesley House at Walmer in Kent, often called "The Duke's House" because the great Duke of Wellington, then Sir Arthur Wellesley, resided there shortly before his departure for the Peninsular War. After five years at Harrow, Mr. Yates went to Oxford, where he received his M.A. World War I interrupted his career as a barrister, and he served with the yeomanry from 1914-1918, eventually attaining the rank of Captain. Following the war he took up writing as his profession, and ever since has been delighting his readers with wonderfully spun yarns of mystery and humor and adventure. Before the outbreak of the war he spent much of his time at his villa at Pau in France. Mr. Yates now lives with his wife in Salisbury, South Africa. His only son served with the British army.

Dornford Yates had had a dozen or more books successfully published in America, and he has a large waiting audience for each new novel. Readers of Yates will long remember such first-rate stories as *Blood Royal*, *Berry & Co.*, *Jonah & Co.*, and *An Eye for a Tooth*.

WERE DEATH DENIED

BY

DORNFORD YATES

PUTNAM

*Dust jacket for the American publication of* Red in the Morning *(1946), a Chandos-Mansel adventure set in France*

lishers considered a growing body of independent or professional women.

While he kept up his legal work, Yates had the satisfaction of seeing a steady stream of his stories appear in the *Windsor Magazine,* some of which were to form the basis of his first published volume, *The Brother of Daphne* (1914). This deals exclusively with the varied adventures of the Pleydells, five childless first cousins – two of whom have the extra complication of being married to each other – who live in the most amicable idleness in a historic stately home, White Ladies. This group of respected gentry, headed by the comic Berry Pleydell, depicts Yates's cherished conception, romanticized by his admiration, of the old English way of life and its traditions in an idyllic countryside undisturbed by the ravages of war, socialism, or economic pressures. The workmanship of the stories is good, though the matter never rises beyond the trivial.

Upon the outbreak of war in 1914, Yates accepted a commission in the third County of London Yeomanry. He served in Egypt and Salonika and was invalided home with chronic rheumatism in 1917, the year his mother died, to serve out the remainder of the hostilities in the Ministry of Labour. Yates did not return to his law practice but stayed with the army, perhaps because of the more-assured income, until being released with the rank of cap-

tain in 1919. On 22 October 1919 he married Bettine Stokes Edwards, an American actress living in London and a devout Roman Catholic. His father did not approve of the union and did not attend the wedding.

Following the birth of a son, Richard, in 1920, Yates moved to southern France, where he hoped to be able to live more frugally, establishing his home in the Villa Maryland at Pau. The decision was dictated by the realization that his law practice, which had suffered a serious interruption, if not in fact a cessation, would be threatened permanently by the specter of continued health problems connected with his rheumatism. In Yates's eyes, too, the quality of postwar life was different, and the fabric of society as he knew it had changed. His father's sudden death in 1921 completed the break from England.

*The Courts of Idleness* (1920), a collection of short stories, shows the deep effects left on Yates by the upheaval of the war years. The book's first section deals with the rather meaningless prewar life of a married couple and their two cousins on an extended holiday to Madeira. It ends with the deaths from an artillery shell of the two men while they are serving together. The dividing piece, "Interlude," also ends tragically in the bloody turmoil of the war. The remaining six stories reintroduce the

Pleydell family, its reunification following the armistice, and the return to the tranquillity of English life.

*Anthony Lyveden* (1921) and its sequel, *Valerie French* (1923), indicate both Yates's unsettled frame of mind and a desire to produce a more serious type of work. A dark, almost grim, tone pervades this bleak love story where madness and the supernatural are studied in relation to their influences on human affairs.

Episodic in style, the two volumes feature Anthony Lyveden, a young, educated gentleman, alone and penniless following distinguished service in the war, who is forced by his circumstances to become an anonymous member of the working classes. In this superficially conventional romance, fate and innumerable coincidences thwart the star-crossed lovers, Lyveden and Valerie French, until Lyveden regains his fortune and these archetypes of Yates's upper-class "Jack and Jill" figures are united happily forever.

While part of the plot hinges on Lyveden's loss of memory, a device Yates reused in an amplified fashion much later as the basis of *Wife Apparent* (1956), the most memorable aspect is the account of "Gramarye," an archaic word for sorcery, which Yates gives to a malevolent, ancient estate, in the full Gothic tradition, that exerts a baleful influence over all who come under its spell — leading several of the characters to death or madness — and is the direct cause of Lyveden's breakdown.

This theme of demonic possession was not Yates's typical material, and although he does create some powerful passages, he seems hesitant in letting a study of black magic dominate the lighter nature of his tale. Intriguingly, the sale of Dennis Wheatley's library in 1979 included two volumes by Yates — one, *And Five Were Foolish* (1924), Yates's next work after *Valerie French,* being autographed by him, which would assume some association between the two writers, and it may be that Yates shared Wheatley's interest not only in the vein of action thrillers but also in the supernatural and occult.

Two more volumes of stories of the Pleydells, *Berry and Co.* (1920) and *Jonah and Co.* (1922), are well-crafted, mellow, light entertainments to the taste of the *Windsor Magazine*. These stories establish the characters of the droll, witty squire, Berry; his dignified wife, Daphne; Boy Pleydell, Mercer's alter ego and an inveterate gallant; his sister, the sweet, innocent Jill; and the somber, capable gentleman adventurer, Jonathan "Jonah" Mansel. Set both in the English countryside and on the Continent, the epi-

sodes are insubstantial but delightful, sentimental yet cheerful romps. The Pleydells, by ingenuity, noblesse oblige, and a certain amount of sheer good fortune, triumph unscathed. They often succeed, at the expense of petty rogues or fools, in the course of various ludicrous or exciting encounters that occasionally threaten the family's privileged and sheltered happiness.

Perhaps thinking that he had found a sure competency in genre and a definite fluency in style, Yates may have felt the need to show his ability in handling more serious matter. *And Five Were Foolish* (1924), *As Other Men Are* (1925), *Maiden Stakes* (1928), and the later volume *Period Stuff* (1942) represent the real core of Yates's talent. These four collections deal with the follies of men and women, the continuing human comedy set against the stern reality of the postwar period. Although uneven, the forty-three stories in these four volumes present the best of Yates's work. Humor abounds, sometimes satiric, and the stories' flavor is often similar to that of Oscar Wilde's comedies, with which Yates would have been familiar. Occasionally, the humor slides into farce, even slapstick and buffoonery, though since his themes are nearly always of the love complications of young men and women, he is at his best with light comedy.

Yates's next novel is another attempt to try his hand at something different. *The Stolen March* (1926) starts realistically, but the opening chapters give subtle clues that he was uncertain of his direction and that it was probably originally intended to be a short tale. In a sudden twist of plot, Yates sends two couples into the Pyrénées, where they find "The Lost Country," Etchechuria, which was hidden by God at the Creation. In this journey through a comic fantasy realm peopled with a kaleidoscope of characters drawn from nursery rhymes, folktales, and allegory, where magic and the illogical rule, Yates recklessly indulges himself in pure, lighthearted fancy that is strongly reminiscent of Lewis Carroll's *Alice* books. Eventually, the four heroes stumble upon the Philosopher's Stone that transmutes anything to gold and escape with it to the outside world to live happily ever after. *The Stolen March* confused Yates's readers, though it would appear from his memoirs, *As Berry and I Were Saying,* that the book was one of his favorites and that he had the intention to write a sequel. Whether discouraged by his publishers or his public's response, Yates never completed the sequel, perhaps unfortunately.

With *Blind Corner* (1927) Yates began the series of fourteen adventure thrillers that was to make

him famous. Often compared to similar action stories involving the gentleman hero – Baroness
Orczy's Scarlett Pimpernel, Sapper's "Bulldog"
Drummond, Leslie Charteris's "The Saint," for
instance – these novels present fast-paced, well-
crafted, exciting tales set in the period after 1918,
often in obscure Carinthian valleys. They sometimes involve fabulous treasures hidden in Gothic
castles and damsels in distress who must be rescued from thugs led by brilliant but amoral villains. There are fast cars, gunfights, acts of daring
initiative executed through strength and endurance, and frequently a final scene of rough justice.
Eight of these adventures are told in the first person by Yates's favorite hero, Richard William
Chandos, the strong, silent man of honor, usually
supported by his brilliant and supremely competent partner, Jonathan Mansel of the Pleydell family.

In *Blind Corner* Chandos and Mansel are pitted
against the evil "Rose" Noble to recover a treasure
hidden in the well of Wagensburg Castle. Though
atypical in its lack of a heroine, it was to set the pattern for more of the hero tales to follow, *Perishable
Goods* (1928), *Blood Royal* (1929), and its sequel, *Fire
Below* (1930). All of these have a heavily Ruritanian
quality about them (in *Blood Royal* Chandos saves
the grand Duchy of Riechtenburg for its rightful
heir); simple, clearcut moral issues; pure and up-
right heroes; thoroughly nasty antagonists; straightforward characterization without internal conflicts;
and well-plotted action enfolded in fantasy that is
redolent of schoolboy escapism.

While Yates was working on these, his marriage was breaking apart. He had achieved fame
and fortune through his success as a writer (together with a substantial legacy from an aunt), and
it is possible that his personality may have changed
somewhat. The demands of his professional career
may have made him appear neglectful, but whatever the reasons, an undefended divorce on the
grounds of adultery, complicated by his expatriate
status, was granted to him in 1933, and it became
absolute that September. Perhaps because of his
pseudonym, the case does not seem to have been
noticed by his reading public. At the time of the separation, his son, Richard, was in preparatory school
in England and was to remain in his father's care,
sheltered from any approaches by Bettine. Later he
attended his father's old school, Harrow. On 10
February 1934 Yates married Doreen Elizabeth
Lucy Bowie, twenty years his junior, the daughter
of a London solicitor; he had met her in 1932 on a
cruise to Madeira.

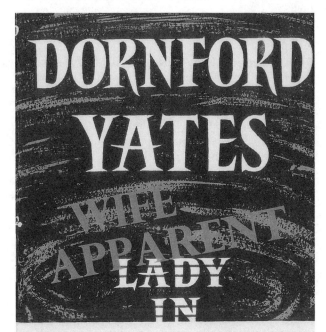

*Dust jacket bearing the original title of Yates's* Wife Apparent
*(1956). The wrap-around band explains the book's title change
(courtesy of the Lilly Library, Indiana University).*

Applying himself even more rigorously to his
work, Yates produced four more adventures: *Adèle
and Co.* (1931), one of his most popular books combining the thriller genre with the Pleydell family in
a neat, finely drawn tale set in France; two superla-
tive pieces in the action genre, *Safe Custody* (1932)
and *Storm Music* (1934), both using his device of fabulous treasure hunts in Central Europe; and *She Fell
Among Thieves* (1935), where Chandos and Mansel
are featured in a skillfully conceived suspense romance. *And Berry Came Too* (1936), another collection of Pleydell stories in the earlier style, was followed by one more Carinthian adventure, *She
Painted Her Face* (1937).

The scars of Yates's divorce show in *This Publican* (1938), a slightly different type of book for the
author but the precursor of others, a grim social
novel in which an innocent young barrister, David
Bohun, is beguiled into marriage with a murderess,
a calculating, hypocritical, tormenting, evil witch
figure, whose true nature has to be revealed so
Bohun can be free to marry his ideal love. A dis-

turbing work in its treatment of harsh marital passions, it is nonetheless engrossing in the tense unfolding of the drama.

Apparently unconcerned by the larger international conflicts developing around him in Europe and Spain, and with the trauma of Bettine purged from his soul, Yates returned to adventure thrillers: *Gale Warning* (1939), another Chandos-Mansel novel, which, apart from a spirited car-chase scene, is weaker and more diffuse than usual; *Shoal Water* (1940), which sees Mansel help Jeremy Solon save his beloved from white slavers; and *An Eye for a Tooth* (1943), a typical piece with Chandos and Mansel once more in action in Central Europe.

On the eve of the outbreak of World War II, Mercer decided to build his dream home, Cockade, on a mountainous slope in the heart of the Pyrénées at Eaux Bonnes, not far from Pau. A full account of its design and undertaking is given in a fictionally disguised form in *The House That Berry Built* (1945), where the Pleydells decide to leave White Ladies and England because of rising costs. No expense was spared on Cockade, which was completed by mid 1939, but it was too late; reality invaded Yates's world with the fall of France in 1940.

Yates, whose long-standing and outspoken dislike for the Germans was later to reach an almost pathological hatred, realized that he was in a dangerous position, especially since he was almost certainly on the Gestapo lists for the pro-British activity he had undertaken in the neighborhood since the start of the war. In as exciting an episode as ever occurred in his own tales, Yates and his wife fled hastily across the border to Spain and then Portugal.

By way of Portuguese East Africa they eventually reached Durban and proceeded to Salisbury, Rhodesia. Yates promptly volunteered his services to the military, who assigned him to light educational duties to foster morale. By the end of the war he had been promoted to the rank of major.

Disillusioned with postwar France and rejecting what he saw as rampantly socialist conditions in England, Yates returned to Southern Rhodesia, settling at Umtali, where he built another new house much in imitation of Cockade. Here, content in a corner of the British Empire where he could preserve his cherished ideals and attitudes, he settled back into writing.

Two more Chandos-Mansel adventures appeared, *Red in the Morning* (1946), set in France, and *Cost Price* (1949), a sequel to *Safe Custody*. Completely in Yates's standard design, *Cost Price* is a combination of knight-errantry and thriller, involv-

ing a stupendous treasure that has to be removed from Central Europe, where it is in danger of falling into the hands of the Nazi forces. Although Yates repeats his usual patterns in the book, it is still as satisfying as any of his previous action novels.

*The Berry Scene* (1947) is another collection of stories of the Pleydell family. They are vintage Yates with their evocations of a happier age, tinged with regret at its loss, and they present a broad panorama that carries the reader from scenes of village life before 1914 through to the epilogue, in which the family is shown as having retired to Portugal following World War II. The nostalgia suffusing these stories is given a fuller treatment in *Lower Than Vermin* (1950), a novel grimly recounting the decline of a noble English family struggling to maintain the old standards against the eroding tides and resulting chaos caused by a collapse of basic values.

Two last works set in the modern period, *Ne'er-Do-Well* (1954), a well-crafted love story, and a murder mystery, *Wife Apparent* (1956), seem to be Yates's attempts to strike out in a new direction. It may be that he was tired of his old material or that he felt his readers needed a more contemporary approach, but in spite of some criticism, neither shows any deterioration in the author's skill.

Although no new stories were to appear, two volumes of thinly disguised memoirs recounted as reminiscences among the Pleydells closed Yates's career. *As Berry and I Were Saying* and *B-Berry and I Look Back* (1958) are chiefly of interest for the views they express of Yates's works and their reception and for their anecdotes, especially the accounts of Yates's early legal experiences and encounters, though at times the author's memory of precise details can be at fault. No great disclosures or confessions are made; instead Yates distances himself quite deliberately, maintaining his pose behind his characters and allowing the reader to see him only as an extension of the fictional roles he has given the Pleydells. By the end of the second volume it is evident that Yates was running out of material, and some space is given to rather dogmatic opinions on a diverse mixture of subjects ranging from old silver to gems, areas in which he regarded himself as an authority. Yates suffered from lung cancer toward the end of his life, and he died from related causes at Umtali on 5 March 1960.

By 1920 Yates's stories had gained such popularity that they could not be ignored by the critics, whose response was largely dismissive, though most sympathetic reviewers recognized the appeal and charm of his romances and remarked on the

polish of his writing: "he is expert in light banter; but some three hundred pages of such entertainment tend to create a sense of surfeit" was *Punch* magazine's judgment of his second book, *The Courts of Idleness.* At a time when each new novel by Yates was advertised in bold type at the head of Ward, Lock's lists, the critic for the *Bookman* was struggling desperately to be favorable in his comments on the first appearance of *Anthony Lyveden* as "an absorbing story which contains some very serious work; and a word or two of praise must go to the style of the prose"; while its sequel, *Valerie French,* was viewed more simply in the same journal as having "a lighter side that will please many readers."

In the midst of the grim social upheavals and stern realities brought by World War II, Yates's old-fashioned period pieces and antique attitudes seemed almost offensively frivolous and out-of-touch with what reviewers saw as the proper concerns and developments of modern, serious fiction. Brian Howard, for example, was forthright in his comments on *Shoal Water* in *The New Statesman and Nation:* "*Shoal Water* is a novel (I suppose) which I find very difficult indeed. It is like reading a study of the habits of some newly discovered tribe of aborigines, with a hitherto unknown behaviour pattern. The language is not unlike English, yet strangely archaic and distorted . . . it is absolutely impossible to decide why anyone in the book acts as he does, unless it is pure ritual."

It is, perhaps, significant that the (London) *Times* obituary of Yates confined itself largely to details of his life, its remarks on his actual writing being restricted to a few telling sentences: "He could write light-hearted farce, but most of his books are fast-moving adventure stories in which right triumphs, sometimes improbably, over wrong. His plots are packed with unexpected twists and turns. . . . His writing has a compulsive enthu-siasm that sweeps readers, especially young readers, along."

In his day Yates was seen as both a novelist of first-rate and absorbing thrillers and a writer of lighter romances. As far as the latter are concerned, his work is negligible and now almost forgotten. His adventure tales, for all their excellent workmanship and easy style, are dated period pieces displaying manners and scenes of a bygone era, though the sheer fantasy of action and setting will always have its attraction. The Berry stories of the Pleydell family are amusing whimsy but again unlikely to appeal to any but those who still hold sentimental views of an idealized English squirearchy in a remote Edwardian world of manor houses and village life. In the content of his books there is a lack of intellectual substance, a complete want of any depth to the themes, and no complexity to the writing itself. Only a few of Yates's short stories give any psychological development to the characters or motivation beyond the demands of the plots themselves. Yates had genuine talent and realized it, but there are indications that in spite of several attempts to achieve a more serious reputation, he failed to break free from the commercial success that he found came so easily.

**Biography:**

A. J. Smithers, *Dornford Yates: A Biography* (London: Hodder & Stoughton, 1982).

**References:**

William Vivian Butler, *The Durable Desperadoes* (London: Macmillan, 1973);

Edward Liveing, *Adventure in Publishing: The House of Ward Lock 1854–1954* (London: Ward, Lock, 1954);

Richard Usborne, *Clubland Heroes* (London: Barrie & Jenkins, 1974), pp. 27–78.

# Checklist of Further Readings

Adcock, Arthur St. John. *The Glory That Was Grub Street*. London: Sampson Low, Marston, 1928; New York: Stokes, 1928.

Adcock. *The Gods of Modern Grub Street*. London: Sampson Low, Marston, 1923.

Allen, Walter. *The English Novel*. New York: Dutton, 1958.

Ardis, Ann. *New Woman, New Novels: Feminism and Early Modernism*. New Brunswick & London: Rutgers University Press, 1990.

Baguley, David. *Naturalist Fiction*. Cambridge: Cambridge University Press, 1990.

Batchelor, John. *The Edwardian Novelists*. London: Duckworth, 1982.

Beauman, Nicola. *A Very Great Profession: the Women's Novel 1914–1939*. London: Virago, 1983.

Beckson, Karl. *London in the 1890's: A Cultural History*. New York: Norton, 1992.

Bennett, Tony. *Popular Fiction*. London: Routledge, 1990.

Bentley, Phyllis. *The English Regional Novel*. London: Allen & Unwin, 1941.

Bergonzi, Bernard. *Heroes' Twilight: A Study of the Literature of the Great War*. London: Constable, 1965.

Bergonzi. *The Turn of a Century: Essays on Victorian and Modern English Literature*. London: Macmillan, 1973.

Bjorhovde, Gerd. *Rebellious Structures. Women Writers and the Crisis of the Novel, 1880–1900*. Oxford: Norwegian University Press, 1987.

Blamires, Harry. *Twentieth Century English Literature*. London: Macmillan, 1982.

Bloom, Clive. *The "Occult" Experience and the New Criticism*. Sussex: Harvester, 1986.

Bradbury, Malcolm. *The Social Context of Modern English Literature*. Oxford: Blackwell, 1971.

Brandon, Ruth. *The New Women and the Old Men*. London: Secker & Warburg, 1990.

Breen, Jennifer. *In Her Own Write: Twentieth-Century Women's Fiction*. London: Macmillan, 1990.

Brewster, Dorothy, and Angus Burrell. *Dead Reckonings in Fiction*. New York: Longmans, Green, 1924.

Brewster and Burrell. *Modern Fiction*. New York: Columbia University Press, 1934.

Britain, Ian. *Fabianism and Culture: A Study in British Socialism and the Arts 1884–1918*. New York: Columbia University Press, 1982.

Bufkin, E. C. *The Twentieth-Century Novel in English*. Athens: University of Georgia Press, 1984.

Buitenhuis, Peter. *The Great War of Words. British, American, and Canadian Propaganda and Fiction, 1914–1933.* Vancouver: University of British Columbia Press, 1987.

Cadogan, Mary, and Wendy Craig. *Women and Children First. Aspects of War and Literature.* London: Gollancz, 1978.

Cavaliero, Glen. *The Rural Tradition in the English Novel 1900–1939.* London: Macmillan, 1977.

Cawelti, John G. *Adventure, Mystery, and Romance: Formula Stories as Art and Popular Culture.* Chicago: University of Chicago Press, 1976.

Chapple, J. A. V. *Documentary and Imaginative Literature, 1880–1920.* New York: Barnes & Noble, 1970.

Chevalley, Abel. *The Modern English Novel,* translated by Ben Ray Redman. New York: Haskell House, 1973.

Church, Richard. *British Authors: A Twentieth-Century Gallery.* London, New York & Toronto: Longmans, Green, 1948.

Church. *The Growth of the English Novel.* London: Methuen, 1951.

Clayton, John J. *Gestures of Healing. Anxiety and the Modern Novel.* Amherst: University of Massachusetts, 1991.

Cockburn, Claud. *Bestseller: The Books That Everyone Read 1900–1939.* London: Sidgwick & Jackson, 1972.

Cox, C. B., and A. E. Dyson, eds. *The Twentieth-Century Mind – 1900–1918.* London: Oxford University Press, 1972.

Crosland, Margaret. *Beyond the Lighthouse. English Women Novelists in the Twentieth Century.* London: Constable, 1981.

Cross, Nigel. *The Common Writer. Life in Nineteenth-Century Grub Street.* Cambridge: Cambridge University Press, 1985.

Cruse, Amy. *After the Victorians.* London: Allen & Unwin, 1938.

Cunningham, A. R. "The 'New Woman Fiction' of the 1890's," *Victorian Studies,* 17 (December 1973): 177–186.

Cunningham, Gail. *The New Woman in Victorian Fiction.* London: Macmillan, 1978.

Dangerfield, George. *The Strange Death of Liberal England.* New York: Capricorn Books/Putnam, 1961.

Delavaney, Emile. *D. H. Lawrence and Edward Carpenter: A Study in Edwardian Transition.* London: Heinemann, 1971.

Drew, Elizabeth A. *The Modern Novel. Some Aspects of Contemporary Fiction.* New York: Harcourt, Brace, 1926.

Ellmann, Richard, ed. *Edwardians and Late Victorians.* New York: Columbia University Press, 1959.

Elwin, Malcolm. *Old Gods Falling.* Freeport, N.Y.: Books for Libraries Press, 1971.

Ensor, R. C. K. *England 1870–1914.* Oxford: Clarendon Press, 1936.

Fisher, Margery. *The Bright Face of Danger: An Exploration of the Adventure Story.* London: Hodder & Stoughton, 1986.

Fraser, G. S. *The Modern Writer and His World.* London: Deutsch, 1964.

Friedman, Alan. *The Turn of the Novel: The Transition to Modern Fiction.* New York & London: Oxford University Press, 1966.

Frierson, William C. *The English Novel in Transition 1885–1940.* Norman: University of Oklahoma Press / New York: Cooper Square, 1965.

Fussell, Paul. *The Great War and Modern Memory.* London: Oxford University Press, 1975.

Gawsworth, John (Terence Ian Fytton Armstrong). *Ten Contemporaries: Notes Towards Their Definitive Bibliographies.* London: Joiner & Steele, 1933.

George, W. L. *A Novelist on Novels.* Port Washington, N.Y.: Kennikat Press, 1970.

Gerber, Richard. *Utopian Fantasy: A Study of English Utopian Fiction Since the End of the Nineteenth Century.* London: Routledge & Kegan Paul, 1955.

Gibbons, Tom. *Rooms in the Darwin Hotel: Studies in English Literary Criticism and Ideas 1880–1920.* Nedlands: University of Western Australia Press, 1973.

Gill, Richard. *Happy Rural Seat: The English Country House and the Literary Imagination.* New Haven: Yale University Press, 1972.

Gillie, Christopher. *Movements in English Literature, 1900–1940.* Cambridge: Cambridge University Press, 1975.

Glicksberg, Charles I. *The Sexual Revolution in Modern English Literature.* The Hague: Nijhoff, 1973.

Gould, Gerald. *The English Novel of Today.* London: Castle, 1924.

Harris, Frank. *Contemporary Portraits (Third Series).* New York: Harris, 1920.

Henkin, Leo J. *Darwinism in the English Novel: 1860–1910.* New York: Russell & Russell, 1963.

Hewitt, Douglas John. *English Fiction of the Early Modern Period 1890–1940.* London: Longman, 1988.

Hibberd, Dominic. *The First World War.* London: Macmillan, 1990.

Hicks, Granville. *Figures of Transition: A Study of British Literature at the End of the Nineteenth Century.* New York: Macmillan, 1939.

Hind, C. Lewis. *More Authors and I.* New York: Dodd, Mead, 1922.

Hochman, Baruch. *The Test of Character from the Victorian Novel to the Modern.* Cranbury, N.J.: Fairleigh Dickinson, 1983.

Hoffman, Frederick J. *Freudianism and the Literary Mind.* Baton Rouge: Louisiana State University Press, 1957.

Hoffman. *The Mortal No: Death and the Modern Imagination.* Princeton: Princeton University Press, 1964.

Homberger, Eric. "Modernists and Edwardians," in *Ezra Pound: The London Years 1908–1920,* edited by Philip

Grover. New York: AMS Press, 1977, pp. 1–14.

Hoops, R. *Der Einflus der Psychoanalyse auf die Englische Literatur.* Heidelburg: Carl Winters Universitatsbuchhandlung, 1934.

Howarth, Patrick. *Play Up and Play the Game: The Heroes of Popular Fiction.* London: Eyre Methuen, 1973.

Hughes, H. Stewart. *Consciousness and Society: The Re-Orientation of European Social Thought 1890–1930.* London: MacGibbon & Kee, 1959.

Humm, Peter, Paul Stigant, and Peter Widdowson, eds. *Popular Fictions.* London: Methuen, 1986.

Hunter, Jefferson. *Edwardian Fiction.* Cambridge, Mass.: Harvard University Press, 1982.

Hynes, Samuel. *Edwardian Occasions: Essays On English Writing in the Early Twentieth Century.* London: Routledge, 1972.

Hynes. *The Edwardian Turn of Mind.* Princeton: Princeton University Press, 1968.

Hynes. *A War Imagined. The First World War and English Culture.* New York: Atheneum, 1991.

Ingle, Stephen. *Socialist Thought in Imaginative Literature.* London: Macmillan, 1979.

Ingram, Angela, and Daphne Patai. *Rediscovering Forgotten Radicals. British Women Writers 1889–1939.* Chapel Hill & London: University of North Carolina Press, 1993.

Jameson, Storm. *The Georgian Novel and Mr. Robinson.* London: Heinemann, 1929.

Johnson, George M. "The Early Influence of Second Wave Psychology on British Prose Fiction," Ph.D. dissertation, McMaster University, 1990.

Johnson, R. Brimley. *Some Contemporary Novelists (Women).* London: Parsons, 1920.

Karl, Frederick R. *Modern and Modernism: The Sovereignty of the Artist 1885–1925.* New York: Atheneum, 1988.

Keating, Peter J. *The Haunted Study: A Social History of the English Novel 1875–1914.* London: Secker & Warburg, 1989.

Keating. *Into Unknown England 1866–1913.* Manchester: Manchester University Press, 1976.

Keating. *The Working Classes in English Fiction.* London: Routledge & Kegan Paul, 1971.

Kennedy, J. M. *English Literature: 1800–1905.* London: Sampson Low, Marston, 1913.

Kenner, Hugh. *A Sinking Island.* London: Barrie & Jenkins, 1988.

Kermode, Frank. "The English Novel, circa 1907," in his *Essays on Fiction 1971–82.* London: Routledge & Kegan Paul, 1983.

Kern, Stephen. *The Culture of Time and Space 1880–1918.* London: Weidenfeld & Nicolson, 1983.

Klaus, H. Gustav. *The Socialist Novel in Britain.* New York: St. Martin's Press, 1982.

Klaus, ed. *The Rise of Social Fiction 1880–1914.* Sussex: Harvester, 1987.

Klein, Holger, ed. *The First World War in Fiction*. London: Macmillan, 1976.

Kunitz, Stanley J., and Howard Haycraft, eds. *Twentieth Century Authors. A Biographical Dictionary of Modern Literature*. New York: Wilson, 1942.

Langbaum, Robert. *The Modern Spirit: Essays on the Continuity of Nineteenth and Twentieth-Century Literature*. New York & London: Oxford University Press, 1970.

Lauterbach, Edward S., and W. Eugene Davies. *The Transitional Age in British Literature, 1880–1920*. Troy, N.Y.: Whitson, 1973.

Lawrence, Margaret. *School of Femininity*. New York: Frederick Stokes, 1936; published as *We Write as Women*. London: M. Joseph, 1936.

Leed, Eric J. *No Man's Land: Combat and Identity in World War I*. Cambridge: Cambridge University Press, 1979.

Leslie, Anita. *Edwardians in Love*. London: Hutchinson, 1972.

Lester, John A. Jr. *Journey Through Despair 1880–1914. Transformations in British Literary Culture*. Princeton: Princeton University Press, 1968.

Lodge, David. *Modernism, Antimodernism and Postmodernism*. Birmingham, U.K.: University of Birmingham, 1977.

Mais, S. P. B. *Some Modern Authors*. London: Richards, 1923.

Markovic, Vida E. *The Changing Face: Disintegration of Personality in the Twentieth-Century British Novel, 1900–1950*. Carbondale: Southern Illinois University Press, 1970.

Marwick, Arthur. *The Deluge: British Society and the First World War*. London: Bodley Head, 1965.

May, Keith. *Out of the Maelstrom. Psychology and the Novel in the Twentieth Century*. London: Elek, 1977.

McNichol, Stella. *The Early Twentieth Century British Novel. A Modern Introduction*. London: Arnold, 1992.

Meyers, Jeffrey. *Homosexuality and Literature: 1890–1930*. London: Athlone, 1977.

Myers, W. L. *The Later Realism*. Chicago: University of Chicago Press, 1927.

Neuberg, Victor E. *Popular Literature: A History and Guide*. Harmondsworth: Penguin, 1977.

Nowell-Smith, Simon, ed. *Edwardian England 1901–1914*. New York: Oxford University Press, 1964.

O'Day, Alan, ed. *The Edwardian Age: Conflict and Stability 1900–1914*. London: Macmillan, 1979.

Orel, Harold. *Popular Fiction in England, 1914–1918*. Lexington: University Press of Kentucky, 1992.

Overton, Grant Martin. *Authors of the Day*. New York: Doran, 1924.

Perl, Jeffrey M. *The Tradition of Return: The Implicit History of Modernism*. Princeton: Princeton University Press, 1984.

Priestley, J. B. *The Edwardians*. London: Sphere, 1972.

Read, Donald, ed. *Edwardian England*. New Brunswick, N.J.: Rutgers University Press, 1982.

Rice, Thomas Jackson. *English Fiction, 1900–1950*, 2 volumes. Detroit: Gale Research, 1979, 1983.

Rose, Jonathan. *The Edwardian Temperament: 1895–1919*. Athens: Ohio University Press, 1986.

Sandison, Alan. *The Wheel of Empire: A Study of the Imperial Idea in Some Late Nineteenth and Early Twentieth Century Fiction*. New York: St. Martin's Press, 1967.

Schwartz, Sanford. *The Matrix of Modernism: Pound, Eliot, and Early Twentieth-Century Thought*. Princeton: Princeton University Press, 1985.

Schwarz, Daniel R. *The Transformation of the English Novel 1890–1930*. London: Macmillan, 1989.

Scott-James, Rolfe A. *Fifty Years of English Literature, 1900–1950; With A Postscript, 1951–1955*. London: Longmans, Green, 1956.

Scott-James. *Modernism and Romance*. London: John Lane/Bodley Head, 1908.

Shaw, G. B. S. *The Sanity of Art: An Exposure of the Current Nonsense about Artists Being Degenerate*. London: New Age Press, 1908.

Showalter, Elaine. *Sexual Anarchy: Gender and Culture at the Fin de Siècle*. New York: Viking, 1990.

Sparrow, Gerald. *Vintage Edwardian Murder*. London: Barker, 1971.

Squillace, Robert. "Bennett, Wells, and the Persistence of Realism," in *The Columbia History of the British Novel*, edited by John Richetti. New York: Columbia University Press, 1994, pp. 658–684.

Stableford, Brian. *Scientific Romance in Britain 1890–1950*. London: Fourth Estate, 1985.

Staley, Thomas. *Twentieth Century Women Novelists*. London: Macmillan, 1982.

Stetz, Margaret Diane. "Life's 'Half-profits': Writers and their Readers in Fiction of the 1890's," in *Nineteenth-Century Lives. Essays Presented to Jerome Hamilton Buckley*, edited by Laurence S. Lockridge, John Maynard, and Donald D. Stone. Cambridge: Cambridge University Press, 1989, pp. 169–187.

Stevenson, Lionel. *The History of the English Novel. Vol. XI – Yesterday and After*. New York: Barnes & Noble, 1967.

Stewart, J. I. M. *Eight Modern Writers*. Oxford: Oxford University Press, 1963.

Street, Brian V. *The Savage in Literature: Representations of 'Primitive' Society in English Fiction 1858–1920*. London: Routledge, 1975.

Swinnerton, Frank. *The Georgian Literary Scene, 1910–1935*. London: Hutchinson, 1935.

Swinnerton. *A London Bookman*. London: Secker, 1928.

Thatcher, David S. *Nietzsche in England 1890–1914*. Toronto: University of Toronto Press, 1970.

Thompson, Paul. *The Edwardians. The Remaking of British Society*. London & New York: Routledge, 1992.

Tindall, William York. *Forces in Modern British Literature, 1885–1956*. New York: Vintage, 1956.

Trodd, Anthea. *A Reader's Guide to Edwardian Literature*. Calgary: University of Calgary Press, 1991.

Trotter, David. "The Avoidance of Naturalism: Gissing, Moore, Grand, Bennett, and Others," in *The Columbia History of the British Novel*, edited by John Richetti. New York: Columbia University Press, 1994, pp. 608–630.

Trotter. "Edwardian Sex Novels," *Critical Quarterly*, 31 (Spring 1989): 92–106.

Trotter. *The English Novel in History 1895–1920*. London & New York: Routledge, 1993.

Verschoyle, Derek, ed. *The English Novelists: A Survey of the Novel by Twenty Contemporary Novelists*. London: Chatto & Windus, 1936.

Ward, Alfred C. *Twentieth-Century English Literature, 1900–1960*. London: Methuen, 1964.

Waters, Chris. *British Socialists and the Politics of Popular Culture, 1884–1914*. Stanford, Cal.: Stanford University Press, 1990.

Waugh, Arthur. *Tradition and Change*. London: Chapman & Hall, 1919; New York: Dutton, 1919.

West, George Cornwallis. *Edwardian Hey-Days*. London & New York: Putnam, 1930.

Williams, Harold. *Modern English Writers, 1890–1914*. London: Sidgwick & Jackson, 1919.

Williams, Raymond. *Culture and Society 1780–1950*. London: Chatto & Windus, 1958.

Williams. *The English Novel from Dickens to Lawrence*. London: Chatto & Windus, 1970.

Wilson, Edmund. *Axel's Castle: A Study in the Imaginative Literature of 1870–1930*. London: Fontana, 1984.

Wohl, Robert. *The Generation of 1914*. Cambridge, Mass.: Harvard University Press, 1979.

# Contributors

Leonard R. N. Ashley ..................... *Brooklyn College of the City University of New York*
Judith Barisonzi.............................*University of Wisconsin Center – Fond du Lac*
Richard Bleiler .................................................*University of Connecticut*
Francis F. Burch ...............................................*Saint Joseph's University*
Ellen Miller Casey.............................................*University of Scranton*
George Allan Cate.............................................*University of Maryland*
Margaret Crosland.............................................*Upper Hartfield, Essex*
James Y. Dayananda...........................................*Lock Haven University*
James M. Decker ............................................*Northern Illinois University*
David Llewellyn Dodds ....................................*Barneveld, The Netherlands*
C. Gordon-Craig ...............................................*University of Alberta*
George J. Johnson.............................................*Waterdown, Ontario*
George M. Johnson ......................................*University College of the Cariboo*
C. J. Keep......................................................*Queen's University*
Richard Kelly ..........................................*University of Tennessee, Knoxville*
Darrell Laird ..........................................*University College of the Cariboo*
Paul A. Love....................................................*Gettysburg College*
Raymond N. MacKenzie.......................................*University of Saint Thomas*
Edward A. Malone...........................................*University of Missouri at Rolla*
Kiernan Ryan ..............................................*University of Cambridge*
Catriona de Scossa .......................................*University of Alberta, Canada*
Maria Aline Seabra Ferreira................................*Universidade de Aveiro*
Michael Douglas Smith ......................................*Germantown, Maryland*
Patricia Thomas Srebrnik ......................................*University of Calgary*
Rebecca J. Sutcliffe ..........................................*Simon Fraser University*
Katherine Sutherland.....................................*University College of the Cariboo*
Eric Thompson ...........................................*Université du Québec à Chicoutimi*
Stephen R. Whited.............................................*Piedmont College*
George Woodcock................................................*Vancouver, B.C.*

# Cumulative Index

*Dictionary of Literary Biography*, Volumes 1-153
*Dictionary of Literary Biography Yearbook*, 1980-1994
*Dictionary of Literary Biography Documentary Series*, Volumes 1-12

# Cumulative Index

**DLB** before number: *Dictionary of Literary Biography,* Volumes 1-153
**Y** before number: *Dictionary of Literary Biography Yearbook,* 1980-1994
**DS** before number: *Dictionary of Literary Biography Documentary Series,* Volumes 1-12

Cumulative Index

## F

# H

Cumulative Index

ISBN 0-8103-5714-3

90000

9 780810 357143

**(Continued from front endsheets)**

## Documentary Series